LEADERSHIP IN
ORGANIZATIONS

Sixth
Edition

LEADERSHIP IN
ORGANIZATIONS

Gary Yukl

University at Albany
State University of New York

PEARSON
Prentice
Hall

UPPER SADDLE RIVER, NJ 07458

Library of Congress Cataloging-in-Publication Data

Yukl, Gary A., [date]
    Leadership in organizations / Gary Yukl.-- 6th ed.
      p. cm.
    Includes bibliographical references and index.
    ISBN 0-13-149484-8 (paperback alk. paper)
  1. Leadership. 2. Decision making. 3. Organization. I. Title.
  HD57.7.Y85 2005
    303.3'4--dc22   2005003244

VP/Editorial Director: Jeff Shelstad
Product Development Manager: Ashley Santora
Marketing Manager: Anke Braun
Marketing Assistant: Patrick Danzuso
Managing Editor: John Roberts
Production Editor: Suzanne Grappi
Permissions Supervisor: Charles Morris
Manufacturing Buyer: Michelle Klein
Production Manager, Manufacturing: Arnold Vila
Cover Design Manager: Jayne Conte
Composition: Laserwords
Full-Service Project Management: Jennifer Welsch, BookMasters, Inc.
Printer/Binder: Courier Stoughton
Typeface: 10/12 Times Ten

Credits and acknowledgments borrowed from other sources and reproduced, with permission, in this textbook appear on appropriate page within text.

Pearson Education LTD.
Pearson Education Singapore, Pte. Ltd
Pearson Education, Canada, Ltd
Pearson Education–Japan
Pearson Education Australia PTY, Limited
Pearson Education North Asia Ltd
Pearson Educación de Mexico, S.A. de C.V.
Pearson Education Malaysia, Pte. Ltd

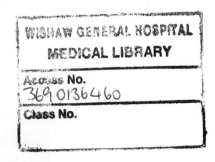

PEARSON
Prentice
Hall

10 9 8 7
ISBN 0-13-149484-8

For her love, support, and understanding, this book is dedicated to Maureen.

Brief Contents

Contents

Preface

This book is about leadership in organizations. Its primary focus is on managerial leadership as opposed to parliamentary leadership, leadership of social movements, or emergent leadership in informal groups. The book presents a broad survey of theory and research on leadership in formal organizations. The topic of leadership effectiveness is of special interest, and the discussion keeps returning to the question of what makes a person an effective leader.

The content of the book reflects a dual concern for theory and practice. I have attempted to satisfy two different audiences with somewhat different preferences. Most academics prefer a book that provides a detailed explanation and critical evaluation of major theories, and a comprehensive review and evaluation of empirical research. They are more interested in how well the research is done and what additional research is needed than in the practical applications. Many academics are skeptical about the value of prescriptions and guidelines for practitioners and consider them premature in the absence of further research. In contrast, most practitioners want some immediate answers about what to do and how to do it in order to be more effective as leaders. They need to deal with the current challenges of their job and cannot wait for decades until the academics resolve their theoretical disputes and obtain definitive answers. Most practitioners are more interested in finding helpful remedies and prescriptions than in finding out how this knowledge was discovered.

These different preferences are a major reason for the much-lamented gulf between scientists and practitioners in management and industrial-organizational psychology. I believe it is important for managers and administrators to understand the complexity of effective leadership, the source of our knowledge about leadership in organizations, and the limitations of this knowledge. Likewise, I believe it is important for academics to think more about how their theories and research can be used to improve the practice of management. Too much of our leadership research is designed only to examine narrow, esoteric questions that are of interest only to a few other scholars who publish in the same journals.

Academics will be pleased to find that major theories are explained and critiqued, empirical research on leadership is reviewed and summarized, and many references are provided to enable them to follow up with additional reading on topics of special interest. The field of leadership is still in a state of ferment, with many continuing controversies about conceptual and methodological issues. The book addresses these issues whenever feasible rather than merely presenting theories and summarizing findings without concern for the quality of research that lies behind the theories. However, the literature review was intended to be incisive, not comprehensive. Rather than detailing an endless series of theories and studies, the book focuses on the ones that are most relevant and informative. The book reviews what we know about leadership effectiveness, and the current edition reflects significant progress in our understanding of leadership since the first edition was published in 1981.

For practitioners, I attempted to convey a better appreciation of the complexity of managerial leadership, the importance of having theoretical knowledge about leadership, and the need to be flexible and pragmatic in applying this knowledge. The current edition provides many guidelines and recommendations for improving managerial effectiveness, but it is not a practitioner's manual of simple techniques and secret recipes that guarantee instant success. The purpose of the guidelines is to help the reader understand the practical implications of leadership theory and research, not to prescribe exactly how things must be done by a leader. Most of the guidelines are based on a limited amount of research, and they are not infallible.

Most chapters have one or two short cases designed to help the reader gain a better understanding of the theories, concepts, and guidelines presented in the chapter. The cases describe events that occurred in real organizations, but some of the cases were modified to make them more useful for learning basic concepts and effective practices. The cases ask a reader to analyze behavioral processes, identify examples of effective and ineffective behavior, and suggest effective ways to handle the situation that is depicted. The cases take from 20 to 30 minutes to discuss.

An instructor's manual is available with detailed analyses of the cases and suggestions on how to use them. The instructor's manual also includes a multiple-choice exam for each chapter with items on the major points in the chapter. The manual includes exercises for use in class (e.g., role plays), and some out-of-class activities that help students to understand how they can apply the theory and guidelines.

With its focus on effective leadership in organizations, this book is especially relevant for people who are currently managers or who expect to become a manager in the near future. The book is appropriate for use as the primary text in an undergraduate or graduate course in leadership. Such courses are found in many different schools or departments, including business, psychology, sociology, educational administration, public administration, and health care administration. The book is also useful for practicing managers who are looking for something more than superficial answers to difficult questions about leadership. The book is widely used in many different countries and has been translated into other languages, including Chinese, Korean, Indonesian, and Greek.

Gary Yukl
Albany, New York
December 2004

LEADERSHIP IN ORGANIZATIONS

CHAPTER

1

INTRODUCTION: THE NATURE OF LEADERSHIP

Learning Objectives

After studying this chapter you should be able to:

- Understand why leadership has been defined in so many different ways.
- Understand the controversy about differences between leadership and management.
- Understand how leadership will be defined in this book.
- Understand why it is so difficult to assess leadership effectiveness.
- Understand the different indicators used to assess leadership effectiveness.
- Understand what aspects of leadership have been studied the most during the past 50 years.
- Understand how leadership can be described as an individual, dyadic, group, or organizational process.
- Understand the organization of this book.

Leadership is a subject that has long excited interest among people. The term connotes images of powerful, dynamic individuals who command victorious armies, direct corporate empires from atop gleaming skyscrapers, or shape the course of nations. The exploits of brave and clever leaders are the essence of many legends and myths. Much of our description of history is the story of military, political, religious, and social leaders who are credited or blamed for important historical events, even though we do not understand very well how the events were caused or how much influence the leader really had. The widespread fascination with leadership may be because it is such a mysterious process, as well as one that touches everyone's life. Why did certain leaders (e.g., Gandhi, Mohammed, Mao Tse-tung) inspire such intense fervor and dedication? How did certain leaders (e.g., Julius Caesar, Alexander the Great) build great

1

empires? Why did some rather undistinguished people (e.g., Adolf Hitler, Claudius Caesar) rise to positions of great power? Why were certain leaders (e.g., Winston Churchill, Indira Gandhi) suddenly deposed, despite their apparent power and record of successful accomplishments? Why do some leaders have loyal followers who are willing to sacrifice their lives, whereas other leaders are so despised that subordinates conspire to murder them?

Questions about leadership have long been a subject of speculation, but scientific research on leadership did not begin until the twentieth century. The focus of much of the research has been on the determinants of leadership effectiveness. Social scientists have attempted to discover what traits, abilities, behaviors, sources of power, or aspects of the situation determine how well a leader is able to influence followers and accomplish task objectives. The reasons why some people emerge as leaders and the determinants of the way a leader acts are other important questions that have been investigated, but the predominant concern has been leadership effectiveness.

Some progress has been made in probing the mysteries surrounding leadership, but many questions remain unanswered. In this book, major theories and research findings on leadership effectiveness will be reviewed, with particular emphasis on managerial leadership in formal organizations such as business corporations, government agencies, hospitals, and universities. This first chapter introduces the subject by considering different conceptions of leadership, different ways of evaluating its effectiveness, and different approaches for studying leadership. The chapter also provides an overview of the book and explains how the subjects are organized.

Definitions of Leadership

The term *leadership* is a word taken from the common vocabulary and incorporated into the technical vocabulary of a scientific discipline without being precisely redefined. As a consequence, it carries extraneous connotations that create ambiguity of meaning (Janda, 1960). Additional confusion is caused by the use of other imprecise terms such as *power, authority, management, administration, control,* and *supervision* to describe similar phenomena. An observation by Bennis (1959, p. 259) is as true today as when he made it many years ago:

> Always, it seems, the concept of leadership eludes us or turns up in another form to taunt us again with its slipperiness and complexity. So we have invented an endless proliferation of terms to deal with it . . . and still the concept is not sufficiently defined.

Researchers usually define leadership according to their individual perspectives and the aspects of the phenomenon of most interest to them. After a comprehensive review of the leadership literature, Stogdill (1974, p. 259) concluded that "there are almost as many definitions of leadership as there are persons who have attempted to define the concept." The stream of new definitions has continued unabated since Stogdill made his observation. Leadership has been defined in terms of traits, behaviors, influence, interaction patterns, role relationships, and occupation of an administrative position. Table 1-1 shows some representative definitions presented over the past 50 years.

TABLE 1-1 Definitions of Leadership

- Leadership is "the behavior of an individual . . . directing the activities of a group toward a shared goal." (Hemphill & Coons, 1957, p. 7)
- Leadership is "the influential increment over and above mechanical compliance with the routine directives of the organization." (Katz & Kahn, 1978, p. 528)
- "Leadership is exercised when persons . . . mobilize . . . institutional, political, psychological, and other resources so as to arouse, engage, and satisfy the motives of followers." (Burns, 1978, p. 18)
- "Leadership is realized in the process whereby one or more individuals succeed in attempting to frame and define the reality of others." (Smircich & Morgan, 1982, p. 258)
- Leadership is "the process of influencing the activities of an organized group toward goal achievement." (Rauch & Behling, 1984, p. 46)
- "Leadership is about articulating visions, embodying values, and creating the environment within which things can be accomplished." (Richards & Engle, 1986, p. 206)
- "Leadership is a process of giving purpose (meaningful direction) to collective effort, and causing willing effort to be expended to achieve purpose." (Jacobs & Jaques, 1990, p. 281)
- Leadership "is the ability to step outside the culture . . . to start evolutionary change processes that are more adaptive." (Schein, 1992, p. 2)
- "Leadership is the process of making sense of what people are doing together so that people will understand and be committed." (Drath & Palus, 1994, p. 4)
- Leadership is "the ability of an individual to influence, motivate, and enable others to contribute toward the effectiveness and success of the organization. . . ." (House et al., 1999, p. 184)

Most definitions of leadership reflect the assumption that it involves a process whereby intentional influence is exerted by one person over other people to guide, structure, and facilitate activities and relationships in a group or organization. The numerous definitions of leadership appear to have little else in common. They differ in many respects, including who exerts influence, the intended purpose of the influence, the manner in which influence is exerted, and the outcome of the influence attempt. The differences are not just a case of scholarly nit-picking; they reflect deep disagreement about identification of leaders and leadership processes. Researchers who differ in their conception of leadership select different phenomena to investigate and interpret the results in different ways. When leadership is defined in a restrictive way by researchers, they are likely to take a narrower perspective on the processes to be studied, and it is less likely they will discover things unrelated to or inconsistent with their initial assumptions about effective leadership.

Because leadership has so many different meanings to people, some theorists question whether it is even useful as a scientific construct (e.g., Alvesson & Sveningsson, 2003; Miner, 1975). Nevertheless, most behavioral scientists and practitioners seem to believe leadership is a real phenomenon that is important for the effectiveness of organizations. The deluge of articles and books about leadership shows no sign of abating.

Specialized Role or Shared Influence Process?

A major controversy involves the issue of whether leadership should be viewed as a specialized role or as a shared influence process. One view is that all groups have role specialization that includes a leadership role with some responsibilities and functions that cannot be shared too widely without jeopardizing the effectiveness of the group. The person expected to perform the specialized leadership role is designated as the "leader." Other members are called "followers" even though some of them may assist the primary leader in carrying out leadership functions. The distinction between leader and follower roles does not mean that a person cannot perform both roles at the same time. For example, a department manager who is the leader of department employees is also a follower of higher-level managers in the organization. Researchers who view leadership as a specialized role are likely to pay more attention to the attributes that determine selection of designated leaders, the typical behavior of designated leaders, and the effects of this behavior on other members of the group or organization.

Another way to view leadership is in terms of an influence process that occurs naturally within a social system and is diffused among the members. Writers with this perspective believe it is more useful to study "leadership" as a social process rather than as a specialized role. According to this view, any member of the social system may exhibit leadership at any time, and there is no clear distinction between leaders and followers. Various leadership functions may be carried out by different people who influence what the group does, how it is done, and the way people in the group relate to each other. Important decisions about what to do and how to do it are made through the use of an interactive process involving many different people who influence each other. Researchers who view leadership as a shared, diffuse process, are likely to pay more attention to the complex influence processes that occur among members, the context and conditions that determine when and how they occur, and the consequences for the group or organization.

Type of Influence Process

Controversy about the definition of leadership involves not only who exercises influence, but also what type of influence is exercised and the outcome. Some theorists would limit the definition of leadership to the exercise of influence resulting in enthusiastic commitment by followers, as opposed to indifferent compliance or reluctant obedience. These theorists argue that a person who uses control over rewards and punishments to manipulate or coerce followers is not really "leading" them and is being unethical with regard to the use of power.

An opposing view is that this definition is too restrictive because it excludes some influence processes that are important for understanding why a manager is effective or ineffective in a given situation. How leadership is defined should not predetermine the answer to the research question of what makes a leader effective. The same outcome can be accomplished with different influence methods, and the same type of influence attempt can result in different outcomes, depending on the nature of the situation. Even people who are forced or manipulated into doing something may become committed to it if they subsequently discover that it really is the best option for them and for the organization. The ethical use of power is a legitimate concern for leadership scholars, but it should not limit the definition of leadership or the type of influence processes that are studied.

Purpose of Influence Attempts

Another controversy about which influence attempts are part of leadership involves their purpose and outcome. One viewpoint is that leadership occurs only when people are influenced to do what is ethical and beneficial for the organization and themselves. This definition of leadership does not include influence attempts that are irrelevant or detrimental to followers, such as a leader's attempts to gain personal benefits at the followers' expense.

An opposing view would include all attempts to influence the attitudes and behavior of followers in an organizational context, regardless of the intended purpose or actual beneficiary. Acts of leadership often have multiple motives, and it is seldom possible to determine the extent to which they are selfless rather than selfish. The outcomes of leader actions usually include a mix of costs and benefits, some of which are unintended, making it difficult to infer purpose. Despite good intentions, the actions of a leader are sometimes more detrimental than beneficial for followers. Conversely, actions motivated solely by a leader's personal needs sometimes result in unintended benefits for followers and the organization. Thus, the domain of leadership processes to be studied should not be limited by their intended purpose.

Influence Based on Reason or Emotions

Most of the leadership definitions listed earlier emphasize rational, cognitive processes. For many years it was common to view leadership as a process wherein leaders influence followers to believe it is in their best interest to cooperate in achieving a shared task objective. Until the 1980s, few conceptions of leadership recognized the importance of emotions as a basis for influence.

In contrast, many recent conceptions of leadership emphasize the emotional aspects of influence much more than reason. According to this view, only the emotional, value-based aspects of leadership influence can account for the exceptional achievements of groups and organizations. Leaders inspire followers to willingly sacrifice their selfish interests for a higher cause. For example, soldiers risk their lives to carry out an important mission or to protect their comrades. The relative importance of rational and emotional processes, and how they interact, are issues to be resolved by empirical research, and the conceptualization of leadership should not exclude either type of process.

Leadership vs. Management

There is a continuing controversy about the difference between leadership and management. It is obvious that a person can be a leader without being a manager (e.g., an informal leader), and a person can be a manager without leading. Indeed, some people with the job title "manager" do not have any subordinates (e.g., a manager of financial accounts). Nobody has proposed that managing and leading are equivalent, but the degree of overlap is a point of sharp disagreement.

Some writers (e.g., Bennis & Nanus, 1985; Zaleznik, 1977) contend that leadership and management are qualitatively different and mutually exclusive. The most extreme distinction involves the assumption that management and leadership cannot occur in the same person. In other words, some people are managers and other people are leaders. The definitions of leaders and managers assume they have incompatible values and different personalities. Managers value stability, order, and efficiency, whereas leaders value flexibility, innovation, and adaptation. Managers are concerned about how things get done, and they try to get people to perform better. Leaders are concerned with what things mean to people, and they try to get people to agree about the most important things to be done. Bennis and Nanus (1985, p. 21) proposed that "managers are people who do things right and leaders are people who do the right thing." However, associating leading and managing with different types of people is not supported by empirical research; people do not sort neatly into these two extreme stereotypes. Moreover, the stereotypes imply that most managers are ineffective. The term *manager* is an occupational title for a large number of people, and it is insensitive to denigrate them with a negative stereotype.

Other scholars (e.g., Bass, 1990; Hickman, 1990; Kotter, 1988; Mintzberg, 1973; Rost, 1991) view leading and managing as distinct processes, but they do not assume that leaders and managers are different types of people. How the two processes are defined varies somewhat, depending on the scholar. For example, Mintzberg (1973) described leadership as one of 10 managerial roles (see Chapter 2). Leadership includes motivating subordinates and creating favorable conditions for doing the work. The other nine roles (e.g., resource allocator, negotiator) involve distinct managing responsibilities, but leadership is viewed as an essential managerial role that pervades the other roles.

Kotter (1990) differentiated between management and leadership in terms of their core processes and intended outcomes. Management seeks to produce predictability and order by (1) setting operational goals, establishing action plans with timetables, and allocating resources; (2) organizing and staffing (establishing structure, assigning people to jobs); and (3) monitoring results and solving problems. Leadership seeks to produce organizational change by (1) developing a vision of the future and strategies for making necessary changes, (2) communicating and explaining the vision, and (3) motivating and inspiring people to attain the vision. According to Kotter, management and leadership both involve deciding what needs to be done, creating networks of relationships to do it, and trying to ensure it happens. However, the two processes have some incompatible elements; strong leadership can disrupt order and efficiency, and strong management can discourage risk taking and innovation. Both processes are necessary for the success of an organization. Strong management alone can create a bureaucracy without purpose, but strong leadership alone can create change that is impractical. The relative importance of the two processes and the best way to integrate them depends on the situation at the time.

Rost (1991) defined management as an authority relationship that exists between a manager and subordinates to produce and sell goods and services. He defined leadership as a multidirectional influence relationship between a leader and followers with the mutual purpose of accomplishing real change. Leaders and followers influence each other as they interact in noncoercive ways to decide what changes they want to make. Managers may be leaders, but only if they have this type of influence relationship. Rost proposed that leading was not necessary for a manager to be effective in producing and selling goods and services. However, even when authority is a sufficient basis for downward influence over subordinates, a leadership relationship seems necessary for influencing people over whom the leader has no authority (e.g., peers). In organizations where change is unavoidable, which today is most organizations, a leadership relationship with subordinates also seems necessary.

Defining managing and leading as distinct roles, processes, or relationships may obscure more than it reveals if it encourages simplistic theories about effective leadership. Most scholars seem to agree that success as a manager or administrator in modern organizations necessarily involves leading. How to integrate the two processes has emerged as a complex and important issue in the organizational literature (Yukl & Lepsinger, 2004). The answer will not come from debates about ideal definitions. Questions about what to include in the domain of essential leadership processes should be explored in empirical research, not predetermined by subjective judgments.

Direct vs. Indirect Leadership

Most definitions of leadership and theories about effective leadership focus on behaviors used to directly influence followers. Most theories and empirical studies deal with direct influence on immediate subordinates, but a middle manager can also directly influence lower-level employees, peers, bosses, or outsiders such as clients and customers. Some theorists make a distinction between direct and indirect leadership (Hunt, 1991; Lord & Mahar, 1991; Yammarino, 1994; Yukl & Lepsinger, 2004). Indirect leadership can take different forms, and some of them provide an opportunity to have a stronger, more lasting influence than is possible with direct leadership.

When the direct influence of a chief executive officer is transmitted down the authority hierarchy of an organization (e.g., from CEO to middle managers to lower-level managers, to regular employees), this "cascading" of effects can be viewed as an example of indirect leadership by the CEO (Bass, Waldman, Avolio, & Bebb, 1987; Waldman & Yammarino, 1999; Yammarino, 1994). It is different from directly influencing lower-level employees by meeting with them, presenting speeches to them on television, sending messages on e-mail, or participating in activities involving them (e.g., attending orientation or training sessions). Direct and indirect types of leadership are not mutually exclusive, and they can be used together in a consistent way to magnify their effects.

Another form of indirect leadership involves influence over formal programs, management systems, and structural forms (Hunt, 1991; Lord & Maher, 1991; Yukl & Lepsinger, 2004). Many large organizations have programs or management systems intended to improve staffing and human resource planning, training and development, compensation and benefits, safety, recognition and rewards, process and quality improvement, quality of worklife, learning and innovation, knowledge management, and employee empowerment. A variety of formal arrangements are used to facilitate control, coordination, innovation, efficiency, growth, and diversification. Examples include specialized subunits, decentralized subunits, standardization of subunits or facilities, formalization (rules and standard procedures), cross-functional teams, self-managed teams, partnering with suppliers, strategic alliances, and acquisitions. In most organizations only top executives have sufficient authority to implement new programs, change the structural forms, or negotiate formal relationships with another organization (see Chapter 12). Here again, the effects of indirect leadership are stronger when supported by consistent forms of direct leadership by managers at all levels. For example, a program to encourage cost reduction is more likely to be successful if top management explains why it is necessary and sets an example through their behavior.

A third form of indirect leadership involves leader influence over the organization culture, which is defined as the shared beliefs and values of members (Trice & Beyer, 1991; Schein, 1992). Leaders may attempt either to strengthen existing cultural beliefs and values or to change them. There are many ways to influence culture, and they may involve direct influence (e.g., communicating a compelling vision or leading by example) or other forms of indirect influence, such as changing the organization structure or reward systems (see Chapter 10).

A Working Definition of Key Terms

It is neither feasible nor desirable at this point in the development of the discipline to attempt to resolve the controversies over the appropriate definition of leadership. Like all constructs in social science, the definition of leadership is arbitrary and subjective. Some definitions are more useful than others, but there is no single "correct" definition that captures the essence of leadership. For the time being, it is better to use the various conceptions of leadership as a source of different perspectives on a complex, multifaceted phenomenon.

In research, the operational definition of leadership depends to a great extent on the purpose of the researcher (Campbell, 1977). The purpose may be to identify leaders, to determine how they are selected, to discover what they do, to discover why they are effective, or to determine whether they are necessary. As Karmel (1978, p. 476) notes, "It is consequently very difficult to settle on a single definition of leadership that is general enough to accommodate these many meanings and specific enough to serve as an operationalization of the variable." Whenever feasible, leadership research should be designed to provide information relevant to the entire range of definitions, so that over time it will be possible to compare the utility of different conceptions and arrive at some consensus on the matter.

In this book, leadership is defined broadly in a way that takes into account several things that determine the success of a collective effort by members of a group or organization to accomplish meaningful tasks. The following definition is used:

> Leadership is the process of influencing others to understand and agree about what needs to be done and how to do it, and the process of facilitating individual and collective efforts to accomplish shared objectives.

The definition includes efforts not only to influence and facilitate the current work of the group or organization, but also to ensure that it is prepared to meet future challenges. Both direct and indirect influences are included. Table 1-2 shows the wide variety of ways leaders can influence the effectiveness of a group or organization.

In this book, leadership is treated as both a specialized role and a social influence process. More than one individual can perform the role (i.e., leadership can be shared or distributed), but some role differentiation is assumed to occur in any group or organization. Both rational and emotional processes are viewed as essential aspects of leadership. No assumptions are made about the actual outcome of the influence processes, because the evaluation of outcomes is difficult and subjective. Thus, the definition of leadership is *not* limited to processes that necessarily result in "successful" outcomes. How leadership processes affect outcomes is a central research question that should not be biased by the definition of leadership. The focus is clearly on the process, not the person, and they are not assumed to be equivalent. Thus, the terms *leader, manager*, and *boss* are used interchangeably in this book to indicate people who occupy positions in

TABLE 1-2 What Leaders Can Influence
• The interpretation of external events by members
• The choice of objectives and strategies to pursue
• The motivation of members to achieve the objectives
• The mutual trust and cooperation of members
• The organization and coordination of work activities
• The allocation of resources to activities and objectives
• The development of member skills and confidence
• The learning and sharing of new knowledge by members
• The enlistment of support and cooperation from outsiders
• The design of formal structure, programs, and systems
• The shared beliefs and values of members

which they are expected to perform the leadership role, but without any assumptions about their actual behavior or success.

The terms *subordinate* and *direct report* are used interchangeably to denote someone whose primary work activities are directed and evaluated by the focal leader. Some writers use the term *staff* as a substitute for subordinate, but this practice creates unnecessary confusion. *Staff* connotes a special type of advisory position, and most subordinates are not staff advisors. Moreover, the term *staff* is used both as a singular and plural noun, which creates a lot of unnecessary confusion. The term *associate* has become popular in business organizations as another substitute for subordinate, because it conveys a relationship in which employees are valued and supposedly empowered. However, *associate* is a vague term that fails to differentiate between a direct authority relationship and other types of formal relationships (e.g., peers, partners). To clarify communication, this text continues to use the term *subordinate* to denote the existence of a formal authority relationship.

The term *follower* is used to describe a person who acknowledges the focal leader as the primary source of guidance about the work, regardless of how much formal authority the leader actually has over the person. Unlike the term *subordinate*, the term *follower* does not preclude leadership processes that can occur even in the absence of a formal authority relationship. Followers may include people who are not direct reports (e.g., coworkers, team members, partners, outsiders). However, the term *follower* is not used to describe members of an organization who completely reject their formal leader and seek to remove the person from office; such people are more appropriately called "rebels" or "insurgents."

Leadership Effectiveness

Like definitions of leadership, conceptions of leader effectiveness differ from one writer to another. The criteria selected to evaluate leadership effectiveness reflect a researcher's explicit or implicit conception of leadership. Most researchers evaluate leadership effectiveness in terms of the consequences of the leader's actions for followers and other organization stakeholders. Many different types of outcomes have been used, including the performance and growth of the leader's group or organization, its preparedness to deal with challenges or crises, follower satisfaction with the leader, follower commitment to the group objectives, the psychological well-being and development of followers, the leader's retention of high status in the group, and the leader's advancement to higher positions of authority in the organization.

The most commonly used measure of leader effectiveness is the extent to which the leader's organizational unit performs its task successfully and attains its goals. Examples of objective measures of performance or goal attainment include net profits, profit margin, sales increase, market share, return on investment, return on assets, productivity, cost per unit of output, and costs in relation to budgeted expenditures. Subjective measures include ratings of effectiveness obtained from the leader's superiors, peers, or subordinates.

The attitude of followers toward the leader is another common indicator of leader effectiveness. How well does the leader satisfy their needs and expectations? Do followers like, respect, and admire the leader? Are followers strongly committed to carrying out the leader's requests, or will they resist, ignore, or subvert them? Follower attitudes are usually measured with questionnaires or interviews. Such aspects of follower behavior also provide an indirect indicator of dissatisfaction and hostility toward the leader. Examples of such indicators include absenteeism, voluntary turnover, grievances, complaints to higher management, requests for transfer, work slowdowns, and deliberate sabotage of equipment and facilities.

Leader effectiveness is occasionally measured in terms of the leader's contribution to the quality of group processes, as perceived by followers or by outside observers. Does the leader enhance group cohesiveness, member cooperation, member motivation, problem solving, decision making, and resolution of conflict among members? Does the leader contribute to the efficiency of role specialization, the organization of activities, the accumulation of resources, and the readiness of the group to deal with change and crises? Does the leader improve the quality of work life, build the self-confidence of followers, increase their skills, and contribute to their psychological growth and development?

It is difficult to evaluate the effectiveness of a leader when there are so many alternative measures of effectiveness, and it is not clear which measure is most relevant. Some researchers attempt to combine several measures into a single, composite criterion, but this approach requires subjective judgments about how to assign a weight to each measure. Multiple criteria are especially troublesome when they are negatively correlated. A negative correlation means that trade-offs occur among criteria, such that as one increases, others decrease. For example, growth in sales and market share (e.g., by reducing price and increasing advertising) is sometimes achieved at the cost of lower profits. An increase in production output (e.g., by inducing people to work faster) is sometimes achieved at the cost of lower product quality. Rapid growth is sometimes achieved (e.g., by financing expansion with excessive debt) at the cost of a weaker financial condition that may result in bankruptcy if economic conditions suddenly worsen. Efficiency may be increased (e.g., by using more specialization) at the expense of flexibility.

Immediate and Delayed Outcomes

Some outcomes are more immediate than others. For example, the immediate result of an influence attempt may be that a follower is willing to do what the leader

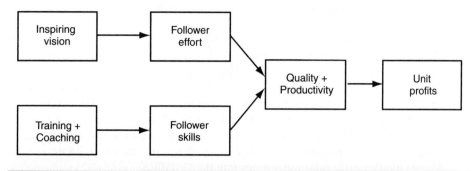

FIGURE 1-1   Causal Chain of Effects from Two Types of Leader Behavior

asks. A more delayed effect of leadership is how well followers actually perform the assignment. The effects of a leader can be viewed as a causal chain of variables, with each "intervening variable" mediating the effects of the preceding one on the next one. An example is provided in Figure 1-1. The farther along in the causal chain, the longer it takes for the effect to occur. For criteria at the end of the causal chain, there is a considerable delay (months or years) before the effects of the leader's actions are evident. Moreover, these end-result criteria are more likely to be influenced by extraneous events (e.g., the economy, market conditions). When the delay is long and there is considerable "contamination" by extraneous events, the end-result criteria are less useful than more immediate outcomes as an indicator of an individual leader's effectiveness.

In many cases a leader has both immediate and delayed effects on the same criterion. The two types of effects may be consistent or inconsistent. When they are inconsistent, the immediate outcome may be very different from the delayed outcomes. For example, profits may be increased in the short run by eliminating costly activities that have a delayed effect on profits, such as equipment maintenance, research and development, investments in new technology, and employee skill training. In the long run, the net effect of cutting these essential activities is likely to be lower profits because the negative consequences slowly increase and eventually outweigh any benefits. The converse is also true. Increased investment in these activities is likely to reduce immediate profits but increase long-term profits.

What Criteria to Use?

There is no simple answer to the question of how to evaluate leadership effectiveness. The selection of appropriate criteria depends on the objectives and values of the person making the evaluation, and people have different values. For example, top management may prefer different criteria than other employees, customers, or shareholders. To cope with the problems of incompatible criteria, delayed effects, and the preferences of different stakeholders, it is usually best to include a variety of criteria in research on leadership effectiveness and to examine the impact of the leader on each criterion over an extended period of time. Multiple conceptions of effectiveness, like multiple conceptions of leadership, serve to broaden our perspective and enlarge the scope of inquiry.

Overview of Major Research Approaches

The attraction of leadership as a subject of research and the many different conceptions of leadership have created a vast and bewildering literature. Attempts to organize the literature according to major approaches or perspectives show only partial success. One of the more useful ways to classify leadership theory and research is according to the type of variable that is emphasized the most. Three types of variables that are relevant for understanding leadership effectiveness include (1) characteristics of leaders, (2) characteristics of followers, and (3) characteristics of the situation. Examples of key variables within each category are shown in Table 1-3. Figure 1-2 depicts likely causal relationships among the variables.

Most leadership theories emphasize one category more than the others as the primary basis for explaining effective leadership. Most theories developed over the past half-century emphasize leader characteristics and it has been common practice to limit the focus to one type of leader characteristic, namely traits, behavior, or power. Therefore, it is helpful to classify the theories and empirical research into the following five approaches: (1) the trait approach, (2) the behavior approach, (3) the power-influence approach, (4) the situational approach, and (5) the integrative approach. Each approach is described briefly in the following sections.

TABLE 1-3   Key Variables in Leadership Theories

Characteristics of the Leader
- Traits (motives, personality, values)
- Confidence and optimism
- Skills and expertise
- Behavior
- Integrity and ethics
- Influence tactics
- Attributions about followers

Characteristics of the Followers
- Traits (needs, values, self-concepts)
- Confidence and optimism
- Skills and expertise
- Attributions about the leader
- Trust in the leader
- Task commitment and effort
- Satisfaction with job and leader

Characteristics of the Situation
- Type of organizational unit
- Size of unit
- Position power and authority of leader
- Task structure and complexity
- Task interdependence
- Environmental uncertainty
- External dependencies

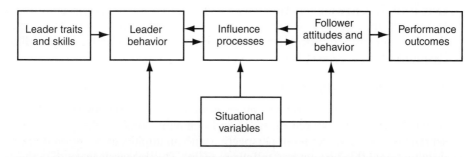

FIGURE 1-2   Causal Relationships Among the Primary Types of Leadership Processes

Trait Approach

One of the earliest approaches for studying leadership was the trait approach. This approach emphasizes leaders' attributes such as personality, motives, values, and skills. Underlying this approach was the assumption that some people are natural leaders, endowed with certain traits not possessed by other people. Early leadership theories attributed managerial success to extraordinary abilities such as tireless energy, penetrating intuition, uncanny foresight, and irresistible persuasive powers. Hundreds of trait studies conducted during the 1930s and 1940s sought to discover these elusive qualities, but this massive research effort failed to find any traits that would guarantee leadership success. One reason for the failure was a lack of attention to intervening variables in the causal chain that could explain how traits could affect a delayed outcome such as group performance or leader advancement. The predominant research method was to look for a significant correlation between individual leader attributes and a criterion of leader success, without examining any explanatory processes. However, as evidence from better designed research slowly accumulated over the years, researchers made progress in discovering how leader attributes are related to leadership behavior and effectiveness.

Behavior Approach

The behavior approach began in the early 1950s after many researchers became discouraged with the trait approach and began to pay closer attention to what managers actually do on the job. The behavior research falls into two general subcategories.

One line of research examines how managers spend their time and the typical pattern of activities, responsibilities, and functions for managerial jobs. Some of the research also investigates how managers cope with demands, constraints, and role conflicts in their jobs. Most research on managerial work uses descriptive methods of data collection such as direct observation, diaries, job description questionnaires, and anecdotes obtained from interviews. Although this research was not designed to directly assess effective leadership, it provides useful insights into this subject. Leadership effectiveness depends in part on how well a manager resolves role conflicts, copes with demands, recognizes opportunities, and overcomes constraints.

Another subcategory of the behavior approach focuses on identifying effective leadership behavior. The preferred research method involves a survey field study with a behavior description questionnaire. In the past 50 years, hundreds of survey studies examined the correlation between leadership behavior and various indicators of leadership effectiveness. A much smaller number of studies used laboratory experiments, field experiments, or critical incidents to determine how effective leaders differ in behavior from ineffective leaders.

Power-Influence Approach

Power-influence research examines influence processes between leaders and other people. Like most research on traits and behavior, some of the power-influence research takes a leader-centered perspective with an implicit assumption that causality is unidirectional (leaders act and followers react). This research seeks to explain leadership effectiveness in terms of the amount and type of power possessed by a leader and how power is exercised. Power is viewed as important not only for influencing subordinates, but also for influencing peers, superiors, and people outside the organization, such as clients and suppliers. The favorite methodology has been the use of survey questionnaires to relate leader power to various measures of leadership effectiveness.

Other power-influence research has used questionnaires and descriptive incidents to determine how leaders influence the attitudes and behavior of followers. The study of influence tactics can be viewed as a bridge linking the power-influence approach and the behavior approach. The use of different influence tactics is compared in terms of their relative effectiveness for getting people to do what the leader wants.

Participative leadership is concerned with power sharing and empowerment of followers, but it is firmly rooted in the tradition of behavior research as well. Many studies have used questionnaires to correlate subordinate perceptions of participative leadership with criteria of leadership effectiveness such as subordinate satisfaction, effort, and performance. Laboratory and field experiments compared autocratic and participative leadership styles. Finally, descriptive case studies of effective managers examined how they use consultation and delegation to give people a sense of ownership for decisions.

Situational Approach

The situational approach emphasizes the importance of contextual factors that influence leadership processes. Major situational variables include the characteristics of followers, the nature of the work performed by the leader's unit, the type of organization, and the nature of the external environment. This approach has two major subcategories. One line of research is an attempt to discover the extent to which leadership processes are the same or unique across different types of organizations, levels of management, and cultures. The primary research method is a comparative study of two or more situations. The dependent variables may be managerial perceptions and attitudes, managerial activities and behavior patterns, or influence processes.

The other subcategory of situational research attempts to identify aspects of the situation that "moderate" the relationship of leader attributes (e.g., traits, skills, behavior) to leadership effectiveness. The assumption is that different attributes will be effective in different situations, and that the same attribute is not optimal in all situations. Theories describing this relationship are sometimes called contingency theories of leadership. A more extreme form of situational theory (leadership substitute) identifies the conditions that can make hierarchical leadership redundant and unnecessary (see Chapter 8).

Integrative Approach

An integrative approach involves more than one type of leadership variable. In recent years it has become more common for researchers to include two or more types of leadership variables in the same study, but it is still rare to find a theory that includes all of them (i.e., traits, behavior, influence processes, situational variables, and outcomes). A good example of the integrative approach is the self-concept theory of charismatic leadership (see Chapter 9), which attempts to explain why the followers of some leaders are willing to exert exceptional effort and make personal sacrifices to accomplish the group objective or mission.

Level of Conceptualization for Leadership

Leadership can be conceptualized as (1) an intra-individual process, (2) a dyadic process, (3) a group process, or (4) an organizational process. The levels can be viewed as a hierarchy, as depicted in Figure 1-3. Most leadership theories are focused on processes at only one of these levels, because it is difficult to develop a multilevel theory that is also parsimonious and easy to apply. What level is emphasized will determine the type of criterion variables used to evaluate leadership and the type of mediating processes used to explain effective leadership. Level of conceptualization also has implications for the methods of analysis used in research on a theory (see Chapter 15).

Intra-Individual Processes

Leadership theories that focus on processes within a single individual are rare, because most definitions of leadership involve influence processes between individuals. Nevertheless, a number of researchers used psychological theories of decision making, motivation, and cognition to explain the behavior of an individual leader. This approach can be found in some of the theories about cognitive decision processes within

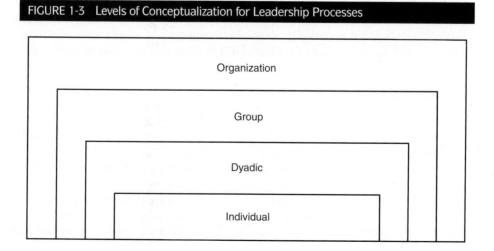

FIGURE 1-3   Levels of Conceptualization for Leadership Processes

Organization

Group

Dyadic

Individual

leaders (see Chapter 2) and in the description of leader traits and skills associated with motivation to become a leader (see Chapter 7). Another example, self-management theory, describes how a person can become more effective as a leader or follower (see Chapter 5). Self-management (sometimes called self-leadership) involves identifying personal objectives and priorities, managing one's time efficiently, monitoring one's own behavior and its consequences, and trying to learn to be more effective in accomplishing personal objectives.

Knowledge of intra-individual processes provides some insights that are helpful for developing better leadership theory. However, the potential contribution of the intra-individual approach to leadership is limited, because it does not include what most theorists consider to be the essential process of leadership, namely influence over others.

Dyadic Processes

The dyadic approach focuses on the relationship between a leader and another individual who is usually a follower. Most dyadic theories view leadership as a reciprocal influence process between the leader and another person. This approach makes an implicit assumption that leadership effectiveness cannot be understood without examining how leader and follower influence each other over time. Key questions are how to develop a cooperative, trusting relationship with a follower, and how to influence a follower to be more motivated and committed. An example is the leader-member exchange theory described in Chapter 5. The theory describes how dyadic relationships evolve over time and take different forms, ranging from a casual exchange to a cooperative alliance with shared objectives and mutual trust. Although the theory recognizes that the leader has multiple dyadic relationships, the focus is clearly on what happens within a single relationship. Much of the research on power and influence tactics (Chapter 6) is also conceptualized in terms of dyadic processes.

Most theories of leadership effectiveness reviewed in Chapters 8 and 9 are conceptualized primarily at the dyadic level. These theories usually acknowledge that group and organizational processes are involved in leadership, but they do not explicitly describe these processes. The research on dyadic processes provides important insights about leadership, but it often underestimates the importance of the context in which a dyadic relationship occurs. For example, developing a cooperative relationship with one subordinate may be dysfunctional if it is done in a way that undermines relationships with other subordinates.

Group Processes

Another perspective on leadership is to view it as a group process. Two key topics include the nature of the leadership role in a task group, and how a leader contributes to group effectiveness. Theories of group effectiveness provide important insights about leadership processes and relevant criteria for evaluating leadership effectiveness. Extensive research on small groups and teams identifies important determinants of effectiveness such as how well the work is organized to utilize personnel and resource, how committed members are to performing their work roles, how confident members are that the task can be accomplished successfully ("potency"), and the extent to which members trust each other and cooperate in accomplishing task objectives. Behavioral theories describing leadership processes in various types of groups and teams are discussed in Chapter 11. Leadership in executive teams is discussed in Chapter 12.

Meetings are a special context for the study of leadership as a group process. Much of a manager's time is spent in formal and informal meetings with people to solve problems and make decisions. The key question for leadership theory and research is what leadership processes make group meetings more effective. This question has been the subject of research by behavioral scientists during the past five decades, and it is described in Chapter 11.

Another key question in the group approach is to explain emergent leadership in formal and informal groups. Why are some members more influential than others, what determines who will be chosen as a leader, and why do some leaders lose the trust and confidence of followers? An example of a theory dealing with these questions is the social exchange theory discussed in Chapter 6.

Organizational Processes

The groups approach provides a better understanding of leadership effectiveness than dyadic or intra-individual approaches, but it has some important limitations. A group usually exists in a larger social system, and its effectiveness cannot be understood if the focus of the research is limited to the group's internal processes. The organizational level of analysis describes leadership as a process that occurs in a larger open system in which groups are subsystems (Fleishman et al., 1991; Katz & Kahn, 1978; Mumford, 1986).

The survival and prosperity of an organization depends on adaptation to the environment and the acquisition of necessary resources. A business organization must be able to market its products and services successfully. Adaptation is improved by anticipating consumer needs and desires, assessing the actions and plans of competitors, evaluating likely constraints and threats (e.g., government regulation, input scarcity, hostile actions by enemies), and identifying marketable products and services that the organization has unique capabilities to provide. Some examples of activities relevant for adaptation include gathering and interpreting information about the environment, identifying threats and opportunities, developing an effective strategy for adapting to the environment, negotiating agreements that are favorable to the organization, influencing outsiders to have a favorable impression of the organization and its products, and gaining cooperation and support from outsiders upon whom the organization is dependent. These activities are aspects of strategic leadership.

Survival and prosperity also depend on the efficiency of the transformation process used by the organization to produce its products and services. Efficiency is increased by finding more rational ways to organize and perform the work, and by deciding how to make the best use of available technology, resources, and personnel. Some examples of leadership responsibilities include designing an appropriate organization structure, determining authority relationships, and coordinating operations across specialized subunits of the organization. Strategic leadership in organizations is described in Chapters 10 and 12.

Other Bases for Comparing Leadership Theories

Key variables and level of conceptualization are not the only ways to compare leadership theories. This section briefly describes three other types of distinctions commonly used in the leadership literature: (1) leader-centered versus follower-centered, (2) descriptive versus prescriptive, and (3) universal versus contingency. Each type of distinction is better viewed as a continuum along which a theory can be located, rather than as a sharp dichotomy. For example, it is possible for a theory to have some descriptive elements as well as some prescriptive elements, some universal elements as well as some contingency elements, and an equal focus on leaders and followers.

Leader- vs. Follower-Centered Theory

The extent to which a theory is focused on either the leader or followers is another useful ways to classify leadership theories. Most leadership theories emphasize the characteristics and actions of the leader without much concern for follower characteristics. The leader focus is strongest in theory and research that identifies traits, skills, or behaviors that contribute to leader effectiveness. Most of the contingency theories (in Chapter 8) also emphasize leader characteristics more than follower characteristics.

Only a small amount of research and theory emphasizes characteristics of the followers. Empowerment theory describes how followers view their ability to influence important events (see Chapter 4). Attribution theory describes how followers view a leader's influence on events and outcomes (see Chapter 5). Some other theories in the same chapter explain how followers can actively influence their work role and relationship with the leader, rather than being passive recipients of leader influence. The leader substitutes theory (see Chapter 8) describes aspects of the situation and follower attributes that make a hierarchical leader less important. The emotional contagion theory of charisma (see Chapter 9) describes how followers influence each other. Finally, theories of self-managed groups emphasize sharing of leadership functions among the members of a group and between an internal coordinator and an external facilitator (see Chapter 11).

Theories that focus almost exclusively on either the leader or the follower are less useful than theories that offer a more balanced explanation. For example, some of the theories in Chapters 8 and 9 include both leader and follower characteristics as important determinants of effective leadership. Most theories of leader power (Chapter 6) emphasize that influence over followers depends on follower perceptions of the leader as well as on objective conditions and the leader's influence behavior.

Descriptive vs. Prescriptive Theory

Another important distinction among leadership theories is the extent to which they are descriptive or prescriptive. Descriptive theories explain leadership processes, describe the typical activities of leaders, and explain why certain behaviors occur in particular situations. Prescriptive theories specify what leaders must do to become effective, and they identify any necessary conditions for using a particular type of behavior effectively.

The two perspectives are not mutually exclusive, and a theory can have both types of elements. For example, a theory that explains why a particular pattern of behavior is typical for leaders (descriptive) may also explain which aspects of behavior are most effective (prescriptive). The two perspectives are not always consistent. For example, the typical pattern of behavior for leaders may or may not be the optimal one. A prescriptive theory is especially useful when a wide discrepancy exists between what leaders typically do and what they should do to be optimally effective.

Universal vs. Contingency Theory

A universal theory describes some aspect of leadership that applies to all types of situations. A universal theory can be either descriptive or prescriptive. A descriptive universal theory may describe typical functions performed to some extent by all types of leader, whereas a prescriptive universal theory may specify functions all leaders must perform to be effective.

A contingency theory describes an aspect of leadership that applies to some situations but not to others. Contingency theories can also be either descriptive or prescriptive. A descriptive contingency theory may explain how leader behavior typically varies from one situation to another, whereas a prescriptive contingency theory may specify the most effective behavior in each type of situation.

The distinction between universal and contingency theories is a matter of degree, not a sharp dichotomy. Some theories fall in between the two extremes. For example, a prescriptive theory may specify that a particular type of leadership (e.g., transformational leadership in Chapter 9) is always effective, but also acknowledge that it is not as effective in some situations as in others.

Organization of the Book

The diversity and complexity of the relevant literature make it difficult to organize a survey book on leadership. No single way of classifying the literature captures all of the important distinctions. Table 1-4 summarizes how these distinctions were used to organize topics into chapters.

TABLE 1-4 Organization of the Book		
Basis for Organization	*Primary Chapter Location*	*Secondary Chapter Location*
Line of Research		
• Leader traits/skills	7	8, 9, 12, 13
• Leader behavior	2, 3	4, 5, 8, 9, 10, 11, 12
• Power/influence	6	4, 8, 9, 10, 12
• Situational	2, 8	6, 9, 12, 14
• Integrative	9, 15	12
Level of Conceptualization		
• Individual	7	2, 4, 5, 12
• Dyadic	5	6, 8, 9
• Group	11	4, 6, 8, 9, 12
• Organization	10, 12	2, 9

The primary basis for organizing chapters is according to type of leadership variable studied. The behavior approach is reviewed first (Chapters 2 and 3), then the power-influence approach (Chapter 6), the trait approach (Chapter 7), and the situational approach (Chapters 2 and 8). Even though the trait approach began before the behavior approach, it is covered later because traits are difficult to understand unless they are linked to behavior and influence processes.

Important lines of research that cut across the primary variables are treated in separate chapters whenever possible. Participative leadership, which involves both the behavior and power-influence approaches, is covered in Chapter 4. The major theories of charismatic and transformational leadership are usually classified as "integrative" because they involve more than one approach, and these theories are covered in Chapter 9.

Level of analysis is used as a secondary basis for organizing the material. Dyadic leadership and follower-based approaches are described in Chapter 5. Group-based approaches are covered in Chapter 11, and organizational approaches are described in Chapters 10 and 12. The transformational and charismatic theories in Chapter 9 are primarily dyadic, but they are sometimes extended to include some group-level and organization-level elements as well. Developing leadership skills is a distinct topic that cuts across levels of analysis, and it is discussed in Chapter 13. Chapter 14 deals with some special issues that apply across approaches, including ethical leadership, gender and leadership, cross-cultural differences in leadership, and management of diversity. Chapter 15 provides an overview that includes a summary of major findings about effective leadership, a critique of conceptual and methodological limitations, and emergent themes about the essence of leadership.

Summary

Leadership has been defined in many different ways, but most definitions share the assumption that it involves an influence process concerned with facilitating the performance of a collective task. Otherwise, the definitions differ in many respects, such as who exerts the influence, the intended beneficiary of the influence, the manner in which the influence is exerted, and the outcome of the influence attempt. Some theorists advocate treating leading and managing as separate roles or processes, but the proposed definitions do not resolve important questions about the scope of each process and how they are interrelated. No single, "correct" definition of leadership covers all situations; what matters is how useful the definition is for increasing our understanding of effective leadership.

Most researchers evaluate leadership effectiveness in terms of the consequences for followers and other organization stakeholders, but the choice of outcome variables has differed considerably from researcher to researcher. Criteria differ in many important respects, including how immediate they are, and whether they have subjective or objective measures. When evaluating leadership effectiveness, multiple criteria should be considered to deal with these complexities and the different preferences of various stakeholders.

Leadership has been studied in different ways, depending on the researcher's methodological preferences and definition of leadership. Most researchers deal only with a narrow aspect of leadership, and most empirical studies fall into distinct lines of research such as the trait, behavior, power, and situational approaches. In recent years there has been an increased effort to cut across and integrate these approaches. The best example is some of the research on charismatic leadership.

Level of analysis is another basis for classifying leadership theory and research. The levels include intra-individual, dyadic, group, and organizational. Each level provides some unique insights, but more research is needed on group and organizational processes, and more integration across levels is needed.

Another basis for differentiating theories is the relative focus on leader or follower. For many years the research focused on leader characteristics, and followers were studied only as the object of leader influence. A more balanced approach is needed, and some progress is being made in that direction.

Leadership theories can be classified as prescriptive versus descriptive, according to the emphasis on "what should be" rather than on "what occurs now." A final basis for differentiation (universal versus contingency) is the extent to which a theory describes leadership processes and relationships that are essentially the same in all situations rather than ones that vary in specified ways across situations.

Review and Discussion Questions

1. What are some similarities and differences in the way leadership has been defined?
2. Does it really matter how you define leadership? Explain and defend the position you take on this question.
3. What are the arguments for and against making a distinction between leaders and managers?
4. Why is it so difficult to measure leadership effectiveness?
5. What criteria have been used to evaluate leadership effectiveness? Are some criteria more useful than others?
6. What are the trait, behavior, and power-influence approaches? What unique insights does each approach provide about effective leadership?
7. Why does it matter whether leadership is described as an intra-individual, dyadic, group, or organizational process? Which level of analysis is emphasized in most leadership theory and research?
8. Compare descriptive and prescriptive theories of leadership. Explain why both types of theory are useful.
9. Compare universal and contingency theories. Is it possible to have a theory with both universal and contingent aspects?

Key Terms

- behavior approach
- contingency theories
- criteria of leadership effectiveness
- delayed effects
- descriptive theory
- dyadic processes
- follower-centered theory
- integrative approach
- intervening variable
- leader-centered theory
- level of conceptualization
- power-influence approach
- prescriptive theory
- shared influence process
- situational approach
- specialized leadership role
- trait approach
- universal theories

2

THE NATURE OF MANAGERIAL WORK

Learning Objectives

After studying this chapter you should be able to:

- Understand what methods have been used to study managerial work.

- Understand the typical activity patterns for people in managerial positions.

- Understand the different roles required for managers and how they are changing.

- Understand how managerial roles and activities are affected by aspects of the situation.

- Understand how managers cope with the demands, constraints, and choices confronting them.

- Understand the importance of external activities and networking for managers.

- Understand the limitations of descriptive research on managerial activities.

- Understand how managers can make effective use of their time.

Leadership is an important role requirement for managers and a major reason why managerial jobs exist. This chapter examines findings from research on the nature of managerial work. The research involves analysis of data from a variety of sources, including observation of managers, diaries in which managers describe their own activities, interviews with managers who explain what they do and why they do it, and job description questionnaires in which managers rate the importance of different types of managerial activities. One major purpose of this research has been to identify patterns of activity that are common to all types of managers. Another major purpose has been to compare activity patterns for different types of managers, or managers in different situations. These comparative studies examine the extent to which the behavior of a manager reflects the unique role requirements of the situation.

Typical Activity Patterns in Managerial Work

To discover what managers do and how they spend their time, researchers used descriptive methods such as direct observation, diaries, and interviews. The researcher attempted to find answers to questions such as how much time managers spend alone or interacting with different people (e.g., subordinates, peers, superiors, outsiders), how often managers use different forms of interaction (e.g., telephone, scheduled meetings, unscheduled meetings, written messages), where the interactions occur, how long they last, and who initiated them. Reviews of this research find some consistent activity patterns for most type of managerial positions (Hales, 1986; McCall, Morrison, & Hannan, 1978; Mintzberg, 1973). This section of the chapter reviews major findings about the nature of managerial work.

Pace of Work Is Hectic and Unrelenting

The typical manager works long hours, and many managers take work home. In part, this workload can be traced to the preferences of people in managerial positions. Having trained their minds to search for and analyze new information continually, most managers do this type of searching automatically and find it difficult to forget about their jobs when at home or on vacation. The typical manager's day seldom includes a break in the workload. Managers receive almost continuous requests for information, assistance, direction, and authorization from a large number of people, such as subordinates, peers, superiors, and people outside the organization. The research on managerial activities contradicts the popular conception of managers as people who carefully plan and orchestrate events, and then sit in their office waiting for the occasional exception to normal operations that may require their attention.

Content of Work Is Varied and Fragmented

Managers typically engage in a variety of activities each day, and many of them are brief in duration. Mintzberg's (1973, p. 33) observations of executives found that "half of the activities were completed in less than nine minutes, and only one-tenth took more than an hour." The activities of managers tend to be fragmented as well as varied. Interruptions occur frequently, conversations are disjointed, and important activities are interspersed with trivial ones, requiring rapid shifts of mood. A manager may go from a budget meeting to decide millions of dollars in spending to a discussion about how to fix a broken water fountain (Sayles, 1979).

Many Activities Are Reactive

The fragmented nature of managerial activity reflects the fact that many interactions are initiated by others, and much of a manager's behavior is reactive rather than proactive in nature. A common stereotype of managers is that they spend a considerable part of their time in careful analysis of business problems and development of elaborate plans to deal with them. However, the descriptive studies find that most managers devote little time to reflective planning. The fragmented activities and continual heavy demands characteristic of managerial work make it difficult for managers to find the long periods of uninterrupted time necessary for this type of activity. Reflective planning and other activities that require large blocks of time, such as team building and training subordinates in complex skills, are usually preempted by "fire fighting" activities involving immediate operational problems. What little time managers spend alone in the office is typically used to read correspondence, check e-mail messages, handle administrative paperwork, write reports or memos, send e-mail messages, and scan journals or technical publications. Most managers gravitate toward the active aspects of their jobs, and they tend to focus on specific, immediate problems rather than general issues or long-term strategies.

Problems occur in a mostly random order, and managers choose to react to some problems as they become aware of them, while others are ignored or postponed. There are more problems than a manager can handle at any given time, and only a few of them will get immediate attention. The importance of a problem is a major determinant of whether it will be recognized and handled, but it is often unclear how important a problem really is.

A manager is more likely to respond to a problem when there is pressure for immediate action due to a crisis, deadline, or expectations of progress by someone important, such as the manager's boss or an external client (McCall & Kaplan, 1985). In the absence of such pressure, a problem is more likely to get action when it is perceived to be similar to other problems that a manager has solved successfully in the past, when the problem is perceived to be clearly within the manager's domain of responsibility, and when the manager perceives that the actions and resources necessary to solve the problem are available. Managers are likely to ignore a problem or postpone dealing with a problem when there is no external pressure for action, it is fuzzy and difficult to diagnose, it is the primary responsibility of other managers or subunits, or it cannot be solved without additional resources and support that would be difficult or impossible to obtain.

Interactions Often Involve Peers and Outsiders

Although much of the leadership literature focuses on the relationship between leader and subordinates, the descriptive research has found that managers typically spend considerable time with persons other than direct subordinates or the manager's boss. These contacts may involve subordinates of subordinates, superiors of the boss, lateral peers, subordinates of lateral peers, and superiors of lateral peers. In addition, many managers spend considerable time with people outside the organization, such as customers, clients, suppliers, subcontractors, people in government agencies, important people in the community, and managers from other organizations. Kotter (1982) found that the network of relationships for general managers often consisted of hundreds of people inside and outside of their organization (see Figure 2-1).

The high incidence of lateral and external interactions can be explained in terms of a manager's need for information about complex and uncertain events that influence the operations of his or her organizational subunit, and the manager's dependence on the cooperation and assistance of numerous people outside the immediate chain of command (Kotter, 1982). A large network of contacts provides information about current events within or outside of the organization that may affect the manager's job performance and career. In addition, networks can be used to obtain assistance for solving problems or making changes. The ability to assemble a coalition of internal and external supporters is especially important to make innovative changes and ensure that they will be implemented successfully (Kanter, 1983). Managers use different parts of their network for different purposes and extend the network as needed to accomplish a particular objective (Kaplan, 1988).

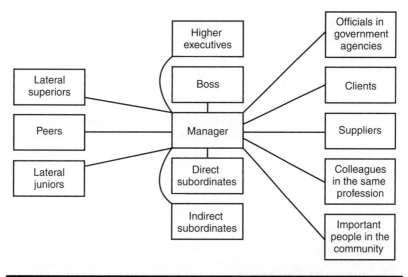

FIGURE 2-1   A Manager's Network of Contacts

Networks are developed in a variety of ways, such as (1) talking with people before, during, and after meetings, ceremonies, and social events in the organization; (2) serving on special committees, interest groups, and task forces; (3) joining civic groups, advisory boards, and social clubs; and (4) attending workshops, trade shows, and meetings of professional associations. Cooperative relationships are established and maintained by showing respect and positive regard, offering unconditional favors (e.g., passing on useful information, offering to help with a problem), keeping in touch, and showing appreciation for favors received, especially those requiring a significant effort on the part of the person doing it. The process of networking is a perpetual activity for managers. Old relationships need to be maintained and new ones established as people in key positions change, the organization changes, and the external environment changes.

Many Interactions Involve Oral Communication

Managers have six principal ways to obtain information: written messages (e.g., memos, letters, reports, work orders, contracts), telephone messages, electronic messages (e.g., e-mail, pagers), scheduled meetings, unscheduled meetings, and observational tours. Managers show a strong preference for the use of oral communication media such as the telephone and informal meetings. The early research on managerial activities found that lower and middle managers spent from 27 to 82 percent of their time engaged in oral communication, and the figure was 65 to 75 percent for higher-level managers. In recent years e-mail has become popular with managers for communication, but like written messages it has limitations. As more advanced forms of electronic communication become readily available (e.g., video conferencing, cell phones with video pictures of the other communicator), they will likely replace many face-to-face meetings.

The research shows that much of the oral communication by managers involves exchange of information and attempts to influence people. Managers tend to prefer current information to old information, and current information is usually obtained directly from people who have access to it, including many people outside the manager's organizational subunit. Informal gossip and rumors contain detailed information about recent events and new developments, whereas written reports usually summarize old information. Neustadt (1960, pp. 153–154) found a preference for recent, detailed information even among U.S. presidents:

> It is not information of a general sort that helps a President see personal stakes; not summaries, not surveys, not the bland amalgams. Rather . . . it is the odds and ends of tangible detail that pieced together in his mind illuminate the underside of issues put before him. To help himself, he must reach out as widely as he can for every scrap of fact, opinion, gossip, bearing on his interests and relationships as President.

Oral communication allows the effect of words to be magnified by the effect of intonation, gestures, and other nonverbal communication. Face-to-face interaction facilitates influence attempts and provides an opportunity to obtain immediate feedback about their effectiveness. This feedback can be used to modify and improve the manager's influence strategy and negotiating effectiveness. The descriptive research found that a manager's oral interactions tend to include a surprising amount of kidding, joking, and discussing of subjects unrelated to the work (e.g., sports, hobbies) or of trivial importance to it. This socializing activity and small talk probably helps managers to build and maintain effective relationships with the large network of people whose cooperation and support are needed.

Decision Processes Are Disorderly and Political

Much of the management literature describes decisions as discrete events made by a single manager or group in an orderly, rational manner. This picture is sharply contradicted by the descriptive research on managerial work and related research on managerial decision making (Cohen & March, 1974; McCall & Kaplan, 1985; Schweiger, Anderson, & Locke, 1985; Simon, 1987). Managers are seldom observed to make major decisions at a single point in time, and they are unable to recall when a decision was finally reached. Some major decisions are the result of many small actions or incremental choices taken without regard to larger strategic issues.

Decision processes are likely to be characterized more by confusion, disorder, and emotionality than by rationality. Instead of careful analysis of likely outcomes in relation to predetermined objectives, information is often distorted or suppressed to serve preconceptions about the best course of action or a self-serving interest in a particular choice. The emotional shock of discovering a serious problem and anxiety about choosing among unattractive alternatives may result in denial of negative evidence, wishful thinking, procrastination, vacillation between choices, and panic reactions by individual managers or by decision groups (Janis & Mann, 1977).

Important decisions in organizations typically require the support and authorization of many different people at different levels of management and in different subunits of the organization. It is common practice for a manager to consult with subordinates, peers, or superiors about important decisions. The person who initiates the decision process may not be the person who makes the final choice among action alternatives. For example, a section supervisor with a problem may point out the need for a decision to his or her boss, the department manager. The department manager may consult with the plant manager or with managers in other departments who would be affected by the decision. Even when not consulted in advance, the plant manager may review the department manager's decision and approve, reject, or modify it.

The different people involved in making a decision often disagree about the true nature of a problem and the likely outcomes of various solutions, due to the different perspectives, assumptions, and values typical of managers from different functional specialties and backgrounds. A prolonged, highly political decision process is likely when decisions involve important and complex problems for which no ready-made, good solutions are available, when many affected parties have conflicting interests, and when a diffusion of power exists among the parties. The decision process may drag on for months or years due to delays and interruptions as a proposal is sidetracked by opponents, preempted by immediate crises, or recycled back to its initiators for revisions necessary to make it suitable to managers whose support is needed (Mintzberg, Raisinghani, & Theoret, 1976). For decisions involving major changes in organizational strategies or policies, the outcome will depend to a great extent on the influence skills and persistence of the individual managers who desire to initiate change and on the relative power of the various coalitions involved in making or authorizing these decisions (Kanter, 1983; Kotter, 1982, 1985).

Not all decisions involve major changes or prolonged political processes. Managers make many less momentous decisions in the process of solving operational problems, setting short-term goals, assigning work to subordinates, setting up work schedules, authorizing the expenditure of funds for supplies or equipment, and approving pay increases. These decisions often involve problems for which low-risk solutions are available, the manager has the authority to make a decision, and pressure is felt for a quick decision due to a deadline or a crisis. Managers usually make this type of decision either alone or after briefly consulting with a few people, and only a short period of problem analysis and search for solutions is likely to occur (McCall & Kaplan, 1985). Although these decisions are less important, they require appropriate technical knowledge by the manager and the capacity to find a good balance between lengthy, systematic analysis and quick, decisive action. A rash analysis may result in a poor decision that fails to solve the problem or makes it worse. On the other hand, if a manager keeps delaying action to get more information about the problem, it may become worse and reflect poorly on the manager's ability to resolve problems.

Most Planning Is Informal and Adaptive

Planning is often described in the managerial literature primarily as a formal process of written objectives, strategies, policies, and budgets, cascading from top management down the hierarchy, with ever more detailed versions at each lower level of management. The descriptive studies find that some planning occurs, but it is often informal and implicit. Kotter (1982) found that general managers develop agendas consisting of goals and plans related to their job responsibilities and involving a variety of short-term and long-term issues. The short-term (1–30 days) objectives and plans are usually quite specific and detailed, but the longer-term (5–20 years) agenda items are usually vague, incomplete, and only loosely connected. A new manager begins the process of developing this agenda immediately, but initially it is likely to be rough and incomplete. Over time, as managers gather more information about their organization or subunit (e.g., operations, people, politics, markets, competitors, problems, and concerns), the agendas are refined and expanded (Gabarro, 1985; Kotter, 1982).

Kotter found that the implementation of agenda items is also a gradual, continuous process. Managers use a variety of influence techniques during their daily interactions with other people to mobilize support and shape events. The agenda guides the manager in making efficient use of random encounters and brief interactions with relevant people in the manager's network of contacts.

In his study of top executives, Quinn (1980) found that most of the important strategic decisions were made outside the formal planning process, and strategies were formulated in an incremental, flexible, and intuitive manner. In response to major unforeseen events, the executives developed tentative, broad strategies that allowed them to keep their options open until they had more opportunity to learn from experience about the nature of the environment and the feasibility of their initial actions. Strategies were refined and implemented simultaneously in a cautious, incremental manner that reflected the need to develop a political coalition in support of a strategy as well as to avoid the risks of an initial, irreversible commitment to a particular course of action. Instead of a top-down, formal process, overall objectives and strategies for the firms were more likely to be the result of a bottom up political process in which the objectives and strategies of powerful individuals and organizational subunits are reconciled and integrated. The formal, annual plans were merely a confirmation of strategic decisions already reached through the informal political process.

The Content of Managerial Work

The early descriptive research on managerial work was concerned primarily with providing a description of activity patterns. Then the focus of descriptive research shifted to classifying the content of managerial activity in terms of its purpose. A major difficulty in this research has been to determine what behavior categories are meaningful, distinct, and relevant for classifying observed activities of managers. In attempting to resolve this question, different researchers have developed different taxonomies of managerial roles or functions. Major lines of research on the content of managerial work are examined in the next two sections.

Job Description Research

Job description research attempts to identify the behavioral requirements for effective performance of a particular type of managerial job. Behavioral requirements are defined in terms of important responsibilities and duties that must be carried out, regardless of who holds the position. Early research on job descriptions for executives was conducted by Hemphill (1959) and Mahoney, Jerdee, and Carroll (1965). An extensive program of research to develop a questionnaire useful for describing managerial jobs and determining appropriate salary levels was started at Control Data Corporation in 1974 (Page & Tornow, 1987; Tornow & Pinto, 1976). The source of the items in the initial version of the job description questionnaire included items from Hemphill's (1959) Executive Position Description Questionnaire, concepts from the management literature, and interviews with managers. The questionnaire is administered to managers, who are asked to rate how important each activity or behavior is in doing the job, or how much time the manager spends on it. The primary approach for identifying behavior categories has been factor analysis. Over a period of 11 years, research was conducted on seven different versions of the questionnaire with more than 10,000 managers in 12 companies, including several hundred managers at facilities in 20 different countries.

The resulting questionnaire is called the Managerial Position Description Questionnaire (MPDQ). Several distinct categories of managerial work content were found fairly consistently across the seven studies. An abbreviated definition of each category, based on Form 2 of the MPDQ, is presented in Table 2-1.

Mintzberg's Managerial Roles

Mintzberg (1973) used observation rather than surveys to learn more about the content of managerial activities. He developed a taxonomy of managerial roles to use for coding content of the activities observed in his study of executives (see Table 2-2). The 10 roles account for all of a manager's activities, and each activity can be explained in

---

TABLE 2-1 Managerial Position Duties and Responsibilities

Supervising: Improving the performance of subordinates by working with them to analyze their strengths and weaknesses, providing training, developing skills, scheduling their work, and setting performance goals.

Planning and Organizing: Formulating short-term plans, carrying out projects, and developing budgets, determining optimal allocation and utilization of resources; translating long-range plans into short-term operational goals; recommending and developing operational policies and procedures.

Decision Making: Making business decisions without hesitation in an unstructured situation; authorizing minor or major deviations from established procedures to meet new or unusual situations.

Monitoring Indicators: Monitoring internal and external forces that may affect the company, including performance indicators, corporate finances and assets, market conditions, and cultural, social, and political climate.

Controlling: Developing schedules and cost-time estimates for producing or delivering products or services, tracking productivity, assuring the quality of products or effectiveness of services, and analyzing operational effectiveness.

Representing: Answering questions and responding to complaints from outsiders; communicating with outsiders to promote company relations; negotiating with outsiders; conducting promotional activities to establish or maintain company image; and convincing others of your point of view.

Coordinating: Communicating with others in the company over whom one has no direct control in order to share information, meet previously established schedules, solve problems, and achieve objectives; maintaining a smooth working relationship with peers; mediating disagreements and conflicts between key individuals.

Consulting: Keeping current with technical developments in one's field, introducing new techniques or technologies into the organization, and acting as expert advisor, consultant, or troubleshooter for other managers.

Administering: Performing basic administrative activities such as locating information on company practices and procedures, analyzing routine information, or maintaining detailed and accurate records and documents.

TABLE 2-2   Mintzberg's Managerial Roles

Interpersonal Roles
- Leader
- Liaison
- Figurehead

Information Processing Roles
- Monitor
- Disseminator
- Spokesperson

Decision-Making Roles
- Entrepreneur
- Disturbance Handler
- Resource Allocator
- Negotiator

terms of at least one role, although many activities involve more than one role. The managerial roles apply to any manager, but their relative importance may vary from one kind of manager to another. The roles are largely predetermined by the nature of the managerial position, but each manager has some flexibility in how to interpret and enact each role. Three roles deal with the interpersonal behavior of managers (leader, liaison, figurehead), three roles deal with information processing behavior (monitor, disseminator, spokesperson), and four roles deal with decision-making behavior (entrepreneur, disturbance handler, resource allocator, negotiator). Each type of role will be described in more detail.

Leader Role.   Managers are responsible for making their organizational subunit function as an integrated whole in the pursuit of its basic purpose. Consequently, the manager must provide guidance to subordinates, ensure that they are motivated, and create favorable conditions for doing the work. A number of managerial activities are expressly concerned with the leader role, including hiring, training, directing, praising, criticizing, promoting, and dismissing. However, the leader role pervades all managerial activities, even those with some other basic purpose.

Liaison Role.   The liaison role includes behavior intended to establish and maintain a web of relationships with individuals and groups outside of a manager's organizational unit. These relationships are vital as a source of information and favors. The essence of the liaison role is making new contacts, keeping in touch, and doing favors that will allow the manager to ask for favors in return.

Figurehead Role.   As a consequence of their formal authority as the head of an organization or one of its subunits, managers are obliged to perform certain symbolic duties of a legal and social nature. These duties include signing documents (e.g., contracts, expense authorizations), presiding at certain meetings and ceremonial events (e.g., retirement dinner for a subordinate), participating in other rituals or ceremonies, and receiving official visitors. The manager must participate in these activities even though they are usually of marginal relevance to the job of managing.

Monitor Role. Managers continually seek information from a variety of sources, such as reading reports and memos, attending meetings and briefings, and conducting observational tours. Some of the information is passed on to subordinates (disseminator role) or to outsiders (spokesperson role). Most of the information is analyzed to discover problems and opportunities, and to develop an understanding of outside events and internal processes within the manager's organizational subunit.

Disseminator Role. Managers have special access to sources of information not available to subordinates. Some of this information is factual, and some of it concerns the stated preferences of individuals desiring to influence the manager, including people at high levels of authority. Some of the information must be passed on to subordinates, either in its original form or after interpretation and editing by the manager.

Spokesperson Role. Managers are also obliged to transmit information and express value statements to people outside their organizational subunit. Middle managers and lower-level managers must report to their superiors; a chief executive must report to the board of directors or owners. Each of these managers is also expected to serve as a lobbyist and public relations representative for the organizational subunit when dealing with superiors and outsiders. As Mintzberg (1973, p. 76) points out, "To speak effectively for his organization and to gain the respect of outsiders, the manager must demonstrate an up-to-the-minute knowledge of his organization and its environment."

Entrepreneur Role. The manager of an organization or one of its subunits acts as an initiator and designer of controlled change to exploit opportunities for improving the existing situation. Planned change takes place in the form of improvement projects such as development of a new product, purchase of new equipment, or reorganization of formal structure. Some of the improvement projects are supervised directly by the manager, and some are delegated to subordinates. Mintzberg (1973, p. 81) offers the following description of the way a manager deals with improvement projects:

> The manager as a supervisor of improvement projects may be likened to a juggler. At
> any one point in time he has a number of balls in the air. Periodically, one comes
> down, receives a short burst of energy, and goes up again. Meanwhile, new balls wait
> on the sidelines and, at random intervals, old balls are discarded and new ones added.

Disturbance Handler Role. In the disturbance handler role, a manager deals with sudden crises that cannot be ignored, as distinguished from problems that are voluntarily solved by the manager to exploit opportunities (entrepreneur role). The crises are caused by unforeseen events, such as conflict among subordinates, the loss of a key subordinate, a fire or accident, a strike, and so on. A manager typically gives this role priority over all of the others.

Resource Allocator Role. Managers exercise their authority to allocate resources such as money, personnel, material, equipment, facilities, and services. Resource allocation is involved in managerial decisions about what is to be done, in the manager's authorization of subordinates' decisions, in the preparation of budgets, and in the scheduling of the manager's own time. By retaining the power to allocate resources, the manager maintains control over strategy formation and acts to coordinate and integrate subordinate actions in support of strategic objectives.

Negotiator Role.   Any negotiations requiring a substantial commitment of resources will be facilitated by the presence of a manager having the authority to make this commitment. Managers may participate in several different types of negotiations, including negotiations with unions involving labor-management contracts or grievances; contract negotiations with important customers, suppliers, or consultants; employment negotiations with key personnel; and other nonroutine negotiations (e.g., acquisition of another firm, application for a large loan).

Role Conflicts

The discussion of characteristic managerial roles emphasizes the types of activities commonly expected of managers, regardless of the type of position. However, many different people (role senders) in an organization exert pressure on the manager to conform with their beliefs about the proper way to behave (role expectations). At times, different people make incompatible demands on the manager, creating "role conflicts" (Kahn, Wolfe, Quinn, & Snoek, 1964; Pfeffer & Salancik, 1975). For example, managers often find themselves beset by conflicting demands from superiors and subordinates. The conflict may involve a disagreement about the relative priority of two different roles, or about the manner in which a particular role should be carried out. In trying to reconcile conflicting role expectations, a manager is likely to be more responsive to the expectations of superiors, because they wield more power over a manager than do subordinates (Kahn et al., 1964). However, the manner in which a role conflict is resolved also depends in part on how important the issue is to each role sender (Salancik et al., 1975). A manager who is able to reconcile successfully the divergent concerns of superiors and subordinates is more likely to be effective (Mann & Dent, 1954; Mann & Hoffman, 1960; Tsui, 1984).

In addition to role expectations from other people, a leader's perception of role requirements will depend on the nature of the task. Role expectations from subordinates or superiors are sometimes inconsistent with objective task requirements, especially when the nature of the task or the external environment changes while norms and beliefs about proper leadership behavior remain the same. Here again, the leader has a role conflict: conform to expectations from role senders and be less effective in facilitating group performance, or do what is necessary to accomplish the task and take a chance on being initially rejected by role senders.

A Theory of Demands, Constraints, and Choices

Mintzberg's 10 managerial roles describe the type of required activities that are common to most managerial and administrative positions. However, descriptive research indicates that managers also have unique role requirements that are specific to a particular type of managerial position in a particular type of organization. Stewart (1967, 1976, 1982) formulated a model for describing different types of managerial jobs and understanding how managers do them. The model was based on extensive research using observation, interviews, and diaries, and it has three core components.

Core Components

Demands, constraints, and choices define the job of a manager and strongly influence the behavior of anyone who occupies the position.

Demands. Demands are the required duties, activities, and responsibilities for someone who occupies a managerial position. Demands include standards, objectives, and deadlines for work that must be met, and bureaucratic procedures that cannot be ignored or delegated, such as preparing budgets and reports, attending certain meetings, authorizing expenditures, signing documents, and conducting performance appraisals. Other demands depend on particular individuals, such as the requirement by the boss that the manager knows operational details, or an important customer's insistence on dealing with the manager instead of a subordinate.

Constraints. Constraints are characteristics of the organization and external environment limiting what a manager can do. They include bureaucratic rules, policies, and regulations that must be observed, and legal constraints such as labor laws, environmental regulations, securities regulations, and safety regulations. Another type of constraint involves the availability of resources, such as facilities, equipment, budgetary funding, supplies, personnel, and support services. The technology used to do the work constrains the options for how the work will be done. The physical location of facilities and distribution of personnel among work sites limits the opportunities for face-to-face interaction. Market considerations such as the preferences of clients and customers are constraints on the type of products and services that may be provided by the manager's organizational unit.

Choices. Choices are the activities that a manager may do but is not required to do. Choices include the opportunities available to someone in a particular type of managerial position to determine what to do and how to do it. Demands and constraints limit choices in the short run, but over a longer time period, a manager has some opportunities to modify demands and remove or circumvent constraints, thereby expanding choices. Examples of major choices include the objectives for the manager's unit, the priorities attached to different objectives, the strategies selected to pursue objectives, the aspects of the work in which the manager gets personally involved, how and with whom the manager spends time, what responsibility is delegated to whom, and how the manager attempts to influence different people. In a sense, these choices can be described in terms of Kotter's (1982) concepts as what agendas to set, what contacts to make to build a network, and how to influence people to implement the agendas.

Managerial jobs differ greatly in the amount and type of demands and constraints the job holder faces. However, even within the same job, the demands and constraints will vary depending on the perception of the job holder. They are not entirely determined by objective conditions but result instead from the dynamic interaction between manager and role senders. By their choices, managers influence demands. For example, agreeing to serve on a committee adds to a manager's demands. Moreover, people differ in the way they interpret role expectations, and one person will perceive a demand where another may not. For example, one operations manager believes that a bureaucratic regulation must be observed exactly, whereas another operations manager in the same company perceives more flexibility in what can be done.

Situational Determinants

There are differences in the pattern of demands, constraints, and choices for different types of managerial jobs, depending on aspects of the situation such as the type of organization and the nature of the work. Based on Stewart's research, three factors were found to be important for comparing managerial jobs with respect to behavioral requirements.

Pattern of Relationships.   The demands made on a manager by superiors, subordinates, peers, and persons outside the organization influence how the manager's time is spent and how much skill is needed to fulfill role requirements. More time is needed to deal with subordinates when they have interlocking jobs requiring coordination, new assignments must be made frequently, it is important but difficult to monitor subordinate performance, and automatic compliance with orders and requests is not assured. More time is needed to deal with superiors when the manager is highly dependent on them for resources or assignments, and they make unpredictable demands. More time is needed to deal with peers when the manager is dependent on them for services, supplies, cooperation, or approval of work outputs. More time is needed for outsiders (e.g., clients, customers, suppliers, subcontractors) when the manager is highly dependent on them and must negotiate agreements, carry out public relations activities, create a good impression, and act discreet. Having to establish relationships with many people for short periods of time, as opposed to dealing with the same people repeatedly, further complicates the manager's job, especially when it is necessary to impress and influence people quickly. The extent to which subordinates, peers, and superiors make incompatible demands on a manager determines how much role conflict the manager will experience.

Work Pattern.   Stewart found that the pattern of role requirements and demands affected managerial behavior, and somewhat different patterns of behavior were associated with different types of managerial jobs. The following factors were useful for classifying managerial jobs: (1) the extent to which managerial activities are either self-generating or a response to the requests, instructions, and problems of other people; (2) the extent to which the work is recurrent and repetitive rather than variable and unique; (3) the amount of uncertainty in the work; (4) the extent of managerial activities requiring sustained attention for long periods of time; and (5) the amount of pressure to meet deadlines. For example, more initiative and planning of activities are required in a predominantly self-generating job (e.g., product manager, research manager, training director) than for a predominantly responding job with unpredictable problems and workload variations that are beyond the manager's control (e.g., production manager, service manager). Stewart suggested that the work pattern associated with some kinds of managerial jobs tends to be habit forming. A person who spends a long time in one position may grow accustomed to acting in a particular way and will find it difficult to adjust to another managerial position with different behavioral requirements.

Exposure.   Another aspect of a managerial job that determines what behavior and skills are required is the amount of responsibility for making decisions with potentially serious consequences, and the amount of time before a mistake or poor decision can be discovered. There is more exposure when decisions and actions have important, highly visible consequences for the organization, and mistakes or poor judgment can result in loss of resources, disruption of operations, and risk to human health and life. There is less exposure when decisions do not have immediate consequences, or when decisions are made by a group that has shared accountability for them. Examples of high exposure jobs include product managers who must recommend expensive marketing programs and product changes that may quickly prove to be a disaster, project managers who may fail to complete projects on schedule and within budget, and managers of profit centers who are held accountable for their unit's costs and profits.

Research on Situational Determinants

Stewart's broad perspective on the demands and constraints is not typical of most research on the situational determinants of leader behavior. Most studies investigate only one or two aspects of the situation at a time, and different aspects of the situation are examined from one study to the next. This narrow approach makes it difficult to determine whether the effects attributed to one situational variable are actually due to another, unmeasured situational variable. Moreover, it is not possible in these studies to evaluate how different aspects of the situation jointly affect leader behavior. Because the research has been so unsystematic, it is difficult to compare and integrate results across studies. Nevertheless, the research provides some useful insights into the manner in which managerial activities and behavior content are shaped by several aspects of the situation, including level of management, size of subunit, lateral interdependence, crisis conditions, and stage in the organization life cycle.

Level of Management

Job responsibilities and the skills necessary to carry them out vary somewhat for managers at different authority levels in the organization (Jacobs & Jaques, 1987; Jacobs & Lewis, 1992; Katz & Kahn, 1978; Lucas & Markessini, 1993). Higher-level managers are usually more concerned with exercise of broad authority in making long-range plans, formulating policy, modifying the organization structure, and initiating new ways of doing things. Decisions at this level usually have a long time perspective, because it is appropriate for top executives to be thinking about what will happen 10 to 20 years in the future. Middle managers are primarily concerned with interpreting and implementing policies and programs, and they usually have a moderately long time perspective (2–5 years). Low-level managers are primarily concerned with structuring, coordinating, and facilitating work activities. Objectives are more specific, issues are less complex and more focused, and managers typically have a shorter time perspective (a few weeks to 2 years).

A manager at a high level in the authority hierarchy of an organization typically has more responsibility for making important decisions, including determination of organizational objectives, planning of strategies to obtain objectives, determination of general policies, design of the organizational structure, and allocation of resources. As one goes down through the authority hierarchy, managers have less discretion and freedom of action. Lower-level managers must operate within the constraints imposed by formalized rules and policy decisions made at higher levels. Blankenship and Miles (1968) found that lower-level managers had less discretion, were required more often to consult with superiors before taking action on decisions, and made the final choice in a decision less often.

Consistent with this difference in job requirements and discretion across levels is the relative importance and amount of time devoted to different managerial activities and roles (Allan, 1981; Luthans, Rosencrantz, & Hennessey, 1985; McCall & Segrist, 1980; Mintzberg, 1973; Paolillo, 1981). The job description research found that planning, strategic decision making, and public relations are more important activities for top managers than for lower-level managers (Hemphill, 1959; Katzell, Barrett, Vann, & Hogan, 1968; Mahoney, Jerdee, & Carroll, 1965; Page & Tornow, 1987; Tornow & Pinto, 1976). The research on managerial roles found that the resource allocator, spokesperson, and figurehead roles are more important for top-level managers than for lower-level managers. High-level managers are usually more dependent on people outside the organization, and research on managerial activities and networking shows that they spend more time interacting with outsiders (Luthans, Rosencrantz, & Hennessey, 1985; McCall, Morrison, & Hannan, 1978; Michael & Yukl, 1993). Lower-level managers tend to be more concerned with technical matters, staffing (personnel selection and training), scheduling work, and monitoring subordinate performance. The number of activities carried out each day is greater for lower-level managers, and the time spent on each activity tends to be less (Kurke & Aldrich, 1983; Mintzberg, 1973; Thomason, 1967; Walker, Guest, & Turner, 1956).

Size of Organizational Unit

The implications of work unit size or "span of control" for leader behavior have been investigated in several types of research, ranging from studies with small groups to studies on chief executives. Kotter studied general managers and concluded that managers of the larger organizational subunits had more demanding jobs in comparison to managers of smaller units. Decisions are more difficult due to the sheer volume of issues and activities and the lack of detailed knowledge a manager is likely to have. Because larger units are likely to have a more bureaucratic structure, managers must cope with more constraints (e.g., rules, standard procedures, and required authorizations). Consistent with this analysis, Kotter (1982) found that general managers in larger organizational units had larger networks and attended more scheduled meetings.

When a manager has a large number of subordinates, it is more difficult to get all of them together for meetings, or to consult individually with each subordinate. Thus, leaders tend to use less participative leadership or to limit it to an "executive committee" or to a few trusted "lieutenants." Heller and Yukl (1969) found that as span of control increased, upper-level managers made more autocratic decisions, but they also used more delegation. Both decision styles allow a manager who is overloaded with responsibilities to reduce the amount of time needed to make decisions. Lower-level managers in this study also made more autocratic decisions as span of control increased, but they did not use more delegation, perhaps because delegation was less feasible for them. Blankenship and Miles (1968) found that as span of control increased, managers relied more on subordinates to initiate action on decisions, and this trend was much more pronounced for upper-level managers than for lower-level managers.

As the size of the group increases, so does the administrative workload. Managers spend more time on planning, coordinating, staffing, and budgeting activities (Cohen & March, 1974; Hemphill, 1950; Katzell et al., 1968). The increase in coordination requirements is magnified when the subordinates have highly uncertain and interdependent tasks. Sometimes part of the increased administrative burden can be delegated to a second in command, to a coordinating committee composed of subordinates, or to new coordinating specialists who serve as staff assistants. In many cases, however, the leader is expected to assume the responsibility for providing direction and integration of group activities.

Managers of large groups have less opportunity for interacting with individual subordinates and maintaining effective interpersonal relationships with them (Ford, 1981). Less time is available to provide support, encouragement, and recognition to individual subordinates (Goodstadt & Kipnis, 1970). Problems with subordinates are likely to be handled in a more formalized, impersonal manner, and managers are more likely to use warnings and punishment (Kipnis & Cosentino, 1969; Kipnis & Lane, 1962). When a subordinate has a performance problem, the manager is less likely to provide individualized instruction and coaching.

As a group grows larger, separate cliques and factions are likely to emerge. These subgroups often compete for power and resources, creating conflicts and posing a threat to group cohesiveness and teamwork. Thus, the leader of a large group needs to devote more time to building group identification, promoting cooperation, and managing conflict. However, the pressure to carry out more administrative activities in a large group may cause the leader to neglect group maintenance activities until serious problems arise.

Lateral Interdependence

The extent to which a leader's subunit is dependent on other subunits in the same organization ("lateral interdependence") or on external groups will affect leader behavior to a considerable extent. As interdependence increases with other subunits, coordination with them becomes more important and there is more need for mutual adjustments in plans, schedules, and activities (Galbraith, 1973; Mintzberg, 1979). Lateral interdependence represents a threat to the subunit because routine activities must be modified more frequently to accommodate the needs of other subunits, with a resulting loss in autonomy and stability (Hunt & Osborn, 1982; Sayles, 1979). Research on activity patterns of managers finds results consistent with this picture. As lateral interdependence increases, the external activities of a leader become more important, managers spend more time in lateral interactions, and they build larger networks with contacts in other parts of the organization (Hammer & Turk, 1987; Kaplan, 1986; Kotter, 1982; Michael & Yukl, 1993; Stewart, 1976; Walker, Guest, & Turner, 1956; Yanouzas, 1964).

The leader's role in lateral relations includes functions such as gathering information from other subunits, obtaining assistance and cooperation from them, negotiating agreements, reaching joint decisions to coordinate unit activities, defending the unit's interests, promoting a favorable image for the unit, and serving as a spokesperson for subordinates. The extent to which a leader emphasizes each of these activities depends on the nature of the lateral relationship. For example, when a unit provides services on demand to other units, acting as a buffer for subordinates against these external demands is a primary concern of the leader (Sayles, 1979).

Just as the leader tries to reconcile demands from above and below, so also is it necessary to make compromises in seeking to reach agreements with other units. Subordinates expect the leader to represent their interests, but it will not be possible to maintain an effective working relationship with other units unless the leader is also responsive to their needs. Salancik and colleagues (1975) conducted a study of managers in an insurance company to investigate this kind of role conflict. They found that to maintain a cooperative effort, managers with interdependent work activities tended to become more responsive to each other's needs. The greater the number of peers a manager had to interact with on a regular basis, the less responsive the manager was to the desires of subordinates.

Crisis Situations

When a group is under extreme pressure to perform a difficult task or to survive in a hostile environment, the role expectations for the leader are likely to change in a predictable manner. In this kind of situation, subordinates expect the leader to be more assertive, directive, and decisive (Mulder & Stemerding, 1963). They look to the leader to show initiative in defining the problem, identifying a solution, directing the group's response to the crisis, and keeping the group informed about events. For example, a study conducted aboard warships showed that navy officers exercised more power in crisis situations and were more directive, autocratic, and goal oriented (Mulder, Ritsema van Eck, & de Jong, 1970). Officers who showed initiative and exercised power in a confident and decisive manner were usually more effective. In a study of bank managers in The Netherlands, Mulder, de Jong, Koppelaar, and Verhage (1986) found that consultation with subordinates was used less in crisis situations than in noncrisis situations. Managers rated effective were more likely than less-effective managers to use consultation in a noncrisis situation, and were less likely to use it in a crisis situation.

Stage in the Organizational Life Cycle

Organizations move along a life cycle similar to biological organisms, with a birth stage, a growth stage, a maturity stage, and a decline or revitalization stage (Quinn & Cameron, 1983). Baliga and Hunt (1988) proposed that by examining what types of processes are important during each stage, it is possible to identify changing leadership demands, constraints, and choices for top management.

In the initial stage of the organization's evolution, a primary management responsibility is to communicate a vision of the proposed organization to potential external stakeholders (e.g., banks, investors, suppliers) who can provide necessary resources to establish the organization. Once the organization is founded, other key responsibilities include identifying and acquiring the technology needed to perform the work, recruiting the key personnel needed to staff the organization, inspiring commitment by the new members, and designing appropriate management systems (e.g., information systems, control systems, reward systems).

As the organization grows rapidly, the management responsibilities concerned with internal demands (e.g., staffing, motivation, organization of work, resource allocation, coordination) become as important as those related to external demands. In the maturity phase, when the organization's key products or services become fully developed and the market stabilizes, a primary management responsibility is to structure the work and develop procedures to increase the efficiency of operations, and to maintain member morale and motivation in a time of increasing controls and declining opportunity for advancement.

Eventually the organization will encounter severe environmental threats (e.g., new competitors, declining demand for its products and services). In this crisis phase the primary responsibility of management is to determine how to adapt and survive. New strategies must be identified, members of the organization must be influenced to support them, resources must be found to finance the changes, credibility must be reestablished with external stakeholders, and the structure of the organization must be changed to be consistent with the new strategy. The success of this effort will determine whether the organization declines or is revitalized (Baliga & Hunt, 1988; Hunt, Baliga, & Peterson, 1988). The behavior of top executives in different evolutionary phases of the organization is discussed in more detail in Chapter 12.

Changes in the Nature of Managerial Work

Managerial work is being altered by sweeping trends in economics, politics, and society (Dess & Picken, 2000). The trend toward globalization continues to accelerate as foreign competition intensifies, foreign markets become more important, and more companies become multinational or participate in cross-national joint ventures. Managerial responsibilities increasingly involve international issues, and managers must be able to understand, communicate with, and influence people from different cultures. Cultural diversity of the workforce within organizations is increasing as well. To build cooperative relationships requires considerable empathy, respect for diversity, and understanding of the values, beliefs, and attitudes of people from different cultures.

New computer and telecommunications technology is changing the nature of work and making it possible to provide more detailed, timely information to anyone who needs it. However, increased information about the organization's operations and environment can be both a blessing and a curse. It takes a clear sense of objectives and priorities and strong cognitive skills to deal with the deluge of information and make sense out of it. Moreover, as electronic communication becomes more important, leaders will need to adjust their behavior to fit the new technologies.

Changes in the structure of organizations present yet another challenge. Many organizations are being decentralized into smaller, semi-autonomous units, flattened by eliminating layers of middle management, or restructured around product teams that cut across functional or geographical lines. Team-based organizations have more shared leadership, and team leaders are expected to be more of a coach and facilitator and less of a director and controller (see Chapter 11).

Another trend is increased reliance on outside suppliers, consultants, and contractors that provide supplies, materials, or services when needed on a just-in-time basis. In many cases the vertically integrated firm that did everything itself is being replaced by a "virtual" or "networked" organization that outsources most activities (e.g., production, marketing, payroll and benefit administration, legal services, and marketing). This type of organization design is typical of many new companies engaged in e-commerce, and leadership scholars have begun to investigate possible differences in managerial skills and role requirements for these dot-coms. Despite many similarities, leaders in virtual organizations are expected to function more like entrepreneurs than traditional managers, and they need more knowledge about information technology and more skills in project management (Horner-Long & Schoenberg, 2002). They must identify strategic opportunities, negotiate joint ventures with people in other organizations, build strategic alliances, and coordinate interdependent activities in dozens of locations spread around the globe.

How Much Discretion Do Managers Have?

The situational research provides strong evidence that aspects of the situation influence the activity pattern and behavior content of managers. A managerial position makes various demands on the person who occupies it, and the actions of the occupant are constrained by laws, policies, regulations, traditions, and scope of formal authority. Despite these demands and constraints, some choice of behavior remains, particularly with respect to what aspects of the job are emphasized, how much time is devoted to various activities, and how much time is spent with different people. The research showed that even for managers with similar jobs, there was considerable variability of behavior (James & White, 1983; Kotter, 1982; Stewart, 1976, 1982). For example, Stewart found that some bank managers emphasized staff supervision, whereas some others delegated much of the internal management to the assistant manager and concentrated on actively seeking out new business.

In part, variability of behavior within the same job occurs because of its multiple performance dimensions. Within the boundaries imposed by the priorities of higher management, a person may choose to devote more effort to some objectives than to others. For example, activities involving development of new products may get more attention than cost reduction, quality improvements, development of new export markets, or improvement of safety practices. Development of subordinates to groom them for promotion may get more attention than team building or training in skills necessary to improve performance in the present job. The trade-offs inherent among performance dimensions and lack of time to do everything well make it inevitable that different people will define the same job in different ways. How this job definition is done will reflect a manager's interests, skills, and values, as well as the changing role expectations of the individuals whose destinies are intertwined with the manager's.

Variability in the same job is also due to the way in which a manager deals with role conflicts. Role expectations for a leader are seldom absolute or comprehensive, and a leader usually has considerable discretion to shape his or her role over time. Given enough time, a skillful leader may be able to reconcile role requirements that were initially incompatible. Leaders with a record of successful decisions and demonstrated loyalty to the organization are given more freedom to redefine their role and initiate innovations (see Chapter 8). However, flexibility is greater for role expectations that do not involve central values of symbolic importance to organization members (Biggart & Hamilton, 1984).

Limitations of the Descriptive Research

Most of the research on managerial activity patterns is dated, and it needs to be redone for organizations with communication technology developed since the early studies (e.g., cellular phones, e-mail, video conferencing). There is also a need for more research is needed on managerial activities that may be affected by new forms of organization (e.g., virtual organizations, team-based organizations, joint venture organizations). More research is also needed to examine how activity patterns for managers are changing in the United States and in other countries.

Most of the observational research on the nature of managerial work was designed to describe the typical pattern and content of managerial activities, not to answer directly the question of what activity patterns or behavior patterns are necessary and effective. Discovering that many managers carry out a particular activity does not tell us whether it is essential for managerial effectiveness. Even the results from the situational research may be misleading. The most prevalent behavior pattern in a particular type of managerial job or situation is not necessarily the most effective one.

Job description studies measure the perceived importance of various activities and responsibilities for the job. This research reveals similarities and differences in skill requirements across various types of managerial positions. The primary purpose of the research is to facilitate development of compensation systems, selection procedures, and performance appraisal procedures, not to determine how managerial behavior is related to managerial effectiveness. The importance ratings made by many managers may be biased by shared stereotypes or implicit theories about effective leaders. As yet there is little evidence to demonstrate that the managerial activities and behaviors rated most important are also the ones related most strongly to criteria of managerial effectiveness.

Other descriptive studies analyzed data from interviews with managers predetermined to be effective (Kanter, 1982; Kotter, 1982; Kotter & Lawrence, 1974), or with managers from organizations designated as effective (Peters & Austin, 1985; Peters and Waterman, 1982). These researchers attempted to find common themes that might explain why the managers were effective. However, the studies did not compare effective managers to ineffective managers. More reliable insights would be gained if researchers compared behavior patterns for effective managers and ineffective managers of the same type and explicitly examined the relation of managerial behavior patterns to the requirements of the managerial job situation.

As for the problem of classifying the content of managerial activities, some convergence is evident among the various descriptive approaches, but only at the level of broad categories or processes. Most managerial activity can be described in terms of four general processes: (1) developing and maintaining relationships, (2) obtaining and providing information, (3) making decisions, and (4) influencing people. These processes are interwoven among a manager's activities, and any specific activity may involve more than one process. The resulting overlap among categories is depicted in Figure 2-2.

Applications for Managers

Even though most descriptive research on managerial activities was not designed to determine how they are related to managerial effectiveness, the research does provide some insights about coping more effectively with the requirements of managerial work. This section summarizes some tentative guidelines for effective managerial leadership. The reader is cautioned to remember that most of these guidelines are patterns and themes inferred from exploratory descriptive research and practitioner insights, not results from research designed to test propositions about effective leader behavior. Guidelines for using time wisely are presented first, followed by guidelines for problem solving.

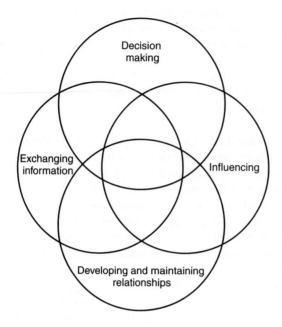

FIGURE 2-2   Four Primary
Processes in Managing

Guidelines for Managing Time

Table 2-3 summarizes some things managers can do to use their time wisely, cope with demands, and handle role conflicts.

- **Understand the reasons for demands and constraints.**

It is essential to learn how others perceive the manager's role and what they expect. Perception of demands and constraints inevitably involves subjective judgments, but many managers fail to take the time necessary to gather sufficient information on which to base these judgments. Do not assume that everyone agrees with your vision,

TABLE 2-3   Guidelines for Performing Managerial Work

- Understand the reasons for demands and constraints.
- Expand the range of choices.
- Determine what you want to accomplish.
- Analyze how you use your time.
- Plan daily and weekly activities.
- Avoid unnecessary activities.
- Conquer procrastination.
- Take advantage of reactive activities.
- Make time for reflective planning.
- Identify important problems that can be solved.
- Look for connections among problems.
- Experiment with innovative solutions.
- Take decisive action to deal with crises.

priorities, or ideas about effective management. Before one can satisfy people or modify their expectations, it is necessary to understand what they really desire. Understanding role expectations requires frequent face-to-face interaction, asking questions, listening to others rather than constantly preaching, being sensitive to negative reactions (including nonverbal cues), and trying to discover the values and needs underlying a person's opinions and preferences.

- **Expand the range of choices.**

Too many managers focus on the demands and constraints and fail to give adequate consideration to opportunities to define the job in different ways. It is essential to step back from the job and see it in a broader strategic perspective. It is usually possible to be proactive with superiors about defining the job in a way that allows more discretion, especially when role ambiguity is already present due to poorly defined responsibilities. Choices may be expanded by finding ways to avoid demands and reduce constraints. A manager's planning and agenda development should include a conscious analysis of the demands and constraints limiting current effectiveness, and how they can be reduced, eliminated, or circumvented.

- **Determine what you want to accomplish.**

Time is a scarce resource that must be used well if the manager is to be effective. The key to effective time management is knowing what you want to accomplish. A person with a clear set of objectives and priorities can identify important activities and plan the best way to use time; without clear objectives, no amount of planning will improve time management. The objectives and priorities may be informal, as with Kotter's (1982) mental agendas, but they need to be identified by a deliberate, conscious process.

- **Analyze how you use your time.**

It is difficult to improve time management without knowing how time is actually spent. Most managers are unable to estimate very accurately how much time they spend on different activities. Most time management systems recommend keeping a daily log of activities for one or two weeks. The log should list each activity in 15-minute blocks of time. It is helpful to indicate the source of control over each activity (e.g., self, boss, subordinates, others, organizational requirements) and whether the activity was planned in advance or an immediate reaction to requests and problems. Typical time wasters should be noted on the log (e.g., unnecessary interruptions, meetings that run too long, searching for misplaced items). The time log should be analyzed to identify how important and necessary each activity is. Consider whether the activity can be eliminated, combined with others, or given less time. Identify whether too many activities are initiated by others, and whether adequate time is allowed for activities that are important but not urgent.

- **Plan daily and weekly activities.**

The extensive practitioner-oriented literature on time management shows considerable agreement about the importance of planning daily and weekly activities in advance (e.g., Webber, 1980). When planning daily activities, the first step is to make a to-do list for the day and assign priorities to each activity. This type of prioritized activity list may be used with a calendar showing required meetings and scheduled appointments to plan the next day's activities. Most of the discretionary time should be allocated to high-priority activities. If insufficient time is available to do important activities with immediate deadlines, reschedule or delegate some activities that are less important. The task of juggling the various activities and deciding which to do is a difficult but essential component of managerial work. Remember that it is more efficient to do a series of similar tasks than to keep switching from one type of task to another. Sometimes it is possible to schedule similar activities (e.g., several telephone calls, several letters) at the same time during the day. In addition, it is wise to take into account natural energy cycles and biorhythms. Peak alertness and efficiency occur at different times of the day for different people, and peak periods should be used for difficult tasks that require creativity.

- **Avoid unnecessary activities.**

Managers who become overloaded with unnecessary tasks are likely to neglect activities that are important for attaining key objectives. Managers may accept unnecessary tasks because they are afraid of offending subordinates, peers, or the boss, and they lack the self-confidence and assertiveness to turn down requests. One way to avoid unnecessary tasks is to prepare and use tactful ways to say no (e.g., say that you could only do the task if the person does some of your work for you; suggest other people who could do the task faster or better; point out that an important task will be delayed or jeopardized if you do what the person requests). Some unnecessary but required tasks can be eliminated by showing how resources will be saved or other benefits attained. Unessential tasks that cannot be eliminated or delegated can be put off until slack times. Sometimes when a task is put off long enough, the person who requested it will discover that it is not needed after all.

- **Conquer procrastination.**

Even when it is obvious that an activity is important, some people delay doing it in favor of a less important activity. One reason for procrastination is the fear of failure. People find excuses for delaying a task because they lack self-confidence. One remedy for a long, complex task is to divide it into smaller parts, each of which is easier and less intimidating. Deadlines are also helpful for overcoming procrastination. When setting deadlines for completion of difficult tasks, it is better to allow some slack and set a deadline that is earlier than the date when the task absolutely must be completed. However, having some slack should not become an excuse for not starting the task. Schedule a definite time early in the day to begin working on unpleasant tasks that tend to be procrastinated. Such tasks are more likely to get done if tackled first before the daily stream of demands provides excuses to avoid them.

- **Take advantage of reactive activities.**

Although some degree of control over the use of one's time is desirable, it is not feasible for a manager to plan in advance exactly how each minute of the day will be spent. The unpredictable nature of the environment makes it essential to view chance encounters, interruptions, and unscheduled meetings initiated by others not just as intrusions on scheduled activities, but rather as opportunities to gain important information, discover problems, influence others, and move forward on implementation of plans and informal agendas. Obligations that might otherwise be time wasters, such as required attendance at some meetings and ceremonial occasions, can be turned to one's advantage (Kotter, 1982; Mintzberg, 1973).

- **Make time for reflective planning.**

Managers face relentless pressures for dealing with immediate problems and responding to requests for assistance, direction, or authorization. Some of these problems require immediate attention, but if managers become too preoccupied with reacting to day-to-day problems, they have no time left for the reflective planning that would help them to avoid many of the problems, or for the contingency planning that would help them cope better with unavoidable problems. Therefore, it is desirable to set aside some time on a regular basis for reflective analysis and planning. Listen to Antonia Bryson, a deputy commissioner in New York City's Department of Environmental Protection (Haas, 1994, p. 60):

> What happens in government is that you always tend to get caught up in crises. . . . But its helpful to sit back at the end of every week and ask, is this part of my long-term plan of what I want to accomplish while I am in this job? . . . The higher up you go, the more you have to constantly examine how you are setting your own priorities. Are you going to the right meetings? Are you going to too many meetings? Are you using your staff members effectively to make sure you yourself are spending time on the right things and accomplishing what you want to get accomplished?

Making time for reflective planning requires careful time management. One approach is to set aside a block of private time (at least 1–2 hours) each week for individual planning. Another approach is to schedule periodic strategy sessions with subordinates to encourage discussion of strategic issues. Still another approach is to initiate a major improvement project, delegate primary responsibility to a subordinate or task force, and schedule regular meetings with the individual or group to review plans and progress.

Guidelines for Problem Solving

Dealing with disturbances and problems is an important activity that requires considerable time for most managers. The following guidelines explain how managers can make better use of the time they spend trying to solve operational problems (see also Table 2-3).

- **Identify important problems that can be solved.**

A manager always faces more problems than can be resolved. Therefore, it is desirable for the manager to evaluate (1) whether a problem can be solved within a reasonable time period with available resources, and (2) whether it is worthwhile to invest the time, effort, and resources on this problem rather than on others (Isenberg, 1984; McCall & Kaplan, 1985). Descriptive research on effective managers suggests that they give priority to important problems that can be solved, rather than ignoring these problems or trying to avoid responsibility for them (e.g., by passing the problem to someone else or involving more people than necessary to diffuse responsibility for decisions) (Peters & Austin, 1985; Peters & Waterman, 1982). Managers should attempt to avoid or postpone action on problems that are either trivial or intractable. Of course, some problems are so important that they should not be postponed even when the initial probability of a successful solution is low.

- **Look for connections among problems.**

In the process of trying to make sense out of the streams of problems, issues, and opportunities encountered by a manager, it is important to look for relationships among them rather than assuming that they are distinct and independent (Isenberg, 1984). A broader view of problems provides better insights for understanding them. By relating problems to each other and to informal strategic objectives, a manager is more likely to recognize opportunities to take actions that contribute to the solution of several related problems at the same time. Finding connections among problems is facilitated if the manager is able to remain flexible and open-minded about the definition of a problem and actively considers multiple definitions for each problem.

- **Experiment with innovative solutions.**

Effective managers are more willing to experiment actively with innovative approaches for solving problems, rather than spending an excessive amount of time studying them. Whenever possible, experiments are conducted initially on a small scale to minimize the risk, and ways are found to obtain the information necessary to evaluate results. In some cases, an action is taken not because the manager believes it is the best way to solve a problem, but rather because taking limited action is the only way to develop an adequate understanding of the problem (Isenberg, 1984; Quinn, 1980). Peters and Waterman (1982, p. 13) found that managers in effective companies had a bias for action characterized as "do it, fix it, try it." One manager described the following approach for quickly introducing innovative products: "Instead of allowing 250 engineers and marketers to work on a new product in isolation for 15 months, they form bands of 5 to 25 and test ideas out on a customer, often with inexpensive prototypes, within a matter of weeks" (Peters & Waterman, 1982, p. 14).

- **Take decisive action to deal with crises.**

In a crisis situation (e.g., financial turmoil, a threatened takeover, health hazards, a serious accident or natural disaster), people are usually anxious and concerned about how they will be affected. The leader is expected to take decisive action to deal with an emergency or crisis situation quickly before it becomes worse. Effective leaders quickly identify the cause of the problem, they take decisive action to direct the work unit's response to it, and they keep people informed about progress in efforts to deal with the crisis (Stewart, 1967, 1976).

Summary

The descriptive research found that managerial work is inherently hectic, varied, fragmented, reactive, disorderly, and political. Brief oral interactions predominate, and many of these involve people outside the manager's immediate work unit and chain of command. Decision processes are highly political, and most planning is informal and adaptive. This activity pattern occurs, in part, because managers face several dilemmas. To carry out their responsibilities, managers need to obtain recent, relevant information that exists only in the heads of people who are widely scattered within and outside the organization; they need to make decisions based on information that is both overwhelming and incomplete; and they need to get cooperation from people over whom they have no formal authority.

Identifying meaningful and widely applicable categories to describe the content of managerial work has been a problem for a long time. One approach is the taxonomy of managerial roles proposed by Mintzberg. Another approach is represented by job description research that asks managers to rate the importance of different activities and responsibilities for their jobs.

Some of the descriptive research has examined differences in behavior related to aspects of the managerial situation. Stewart identified several situational influences on leader behavior. The pattern of interactions with subordinates, peers, superiors, and outsiders is affected by a manager's dependency on these people and by the demands they make on a manager. The type of work pattern depends on the nature of the work itself: self-generating or responding, repetitive or variable, uncertain or predictable, fragmented or sustained, and subject to tight deadlines or relatively unhurried.

Comparative research on managers in different situations reveals several other aspects of the situation that affect managerial behavior, including level of management, size of the organizational unit, lateral interdependence, crisis conditions, and stage in the organizational life cycle. Managerial work is being altered by sweeping societal trends such as globalization, workforce diversity, the pace of technological change, and the emergence of new forms of organizations.

Despite all the demands and constraints a manager faces, some choice of behavior remains. Even managers in similar positions define their roles differently. There are choices in what aspects of the job to emphasize, how to allocate one's time, and with whom to spend it. Managers will be more effective if they understand the demands and constraints in their job situation, and work to expand their choices. Finally, effective managers are more proactive about identifying emerging problems, and even when reacting to unforeseen events, their behavior more closely reflects their objectives and priorities.

The descriptive research suggests that managerial work includes four general types of activities: (1) building and maintaining relationships, (2) getting and giving information, (3) influencing people, and (4) decision making. The next chapter examines leadership behavior embedded in these activities or occurring in conjunction with them.

Review and Discussion Questions

1. Briefly describe typical activity patterns in managerial work.
2. What does descriptive research tell us about managerial decision making, planning, and problem solving?
3. Briefly describe Mintzberg's 10 managerial roles. Are some roles more important than others?
4. Briefly describe how managerial behavior is influenced by the nature of the job situation, according to Stewart.
5. How are managerial activities and behavior affected by level of management, unit size, and lateral interdependence?
6. How is a crisis likely to affect managerial activities and behavior?
7. How does the organizational life cycle affect the relative importance of different managerial functions and activities?
8. How much latitude do managers have in what they do and how they do it? Is it more accurate to view managers as "captains of their destiny" or "prisoners of their fate"?
9. Why do managers have so much difficulty managing their time?
10. What can be done to improve time management and problem solving?

Key Terms

- constraints
- demands
- dependence
- exposure

- job description research
- lateral interdependence
- managerial activities
- managerial roles

- networks
- role conflicts
- role expectations

CASE

Acme Manufacturing Company

When Steve Arnold, a production manager at Acme Manufacturing Company, drove into the parking lot Tuesday morning at 8:45, he was already 45 minutes late for work. Steve had overslept that morning because he was up late the night before finishing the monthly production report for his department. He parked his car and entered the rear of the plant building. Passing through the shipping area, Steve spotted his friend George Summers and stopped to ask how work was progressing on the new addition to George's house.

Entering the office at 9:05, Steve greeted his secretary, Ruth Sweeney, and asked whether anything urgent needed his immediate attention. Ruth reminded him of the staff meeting at 9:30 with Steve's boss—Frank Jones, the vice president for Production—and the other production managers. Steve thanked Ruth for reminding him (he had forgotten about the meeting) and continued on to his adjoining inner office. He went to his desk and began looking through the piles of papers to find the memo announcing the meeting. He vaguely remembered getting the memo last week, but had not had time to read it or look at the attached materials.

The phone rang and it was Sue Bradley, the Sales vice president, who was inquiring about the status of a rush order for one of the company's important clients. Steve promised to look into the matter and get back to her

later in the day with an answer. Steve had delegated the rush order last week to Lucy Adams, one of his production supervisors, and he had not thought about it since then. Stepping back into the outer office, Steve asked Ruth if she had seen Lucy today. Ruth reminded him that Lucy was out of town at a training workshop and would be difficult to reach. Steve asked Ruth to leave a message for Lucy to call him during a break in the training.

Going back into his office, Steve resumed his search for the memo about the meeting with his boss and the other production managers. After 10 minutes of frantic searching, he finally found it. The purpose of the meeting was to discuss a proposed change in quality control procedures. By now it was 9:25, and there was no time to read the proposal. He hurried out to get to the meeting on time. During the meeting, the other production managers participated in the discussion and made helpful comments or suggestions. Steve was not prepared for the meeting and did not contribute much except to say that he did not anticipate any problems with the proposed changes.

The meeting ended at 10:30, and Steve returned to his office, where he found Paul Chen, one of his production supervisors, waiting for him. Paul wanted to discuss a problem caused in the production schedules by a major equipment breakdown. Steve called Glenda Brown, his assistant manager, on the telephone and asked her to join them to help rearrange the production schedules for the next few days. Glenda came in shortly and the three of them worked on the production schedules. At 11:25, Ruth came in to announce that a Mr. Ferris was waiting and he claimed to have an appointment with Steve at 11:30. Steve looked at his calendar but could not find any entry for the appointment. Steve asked Ruth to tell Mr. Ferris that he would be ready shortly.

The schedules were completed around 11:40. Since it was nearly noon, Steve invited Mr. Ferris to join him for lunch at a nearby restaurant. During lunch Steve learned that Mr. Ferris was from one of the firms that provided materials used in the production process at Acme, and the purpose of the meeting was to inquire about some changes in material specifications the company had requested. As Mr. Ferris talked, Steve realized that he would not be able to answer some of the technical questions. When they returned to the plant at 1:15, Steve introduced Mr. Ferris to an engineer who could answer his questions.

Steve walked back to his office, where his secretary informed him that Lucy had returned his call while he was out to lunch. Just then, Steve's boss (Frank Jones) stopped in to ask about the quality figures he had asked Steve to assemble for him last week. Steve explained that he had given top priority to finishing the monthly production report the last few days and would do the quality information next. Frank was irritated, because he needed the quality data to finalize his proposal for new procedures, and he had made it clear to Steve that this task was more urgent then the production report. He told Steve to get the quality data to him as soon as possible and left. Steve immediately called Glenda Brown and asked her to bring the quality data to his office. The task of reviewing the data and preparing a short summary was not difficult, but it took longer than he anticipated. It was 2:40 by the time Steve completed the report and attached it to an e-mail to his boss.

Looking at his calendar, Steve noticed that he was already late for a 2:30 meeting of the plant safety committee. The committee meets weekly to review safety problems, and each department sends a representative. Steve rushed out to the meeting, which was held in another part of the plant. The meeting was dull this week, without any important issues or problems to discuss.

The meeting ended at 3:30, and as Steve walked back through his section of the plant, he stopped to talk to his assistant manager. Glenda wanted some advice on how to resolve a problem in the production assignments for the next day. They discussed the problem for about a half-hour. When Steve returned to his office at 4:05, his secretary was just leaving. She reported that Lucy had called again at 4:00 before leaving to fly home from the conference.

Steve was feeling tired and decided it was time for him to go home also. As he drove out of the parking lot, Steve reflected that he was getting further behind in his work. He wondered what he could do to get better control over his job. ■

SOURCE: Copyright © 1988 by Gary Yukl

QUESTIONS

1. What specific things did Steve do wrong, and what should have been done in each instance?

2. What should Steve do to become more effective as a manager?

CHAPTER

3

PERSPECTIVES ON EFFECTIVE LEADERSHIP BEHAVIOR

Learning Objectives

After studying this chapter you should be able to:

- Understand what research methods have been used to study leadership behavior.

- Understand the findings in the early research on leadership behavior.

- Understand how leadership behavior can be described with either broad or specific categories.

- Understand the different methods for developing taxonomies of leadership behavior.

- Understand why task, relations, and change-oriented behaviors are important for leadership effectiveness.

- Understand how specific types of task and relations behavior can be used effectively.

- Understand why it is useful to classify leadership behavior in terms of a three-dimensional model.

- Understand the contributions and limitations of the behavior approach.

The preceding chapter reviewed descriptive research that was designed to identify typical activity patterns of managers, not to determine how effective leaders differ in behavior from ineffective leaders. The current chapter will review research on the types of leadership behavior most likely to influence subordinate satisfaction and performance. The methods used for this research include behavior description questionnaires, laboratory and field experiments, and critical incidents.

The chapter begins by examining some of the early research on leader behavior conducted by psychologists in the 1950s and 1960s. Much of the research on leadership behavior during the past five decades has followed the pattern set by the pioneering research programs at Ohio State University and the University of Michigan. These programs and subsequent research are briefly discussed. The methods used to develop taxonomies of leadership behavior are also described, as well as important findings from research on this subject. The final part of the chapter describes some aspects of task-oriented and relationship-oriented behaviors that are important for effective leadership.

Ohio State Leadership Studies

Questionnaire research on effective leadership behavior was strongly influenced by the early research at Ohio State University during the 1950s. The initial task of the researchers was to identify categories of relevant leadership behavior and develop questionnaires to measure how often a leader used these behaviors. The researchers compiled a list of about 1800 examples of leadership behavior, then reduced the list to 150 items that appeared to be good examples of important leadership functions. A preliminary questionnaire composed of these items was used by samples of military and civilian personnel to describe the behavior of their supervisors (Fleishman, 1953; Halpin & Winer, 1957; Hemphill & Coons, 1957).

Leadership Behaviors

Factor analysis of the questionnaire responses indicated that subordinates perceived their supervisor's behavior primarily in terms of two broadly defined categories labeled "consideration" and "initiating structure." The two types of behavior were relatively independent, which means that a leader's use of one behavior was not necessarily the same as his or her use of the other behavior.

Consideration.   This category of behavior involves leader concern for people and interpersonal relationships. The leader acts in a friendly and supportive manner and shows concern for the needs and feelings of subordinates. Examples include doing personal favors for subordinates, finding time to listen to a subordinate with a problem, backing up or defending a subordinate, consulting with subordinates on important matters, being willing to accept suggestions from subordinates, and treating a subordinate as an equal.

Initiating Structure.   This category of behavior involves leader concern for accomplishing the task. The leader defines and structures his or her own role and the roles of subordinates toward attainment of task goals. Examples include criticizing poor work, emphasizing the importance of meeting deadlines, assigning subordinates to tasks, maintaining definite standards of performance, asking subordinates to follow standard procedures, offering new approaches to problems, and coordinating the activities of different subordinates.

Based on the results of the initial studies, two revised and shortened questionnaires were constructed to measure consideration and initiating structure: the Leader Behavior Description Questionnaire (LBDQ), and the Supervisory Behavior Description (SBD or SBDQ). Although these two questionnaires are often treated as equivalent, they differ somewhat with regard to the content of the behavior scales (Schriesheim & Stogdill, 1975). A third questionnaire, called the Leader Opinion Questionnaire (LOQ), has been treated by some researchers as a measure of behavior, but it is viewed more appropriately as a measure of leader attitudes.

Eventually, researchers at the Ohio State University developed a fourth questionnaire, called the Leader Behavior Description Questionnaire, Form XII. In the LBDQ XII, the scope of consideration and initiating structure was narrowed, and 10 additional scales were added (Stogdill, Goode, & Day, 1962). Some of the new scales measured aspects of leadership behavior (e.g., representation, integration), but other scales measured traits (e.g., uncertainty tolerance) or skills (i.e., predictive accuracy, persuasiveness). It is interesting to note that, even after the new scales were added, most researchers continued to use only the consideration and initiating structure scales.

Example of a Survey Study

A study by Fleishman and Harris (1962) provides one of the best examples of correlational field research on consideration and initiating structure. The study was conducted in a truck manufacturing plant of the International Harvester Company. The behavior of 57 production supervisors was described by subordinates who filled out the SBDQ. The criteria of leadership effectiveness included the number of written grievances and the amount of voluntary turnover during an 11-month period. Supervisors who were considerate had fewer grievances and less turnover in their work units than supervisors who were low on consideration. The relationship was in the opposite direction for initiating structure; supervisors who used a lot of structuring behavior had more turnover and grievances. Statistical analyses confirmed the existence of a significant curvilinear relationship. As noted by Fleishman and Harris (1962, p. 53), "There appear to be certain critical levels beyond which increased consideration or decreased initiating structure have no effect on turnover or grievance rate." The relationship between leader behavior and turnover is shown in Figures 3-1 and 3-2. The results in this study were mostly corroborated by Skinner (1969) in a study of supervisors in a textile firm.

Results in Survey Research

The Ohio State leadership questionnaires and modified versions of them have been used in hundreds of survey studies by many different researchers. The results have been weak and inconsistent for most criteria of leadership effectiveness (Bass, 1990; Fisher & Edwards, 1988). In some studies, subordinates were more satisfied and performed better with a structuring leader, whereas other studies found the opposite relationship or no significant relationship at all. The findings were also inconsistent for the relationship between consideration and subordinate performance. The only consistent finding was a positive relationship between consideration and subordinate satisfaction. As suggested by the Fleishman and Harris study, subordinates are usually more satisfied with a leader who is at least moderately considerate. However, unlike Fleishman and Harris, most researchers neglected to test for the possibility of curvilinear relationships or an interaction between consideration and initiating structure.

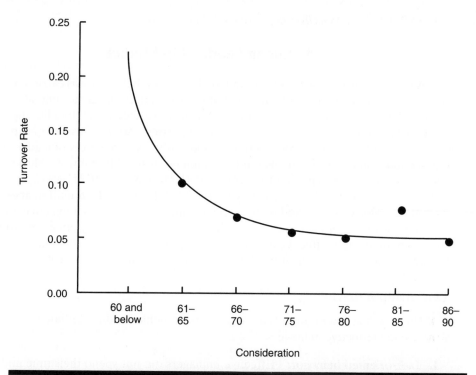

FIGURE 3-1   Relation Between Consideration and Turnover Rate

Source: From E.A Fleishman and E.F. Harris "Patterns of Leadership Behavior Related to Employee Grievances and Turnover. " *Personnel Psychology*, 1962, 15, 43–56.

FIGURE 3-2   Relation Between Initiating Structure and Turnover Rate

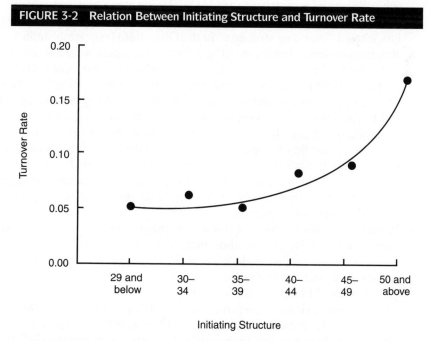

Source: From E.A Fleishman and E.F. Harris "Patterns of Leadership Behavior Related to Employee Grievances and Turnover. " *Personnel Psychology*, 1962, 15, 43–56.

Michigan Leadership Studies

A second major program of research on leadership behavior was carried out by researchers at the University of Michigan at approximately the same time as the Ohio State leadership studies. The focus of the Michigan research was the identification of relationships among leader behavior, group processes, and measures of group performance. The initial research was a series of field studies with a variety of leaders, including section managers in an insurance company (Katz, Maccoby, & Morse, 1950), supervisors in a large manufacturing company (Katz & Kahn, 1952), and supervisors of railroad section gangs (Katz, Maccoby, Gurin, & Floor, 1951). Information about managerial behavior was collected with interviews and questionnaires. Objective measures of group productivity were used to classify managers as relatively effective or ineffective. A comparison of effective and ineffective managers revealed some interesting differences in managerial behavior, which were summarized by Likert (1961, 1967).

Leadership Behaviors

The research found three types of leadership behavior differentiated between effective and ineffective managers.

1. **Task-oriented behavior.**   Effective managers did not spend their time and effort doing the same kind of work as their subordinates. Instead, the more effective managers concentrated on task-oriented functions such as planning and scheduling the work, coordinating subordinate activities, and providing necessary supplies, equipment, and technical assistance. Moreover, effective managers guided subordinates in setting performance goals that were high but realistic. The task-oriented behaviors identified in the Michigan studies appear similar to the behaviors labeled "initiating structure" in the Ohio State leadership studies.
2. **Relations-oriented behavior.**   The effective managers were also more supportive and helpful with subordinates. Supportive behaviors that were correlated with effective leadership included showing trust and confidence, acting friendly and considerate, trying to understand subordinate problems, helping to develop subordinates and further their careers, keeping subordinates informed, showing appreciation for subordinates' ideas, allowed considerable autonomy in how subordinates do the work, and providing recognition for subordinates' contributions and accomplishments. These behaviors are similar to the behaviors labeled "consideration" in the Ohio State leadership studies. Likert proposed that a manager should treat each subordinate in a supportive way that will build and maintain the person's sense of personal worth and importance.
3. **Participative leadership.**   Effective managers used more group supervision instead of supervising each subordinate separately. Group meetings facilitate subordinate participation in decision making, improve communication, promote cooperation, and facilitate conflict resolution. The role of the manager in group meetings should be primarily to guide the discussion and keep it supportive, constructive, and oriented toward problem solving. However, use of participation does not imply abdication of responsibilities, and the manager remains responsible for all decisions and their results. Participative leadership will be examined more closely in Chapter 4.

Peer Leadership

Bowers and Seashore (1966) extended the investigation of leadership behavior by suggesting that most leadership functions can be carried out by someone besides the designated leader of a group. Sometimes a manager asks subordinates to share in performing certain leadership functions, and sometimes subordinates perform these functions on their own initiative. Group effectiveness will depend more on the overall quality of leadership in a work unit than on who actually performs the functions. However, the possibility of shared leadership does not imply that it is unnecessary to have a designated leader. According to Bowers and Seashore (1966, p. 249), "There are both common sense and theoretical reasons for believing that a formally acknowledged leader through his supervisory leadership behavior sets the pattern of the mutual leadership which subordinates supply each other."

Bowers and Seashore were the first researchers to survey peer leadership as well as leadership behavior by the manager. The Survey of Organizations (Taylor & Bowers, 1972), a standardized questionnaire used extensively in organizations by researchers at the University of Michigan, has scales measuring two task-oriented behaviors (goal emphasis, work facilitation), and two relations-oriented behaviors (supportive leadership, interaction facilitation). In a review of results from research on 21 organizations, Bowers (1975) found that leadership behavior (by leaders and peers) was related to subordinate satisfaction and group processes, but the pattern of results varied, depending on the type of industry and the authority level of the manager.

Limitations of Survey Research

Survey research with questionnaires is by far the most common method used to study the relationship between leadership behavior and various antecedents (e.g., leader traits, attitudes) or outcomes of this behavior (e.g., subordinate satisfaction and performance). However, it is often difficult to interpret the meaning of the results in these survey studies. Two sources of error include limitations of the questionnaires and problems of determining causality.

Biases in Behavior Description Questionnaires

Behavior description questionnaires are susceptible to several types of bias and error (Luthans & Lockwood, 1984; Schriesheim & Kerr, 1977; Uleman, 1991). One source of error is the use of ambiguous items that can be interpreted in different ways by different respondents. Most leadership questionnaires have a fixed-response format that requires respondents to think back over a period of several months or years and indicate how often or how much a leader used the behavior described in an item. An accurate judgment is difficult to make, because the respondent may not have noticed the behavior at the time it occurred or may be unable to remember how many times it occurred during the specified time period (Shipper, 1991).

Another source of error for questionnaire items is response bias. For example, some respondents answer each item much the same way despite real differences in the leader's behavior, because the respondent likes (or dislikes) the leader (Schriesheim, Kinicki, & Schriesheim, 1979). Responses may also be distorted by stereotypes and implicit theories about what behaviors occur together. Respondents may attribute desirable behavior to a leader who is perceived to be effective, even though the behavior was not actually observed (Green & Mitchell, 1979; Lord, Binning, Rush, & Thomas, 1978; Mitchell, Larson, & Green, 1977).

Additional problems in behavior description questionnaires involve the way items are aggregated into scales, which is discussed later in this chapter. When the many sources of error are taken into account, it is easy to understand why retrospective behavior description questionnaires are not highly accurate measures of behavior.

Interpreting Causality in Survey Studies

Most of the research on effects of leadership behavior has measured behavior with questionnaires filled out by subordinates, and the resulting behavior scores have been correlated with criterion measures obtained at the same point in time. When a significant correlation is found, it is not possible to determine the direction of causality. There is often more than one plausible interpretation of causality, and more than one form of causality may occur at the same time.

When a positive correlation is found in a survey study, researchers usually assume that causality is from leader behavior to the criterion variable (Figure 3-3A). For example, a correlation between consideration and subordinate performance is usually interpreted as showing that considerate leaders cause subordinates to be more motivated

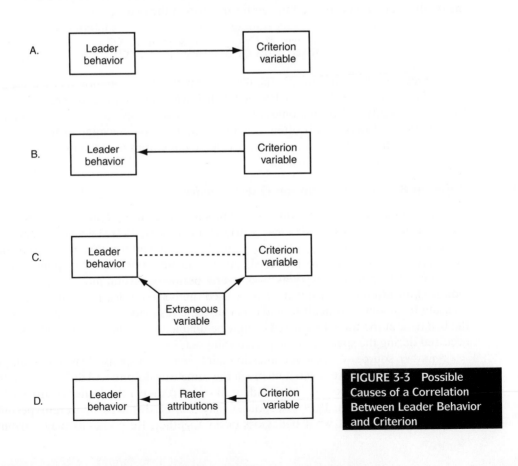

FIGURE 3-3 Possible Causes of a Correlation Between Leader Behavior and Criterion

and productive. However, it is also possible that causality is in the opposite direction (Figure 3-3B). This reverse causality occurs when leader behavior is influenced by the criterion variable. For example, the leader is more supportive to subordinates who demonstrate high performance.

Another possibility is that both leader behavior and the criterion variable are affected in the same way by a third variable (Figure 3-3C). In many studies the measures of leader behavior and the criterion variable are obtained from the same respondents. The correlation will be inflated if both measures are biased in the same way. For example, well-liked leaders are rated high on both consideration and effectiveness, whereas disliked leaders are rated low on both variables. This possibility is not likely when the criterion variable is measured independently of leader behavior. However, even when an independent criterion is used, the correlation between it and ratings of leader behavior may be inflated by rater attributions (Figure 3-3D). For example, raters who know the leader has a high-performing group may rate the leader higher on behaviors they perceive to be relevant for effective leadership (see section on follower attributions and implicit theories in Chapter 5).

Experiments on Task and Relations Behavior

The best way to determine causality is to conduct an experiment in which leader behavior is manipulated by the researcher. Several experiments were conducted in a laboratory setting with university students (Day, 1971; Day & Hamblin, 1964; Farris & Lim, 1969; Herold, 1977; Lowin & Craig, 1968; Misumi & Shirakashi, 1966; Sims & Manz, 1984). This research demonstrated that causality operates in both directions, from behavior to outcomes, and vice versa.

A limitation of most laboratory experiments on leadership is that they are unrealistic, which makes it difficult to generalize the findings to employees in real organizations. In an attempt to overcome this limitation, two studies were conducted with students hired to work in temporary, part-time jobs for a supervisor who was actually one of the researchers. Consideration and initiating structure were manipulated independently by having the supervisors display either high or low amounts of each leadership behavior to different subordinates. In one study (Lowin, Hrapchak, & Kavanagh, 1969), considerate leaders had more satisfied and productive subordinates, but there was no significant effect of leader structuring behavior. In the other study (Gilmore, Beehr, & Richter, 1979), neither type of leadership behavior had a consistent, significant effect on subordinate productivity or quality, perhaps because the manipulation of leader behavior was very weak.

Field experiments are difficult to conduct in real organizations, and only a small number of them have been used to investigate the effects of leadership behavior. In these field experiments, leadership behavior is usually manipulated with a training program. One study in a steel plant found that training increased the use of consideration by managers in the experimental group, and 18 months after the training was completed these managers were rated more effective than managers in the control group (Hand & Slocum, 1972). The results for task-oriented behavior were inconclusive. In a study of hospital supervisors, training increased consideration behavior, which resulted in higher subordinate satisfaction and attendance measured two months after training (Wexley & Nemeroff, 1975). In a study of first-line production supervisors, training increased the use of some relationship-oriented behaviors (e.g., active listening, use of praise), and there was a significant increase in performance ratings for these supervisors one year after training (Latham & Saari, 1979). In another study of supervisors, human relations training resulted in more use of some relationship-oriented behaviors (e.g., active listening, praise, consultation), including a significant 17 percent increase in worker productivity (production per hour) six months after training was completed (Porras & Anderson, 1981). Finally, in a study of production supervisors in a furniture factory, productivity improved (for six months to two years after training) in three of the four departments in which supervisors were trained to use more praise with subordinates (Wikoff, Anderson, & Crowell, 1983).

In summary, the experimental research in laboratory and field settings found that increases in relations-oriented leadership behavior usually resulted in higher subordinate satisfaction and productivity. Task-oriented leadership was seldom manipulated in the experimental studies, and when it was manipulated, the results were mixed and inconclusive.

Research Using Critical Incidents

Another type of research on managerial behavior uses the critical incident approach (Flanagan, 1951). This method represents a bridge between descriptive research on what managers do and research on effective behavior. The method is based on the assumption that respondents such as subordinates, peers, and superiors can provide descriptions of effective and ineffective behavior for a particular type of manager (e.g., production supervisors, retail store managers, military officers). The behavior incidents are collected by interview or open-ended questionnaire from a large sample of respondents. Critical incidents are especially useful in exploratory research designed to examine specific, situationally relevant aspects of managerial behavior. The following examples of critical incidents for production supervisors are from a study by Kay (1959, pg. 26):

> Aware that a change in setup was scheduled for the next day, a foreman checked a machine, noted a missing part, and ordered it. (positive incident)

> A foreman failed to notify the relief shift foreman that a machine was in need of repair before it could be operated again. (negative incident)

In most critical incident studies, the incidents are grouped together on the basis of similar behavior content, either by the researchers or by a panel of the respondents. The resulting behavior categories differ greatly from study to study. These differences are due in part to the large variety of leaders who have been studied, including production supervisors (Gellerman, 1976; Heizer, 1972), grocery store managers (Anderson & Nilsson, 1964), department managers in retail stores (Campbell, Dunnette, Arvey, & Hellervik, 1973), and logging crew supervisors (Latham & Wexley, 1977). The differences in behavior categories are also due to the arbitrary and subjective nature of the classification process. Even so, a close examination of the results reveals a moderate degree of communality across studies. The following types of leader behavior were represented in most of the studies:

1. Planning, coordinating, and organizing operations
2. Supervising subordinates (directing, instructing, monitoring performance)

3. Establishing and maintaining good relations with subordinates
4. Establishing and maintaining good relations with superiors, peers, and outsiders
5. Assuming responsibility for observing organizational policies, carrying out required duties, and making necessary decisions

Limitations of Critical Incident Research

The critical incident method has a number of limitations. It assumes that most respondents know what behaviors are relevant for leadership effectiveness, and it assumes a behavior is important if it appears frequently in incidents reported by many different people. However, the respondents may be biased in their perception of what is effective, and respondents may tend to remember and report incidents that are consistent with their stereotypes or implicit theories about effective leaders. Researchers rarely follow up a critical incident study with additional research to verify that the behaviors differentiate between effective and ineffective leaders selected on the basis of an independent criterion, such as group performance. This follow-up approach was used successfully in one study by Latham and Wexley (1977) on logging crew supervisors.

Many of the behavior categories found in research with critical incidents are defined in terms that relate the behavior to the specific requirements of the job for the type of leader studied. Defining behavior categories at this level of specificity facilitates objectives such as developing a performance appraisal instrument or determining training needs, but it is difficult to compare the categories across studies with different types of leaders. This limitation can be overcome by coding the incidents into predetermined behavior categories that are widely applicable, as was done in the study by Yukl and Van Fleet (1982). The use of both situation-specific and more generic behavior categories makes it possible for critical incident research to serve multiple purposes.

The High-High Leader

The extensive research on task-oriented and relations-oriented leadership during the 1960s gave rise to the idea of the high-high leader. Blake and Mouton (1964) proposed a model called the *managerial grid* to describe managers in terms of concern for people and concern for production. According to the model, effective managers have a high concern for both people and production. Many researchers who were influenced by the managerial grid and the early Ohio State leadership studies decided to test the idea that effective leaders make frequent use of task-oriented and person-oriented behaviors. In Japan, a parallel program of behavior research led to the formulation of a similar, two-factor model called PM Leadership Theory (Misumi & Peterson, 1985). According to that theory, effective leaders are high in both performance behavior and maintenance behavior (the PM leader).

Even though most theorists agree that task and relations behavior are both important for effective leadership, there is disagreement about the way the two types of leadership behavior jointly affect subordinates (Larson, Hunt, & Osborn, 1976). Some theorists assumed that a leader's task-oriented behavior and person-oriented behavior have independent, additive effects on subordinates. In this additive model, a particular type of leadership behavior is relevant only for accomplishing the task or maintaining harmonious, cooperative relationships, but not for both concerns simultaneously. Person-oriented behavior may result in higher job satisfaction, teamwork, and organizational commitment, whereas task-oriented behavior may result in better understanding of role requirements, better coordination among subordinates, and more efficient utilization of resources and personnel. Both types of outcomes are important for the overall performance of a work unit, and both types of behaviors are necessary to be an effective leader.

Other theorists have assumed that the two types of behavior interact and are mutually facilitative in their effects on subordinates. In this multiplicative version of the high-high leader model, one type of behavior enhances the effects of the other type of behavior. The reasons for a facilitative interaction were not well developed, but a number of plausible explanations have been provided over the years, and they are not mutually exclusive. One explanation involves the effect of supportive behavior on subordinate perception of task-oriented behavior. For example, detailed instruction and frequent monitoring may be perceived as helpful behavior from a leader who is supportive, but as punitive behavior from a leader who is not supportive (Fleishman & Harris, 1962; Misumi, 1985). A second explanation involves the effect of supportive behavior on the leader's potential influence over a subordinate. A supportive leader will have more referent power (see Chapter 6), which can be used to influence subordinates to improve their performance (Yukl, 1981).

Research on the High-High Leader

In most survey studies on leadership behavior, researchers have used measures and analyses that assume an additive model. In Western countries, results for the additive model have been inconclusive. Task and relations behavior tend to be correlated positively with subordinate performance, but the correlation is usually weak (Fisher & Edwards, 1988). Only a small number of studies have actually tested for an interaction between task-oriented and person-oriented behavior, and the results were inconsistent (e.g., Evans, 1970; Fleishman & Harris, 1962; Larson, Hunt, & Osborn, 1976). In Japan, survey and quasi-experimental studies have provided more consistent support for the additive model (Misumi, 1985), but the multiplicative model was not tested.

In summary, the survey research provides only limited support for the universal proposition that high-high leaders are more effective. In contrast, the research based on critical incidents and interviews strongly suggests that effective leaders guide and facilitate the work to accomplish task objectives while at the same time maintaining cooperative relationships and teamwork.

Evaluation of the Model and Research

The survey research on consequences of leader behavior does not provide an adequate test of the high-high model. Few studies have directly investigated whether the two types of leader behavior interact in a mutually facilitative way. Even when such an analysis is made, it is doubtful that the questionnaires used in the research provide an adequate basis for evaluating the theory (Blake & Mouton, 1982; Sashkin & Fulmer, 1988; Yukl, 1989).

Blake and Mouton (1982) proposed that an effective leader is not someone who merely uses a mix of task and relations behaviors, but rather someone who selects specific forms of behavior that simultaneously reflect a concern for both task and people. As we saw in Chapter 2, managers are overloaded with demands and must ration their time and select relevant behaviors. Whenever possible, an effective manager will select behaviors that accomplish task and relations concerns simultaneously. To determine whether a leader uses these high-high behaviors requires a questionnaire that includes them. Unfortunately, behavior items that reflect a high concern for both task and relations are unlikely to survive the procedures (e.g., factor analysis) used to select items for the scales.

Blake and Mouton (1982) also recognized the need for leaders to select specific forms of behavior that are appropriate for a particular time or situation. The usual assumption made with the behavior questionnaires is that all items in a scale are equally relevant regardless of the situation. This assumption fails to recognize the need for leaders to be flexible and adaptive in their behavior. A leader who uses only the most relevant forms of task and relations behavior will not get high mean scores on both scales, even though the leader fits the conception of a high-high leader.

The limitations of the survey research suggest that it may be more appropriate to test the model with other research methods such as experiments and behavior descriptions obtained from diaries or interviews. An example is provided by a recent study of 26 project teams using content coding of diary incidents recorded by team members for many weeks. The study found that specific types of task and relations behaviors were intertwined in complex ways (Amabile, Schatzel, Moneta, & Kramer, 2004). Effective leaders used more relations-oriented behaviors such as providing psychological support, consulting with team members, and providing recognition, but they also used more task behaviors such as clarifying roles and objectives, monitoring progress, and dealing with work-related problems. An analysis of positive and negative incidents showed that when and how the behavior was done was often more important than what type of behavior was done. Negative behavior (inappropriate or inept actions or failure to take appropriate action when it was needed) usually had a stronger influence on subordinate affect than positive behavior and could result in a negative spiral of actions and reactions between the leader and subordinates. This study and other descriptive research on effective leaders show that effective leadership requires the integration of relevant task and relations behaviors in a skillful and timely way.

The way in which leader behavior is conceptualized and measured is relevant for the controversy about universal versus situational models of leadership effectiveness. As noted in Chapter 1, universal models postulate that a particular leadership attribute is optimal in all situations, whereas situational models specify different attributes in different situations. The managerial grid has both universal and situational aspects. The universal aspect is the manager's dual concern for task and people, and the situational aspect is the selection of behaviors that are relevant for the situation as well as for these concerns. Unfortunately, Blake and Mouton did not develop propositions about appropriate behaviors for different situations.

We will make faster progress in understanding managerial effectiveness when specific aspects of managerial behavior are examined in the context of the situational requirements and constraints faced by a manager. The next section of this chapter reviews research to develop more complex taxonomies of leadership behavior.

Leadership Behavior Taxonomies

A major problem in research on the content of leadership behavior has been the identification of behavior categories that are relevant and meaningful for all leaders. In the research on managerial activities in Chapter 2, we saw that each study produced a somewhat different set of behavior categories, making it difficult to compare and integrate the results across studies. A similar condition exists for the behavior research described in this chapter. As a consequence, the past half-century of research has produced a bewildering variety of behavior concepts pertaining to managers and leaders (see Bass, 1990; Fleishman et al., 1991). Sometimes different terms have been used to refer to the same type of behavior. At other times, the same term has been defined differently by various theorists. What is treated as a general behavior category by one theorist is viewed as two or three distinct categories by another theorist. What is a key concept in one taxonomy is absent from another. Different taxonomies have emerged from different research disciplines, and it is difficult to translate from one set of concepts to another. Table 3-1 lists several behavior taxonomies proposed during the past half-century.

TABLE 3-1   Overview of Behavior Taxonomies

Authors and Date	Categories	Primary Purpose	Primary Method
Fleishman (1953)	2	Describe effective behavior	Factor analysis
Stogdill (1963)	12	Describe effective behavior	Theoretical-deductive
Mahoney et al. (1963)	8	Describe job requirements	Theoretical-deductive
Bowers & Seashore (1966)	4	Describe effective behavior	Theoretical-deductive
Mintzberg (1973)	10	Classify observed activities	Judgmental classification
House & Mitchell (1974)	4	Describe effective behavior	Theoretical-deductive
Morse & Wagner (1978)	6	Describe effective behavior	Factor analysis
Yukl & Nemeroff (1979)	13	Describe effective behavior	Factor analysis
Luthans & Lockwood (1984)	12	Classify observed activities	Judgmental classification
Page (1985)	10	Describe job requirements	Factor analysis
Yukl et al. (1990)	14	Describe effective behavior	Factor analysis
Bass & Avolio (1990)	7	Describe effective behavior	Factor analysis
Wilson et al. (1990)	15	Describe effective behavior	Factor analysis
Podsakoff et al. (1990)	6	Describe effective behavior	Factor analysis
Fleishman et al. (1991)	13	Describe effective behavior	Theoretical-deductive
Conger & Kanungo (1994)	6	Describe effective behavior	Factor analysis
Yukl, Gordon, & Taber (2002)	12	Describe effective behavior	Factor analysis

Sources of Diversity Among Taxonomies

There are several reasons why taxonomies developed to describe leadership behavior are so diverse (Fleishman et al., 1991; Yukl, 1989). Behavior categories are abstractions rather than tangible attributes of the real world. The categories are derived from observed behavior in order to organize perceptions of the world and make them meaningful, but they do not exist in any objective sense. No absolute set of "correct" behavior categories can be established. Thus, taxonomies that differ in purpose can be expected to have somewhat different constructs. For example, taxonomies designed to facilitate research and theory on managerial effectiveness have a somewhat different focus from taxonomies designed to describe observations of managerial activities, or taxonomies designed to catalog position responsibilities of managers and administrators.

Another source of diversity among taxonomies, even for those with the same purpose, is the possibility that behavior constructs can be formulated at different levels of abstraction or generality. Some taxonomies contain a small number of broadly defined behavior categories, whereas other taxonomies contain a larger number of narrowly focused behavior categories. For example, initiating structure as defined by Fleishman (1953) is a broad category, clarifying work roles is a mid-range category, and setting concrete goals is a concrete, narrowly focused category. All three are abstract behavior categories, but goal setting is a component of clarifying, which is a component of initiating structure (see Table 3-2). The optimal level of abstraction for the behavior categories in a taxonomy depends upon the purpose of the taxonomy. Some taxonomies of leader or manager behavior contain a mix of constructs at different levels of abstraction, thereby creating additional confusion.

A third source of diversity among behavior taxonomies is the method used to develop them. Some taxonomies are developed by examining the pattern of covariance among behavior items on a behavior description questionnaire describing actual managers (factor analysis method); some taxonomies are developed by having judges group behavior examples according to perceived similarity in content or purpose (judgmental classification); and some taxonomies are developed by deduction from theory (theoretical-deductive approach). Each method has its own associated biases, and the use of different methods results in somewhat different taxonomies, even when the purpose is the same. When a combination of methods has been used, one method is usually more important than others for selecting the behavior categories.

When different taxonomies are compared, it is obvious that there are substantial differences in the number of behaviors, the range of behaviors, and the level of abstraction of the behavior concepts. Some taxonomies focus on a few, broadly defined behaviors, whereas other taxonomies have a larger number of behavior categories that

TABLE 3-2 Examples of Behaviors at Different Levels of Abstraction

Broad, Abstract Categories	Task-Oriented Behavior	
Mid-Range Categories	Clarifying	Monitoring
Concrete, Narrow Categories	Goal setting	Visiting facilities
Observed Incidents	The manager set a goal to increase sales 10% by March 1.	The manager walked through the new store to see if it was ready for the opening.

are more narrowly defined. Some taxonomies are intended to cover the full range of leader behaviors, whereas others only include the behaviors identified in a leadership theory (e.g., theories of charismatic or transformational leadership).

Limitations of Factor-Based Taxonomies

Factor analysis of survey questionnaires has been used to develop most of the behavior taxonomies. It is a useful statistical tool, but it has some serious limitations, which helps to explain the lack of consistency even among the taxonomies that were developed with the same method for the same purpose. The results are affected by subjective choices among the various factor analysis procedures. The results are also affected by the content of the item pool, the amount of ambiguity in the behavior items, the format and response choices used in the questionnaire, the sample size and identity of the respondents, the experience and cognitive complexity of the respondents, the intended use and confidentiality of the data, and the initial expectations of the researcher.

The content of the behavior questionnaire can affect the factor structure in significant ways. When a wide variety of leadership behavior is well represented in the item pool, a simple factor solution is less likely to be found. When the initial questionnaire includes sets of similarly worded items, a separate factor is more likely to be found for each set. However, it is difficult to conclude that these factors represent distinct and meaningful behavior categories, especially when the resulting scales are highly intercorrelated.

The results from factor analysis of behavior description questionnaires are also affected by the experience of respondents and their implicit theories about leadership (see Chapter 5). It is difficult to rate leadership behavior even under the best of conditions. People with limited experience and simple ideas about effective leadership are unlikely to notice and remember subtle aspects of leader behavior that happened months or years earlier. When people are asked to rate behaviors that are difficult to understand and remember, the ratings are more likely to be biased by general impressions of leader competence and how satisfied respondents are with the leader.

A Three-Dimensional Taxonomy

The large number of specific behaviors identified in leadership research makes it difficult integrate results across studies. Metacategories make it easier to "see the forest for the trees." The distinction made between task-oriented and people-oriented behaviors during the 1950s has been helpful for organizing specific types of leadership behavior into broader categories. However, something important was still missing. The two metacategories do not include behaviors directly concerned with encouraging and facilitating change. By the 1980s, change-oriented behavior was implicit in some theories of charismatic and transformational leadership, but it was still not explicitly recognized as a separate dimension or metacategory. That discovery was made independently in the 1990s by researchers in Sweden (Ekvall & Arvonen, 1991) and the United States (Yukl, 1997, 1999a).

Verification that change-oriented behavior is a distinct and meaningful metacategory extended the earlier research and provided important insights about effective leadership. Each of the three metacategories was not clearly linked to a different outcome, and each outcome was relevant for effective leadership (see Chapter 12). Task-oriented behavior is primarily concerned with accomplishing the task in an efficient and reliable way. Relations-oriented behavior is primarily concerned with increasing mutual trust, cooperation, job satisfaction, and identification with the organization. Change-oriented behavior is primarily concerned with understanding the environment, finding innovative ways to adapt to it, and implementing major changes in strategies, products, or processes.

Figure 3-4 provides two alternative ways to graphically show how the three meta-categories relate to specific types of leadership behavior. A *categorical model* is most useful when specific behaviors have a single objective or an obvious primary objective. This model is consistent with a hierarchical taxonomy in which each specific behavior is a component of only one metacategory. Table 3-3 lists specific leader behaviors that represent each metacategory.

A *multidimensional model* is more useful when many leader behaviors strongly affect more than one objective. For example, when a leader consults with team members about the action plan for a project, the result may be more commitment to the project (human relations), better use of available personnel and resources (task efficiency), and discovery of more innovative ways to satisfy the client (adaptation). When a leader provides coaching for an employee, the result may be improved productivity (task efficiency), an increase in employee skills relevant for career advancement (human relations), and better implementation of an innovative new program (adaptive change). In the dimensional model shown in the figure, any specific behavior can be located in three-dimensional space in order to show how much the behavior reflects a concern for task efficiency, human relations, and adaptive change. Note that unlike managerial grid theory (Blake & Mouton, 1982), this model is used to classify specific leadership behaviors rather than to classify managers in terms of their general concern for tasks and relationships.

Yukl, Gordon, and Taber (2002) recently conducted a study to assess support for the hierarchical taxonomy and the three-dimensional model. They constructed a questionnaire

A. Three-Factor Model

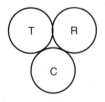

B. Three-Dimensional Model

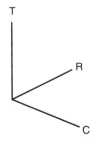

FIGURE 3-4 Two Alternative Conceptions of Task-, Relations-, and Change-Oriented Behavior

TABLE 3-3   Examples of Task-, Relations-, and Change-Oriented Behaviors

Task-Oriented Behaviors

- Organize work activities to improve efficiency.
- Plan short-term operations.
- Assign work to groups or individuals.
- Clarify what results are expected for a task.
- Set specific goals and standards for task performance.
- Explain rules, policies, and standard operating procedures.
- Direct and coordinate work activities.
- Monitor operations and performance.
- Resolve immediate problems that would disrupt the work.

Relations-Oriented Behaviors

- Provide support and encouragement to someone with a difficult task.
- Express confidence that a person or group can perform a difficult task.
- Socialize with people to build relationships.
- Recognize contributions and accomplishments.
- Provide coaching and mentoring when appropriate.
- Consult with people on decisions affecting them.
- Allow people to determine the best way to do a task.
- Keep people informed about actions affecting them.
- Help resolve conflicts in a constructive way.
- Use symbols, ceremonies, rituals, and stories to build team identity.
- Recruit competent new members for the team or organization.

Change-Oriented Behaviors

- Monitor the external environment to detect threats and opportunities.
- Interpret events to explain the urgent need for change.
- Study competitors and outsiders to get ideas for improvements.
- Envision exciting new possibilities for the organization.
- Encourage people to view problems or opportunities in a different way.
- Develop innovative new strategies linked to core competencies.
- Encourage and facilitate innovation and entrepreneurship in the organization.
- Encourage and facilitate collective learning in the team or organization.
- Experiment with new approaches for achieving objectives.
- Make symbolic changes that are consistent with a new vision or strategy.
- Encourage and facilitate efforts to implement major change.
- Announce and celebrate progress in implementing change.
- Influence outsiders to support change and negotiate agreements with them.

with scales for specific behaviors identified in earlier research on effective leadership. A confirmatory factor analysis was used to determine whether each specific behavior could be sorted into one of the three metacategories in a way that is consistent with assumptions about the primary objective of the behavior. The study found support for 12 specific behaviors, but results were inconclusive for some other behaviors included in the questionnaire.

The results provided moderate support for the proposed hierarchical taxonomy, which is a categorical model. However, the pattern of factor results for items and scales also indicated that some of the specific behaviors were relevant for more than one ob-jective, which is consistent with a dimensional model. At the present time it appears that both the categorical and dimensional models can be useful for describing the com-plex interrelationships among different types of leadership behavior.

Comparison of Recent Taxonomies

Because most of the behaviors identified in earlier research on effective leadership were also included in the study by Yukl and colleagues (2002), the results from that study provide insights about similarities and differences among the behavior taxonomies. Table 3-4 shows how the 12 behaviors identified in the survey research correspond to

TABLE 3-4	Approximate Correspondence Among Leadership Behaviors in Four Taxonomies		
TRCQ	*MLQ*	*CK Inventory*	*MPS*
Supporting	Individualized consideration	Sensitivity to members	Supporting
Developing	Individualized consideration	NI	Developing & Mentoring
Recognizing	Contingent rewarding	NI	Recognizing & Rewarding
Consulting	NI	NI	Consulting
Delegating & Empowering	NI	NI	Delegating
Clarifying roles & objectives	NI	NI	Clarifying roles & objectives
Short-term planning	NI	NI	Planning
Monitoring	Active managing by exception	NI	Monitoring
Envisioning Change	Inspirational motivation	Strategic vision articulation	Inspiring & Motivating
Encouraging innovative thinking	Intellectual stimulation	NI	NI
External monitoring	NI	Environmental Sensitivity	Networking & interfacing
Taking risks & leading by example	Idealized influence behaviors	Personal risk taking	NI

Note: NI means that a behavior is not explicitly included in a taxonomy. The heavy lines indicate the classification and sorting of behaviors into relations-, task-, or change-oriented metacategories.

observable effective behaviors in three other taxonomies, and how each behavior is related to the three metacategories. The table does not include behaviors that are ineffective (e.g., laissez-faire leadership, passive monitoring by exception), or behaviors that are vague and difficult for subordinates to observe (e.g., nontraditional behavior, attributed idealized influence).

The Managerial Practices Survey (MPS) is used primarily for multisource feedback to managers (Yukl, Wall, & Lepsinger, 1990), but it has also been used for research on effective leadership (e.g., Kim & Yukl, 1995). The MPS has good representation of task and relations behaviors, but it does not measure some strategic change-oriented behaviors. The C-K inventory (Conger & Kanungo, 1994) is used for research on charismatic leadership, and it has the narrowest range of behaviors. The the Multifactor Leadership Questionnaire (MLQ) is used for research on transformational leadership (Bass & Avolio, 2000). The taxonomy of behaviors measured by the MLQ has been labeled the "full-range model" (Avolio, 1999), but it does not include several task-, relations-, and change-oriented behaviors found to be relevant in the past half-century of behavior research (Yukl, 1998; Yukl et al., 2002).

The remaining two sections of this chapter describe in greater detail several specific leadership behaviors that are primarily task-oriented or relations-oriented. Change-oriented behaviors are described in Chapters 9 and 10. The challenge for leaders of balancing and integrating all three types of behavior is discussed in Chapter 12.

Specific Task Behaviors

This section of the chapter describes three specific types of task-oriented behaviors that are especially relevant for effective leadership. The behaviors include (1) short-term planning, (2) clarifying roles and objectives, and (3) monitoring operations and performance. The behaviors are explained and research on each type of behavior is briefly reviewed.

Planning Work Activities

Short-term planning of work activities means deciding what to do, how to do it, who will do it, and when it will be done. The purpose of planning is to ensure efficient organization of the work unit, coordination of activities, and effective utilization of resources. Planning is a broadly defined behavior that includes making decisions about objectives, priorities, strategies, organization of the work, assignment of responsibilities, scheduling of activities, and allocation of resources among different activities according to their relative importance. Special names are sometimes used for subvarieties of planning. For example, *operational planning* is the scheduling of routine work and determination of task assignments for the next day or week. *Action planning* is the development of detailed action steps and schedules for implementing a new policy or carrying out a project (see guidelines in Table 3-5). *Contingency planning* is the development of procedures for avoiding or coping with potential problems or disasters. Finally, planning also includes determining how to allocate time to different responsibilities and activities ("time management").

Planning is largely a cognitive activity involving processing of information, analyzing, and deciding. Planning seldom occurs in a single behavior episode; rather it tends to be a prolonged process that occurs over a period of weeks or months. We saw in Chapter 2

TABLE 3-5   Guidelines for Action Planning
• Identify necessary action steps.
• Identify the optimal sequence of action steps.
• Estimate the time needed to carry out each action step.
• Determine starting times and deadlines for each action step.
• Estimate the cost of each action step.
• Determine who will be accountable for each action step.
• Develop procedures for monitoring progress.

that most planning involves formulation of informal and implicit agendas, rather than formal, written documents and agreements. Because planning is a cognitive activity that seldom occurs as a single discrete episode, it is difficult to observe (Snyder & Glueck, 1980). Nevertheless, some observable aspects include writing plans, preparing written budgets, developing written schedules, and meeting with others to formulate objectives and strategies. Planning is most observable when a manager takes action to implement plans by communicating them to others and making specific task assignments.

The importance of planning and organizing has long been recognized in the management literature (Carroll & Gillen, 1987; Drucker, 1974; Fayol, 1949; Quinn, 1980; Urwick, 1952). Evidence of a relationship between planning and managerial effectiveness is provided by a variety of different types of studies (e.g., Boyatzis, 1982; Carroll & Gillen, 1987; Kim & Yukl, 1995; Kotter, 1982; Morse & Wagner, 1978; Shipper & Wilson, 1992; Yukl, Wall, & Lepsinger, 1990).

Clarifying Roles and Objectives

Clarifying is the communication of plans, policies, and role expectations. Major subcategories of clarifying include (1) defining job responsibilities and requirements, (2) setting performance goals, and (3) assigning specific tasks. Guidelines for each type of clarifying are shown in Table 3-6. The purpose of this clarifying behavior is to guide and coordinate work activity and make sure people know what to do and how to do it. It is essential for each subordinate to understand what duties, functions, and activities are required in the job and what results are expected. Even a subordinate who is highly competent and motivated may fail to achieve a high level of performance if confused about responsibilities and priorities. Such confusion results in misdirected effort and neglect of important responsibilities in favor of less important ones. The more complex and multifaceted the job, the more difficult it is to determine what needs to be done.

Clarifying behavior is likely to be more important when there is substantial role ambiguity or role conflict for members of the work unit. Less clarifying is necessary if the organization has elaborate rules and regulations dictating how the work should be done and subordinates understand them, or if subordinates are highly trained professionals who have the expertise to do their jobs without much direction from superiors. Contingency theories about the amount of clarifying behavior needed in different situations are described in Chapter 8.

Clarifying is a core component of initiating structure. As noted earlier, the research on broadly defined measures of task-oriented behavior was mostly inconclusive. However, research on specific aspects of clarifying behavior has found stronger results. A number

TABLE 3-6   Guidelines for Clarifying Roles and Objectives

Defining Job Responsibilities
- Explain the important job responsibilities.
- Clarify the person's scope of authority.
- Explain how the job relates to the mission of the unit.
- Explain important policies, rules, and requirements.

Assigning Work
- Clearly explain the assignment.
- Explain the reasons for an assignment.
- Clarify priorities and deadlines.
- Check for comprehension.

Setting Performance Goals
- Set goals for relevant aspects of performance.
- Set goals that are clear and specific.
- Set goals that are challenging but realistic.
- Set a target date for attainment of each goal.

of different types of studies have found a positive relationship between clarifying and managerial effectiveness (Alexander,1985; Bauer & Green, 1998; Kim & Yukl, 1995; Van Fleet & Yukl, 1986b; Wilson et al., 1990; Yukl, Wall, & Lepsinger,1990). Strong evidence from many studies (including some field experiments) indicates that setting specific, challenging goals results in higher performance (see Locke & Latham, 1990).

Monitoring Operations and Performance

Monitoring involves gathering information about the operations of the manager's organizational unit, including the progress of the work, the performance of individual subordinates, the quality of products or services, and the success of projects or programs. Monitoring behavior can take many forms, including observation of work operations, reading written reports, watching computer screen displays of performance data, inspecting the quality of samples of the work, and holding progress review meetings with an individual or group. The appropriate type of monitoring depends on the nature of the task and other aspects of the situation. Some guidelines for monitoring operations are provided in Table 3-7.

Monitoring provides much of the information needed for planning and problem solving, which is why it is so important for managerial effectiveness (Meredith & Mantel, 1985). Information gathered from monitoring is used to identify problems and opportunities, as well as to formulate and modify objectives, strategies, plans, policies, and procedures. Monitoring provides the information needed to evaluate subordinate performance, recognize achievements, identify performance deficiencies, assess training needs, provide coaching and assistance, and allocate rewards such as a pay increase or promotion. When monitoring is insufficient, a manager will be unable to detect problems before they become serious (problems such as declining quality, low productivity, cost overruns, behind-schedule projects, employee dissatisfaction, and conflicts among employees).

The appropriate degree of monitoring will depend on the competence of the subordinate and the nature of the work. More frequent monitoring is desirable when

TABLE 3-7	Guidelines for Monitoring Operations

- Identify and measure key performance indicators.
- Monitor key process variables as well as outcomes.
- Measure progress against plans and budgets.
- Develop independent sources of information about performance.
- Observe operations directly when it is feasible.
- Ask specific questions about the work.
- Encourage reporting of problems and mistakes.
- Conduct periodic progress review meetings.

subordinates are inexperienced and insecure, when mistakes have serious consequences, when the tasks of subordinates are highly interdependent and require close coordination, and when disruptions in the workflow are likely, due to equipment breakdowns, accidents, materials shortages, personnel shortages, and so forth. Monitoring of performance is most difficult when the work involves unstructured, unique tasks for which results can be determined only after a long time interval. For example, it is more difficult to evaluate the performance of a research scientist or human resource manager than the performance of a sales representative or production manager. Monitoring too closely or in ways that communicate distrust can undermine subordinate self-confidence and reduce intrinsic motivation.

As noted previously, monitoring indirectly affects a manager's performance by facilitating the effective use of other behaviors. Some evidence also shows that monitoring affects performance directly. In a laboratory experiment, Larson and Callahan (1990) found that performance increased on a task that was monitored closely but not on a task that was subject to little monitoring. The effect on performance was greater when monitoring was followed by praise or criticism, but it occurred even when there were no associated consequences for the workers. The amount of research on the effects of monitoring by leaders is still limited. Some evidence that monitoring is related to managerial effectiveness is provided by several studies and a variety of research methods including field surveys, observation, and diary incidents (e.g., Amabile et al., 2004; Jenster,1987; Kim & Yukl, 1995; Komaki, 1986; Komaki, Desselles, & Bowman, 1989; Komaki & Minnich, 2002; Yukl, Wall, & Lepsinger, 1990).

Specific Relations Behaviors

This section of the chapter describes three specific types of relations-oriented behaviors that are especially relevant for effective leadership. The behaviors include (1) supporting, (2) developing, and (3) recognizing. The behaviors are explained and research on the behaviors is briefly reviewed. Other relations-oriented behaviors are described in subsequent chapters, including consulting (Chapter 4) and team building (Chapter 11).

Supporting

Supporting includes a wide variety of behaviors that show consideration, acceptance, and concern for the needs and feelings of other people. Supporting is the core

TABLE 3-8   Guidelines for Supporting
• Show acceptance and positive regard.
• Be polite and considerate, not arrogant and rude.
• Treat each subordinate as an individual.
• Remember important details about the person.
• Be patient and helpful when giving instructions or explanations.
• Provide sympathy and support when the person is anxious or upset.
• Express confidence in the person when there is a difficult task.
• Provide assistance with the work when it is needed.
• Be willing to help with personal problems.

component of consideration, as defined by Fleishman (1953) and Stogdill (1974), and it is also the core component of supportive leadership, as defined by Bowers and Seashore (1966) and House and Mitchell (1974). Table 3-8 shows guidelines for supportive behavior by leaders.

Supportive leadership helps to build and maintain effective interpersonal relationships. A manager who is considerate and friendly toward people is more likely to win their friendship and loyalty. The emotional ties that are formed make it easier to gain cooperation and support from people on whom the manager must rely to get the work done. It is more satisfying to work with someone who is friendly, cooperative, and supportive than with someone who is cold and impersonal, or worse, hostile and uncooperative. Some forms of supporting behavior reduce the amount of stress in the job, and other forms help a person cope with stress. Higher job satisfaction and stress tolerance are likely to result in less absenteeism, less turnover, less alcoholism, and less drug abuse (Brief, Schuler, & Van Sell, 1981; Ganster, Fusilier, & Mayes, 1986; Kessler, Price, & Wortman, 1985).

As noted earlier in this chapter, the effects of supportive leadership have been studied extensively with a variety of research methods. The studies show that subordinates of supportive leaders are usually more satisfied with their leader and with their job. The findings regarding the effects of supporting behavior on subordinate performance are less consistent, especially when controlling for the effects of other person-oriented behaviors such as developing and recognizing. Although no firm conclusions can be drawn, supportive leadership probably has a weak positive effect on subordinate performance. Unfortunately, few studies have measured the mediating processes that could explain the reasons for this effect or when it is most likely to occur. Supportive leadership may increase a subordinate's self-confidence, stress resistance, acceptance of the leader, trust of the leader, and willingness to do extra things for the leader. How these mediating processes can contribute to effective performance by a subordinate is described in more detail in subsequent chapters.

Developing

Developing includes several managerial practices that are used to increase a person's skills and facilitate job adjustment and career advancement. Component behaviors include coaching, mentoring, and career counseling. Guidelines for coaching are shown in Table 3-9, and guidelines for mentoring appear in Table 3-10.

TABLE 3-9   Guidelines for Coaching

- Help the person analyze his or her performance by asking questions or suggesting aspects to examine more closely.
- Provide constructive feedback about effective and ineffective behaviors exhibited by the person.
- Suggest specific things that could help to improve the person's performance.
- Demonstrate a better way to do a complex task or procedure.
- Express confidence the person can learn a difficult task or procedure.
- Provide opportunities to practice difficult procedures before they are used in the work.
- Help the person learn how to solve a problem rather than just providing the answer.

TABLE 3-10   Guidelines for Mentoring

- Help the person identify relevant strengths and weaknesses.
- Help the person find ways to acquire necessary skills and knowledge.
- Encourage attendance at relevant training courses.
- Provide opportunities to learn from experience.
- Provide helpful career advice.
- Promote the person's reputation.
- Serve as a role model (demonstrate appropriate behavior).

Developing is usually done with a subordinate, but it may also be done with a peer, a colleague, or even with a new, inexperienced boss. Responsibility for developing subordinates can be shared with other members of the work unit who are competent and experienced. For example, some leaders assign an experienced subordinate to serve as a mentor and coach for a new employee.

Developing offers a variety of potential benefits for the manager, the subordinate, and the organization. One benefit is to foster mutually cooperative relationships. Potential benefits for subordinates include better job adjustment, more skill learning, greater self-confidence, and faster career advancement. The leader can gain a sense of satisfaction from helping others grow and develop. Potential benefits for the organization include higher employee commitment, higher performance, and better preparation of people to fill positions of greater responsibility in the organization as openings occur.

There has been extensive research on the effects of skill training in organizations (see reviews by Goldstein, 1992). This literature suggests that skill development usually increases the satisfaction and performance. Managers play an important role in the development of subordinates. Empirical research on the effects of coaching and mentoring by managers is still limited. A few survey studies have examined the correlation between developing behavior and an independent criterion of leadership effectiveness, but the results were not consistent across samples (e.g., Javidan, 1992; Kim & Yukl, 1995; Wilson, O'Hare, & Shipper, 1990; Yukl, Wall, & Lepsinger, 1990). Descriptive research involving effective managers suggests that they take a more active role in developing the skills and confidence of subordinates (Bradford & Cohen, 1984; McCauley, 1986). Additional research on coaching and mentoring is described in Chapter 13.

Recognizing

Recognizing involves giving praise and showing appreciation to others for effective performance, significant achievements, and important contributions to the organization. Although it is most common to think of recognition as being given by a manager to subordinates, this managerial practice can also be used with peers, superiors, and people outside the work unit. The primary purpose of recognizing, especially when used with subordinates, is to strengthen desirable behavior and task commitment. Some guidelines for recognizing are presented in Table 3-11.

Three major forms of recognizing are praise, awards, and recognition ceremonies. Praise consists of oral comments, expressions, or gestures that acknowledge a person's accomplishments and contributions. It is the easiest form of recognition to use. Most praise is given privately, but it can be used in a public ritual or ceremony as well.

Awards include things such as a certificate of achievement, a letter of commendation, a plaque, a trophy, a medal, or a ribbon. Awards can be announced in many different ways, including an article in the company newsletter, a notice posted on the bulletin board, a picture of the person (e.g., "employee of the month") hung in a prominent place, over a public address system, in regular meetings, and at special ceremonies or rituals. Giving formal awards is a symbolic act that communicates a manager's values and priorities to people in the organization. Thus, it is important for awards to be based on meaningful criteria rather than favoritism or arbitrary judgments. An award that is highly visible allows others to share in the process of commending the recipient and showing appreciation for his or her contributions to the success of the organization. The basis for making the award is more important than the form of the award. Some managers are creative about using awards, and they look for new and unusual awards to use with "planned spontaneity." Examples include donuts, home-baked bread, flowers, a bottle of champagne, a new chair, and a picture of the employee shaking hands with the CEO.

A recognition ceremony ensures that an individual's achievements are acknowledged not only by the manager but also by other members of the organization. Recognition ceremonies can be used to celebrate the achievements of a team or work unit as well as those of an individual. Special rituals or ceremonies to honor particular employees or teams can have strong symbolic value when attended by top management, because they demonstrate their concern for the aspects of behavior or performance being recognized. A rather unique version of a recognition ceremony is used by Milliken and Company (Peters & Austin, 1985).

TABLE 3-11   Guidelines for Recognizing

- Recognize a variety of contributions and achievements.
- Actively search for contributions to recognize.
- Recognize specific contributions and achievements.
- Recognize improvements in performance.
- Recognize commendable efforts that failed.
- Provide recognition that is sincere.
- Provide recognition that is timely.
- Use a form of recognition appropriate for the person and situation.

Once each quarter a Corporate Sharing Rally is held to allow work teams to brag about their achievements and contributions. Each of the "fabulous bragging sessions" has a particular theme such as improved productivity, better product quality, or reduced costs. Attendance is voluntary, but hundreds of employees show up to hear teams make short five-minute presentations describing how they have made improvements relevant to the theme. Every participant receives a framed certificate, and the best presentations (determined by peer evaluation) get special awards. In addition to celebrating accomplishments and emphasizing key values (represented by the themes), these ceremonies increase the diffusion of innovative ideas within the company.

Praise is often given along with tangible rewards, and it is difficult to separate their effects on subordinate effort and satisfaction in much of the research literature. Most studies that measure contingent reward behavior with leader behavior questionnaires find a positive correlation with subordinate satisfaction, but results for performance are not consistent (e.g., Kim & Yukl, 1995; Lowe, Kroeck & Sivasubramaniam,1996; Podsakoff & Todor, 1985; Podsakoff, Todor, Grover, & Huber, 1984; Yukl et al., 1990). A meta-analysis of laboratory and field studies on praise as a form of feedback found little support for its effectiveness; praise was more likely to have a negative effect on performance than a positive effect (Kluger & DeNisi, 1996). In contrast, descriptive studies in organizations (Kouzes & Posner, 1987; Peters & Austin, 1985) suggest that effective leaders provide extensive recognition to subordinates for their achievements and contributions. A rare field experiment by Wikoff, Anderson, and Crowell (1983) found that praise by the supervisor increased subordinate performance. In summary, the results of empirical research on the effects of praise are inconsistent, but they suggest that it can be beneficial when used in a skillful way under favorable conditions.

Evaluation of the Behavior Approach

The early fixation on consideration and initiating structure appears to have ended, and most researchers now examine a broader range of behavior and more specific types of behaviors. Additional research on specific leadership behaviors is reviewed in later chapters of this book. Unfortunately, there are serious weaknesses in much of the behavior research conducted during the past two decades. The proliferation of taxonomies and lack of agreement about what behaviors to study has made it more difficult to integrate the research on leader behavior. Most researchers continue to use an available, "validated" questionnaire for their research without careful consideration about the relevance of the content for their research question and sample. Field studies that measure only the behaviors included in an available questionnaire (or selected scales from it) usually miss the opportunity to examine a wide range of behaviors, or to collect rich, descriptive information about leadership behavior. When the analysis involves only scale scores from questionnaires, it is often difficult to interpret the results, and there is little opportunity for inductive discoveries about effective leadership.

Like the trait research (see Chapter 7), the behavior research suffers from a tendency to look for simple answers to complex questions. Most research on leadership effectiveness has examined behaviors individually rather than examining how effective leaders use patterns of specific behaviors to accomplish their agendas. It is likely that specific behaviors interact in complex ways, and that leadership effectiveness cannot be understood unless these interactions are studied. For example, monitoring is useful for discovering problems, but unless something is done to solve the problems monitoring will not contribute to leader effectiveness. Planning is likely to be ineffective unless it is based on timely, accurate information gathered from monitoring, consulting, and networking, and developing plans is pointless unless the leader also influences people to support and implement them. Delegating is not likely to be effective unless the leader clarifies the subordinate's new responsibilities; ensures that the subordinate accepts them; monitors progress in an appropriate way; and provides necessary support, resources, and assistance.

Descriptive studies of managerial work suggest that complementary behaviors are woven together into a complex tapestry such that the whole is greater than the sum of the parts (Kaplan, 1986). A leader's skill in selecting and enacting appropriate behaviors is related to the success of the outcome, but different patterns of behavior may be used to accomplish the same outcome (the idea of equifinality). In future research it is essential to pay more attention to the overall pattern of leadership behavior rather than becoming too preoccupied with any particular component of it. Measures of how often a particular type of behavior is used are not enough; it is also essential to consider whether the behavior is used when and where it is appropriate, and in a skillful way.

Summary

From the 1950s to the mid-1980s, research on leader behavior was dominated by a focus on two broadly defined categories of behavior. Most studies of leadership behavior during this period used questionnaires measuring leader consideration and initiating structure. Hundreds of studies were conducted to see how these behaviors were correlated with criteria of leadership effectiveness such as subordinate satisfaction and performance. Other researchers used critical incidents, laboratory experiments, or field experiments to investigate how leader behavior affects subordinate satisfaction and performance. Results from this massive research effort have been mostly inconclusive. However, the overall pattern of results suggests that effective leaders use a pattern of behavior that is appropriate for the situation and reflects a high concern for task objectives and a high concern for relationships.

Recent research has identified a third general category of leadership behavior that is concerned primarily with change and innovation. This type of leadership behavior was not explicitly represented in the early research and theory about leadership behavior, and it is an essential element in more recent theory and research (see Chapters 9, 10, and 12). However, a more comprehensive set of metacategories does not mean that specific behaviors can be ignored in leadership theory and research. Much of the research on leader effectiveness indicates that for a given situation some specific behaviors are more relevant than others. Thus, to determine what form of leadership is appropriate in a particular situation, it is still necessary to study the specific behaviors rather than merely looking at the metacategories.

Behavior taxonomies are descriptive aids that may help us analyze complex events and understand them better. However, it is important to remember that all leader behavior constructs are subjective. Despite claims of validity for widely used scales, the type of research needed to assess whether behavior constructs are accurately measured (free of respondent bias) and meaningful for explaining effective leadership is seldom done. In the research on leader behavior there has been too much reliance on a small number of well-known questionnaires that measure a limited range of behaviors. This strategy is equivalent to assuming that we already know what types of behavior will be most useful for studying leadership. To facilitate interpretation of results and inductive discoveries, it is essential to be more flexible about what behaviors are examined in the research and the methods used to measure them.

Planning, clarifying, and monitoring are specific task-oriented behaviors that jointly affect subordinate performance. Planning involves deciding about objectives, priorities, strategies, allocation of resources, assignment of responsibilities, scheduling of activities, and allocation of the manager's own time. Clarifying includes assigning tasks, explaining job responsibilities, explaining rules and procedures, communicating priorities, setting specific performance goals and deadlines, and giving instructions in how to do a task. Monitoring involves getting information needed to evaluate the operations of the work unit and the performance of individual subordinates.

Supporting, developing, and recognizing are key relations-oriented behaviors. Supporting includes a wide range of behaviors by which a manager shows consideration, acceptance, and concern for someone's needs and feelings. A manager who is considerate and personable toward people is more likely to win their friendship and loyalty. Developing includes behavior that is intended to increase job-relevant skills and facilitate a person's job adjustment and career advancement. Examples include coaching, mentoring, and career counseling. Recognizing involves giving praise and showing appreciation to others for effective performance, significant achievements, and important contributions to the organization. Recognizing helps to strengthen desirable behavior, improve interpersonal relationships, and increase job satisfaction.

Review and Discussion Questions

1. What did we learn about leadership effectiveness from the early Ohio State and Michigan leadership studies?
2. What problems have impeded questionnaire research on leadership behavior?
3. What are critical incident studies, and what do they tell us about the behavior of effective leaders?
4. Explain the high-high theory of leadership effectiveness, and evaluate the research evidence for this theory.
5. How can a leader's behavior reflect a high concern for both task and relations at the same time?
6. Why are taxonomies of behavior constructs important for research and theory on managerial effectiveness?
7. Why do the taxonomies proposed by different theorists show so many differences?
8. Why are planning, clarifying, and monitoring relevant for leadership effectiveness?
9. Why are supporting, developing, and recognizing important for leadership effectiveness?
10. In general, what has been learned from research on effective leadership behavior?
11. To what extent are the findings consistent for this chapter and the previous one?

Key Terms

- behavior taxonomies
- change-oriented behavior
- clarifying
- consideration
- critical incidents
- developing

- high-high leader
- initiating structure
- Leader Behavior Description Questionnaire (LBDQ)
- monitoring

- Multifactor Leadership Questionnaire (MLQ)
- participative leadership
- peer leadership
- planning

- recognizing
- relations-oriented behavior
- supportive leadership
- task-oriented behavior

CASES

Consolidated Products

Consolidated Products is a medium-sized manufacturer of consumer products with nonunionized production workers. Ben Samuels was a plant manager for Consolidated Products for 10 years, and he was well liked by the employees. They were grateful for the fitness center he built for employees, and they enjoyed the social activities sponsored by the plant several times a year, including company picnics and holiday parties. He knew most of the workers by name, and he spent part of each day walking around the plant to visit with them and ask about their families or hobbies.

Ben believed that it was important to treat employees properly so they would have a sense of loyalty to the company. He tried to avoid any layoffs when production demand was slack, figuring that the company could not afford to lose skilled workers that are so difficult to replace. The workers knew that if they had a special problem, Ben would try to help them. For example, when someone was injured but wanted to continue working, Ben found another job in the plant that the person could do despite having a disability. Ben believed that if you treat people right, they will do a good job for you without close supervision or prodding. Ben applied the same principle to his supervisors, and he mostly left them alone to run their departments as they saw fit. He did not set objectives and standards for the plant, and he never asked the supervisors to develop plans for improving productivity and product quality.

Under Ben, the plant had the lowest turnover among the company's five plants, but the second worst record for costs and production levels. When the company was acquired by another firm, Ben was asked to take early retirement, and Phil Jones was brought in to replace him.

Phil had a growing reputation as a manager who could get things done, and he quickly began making changes. Costs were cut by trimming a number of activities such as the fitness center at the plant, company picnics and parties, and the human relations training programs for supervisors. Phil believed that training supervisors to be supportive was a waste of time. His motto was: "If employees don't want to do the work, get rid of them and find somebody else who does."

Supervisors were instructed to establish high performance standards for their departments and insist that people achieve them. A computer monitoring system was introduced so that the output of each worker could be checked closely against the standards. Phil told his supervisors to give any worker who had substandard performance one warning, then if performance did not improve within two weeks, to fire the person. Phil believed that workers don't respect a supervisor who is weak and passive. When Phil observed a worker wasting time or making a mistake, he would reprimand the person right on the spot to set an example. Phil also checked closely on the performance of his supervisors. Demanding objectives were set for each department, and weekly meetings were held with each supervisor to review department performance. Finally, Phil insisted that supervisors check with him first before taking any significant actions that deviated from established plans and policies.

As another cost-cutting move, Phil reduced the frequency of equipment maintenance, which required machines to be idled when they could be productive. Because the machines had a good record of reliable operation, Phil believed that the current maintenance schedule was excessive and was cutting into production. Finally, when business was slow for one of the product lines, Phil laid off workers rather than finding something else for them to do.

By the end of Phil's first year as plant manager, production costs were reduced by 20 percent and production output was up by 10 percent. However, three of his seven supervisors left to take other jobs, and turnover was also high among the machine operators. Some of the turnover was due to workers who were fired, but competent machine operators were also quitting, and it was becoming increasingly difficult to find any replacements for them. Finally, talk of unionizing was increasing among the workers. ■

SOURCE: Copyright © 1987 by Gary Yukl.

QUESTIONS

1. Describe and compare the managerial behavior of Ben and Phil. To what extent does each manager display specific relations behaviors (supporting, developing, recognizing) and specific task behaviors (clarifying, planning, monitoring)? To what extent does each manager use participative or inspirational leadership?
2. Compare Ben and Phil in terms of their influence on employee attitudes, short-term performance, and long-term plant performance, and explain the reasons for the differences.
3. If you were selected to be the manager of this plant, what would you do to achieve both high employee satisfaction and performance?

Air Force Supply Squadron

Colonel Pete Novak was assigned to command an air force squadron that airlifted supplies to combat units during the Korean War. The squadron had more than 200 men and several cargo planes. When he assumed command, the situation was bleak. They were short of supplies, personnel, and replacements. Organization and coordination were poor, and there was little cooperation and teamwork among different sections. Morale was low due to the unrelenting workload, the constant bickering and disagreements, and the stress of flying into combat zones.

Colonel Novak held a meeting of the squadron to introduce himself and talk about how important their mission was to the success of the war effort. He talked about how the men in the front lines were counting on the squadron to bring them the supplies and ammunition they needed to keep the enemy from overrunning the country. He reminded them that every man had a vital function in the operation of the squadron.

Then Colonel Novak set out to learn more about the men in his unit, beginning with the officers. He held frequent staff meetings with the section heads and some key noncommissioned officers (NCOs) to discuss the methods used to carry out the mission of the squadron. He visited the enlisted men at work and off duty, talking to them and showing a personal interest in them. He listened to their complaints, and whenever possible tried to deal with their concerns about the poor living conditions at the base. He flew along with the airplane crews on some of the supply missions. On one occasion when supplies were desperately needed at the front lines and the squadron was shorthanded, he pitched in and worked beside the men all during the night to load the planes.

It was not long before Colonel Novak had learned each person's name, what his job was, and something about his background. As he found out more about the capabilities of the men, he reorganized the squadron to place people where the best use could be made of their skills and experience. In staff meetings, disagreements were discussed and worked out, and responsibilities were assigned when all concerned were present. Authority was clearly delegated to reduce confusion and duplication of orders. The NCOs were held responsible for the actions of their men and, within limits, their decisions were enforced without question.

Within two months the effects of the changes were evident. The officers and enlisted men learned what was expected of them and began to see themselves as an essential part of a well-run organization. They began to take pride in their ability to accomplish their mission despite the hardships. Morale and teamwork improved. Before long the squadron became one of the most efficient in Korea. ■

SOURCE: Copyright © 1985 by Gary Yukl.

QUESTIONS

1. What effective leadership behaviors were exhibited by Colonel Novak?

2. What does this case illustrate about effective leadership?

3. Compare the leadership behavior in this case with the leadership behavior in the preceding case.

4

PARTICIPATIVE LEADERSHIP, DELEGATION, AND EMPOWERMENT

Learning Objectives

After studying this chapter you should be able to:

- Understand what research methods have been used to study participative leadership.

- Understand the major findings in research on consequences of participative leadership.

- Understand the situations in which participative leadership is most likely to be effective.

- Understand the major findings in research on the normative theory of leader decision making.

- Understand procedures for the effective use of consultation.

- Understand the potential benefits and risks of delegation.

- Understand when and how to use delegation effectively.

- Understand why follower perceptions of empowerment are important.

Making decisions is one of the most important functions performed by leaders. Many of the activities of managers and administrators involve making and implementing decisions, including planning the work, solving technical problems, selecting subordinates, determining pay increases, making job assignments, and so forth. Participative leadership involves efforts by a leader to encourage and facilitate participation by others in making important decisions. Democratic societies uphold the right of people to influence decisions that will affect them in important ways. Involving others in making decisions is often a necessary part of the political process for getting decisions approved and implemented in organizations. Delegation is a distinct type of power-sharing process that occurs when a manager gives subordinates the responsibility and authority for making some types of decisions formerly made by the manager. Empowerment involves the perception by members of an organization that they have the opportunity to determine their work roles, accomplish meaningful work, and influence important events.

Participative leadership, delegation, and empowerment are subjects that bridge the power and behavior approaches to leadership. The research on participative leadership and delegation emphasizes the leader's perspective on power sharing. The research on empowerment is a more limited and recent addition to the leadership literature, and it emphasizes the follower's perspective. Taken together, the two different perspectives provide a better understanding of the reasons why effective leadership is so important in organizations. This chapter describes the theory and research findings on this important aspect of leadership.

Nature of Participative Leadership

Participative leadership involves the use of various decision procedures that allow other people some influence over the leader's decisions. Other terms commonly used to refer to aspects of participative leadership include *consultation, joint decision making, power sharing, decentralization, empowerment*, and *democratic management*. Participative leadership can be regarded as a distinct type of behavior, although it may be used in conjunction with specific task and relations behaviors (Likert, 1967; Yukl, 1971). For example, consulting with employees about the design of a flextime system may simultaneously involve planning better work schedules and showing concern for employee needs.

Varieties of Participation

Participative leadership can take many forms. A variety of different decision procedures may be used to involve other people in making decisions. A number of leadership theorists have proposed different taxonomies of decision procedures, but there is no agreement about the optimal number of decision procedures or the best way to define them (Heller & Yukl, 1969; Strauss, 1977; Tannenbaum & Schmidt, 1958; Vroom & Yetton, 1973). However, most theorists would acknowledge the following four decision procedures as distinct and meaningful:

1. **Autocratic Decision:** The manager makes a decision alone without asking for the opinions or suggestions of other people, and these people have no direct influence on the decision; there is no participation.
2. **Consultation:** The manager asks other people for their opinions and ideas, then makes the decision alone after seriously considering their suggestions and concerns.
3. **Joint Decision:** The manager meets with others to discuss the decision problem and make a decision together; the manager has no more influence over the final decision than any other participant.

4. **Delegation:** The manager gives an individual or group the authority and responsibility for making a decision; the manager usually specifies limits within which the final choice must fall, and prior approval may or may not be required before the decision can be implemented.

The four decision procedures can be ordered along a continuum ranging from no influence by other people to high influence (see Figure 4-1). Some researchers differentiate between subvarieties of these basic four procedures. For example, Tannenbaum and Schmidt (1958) distinguish two varieties of autocratic decision, one in which the leader merely announces an autocratic decision ("tell" style), and the other in which the leader uses influence tactics such as rational persuasion ("sell" style). The same writers also distinguished three varieties of consultation: (1) the leader presents a decision made without prior consultation, but is willing to modify it in the face of strong objections and concerns; (2) the leader presents a tentative proposal and actively encourages people to suggest ways to improve it; and (3) the leader presents a problem and asks others to participate in diagnosing it and developing solutions, but then makes the decision alone. Vroom and Yetton (1973) distinguish between consulting with individuals and consulting with a group.

The distinctions among decision procedures are useful, but Strauss (1977) reminds us that it is important to distinguish between overt procedures and actual influence. Sometimes what appears to be participation is only pretense. For example, a manager may solicit ideas and suggestions from others but ignore them when making the decision. Likewise, the manager may ask subordinates to make a decision, but do it in such a way that the subordinates are afraid to show initiative or deviate from the choices they know the boss prefers.

Decision procedures are abstract descriptions of pure or ideal types; the actual behavior of managers seldom occurs in ways that neatly fit these descriptions. The research discussed in Chapter 2 suggests that consultation often occurs informally during the course of repeated interactions with other people rather than at a single point of time in a formal meeting. Consultation may occur during brief contacts in the hall, after a meeting or social event, at lunch, or on the golf course. Actual behavior may involve a mix of elements from different decision procedures, such as consulting about problem diagnosis but not about final choice among solutions, or consulting about final choice among a limited set of predetermined solutions. Participative behavior has a dynamic quality and may change over time. For example, what was initially consultation may become a joint decision as it becomes evident that subordinates agree with the leader's preferred choice. What was initially a group decision may become

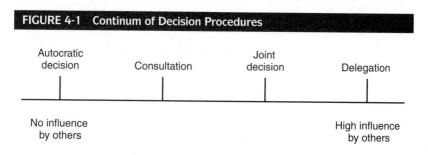

FIGURE 4-1   Continuum of Decision Procedures

consultation when it becomes obvious that the group is deadlocked and the leader must make the final decision.

Consequences of Participative Leadership

This section of the chapter examines the potential benefits of participation and explanatory processes for the effects of participation (see Figure 4-2). Situational variables that enhance or limit the effects of participation are discussed later in the chapter as part of the theories developed to explain why this form of leadership is not effective in all situations.

Potential Benefits of Participation

Participative leadership offers a variety of potential benefits, but whether the benefits occur depends on who the participants are, how much influence they have, and other aspects of the decision situation. Four potential benefits include higher decision quality, higher decision acceptance by participants, more satisfaction with the decision process, and more development of decision making skills. Several explanations have been proposed for the positive effects of participation (Anthony, 1978; Cooper & Wood, 1974; Maier, 1963; Mitchell, 1973; Strauss, 1963; Vroom & Yetton, 1973).

Decision Quality.   Involving other people in making a decision is likely to increase the quality of a decision when participants have information and knowledge lacked by the leader and are willing to cooperate in finding a good solution to a decision problem. Cooperation and sharing of knowledge will depend on the extent to which participants trust the leader and view the process as legitimate and beneficial. If participants and the leader have incompatible goals, cooperation is unlikely to occur. In the absence of cooperation, participation may reduce rather than increase decision

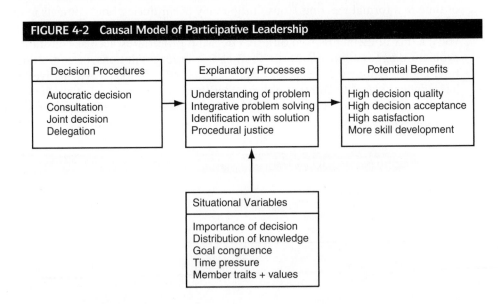

FIGURE 4-2   Causal Model of Participative Leadership

Decision Procedures	Explanatory Processes	Potential Benefits
Autocratic decision Consultation Joint decision Delegation	Understanding of problem Integrative problem solving Identification with solution Procedural justice	High decision quality High decision acceptance High satisfaction More skill development

Situational Variables
Importance of decision Distribution of knowledge Goal congruence Time pressure Member traits + values

quality. Even high cooperation does not guarantee that participation will result in a better decision. The decision process used by the group will determine whether members are able to reach agreement, and it will determine the extent to which any decision incorporates the members' expertise and knowledge (see Chapter 11). When members have different perceptions of the problem or different priorities for the various outcomes, it is difficult to discover a high-quality decision. The group may fail to reach agreement or settle for a poor compromise. Finally, other aspects of the decision situation such as time pressures, the number of participants, and formal policies may make some forms of participation impractical.

Decision Acceptance. People who have considerable influence in making a decision tend to identify with it and perceive it to be their decision. This feeling of ownership increases their motivation to implement it successfully. Participation also provides a better understanding of the nature of the decision problem and the reasons why a particular alternative was accepted and others rejected. Participants gain a better understanding of how they will be affected by a decision, which is likely to reduce any unwarranted fears and anxieties about it. When adverse consequences are likely, participation allows people an opportunity to express their concerns and help to find a solution that deals with these concerns. Finally, when a decision is made by a participative process considered legitimate by most members, then the group is likely to apply social pressure on any reluctant members to do their part in implementing the decision.

Satisfaction with the Decision Process. Research on procedural justice (e.g., Earley & Lind, 1987; Lind & Tyler, 1988) found that the opportunity to express opinions and preferences before a decision is made (called "voice") can have beneficial effects regardless of the amount of actual influence participants have over the final decision (called "choice"). People are more likely to perceive that they are being treated with dignity and respect when they have an opportunity to express opinions and preferences about a decision that will affect them. The likely result is more perception of procedural justice and stronger satisfaction with the decision process (Roberson, Moye, & Locke, 1999). However, in the absence of real influence over a decision, voice alone may not result in strong commitment to implement the decision. Furthermore, the process may reduce rather than increase satisfaction if participants perceive that the leader is attempting to manipulate them into supporting an undesirable decision.

Development of Participant Skills. The experience of helping to make a complex decision can result in the development of more skill and confidence by participants. Whether the potential benefits are realized depends on how much involvement participants actually have in the process of diagnosing the cause of the problem, generating feasible solutions, evaluating solutions to identify the best one, and planning how to implement it. Participants who are involved in all aspects of the decision process learn more than participants who merely contribute to one aspect. For participants with little experience in making complex decisions, learning also depends on the extent to which participants receive coaching and encouragement from the leader during difficult stages of the decision process (see Chapter 13).

Objectives for Different Participants

The potential benefits of participation are not identical for all types of participants. The leader's objectives for using participation may differ depending on whether participants are subordinates, peers, superiors, or outsiders.

Downward consultation may be used to increase the quality of decisions by drawing on the knowledge and problem-solving expertise of subordinates. Another objective is to increase subordinate acceptance of decisions by providing a sense of ownership. A third objective may be to develop the decision-making skills of subordinates by giving them experience in helping to analyze decision problems and evaluate solutions. A fourth objective is to facilitate conflict resolution and team building.

Lateral consultation with people in different subunits may be used to increase decision quality when peers have relevant knowledge about the cause of a problem and likely solutions. When cooperation from other managers is necessary to implement a decision, consultation is a way to increase their understanding and commitment. Lateral consultation facilitates coordination and cooperation among managers of different organizational subunits with interdependent tasks. However, consultation should be limited to decisions for which it is appropriate, so that time is not wasted in unnecessary meetings.

Upward consultation allows a manager to draw on the expertise of the boss, which may be greater than the expertise of the manager. In addition, upward consultation allows a manager to find out how the boss feels about a problem and is likely to react to various proposals. On the other hand, excessive consultation with a boss suggests a lack of self-confidence and initiative on the part of the subordinate. A manager with the authority to make the final choice in decisions is wise to avoid becoming too dependent on the boss when making these decisions.

Consulting with outsiders such as clients and suppliers helps ensure that decisions affecting them are understood and accepted. Consultation with outsiders is a way to learn more about their needs and preferences, strengthen external networks, improve coordination, and solve mutual problems related to the work.

Research on Effects of Participative Leadership

Since the pioneering studies by Lewin, Lippitt, and White (1939) and Coch and French (1948), social scientists have been interested in studying the consequences of participative leadership. After supportive and task-oriented behavior, the largest amount of behavior research has been on participative leadership. The research has employed a variety of methods, including laboratory experiments, field experiments, correlational field studies, and qualitative case studies involving interviews with effective leaders and their subordinates. Most of the studies involved participation by subordinates, and the criteria of leader effectiveness were usually subordinate satisfaction and performance.

Example of Research on Participation

Bragg and Andrews (1973) conducted a quasi-experimental study on participation in a hospital laundry department. Following is a detailed description of the way participation was introduced into the department and the consequences for worker satisfaction and productivity.

> The foreman of the laundry department typically made decisions in an autocratic manner, and he was persuaded by the chief administrator to try a participative approach. The 32 workers in the laundry department were told that the purpose of the group meetings was to make their jobs more interesting, not to increase productivity, which was already high. The workers and union were told that the participation program would be discontinued if they found it unsatisfactory. Over the next 18 months, meetings were held whenever the workers wanted to discuss specific proposals about hours of work, working procedures, working conditions, minor equipment modifications, and safety matters. In addition to these group meetings, the foreman consulted regularly with individuals and smaller groups of workers to discuss problems and new ideas.
>
> Worker attitudes were measured at two-month intervals for 14 months with a questionnaire. The attitude data showed some initial doubts about the participation program, after which workers became increasingly more favorable toward it. Productivity during the first 18 months of the program increased 42 percent over that for the department during the prior year, whereas for similar departments in two other hospitals (the comparison groups), productivity declined slightly during the same period of time. Attendance in the department, which was high initially, became even better after the participation program was introduced, whereas for other non-medical departments in the same hospital (the comparison groups), it became worse. The results were statistically significant and showed that the participation program was highly successful.
>
> After the program had been in effect for three years, neither the workers nor the supervisor had any desire to return to the old autocratic style of management. The success of the program encouraged the introduction of participation in the medical records section, where it resulted in elimination of grievances and a sharp reduction in turnover. However, an attempt to introduce a participation program in the nursing group was much less successful, due primarily to lack of support by the head nurse and resistance by administrative medical personnel.

Effects of Participation

The results of quantitative research (i.e., questionnaire studies, field experiments, laboratory experiments) on the effects of participation are summarized in several literature reviews and meta-analyses (Cotton et al., 1988; Leana, Locke, & Schweiger, 1990; Miller & Monge, 1986; Sagie & Koslowsky, 2000; Spector, 1986; Wagner & Gooding, 1987). The various reviewers did not agree in their conclusions, but they all noted the lack of consistent strong results in the research. One reason for the inconsistency seemed to be the type of methodology used in the research.

Studies that used questionnaire data from the same respondents usually found positive effects for participation, whereas studies with independent measures of outcome variables had results that were weaker and less consistent. Experiments and quasi-experimental studies in field settings showed positive results in most cases, whereas laboratory experiments did not support the effectiveness of participation in decision making. In experiments on goal setting, the effect of participation depended in part on other factors such as goal difficulty and supportive leadership. Assigned goals were as effective as participative goals when goal difficulty was held constant and the leaders who assigned goals were supportive and persuasive (Latham, Erez, & Locke, 1988). Overall, the evidence from the quantitative studies is not sufficiently strong and consistent to draw any firm conclusions, but the results suggest that participation can be effective in some situations.

The findings from qualitative research, including case studies of effective managers, have been more consistently supportive of the benefits of participative leadership (Bradford & Cohen, 1984; Kanter, 1983; Kouzes & Posner, 1987; Peters & Austin, 1985; Peters & Waterman, 1982). This research found that effective managers used a substantial amount of consultation and delegation to empower subordinates and give them a sense of ownership for activities and decisions.

In summary, after more than 40 years of research on participation, we are left with the conclusion that participative leadership sometimes results in higher satisfaction, effort, and performance, and at other times it does not.

Limitations of Participation Research

The lack of strong, consistent results in the research on participative leadership may be a result of methodological problems in much of the research. Weak methods have been used in much of the research, and even the studies using stronger methods such as experiments have serious limitations.

The survey field studies are limited by measurement problems and difficulty of determining direction of causality (see Chapter 3). In most of these studies, subordinates were asked to rate how much involvement they had in decisions, or to rate the leader's general use of participative decision procedures. No effort was made to identify the particular mix of decision procedures that were used or to determine whether these procedures were appropriate for the types of decisions being made. In effect, these studies tested only the general hypothesis that more is better when it comes to participation.

The field experiments and quasi-experimental studies also have limitations. Many of them involved a participation program introduced by the organization rather than participative behavior by an individual manager. In some studies, participation was combined with other types of interventions (e.g. more supportive behavior by the leader, better training of subordinates, or use of better procedures for planning and problem solving), making it difficult to determine what consequences were due to participation. The short-term nature of many field experiments raises the possibility that improved satisfaction and effort for people in the participation condition is the result of temporary elation from being singled out for special attention by the organization (the Hawthorne effect). In some studies the nonparticipation control group knew about the participation group, which could have led to resentment about not getting the "special" treatment, thereby lowering satisfaction and making the participation group appear better. Finally, most lab and field experiments only compared two decision procedures, and the definition of high and low participation varied from study to study, making it difficult to compare results across studies. For example, in some studies participation was a joint decision, whereas in others it was consultation.

The measure of participation consequences in most of the studies was overall satisfaction and performance of subordinates, not satisfaction with the way a particular decision was handled or commitment to implement that decision effectively. Thus, most studies failed to measure the most relevant and immediate outcomes, and instead used a relatively insensitive criterion that is influenced by many things besides participative leadership. Most studies also failed to measure the underlying influence and motivational processes that could explain how participation affects decision acceptance.

Lack of consistent results about the effectiveness of participative leadership may also reflect the fact that various forms of participation are effective in some situations but not in others. In most studies of participation, researchers either ignored the situation entirely or identified limiting conditions only on a post hoc basis to explain discrepant results or lack of success. Few studies incorporated situational variables in a systematic manner or investigated whether different procedures are more effective for different types of decisions. This question is the subject of a contingency theory developed by Vroom and Yetton (1973).

Normative Decision Model

The importance of using decision procedures that are appropriate for the situation has been recognized for some time. Tannenbaum and Schmidt (1958) noted that a leader's choice of decision procedures reflects forces in the leader, forces in the subordinates, and forces in the situation. Maier (1963) pointed out the need for leaders to consider both the quality requirements of a decision and the likelihood of subordinate acceptance before choosing a decision procedure. Vroom and Yetton (1973) built upon these earlier approaches but went further in specifying which decision procedures will be most effective in each of several specific situations. Vroom and Jago (1988) subsequently revised the initial model to include some additional variables and decision rules.

Vroom and Yetton Model

The decision procedure used by a leader affects the quality of a decision and decision acceptance by the people who are expected to implement the decision. These two mediating variables jointly determine how effective the decision will be after it is implemented, which has obvious implications for the performance of the unit or team. However, the effect of the decision procedures on decision quality and acceptance depends on various aspects of the situation, and a procedure that is effective in some situations may be ineffective in other situations.

Decision Procedures. Vroom and Yetton identify five decision procedures for decisions involving multiple subordinates, including two varieties of autocratic decision (AI and AII), two varieties of consultation (CI and CII), and one variety of joint decision making by leader and subordinates as a group (GII). Each of these decision procedures is defined as follows (Vroom & Yetton, 1973, p. 13):

AI. You solve the problem or make the decision yourself, using information available to you at the time.
AII. You obtain the necessary information from your subordinates, then decide the solution to the problem yourself. You may or may not tell

your subordinates what the problem is in getting the information from them. The role played by your subordinates in making the decision is clearly one of providing necessary information to you, rather than generating or evaluating alternative solutions.

CI. You share the problem with the relevant subordinates individually, getting their ideas and suggestions, without bringing them together as a group. Then you make the decision, which may or may not reflect your subordinates' influence.

CII. You share the problem with your subordinates as a group, obtaining their collective ideas and suggestions. Then you make the decision, which may or may not reflect your subordinates' influence.

GII. You share the problem with your subordinates as a group. Together you generate and evaluate alternatives and attempt to reach agreement (consensus) on a solution. Your role is much like that of chairman. You do not try to influence the group to adopt your preferred solution, and you are willing to accept and implement any solution that has the support of the entire group.

Situational Variables.   The effectiveness of a decision procedure depends on several aspects of the decision situation: (1) the amount of relevant information possessed by leader and subordinates, (2) the likelihood that subordinates will accept an autocratic decision, (3) the likelihood that subordinates will cooperate if allowed to participate, (4) the amount of disagreement among subordinates with respect to their preferred alternatives, and (5) the extent to which the decision problem is unstructured and requires creative problem solving. The model also takes into account (1) whether the decision is important or trivial, and (2) whether the decision will be accepted by subordinates even if they are not involved in making it. The causal relationships among the variables are shown in Figure 4-3.

Decision Acceptance.   Decision acceptance is the degree of commitment to implement a decision effectively. Acceptance is important whenever a decision must be implemented by subordinates or has implications for their work motivation. In some cases, subordinates are highly motivated to implement a decision made by the

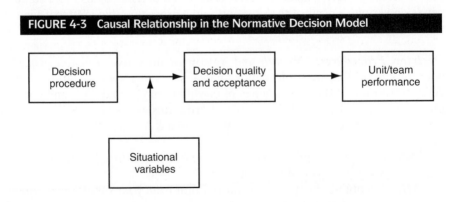

FIGURE 4-3   Causal Relationship in the Normative Decision Model

leader because it is clearly beneficial to them or because the leader uses influence tactics to gain their commitment to the decision. However, subordinates may not accept an autocratic decision for other reasons. For example, subordinates may resent not being consulted, they may not understand the reasons for the decision, and they may see it as detrimental to their interests. A basic assumption of the model is that participation increases decision acceptance if it is not already high, and the more influence subordinates have in making a decision, the more they will be motivated to implement it successfully. Thus, decision acceptance is likely to be greater for joint decision making than for consultation, and for consultation than for an autocratic decision.

Decision Quality. Decision quality refers to the objective aspects of the decision that affect group performance aside from any effects mediated by decision acceptance. The quality of a decision is high when the best alternative is selected. For example, an efficient work procedure is selected instead of less efficient alternatives, or a challenging performance goal is set instead of an easy goal. Decision quality is important when there is a great deal of variability among alternatives and the decision has important consequences for group performance. If the available alternatives are approximately equal in consequences, or if the decision has no important consequences for group performance, then decision quality is not important. Examples of task decisions that are usually important include determination of goals and priorities, assignment of tasks to subordinates who differ in skills, determination of work procedures for complex tasks, and determination of ways to solve technical problems.

The effect of participation on decision quality depends on the distribution of relevant information and problem-solving expertise between leader and subordinates. The model assumes that participation will result in better decisions if subordinates possess relevant information and are willing to cooperate with the leader in making a good decision. Cooperation, however, depends in turn on the extent to which subordinates share the leader's task objectives and have a relationship of mutual trust with the leader. The model assumes that consultation and joint decision making are equally likely to facilitate decision quality when subordinates share the leader's objectives. However, when subordinates have incompatible objectives, consultation usually results in higher-quality decisions than joint decision making, because the leader retains control over the final choice.

Decision Rules. The model provides a set of rules for identifying any decision procedure that is inappropriate in a given situation because decision quality and/or acceptance would be jeopardized by using that procedure. The rules are based on the assumptions discussed earlier about the consequences of different decision procedures under different conditions. The decision rules are summarized briefly in Table 4-1.

For some decision situations, the model prescribes more than one feasible decision procedure. In this case, the choice among decision procedures in the "feasible set" should be based on other criteria, such as time pressure, desire to develop subordinates, or a leader's personal preferences among the procedures. Vroom and Yetton developed decision process flow charts to simplify the application of the rules and assist managers in identifying the feasible set of decision procedures for each situation.

TABLE 4-1   Decision Rules in Vroom-Yetton Decision Model

1. When the decision is important and subordinates possess relevant information lacked by the leader, an autocratic decision (AI, AII) is not appropriate because an important decision would be made without all of the relevant, available information.

2. When decision quality is important and subordinates do not share the leader's concern for task goals, a group decision (GII) is not appropriate because these procedures would give too much influence over an important decision to uncooperative or even hostile people.

3. When decision quality is important, the decision problem is unstructured, and the leader does not possess the necessary information and expertise to make a good decision, then the decision should be made by interaction among the people who have the relevant information (CII, GII).

4. When decision acceptance is important and subordinates are unlikely to accept an autocratic decision, then an autocratic decision (AI, AII) is not appropriate because the decision may not be implemented effectively.

5. When decision acceptance is important and subordinates are likely to disagree among themselves about the best solution to an important problem, autocratic procedures (AI, AII) and individual consultation (CI) are not appropriate because they do not provide the opportunity to resolve differences through discussion and negotiation among subordinates and between the subordinates and the leader.

6. When decision quality is not important but acceptance is important and unlikely to result from an autocratic decision, then the only appropriate procedure is a group decision (GII), because acceptance is maximized without risking quality.

7. When decision acceptance is important and not likely to result from an autocratic decision, and subordinates share the leader's task objectives, subordinates should be given equal partnership in the decision process (GII), because acceptance is maximized without risking quality.

Source: Based on V. H. Vroom and P. W. Yetton, *Leadership and Decision Making* (Pittsburgh: University of Pittsburgh Press, 1973).

The Revised Model

Vroom and Jago (1988) reviewed the research findings on the model and offered a revised version of it. The revised model was designed to correct some of the weaknesses in the earlier version. The Vroom-Yetton model eliminates some of the procedures from the feasible set, but it does not indicate which of the remaining procedures is best. The Vroom-Jago model incorporates features that allow a manager to determine the relative priority of different criteria and reduce the feasible set to a single procedure by applying the criteria.

The Vroom-Yetton model fails to include some important aspects of the situation, such as severe time constraints, amount of subordinate information, and geographical dispersion of subordinates. These attributes are incorporated in the Vroom-Jago model. The Vroom-Yetton model uses only two outcome criteria—decision acceptance and decision quality—in the decision rules. The new model adds concern for subordinate development and concern for decision time as explicit criteria for determining optimal decision procedures. Managers are given more choice in setting priorities for the criteria in the new model, and there are different versions of the model for different priorities.

The Vroom-Yetton model fails to capture some differences among situations by requiring a definite yes-no answer to the situational questions. The new model corrects this deficiency by requiring managers to differentiate among five choices in describing each aspect of the situation. For example, to the question "Do subordinates share the organizational goals to be attained in solving this problem?" managers select one of the following choices: no, probably no, maybe, probably yes, yes. Decision rules are replaced by mathematical functions. The result of the various changes is to make an already complex model even more complex, and a computer software program is recommended to apply the model in its complete form.

Over the years various theorists have attempted to simplify the normative decision model to make it easier for managers to use (e.g., Yukl, 1990). One example is shown in Table 4-2. This simplified model involves three decision procedures (autocratic, consultation, joint decision), and it shows the optimal procedure when the priorities are (1) protect decision quality, (2) gain decision acceptance, and (3) save time.

Research on the Models

Several field studies have been conducted to test the Vroom-Yetton model since it first appeared (e.g., Ettling & Jago, 1988; Jago & Vroom, 1980; Margerison & Glube, 1979; Paul & Ebadi, 1989: Tjosvold, Wedley, & Field, 1986; Vroom & Jago, 1978). The most common research method was to collect incidents in which managers described a successful or unsuccessful decision. The researchers classified the situation and decision procedure for each incident, then determined how often successful decisions involved the use of a decision procedure consistent with the model. Vroom and Jago (1988) computed the mean rate of success across five studies and found that for decisions made in accordance with the model, the mean success rate was 62 percent, versus 37 percent for decisions made using a decision procedure outside of the feasible set.

TABLE 4-2   Simplified Version of the Normative Decision Model

	Subordinate Acceptance of Decision	
Decision Quality	*Not Important or Assured with Autocratic Decision*	*Important and Not Assured with Autocratic Decision*
Not important	Autocratic	Group
Important, but leader has sufficient information; members share leader's goals	Autocratic	Group
Important, but leader has sufficient information; members do not share the leader's goals	Autocratic	Consultation
Important and the leader lacks essential information; members share leader goals	Consultation	Group
Important and the leader lacks essential information; members don't share leader goals	Consultation	Consultation

Source: Based on G. Yukl, *Skills for Managers and Leaders* (Upper Saddle River, NJ: Prentice Hall, 1990).

Four studies that tested the decision rules separately found some decision rules were supported much better than others (Vroom & Jago, 1988). In a subsequent field study, the researchers obtained information about decisions from two different sources (Field & House, 1990), and the data from subordinates provided much less support for the model than data from managers. The normative decision model was also tested in laboratory experiments in which researchers manipulated the situation and the decision procedure used by the leader and measured the consequences for the group (e.g., Crouch & Yetton, 1987; Field, 1982; Heilman, Hornstein, Cage, & Herschlag, 1984; Liddel et al., 1986, cited in Vroom & Jago, 1988). The results were weaker and less consistent in the experiments than in the field studies.

In summary, the empirical research on the initial version of the normative decision model provides some support for it, but more research is needed to adequately test the model and each of the decision rules. The extended version of the model has not been extensively tested. Vroom and Jago (1988) reported some positive findings in their research on managers, and positive results were also found in a laboratory experiment with scenarios (Field, Read, & Louviere, 1990). The initial results are promising, but more research is needed to test the extended version of the model.

Conceptual Weaknesses

Critics of the model have identified several conceptual weaknesses. Decision processes are treated as a single, discrete episode that occurs at one point in time, but most important decisions are not made in this way. As we saw in Chapter 2, important decisions typically involve multiple meetings with a variety of different people at different times, and repeated cycles occur as decisions are returned for revisions necessary for approval by powerful people not directly involved in the initial process. Thus, the leader may have to use a sequence of different decision procedures with different people at different times before the matter is resolved.

The theory is not parsimonious (Field, 1979). The distinction between autocratic, consultative, and joint decision procedures is more important than the distinction made among subvarieties of each procedure (AI vs. AII, and CI vs. CII). The theory would be much easier to understand and apply if the primary model focused on the choice among these three decision styles. Supplementary models could be developed to guide a manager in selecting among the major variations of each decision procedure. The distinction made between AI and AII is unnecessary; the descriptive research shows that managers are continually gathering factual information from a variety of sources. The distinction between CI and CII is important, but other variations are possible. For example, sometimes different people are consulted individually followed by consultation with the entire group.

Leaders are assumed to have the skills necessary to use each of the decision procedures, and leader skill is not a factor in determining which procedure is most appropriate (Crouch & Yetton, 1987; Field, 1979). Crouch and Yetton showed that some assumptions of the model are not valid for unskilled leaders. Their study found that in situations with conflict among subordinates, group procedures (CII or GII) were effective for leaders who had conflict management skills, but not for leaders lacking these skills. Leaders without these skills are better off using individual consultation (CI), which does not require direct confrontation between subordinates who disagree with each other.

Summary

The normative decision model is probably the best supported of the contingency theories of effective leadership (see Chapter 8). It focuses on specific aspects of behavior, it includes meaningful intervening variables, and it identifies important aspects of the situation moderating the relationship between behavior and outcomes. However, the model deals with only a small part of leadership, and several conceptual weaknesses need to be corrected.

Applications: Guidelines for Participative Leadership

Building on the participation research and the Vroom-Yetton model, some tentative guidelines are proposed for using participative leadership. Guidelines for diagnosing the situation are presented first, followed by some guidelines for encouraging participation (see Table 4-3).

Diagnosing Decision Situations

The following sequence is a relatively easy way to determine whether a participative procedure is feasible and appropriate for a particular decision situation.

- **Evaluate how important the decision is.**

Decision quality is likely to be important if the decision has important consequences for the manager's work unit or the overall organization, and some of the alternatives are much better than others. Decision quality is also more important when the manager's position is one with high exposure (i.e., mistakes are very visible and will reflect poorly on the manager).

TABLE 4-3 Guidelines for Participative Leadership

How to Diagnose Decision Situations
- Evaluate how important the decision is.
- Identify people with relevant knowledge or expertise.
- Evaluate likely cooperation by participants.
- Evaluate likely acceptance without participation.
- Evaluate whether it is feasible to hold a meeting.

How to Encourage Participation
- Encourage people to express their concerns.
- Describe a proposal as tentative.
- Record ideas and suggestions.
- Look for ways to build on ideas and suggestions.
- Be tactful in expressing concerns about a suggestion.
- Listen to dissenting views without getting defensive.
- Try to utilize suggestions and deal with concerns.
- Show appreciation for suggestions.

- **Identify people with relevant knowledge or expertise.**

  Participative decision procedures are appropriate when a manager lacks relevant information possessed by others such as subordinates, peers, or outsiders. This situation is likely when the decision problem is complex and the best way to resolve the problem is not evident from the data or from the manager's prior experience with similar problems. A decision is more complex when it involves many possible alternatives, the outcomes of each alternative are difficult to predict, and the alternatives involve trade-offs among several important criteria. For complex decisions, it is essential to identify people who have relevant knowledge and expertise, and a good network of contacts is invaluable for identifying such people.

- **Evaluate likely cooperation by participants.**

  Participation is unlikely to be successful unless the prospective participants are willing to cooperate in finding a good solution to the decision problem. Cooperation is more likely when the decision is important to followers and they perceive that they will actually have some influence over the final decision. If people perceive that a leader is trying to manipulate them, then consultation is unlikely to increase either decision quality or decision acceptance.

  Cooperation is also unlikely if potential participants have task objectives that are incompatible with those of the manager. When there is doubt about the motives of potential participants, it is advisable to consult with a few of them individually to determine whether a group meeting would be productive. It is unwise to hold a meeting with a hostile group of people who will use it as an opportunity to make decisions that are contrary to the interests of the manager. When people with relevant information have different objectives, then some consultation may be useful to diagnose the cause of a problem and identify promising alternatives, but the final choice of an alternative must remain with the manager.

  Another reason for lack of cooperation is that the potential participants simply do not want to become involved in making decisions they view as the manager's responsibility. Opportunities to participate may be rejected by followers who are already overloaded with work, especially when the decisions do not affect them in any important way. Just as many people decline to vote in local elections, not everyone will be enthusiastic about the opportunity for participation in organizational decisions.

- **Evaluate likely acceptance without participation.**

  A time-consuming participative procedure is not necessary if the manager has the knowledge to make a good decision and it is likely to be accepted by subordinates or others who must implement it or who will be affected by it. An autocratic decision is more likely to be accepted if the manager has considerable position and personal power over group members or has the persuasive skills to sell the decision successfully. Acceptance of an autocratic decision is also likely if the decision is to do something people already want to do, or the decision appears to be a reasonable response to a crisis situation. Finally, acceptance of autocratic decisions is more likely when people have cultural values that emphasize obedience to authority figures (see Chapter 14).

- **Evaluate whether it is feasible to hold a meeting.**

Consulting with people separately or holding a group meeting usually requires more time than making an autocratic decision and telling people to implement it. It is especially difficult to hold a meeting if the number of people who need to be involved is large and they are widely dispersed. In many crisis situations time is not available either for extensive consultation with individuals or for a lengthy group meeting to decide how to react to the crisis. In this situation, a leader who takes charge in a decisive way is likely to be more effective than one who is very participative. Nevertheless, even in a crisis situation a leader should remain responsive to suggestions made by knowledgeable subordinates. Under the stress of a crisis, a leader is unlikely to notice all of the problems that require attention or to think of all the actions that need to be taken.

Encouraging Participation

Consulting will not be effective unless people are actively involved in generating ideas, making suggestions, stating their preferences, and expressing their concerns. Some guidelines for encouraging more participation include the following.

- **Encourage people to express their concerns.**

Before making changes that will affect people in significant ways, it is useful and considerate to consult with them. This guideline applies to peers and outsiders as well as subordinates. One form of consultation that is often appropriate is to hold special meetings with people who will be affected by a change to identify their concerns and deal with them.

- **Describe a proposal as tentative.**

More participation is likely if you present a proposal as tentative and encourage people to improve it, rather than asking people to react to an elaborate plan that appears complete. In the latter case, people will be more inhibited about expressing concerns that appear to be criticism of the plan.

- **Record ideas and suggestions.**

When someone makes a suggestion, it is helpful to acknowledge the idea and show that it is not being ignored. One approach is to list ideas on a flipchart or blackboard when they are expressed. In an informal meeting, if no flipchart or blackboard is available, make some written notes to avoid forgetting a person's ideas and suggestions.

- **Look for ways to build on ideas and suggestions.**

Most people quickly focus on the weaknesses of an idea or suggestion made by someone else without giving enough consideration to its strengths. It is helpful to make a conscious effort to find positive aspects of a suggestion and mention them before mentioning negative aspects. Many times an initial idea is incomplete, but it can be turned into a much better idea with a little conscious effort. Thus, rather than automatically rejecting a suggestion with obvious weaknesses, it is useful to discuss how the weaknesses could be overcome and to consider other, better ideas that build on the initial one.

- **Be tactful in expressing concerns about a suggestion.**

If you have concerns about a suggestion, express them tactfully to avoid threatening the self-esteem of the person who made the suggestion and discouraging future suggestions. Some negative examples include the following:

You aren't serious about that?

That has been tried before and it doesn't work.

Concerns should be expressed in a way that indicates qualified interest rather than outright rejection. It is usually possible to express concerns in the form of a question using the terms *we* and *us* to emphasize a shared effort, as shown in the following example:

Your suggestion is promising, but I am concerned about the cost. Is there any way we could do it without exceeding our budget?

- **Listen to dissenting views without getting defensive.**

In order to encourage people to express concerns and criticisms of your plans and proposals, it is essential to listen carefully without getting defensive or angry. Use restatement of a person's concerns in your own words to verify that you understand them and to show you are paying attention. Avoid making excuses, and instead try to consider objectively whether revisions are needed.

- **Try to utilize suggestions and deal with concerns.**

People will stop making suggestions if you dismiss them without serious consideration or simply ignore them in making a final decision. It is important to make a serious effort to utilize suggestions and deal with concerns expressed by people with whom you have consulted. The potential benefits from participation will not occur if people perceive that a request for suggestions was done just to manipulate them.

- **Show appreciation for suggestions.**

People will be more likely to cooperate in making decisions and solving problems if they receive appropriate credit for their helpful suggestions and ideas. Compliment someone for good ideas and insights. It is important to thank people and show appreciation for helpful suggestions. Explain how an idea or suggestion was used in the final decision or plan. Explain how the proposal or plan was modified to incorporate a person's suggestion or respond to his or her concerns. If a suggestion is not used, thank the contributor and explain why it was not feasible to use the suggestion.

Delegation

As noted earlier, delegation involves the assignment of new responsibilities to subordinates and additional authority to carry them out. Although delegation is sometimes regarded as a variety of participative leadership, there is ample justification for treating delegation as a separate category of managerial behavior. Delegation is qualitatively different in some ways from the other forms of participative leadership such as consulting and joint decision making. A manager may consult with subordinates, peers, or superiors, but in most cases delegation is appropriate only with subordinates. Delegation has somewhat different situational determinants than consultation (Leana, 1987). For example, a manager who is overloaded with work is likely to use more delegating but less consulting. Thus, it is not surprising that factor analysis of leadership questionnaires typically yields distinct factors for consulting and delegating (Yukl & Fu, 1999).

Varieties of Delegation

The term *delegation* is commonly used to describe a variety of different forms and degrees of power sharing with individual subordinates. Major aspects of delegation include the variety and magnitude of responsibilities, the amount of discretion or range of choice allowed in deciding how to carry out responsibilities, the authority to take action and implement decisions without prior approval, the frequency and nature of reporting requirements, and the flow of performance information (Sherman, 1966; Webber, 1981).

In its most common form, delegation involves assignment of new and different tasks or responsibilities to a subordinate. For example, a person who is responsible for manufacturing something is also given responsibility for inspecting the product and correcting any defects that are found. When new tasks are assigned, the additional authority necessary to accomplish the tasks is usually delegated also. For example, a production worker who is given new responsibility for ordering materials is given the authority (within specified constraints) to sign contracts with suppliers.

Sometimes delegation involves only the specification of additional authority and discretion for the same tasks and assignments already performed by the subordinate. For example, a sales representative is allowed to negotiate sales within a specified range of prices, quantities, and delivery dates, but cannot exceed these limits without prior approval from the sales manager. Delegation is increased by giving the sales representative more latitude in setting prices and delivery dates.

The extent to which a subordinate must check with the boss before taking action is another aspect of delegation. There is little or no delegation for someone who must ask the boss what to do whenever there is a problem or something unusual occurs. There is moderate delegation when the subordinate is allowed to determine what to do but must get approval before implementing decisions. There is substantial delegation when the subordinate is allowed to make important decisions and implement them without getting prior approval. For example, a sales representative who was not allowed to make adjustments for damaged goods and late deliveries without checking first is given permission to resolve these matters in the future without getting prior approval.

Reporting requirements are another aspect of delegation that is subject to considerable variation. The amount of subordinate autonomy is greater when reports are required only infrequently. For example, a department manager must report department performance on a weekly basis rather than on a daily basis. Autonomy is also greater when reports describe only results rather than describing both the results and the procedures used to accomplish them. For example, a training director must report to the vice president for human resources the number of employees who were trained in each subject area and the overall training expenses for the month, but not the types of training methods used, the number of trainers, or the breakdown of training expenses in different categories.

The flow of performance information involved in monitoring a subordinate's activities is also subject to variation. Subordinate autonomy is greater when detailed information about subordinate performance goes directly to the subordinate, who is then allowed to correct any problems. A subordinate is likely to have less autonomy when detailed performance information goes first to the boss and is subsequently passed on to the subordinate. There is an intermediate amount of subordinate autonomy when detailed performance information goes to both parties simultaneously.

Potential Advantages of Delegation

There are many different reasons for delegating (Leana, 1986; Newman & Warren, 1977; Preston & Zimmerer, 1978; Yukl & Fu, 1999). Table 4-4 shows the results found in a study that asked managers in several organizations about the importance of various reasons for delegation to a subordinate.

Delegation offers a number of potential advantages if carried out in an appropriate manner by a manager. One potential advantage of delegation, like other forms of participation and power sharing, is the improvement of decision quality. Delegation is likely to improve decision quality if a subordinate has more expertise in how to do the task than the manager. Decision quality is likely to improve also if the subordinate's job requires quick responses to a changing situation and the lines of communication do not permit the manager to monitor the situation closely and make rapid adjustments. A subordinate who is closer to the problem than the manager and has more relevant information can make quicker and better decisions about how to resolve the problem. The result may be better customer service and reduced administrative costs. However, delegation is not likely to improve decision quality if the subordinate lacks the skills to make good decisions, fails to understand what is expected, or has goals incompatible with those of the manager.

Another potential advantage of delegation is greater subordinate commitment to implement decisions effectively. The commitment results from identification with the decision and a desire to make it successful. However, commitment is unlikely to improve if a subordinate views delegation as a manipulative tactic by the manager, considers the task impossible to do, or believes the newly delegated responsibilities are an unfair increase in workload.

Delegation of additional responsibilities and authority can make a subordinate's job more interesting, challenging, and meaningful. Enriched jobs are sometimes necessary to attract and retain competent employees, especially when the organization has limited

TABLE 4-4   Percentage of Managers Who Rated a Reason for Delegating As Moderately or Very Important

Reason	%
Develop subordinate skills and confidence	97%
Enable subordinates to deal with problems quickly	91
Improve decisions by moving them close to the action	89
Increase subordinate commitment to a task	89
Make the job more interesting for subordinates	78
Reduce your workload to manage time better	68
Satisfy superiors who want you to delegate more	24
Get rid of tedious tasks you don't want to do	23

Source: Adapted from G. Yukl and P. Fu, "Determinants of delegation and consultation by managers," *Journal of Organizational Behavior*, 20 (1999), pp. 219–232.

opportunities for advancement to higher-level positions. Giving junior managers more responsibility and authority, with a commensurate increase in salary, reduces the likelihood that they will be lured away to other companies in times of stiff competition for managerial talent. However, delegation will only increase the satisfaction of a subordinate who desires more responsibility, has the skills necessary to handle new responsibilities, and is able to experience some success in accomplishing a challenging task. Delegation will decrease job satisfaction if the subordinate is constantly frustrated due to a lack of sufficient authority and resources to carry out new responsibilities, or to a lack of ability to do the work.

Delegation is an important form of time management for a manager who is overloaded with responsibilities. By delegating less important duties and functions to subordinates, a manager frees additional time for more important responsibilities. Even when a manager could do the delegated tasks better than subordinates, it is a more efficient use of the manager's time to concentrate on those functions that will have the greatest influence on the performance of the manager's organizational unit. Without delegation, a manager is unlikely to have sufficient discretionary time to do some important tasks that require larger blocks of time and are not immediately urgent.

Delegation can be an effective method of management development. Organizations need to develop managerial talent to fill vacant positions at higher levels of authority. Delegation is a way to facilitate development of the skills necessary to perform key responsibilities in a higher position. When delegation is used for developmental purposes, however, it is usually necessary for the manager to do more monitoring and coaching. Thus, when used for this purpose, delegation is unlikely to reduce a manager's workload much.

Reasons for Lack of Delegation

With all of these potential advantages from delegation, it would seem as if it should occur whenever appropriate. However, for a number of reasons some managers fail to delegate as much as they should (Leana, 1986; Newman & Warren, 1977; Preston & Zimmerer, 1978; Yukl & Fu, 1999). Results from a study that asked managers in several companies about the importance of different reasons for not delegating are shown in Table 4-5.

TABLE 4-5 Percentage of Managers Who Rated a Reason for Not Delegating As Moderately or Very Important

Keep decisions involving confidential information	87%
Keep tasks and decisions that are very important	76
Keep tasks and decisions central to your role	73
Keep tasks for which mistakes are highly visible	58
Keep tasks you can do better than subordinates	51
Keep tasks that are difficult to explain to subordinates	43
Keep tasks that are difficult to monitor	39
Keep tasks that are interesting and enjoyable	24

Source: Adapted from G. Yukl and P. Fu, "Determinants of delegation and consultation by managers," *Journal of Organizational Behavior*, 20 (1999), pp. 219–232.

Several aspects of personality are associated with failure to delegate, including a strong need for power, insecurity, a high need for achievement, and difficulty in forming relationships. Some managers enjoy the exercise of power over subordinates and the feeling of being in charge. Delegation would require sharing power with subordinates and reducing their dependence.

Delegation is never absolute, because a manager continues to be responsible for the work activities of subordinates. To avoid the risk of mistakes, a manager who is insecure may delegate sensitive tasks only to a few trusted subordinates, or not at all. Furthermore, allowing a subordinate to demonstrate competence in performing managerial responsibilities may create a competitor for the manager's job.

Managers with a high need for achievement often prefer to retain important, challenging tasks rather than delegating them to subordinates (Miller & Toulouse, 1982). Managers who take pride in solving important problems may be reluctant to relinquish that activity or admit others could do it as effectively. Reluctance to delegate may be supported by biases in perception of one's own performance. One experiment found that managers rated quality of performance higher when they were directly involved in supervising a task, even though actual quality was the same as for a delegated task (Pfeffer, Cialdini, Hanna, & Knopoff, 1998).

Failure to delegate is also related to characteristics of the subordinates, such as task expertise and shared objectives. Managers are reluctant to delegate significant responsibilities to subordinates who lack the necessary expertise (Ashour & England, 1972; Leana, 1986; Yukl & Fu, 1999). Even if a subordinate has the expertise, delegation of significant responsibility is unlikely if the person seems indifferent about task objectives (McGregor, 1960). This perception may be inaccurate initially, but distrust by the manager may eventually make it a self-fulfilling prophecy (Argyris, 1964). Sometimes distrust of subordinates is determined more by personality problems in the manager than by the actual characteristics of the subordinates (Johnston, 2000).

The reader should not assume that only insecure, power hungry managers are reluctant to delegate. Even managers who become successful at empowering people often say it was personally difficult. Consider Ben Cohen, the cofounder of Ben and Jerry's (Ice Cream), who believes strongly in empowerment. When describing how difficult it was, he explained how it was not natural to ask questions of employees when he already knew the answer, to listen patiently when they said something that wasn't right, or to ask them for ideas when he was eager to express ideas of his own (O'Toole, 1995).

The potential for delegation also depends on the nature of the work and the amount of authority possessed by the leader. A lack of leader authority to make decisions or change how the work is done limits the potential for delegation. Another constraint is when subordinates have highly interdependent jobs. Even if people have shared objectives, they may disagree about priorities and the best way to accomplish the objectives. In this situation empowering individuals to act on their own increases the danger they will be working at cross-purposes. To achieve coordination and avoid destructive conflicts, it will be necessary to devote more time to meetings to plan joint activities and solve operational problems. In this type of situation it is more feasible to use consultation or to delegate authority for a task to a team rather than to individual subordinates. Self-managed teams are discussed in Chapter 11.

Research on Consequences of Delegation

Much less empirical research is available on leader delegation than on leader consultation with individuals or a group. Studies on the amount of delegation used by supervisors find that it is correlated with subordinate performance (e.g., Bauer & Green, 1996; Leana,1986; Schriesheim, Neider, & Scandura,1998). Miller and Toulouse (1986) found that the amount of delegation by top executives in 97 small businesses was related to their profitability and sales growth. Descriptive research on effective management also tends to support the effectiveness of delegation (Bradford & Cohen, 1984; Kanter, 1983; Kouzes & Posner, 1987; Peters & Austin, 1985; Peters & Waterman, 1982). However, the direction of causality is difficult to determine in the existing research. It is not clear whether delegation improves performance, improved performance results in more delegation, or both effects are occurring simultaneously. More longitudinal, experimental research is needed to investigate direction of causality and the mediating processes (e.g., mutual trust, shared objectives, leader self-confidence, subordinate desire for more responsibility).

Applications: Guidelines for Delegating

This section of the chapter provides some tentative guidelines for effective use of delegation by managers. Although research on delegation is still very limited, there is considerable agreement in the practitioner literature about when and how to use delegation effectively. Guidelines for what to delegate are presented here first, followed by guidelines on how to delegate (see Table 4-6 for summary).

TABLE 4-6   Guidelines for Delegation

What to Delegate
- Tasks that can be done better by a subordinate.
- Tasks that are urgent but not high priority.
- Tasks relevant to a subordinate's career.
- Tasks of appropriate difficulty.
- Both pleasant and unpleasant tasks.
- Tasks not central to the manager's role.

How to Delegate
- Specify responsibilities clearly.
- Provide adequate authority and specify limits of discretion.
- Specify reporting requirements.
- Ensure subordinate acceptance of responsibilities.
- Inform others who need to know.
- Monitor progress in appropriate ways.
- Arrange for the subordinate to receive necessary information.
- Provide support and assistance, but avoid reverse delegation.
- Make mistakes a learning experience.

What to Delegate

The selection of tasks to delegate depends in part on the purpose of the delegation. Some guidelines on what to delegate are the following.

- **Delegate tasks that can be done better by a subordinate.**

Some responsibilities can be done better by a subordinate than by a manager. Better performance by a subordinate is likely when the person has more expertise, when the person is closer to the problem and can obtain more timely information about it, or because the manager simply does not have the time necessary to do the task properly. Such responsibilities are usually good candidates for delegation, regardless of the purpose.

- **Delegate tasks that are urgent but not high priority.**

When the purpose is to reduce excessive workload, the best tasks for delegation are ones that are urgent but not high priority. These tasks must get done quickly, but the manager does not have time to do all of them. Some of the tasks may be things that a subordinate cannot do as well as the manager, but it is better for them to be done by a subordinate than not at all. Delegation of these tasks frees more time for a manager to do higher priority tasks.

- **Delegate tasks relevant to a subordinate's career.**

If the purpose of delegation is to develop subordinate skills, the responsibilities must be ones relevant to the subordinate's career objectives. Developmental delegation is likely to include special projects that allow a subordinate the opportunity to struggle with a challenging task and exercise initiative and problem solving. Preparation of a subordinate to take over the manager's job or to advance to a similar job in another unit requires delegating some important managerial responsibilities, including ones the subordinate initially may not do as well as the manager. Some of these delegated tasks may be irrelevant to the subordinate's current job and, in fact, may take time away from the subordinate's regular work.

- **Delegate tasks of appropriate difficulty.**

Delegated tasks should be challenging for a subordinate, but not so difficult as to offer little hope of doing them successfully. The tasks should be difficult enough so that some mistakes are likely to occur, because mistakes are an integral part of the learning experience. However, the task should not be so difficult and important that mistakes will undermine the subordinate's self-confidence and ruin his or her reputation. Delegation for developmental purposes should be carried out gradually. As the subordinate learns how to handle the initial responsibilities, additional responsibilities can be delegated.

- **Delegate both pleasant and unpleasant tasks.**

Some managers keep all of the pleasant tasks for themselves and delegate only tedious, boring tasks to subordinates. Such tasks will not enrich subordinate jobs and are likely to reduce rather than increase subordinate job satisfaction. On the other hand, some managers with a martyr complex delegate only pleasant tasks and retain for themselves all of the disagreeable ones. This approach leaves a gap in the development of subordinates and is likely to make the manager's job more stressful than it should be. Delegation should include both pleasant and unpleasant tasks. The unpleasant tasks should be shared by subordinates or rotated among them to avoid perceptions of favoritism and inequity in work assignments.

- **Delegate tasks not central to the manager's role.**

Tasks that are symbolically important and central to a manager's role should not be delegated. These responsibilities include such things as setting objectives and priorities for the work unit, allocating resources among subordinates, evaluating the performance of subordinates, making personnel decisions about pay increases and promotions for subordinates, directing the group's response to a crisis, and various figurehead activities for which an appearance by the manager is expected (Mintzberg, 1973). When it is necessary to develop subordinate skills related to these responsibilities, another form of participation such as consultation and group decisions can be used rather than delegation. For example, strategic planning may be carried out in planning meetings in which subordinates provide ideas and suggestions, but the responsibility for strategic decisions is not delegated to individual subordinates.

How to Delegate

The success of delegation depends as much on how it is carried out as on what is delegated. The following guidelines are designed to minimize problems and avoid common pitfalls related to assignment of tasks and delegation of authority. The first four guidelines are for the meeting to delegate responsibilities to a subordinate.

- **Specify responsibilities clearly.**

When delegating, it is essential to make sure the subordinate understands the new responsibilities. Explain the results expected for a delegated task or assignment, clarify objectives and priorities, and inform the person about any deadlines that must be met. Check for comprehension by asking the subordinate to restate your expectations, or by questioning the subordinate about important aspects of the task. In the case of an inexperienced subordinate, you may want to ask the person to prepare action plans for you to review before they are implemented.

- **Provide adequate authority and specify limits of discretion.**

Unless adequate resources are provided, the subordinate is unlikely to be successful in carrying out a delegated task. When assigning new responsibilities, determine the appropriate amount of authority needed by the subordinate to carry them out. Specify clearly the subordinate's scope of authority and limits of discretion. Authority includes funds that can be committed, resources that can be used, decisions that can be made without prior approval, and agreements that can be negotiated directly with outsiders or other units in the organization.

- **Specify reporting requirements.**

It is important for a subordinate to understand the types of information that must be reported, how often reports are expected, and the manner in which progress will be monitored (e.g., written reports, progress review meetings, presentations in department meetings, formal performance evaluations). The frequency and timing of progress reviews will depend on the nature of the task and the competence of the subordinate. More frequent checking is appropriate for critical tasks with high exposure and high cost of mistakes, and for subordinates who lack experience and confidence. As a subordinate demonstrates competence in doing delegated tasks, the frequency of reporting can be reduced. Progress reports should emphasize results, but the means for accomplishing delegated tasks should not be ignored entirely. It is important to ensure use of procedures that are legal, ethical, and consistent with organizational policy.

- **Ensure subordinate acceptance of responsibilities.**

If delegation is to be successful, the subordinate must accept the new assignments and be committed to carrying them out. In some cases acceptance is not a problem, because the assignments are interesting and important for the subordinate's career advancement. However, a subordinate may be reluctant to admit doubts and concerns about new assignments. It is useful to allow the subordinate to participate in determining what tasks will be assigned and how much authority will be delegated. With developmental delegation, it is useful to discuss how the delegated tasks are relevant to the person's career advancement. If the subordinate lacks self-confidence, it is helpful to express confidence in the person's ability to do a good job.

How to Manage Delegation

The next five guidelines describe steps the manager should take after delegating responsibilities to a subordinate. These steps help to ensure that delegation will be successful.

- **Inform others who need to know.**

People who are affected by the delegation and people whose cooperation and assistance are necessary for the subordinate to do the delegated tasks should be informed about the subordinate's new responsibilities and authority. Unless informed about the delegation by you, these people may doubt the subordinate's authority and ignore his or her requests and directions. The people who need to be informed may include other subordinates, subordinates of your subordinate, peers in other units, outsiders such as clients and suppliers, and your boss.

- **Monitor progress in appropriate ways.**

With delegated tasks, as with all tasks, it is important to monitor progress and provide feedback to the subordinate. It is difficult to achieve an optimal balance between control and delegation, and progress review meetings enable a manager to monitor subordinate progress without having to supervise too closely on a day-to-day basis. The subordinate is given considerable latitude to deal with problems without interference, yet is free to ask for advice and assistance whenever it is needed. When authority is delegated, a manager and subordinate should decide on the type of performance measures and progress indicators to collect.

- **Arrange for the subordinate to receive necessary information.**

It is usually best to have all detailed information about the subordinate's performance flow directly to the subordinate, with less detailed summary information coming to the manager at less frequent intervals. However, in the case of developmental delegation with an inexperienced subordinate, detailed information may be collected more frequently to check closely on the progress of the subordinate. In addition to performance information, the subordinate will need various types of technical and general information to carry out the delegated tasks effectively. Keep the subordinate informed about changes that affect his or her plans and schedules. If possible, arrange for relevant technical information to flow directly to the subordinate and help the subordinate establish his or her own sources of essential information.

- **Provide support and assistance, but avoid reverse delegation.**

A manager should provide psychological support to a subordinate who is discouraged or frustrated, and encourage the person to keep going. For newly delegated tasks, it may be necessary to provide more advice and coaching about procedures for doing some aspect of the work. However, it is important to avoid reverse delegation, in which control is reasserted over a task that was previously delegated. When a subordinate asks for help with problems, he or she should be asked to recommend a solution. The manager can help the person evaluate whether the solution is feasible and appropriate.

- **Make mistakes a learning experience.**

It is important to recognize that mistakes are inevitable for delegated tasks. Mistakes and failures should be treated seriously, but the response should not be one of criticism and blame. Instead, the episode should become a learning experience for both parties as they discuss the reason for the mistake and identify ways to avoid similar mistakes in the future. If it becomes obvious that the subordinate does not know how to do some essential aspect of the work, the manager should provide additional instruction and coaching.

Perceived Empowerment

The theory and research reviewed earlier in this chapter examines power sharing and participation from the perspective of leader behavior, decision procedures, and the formal structure of the organization. The emphasis has been on what is done to give people more influence over work-related decisions and to create conditions that foster initiative and self-determination. Leader actions and decision processes are an important determinant of empowerment, but by themselves they do not explain when and why people will actually feel empowered. Additional insights can be gained by examining follower perceptions, needs, and values.

Nature of Psychological Empowerment

The term *psychological empowerment* describes how the intrinsic motivation and self-efficacy of people are influenced by leadership behavior, job characteristics, organization structure, and their own needs and values. One reason it is important to consider psychological processes is that participative practices and employee involvement programs do not necessarily reduce feelings of powerlessness or leave people feeling that their work is meaningful and worthwhile (Conger & Kanungo, 1988). For example, allowing people to determine how to do a trivial and demeaning task is unlikely to increase their feelings of self-worth and self-fulfillment. Delegating responsibility for a more significant task will not be empowering if people lack the skills and knowledge required to perform the task successfully and are worried about failure. The opportunity to elect a leader may do little to reduce feelings of powerlessness if the choice is between candidates who are equally unsatisfactory. Theories of psychological empowerment attempt to explain when and why efforts to empower people are likely to be successful.

Theories about the defining elements of psychological empowerment have been proposed by various scholars (e.g., Bowen & Lawler, 1992; Conger & Kanungo, 1988; Kanter, 1983; Thomas & Velthouse, 1990), but as yet there has been only limited research on this question. A study by Spreitzer (1995) found support for the proposition that psychological empowerment includes four defining elements: (1) meaning, (2) self-determination, (3) self-efficacy, and (4) impact. A person will feel more empowered if the content and consequences of the work are consistent with a person's values and ideals, the person has the capability to determine how and when the work is done, the person has high confidence about being able to do it effectively, and the person believes it is possible to have a significant impact on the job and work environment. The emphasis on these four elements links psychological empowerment to earlier theory and research on work motivation (e.g., Bandura, 1986; Shamir, 1991), job design (e.g., Hackman & Oldham, 1980; Fried & Ferris, 1987), participative leadership (e.g., Vroom & Jago, 1978; Sagie & Koslowsky, 2000), and organizational programs for employee involvement (e.g., Cotton, 1993; Lawler, 1986).

Consequences of Empowerment

Psychological empowerment probably has the same type of consequences as high intrinsic motivation and self-efficacy. A number of potential benefits have been identified (Block, 1987; Howard, 1998; Thomas & Velthouse, 1990). The beneficial consequences include (1) stronger task commitment, (2) greater initiative in carrying out role responsibilities, (3) greater persistence in the face of obstacles and temporary setbacks, (4) more innovation and learning, and stronger optimism about the eventual success of the work, (5) higher job satisfaction, (6) stronger organizational commitment, and (7) less turnover. Some potential costs and risks have also been identified (e.g., Baloff & Doherty, 1989; Bowen & Lawler, 1992; Eccles, 1993). Examples include (1) higher costs for selection and training, (2) higher labor costs for skilled employees, (3) inconsistent service quality, (4) expensive giveaways and bad decisions by some employees, (5) customer feelings of inequity about unequal treatment, (6) opposition by middle managers who feel threatened, and (7) conflicts from raising employee expectations beyond what top management is willing to concede. As yet only a few studies have examined the consequences of psychological empowerment (e.g., Howard & Wellins, 1994; Koberg, Boss, Senjem, & Goodman, 1999; Konczak, Stelly, & Trusty, 2000; Spreitzer, 1995; Spreitzer, Kizilos, & Nason, 1997). It is too early to reach any firm conclusions, but the combined evidence from these studies and related lines of research suggest that the potential benefits are likely to occur when conditions are favorable for empowerment.

Facilitating Conditions for Empowerment

The conditions that encourage and strengthen feelings of empowerment have been suggested by a number of writers (e.g., Ackoff, 1994; Argyris, 1998; Bowen & Lawler, 1992; Conger, 1989; Forrester, 2000; Gratton, 2004; Howard, 1998; Leadbeater, 2000;

TABLE 4-7 Conditions Facilitating Psychological Empowerment

Condition	Unfavorable	Favorable
Organization structure	High centralization and formalization	Very decentralized, low formalization
Competitive strategy	Low cost, standard product or service	Customized, highly differentiated product/service
Task design and technology	Simple, repetitive task and reliable technology	Complex, nonroutine task, unreliable technology
Duration of relation with customers/clients	Brief transactions during a short time interval	Repeated interaction in a continuing relationship
Dominant cultural values in the organization	Reliable, efficient operations without any mistakes	Flexibility, learning, and participation
Employee traits	Low achievement motivation, external locus of control, and emotional stability	High need for achievement, internal locus of control, and emotional stability
Employee ability	Unskilled, inexperienced	Highly skilled professional
Employee tenure	Temporary employee	Regular, continuing employee
Employee ownership and rewards for success	None or very little	Employees are shareholders or co-owners
Employee involvement programs	None	Extensive programs strongly supported by top management
Mutual trust	Low	High

Randolph, 1995; Spreitzer, 1996). Characteristics of the organization, the members, and the work can encourage or discourage leaders from attempting to empower subordinates, and they can facilitate or limit the success of efforts to empower subordinates (see Table 4-7). Some aspects of the situation that can be facilitating conditions for empowerment are described in more detail next.

Job Design. Employees have little opportunity for empowerment when they perform routine, repetitive production jobs, or jobs where they interact only briefly with customers. There is more potential for meaningful work and self-determination in a job that has complex tasks, longer interactions, and continuing relationships with the same customers. Access to information and resources needed to do the work increases self-determination and self-efficacy.

Organization Structure. In organizations with high centralization of power in top management, the middle and lower-level managers have little power or authority, which severely limits their opportunity to use delegation or job enrichment. Likewise, delegation to lower-level managers and employees is less likely when the organization has extensive formalization and standardization, with lots of detailed rules and procedures for doing the work the same efficient way in every location (e.g., fast-food restaurants). In contrast, decentralized organizations that compete on the basis of customized products or services provide more opportunities for employees to determine how to do the work and exercise initiative in solving problems.

Organization Culture.   The term *organization culture* is used to describe the shared values and beliefs of members about the activities of the organization and interpersonal relationships (see Chapter 10). A culture that emphasizes reliable, efficient operations without any mistakes will discourage members from taking initiative in solving problems. Even the middle managers may fear mistakes that will jeopardize their career in the organization. In contrast, a culture with strong values for flexibility, learning, and participation will support employee empowerment.

Leader Selection and Assessment.   More empowerment is likely when members elect their leaders for limited terms, which is a common practice in voluntary organizations, professional associations, and democratic political units (e.g., city councils, school boards, state legislatures). Most private business organizations have leaders who are appointed rather than elected, but some companies use a hybrid form of selection. The leaders are selected by a council of representatives who were elected by the members (c.f., de Jong & van Witteloostuijn, 2004). Regardless of how a leader is selected, the influence of members' is greater when they participate actively in assessing leader performance, especially if they are able to remove a leader with unsatisfactory performance.

Procedures for Influencing Decision.   Empowerment is also increased when the formal procedures for making important decisions give members significant influence over these decisions. In some organizations the charter specifies that a meeting or referendum must be held to allow members to decide important matters by a majority vote. In large organizations where direct participation is not feasible, an alternate form of empowerment that is sometimes used is to have elected representatives from each major subunit on the governing council, or to allow lower-level members to elect one or more representatives to serve on the board of directors. In many public sector organizations members also have the right to attend open meetings of the board or council to express opinions about important issues before a decision is made. The election of leaders and the use of policy-making councils or boards with elected members are common in public sector organizations and professional associations, but they are rare in private sector business organizations in the United States.

The success of formal structures and procedures for increasing member influence over strategic decisions is a subject of continuing controversy (Kerr, 2004). Within the many different forms of industrial democracy, the implications for organizational performance and member satisfaction depend on the type of organization and society in which they are used. Many obstacles to success must be overcome in order to realize the potential benefits.

Shared Leadership.   Empowerment is also increased when leadership responsibilities are shared by members of a small organization or team rather than invested in a single leader. One example is the growing use of self-managed teams in business organizations (see Chapter 11). The most extreme form of shared leadership occurs when all important decisions are made collectively, and leadership responsibilities for daily operations are distributed among the members and rotated frequently. This form of empowerment is most likely to be found in small employee-owned businesses, cooperatives, and voluntary organizations. An example of a bossless organization is provided by Vanderslice (1988) in her case study of the Moosewood Restaurant.

> Moosewood is a small, collectively owned organization that has been financially sound for the 15 years it has existed. The restaurant has 18 members, and all of them are involved in making important decisions such as policy changes, selection and dismissal of members, financial issues, wages and benefits, and selection of suppliers. In addition, there are usually 4 to 6 temporary workers who are not involved in decision making but who may be accepted as regular members after a year of apprenticeship. Areas of responsibility are rotated among the members. The time an individual remains responsible for a particular job depends on the logical cycle of the task and the individual's interest in doing it. All jobs are open to any member who wants to learn to do them, and members are encouraged to take a turn at every job. Job rotation spreads expertise and responsibility among collective members rather than lodging it in one or two managers. All jobs pay the same hourly rate, and income from the 15% service charge is shared by all members. Some power differences exist, but they are based on demonstrated expertise and commitment to the organization. Accountability is regulated through internalized values and group pressure. However, confronting a member about inappropriate behavior is still an unresolved problem.

How Leaders Can Increase Empowerment

The theory and research on psychological empowerment makes it evident that participative leadership and delegation are not the only types of leadership behavior that can make people feel empowered. Other types of leadership behavior can directly affect psychological empowerment, and these behaviors may also enhance the effects of participative leadership and delegation (Forrester, 2000; Howard, 1998; Konczak et al., 2000). Table 4-8 provides guidelines on how to empower subordinates. The behaviors are explained in more detail in other parts of this book.

TABLE 4-8 Guidelines for Empowering

- Clarify objectives and explain how the work supports them.
- Involve people in making decisions that affect them.
- Delegate responsibility and authority for important activities.
- Take into account individual differences in motivation and skills.
- Provide access to relevant information.
- Provide resources needed to carry out new responsibilities.
- Change management systems to be consistent with empowerment.
- Remove bureaucratic constraints and unnecessary controls.
- Express confidence and trust in people.
- Provide coaching and advice when requested.
- Encourage and support initiative and problem solving.
- Recognize important contributions and achievements.
- Ensure that rewards are commensurate with new responsibilities.
- Ensure accountability for the ethical use of power.

Summary

Participative leadership involves efforts by a manager to encourage and facilitate participation by others in making decisions that would otherwise be made by the manager alone. Participation can take many forms, ranging from revising a tentative decision after receiving protests, to asking for suggestions before making a decision, to asking an individual or group to jointly make a decision, to allowing others to make a decision subject to the manager's final authorization. Involving others in making decisions is often necessary for getting decisions approved and implemented in organizations. Even when it is not necessary to consult with others before making a decision, a manager may still prefer to do so in order to obtain the potential benefits, which include better decisions and greater acceptance of decisions.

Many studies have been conducted on the outcomes of using participation, but the research evidence is not sufficiently strong and consistent to draw any firm conclusions. Lack of consistent results about the effectiveness of participative leadership probably means that various forms of participation are effective in some situations but not in others. Participation is unlikely to be effective if potential participants do not share the leader's objectives, if they do not want to take responsibility for helping to make decisions, if they distrust the leader, or if time pressures and the dispersion of participants make it impractical to consult with individuals or hold group meetings. Group forms of participation are unlikely to be effective unless the manager has sufficient skill in managing conflict, facilitating constructive problem solving, and dealing with common process problems that occur in groups (see Chapter 11).

Vroom and Yetton developed a model of participative leadership to help managers identify the appropriate decision procedures in different situations. The situational variables are characteristics of the decision situation that determine whether a particular decision procedure will increase or decrease decision quality and acceptance. The model was extended by Vroom and Jago to include other criteria and aspects of the situation. Research on these models is limited, but it provides moderate support for them. The findings suggest that managers are likely to be more effective if they use decision procedures that are appropriate for the situation.

Delegation involves the assignment of new responsibilities and additional authority to individual subordinates or to a team. The potential benefits of delegation include better decisions, increased subordinate motivation, more satisfying jobs for subordinates, development of subordinate skills, and reduction of work overload for a manager. Lack of confidence in subordinates and desire to consolidate power prevent some managers from delegating as much as they should. Research on the consequences of using delegation is still limited, but the findings suggest it can be effective when used for appropriate decisions and carried out in a competent manner.

Psychological empowerment involves a combination of meaningful work, high self-efficacy, self-determination, and ability to influence relevant events. Leaders can affect the psychological empowerment of followers in many ways, and participative leadership and delegation are only two of the relevant behaviors. Whether an employee feels powerful or powerless also depends on aspects of the job, the organization, and the employees.

Review and Discussion Questions

1. What are the potential benefits and risks of using participative leadership?
2. What have we learned from the research on participative leadership?
3. What conditions determine whether a participative decision procedure is likely to be successful?
4. Briefly explain the Vroom-Yetton normative model of leadership and the Vroom-Jago extension of the model.
5. How useful are these prescriptive models if a leader does not know the answers to some of the situational questions?
6. What are some guidelines on how to encourage participation?
7. What are the potential benefits and risks of delegation?
8. Under what conditions is delegation most likely to be successful?
9. What are some guidelines on what to delegate?
10. Why do some managers find it so difficult to delegate or share power?
11. What are essential elements of psychological empowerment?
12. What are some facilitating conditions for employee empowerment?
13. What types of leadership behavior contribute to high empowerment?

Key Terms

- autocratic decision
- consultation
- decision acceptance
- decision quality
- decision procedure

- delegation
- employee involvement programs
- normative decision model
- participation

- psychological empowerment
- self-determination
- self-efficacy
- trust

CASES

Echo Electronics

Paul Sanchez is the production manager for Echo Electronics, a small company that makes and distributes communications equipment. Paul's direct subordinates are the supervisors of the four production departments in the company's manufacturing plant. Six months ago, the engineering manager at Echo Electronics proposed a plan to install new computerized work stations to increase productivity in the plant. It seemed to be a good idea to Paul, and he welcomed the change. The CEO also approved the plan, and the new equipment was installed immediately.

Three months later, Paul was surprised and disappointed to find that the expected increase in productivity did not occur. In fact, productivity and quality actually decreased. The marketing manager told Paul that several of their best customers complained about receiving Echo equipment that was defective. Paul does not believe that the problem lies with the new workstations. Technicians from the firm that built the workstations recently checked them and found that they were operating properly. Paul talked to someone at another company that uses the workstations, and his contact reported that they were having great success with them.

When Paul discussed the problem with his four production supervisors, he found that they shared his concern but did not agree among themselves about the cause of the problem. Reasons given for the decline in performance included poor design of the workstations, inadequate training of the production workers who operate them, and lack of financial incentives for increasing productivity. The supervisors also told Paul that the production workers have strong feelings about the workstations. Morale declined, and two employees quit because they were upset about the changes made in the way the work is done.

This morning Paul received a phone call from the CEO who just received the production figures for last month and was calling to express concern about them. The CEO indicated that the problem was Paul's to solve, and he must take immediate steps to deal with it. The CEO wants to know by next week what steps Paul will take to reverse the decline in productivity and product quality. ∎

SOURCE: Adapted from a case by Timothy R. Hinkin and used with his permission.

QUESTIONS

1. What actions could Paul have taken to prevent the problem?

2. What steps should Paul take now to deal with the problem?

Alvis Corporation

Kathy McCarthy was the manager of a production department in Alvis Corporation, a firm that manufactures office equipment. The workers are not unionized. After reading an article that stressed the benefits of participative management, Kathy believed that these benefits could be realized in her department if the workers were allowed to participate in making some decisions that affect them. Kathy selected two decisions for an experiment in participative management.

The first decision involved vacation schedules. Each summer the workers are given two weeks vacation, but no more than two workers can go on vacation at the same time. In prior years, Kathy made this decision herself. She would first ask the workers to indicate their preferred dates, then she considered how the work would be affected if different people were out at the same time. It was important to plan a vacation schedule that would ensure adequate staffing for all of the essential operations performed by the department. When more than two workers wanted the same time period, and they had similar skills, she usually gave preference to the workers with the highest productivity.

The second decision involved production standards. Sales had been increasing steadily over the past few years, and the company recently installed some new equipment to increase productivity. The new equipment would make it possible to produce more with the same number of workers. The company had a pay incentive system in which workers received a piece rate for each unit produced above a standard amount. Separate standards existed for each type of product, based on an industrial engineering study conducted a few years earlier. Top management wanted to read just the production standards to reflect the fact that the new equipment made it it possible for the workers to earn more without working any harder. The savings from higher productivity were needed to help pay for the new equipment.

Kathy called a meeting of her 15 workers an hour before the end of the work day and explained that she wanted them to discuss the two issues and make recommendations. Kathy figured that the workers might be inhibited about participating in the discussion if she were present, so she left them alone to discuss the issues. Besides, Kathy had an appointment to meet with the quality control manager. Quality problems had increased after the new equipment was installed, and the industrial engineers were studying the problem in an attempt to determine why quality had gotten worse rather than better.

When Kathy returned to her department just at quitting time, she was surprised to learn that the workers recommended keeping the standards the same. She had assumed they knew the pay incentives were no longer fair and would set a higher standard. The worker speaking for the group explained that their base pay had not kept up with inflation and the higher incentive pay restored their real income to its prior level.

On the vacation issue, the group was deadlocked. Several of the workers wanted to take their vacations during the same two week period and could not agree on who should go. Some workers argued that they should have priority because they had more seniority, while others argued that priority should be based on productivity, as in the past. Because it was quitting time, the group concluded that Kathy would have to resolve the dispute herself. After all, wasn't that what she was being paid for? ∎

SOURCE: Copyright © 1987 by Gary Yukl.

QUESTIONS

1. Were the two decisions appropriate for a group decision procedure according to the Vroom-Yetton model?

2. What mistakes were made in using participation, and what could have been done to avoid the difficulties the manager encountered?

3. Were these two decisions appropriate ones for introducing participation into the department?

5

DYADIC ROLE MAKING, ATTRIBUTIONS, AND FOLLOWERSHIP

Learning Objectives

After studying this chapter you should be able to:

- Understand how attributions and implicit theories influence follower perception and evaluation of a leader.

- Understand how leader behavior is influenced by attributions about the motives and skills of subordinates.

- Understand why different dyadic relationships develop between a leader and individual subordinates.

- Understand the major findings in research on leader-member exchange theory and the limitations of this research.

- Understand appropriate ways to manage a subordinate who has performance deficiencies.

- Understand what followers can do to have a more effective dyadic relationship with their leader.

- Understand how follower self-management can substitute for some aspects of leadership.

- Understand why it is important for managers to integrate their leader and follower roles.

Most of the early theory and research on leadership behavior did not consider how much leaders vary their behavior with different subordinates. However, the discussion of delegation in the preceding chapter makes it clear that dyadic relationships are not identical for all of a leader's direct subordinates. This chapter begins with a theory (LMX) that describes how a leader develops an exchange relationship over time with each subordinate as the two parties influence each other and negotiate the subordinate's role in the organization. Next, attribution theory is examined to discover how leaders interpret subordinate performance and decide how to react to it. Research on upward impression management is examined to see how subordinates attempt to influence a leader's perception of their competence and motivation. This part of the chapter also has some guidelines on how leaders can deal with unsatisfactory performance and improve the quality of the exchange relationship.

The chapter then turns to follower-based approaches to leadership. Most leadership literature over the past half-century has focused on leaders. The attitudes and behavior of leaders have been examined in detail, but until recently, follower attitudes and behavior have been of interest only as an indicator of leader influence and effectiveness. Chapter 4 described research on follower perceptions of empowerment, and the present chapter describes research on follower evaluation of leader effectiveness. The chapter also examines self-management processes that enable followers to become more effective as individual contributors, even in the absence of good leaders. The chapter includes guidelines on how to be an effective follower while remaining true to one's values. Finally, the chapter includes a brief discussion about integrating leader and follower roles in organizations.

Leader-Member Exchange Theory

Leader-member exchange (LMX) theory, describes the role-making processes between a leader and each individual subordinate and the exchange relationship that develops over time (Dansereau, Graen, & Haga, 1975; Graen & Cashman, 1975). LMX theory was formerly called the vertical dyad linkage theory because of its focus on reciprocal influence processes within vertical dyads composed of one person who has direct authority over another person.

Initial Version of LMX Theory

The basic premise of the theory is that leaders develop a separate exchange relationship with each subordinate as the two parties mutually define the subordinate's role. Graen and Cashman (1975) suggested that exchange relationships are formed on the basis of personal compatibility and subordinate competence and dependability. Over time, a leader is likely to establish either a high-exchange relationship or a low-exchange relationship with each subordinate.

According to the theory, most leaders develop a high-exchange relationship with a small number of trusted subordinates who function as assistants, lieutenants, or advisors. The basis for establishing a high-exchange relationship is the leader's control over outcomes that are desirable to a subordinate. These outcomes include such things as assignment to interesting and desirable tasks, delegation of greater responsibility and authority, more sharing of information, participation in making some of the leader's decisions, tangible rewards such as a pay increase, special benefits (e.g., better work schedule, bigger office), personal support and approval, and facilitation of the subordinate's career (e.g., recommending a promotion, giving developmental assignments with high visibility). In return for greater status, influence, and benefits, a high-exchange subordinate has additional obligations and costs. The subordinate is expected to work harder, to be more committed to task objectives, to be loyal to the leader, and to share some of the leader's administrative duties. The development of high-exchange relationships occurs gradually over a period of time, through reciprocal reinforcement of behavior as the exchange cycle is repeated over and over again. Unless the cycle is broken, the relationship is likely to develop a high degree of mutual dependence, loyalty, and support.

The benefits to the leader from a high-exchange relationship are evident. Subordinate commitment is important when the leader's work unit has tasks that require considerable initiative and effort on the part of some members to be carried out successfully. The assistance of committed subordinates can be invaluable to a manager who lacks the time and energy to carry out all of the administrative duties for which he or she is responsible. However, the high-exchange relationships create certain obligations and constraints for the leader. To maintain these relationships, the leader must provide attention to the subordinates, remain responsive to their needs and feelings, and rely more on time-consuming influence methods such as persuasion and consultation. The leader cannot resort to coercion or heavy-handed use of authority without endangering the special relationship.

The exchange relationship established with the remaining subordinates is substantially different. A low-exchange relationship is characterized by a relatively low level of mutual influence. To satisfy the terms of this "outgroup" relationship, subordinates need only comply with formal role requirements (e.g., duties, rules, standard procedures, and legitimate directions from the leader). As long as such compliance is forthcoming, the subordinate receives the standard benefits for the job (such as a salary).

Role-Making Stages

In a revision of LMX theory, the development of relationships in a leader-subordinate dyad was described in terms of a "life cycle model" with three possible stages (Graen & Scandura, 1987; Graen & Uhl-Bien, 1991). The relationship begins with an initial testing phase in which the leader and subordinate evaluate each other's motives, attitudes, and potential resources to be exchanged, and mutual role expectations are established. Some relationships never go beyond this first stage. If the relationship proceeds to the second stage, the exchange arrangement is refined, and mutual trust, loyalty, and respect are developed. Some exchange relationships advance to a third ("mature") stage wherein exchange based on self-interest is transformed into mutual commitment to the mission and objectives of the work unit. According to Graen and Uhl-Bien (1991), the third stage corresponds to transformational leadership, whereas the first stage corresponds to transactional leadership (see Chapter 9).

Measurement of LMX

The way in which LMX has been defined has varied substantially from study to study. Quality of exchange relationship is usually assumed to involve such things as mutual trust, respect, affection, support, and loyalty. However, sometimes LMX is defined to include other aspects of the relationship (e.g., negotiating latitude, incremental influence, shared values), or individual attributes of the leader and subordinate (see Schriesheim, Castro, & Cogliser, 1999). Several different measures of LMX have been

TABLE 5-1 Sample Items from the LMX-7				
1. How well does your leader understand your job problems and needs?				
Not a Bit	A Little	A Fair Amount	Quite a Bit	A Great Deal
2. How well does your leader recognize your potential?				
Not at All	A Little	Moderately	Mostly	Fully
3. How would you characterize your working relationship with your leader?				
Extremely Ineffective	Worse Than Average	Average	Better Than Average	Extremely Effective
4. What are the chances that your leader would use his/her power to help you solve problems in your work?				
None	Small	Moderate	High	Very High

Source: G. B. Graen and M. Uhl-Bien, "Relationship-based approach to leadership: Development of leader-member exchange (LMX) theory of leadership over 25 years: Applying a multilevel multi-domain approach," *Leadership Quarterly*, 6 (1995), pp. 219–247.

used since the theory was first proposed. The most widely used measure in recent years is a seven-item scale called LMX-7, and sample items from it are shown in Table 5-1. Some researchers have used longer, more diverse questionnaires in an attempt to identify separate dimensions of LMX (e.g., Liden & Maslyn, 1998; Schrieshein, Neider, Scandura, & Tepper, 1992). It is not clear yet whether the multidimensional scales offer any advantages over a unidimensional scale. More research is needed to determine the implications of using a multidimensional measure of LMX.

Only a small number of studies have measured LMX from the perception of both the leader and the follower (e.g., Deluga & Perry, 1994; Liden, Wayne, & Stilwell, 1993; Phillips & Bedeian, 1994; Scandura & Schriesheim, 1994). It is reasonable to expect the two parties to agree about something as important and salient as the quality of their relationship. Contrary to this expectation, the correlation between leader-rated LMX and subordinate-rated LMX is low enough to raise questions about scale validity for one or both sources (see Gerstner & Day, 1997). It is not clear whether the low correlation reflects measurement problems in the scales or actual differences in perception. More research is needed to determine the answer and to clarify the implications of measuring LMX from different (leader and subordinate) perspectives.

Research on Correlates of LMX

Most of the research on LMX theory since the initial studies in the 1970s has examined how LMX is related to other variables. This research includes a large number of survey field studies, a smaller number of laboratory experiments, and a couple of field experiments. In addition, a few studies have used observation and analysis of communication patterns within high versus low LMX relationships (e.g., Fairhurst, 1993; Kramer, 1995). Detailed reviews of research on the correlates of LMX can be found in various articles (e.g., Erdogan & Liden, 2002; Gerstner & Day, 1997; Liden, Sparrowe, & Wayne, 1997; Schriesheim et al., 1999). A summary of major findings is presented in the remainder of this section.

One set of studies examined factors that predict the quality of the exchange relationship for a dyad. A favorable relationship is more likely when the subordinate is perceived to be competent and dependable, and the subordinate's values and attitudes are similar to those of the leader. Some aspects of subordinate personality and leader personality may also be related to LMX, but the number of studies on this question is too small to reach any firm conclusions.

Another set of studies examined how LMX is related to leader and subordinate behavior. When the exchange relationship is favorable, behavior by the leader is more supportive and includes more consultation and delegation, more mentoring, less close monitoring, and less domination of conversations. The subordinate demonstrates organizational citizenship behavior, more support of the leader, more open communication with the leader, and less use of pressure tactics (e.g., threats, demands) to influence the leader. It is not clear how much a new subordinate can directly influence the role-making process, for example by using impression management behavior, but it is likely that some subordinates are proactive about developing a favorable relationship rather than passively accepting whatever the leader decides to do.

A substantial body of research has now examined the relationship between LMX and outcomes such as subordinate satisfaction and performance. This body of research found that a favorable downward exchange relationship was usually correlated with more role clarity, higher satisfaction, stronger organizational commitment, and better subordinate performance. In a rare field experiment (Graen, Novak, & Sommerkamp, 1982; Scandura & Graen, 1984), leaders trained to develop favorable exchange relationships with their subordinates had subsequent gains in the objective performance and satisfaction of their subordinates. To incorporate the results of the research on outcomes, the revised theory (Graen & Uhl-Bien, 1995) included the prescription that the leader should try to establish a special exchange relationship with all subordinates if possible, not just with a few favorites.

The early research found that a leader's upward dyadic relationship affects downward dyadic relationships (Cashman, Dansereau, Graen, & Haga,1976; Graen, Cashman, Ginsburgh, & Schiemann, 1977). A manager who has a favorable exchange relationship with the boss is more likely to establish favorable exchange relationships with subordinates. A favorable upward relationship enables a manager to obtain more benefits for subordinates and to facilitate their performance by obtaining necessary resources, cutting red tape, and gaining approval of changes desired by subordinates. Subordinates feel less motivation to incur the extra obligations of a special exchange relationship if the leader has little to offer in the way of extra benefits, opportunities, and empowerment. The research found that the effects of a manager's upward relationship were felt by subordinates regardless of their own relationship with the manager. Managers with a favorable upward relationship with their own boss were described by subordinates as having more technical skill, providing more outside information, allowing more participation in decision making, allowing more subordinate autonomy, and providing more support and consideration.

Evaluation of LMX Theory and Research

LMX theory began as a descriptive theory, but over time it has become more prescriptive. Refinement of theories can be an advantage if they become more precise, parsimonious, and comprehensive. Unfortunately, the revisions of LMX theory have not always produced these benefits. LMX theory still has a number of conceptual weaknesses that limit its utility. Early versions of the theory did not adequately explain how dyadic relationships develop over time, how the leader's different dyadic relationships affect each other, and how differentiated relationships affect overall performance by the leader's work unit (Dienesh & Liden, 1986; Schriesheim et al., 1999, Vecchio & Gobdel, 1984). Revisions of the theory have attempted to remedy some of these deficiencies, but additional improvements are needed.

A continuing problem over the years has been ambiguity about the nature of the exchange relationship (Schriesheim et al., 1999). The proliferation of LMX definitions and scales has not helped to reduce the ambiguity. It is still not evident whether the LMX scales measure a theoretical construct (quality of relationship) that is conceptually meaningful and distinct from more traditional constructs such as satisfaction with the leader, trust of the leader, and identification with the leader. The low agreement between dyad members in their ratings of LMX may mean that the scales measure biased individual perceptions that are highly confounded with other variables. These problems in the definition and measurement of LMX need to be resolved.

The theory needs more elaboration about the way exchange relationships evolve over time. Despite the growing body of research on LMX, we still know little about how the role-making process actually occurs. The theory implies that exchange relationships evolve in a continuous, smooth fashion, starting from initial impressions. The few longitudinal studies suggest that LMX relationships may form quickly and remain stable. Evidence from other types of research suggest that dyadic relationships typically progress through a series of ups and downs, with shifts in attitudes and behavior as the two parties attempt to reconcile their desire for autonomy with their desire for closer involvement (see Fairhurst, 1993). To resolve these inconsistencies, longitudinal research is needed, with methods that can record the pattern of interactions over time in more detail and probe more deeply into each party's changing perceptions of the relationship.

The theory would be improved by a clear description of the way a leader's different dyadic relationships affect each other and overall group performance. At some point, increasing differentiation of dyadic relationships probably begins to create feelings of resentment among the low-exchange members (McClane, 1991; Yukl, 1989). The minimal level of compliance expected of them may fail to occur if the leader's favorites appear to be getting more benefits than they deserve. The negative effects of extreme differentiation will be greater when the work unit is an interacting team, because hostility among members undermines necessary cooperation. The challenge for a leader is to develop differentiated relationships with some subordinates to facilitate achievement of the team's mission, while maintaining a relationship of mutual trust, respect, and loyalty with the other subordinates. It is not necessary to treat all subordinates exactly the same, but each person should perceive that he or she is an important and respected member of the team rather than a second class citizen. Not every subordinate may desire more responsibility, but each person should perceive an equal opportunity based on competence rather than arbitrary favoritism.

LMX theory can be improved by incorporation of attributional processes that explain how leaders interpret subordinate actions and subordinates interpret leader actions (Dienesch & Liden, 1986; Steiner, 1997). These attributional processes are described later in the chapter. Another way to enrich the theory is to include conceptions about procedural and distributive justice (Scandura, 1999). Subordinate perception of fairness in the assignment of responsibilities and the allocation of rewards can help to explain the development of exchange relationships.

LMX theory has been almost exclusively about vertical dyadic relationships. Graen and Uhl-Bien (1995) proposed that the theory can be extended to other types of dyadic relationships, such as those with lateral peers or members of one's informal network. Sparrowe and Liden (1997) proposed that insights from social network theory may help to explain how dyadic relations develop within a broader social context. However, as yet only a small amount of research has been conducted on exchange processes in nonhierarchical dyadic relationships.

Leader-member exchange is mostly a universal theory, with minimal effort to explain how situational variables may affect the exchange process (Green, Anderson, & Shivers, 1996). Some aspects of the situation that are likely to be relevant include demographic attributes of work unit members, job characteristics, work unit characteristics (e.g., size, function, stability of membership), and type of organization. These organizational variables may affect the type of dyadic relationships that occur, the underlying exchange processes, and their implications for individuals and the organization. In general there has been little research on situational conditions affecting development of exchange relationships. One exception is a study by Green, Anderson, and Shivers (1996) that investigated how leader-member exchange relationships are affected by demographic and organizational variables.

The research on leader-subordinate exchange has relied too much on static field studies with questionnaires. Only a few studies on LMX used a longitudinal design (e.g., Bauer & Green, 1996; Duchon, Green, & Taber, 1986; Liden et al., 1993; Major, Kozlowski, Chao, & Gardner, 1995). More longitudinal research is needed to discover how exchange relationships evolve over time, and the research should include more intensive measures (e.g., observation, diaries, interviews, analysis of communications) to supplement the usual questionnaires.

Leader Attributions About Subordinates

As we already discussed, how a leader acts toward a subordinate varies depending on whether the subordinate is perceived as competent and loyal, or incompetent and untrustworthy. The assessment of competence and dependability is based on interpretation of the subordinate's behavior and performance. Attribution theory describes the cognitive processes used by leaders to determine the reasons for effective or ineffective performance and the appropriate reaction (Green & Mitchell, 1979; Martinko & Gardner, 1987).

Two-Stage Attribution Model

Green and Mitchell (1979) described the reaction of a manager to poor performance as a two-stage process. In the first stage the manager tries to determine the cause of the poor performance; in the second stage the manager tries to select an appropriate response to correct the problem.

Managers attribute the major cause of poor performance either to something internal to the subordinate (e.g., lack of effort or ability) or to external problems beyond the subordinate's control (e.g., the task had inherent obstacles, resources were inadequate, information was insufficient, other people failed to provide necessary support, or it was just plain bad luck). An external attribution is more likely when (1) the subordinate has no prior history of poor performance on similar tasks;

(2) the subordinate performs other tasks effectively; (3) the subordinate is doing as well as other people who are in a similar situation; (4) the effects of failures or mistakes are not serious or harmful; (5) the manager is dependent on the subordinate for his or her own success; (6) the subordinate is perceived to have other redeeming qualities (popularity, leadership skills); (7) the subordinate has offered excuses or an apology; or (8) evidence indicates external causes. In addition, managers with prior experience doing the same kind of work as the subordinate are more likely to make external attributions than managers without such experience, perhaps because they know more about the external factors that can affect performance (Mitchell & Kalb, 1982).

The type of attribution made by a manager influences the response to the problem. When an external attribution is made, the manager is more likely to respond by trying to change the situation, such as providing more resources, providing assistance in removing obstacles, providing better information, changing the task to reduce inherent difficulties, or in the case of bad luck, by showing sympathy or doing nothing. When an internal attribution is made and the manager determines that the problem is insufficient ability, the likely response is to provide detailed instruction, monitor the subordinate's work more closely, provide coaching when needed, set easier goals or deadlines, or assign the subordinate to an easier job. If the problem is perceived to be lack of subordinate effort and responsibility, then the likely reaction is to give directive or nondirective counseling, give a warning or reprimand, punish the subordinate, monitor subsequent behavior more closely, or find new incentives.

Research on the Model

Several studies confirm the major propositions of the model (e.g., Ashkanasy & Gallois, 1994; Crant & Bateman, 1993; Dugan, 1989; Gioia & Sims, 1985; Green & Liden, 1980; Ilgen, Mitchell, & Fredrickson, 1981; Mitchell, Green, & Wood, 1981; Mitchell & Kalb, 1981; Mitchell & Liden, 1982; Mitchell & Wood, 1980; Offermann, Schroyer, & Green, 1998; Trahan & Steiner, 1994; Wood & Mitchell, 1981). The attribution model is also supported by research on the effect of position power on a leader's treatment of subordinates (Kipnis, Schmidt, Price, & Stitt, 1981; McFillen & New, 1979). The more position power a leader has, the more likely the leader will attribute appropriate behavior by a subordinate to a desire to gain rewards or avoid punishments rather than to intrinsic motivation.

Attributions and LMX

Research on attributions also points out another danger of having low-exchange relationships with some subordinates (Lord & Mahar, 1991). The type of exchange relationship that has been formed influences the manager's subsequent interpretation of the person's behavior. Leaders appear to be less critical in evaluating the performance of subordinates with whom they have established a high-exchange relationship (Duarte, Goodson, & Klich, 1994; Heneman, Greenberger, & Anonyuo, 1989). Moreover, attributions about reasons for performance appear to differ. Effective performance is more likely to be attributed to internal causes for a high-exchange member and to external causes for a low-exchange member. In contrast, poor performance is attributed to external causes for a high-exchange member and to internal causes for a low-exchange member.

The leader's behavior toward the subordinate is consistent with the attribution about performance. For example, effective behavior by a high-exchange subordinate is more likely to be praised, and mistakes by a low-exchange subordinate are more likely to be criticized. Thus, the leader's stereotype for a subordinate tends to become a self-fulfilling prophecy that perpetuates the stereotype. Low-exchange subordinates get less support, coaching, and resources, yet when they make mistakes or have performance difficulties, the manager blames them rather than recognizing situational causes and his or her own contribution to the problem.

The bias of many managers toward making internal attributions about poor performance by a subordinate is in sharp contrast to the self-serving bias of subordinates to blame external factors for their mistakes or failures. These incompatible biases make it especially difficult for the manager to handle performance problems effectively. The manager's bias results in greater use of punitive actions, which are resented all the more by subordinates who do not feel responsible for the problem. Thus, a major implication of the attribution research is the need to help managers become more careful, fair, and systematic about evaluating subordinate performance. Managers need to become more aware of the many options available for dealing with different causes of performance problems and the importance of selecting an appropriate one.

Applications: Correcting Performance Deficiencies

Correcting performance deficiencies is an important but difficult managerial responsibility. People tend to be defensive about criticism, because it threatens their self-esteem and may imply personal rejection. Many managers avoid confronting subordinates about inappropriate behavior or poor performance, because such confrontations often degenerate into an emotional conflict that fails to deal with the underlying problem, or does so only at the cost of lower respect and trust between the parties. Corrective feedback may be necessary to help a subordinate improve, but it should be done in a way that will preserve a favorable relationship or improve a relationship that is already strained.

Insights about the most effective way to provide corrective feedback are provided by the research on dyadic leadership processes, together with related research on counseling, feedback, and conflict. Effective managers take a supportive, problem-solving approach when dealing with inappropriate behavior or deficient performance by a subordinate. The following guidelines show how to improve communication and problem solving while reducing defensiveness and resentment (see also Table 5-2).

- **Gather information about the performance problem.**

Before confronting a subordinate about a performance deficiency, it is helpful to have the facts straight. It is especially important to do some fact finding when you did not directly observe the subordinate doing something improper. Gather information about the timing (when did problems occur, how many times), magnitude (what were the negative consequences, how serious were they), antecedents (what led up to the problems, what was the subordinate's involvement), and scope (did the problems occur only for the subordinate, or did others experience the same problems). If information about a subordinate's unsatisfactory behavior is second hand (passed on by somebody

---

TABLE 5-2   Guidelines for Correcting Performance Deficiencies

- Gather information about the performance problem.
- Try to avoid attributional biases.
- Provide corrective feedback promptly.
- Describe the deficiency briefly in specific terms.
- Explain the adverse impact of ineffective behavior.
- Stay calm and professional.
- Mutually identify the reasons for inadequate performance.
- Ask the person to suggest remedies.
- Express confidence in the person.
- Express a sincere desire to help the person.
- Reach agreement on specific action steps.
- Summarize the discussion and verify agreement.

---

else), try to obtain a detailed account from the party who initiated the complaint. If the problem occurred previously, identify any prior actions that were taken to deal with it.

- **Try to avoid attributional biases.**

In view of the attributional biases described earlier, it is essential to avoid assuming that the problem is due to a lack of subordinate motivation or competence. There may be more than one reason for inadequate performance. As noted previously, a performance deficiency may be due to situational causes, internal causes, or a combination of both. Situational causes that are usually beyond the control of the subordinate include the following: shortages in supplies, materials, or personnel; unexpected or unusual events (e.g., accidents, bad weather, sabotage, lawsuits, new regulations); resource levels below budgeted levels due to last-minute cuts or shifts in priorities; and failure by people in other parts of the organization or outsiders to carry out their part of a project properly and on time. Internal causes for poor performance usually involve low motivation or deficiencies in subordinate skill. Examples of this type of problem include the following: failure to carry out a major action step on schedule, failure to monitor progress to detect a problem before it becomes serious, showing poor judgment in dealing with a problem, procrastinating in dealing with a problem until it gets worse, failure to notify superiors about a problem that requires their attention, making an avoidable error in the performance of a task, failure to follow standard procedures and rules, and acting in an unprofessional or improper manner.

- **Provide corrective feedback promptly.**

Corrective feedback should be provided soon after the problem is noticed rather than waiting until a later time when the person may not remember the incident. Deal immediately with improper behavior that you observe yourself, and handle other performance problems (complaints about a subordinate, substandard quality or productivity) as soon as you can conduct a preliminary investigation. Some managers save up criticisms for the annual appraisal meeting or scheduled progress review meetings. This practice is likely to be ineffective. By delaying feedback, you lose the opportunity to deal with the problem immediately before it becomes worse. Moreover, by not responding to inappropriate or ineffective behavior, the wrong message may be sent, namely that the behavior is acceptable or not of any consequence. Finally, a person is likely to be more defensive after hearing a barrage of criticisms at the same time.

- **Describe the deficiency briefly in specific terms.**

Feedback is more effective if it involves specific behavior or specific examples of performance deficiencies. Vague, general criticism ("Your work is sloppy") may not communicate what the person is doing wrong and is easier for the person to deny. Provide specific examples of what was done, where it occurred, and when it occurred. For example, instead of saying a person is rude, point out that he interrupted you twice this week with trivial questions when you were talking to other people (identify them and when the incident happened). When criticizing performance, cite specific examples of unsatisfactory performance. For example, point out that two customers complained about slow service by the person's department. Avoid exaggeration such as "You are always late." Keep the description of ineffective behavior brief. The longer the person has to listen to criticism, even when constructive, the more defensive the person is likely to get.

- **Explain the adverse impact of ineffective behavior.**

Corrective feedback is more useful if it includes an explanation of the reason why a person's behavior is inappropriate or ineffective. For example, describe how the behavior causes problems for others and interferes with their work. Describe the discomfort and distress you or others experienced as a result of the person's inappropriate behavior. Describe how the person's behavior jeopardizes the success of an important project or mission and express your personal concern about it.

- **Stay calm and professional.**

It is appropriate to show concern about a performance problem or mistake, but corrective feedback should be provided without expressing anger or personal rejection. A manager who blows up, yells at the person, and makes insulting remarks (e.g., calling the person stupid and lazy) is unlikely to motivate the person to improve his or her performance. Moreover, this type of behavior impedes problem solving and undermines the relationship between manager and subordinate. Avoid accusations and insults ("Why did you do such a stupid thing?") that will make the person defensive. Criticize behavior instead of the person. Make it clear that you value the person and want to help him or her to deal with the performance problem.

- **Mutually identify the reasons for inadequate performance.**

Even after a preliminary investigation into the causes of a performance problem, you may lack important information about the problem that would change your perception of it. It is essential to listen to the subordinate's explanation for the problem, rather than jumping to conclusions about the causes. Give the person an opportunity to explain errors, inadequate performance, or inappropriate behavior. Sometimes the person may not know the reason or may make excuses rather than admitting responsibility. Be careful to differentiate between situational causes and personal causes. Personal causes of inadequate performance are harder to detect than situational causes, because a subordinate is usually reluctant to admit mistakes and failures. When probing to discover these causes, ask what types of things the subordinate would do differently with the benefit of hindsight, and what lessons were learned from the experience. Keep the discussion of personal causes focused on specific behavior that was ineffective or inappropriate rather than on personal attributes such as poor judgment, irresponsibility, or lack of motivation. Mutually identify all of the important reasons in a careful, systematic manner, rather than moving immediately to a discussion of corrective actions.

- **Ask the person to suggest remedies.**

It is essential to get the person to take responsibility for dealing with a performance deficiency. Improvement is unlikely if the person makes excuses and denies responsibility for the problem. Commitment to improve is more likely if the person suggests ways to deal with the problem. Thus, when discussing how to correct performance deficiencies, begin by asking for suggestions rather than telling the person what to do. Use open-ended questions such as "What ideas do you have for improving performance? and "What can we do to avoid this problem in the future?" Encourage the person to consider a variety of possible remedies, rather than focusing quickly on one narrow remedy. Try to build on the subordinate's ideas rather than merely pointing out limitations. If the subordinate fails to identify some promising remedies, try to present your own ideas as variations of the subordinate's ideas. State your ideas in a general, tentative way ("What about the possibility of . . . ?") and let the subordinate develop the details so he or she feels some ownership of the improvement plans.

- **Express confidence in the person.**

A subordinate who lacks self-confidence and is discouraged about doing poorly on a task is less likely to improve. One important leadership function is to increase a person's confidence that difficult things can be achieved with a concerted effort, despite past failures. Mention the person's beneficial qualities that can help him or her do better. Describe how others overcame similar failures or setbacks. Express confidence that the person will succeed. Research shows that subordinates perform better when the leader has high expectations for them (Eden, 1990; McNatt, 2000).

- **Express a sincere desire to help the person.**

It is essential to communicate your intention to help the person do better. Be alert for opportunities to provide assistance to the subordinate by using your knowledge, influence, or contacts. Subordinates may be reluctant to ask for help if they believe that it is an admission of weakness. If a person's performance is being affected by personal problems (e.g., family problems, financial problems, substance abuse), be prepared to offer assistance if it is requested or is clearly needed. Examples of things that a leader can do include the following: help the person identify and express concerns and feelings, help the person understand the reasons for a personal problem, provide new perspectives on the problem, help the person identify alternatives, offer advice on how to deal with the problem, and refer the person to professionals who can provide assistance.

- **Reach agreement on specific action steps.**

It is essential to identify concrete action steps to be taken by the subordinate. If you discuss possible remedies but end the discussion without agreement on specific action steps, the person may walk away from the meeting without a clear understanding of what he or she is expected to do. Likewise, it is not enough to tell the subordinate to try to do better. Unless the person makes an explicit promise to carry out specific action steps, he or she may quickly forget about the discussion. As part of the explicit agreement, you should clearly state any action steps you will take to help the subordinate improve performance.

- **Summarize the discussion and verify agreement.**

After agreement has been reached, summarize the essence of the discussion. The purpose of a summary is to check for agreement and mutual understanding. As you end the meeting, repeat your willingness to provide assistance and indicate that you are available to discuss any additional problems or complications that may arise. You may also want to set a tentative date and time for a follow-up meeting to review progress.

Follower Attributions and Implicit Theories

How followers perceive a leader has important implications for the organization. Leaders perceived to be competent are likely to retain their position or be advanced to a higher position, whereas leaders perceived to be incompetent are likely to be replaced. Leaders who are judged to be competent gain more power and have more discretion to make changes. Followers use information about leader actions, changes in the performance of the team or organization, and external conditions to reach conclusions about responsibility for success or failure. Just as leaders make attributions about follower competence, followers make attributions about leader competence and intentions. More attributions are made for someone who occupies a high-level position with substantial prestige and power, especially in cultures where leaders are viewed as heroic figures (Calder, 1977; Konst, Vonk, & Van der Vlist, 1999; Meindl, Ehrlich, & Dukerich, 1985; Pfeffer, 1977b).

Determinants of Follower Attributions

Several interrelated factors determine how followers assess leader effectiveness (Awamleh & Gardner, 1999; Choi & Mai-Dalton, 1999; Ferris, Bhawuk, Fedor & Judge, 1995; Lord & Mahar, 1991; Meindl, Ehrlick, & Dukerich,1985). One factor is the extent to which clear, timely indicators of performance are available for the leader's team or organization. A leader is usually judged more competent if his or her unit is successful than if it is unsuccessful. The performance trend will also influence follower assessment of the leader. A leader is more likely to be judged competent if performance is improving than if it is declining. Moreover, if performance suddenly increases (or decreases) soon after the leader's term of office begins, more credit or blame for the change will be attributed to the person than if performance remains stable.

Followers also consider the leader's actions. A leader who has done something that could explain a change in performance will be attributed more responsibility for it. Leaders who take direct actions that appear relevant get more credit for performance improvements than leaders who do not. Direct actions that are highly visible to followers influence attributions more than indirect actions that are not visible. The importance of direct action is increased when followers perceive an immediate crisis. A leader who acts decisively to resolve an obvious crisis is considered highly competent, whereas a leader who fails to take direct action in a crisis, or whose action has no apparent effect is likely to be judged incompetent. The uniqueness of changes made by a leader also influences attributions about the leader's competence. Leaders who make innovative changes in the strategy (what is done or how it is done) get more credit for success and more blame for failure than leaders who stick with a traditional strategy.

Followers also use information about the situation to reach conclusions about responsibility for success or failure. Improving performance is less likely to be credited to the leader when external conditions are favorable (e.g., the economy is improving and sales are up for all firms in the industry). Likewise, declining performance is less likely to be blamed on the leader when external conditions are unfavorable (e.g., a new competitor enters the market). Followers may also consider constraints on the leader's decisions and actions (e.g., new government regulations, pressure from superiors). A leader who appears to have considerable power and discretion in deciding what to do is attributed more responsibility for success or failure than a leader who is viewed as a puppet or figurehead.

Followers judge leader intentions as well as leader competence. A leader who appears to be more concerned about followers and the mission than about personal benefit or career advancement will gain more follower approval. Credibility is increased when the leader expresses strong and consistent convictions about a program or change and explains why it is necessary without exaggerating the benefits or ignoring the costs. Dedication to the organization is indicated when the leader takes personal risks to accomplish important objectives and does not benefit materially from them (Yorges, Weiss, & Strickland, 1999). A leader who makes visible self-sacrifices in the service of the organization will be viewed as more sincere and committed. When a clear display of dedication is combined with demonstrated competence, it may result in follower perception that the leader is extraordinary (Choi & Mai-Dalton, 1999). This attribution of charisma to a leader is a source of additional influence over followers (see Chapter 9). In contrast, leaders who appear insincere or motivated only by personal gain get less credit for making changes that are successful, and receive more blame for making changes that are unsuccessful. The mood of the followers can also affect attributions about leader intentions. Leaders are more likely to be seen as manipulative and self-serving if followers are in a negative mood (Dasborough & Ashkanasy, 2002).

It is more difficult to assess leader competence when reliable indicators of performance are absent, the opportunity to observe the leader's actions is not available, or a long delay occurs before leader actions affect performance. Just as leaders tend to be biased toward making internal attributions about followers, followers seem to have a bias toward making internal attributions about leaders, especially when information is ambiguous. Followers usually attribute success or failure more to the leader's personal qualities (e.g., expertise, initiative, creativity, dedication) than to situational factors beyond the control of the leader. Coaches are praised when the team is winning consistently and blamed for repeated losses. The CEO of a company gets credit for increasing profits and is blamed for declining profits. The implications of follower attributions for leadership effectiveness are discussed in Chapters 9 and 12.

Implicit Leadership Theories

How leaders are evaluated is affected by implicit leadership theories, which are beliefs and assumptions about the characteristics of effective leaders (Eden & Leviatan,

1975; Gioia & Sims, 1985; Lord, Foti, & Devader, 1984; Offerman, Kennedy, & Wirtz, 1994; Rush, Thomas, & Lord, 1977). The implicit theories involve stereotypes and prototypes about the traits, skills, or behaviors that are relevant for a particular type of position (e.g., executive vs. lower-level leader, manager vs. military officer), context (e.g., crisis vs. noncrisis situation), or individual (e.g., male vs. female leader, experienced vs. new leader). Implicit theories are developed and refined over time as a result of actual experience, exposure to literature about effective leaders, and other social-cultural influences (Lord, Brown, Harvey, & Hall, 2001). The implicit theories are influenced by individual beliefs, values, and personality traits, as well as by shared beliefs and values about leaders in the organizational culture and the national culture (Gerstner & Day, 1997; Keller, 1999). Some differences in implicit theories are likely among countries with diverse cultures (see Chapter 14).

Implicit theories are important because they influence the expectations people have for leaders and their evaluation of the leader's actions. Implicit theories about effective leadership determine the perceived relevance of various types of leader behavior (Lord & Maher, 1991). Leaders who do things that are relevant for the situation but inconsistent with follower expectations may be evaluated less favorably than leaders who conform to role expectations.

Implicit leadership theories can also be a source of biased ratings on leadership behavior questionnaires. A respondent's implicit theory may interact with other factors (e.g., perceived leader competence, satisfaction with the leader) to jointly influence ratings of leader behavior. For example, a leader who is liked or perceived to be effective may be rated higher on behaviors in the rater's conception of an ideal leader than on behaviors not included in this prototype, regardless of the leader's actual use of the behaviors. Effective performance by a leader's group or organization may be attributed to behaviors assumed to be relevant for performance, even though the respondent did not have an opportunity to observe the behaviors or did not remember them clearly. If most respondents in a survey study have a similar implicit theory, their biases may influence the factor structure found for a leader behavior questionnaire. When relevant and irrelevant aspects of behavior are confounded in the same questionnaire, it is difficult to interpret the results from research that uses it. This problem has been evident in much of the research on transformational leadership (see Chapter 9).

Impression Management

Impression management is the process of influencing how others perceive you, and the behaviors used for this purpose are called *impression management tactics*. Tactics such as excuses and apologies are used in a defensive way to avoid blame for weak performance or to seek forgiveness for a mistake. Scholars of organizational behavior have been especially interested in impression management tactics that are used to elicit positive affect and respect from others (e.g., Gardner & Martinko, 1988; Godfrey, Jones, & Lord, 1986; Jones & Pittman, 1982; Tedeschi & Melburg, 1984; Wayne & Ferris, 1990; Wortman & Linsenmeier, 1977). Four impression tactics seem especially relevant for the study of leadership: exemplification, ingratiation, self-promotion, and intimidation.

Exemplification.   This tactic involves behavior intended to demonstrate dedication and loyalty to the mission, to the organization, or to followers. Exemplification tactics used to influence bosses include arriving early and staying late to work extra hours, demonstrating effective behavior when you know the person is watching, and doing voluntary tasks that are highly visible organizational citizenship behaviors. Exemplification tactics used to influence subordinates or peers include acting in a way that is consistent with espoused values (walking the talk) and making self-sacrifices to achieve a proposed objective, change, or vision.

Ingratiation. This tactic involves behavior intended to influence the target person to like the agent and perceive the agent as someone who has desirable social qualities (e.g., friendly, considerate, caring, charming, interesting, attractive). Ingratiating behavior can take many different forms. Some examples include providing praise, agreeing with the target person's opinions, showing appreciation for the target's accomplishments, laughing at the target's jokes, showing an interest in the target's personal life, and showing deference and respect for the target person.

Self-Promotion. This tactic involves behavior intended to influence favorable impressions about your competence and value to the organization. The behavior may take the form of informing people about your achievements and talking about your skills. A more subtle form of self-promotion is to display diplomas, awards, and trophies in one's office or workspace for others to see. An indirect form of self-promotion that is similar to a coalition tactic is to get other people to talk about your skills and loyalty.

Intimidation. This tactic involves behavior intended to influence the target person to perceive the agent as a dangerous person who is able and willing to use power to harm others who fail to do what the person wants. The behavior used to arouse fear and respect for the coercive power of the agent can take a variety of forms, including use of warnings that any unacceptable behavior will be punished, making an example of someone punished for transgressions, incompetence, or disloyalty, and using punishment in a limited but highly visible way to demonstrate that you are prepared to use coercive power. Some scholars do not consider intimidation relevant for impression management by leaders, because the use of fear as a motivator can be dysfunctional. However, because intimidation is used by many political and business leaders and can serve an important purpose (e.g., to deter illegal or unethical activities), it should be not be ignored by leadership researchers.

Impression Management by Followers

Most studies on impression management have examined how followers attempt to influence bosses. Wayne and Ferris (1990) developed a self-report agent questionnaire to measure how subordinates use impression management tactics for upward influence in organizations. Their study found support for a three-factor model that included supervisor-focused tactics (similar to ingratiation), job-focused tactics (similar to exemplification), and self-focused tactics (similar to self-promotion).

The usual measure in research on the effectiveness of upward impression management is how the boss evaluates the subordinate's competence, or the extent to which the subordinate gets favorable career outcomes such as a pay increase or promotion. The research indicates that ingratiation is often effective as an impression management tactic for upward influence (Higgins, Judge, & Ferris, 2003; Leary & Kowalski, 1990). Ingratiation can increase positive affect for the subordinate, which in turn is positively related to the quality of the exchange relationship and the manager's appraisal of subordinate performance (Ferris, Judge, Rowland, & Fitzgibbons, 1994; Wayne & Ferris, 1990; Wayne & Kacmar, 1991; Wayne & Liden, 1995). However, to be effective as an impression management tactic ingratiation must appear to be sincere, and it may be counterproductive if viewed as manipulative.

The results for self-promotion tactics are less consistent, but they suggest that a negative reaction is more likely than a positive reaction (Higgins, Judge, & Ferris, 2003). A subordinate who uses this tactic too often or in an annoying way will be liked less by the boss and given a lower performance appraisal. Self-promotion is a more difficult form of impression management to pull off successfully. Unless done only infrequently and in a subtle way, self-promotion tactics are usually seen as bragging and conceit.

Research on the effects of upward impression management on job outcomes has some limitations that complicate interpretation of the results. An outcome such as a pay increase or promotion may be based more on a subordinate's actual job performance than on how often the subordinate uses an impression management tactic. Moreover, the effectiveness of impression management tactics depends to a great extent on the interpersonal skills of the agent (Ammeter et al., 2002; Turnley & Bolino, 2001), and these skills are also a determinant of performance. It is difficult to determine the independent effects of impression management tactics unless these other likely determinants of job outcomes are also measured, which seldom occurs in the research.

Impression Management by Leaders

Many leaders attempt to create the impression that they are important, competent, and in control of events (Pfeffer, 1977b, 1981). Successes are announced and celebrated, and failures are suppressed or downplayed. Salancik and Meindl (1984) analyzed annual reports for a sample of corporations over a period of 18 years and found that top management consistently credited themselves for positive outcomes and blamed negative outcomes on aspects of the environment.

Impression management is especially important when constraints and unpredictable events make it difficult for leaders to exert much influence over organizational performance. Highly visible symbolic actions are one way to create the impression that a leader is dealing with problems and making progress toward attaining organizational objectives, despite some delays and setbacks. Examples include visiting a disaster site to demonstrate active involvement and personal interest, implementing a new policy or program to deal with a serious problem, replacing people who are blamed for a failure, creating a blue ribbon commission to study a problem and make recommendations, and creating new subunits or positions that will be responsible for dealing with a serious problem. Dramatic changes in structure, policies, programs, and personnel may be relevant for solving problems and improving performance. However, it is often difficult to determine whether such changes will be beneficial, and the effects may not be known for months or years. In an effort to maintain a favorable impression, leaders may be tempted to use symbolic actions that are irrelevant or even detrimental.

Impression management is also used by leaders to avoid the appearance of failure, or to shift the blame for it to other people or uncontrollable events. Some leaders seek to distort or cover up evidence that a prior strategy is not succeeding (Pfeffer, 1981; Staw, McKechnie, & Puffer, 1983). In the early stage of a developing crisis, many leaders discount the seriousness of the problem and continue with incremental approaches for dealing with it rather than proposing innovative, dramatic remedies. In part, the avoidance of dramatic action may be due to their own denial of negative evidence and wishful thinking that things will get better. However, even leaders who recognize an impending crisis may not have the courage to acknowledge the weakness of previous strategies and take dramatic new actions for which they will be held accountable. Many leaders with a limited term of office, such as elected officials, are tempted to put off problems and leave them to the next person who holds the office.

Impression management tactics can be manipulative, but some of the same behaviors can also be used in a positive way by leaders. Praise (a form of ingratiation) can be used to build the confidence of subordinates and improve their performance. Announcing achievements that demonstrate progress in implementing a change initiated by the leader (a form of self-promotion) can increase follower optimism and commitment to make the change successful. Forms of exemplification such as showing courage, making personal sacrifices, and acting consistent with espoused values are also a way to lead by example and inspire follower commitment to a vision or strategy. These forms of leader behavior are discussed in more detail in Chapters 9 and 10.

Follower Contributions to Effective Leadership

Our tendency to credit successful events to leaders obscures the significant contributions of followers. Motivated, competent followers are necessary for the successful performance of work carried out by the leader's unit. Consider the role of Thomas Jefferson in writing the Declaration of Independence. Today most people regard it as an example of effective leadership by a person who became one of our most famous presidents. At the time, however, Jefferson was in a follower role. He was a junior member of the committee and was assigned the task by John Adams and Benjamin Franklin. Few people outside the Continental Congress knew that Jefferson was the principal author, and he received no public recognition until eight years later when his role was explained in a newspaper article (Kelley, 1992).

Followers can also contribute to the effectiveness of the group in other ways, such as by maintaining cooperative working relationships, providing constructive dissent, sharing leadership functions, and supporting leadership development. This section examines alternative conceptions of the follower role and describes how followers can actively contribute to the effectiveness of their leader.

The Courageous Follower

Chaleff (1995) noted that many people define the role of follower in terms of conformity, weakness, and passivity. This negative conception is strongly influenced by early childhood experiences at home and in school, where others are responsible for our behavior but we are not responsible for their behavior. As adults, passivity in follower roles is encouraged by the fact that leaders typically are more powerful, have higher status, are older, and have more experience. The inhibitions to challenge a leader are even worse for an established leader who is widely seen as brilliant and successful. Chaleff argues that it is essential to replace this negative conception of followers with a positive conception. In short, effective followers are courageous, responsible, and proactive.

The reason why such followers are more effective stems from the fact that all leaders have weaknesses as well as strengths. Followers can influence whether the strengths are fully utilized and the weaknesses overcome. Some of the qualities that contribute to leadership effectiveness (e.g., self-confidence, strong convictions, a passion for change) also make a leader prone to excessive ambition, risk taking, or righteousness. Followers can help the leader avoid these excesses. Rather than complaining about the leader, followers should help the leader to do better.

To be effective as a follower, it is necessary to find a way to integrate two different follower roles, namely to implement decisions made by a leader and to challenge decisions that are misguided or unethical. Followers must be willing to risk the leader's displeasure, but the risk can be reduced by developing a high level of mutual trust and respect. In such a relationship, a leader is likely to view criticism and dissent as an honest effort to facilitate attainment of shared objectives and values, rather than as an expression of personal rejection or disloyalty.

It takes time and effort to help a leader grow and succeed. If the leader is less competent than you or has been elevated to a position you really deserved, it is especially difficult to make this extra effort. Thus, effective followers are more likely to be people with a strong commitment to the organization and its mission. However, mentoring a weak leader is not without its benefits. In the process of helping the leader, the follower will also learn and develop.

Self-Management

Self-management is a set of strategies a person uses to influence and improve his or her own behavior (Manz & Sims, 1980; Sims & Lorenzi, 1992). Self-management, which is sometimes called self-leadership or self-control, is based primarily on social learning theory. Self-management is more appropriately viewed as a motivation theory than as a leadership theory, but it can serve as a partial substitute for leadership (see Chapter 8). By taking more responsibility for their own lives, followers do not need to depend so much on leaders to direct and motivate them.

Self-Management Strategies

Self-management includes both behavior and cognitive strategies (Sims & Lorenzi, 1992). Behavioral self-management strategies (see Table 5-3) are useful when you are reluctant to do a necessary task or want to change your behavior. For example, set realistic goals to accomplish a task or change a behavior, including subgoals that can be achieved quickly (e.g., a goal to write the first page of a report today; a goal to get through the next hour without saying "you know" to anyone). Then, monitor your own behavior to note what you did and how others reacted (e.g., noticing each time you say something that annoys others; trying different ways of communicating ideas to see which one people respond to most favorably). Compliment yourself for doing something correctly, and reward yourself when you complete a difficult task or accomplish a

---

TABLE 5-3   Strategies for Self-Management

Behavioral Strategies
- Self-reward
- Self-punishment
- Self-monitoring
- Self-goal setting
- Self-rehearsal
- Cue modification

Cognitive Strategies
- Positive self-talk
- Mental rehearsal

---

goal or subgoal (e.g., go to a movie, purchase something you want). Use self-criticism or self-punishment after acting in an inappropriate way or relapsing into behavior you want to change; for example, after making a careless mistake, work extra hours to correct it. Rehearse a difficult behavior by yourself to improve skill and build confidence you can do it (e.g., practice a presentation in front of the mirror with a tape recorder). Rearrange cues in the immediate physical environment; remove cues that encourage undesirable behavior and replace them with cues that encourage desirable behavior (e.g., go to a quiet place where you will not be disturbed to write a report; purchase only healthy food to avoid being tempted to eat junk food).

Cognitive self-management strategies help you to build self-confidence and optimism about doing a difficult task. One helpful cognitive strategy is positive self-talk, which means emphasizing positive, optimistic thoughts and avoiding negative, pessimistic thoughts (Manz, 1992). An example is to interpret a difficult situation as an opportunity rather than as a problem. The confidence and determination needed to improve are more likely to be found by concentrating on what can be done to make things better rather than by dwelling on the difficulties or what can go wrong.

To increase positive self-talk, it is necessary to do more than just look for the silver lining in a dark cloud. It is essential to identify and suppress destructive thinking patterns, such as viewing success and failure as extreme conditions with nothing in between, exaggerating the significance of a mistake or setback, stereotyping yourself negatively, dismissing positive feedback as irrelevant ("She's just saying that to be kind"), and assuming blame for something that is not your responsibility. This type of thinking encourages overreaction to mistakes, setbacks, or periods of slow improvement in performance, all of which are common in learning a complex activity. A more constructive pattern of thinking is to view performance as a continuum rather than a dichotomy, understand the process involved in learning a complex activity, look for and celebrate signs of progress, accept positive feedback, and be careful about attributing responsibility for failure. Identify destructive thoughts (e.g., "It's hopeless; even after practicing for a week I still made several mistakes") and replace them with constructive thoughts (e.g., "I improved by 20 percent this week, and with additional practice I will do even better").

Another cognitive strategy for self-management is mental imagery, which can be used instead of behavioral rehearsal to practice doing a difficult task. First you visualize yourself doing the task. Then you imagine how it would feel to experience the satisfaction of performing it successfully. Many professional athletes mentally rehearse an activity, carefully visualizing each movement and how it will feel, before actually performing the activity (Sims & Lorenzi, 1992).

How Leaders Encourage Self-Management

A leader can do several things to encourage and facilitate self-management by followers. Encouragement is especially important when followers are dependent on the leader for direction and are not intrinsically motivated by the work. According to some theorists (Manz & Sims, 1991; Sims & Lorenzi, 1992), a primary role of the leader is to help subordinates develop skills in self-management. Leadership activities include explaining the rationale for self-management, explaining how to use behavioral and cognitive self-management strategies, encouraging efforts to use these techniques, and providing enough autonomy to make self-management feasible. The leader should model the use of self-management strategies to set an example for subordinates. The leader should also share information subordinates need to do the work, including sensitive information about strategic plans and the financial performance of the organization. As subordinates develop skills and confidence in self-management, the leader should encourage them to take more responsibility for their own work activities.

Applications: Guidelines for Followers

The theory and research on followers has some practical applications. The following guidelines (based on Chaleff, 1995; Kelley, 1992; Whetton & Cameron, 1991) deal with issues such as how to improve one's relationship with a leader, how to resist improper influence from the leader, how to provide advice and coaching to the leader, and how to challenge flawed plans and policies (see Table 5-4 for a summary). Underlying themes in the guidelines include maintaining credibility and trust, taking responsibility for your own life, and remaining true to your own values and convictions.

- **Find out what you are expected to do.**

It is difficult to be viewed as competent and reliable if you have role ambiguity and are unsure what you are expected to do. You may be working very hard, but doing the wrong things or doing things the wrong way. Earlier in the book we saw that it is an

---

TABLE 5-4   Applications: Guidelines for Followers

- Find out what you are expected to do.
- Take the initiative to deal with problems.
- Keep the boss informed about your decisions.
- Verify the accuracy of information you give the boss.
- Encourage the boss to provide honest feedback to you.
- Support leader efforts to make necessary changes.
- Show appreciation and provide recognition when appropriate.
- Challenge flawed plans and proposals made by leaders.
- Resist inappropriate influence attempts by the boss.
- Provide upward coaching and counseling when appropriate.

---

important leader responsibility to clearly communicate role expectations for subordinates. Nevertheless, many leaders fail to explain job responsibilities, scope of authority, performance standards that must be attained, and the relative priority of different aspects of performance. Sometimes the message is inconsistent, such as when the leader says something is important but acts as if it is not. Sometimes the leader asks for something that is inconsistent with the needs of the client or customer. Followers should be assertive but diplomatic about resolving role ambiguity and conflict.

- **Take the initiative to deal with problems.**

Effective followers take initiative to deal with serious problems that prevent the attainment of task objectives. These problems can take many forms, such as rules that prevent attainment of task objectives, a process that does not achieve the desired results, traditions that are obsolete, conflicts between individuals with interrelated jobs, and unsatisfactory performance by someone over whom you have no authority. Taking initiative may mean pointing out the problem to the boss, suggesting ways to deal with the problem, or, if necessary, handling the problem yourself. One way to gain support for changing a flawed process is to conduct a pilot demonstration to show the superiority of a different approach. Taking initiative often involves risks, but if done carefully it can make you a more valuable follower.

- **Keep the boss informed about your decisions.**

Followers who take more initiative to deal with problems also have a responsibility to keep the leader informed about their actions and decisions. It is embarrassing for a leader to hear from someone else that changes have been made. The leader may appear incompetent to others, and lack of knowledge about ongoing changes may also adversely affect the leader's own actions and decisions. How much and how often you inform the boss about your decisions and actions is a complex issue that may be a subject of continuing discussion and revision as conditions change. Finding the right balance is much easier within a relationship of mutual trust and respect.

- **Verify the accuracy of information you give to the boss.**

An important role of followers is to relay information to their leader. Control over what information is passed on and how it is depicted gives a follower power over the leader's perception of events and choices. It is an important responsibility for followers to provide accurate, timely information needed by the leader to make good decisions. The responsibility includes relaying bad news as well as good news. It is important to verify the accuracy of information you are trusted to obtain for the leader. Rumors, complaints, and reports of problems can have a disproportionate effect if the leader assumes incorrectly that you took the time to substantiate them. It is also important to acknowledge when your information is limited or questionable. Rather than pretending to have expertise about a matter, say that you will look into it immediately and get back to the leader as soon as possible.

- **Encourage the boss to provide honest feedback.**

One way to improve mutual trust with the leader is to encourage honest feedback about his or her evaluation of your performance. The leader may be uncomfortable about expressing concerns about a subordinate's performance. It may be necessary to probe for more information. For example, ask the leader to identify the strongest and weakest aspects of your work. Ask what you can do to be more effective. After an initial response, ask if the leader has concerns about any other aspects of your performance.

- **Support leader efforts to make necessary changes.**

Contrary to the myth of heroic leaders, most major changes require a cooperative effort of many people in the organization. Leaders need the encouragement and support of loyal followers to overcome resistance to change in organizations. Look for opportunities to express support and encouragement to a leader who is frustrated by difficulties encountered in trying to implement necessary change. Offer to provide assistance to a leader who is temporarily overwhelmed with new work or too preoccupied with an immediate crisis to handle other work that still must be done.

- **Show appreciation and provide recognition when appropriate.**

Leaders can feel unappreciated and taken for granted. It is appropriate to express appreciation when a leader makes a special effort to help you with a problem, represent your interests, or promote your career in the organization. It is also helpful to provide praise when the leader carries out a difficult activity successfully (e.g., negotiating a favorable contract with a client, lobbying successfully for a larger budget, finding a solution to a difficult problem, persuading superiors to authorize a proposed change). These forms of supporting are one way followers can provide feedback to the leader and reinforce desirable leadership practices. Although praising the leader is a form of ingratiation that is sometimes used in a manipulative way, when sincere it can help to promote a more favorable relationship with a leader.

- **Challenge flawed plans and proposals made by leaders.**

One of the most valuable contributions a follower can make is to provide accurate feedback about the leader's plans and proposals. To minimize defensiveness, begin with a comment that shows respect and a desire to be helpful in accomplishing shared objectives. For example:

> You know I respect what you are trying to accomplish, and I hope you won't mind if I express some honest concerns about this proposal.

If the issue is obvious faults, describe them in specific terms rather than vague generalities, and avoid making the critique personal. If you are unable to identify specific weaknesses in a proposed change, suggest getting reactions from other credible people before going ahead with it. Following is an example:

> This change may cause some serious problems for the operations group. Shouldn't we consult with them first before going ahead with it? They are likely to have some good ideas on how to avoid problems that are not obvious to us.

Sometimes a boss may be unwilling to listen to concerns about a decision or policy that is unethical, illegal, or likely to have adverse consequences for the organization. In this situation it may be necessary to escalate your influence attempt and use pressure tactics such as threats and warnings. Threatening to resign is one way followers can express deep concern over a controversial decision. However, such threats should not be used lightly, and they are appropriate only after a serious effort has been made to influence the boss in other ways, such as rational persuasion and use of coalitions. The threat should be expressed with conviction but not personal hostility. Following is a specific example:

> I cannot live with this decision, because it violates our basic principles and poses a serious risk to our people. Unless the decision can be changed, I will have no choice but to resign from my position.

- **Resist inappropriate influence attempts by the boss.**

Despite the obvious power advantage a boss holds over a subordinate, it is not necessary to comply with inappropriate influence attempts or be exploited by an abusive leader. Followers often have more counterpower than they realize, and there are things they can do to deter a leader accustomed to exploiting people who are unassertive. It is essential to challenge abuse early before it becomes habitual, and the challenge must be firm but diplomatic. Point out use of inappropriate or manipulative influence tactics (e.g., "I don't respond well to threats" or "This offer might be misconstrued by some people as a bribe"). Insist on your rights ("It's not right to ask me to cancel my vacation plans at the last minute to do this job when other people around here have the time and skills to do it."). Remind the leader of a promise about to be violated ("Didn't you promise that assignment to me just last month?"). Point out the negative consequences of complying with an inappropriate request. For example, explain how compliance with a demand to do something immediately will interfere with your other work or jeopardize an important project.

- **Provide upward coaching and counseling when appropriate.**

Coaching is usually viewed as a leader behavior, but subordinates also have opportunities to coach the boss, especially one who is new and inexperienced. Upward coaching is easier to do when a follower has already developed a deep and trusting exchange relationship with the leader. Be alert for opportunities to provide helpful advice on technical matters (the leader may be reluctant to ask for help). Model effective behaviors the leader can learn from and imitate.

Upward counseling is awkward, but at times it is appropriate and even appreciated by a boss. One form of counseling is to help the leader understand actions that are ineffective. For example, describe how inappropriate behavior is having a different effect than the leader intended ("I'm sure you didn't mean to imply Sue is unreliable when you said . . . , but that's how she took it"). Another form of counseling is to be a good listener when the leader needs someone in whom to confide about worries and concerns. Look for opportunities to ask questions about things the leader should consider in handling a difficult problem.

Integrating Leader and Follower Roles

Many members of an organization have the dual roles of leader and follower. For example, a middle manager is the leader of an organizational unit, but also a follower of a higher-level manager. How to integrate these two diverse roles is an interesting question with important implications for leadership effectiveness.

To be effective in both roles simultaneously, it is necessary to find a way to integrate them. Inevitable role conflicts and dilemmas make integration of the two roles difficult. The leader in the middle is expected to represent the interests of superiors to subordinates, and to represent the interests of subordinates to superiors. He or she is expected to implement decisions made at a higher level of authority, but also to challenge weak decisions. Leaders are expected to initiate and guide change, but they are also expected to encourage and support bottom-up changes suggested by followers. A leader is held responsible for everything that happens in his or her team or work unit, but encouraged to empower followers to act on their own in resolving problems. Leaders are also expected to develop followers, which may involve gradually turning over most leadership responsibilities to one or two subordinates designated as likely successors. How to balance these competing interests and resolve the role conflicts is a subject that deserves much more attention than it has received in the leadership literature.

Summary

Leader-member exchange theory describes how leaders develop exchange relationships over time with different subordinates. A favorable exchange relationship is more likely when a subordinate is perceived to be competent, reliable, and similar to the leader in values and attitudes. A leader's upward influence is another important determinant of the potential for establishing a favorable exchange relationship with subordinates. The behavior of both leader and subordinate is different in favorable exchange relationships than in unfavorable exchange relationships. The exchange relationships with subordinates have implications for leadership effectiveness. Subordinate satisfaction, commitment, and performance are usually higher when the relationship is favorable. Some differentiation of exchange relationships with subordinates may be necessary, but too much can be detrimental.

A manager's reaction to mistakes or failures by a subordinate depends in part on attributions about the reason for poor performance. Attribution theory explains how managers interpret performance information and make judgments about the competence and motivation of a subordinate. Managers may unwittingly create a self-fulfilling prophecy if their behavior is based on a biased perception about the ability and motivation of individual subordinates. For their part, subordinates can use impression management tactics to influence the leader to view them more favorably. Followers often do things to appear competent, loyal, and reliable. The difficult responsibility of providing corrective feedback to a subordinate is more likely to be successful if the leader is supportive rather than hostile and encourages the subordinate to take ownership of the problem.

How followers view leader competence and intentions has implications for leadership effectiveness. Followers are susceptible to the same types of attributions as leaders. A leader who takes visible actions that are followed by improvements in group performance will be viewed as more competent than one who takes no action or acts without apparent success. Leaders use impression management tactics in an effort to appear more decisive, competent, powerful, and trustworthy.

Followers are more likely to be effective if they view themselves as active and independent rather than passive and dependent on the leader. Followers can help make their leader more effective by providing accurate information, challenging weak decisions, resisting inappropriate influence attempts, giving support and encouragement, and providing coaching and advice.

Self-management is a way for followers to become more effective as individual contributors. Self-management strategies can be used to increase confidence, spur greater effort, and manage time more effectively. One way for a leader to empower subordinates is to encourage and facilitate their self-management activities.

All leaders are also followers, and to be effective in both roles, it is essential to find a way to integrate them. Moreover, it is essential to find appropriate ways to share leadership functions within teams, across levels of the authority hierarchy, and between interdependent subunits of the organization. We will return to this subject in later chapters of the book.

Review and Discussion Questions

1. Briefly explain LMX theory.
2. What are some predictors and consequences of LMX?
3. What are some possible benefits and costs of developing different relationship with different subordinates?
4. Is it possible to develop different dyadic relationships with individual subordinates and still treat everyone fairly?
5. Use attribution theory to explain how leaders interpret the reason for poor performance by a subordinate.
6. How can subordinates influence a leader's perceptions about them?
7. What are some guidelines for corrective feedback?
8. What factors influence follower attributions about leader competence?
9. How are exemplification, ingratiation, self-promotion, and intimidation used to manage impressions?
10. What are some guidelines for improving effectiveness as a follower?
11. Describe the strategies for behavioral and cognitive self-management.
12. How can a leader encourage more self-management by subordinates?
13. What are some potential risks of an extensive amount of self-management in a team or organization?

Key Terms

- empowerment
- exchange relationship
- external attribution
- implicit theories of leadership
- impression management
- internal attribution
- leader-member exchange
- LMX-7 scale
- reciprocal influence
- self-management
- self-talk
- vertical dyads

CASES

Cromwell Electronics

Dan Dalton was the marketing VP for Cromwell Electronics. Ten months earlier he had appointed Ed Corelli as the manager of a newly formed marketing unit for the eastern region. The unit was responsible for developing marketing presentations, advertising campaigns, and promotions for the sale of Cromwell products in the eastern region.

The unit had six marketing specialists; two were long-time employees, and the other four were newly hired. Ed was promoted to the position based on a good reputation as a marketing specialist. Even though the marketing unit was new, Dan expected its performance to be better by now. The marketing unit for the western region was formed at the same time, and it had higher performance. Dan reflected on the comments made by two of Ed's subordinates when asked how they liked working for him.

Pat Posner had worked for the company for nearly 10 years. He commented that Ed was "a great manager." Pat especially liked the high level of autonomy he was allowed. Pat said, "Ed gives me complete discretion to plan the marketing campaigns for my set of products. If I have a problem, he encourages me to look at it from different perspectives, but he doesn't say what he wants me to do about it. He trusts me to solve my own problems. When I make a mistake, which seldom happens, he doesn't get upset. Instead, he expects me to learn from it." Pat also noted that Ed showed sincere appreciation for good performance. "My marketing campaign for the new product was very successful, and I really appreciated the recognition Ed gave me in the monthly unit meeting. He also told me that he would try to get me a pay increase."

Katie O'Toole, one of the new employees, was less satisfied with Ed as a manager. "Sometimes I wish Ed would give me more direction. He is always pushing me to make my own decisions. Maybe if I had more experience I would like it, but right now it makes me feel very insecure. I never really know if I am doing what he expects. When I go to him for help with a problem, he turns the question around and asks what I would do. He doesn't seem to understand that I wouldn't ask if I already knew the answer. And when I do something wrong, he doesn't seem to care. Ed likes to pretend that mistakes will go away if you don't talk about them." Katie had another complaint as well. She said, "He seems to favor the two employees who have been with the company longer. He gives them the most interesting assignments, he consults with them more about his plans for the unit, and he recommends them for larger pay increases." Katie noted that Sally and George, both new employees, agreed with her complaints about Ed.

At lunch later that day, Dan asked Ed how things were going in his unit. Ed replied that he was disappointed in some of the new marketing specialists. Only one of the new employees (Linda) was performing well. The others seemed to lack drive and initiative. Ed emphasized that he tried to avoid any favoritism, which had been a serious problem for a former boss. Although he gave the most complex assignments to the marketing specialists with more experience, everyone had challenging assignments and opportunities to excel. Ed had attended the company workshop on empowerment, and he was trying to give employees the autonomy they needed to learn and develop new skills on the job. He was careful not to supervise too closely or criticize mistakes. He provided recognition for outstanding achievements, and he tried to base recommendations for a pay raise on performance. Ed asked his boss, "What am I doing wrong?" ■

SOURCE: Copyright © 1990 by Gary Yukl.

QUESTIONS

1. What theories from this chapter are relevant for analyzing the case?

2. Evaluate Ed's behavior as a manager, and identify effective and ineffective actions.

3. What should Dan say or do now?

American Financial Corporation

Betty Powell is the manager of human resources for American Financial Corporation, a large financial services company. When she arrived back in her office Monday after being away for a week, she discovered that a staffing report due the day before was still not finished. The report was for the vice president of the company's brokerage division, and Betty was supposed to give him the report by Wednesday.

Six weeks earlier Betty had asked Don Adams, one of her subordinates to collect the information and to write the staffing report. At that time she told him what should be included in the report and when it was due. It is not the first time Don has missed a deadline. His work is careful and meticulous, but he appears to be compulsive about checking and rechecking everything several times to avoid any mistakes.

Betty called Don and asked him to meet with her immediately. When Don came into her office, she greeted him and asked him to sit down. The following dialogue occurred.

"Don, I understand the staffing report for the brokerage division is not completed yet. The division vice president needs that report to prepare his annual budget, and he is putting a lot of pressure on me to get it to him immediately. When I gave you this assignment, you assured me that six weeks was ample time to do it."

"I'm sorry that the report wasn't ready on schedule," responded Don, "but it turned out to be much more complex than I initially expected. I had to spend extra time verifying the figures from the branch offices, because they just didn't look right. Just when I thought . . ."

"Look Don," interrupted Betty, "this is not the first time you have been late on an important project. You're supposed to be a professional, and professionals plan their work and get it done on time."

"It would not be very professional to do a report full of mistakes," replied Don. "It's important to me to do quality work that I can be proud of. It's not my fault that the branch managers don't keep accurate records."

"What types of mistakes did you find when you checked their records?" asked Betty.

"Well . . . , I didn't actually find any mistakes," replied Don, looking embarrassed, "but after I entered the information into the computer and did the preliminary analysis, I discovered that the records were missing for one of the branch offices. I lost a week waiting to get the missing information, but without it the report would not provide an accurate picture of the division's staffing needs. It's a good thing I noticed the . . ."

Betty interrupted impatiently, "Don, we have clerical workers to do things like checking records and making sure they are complete. It sounds to me like you are not very efficient about managing your time. If you delegated some of these simple tasks to other people, you wouldn't get so far behind in your work."

"The clerical workers were tied up finishing the new employee manual," Don protested. "I don't get enough clerical help on any of my projects, and that's why they are sometimes late."

"Why didn't you inform me there were problems that might delay the report?" asked Betty, her voice showing she was becoming very annoyed. "I could have found you some clerical support."

Don was now becoming more defensive. "I tried to let you know last week, but you were on the West Coast for the management training workshop. I left a message for you to call me."

"Don, you have an excuse for everything, and nothing is ever your fault," Betty said sarcastically. "You seem to be incapable of planning the action steps needed to do a project like this one. You should have checked the records before you began the data analysis. As for the missing records, it wouldn't surprise me if they are buried somewhere under the piles of stuff laying around your office. You have the messiest office in the company."

Don looked sullen but did not reply. Betty continued her tirade.

"Don, your career in this company is going to be very short unless you get your act together. I want that report in my hands by noon tomorrow, and no more excuses." ∎

SOURCE: Copyright © 1988 By Gary Yukl.

QUESTIONS

1. What did Betty do wrong prior to the meeting, and what could have been done to avoid missing the deadline?

2. What did Betty do wrong in the meeting itself, and what could have been done to make the meeting more effective?

3. What should Don have done to be more effective?

CHAPTER 6

POWER AND INFLUENCE

Learning Objectives

After studying this chapter you should be able to:

- Understand how position and personal attributes can be a source of power for leaders.

- Understand the process by which power is acquired or lost in organizations.

- Understand the consequences of power for leadership effectiveness.

- Understand some of the psychological processes that explain how leaders influence people.

- Understand the different types of influence tactics used in organizations.

- Understand how proactive tactics are typically used in influence attempts with subordinates, peers, or superiors.

- Understand the relative effectiveness of different proactive tactics.

Influence is the essence of leadership. To be effective as a leader, it is necessary to influence people to carry out requests, support proposals, and implement decisions. In large organizations, the effectiveness of managers depends on influence over superiors and peers as well as influence over subordinates. Influence in one direction tends to enhance influence in other directions. As noted by Bradford and Cohen (1984, p. 280), "Having clout with your boss gains respect from subordinates and peers; being influential with colleagues lets you deliver what your boss wants and your subordinates need; and high-performing subordinates increase your power sideways and upwards because you can deliver on your obligations and promises."

To understand what makes managers effective requires an analysis of the complex web of power relationships and influence processes found in all organizations. The first part of this chapter explains key concepts, describes different sources of power, examines the relevance of power for leadership effectiveness,

145

and describes the processes by which power is gained or lost. The second part of the chapter examines how power is enacted in different forms of influence behavior, and it describes how power and influence behavior jointly determine leadership effectiveness.

Conceptions of Power and Influence

Terms such as *power* and *authority* have been used in different ways by different writers, thereby creating considerable conceptual confusion. It is worthwhile to begin by reviewing some of the interpretations and clarifying how the terms will be used in this chapter.

Power

The concept of power is useful for understanding how people are able to influence each other in organizations (Mintzberg, 1983; Pfeffer, 1981, 1992). Power involves the capacity of one party (the agent) to influence another party (the target). This flexible concept can be used in many different ways. The term may refer to the agent's influence over a single target person, or over multiple target persons. Sometimes the term refers to potential influence over things or events as well as attitudes and behavior. Sometimes the agent is a group or organization rather than an individual. Sometimes power is defined in relative rather than absolute terms, in which case it means the extent to which the agent has more influence over the target than the target has over the agent. Finally, different types of power exist, and an agent may have more of some types than of others.

It is difficult to describe the power of an agent without specifying the target person(s), the influence objectives, and the time period. An agent will have more power over some people than over others and more influence for some types of issues than for others. Furthermore, power is a dynamic variable that changes as conditions change. How power is used and the outcomes of influence attempts can increase or undermine an agent's subsequent power. In this book, the term *power* is usually used to describe the absolute capacity of an individual agent to influence the behavior or attitudes of one or more designated target persons at a given point in time.

Authority

Authority involves the rights, prerogatives, obligations, and duties associated with particular positions in an organization or social system. A leader's authority usually includes the right to make particular types of decisions for the organization. A leader with direct authority over a target person has the right to make requests consistent with this authority, and the target person has the duty to obey. For example, a manager usually has the legitimate right to establish work rules and give work assignments to subordinates. Authority also involves the right of the agent to exercise control over things, such as money, resources, equipment, and materials, and this control is another source of power.

The *scope of authority* for the occupant of a managerial position is the range of requests that can properly be made and the range of actions that can properly be taken. Scope of authority is much greater for some managers than for others, and it depends in large part on the influence needed to accomplish recognized role requirements and organizational objectives (Barnard, 1952).

Outcomes of Influence Attempts

One useful basis for evaluating the success of an influence attempt is whether the immediate outcome is what the agent intended. The agent may achieve the intended effect on the target, or the effect may be less than was intended. For a proactive influence attempt that involves a specific request by a single agent to a single target person, it is useful to differentiate among three distinct outcomes.

Commitment. The term *commitment* describes an outcome in which the target person internally agrees with a decision or request from the agent and makes a great effort to carry out the request or implement the decision effectively. For a complex, difficult task, commitment is usually the most successful outcome from the perspective of the agent who makes an influence attempt.

Compliance. The term *compliance* describes an outcome in which the target is willing to do what the agent asks but is apathetic rather than enthusiastic about it and will make only a minimal effort. The agent has influenced the target person's behavior but not the person's attitudes. The target person is not convinced that the decision or action is the best thing to do or even that it will be effective for accomplishing its purpose. For a complex, difficult task, compliance is clearly a less successful outcome than commitment. However, for a simple, routine request, compliance may be all that is necessary for the agent to accomplish task objectives.

Resistance. The term *resistance* describes an outcome in which the target person is opposed to the proposal or request, rather than merely indifferent about it, and actively tries to avoid carrying it out. The target person will respond in one or more of the following ways: (1) refuse to carry out the request, (2) make excuses about why the request cannot be carried out, (3) try to persuade the agent to withdraw or change the request, (4) ask higher authorities to overrule the agent's request, (5) delay acting in the hope that the agent will forget about the request, or (6) make a pretense of complying but try to sabotage the task.

The target person's reaction to the agent's request is not the only basis for evaluating success. Influence attempts can also affect interpersonal relationships and the way other people perceive the agent (e.g., ethical, supportive, likable, competent, trustworthy, strong). How a leader attempts to influence someone may improve the relationship or make it less friendly and cooperative. In fact some types of influence attempts are intended primarily to change how people perceive the agent, rather than to achieve an immediate task objective. For example, to increase the chance of promotion in the organization, a person may seek to create the impression that he or she is highly competent and loyal.

Influence Processes

The psychological explanation for the influence of one person on another involves the motives and perceptions of the target in relation to the actions of the agent and the context in which the interaction occurs. Kelman (1958) proposed three different types of influence processes, called instrumental compliance, internalization, and personal identification. The influence processes are qualitatively different from each other, but more than one process may occur at the same time. For example, a target may become committed to implement a new program proposed by the agent, because the target identifies with the agent, believes in the ideals of the program, and expects to gain tangible benefits from supporting it.

Instrumental Compliance.   The target person carries out a requested action for the purpose of obtaining a tangible reward or avoiding a punishment controlled by the agent. The motivation for the behavior is purely instrumental; the only reason for compliance is to gain some tangible benefit from the agent. The level of effort is likely to be the minimum amount necessary to gain the rewards or avoid the punishment.

Internalization.   The target person becomes committed to support and implement proposals espoused by the agent because they appear to be intrinsically desirable and correct in relation to the target's values, beliefs, and self-image. In effect, the agent's proposal (e.g., an objective, plan, strategy, policy, procedure) becomes linked to the target person's underlying values and beliefs. Commitment occurs regardless of whether any tangible benefit is expected, and the target's loyalty is to the ideas themselves, not to the agent who communicates them.

Personal Identification.   The target person imitates the agent's behavior or adopts the same attitudes to please the agent and to be like the agent. The motivation for the target probably involves the target person's need for acceptance and esteem. By doing things that gain approval from the agent, the target is able to maintain a relationship that satisfies a need for acceptance. Maintaining a close relationship with an attractive agent may help to satisfy the target person's need for esteem from other people, and becoming more like an attractive agent helps the target person maintain a more favorable self-image.

Power Types and Sources

Efforts to understand power usually involve distinctions among different types of power. French and Raven (1959) developed a taxonomy to classify different types of power according to their source. This taxonomy includes five different types of power (see Table 6-1). The French and Raven taxonomy influenced much of the subsequent research on power, but it did not include all of the power sources relevant to managers. For example, control over information is also a relevant power source for managers (Pettigrew, 1972; Yukl & Falbe, 1991).

TABLE 6-1   French and Raven Power Taxonomy

Reward Power: The target person complies in order to obtain rewards controlled by the agent.

Coercive Power: The target person complies in order to avoid punishments controlled by the agent.

Legitimate Power: The target person complies because he/she believes the agent has the right to make the request and the target person has the obligation to comply.

Expert Power: The target person complies because he/she believes that the agent has special knowledge about the best way to do something.

Referent Power: The target person complies because he/she admires or identifies with the agent and wants to gain the agent's approval.

Another conceptualization of power sources that is widely accepted is the dichotomy between position power and personal power (Bass, 1960; Etzioni, 1961). According to this two-factor conceptualization, power is derived in part from the opportunities inherent in a person's position in the organization, and in part from attributes of the agent and agent-target relationship. Research by Yukl and Falbe (1991) showed that these two types of power are relatively independent, and each includes several distinct but partially overlapping components (see Table 6-2). Position power includes potential influence derived from legitimate authority, control over resources and rewards, control over punishments, control over information, and control over the physical work environment. Personal power includes potential influence derived from task expertise, and potential influence based on friendship and loyalty. Position and personal determinants of power interact in complex ways, and sometimes it is difficult to distinguish between them. The various types of position and personal power will be described in the following sections of this chapter.

Legitimate Power

Power stemming from formal authority over work activities is sometimes called legitimate power (French & Raven, 1959). The influence processes associated with legitimate power are complex. Some theorists emphasize the downward flow of authority from owners and top management, but the potential influence derived from authority depends as much on the consent of the governed as on the ownership and control of property (Jacobs, 1970). Members of an organization usually agree to comply with rules and directions from leaders in return for the benefits of membership (March & Simon, 1958). However, this agreement is usually an implicit mutual understanding rather than an explicit formal contract.

Compliance with legitimate rules and requests is more likely for members who identify with the organization and are loyal to it. Compliance is also more likely for members who have an internalized value that it is proper to obey authority figures, show respect for the law, and follow tradition. Acceptance of authority also depends on whether the agent is perceived to be a legitimate occupant of his or her leadership position. The specific procedures for selecting a leader are usually based on tradition and the provisions of a legal charter or constitution. Any deviation from the selection process considered legitimate by members will weaken a new leader's authority.

The amount of legitimate power is also related to one's scope of authority. Higher-level managers usually have more authority than lower-level managers, and a manager's authority is usually much stronger in relation to subordinates than in relation to peers, superiors, or outsiders. However, even for a target person outside of the chain of command

TABLE 6-2 Different Types of Power	
Position Power	*Personal Power*
Legitimate power	Referent power
Reward power	Expert power
Coercive power	
Information power	
Ecological power	

(e.g., a peer or outsider), the agent may have the legitimate right to make requests necessary to carry out job responsibilities, such as requests for information, supplies, support services, technical advice, and assistance in carrying out interrelated tasks.

A manager's scope of authority is usually delineated by documents such as an organization charter, a written job description, or an employment contract, but considerable ambiguity about it often remains (Davis, 1968; Reitz, 1977). People evaluate not only whether a request or order falls within a leader's scope of authority, but also whether it is consistent with the basic values, principles, and traditions of the organization or social system. The legitimacy of a request may be questioned if it contradicts basic values of the organization or the larger society to which members of the organization belong. For example, soldiers may disobey an order to shoot everyone who lives in a village that has aided insurgents, because the soldiers perceive this use of excessive force to be contrary to basic human rights.

Authority is usually exercised with a request, order, or instruction that is communicated orally or in writing. The way in which legitimate power is exercised affects the outcome (see Table 6-3). A polite request is more effective than an arrogant demand, because it does not emphasize a status gap or imply target dependence on the agent. Use of a polite request is especially important for people who are likely to be sensitive about status differentials and authority relationships, such as someone who is older than the agent or who is a peer rather than a direct subordinate. Making a polite request does not imply that the agent should plead or appear apologetic about the request. To do so risks the impression that the request is not worthy or legitimate, and it may give the impression that compliance is not really expected (Sayles, 1979). A legitimate request should be made in a firm, confident manner. In an emergency situation, it is more important to be assertive than polite. A direct order by a leader in a command tone of voice is sometimes necessary to shock subordinates into immediate action in an emergency. In this type of situation, subordinates associate confident, firm direction with expertise as well as authority (Mulder, Ritsema van Eck, & de Jong, 1970). To express doubts or appear confused risks the loss of influence over subordinates.

Instances of outright refusal by subordinates to carry out a legitimate order or request undermine the leader's authority and increase the likelihood of future disobedience. Orders that are unlikely to be carried out should not be given. If the agent's authority to make a request is in doubt, it should be verified with legitimating tactics, which are explained later in this chapter. Sometimes a subordinate will delay in complying with an unusual or unpleasant request to test whether the leader is really serious about it. If the leader does not follow up the initial request to check on compliance, the subordinate is likely to conclude that the request may be ignored.

TABLE 6-3   Guidelines for Using Legitimate Authority

- Make polite, clear requests.
- Explain the reasons for a request.
- Do not exceed your scope of authority.
- Verify authority if necessary.
- Follow proper channels.
- Follow up to verify compliance.
- Insist on compliance if appropriate.

Reward Power

Reward power is the perception by the target person that an agent controls important resources and rewards desired by the target person. Reward power stems in part from formal authority to allocate resources and rewards. This authority varies greatly across organizations and from one type of management position to another within the same organization. More control over scarce resources is usually authorized for high-level executives than for lower-level managers. Executives have authority to make decisions about the allocation of resources to various subunits and activities, and in addition they have the right to review and modify resource allocation decisions made at lower levels.

Reward power depends not only on a manager's actual control over resources and rewards, but also on the target person's perception that the agent has the capacity and willingness to follow through on promises. An attempt to use reward power will be unsuccessful if the agent lacks credibility as a source of resources and rewards.

Managers usually have much more reward power over subordinates than over peers or superiors (Yukl & Falbe, 1991). One form of reward power over subordinates is the authority to give pay increases, bonuses, or other economic incentives to deserving subordinates. Reward power is derived also from control over tangible benefits such as a promotion, a better job, a better work schedule, a larger operating budget, a larger expense account, and status symbols such as a larger office or a reserved parking space. Possible constraints on a manager's reward power include any formal policies or agreements that specify how rewards must be allocated (Podsakoff, 1982).

A source of reward power in lateral relations is dependence of a peer on the agent for resources, information, assistance, or support needed to carry out the peer's work. Trading of favors needed to accomplish task objectives is a common form of influence among peers in organizations, and research indicates that it is important for the success of middle-level managers (Cohen & Bradford, 1989; Kaplan, 1984; Kotter, 1982; Strauss, 1962). Another source of lateral reward power in some organizations is a performance appraisal system that includes evaluations by peers as input for decisions about pay increases or promotions for managers.

Upward reward power of subordinates over their boss is limited in most organizations. Few organizations provide a formal mechanism for subordinates to evaluate leaders. Nevertheless, subordinates usually have some indirect influence over the leader's reputation and prospects for a pay increase or promotion. If subordinates perform well, the reputation of their manager will usually be enhanced. Some subordinates may also have upward reward power based on their ability to acquire resources outside of the formal authority system of the organization. For example, a department chairperson in a state university was able to obtain discretionary funds from grants and contracts, and these funds were used as a basis for influencing the decisions made by the college dean, whose own discretionary funds were limited.

Reward power is most commonly exercised with an explicit or implicit promise to give the target person something under the agent's control for carrying out a request or performing a task. How reward power is exercised affects the outcome (see Table 6-4). Compliance is most likely if the reward is something valued by the target person, and the agent is perceived as a credible source of the reward. Thus, it is essential to determine what rewards are valued by the people one wants to influence, and agent credibility should not be risked by making unrealistic promises or failing to deliver on a promise after compliance occurs.

TABLE 6-4   Guidelines for Using Reward Power
• Offer the type of rewards that people desire.
• Offer rewards that are fair and ethical.
• Do not promise more than you can deliver.
• Explain the criteria for giving rewards and keep it simple.
• Provide rewards as promised if requirements are met.
• Use rewards symbolically (not in a manipulative way).

Even when the conditions are favorable for using rewards, they are more likely to result in compliance rather than commitment. A promised reward is unlikely to motivate someone to put forth extra effort beyond what is required to complete the task. The target person may be tempted to neglect aspects of the task not included in the specification of performance criteria or aspects not easily monitored by the agent. If rewards are used in a manipulative manner they may result in resistance rather than compliance. The power to give or withhold rewards may cause resentment among people who dislike being dependent on the whims of a powerful authority figure, or who believe that the agent is manipulating them to his or her own advantage. Even when the reward is attractive, resistance may occur if the reward is seen as a bribe to get the target person to do something improper or unethical.

When rewards are used frequently as a source of influence, people may come to perceive their relationship to the leader in purely economic terms. They will expect a reward every time they are asked to do something new or unusual. It is more satisfying for both parties to view their relationship in terms of mutual loyalty and friendship. Rather than using rewards as incentives in an impersonal, mechanical way, they should be used in a more symbolic manner to recognize accomplishments and express personal appreciation for special contributions or exceptional effort. Used in this way, reward power can be a source of increased referent power over time (French & Raven, 1959).

Coercive Power

A leader's coercive power over subordinates is based on authority over punishments, which varies greatly across different types of organizations. The coercive power of military and political leaders is usually greater than that of corporate managers. Over the last two centuries, there has been a general decline in use of legitimate coercion by all types of leaders (Katz & Kahn, 1978). For example, managers once had the right to dismiss employees for any reason they thought was justified. The captain of a ship could flog sailors who were disobedient or who failed to perform their duties diligently. Military officers could execute a soldier for desertion or failure to obey an order during combat. Nowadays, these forms of coercive power are prohibited or sharply restricted in most nations.

Lateral relations provide few opportunities for using coercion. If the peer is dependent on the manager for assistance in performing important tasks, the manager may threaten to withhold cooperation if the peer fails to carry out a request. However, because mutual dependencies usually exist between managers of different subunits, coercion is likely to elicit retaliation and escalate into a conflict that benefits neither party.

The coercive power subordinates have over superiors varies greatly from one kind of organization to another. In many organizations subordinates have the capacity to indirectly influence the performance evaluation of their boss. Subordinates in these organizations can damage the reputation of the boss if they restrict production, sabotage operations, initiate grievances, hold demonstrations, or make complaints to higher management. In organizations with elected leaders, subordinates may have sufficient counterpower to remove a leader from office or to prevent the leader's reelection. Occasionally, the coercive power of subordinates involves more extreme methods of removing a leader from office. In fragging incidents during the Vietnam War, subordinates killed a despised leader by throwing a grenade at him during a firefight where the cause of death could not be determined. In the case of political leaders, the ultimate form of coercive power for subordinates is a violent revolution that results in the imprisonment, death, or exile of the leader.

Coercive power is invoked by a threat or warning that the target person will suffer undesirable consequences for noncompliance with a request, rule, or policy. The threat may be explicit, or it may be only a vague comment that the person will be sorry for failing to do what the agent wants. The likelihood of compliance is greatest when the threat is perceived to be credible, and the target person strongly desires to avoid the threatened punishment. Credibility will be undermined by rash threats that are not carried out despite noncompliance by the target person. Sometimes it is necessary to establish credibility by demonstrating the will and ability to cause unpleasant consequences for the target person. However, even a credible threat may be unsuccessful if the target person refuses to be intimidated or believes that a way can be found to avoid compliance without being detected by the agent.

It is best to avoid using coercion except when absolutely necessary, because it is difficult to use and likely to result in undesirable side effects. Coercion often arouses anger or resentment, and it may result in retaliation. In work organizations, the most appropriate use of coercion is to deter behavior detrimental to the organization, such as illegal activities, theft, violation of safety rules, reckless acts that endanger others, and direct disobedience of legitimate requests. Coercion is not likely to result in commitment, but when used skillfully in an appropriate situation, there is a reasonably good chance that it will result in compliance. A number of writers have proposed guidelines for coercion when it is used primarily to maintain discipline with subordinates (Arvey & Ivancevich, 1980; Preston & Zimmerer, 1978; Schoen & Durand, 1979). These guidelines, which are summarized in Table 6-5, are similar to guidelines presented in Chapter 5 for correcting performance deficiencies.

Referent Power

Referent power is derived from the desire of others to please an agent toward whom they have strong feelings of affection, admiration, and loyalty (French & Raven, 1959). People are usually willing to do special favors for a friend, and they are more likely to carry out requests made by someone they greatly admire. The strongest form of referent power involves the influence process called personal identification. To gain and maintain the agent's approval and acceptance, the target person is likely to do what the agent asks, imitate the agent's behavior, and develop attitudes similar to those expressed by the agent.

Referent power is usually greater for someone who is friendly, attractive, charming, and trustworthy. Some specific ways to acquire and maintain referent power are

TABLE 6-5   Guidelines for Using Coercive Power to Maintain Discipline

1. Explain rules and requirements, and ensure that people understand the serious consequences of violations.
2. Respond to infractions promptly and consistently without showing favoritism to particular individuals.
3. Investigate to get the facts before using reprimands or punishment, and avoid jumping to conclusions or making hasty accusations.
4. Except for the most serious infractions, provide sufficient oral and written warnings before resorting to punishment.
5. Administer warnings and reprimands in private, and avoid making rash threats.
6. Stay calm and avoid the appearance of hostility or personal rejection.
7. Express a sincere desire to help the person comply with role expectations and thereby avoid punishment.
8. Invite the person to suggest ways to correct the problem, and seek agreement on a concrete plan.
9. Maintain credibility by administering punishment if noncompliance continues after threats and warnings have been made.
10. Use punishments that are legitimate, fair, and commensurate with the seriousness of the infraction.

summarized in Table 6-6. Referent power is increased by showing concern for the needs and feelings of others, demonstrating trust and respect, and treating people fairly. However, to achieve and maintain strong referent power usually requires more than just flattery, favors, and charm. Referent power ultimately depends on the agent's character and integrity. Over time, actions speak louder than words, and someone who tries to appear friendly but manipulates and exploits people will lose referent power. Integrity is demonstrated by being truthful, expressing a consistent set of values, acting in a way that is consistent with one's espoused values, and carrying out promises and agreements.

Strong referent power will tend to increase the agent's influence over the target person even without any explicit effort by the agent to invoke this power. When the relationship is characterized by a strong bond of love or friendship, it may be sufficient merely to ask the target person to do something. However, when referent power is not this strong, it may be necessary to invoke the salience of the relationship during an influence attempt. This type of personal appeal is a proactive influence tactic that will be discussed later in the chapter.

TABLE 6-6   Ways to Acquire and Maintain Referent Power

- Show acceptance and positive regard.
- Act supportive and helpful.
- Use sincere forms of ingratiation.
- Defend and back up people when appropriate.
- Do unsolicited favors.
- Make self-sacrifices to show concern.
- Keep promises.

Referent power is an important source of influence over subordinates, peers, and superiors, but it has limitations. A request based solely on referent power should be commensurate with the extent of the target person's loyalty and friendship toward the leader. Some things are simply too much to ask, given the nature of the relationship. When requests are extreme or made too frequently, the target person may feel exploited. The result of such behavior may be to undermine the relationship and reduce the agent's referent power.

Another way to exercise referent power is through role modeling. A person who is well liked and admired can have considerable influence over others by setting an example of proper and desirable behavior for them to imitate. When identification is strong, imitation is likely to occur even without any conscious intention by the agent. Because people also imitate undesirable behavior in someone they admire, it is important to be aware of the examples one sets.

Expert Power

Task-relevant knowledge and skill are a major source of personal power in organizations. Unique knowledge about the best way to perform a task or solve an important problem provides potential influence over subordinates, peers, and superiors. However, expertise is a source of power only if others are dependent on the agent for advice. The more important a problem is to the target person, the greater the power derived by the agent from possessing the necessary expertise to solve it. Dependency is increased when the target person cannot easily find another source of advice besides the agent (Hickson et al., 1971; Patchen, 1974).

It is not enough for the agent to possess expertise, the target person must recognize this expertise and perceive the leader to be a reliable source of information and advice. In the short run, perceived expertise is more important than real expertise, and an agent may be able to fake it for a time by acting confident and pretending to be an expert. However, over time, as the agent's knowledge is put to the test, target perceptions of the agent's expertise are likely to become more accurate. Thus, it is essential for leaders to develop and maintain a reputation for technical expertise and strong credibility.

Actual expertise is maintained through a continual process of education and practical experience. For example, in many professions it is important to keep informed about new developments by reading technical publications and attending workshops and seminars. Evidence of expertise can be displayed in the forms of diplomas, licenses, and awards. However, the most convincing way to demonstrate expertise is by solving important problems, making good decisions, providing sound advice, and successfully completing challenging but highly visible projects. An extreme tactic is to intentionally but covertly precipitate crises just to demonstrate the ability to deal with them (Goldner, 1970; Pfeffer, 1977a).

Specialized knowledge and technical skill will remain a source of power only as long as dependence on the person who possesses them continues. If a problem is permanently solved or others learn how to solve it by themselves, the agent's expertise is no longer valuable. Thus, people sometimes try to protect their expert power by keeping procedures and techniques shrouded in secrecy, by using technical jargon to make the task seem more complex and mysterious, and by destroying alternate sources of information about task procedures such as written manuals, diagrams, blueprints, and computer programs (Hickson et al., 1971).

When the agent has a lot of expert power and is trusted as a reliable source of information and advice, the target person may carry out a request without receiving any explanation for it. One example is a patient who takes medicine prescribed by a doctor without knowing much about the medicine. Another example is an investor who purchases stocks recommended by a financial consultant without knowing much about the companies that issued the stocks. It is rare to possess this much expert power. In most cases, the agent must support a proposal or request by making logical arguments and presenting evidence that appears credible. Successful influence depends on the leader's credibility and persuasive communication skills in addition to technical knowledge and analytical ability.

Some guidelines for exercising expert power are shown in Table 6-7. Proposals or requests should be made in a clear, confident manner, and the agent should avoid making contradictory statements or vacillating between inconsistent positions. However, it is important to remember that superior expertise can also cause resentment if used in a way that implies the target person is ignorant or helpless. In the process of presenting rational arguments, some people lecture in an arrogant, condescending manner. In their efforts to sell a proposal, they fire a steady stream of arguments, rudely interrupting any attempted replies and dismissing any objections or concerns without serious consideration. Even when the agent is acknowledged to have more expertise, the target person usually has some relevant information, ideas, and concerns that should be considered.

Information Power

Another important source of power is control over information. This type of power involves both the access to vital information and control over its distribution to others (Pettigrew, 1972). Some access to information results from a person's position in the organization's communication network. Managerial positions often provide opportunities to obtain information that is not directly available to subordinates or peers (Mintzberg, 1973, 1983). Boundary role positions (e.g., marketing, purchasing, public relations) provide access to important information about events in the external environment of an organization. However, it is not merely a matter of occupying a particular position and having information appear as if by magic; a person must be actively involved in cultivating a network of information sources and gathering information from them (Kotter, 1982).

A leader who controls the flow of vital information about outside events has an opportunity to interpret these events for subordinates and influence their perception and attitudes (Kuhn, 1963). Some managers distort information to persuade people that a particular course of action is desirable. Examples of information distortion

---

TABLE 6-7 Ways to Use and Maintain Expert Power

- Explain the reasons for a request or proposal and why it is important.
- Provide evidence that a proposal will be successful.
- Do not make rash, careless, or inconsistent statements.
- Do not lie, exaggerate, or misrepresent the facts.
- Listen seriously to the person's concerns and suggestions.
- Act confident and decisive in a crisis.

include selective editing of reports and documents, biased interpretation of data, and presentation of false information. Some managers use their control over the distribution of information as a way to enhance their expert power and increase subordinate dependence. If the leader is the only one who knows what is going on, subordinates will lack evidence to dispute the leader's claim that an unpopular decision is justified by circumstances. Moreover, control of information makes it easier for a leader to cover up failures and mistakes that would otherwise undermine a carefully cultivated image of expertise (Pfeffer, 1977a).

Control over information is a source of upward influence as well as downward and lateral influence. When subordinates have exclusive access to information needed by superiors to make decisions, this advantage can be used to influence the superior's decisions. Some subordinates actively seek this type of influence by gradually assuming more responsibility for collecting, storing, analyzing, and reporting operating information. If a leader is completely dependent on a subordinate to interpret complex analyses of operating information, the subordinate may be invited to participate directly in making decisions based on these analyses (Korda, 1975). However, even without direct participation, a subordinate with information control will be able to influence a superior's decisions. For example, in a study by Pettigrew (1972), a manager was able to influence the selection of a new computer by providing the board of directors with information that favored one option and discredited others. Control over the flow of operating information also enables subordinates to magnify their accomplishments, cover up mistakes, and exaggerate the amount of expertise and resources needed to do their work.

Ecological Power

Control over the physical environment, technology, and organization of the work provides an opportunity for indirect influence over other people. Because behavior is determined in part by perception of opportunities and constraints, it can be altered in subtle ways by rearranging the situation (Cartwright, 1965). This form of influence is sometimes called *situational engineering* or *ecological control.*

One form of situational engineering is to modify the design of subordinate jobs to increase subordinate motivation (Oldham, 1976). Research on job enrichment suggests that significant improvements in work quality and job satisfaction are sometimes possible (Hackman & Oldham, 1980; Lawler, 1986). The organization of work activities and design of formal structure is another form of situational engineering. The grouping of activities into subunits, determination of reporting relationships, and design of information systems are all sources of influence over employee behavior (Lawrence & Lorsch, 1967; Mintzberg, 1983).

Another form of situational engineering is control over the physical work environment. For example, lights or auditory signals on equipment can be used to inform the operator that it is time for necessary maintenance, or to warn the operator to discontinue doing something that will cause an accident or breakdown. The workflow design and layout of physical facilities determine which employees interact with each other and who initiates action for whom. Machine-paced assembly lines set the speed at which employees work.

A final form of ecological power is *cultural engineering.* The culture of an organization consists of the shared norms, values, and beliefs of members. By establishing a strong culture, leaders can indirectly influence the attitudes and behavior of members (Schein, 1992). Culture provides a way to control and coordinate the actions of people without the need for elaborate formal control systems or continuous use of direct influence attempts (Tushman & O'Reilly, 1996). It is much easier for leaders to influence culture in small, newly formed organizations than in large, established ones, and once a strong culture has been established it is difficult to change (see Chapter 10). Thus, culture can be an obstacle rather than an enhancer of leader influence if the shared values and beliefs of organization members are inconsistent with the leader's influence objectives.

How Power Is Acquired or Lost

Power is not a static condition; it changes over time due to changing conditions and the actions of individuals and coalitions. Two theories that describe how power is acquired or lost are social exchange theory and the strategic contingencies theory. *Social exchange theory* explains how power is gained and lost as reciprocal influence processes occur over time between leaders and followers in small groups. *Strategic contingencies theory* explains the acquisition and loss of power by different subunits of an organization (e.g., functional departments or product divisions) and the implications of this power distribution for the effectiveness of the organization in a changing environment. Although the two theories focus on power processes at different levels of analysis, they share many similar features and appear mostly compatible. Both theories emphasize the importance of demonstrated expertise for the acquisition of authority.

Social Exchange Theory

The most fundamental form of social interaction is an exchange of benefits or favors, which can include not only material benefits but also psychological benefits such as expressions of approval, respect, esteem, and affection. Individuals learn to engage in social exchanges early in their childhood, and they develop expectations about reciprocity and equity in these exchanges. Several versions of social exchange theory have been proposed (Blau, 1974; Homans, 1958; Thibaut & Kelley, 1959), but the versions by Hollander (1958, 1980) and Jacobs (1970) are most relevant because they are explicitly concerned with leadership.

Member expectations about what leadership role a person should have in the group are influenced by the person's loyalty and demonstrated competence. The amount of status and power accorded a person is proportionate to the group's evaluation of the person's potential contribution relative to that of other members. The contribution may involve control over scarce resources, access to vital information, or skill in dealing with critical task problems. In addition to increased status and influence, a person who has demonstrated good judgment accumulates idiosyncrasy credits and is allowed more latitude than other members to deviate from nonessential group norms. Group members are usually willing to suspend immediate judgment and go along with the person's innovative proposals for attaining group goals. When a leader makes an innovative proposal that proves to be successful, the group's trust in the person's expertise is confirmed, and even more status and influence may be accorded to the person.

On the other hand, if the leader's proposals prove to be a failure, then the terms of the exchange relationship are likely to be reassessed by the group. The negative effects are greater if failure appears to be due to poor judgment or incompetence rather than to circumstances beyond the leader's control. A more negative evaluation will be made if the leader is perceived to have pursued selfish motives rather than loyally serving the group. Selfish motives and irresponsibility are more likely to be attributed to a leader who willingly deviates from group norms and traditions. Thus, innovation by the leader can be a double-edged sword. Success resulting from innovation leads to greater credit, but failure leads to greater blame. The extent of a leader's loss of status and influence following failure depends in part on how serious the failure is to the group. A major disaster results in greater loss of esteem than a minor setback. Loss of status also depends on amount of status the leader had prior to the failure. More is expected of a leader with high status, and such a leader will lose more status if perceived to be responsible for failure.

According to social exchange theory, innovation is not only accepted but expected of leaders when necessary to deal with serious problems and obstacles. A leader who fails to show initiative and deal decisively with serious problems will lose esteem and influence, just as a leader who proposes actions that are unsuccessful.

The exchange process by which leaders gain influence from repeated demonstration of expertise and loyalty is probably much the same for formal leaders in large organizations as for emergent leaders in small groups. However, the authority and position power that comes with appointment by superiors makes formal leaders less dependent on subordinate evaluation of their competence. Nevertheless, an incompetent leader will lose status and expert power with subordinates, and demonstrated incompetence may eventually undermine the leader's legitimate authority as well (Evans & Zelditch, 1961).

Social exchange theory emphasizes expert power and authority, and other forms of power do not receive much attention. For example, the theory does not explain how reciprocal influence processes affect a leader's reward and referent power. The supporting evidence for the theory was found in research with small groups in a laboratory setting (Hollander, 1960, 1961, 1980), but longitudinal field research is needed on social exchange processes for leaders in large organizations to verify that the process is the same.

Strategic Contingencies Theory

Strategic contingencies theory explains how some organizational subunits gain or lose power to influence important decisions such as selection of the chief executive, determination of the organization's competitive strategy, and the allocation of resources among subunits and activities (Hickson et al., 1971). The theory postulates that the power of a subunit depends on three factors: (1) expertise in coping with important problems, (2) centrality of the subunit within the workflow, and (3) the extent to which the subunit's expertise is unique rather than substitutable.

All organizations must cope with critical contingencies, especially problems in the technological processes used to carry out operations and problems in adapting to unpredictable events in the environment. Success in solving important problems is a source of expert power for subunits, just as it is for individuals. The opportunity to demonstrate expertise and gain power from it is much greater for a subunit that has responsibility for dealing with critical problems. A problem is critical if it is clearly essential for the survival and prosperity of the organization. The importance of a particular type of problem is greater as the degree of interdependence among subunits increases; other subunits cannot perform their own functions unless this type of problem is handled effectively. An individual or subunit will gain more power over important decisions if the critical functions cannot be performed by someone else or made easier by development of standard procedures. In other words, the more unique and irreplaceable the expertise required to solve critical problems, the more power is gained from possessing this expertise.

Increased expert power can result in increased legitimate power. People with valuable expertise are more likely to be appointed or elected to positions of authority in the organization. Subunits with critical expertise are likely to have more representation on boards or committees that make important decisions for the organization.

Some support for the theory was found in several studies (Brass, 1984, 1985; Hambrick, 1981a; Hinings, Hickson, Pennings, and Schneck, 1974; Hills & Mahoney, 1978; Pfeffer & Moore, 1980; Pfeffer & Salancik, 1974). However, the theory fails to take into account the possibility that a powerful subunit or coalition can use its power to protect its dominant position in the organization by enhancing its perceived expertise and by denying potential rivals an opportunity to demonstrate their greater expertise. These political processes and the implications for organizational change are described in Chapter 12.

Consequences of Position and Personal Power

Most of the research on different types of power used the power taxonomy proposed by French and Raven (1959) or a variation of it. In several studies, questionnaires were administered to subordinates to measure how each type of power was related to subordinate satisfaction or performance (e.g., Hinkin & Schriesheim, 1989; Rahim, 1989; Schriesheim, Hinkin, & Podsakoff, 1991). Most of the power studies found that expert and referent power were positively correlated with subordinate satisfaction and performance. The results for legitimate, reward, and coercive power were inconsistent, and the correlations with criteria were usually negative or non-significant rather than positive. Overall, the results suggest that effective leaders rely more on expert and referent power to influence subordinates.

Most of the early power studies asked respondents to rank or rate the importance of different types of power as a reason for compliance with leader requests. Methodological limitations in these studies raise serious doubts about the findings (Podsakoff & Schriesheim, 1985). In most subsequent studies, respondents rated a leader on various position or personal attributes that provide a source of power (Hinkin & Schriesheim, 1989; Rahim, 1989; Yukl & Falbe, 1991). However, the results from all of the power studies may be biased due to attributions, social desirability, and stereotypes. For example, subordinates in high-performing groups are likely to attribute more expert power to their leader than subordinates in low-performing groups. Due to these biases, the importance of less socially desirable forms of power such as rewards and coercion may be underestimated.

The field survey research may have underestimated the utility of other forms of power, especially when compliance is an acceptable outcome. Only a few studies have related power to immediate influence outcomes such as changes in subordinate attitudes and behavior. Warren (1968) found that expert, referent, and legitimate power were correlated positively with attitudinal commitment by subordinates, whereas reward and coercive power were correlated with behavioral compliance. In a study by Thambain and Gemmill (1974), the primary reason given for compliance was the leader's legitimate power, and reward power was also an important reason for compliance, even though neither type of power was associated with commitment. Yukl and Falbe (1991) found that legitimate power was the most common reason given for compliance with requests from the boss, even though it was not correlated with task commitment. For many routine requests or orders, exerting legitimate power in the form of a simple request or command is likely to produce target compliance.

The relevance of reward and coercive power when used in an appropriate way is supported by research on a leader's use of contingent reward behavior. In a review of this research, Podsakoff, Todor, Grover, and Huber (1984) concluded that making desirable rewards contingent on subordinate performance leads to higher subordinate satisfaction and performance. Some of this research also suggests that contingent punishment can have a positive effect on subordinate performance when used in combination with rewards (Arvey & Ivancevich, 1980; Podsakoff, Todor, & Skov, 1982).

Another limitation of most power studies is their failure to deal with relationships among different sources of power. French and Raven (1959) proposed that different types of power are likely to be interrelated in complex ways. For example, leaders with considerable authority are likely to have more reward and coercive power, and use of these forms of power may affect a leader's referent power. The power studies did not attempt to separate the effects of different types of power, nor did they examine the interactions among different types of power.

How Much Power Should Leaders Have?

It is obvious that leaders need some power to be effective, but it does not follow that more power is always better. The amount of overall power that is necessary for effective leadership and the mix of different types of power are questions that research has only begun to answer. Clearly the amount of necessary power will depend on what needs to be accomplished and on the leader's skill in using the available power. Less power is needed by a leader who has the skills to use power effectively and who recognizes the importance of concentrating on essential objectives. Bauer (1968, p. 17) explains the wisdom of using power selectively and carefully.

> In any ongoing institution, the ability to get important things done is dependent upon maintaining a reservoir of goodwill. The person who fights every issue as though it were vital exhausts his resources, including, most especially, the patience and goodwill of those on whom he has to depend to get things done. Therefore, it should be considered neither surprising nor immoral that, when an issue is of low salience, the sensible individual may use it to build goodwill for the future, or pay off past obligations, by going along with some individual for whom the issue is of high salience.

Some leadership situations require more power than others for the leader to be effective. More influence is necessary in an organization where major changes are required, but there is strong initial opposition to the leader's proposals for change. It is especially difficult for a leader who recognizes that the organization will face a major crisis in coming years, a crisis that can be overcome only if preparations are begun immediately, but the evidence of the coming crisis is not yet sufficiently strong to persuade members to act now. A similar situation is the case where a leader desires to make changes that will require short-term sacrifices and a long period of implementation before the benefits are realized, but there is opposition by factions with a short-term perspective. In such situations, a leader will need sufficient expert and referent power to persuade people that change is necessary and desirable, or sufficient position and political power to overcome the opposition and buy time to demonstrate that the proposed changes are necessary and effective. A combination of personal and position power increases the likelihood of success, but forcing change is always risky. Maurer (1996, p. 177) describes one successful example:

> When Leonard Bernstein became conductor of the Vienna Philharmonic, he reintroduced the symphonies of Gustav Mahler. The orchestra hated Mahler; they felt his music was overblown and pompous. Bernstein was undeterred. He scheduled the symphonies into programs. Although Bernstein certainly had the power to program whatever he wished, it was a risky move. Orchestras notoriously show their disdain for conductors they disrespect by engaging in malicious compliance. All the notes are correct—so no one can be reprimanded—but they play without spirit.... Although Bernstein did not enjoy support for the decision to play Mahler, he was highly respected by the members of the orchestra.... He was a world class musician. So, for Leonard Bernstein they played Mahler beautifully. Eventually, it seems, most of the orchestra grew to enjoy playing the music of their hometown boy.

Questions about the optimal mix of power for leaders are complicated by the interdependence among different sources of power. The distinction between position and personal power is sometimes convenient, but it should not be overdrawn. Position power is important, not only as a source of influence but also because it can be used to enhance a leader's personal power. Control over information complements expert power based on technical skill by giving the leader an advantage in solving important problems and by enabling a leader to cover up mistakes and exaggerate accomplishments. Reward power facilitates development of a deeper exchange relationship with subordinates, and when used skillfully it enhances a leader's referent power. The authority to make decisions and the upward influence to get them approved enables a leader to demonstrate expertise in problem solving, and it also facilitates development of stronger exchange relationships with subordinates. Some coercive power is necessary to buttress legitimate and expert power when a leader needs to influence compliance with rules and procedures that are unpopular but necessary to do the work and avoid serious accidents. Likewise, coercive power is needed by a leader to restrain or banish rebels and criminals who would otherwise disrupt operations, steal resources, harm other members, and cause the leader to appear weak and incompetent.

However, too much position power may be as detrimental as too little. Leaders with a great deal of position power may be tempted to rely on it instead of developing personal power and using other approaches (e.g., consultation, persuasion) for influencing people to comply with a request or support a change. The notion that power corrupts is especially relevant for position power. Throughout history many political leaders with strong position power have used it to dominate and exploit subordinates. The ethical use of power is discussed in more detail in Chapter 14.

How easily power can corrupt leaders is demonstrated in an experiment conducted by Kipnis (1972). He found that leaders with greater reward power perceived subordinates as objects of manipulation, devalued the worth of subordinates, attributed subordinate efforts to the leader's power, maintained more social distance from subordinates, and used rewards more often to influence subordinates. Although only a laboratory experiment with students, the research clearly points out the dangers of excessive position power. In general, a leader should have only a moderate amount of position power, although the optimal amount will vary somewhat depending on the situation.

What about personal power? Are there also dangers from having a great deal of expert and referent power? Personal power is less susceptible to misuse, because it erodes quickly when a leader acts contrary to the interests of followers. Nevertheless, the potential for corruption remains. A leader with extensive expert power or charismatic appeal will be tempted to act in ways that will eventually lead to failure (Zaleznik, 1970). McClelland (1975, p. 266) describes this phenomenon:

> How much initiative he should take, how persuasive he should attempt to be, and at what point his clear enthusiasm for certain goals becomes personal authoritarian insistence that those goals are the right ones whatever the members of the group may think, are all questions calculated to frustrate the well-intentioned leader. If he takes no initiative, he is no leader. If he takes too much, he becomes a dictator, particularly if he tries to curtail the process by which members of the group participate in shaping group goals. There is a particular danger for the man who has demonstrated his competence in shaping group goals and in inspiring group members to pursue them. In time both he and they may assume that he knows best, and he may almost imperceptibly change from a democratic to an authoritarian leader.

Studies of the amount of influence exercised by people at different levels in the authority hierarchy of an organization reveal that the most effective organizations have a high degree of reciprocal influence (Bachman, Smith, & Slesinger, 1966; Smith & Tannenbaum, 1963). The results suggest that leaders in effective organizations create relationships in which they have strong influence over subordinates but are also receptive to influence from them. Instead of using their power to dictate how things will be done, effective executives empower members of the organization to discover and implement new and better ways of doing things.

One of the best ways to ensure that leaders remain responsive to follower needs is to provide formal mechanisms to promote reciprocal influence and discourage arbitrary actions by the leader. Rules and policies can be enacted to regulate the exercise of position power, especially reward and coercive power. Grievance and appeals procedures can be enacted and independent review boards established to protect subordinates against misuse of power by leaders. Bylaws, charter provisions, and official policies can be drafted to require leaders to consult with subordinates and obtain their approval on specified types of decisions. Regular attitude surveys can be conducted to measure subordinate satisfaction with their leaders. In types of organizations where it is appropriate, periodic elections or votes of confidence can be held to determine whether the leader should continue in office. Recall procedures can be established to remove incompetent leaders in an orderly manner. Finally, leaders themselves can facilitate reciprocal influence by encouraging subordinates to participate in making important decisions, and by fostering and rewarding innovation.

Influence Tactics

For the past two decades, rather than focusing exclusively on power as a source of potential influence, researchers have begun to examine the specific types of behavior used to exercise influence. The type of behavior used intentionally to influence the attitudes and behavior of another person is usually called an *influence tactic*. Three general types of influence tactics can be differentiated according to their primary purpose (Yukl & Chavez, 2002).

Impression management tactics are intended to influence people to like the agent or to have a favorable evaluation of the agent. Examples include providing praise or offering unconditional help (ingratiation), and talking about one's achievements or qualifications (self-promotion). These tactics can be used by leaders to influence followers, or by followers to influence a leader. Impression management by leaders and followers is discussed in Chapter 5.

Political tactics are used to influence organizational decisions or otherwise gain benefits for an individual or group. Several scholars have identified political tactics used in organizations (e.g., Fairhurst, 1993; Kacmar & Baron, 1999; Pfeffer, 1992; Porter, Allen, & Angle, 1981). One type of political tactic involves an attempt to influence how important decisions are made and who makes them. Examples include selecting decision makers who will favor you, influencing the agenda of meetings, or getting decision makers to use criteria that will bias decisions in your favor. Political tactics are also used to defend against opponents and silence critics (Valle & Perrewe, 2000). Some political tactics involve deception, manipulation, and abuse of power (Zanzi & O'Neill, 2001). How political tactics are used to avoid organizational change is discussed in Chapter 12, and ethical aspects of power and influence are discussed in Chapter 14.

Proactive influence tactics have an immediate task objective, such as getting the target person to carry out a new task, change the procedures used for a current task, provide assistance on a project, or support a proposed change. If a request is clearly legitimate, relevant for the work, and something the target person knows how to do, then it is often possible to get target compliance by using a simple request based on legitimate power. However, when target resistance is likely the agent may need to use a proactive influence tactic such as rational persuasion.

Some specific types of influence tactics can be used for more than one purpose, but the effectiveness of a tactic will depend on the purpose and the context in which it is used. For example, ingratiation is more effective for impression management than for influencing someone to carry out a task. Literature reviews and meta-analyses are likely to reach incorrect conclusions about tactic effectiveness if they fail to consider the purpose for which a tactic was used.

Research to Identify Proactive Tactics

Two research programs have used inductive and deductive approaches to identify distinct types of proactive tactics. Kipnis, Schmidt, and Wilkinson (1980) developed a preliminary taxonomy by analyzing critical incidents that described successful and unsuccessful influence attempts. Then the tactics identified with this inductive approach were used to develop a self-report agent questionnaire called the Profiles of Organizational Influence Strategies (POIS). Schriesheim and Hinkin (1990) later conducted a factor analysis of the POIS using data from samples of agents who rated their own use of the tactics in upward influence attempts with their boss. This study found support for six of the proposed tactics (i.e., rationality, exchange, ingratiation, assertiveness, coalition, and upward appeal), but not for the remaining two tactics (blocking and sanctions). The revised version of the questionnaire was supported in a subsequent study (Hochwarter, Pearson, Ferris, Perrewe, & Ralston, 2000). However, there has been no systematic research to validate the questionnaire as a measure of tactics used to influence subordinates and peers. Both the original and revised versions of the POIS have been used in many studies on determinants and consequences of the proactive tactics (see Ammeter et al., 2002).

A research program on proactive tactics was carried out by Yukl and his colleagues. The Influence Behavior Questionnaire (IBQ) was developed to provide multisource feedback to managers (Yukl, Lepsinger, & Lucia, 1991). The target version of the questionnaire has been used in most of the research, because target ratings of agent influence behavior are usually more accurate than agent self-ratings. The initial version of the IBQ included scales to measure the six primary tactics from the POIS. However, instead of merely revising POIS items to make them appropriate for targets, a new set of items was developed, and some scale names were changed to reduce ambiguity. The IBQ also included scales to measure tactics identified by a deductive approach from theories about leadership and power. A factor analysis (Yukl et al., 1991) found support for nine distinct tactics, including four not represented in the POIS (i.e., consultation, inspirational appeals, personal appeals, and legitimating). Upward appeals and coalition tactics were combined into a single coalition scale, because many respondents failed to differentiate between them, especially when rating downward influence behavior by a boss or lateral influence behavior by a peer. Subsequent use of the IBQ in feedback workshops with managers resulted in the identification of two additional tactics called collaboration and apprising (Yukl & Seifert, 2002). The 11 proactive tactics from the research by Yukl and his colleagues are defined in Table 6-8. Table 6-9 compares tactics resulting from the two research programs. The proactive tactics found by Yukl and his colleagues will be explained next, as well as the conditions where each tactic is most likely to be successful.

Rational Persuasion

Rational persuasion involves the use of explanations, logical arguments, and factual evidence to show that a request or proposal is feasible and relevant for attaining task objectives. A weak form of rational persuasion may include only a brief explanation of the reason for a request, or an undocumented assertion that a proposed change is desirable and feasible. Stronger forms of rational persuasion include a detailed explanation of the reasons why a request or proposed change is important, and presentation of concrete evidence that the proposal is feasible.

Rational persuasion is most appropriate when the target person shares the same task objectives as the manager but does not recognize the proposal is the best way to attain the objectives. If the agent and target person have incompatible objectives, then rational persuasion is unlikely to be successful for obtaining target commitment or

TABLE 6-8   Definition of the 11 Proactive Influence Tactics

Rational Persuasion: The agent uses logical arguments and factual evidence to show a proposal or request is feasible and relevant for attaining important task objectives.

Apprising: The agent explains how carrying out a request or supporting a proposal will benefit the target personally or help advance the target person's career.

Inspirational Appeals: The agent makes an appeal to values and ideals or seeks to arouse the target person's emotions to gain commitment for a request or proposal.

Consultation: The agent encourages the target to suggest improvements in a proposal or to help plan an activity or change for which the target person's support and assistance are desired.

Collaboration: The agent offers to provide relevant resources and assistance if the target will carry out a request or approve a proposed change.

Ingratiation: The agent uses praise and flattery before or during an influence attempt, or expresses confidence in the target's ability to carry out a difficult request.

Personal Appeals: The agent asks the target to carry out a request or support a proposal out of friendship, or asks for a personal favor before saying what it is.

Exchange: The agent offers an incentive, suggests an exchange of favors, or indicates willingness to reciprocate at a later time if the target will do what the agent requests.

Coalition Tactics: The agent seeks the aid of others to persuade the target to do something, or uses the support of others as a reason for the target to agree.

Legitimating Tactics: The agent seeks to establish the legitimacy of a request or to verify the authority to make it by referring to rules, policies, contracts, or precedent.

Pressure: The agent uses demands, threats, frequent checking, or persistent reminders to influence the target to carry out a request.

Source: Copyright © 2001 by Gary Yukl.

even compliance. Along with facts and logic, a rational appeal usually includes some opinions or inferences that the agent asks the target person to accept at face value because there is insufficient evidence to verify them. Thus, the success of the influence attempt also depends in part on whether the target person perceives the agent to be a credible and trustworthy source of information, inferences, and predictions.

TABLE 6-9   Comparison of Influence Tactics Found in Two Research Programs

Based on the POIS	*Based on the IBQ*
Rationality	Rational persuasion
Exchange	Exchange
Ingratiation	Ingratiation
Assertiveness	Pressure
Coalition	Coalition
Upward Appeal	(tactic is included in coalition)
	Consultation
	Inspirational appeals
	Personal appeals
	Legitimating
	Collaboration
	Apprising

Apprising

With this tactic the agent explains why a request or proposal is likely to benefit the target person as an individual. One type of benefit involves the target person's career, which could be aided by opportunities to learn new skills, meet important people, or gain more visibility and a better reputation. Another type of benefit is to make the target person's job easier or more interesting. Like rational persuasion, apprising often involves the use of facts and logic, but the benefits described are for the target person rather than for the organization. Unlike exchange tactics, the benefits to be obtained by the target person are a by-product of doing what the agent requests, not something the agent will provide. Use of apprising is more likely to be successful if the agent understands the target's needs and how a request or proposal may be relevant for satisfying them. Apprising is more likely to be effective if the agent has credibility as a source of information about career issues.

Inspirational Appeals

This tactic involves an emotional or value-based appeal, in contrast to the logical arguments used in rational persuasion. An inspirational appeal is an attempt to develop enthusiasm and commitment by arousing strong emotions and linking a request or proposal to a person's needs, values, hopes, and ideals. Some bases for appealing to most people include their desire to be important, to feel useful, to develop and use their skills, to accomplish something worthwhile, to perform an exceptional feat, to be a member of the best team, or to participate in an exciting effort to make things better. Some ideals that may be the basis for an inspirational appeal include patriotism, loyalty, liberty, freedom, self-fulfillment, justice, fairness, equality, love, tolerance, excellence, humanitarianism, and progress. For example, soldiers are asked to volunteer for a dangerous mission as an expression of their patriotism, or a group of employees is asked to work extra hours on a special project because it may save many lives. No tangible rewards are promised, only the prospect that people will feel good as a result of doing something that is noble and just, making an important contribution, performing an exceptional feat, or serving God and country. To formulate an effective appeal, the agent must have insight into the values, hopes, and fears of the person or group to be influenced. Effectiveness also depends on communication skills, such as the agent's ability to use vivid imagery and metaphors, manipulate symbols, and employ voice and gestures to generate enthusiasm and excitement.

Consultation

Consultation occurs when the target person is invited to participate in planning how to carry out a request or implement a proposed change. There are several reasons for using consultation as a decision procedure (see Chapter 4), but when used as a proactive influence tactic, the primary purpose is to influence the target person to support a decision already made by the agent. Consultation can take a variety of forms when used as an influence tactic. In one common form of consultation, the manager presents a proposed policy or plan to a person who will be involved in implementing it to discover whether the person has any doubts or concerns. In the discussion, which is really a form of negotiation and joint problem solving, the manager tries to find ways to modify the proposal to deal with the person's major concerns. In another common variation of consultation, the manager presents a general strategy or objective to the other person rather than a detailed proposal and asks the person to suggest specific action steps for implementing it. The suggested action steps are discussed until the parties reach an agreement.

Exchange Tactics

This type of influence tactic involves the explicit or implicit offer to provide something the target person wants in return for carrying out a request. This tactic is especially useful when the target person is indifferent or reluctant about complying with a request because it offers no important benefits and would involve considerable effort and inconvenience. Exchange tactics are a way to increase the benefits enough to make it worthwhile for a target person to comply with the request. An essential condition for effective use of this tactic is control over something the target person desires enough to justify compliance. The incentive may involve a wide range of tangible or intangible benefits (e.g., a pay increase or promotion, scarce resources, information, assistance on another task, assistance in advancing the target's career). Sometimes the promise may be implicit rather than explicit; that is, the agent suggests returning the favor in some unspecified way at a future time. An offer to exchange benefits will not be effective unless the target person perceives that the agent is able and willing to provide the promised benefit.

Collaboration

This influence tactic involves an offer to provide necessary resources or assistance if the target person will carry out a request or approve a proposal. Examples include offering to show the target person how to do a requested task, offering to provide the equipment or technical assistance needed to perform a requested task, and offering to help the target person deal with a problem that would be caused by carrying out the request. Collaboration may seem similar to exchange in that both tactics involve an offer to do something for the target person. However, there are important differences in the underlying motivational processes and facilitating conditions. Exchange usually involves an impersonal trade of unrelated benefits, whereas collaboration usually involves a joint effort to accomplish the same task or objective.

Personal Appeals

A personal appeal involves asking someone to do a favor out of friendship or loyalty to the agent. This influence tactic is not feasible when the target person dislikes the agent or is indifferent about what happens to the agent. The stronger the friendship or loyalty, the more one can ask of the target person. Of course, if referent power is very strong, a personal appeal should not be necessary. Personal appeals are most likely to be used when asking for something that is not part of the target person's regular job responsibilities (e.g., provide assistance, do a personal favor).

Ingratiation

Ingratiation is an attempt to make the target person feel better about the agent. Examples include giving compliments, doing unsolicited favors, acting deferential and respectful, and acting especially friendly. When ingratiation is perceived to be sincere, it tends to strengthen positive regard and make a target person more willing to consider the agent's request. However, ingratiation is likely to be viewed as manipulative when it is used just before asking for something. Therefore, ingratiation is less useful for an immediate influence attempt than as a longer-term strategy to improve relationships with people.

Legitimating Tactics

Legitimating tactics involve attempts to establish one's authority or right to make a particular type of request. Legitimacy is unlikely to be questioned for a routine request that has been made and complied with many times before. However, a legitimating tactic may be needed when a request is unusual, it clearly exceeds your authority, or the target person does not know who you are or what authority you have. There are several different types of legitimating tactics, most of which are mutually compatible. Examples include providing evidence of prior precedent, showing consistency with organizational policies and rules, showing consistency with professional role expectations, and showing that the request is consistent with the terms of a contract or prior agreement.

Pressure

Pressure tactics include threats, warnings, and assertive behavior such as repeated demands or frequent checking to see whether the person has complied with a request. Pressure tactics are sometimes successful in inducing compliance with a request, particularly if the target person is just lazy or apathetic rather than strongly opposed to it. However, pressure tactics are unlikely to result in commitment, and they may have serious side effects. The harder forms (e.g., threats, warnings, demands) are likely to cause resentment and undermine working relationships. In response, the target person may try to avoid, discredit, or restrict the power of the agent. Sometimes hard pressure tactics are necessary to obtain compliance with a rule or policy that is important to the organization, such as safety rules and ethical practices. However, in most cases, the softer forms of pressure (e.g., persistent requests, reminders that the target person promised to do something) are more likely to gain compliance without undermining the relationship with the target person.

Coalition Tactics

Coalition tactics involve getting help from other people to influence the target person. The coalition partners may be peers, subordinates, superiors, or outsiders. When assistance is provided by the superior of the target person, the tactic may be called an upward appeal. Another distinct coalition tactic is to use a prior endorsement by other people to help influence the target person to support your proposal. To be helpful, the endorsement should be provided by someone the target person likes or respects. Coalition tactics are usually used in combination with other influence tactics. For example, the agent and a coalition partner may both use rational persuasion to influence the target person.

Power and Influence Behavior

Studies using survey questionnaires (Hinkin & Schriesheim, 1990; Kapoor & Ansari, 1988) or influence incidents (Yukl, Kim, & Falbe, 1996) find that power and influence behavior are distinct constructs. However, the relationship among specific forms of power, specific influence behaviors, and influence outcomes is complex and not well understood. Several types of effects are possible, and they are not mutually exclusive (see Figure 6-1).

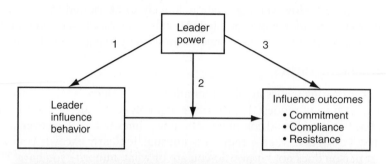

FIGURE 6-1   Effects of Agent Power and Influence Behavior on Influence Outcomes

Agent power may directly affect the agent's choice of influence tactics (as depicted by arrow #1). Some tactics require a particular type of power to be effective, and a leader with relevant power is more likely to use these tactics. For example, exchange tactics require reward power, which provides an agent with something of value to exchange with the target person. Strong forms of pressure such as warnings and threats are more likely to be used by an agent who has some coercive power over the target person. Rational persuasion is more likely to be used when the agent has the knowledge necessary to explain why a request is important and feasible.

Some influence tactics may have a direct effect on target attitudes and/or behavior, regardless of the agent's power. However, in the majority of influence attempts, it is likely that power acts as a moderator variable to enhance or diminish the effectiveness of the tactics used by the agent. This moderator effect of power (depicted by arrow #2) is most likely to occur for types of the power directly relevant to the tactics used in an influence attempt. For example, expert power probably moderates the effect of rational persuasion. A proposal explaining why it is important to change operating procedures is more likely to be successful if made by someone perceived to have relevant expertise. A similar moderating effect probably occurs for reward power and exchange tactics. An agent with high reward power is likely to have more success offering an exchange than an agent with little reward power. Note that the target person's perception of agent reward power is more important than the agent's actual control over rewards. In a classic movie theme, a shabbily dressed millionaire offers a stranger a lot of money to do something, and believing that the agent is poor the stranger refuses. In contrast, well-dressed con artists with little money are sometimes able to influence people to extend credit or lend valuable items on the (unfulfilled) hope they will result in later purchases.

It is also possible that agent power can enhance the success of an influence tactic for which the power is not directly relevant (also depicted by arrow #2). An agent with strong referent power may be more successful when using rational persuasion to gain support for a proposal. An agent with strong coercive power may be more successful in gaining compliance with a simple request, even though no pressure or exchange tactics are used. Strong expert power may increase the credibility of a request unrelated to the agent's expertise. For example, a famous scientist influences people to participate in a risky financial venture that does not involve the scientist's field of expertise.

Another possibility (depicted by arrow #3) is that agent power can influence the target person regardless of whether the agent makes any overt influence attempt. For example, people may cooperate more with an agent who has substantial reward power in the hopes of getting some rewards in the future. A classic example is provided by the case of relatives who are especially friendly and helpful to a rich old uncle, but ignore another uncle whom they believe to be poor. In organizations, people act more deferential toward somebody who has high position power, because they are aware of the possibility that the person can affect their job performance and career advancement. People are less likely to criticize or contradict a powerful agent, because they do not want to risk the agent's displeasure. People are more likely to cooperate with an agent who has strong referent power, even though the agent does nothing to encourage such behavior.

Only a small amount of research has been conducted to investigate the relationships between power and influence. There is only limited evidence for the proposition that power influences the choice of influence tactics. There is no supporting evidence that power moderates the effectiveness of a specific influence tactic. There is only anecdotal evidence that power increases compliance or changes target behavior independently of the use of tactics based on this power. Clearly these important research questions deserve more attention.

Use and Effectiveness of Influence Tactics

A number of studies examined how the agent's use of influence tactics varies depending on the direction of influence (i.e., with subordinates, peers, or superiors). A few studies examined how different tactics are used together in combinations and sequences. Other studies assessed the relative effectiveness of different tactics or tactic combinations. This section of the chapter briefly reviews major findings in the research on proactive influence tactics.

Directional Differences in Use of Tactics

One research question is whether managers use different tactics depending on the relative status of the agent and target. Yukl and Tracey (1992) developed a model in which the following interrelated factors determine the selection of influence tactics for a particular influence attempt: (1) consistency with prevailing social norms and role expectations about use of the tactic in that context, (2) agent possession of an appropriate power base for use of the tactic in that context, (3) appropriateness for the objective of the influence attempt, (4) level of target resistance encountered or anticipated, and (5) costs of using the tactic in relation to likely benefits. The underlying assumption is that most agents prefer to use tactics that are socially acceptable, that are feasible in terms of the agent's position and personal power in relation to the target, that are not costly (in terms of time, effort, loss of resources, or alienation of the target), and that are likely to be effective for a particular objective given the anticipated level of target resistance.

The model was used to derive specific hypotheses about directional differences in how often each type of tactic is used. For example, it was hypothesized that exchange, pressure, ingratiation, and legitimating tactics are used more in a downward and lateral direction than upward. The reason was that these tactics are more consistent with the power base and role expectations for a boss in relation to a subordinate than for a subordinate in relation to a boss. Support for most of the hypotheses was found in three studies using survey questionnaires or descriptions of influence incidents (Yukl & Falbe, 1990; Yukl, Falbe, & Youn, 1993; Yukl & Tracey, 1992). The results are summarized in Table 6-10. Other studies that examined directional differences in the use of various influence tactics found moderately consistent results, and the few discrepancies may reflect differences in how the tactics were operationally defined and measured (Gravenhorst & Boonstra, 1998; Erez et al., 1986; Kipnis et al., 1980; Savard & Rogers, 1992; Xin & Tsui, 1996).

The research on directional differences in tactic selection is complicated by the complex interrelationships among situational determinants of agent behavior, such as the authority relationship between the agent and target, their relative power bases, and the agent's influence objectives. The objective of an agent's influence attempt (e.g., assign a task, make changes, get resources or approvals) may differ considerably depending on whether the target is a subordinate, peer, or superior (Erez, Rim, & Keider, 1986; Kipnis, Schmidt, & Wilkinson, 1980; Yukl & Falbe, 1990). The confounding of influence objectives with direction of influence makes it difficult to interpret results from research on these situational determinants of an agent's choice of tactics (Ansari & Kapoor, 1987; Kipnis et al., 1980; Erez et al., 1986; Schmidt & Kipnis, 1984; Yukl, Guinan, & Sottolano, 1995).

TABLE 6-10   Summary of Findings for Proactive Influence Tactics

Influence Tactic	Directional Use of Tactic	Sequencing Results	Used Alone or in Combination	General Effectiveness
Rational Persuasion	Widely used in all directions	Used more for initial request	Used frequently both ways	High
Inspirational Appeal	More down than up or lateral	No difference	Used most with other tactics	High
Consultation	More down and lateral than up	No difference	Used most with other tactics	High
Collaboration	More down and lateral than up	Not studied	Used most with other tactics	High
Apprising	More down than lateral or up	Not studied	Used most with other tactics	Moderate
Ingratiation	More down and lateral than up	Used more for initial request	Used most with other tactics	Moderate
Exchange	More down and lateral than up	Used most for immed. follow-up	Used both ways equally often	Moderate
Personal Appeal	More lateral than down or up	Used more for initial request	Used both ways equally often	Moderate
Coalition Tactic	More lateral and up than down	Used most for delayed follow-up	Used both ways equally often	Low to moderate
Legitimating Tactic	More down and lateral than up	Used most for immed. follow-up	Used most with other tactics	Low
Pressure	More down than lateral or up	Used most for delayed follow-up	Used both ways equally often	Low

Sequencing of Tactics in an Influence Attempt

Influence attempts often involve a series of separate influence episodes that occur over a period of days or weeks. Some tactics are used more in initial influence attempts, whereas other tactics are used more in follow-up influence attempts. The model of tactic selection described earlier can be used to explain sequencing differences in the use of different influence tactics. In general, it is reasonable to assume that a manager will initially select tactics that are likely to accomplish an objective with the least effort and cost. Support for this proposition was found in a study of influence incidents described from the perspective of either the agent or the target (Yukl, Falbe, & Youn, 1993), and the results found in this study are summarized in Table 6-10. Other studies on sequencing differences found mostly consistent results (e.g., Savard & Rogers, 1992).

Most initial influence attempts involve either a simple request or a relatively weak form of rational persuasion. These tactics are easy to use and entail little in the way of agent costs. However, if some target resistance is anticipated, then the agent is likely to use a stronger form of rational persuasion, and soft tactics such as personal appeals, ingratiation, consultation, collaboration, and inspirational appeals. In the face of continued resistance by a target, the agent will either escalate to harder tactics or abandon the effort if the request does not justify the risks entailed by escalation. Pressure, exchange, and coalitions are likely to be saved for follow-up influence attempts, because they involve the greatest costs and risks.

Effectiveness of Individual Tactics

Yukl and Tracey (1992) proposed a model to predict the outcomes of using different influence tactics. The effectiveness of an influence tactic used by a particular agent in a particular context appears to depend on several factors: (1) amount of intrinsic resistance by the target due to the nature of the request, (2) potential of the tactic to influence target attitudes about the desirability of the requested action, (3) agent possession of an appropriate power base for use of the tactic in that context, (4) agent skill in using the tactic, and (5) prevailing social norms and role expectations about use of the tactic in that context. A tactic is more likely to be successful if the target perceives it to be a socially acceptable form of influence behavior, if the agent has sufficient position and personal power to use the tactic, if the tactic has the capability to affect target attitudes about the desirability of the request, if it is used in a skillful way, and if it is used for a request that is legitimate and consistent with target values and needs.

The relative effectiveness of the proactive influence tactics has been examined in field studies with questionnaires (e.g., Barry & Bateman, 1992; Kipnis & Schmidt, 1988; Yukl & Tracey, 1992), in incident studies (e.g., Falbe & Yukl, 1992; Schilit & Locke, 1982; Yukl, Kim, & Falbe, 1996), in laboratory experiments (e.g., Barry & Shapiro, 1992; Yukl, Kim, & Chavez, 1999), and in scenario studies (e.g., Yukl et al., 2003; Fu & Yukl, 2000). The limited number of studies, the use of different research methods, and the choice of different tactics to assess make it difficult to integrate the findings from this research. Nevertheless, some tentative conclusions can be drawn about the effectiveness of each influence tactic (see also Table 6-10).

The most effective tactics for influencing target commitment to carry out a request or support a proposal (sometimes called core tactics) are rational persuasion, consultation, collaboration, and inspirational appeals. How a tactic is actually used is one determinant of its effectiveness. For example, a strong form of rational persuasion (e.g., a detailed proposal, elaborate documentation) is much more effective than a weak form of rational persuasion (e.g., a brief explanation, an assertion without supporting evidence).

Ingratiation, exchange, and apprising are moderately effective for influencing subordinates and peers, but these tactics are difficult to use for proactive influence attempts with superiors. Agents have little to exchange in an upward direction, because most rewards and resources are controlled by the superior rather than by subordinates. Successful use of apprising requires unique knowledge about the likely personal benefits associated with an activity or change, and a subordinate is much less likely than a superior to be a credible source of such knowledge. Ingratiation is likely to be viewed as manipulative when used as part of a proactive influence attempt with a superior. In general, it is more effective to use ingratiation as part of a long-term strategy for building cooperative relations than as a proactive influence tactic.

Personal appeals can be useful for influencing a target person with whom the agent has a friendly relationship. However, this tactic is only relevant for certain types of requests (e.g., get assistance, get a personal favor, change a scheduled meeting or deadline), and it is likely to result in target compliance rather than commitment.

Pressure and legitimating tactics are not likely to result in target commitment, but these tactics can be useful for eliciting compliance. As noted earlier, compliance is sometimes all that is needed to accomplish the objective of an influence attempt.

A coalition can be effective for influencing someone to support a change or innovation, especially if the coalition partners use direct tactics such as rational persuasion and inspirational appeals. However, use of a coalition is not likely to be effective for influencing someone to carry out an assignment or improve performance, especially when viewed as an attempt to gang up on the target person.

Overall, the results are consistent with the proposition that each tactic can be useful in an appropriate situation. Some tactics tend to be more effective than others, but the best tactics do not always result in task commitment and the worst tactics do not always result in resistance. The outcome of any particular influence attempt is affected strongly by other factors in addition to the type of influence tactics used by the agent (e.g., the power and authority of the agent, the type of influence objective, the perceived importance of the request, the relationship between agent and target, cultural values and norms about the use of the tactics). Any tactic can result in resistance if it is not used in a skillful manner, or if it is used for a request that is improper or unethical.

Effectiveness of Tactic Combinations

As noted earlier, different tactics can be used together in the same influence attempt. Only a few studies have examined use of tactic combinations, and some of the research was done with abstract metacategories (e.g., soft vs. hard tactics) rather than the specific tactics (Barry & Shapiro, 1992; Case, Dosier, Murkinson, & Keys, 1988; Emans, Klaver, Munduate, & Van de Vliert, 1999; Falbe & Yukl, 1992). Nevertheless, some tentative conclusions can be drawn from the available research.

Whether a combination of two or more tactics is better than a single tactic depends on what tactics are combined. The effectiveness of a combination seems to depend in part on the potency of the individual tactics and how compatible they are with each other. Compatible tactics are easy to use together, and they enhance each other's effectiveness.

Rational persuasion is a very flexible tactic that is usually compatible with any of the other tactics. Some other tactics are clearly incompatible. For example, pressure tactics are likely to be incompatible with personal appeals or ingratiation. Knowing how to successfully combine different influence tactics appears to require considerable insight and skill.

Tactics for Resisting Influence Attempts

In proactive influence attempts the agent initiates the interaction, but effective leaders must also be able to respond in appropriate ways to an unwanted influence attempt initiated by someone else. The response involves reactive tactics rather than proactive tactics. The target person tries to avoid doing what the agent requests, or to influence the agent to modify the request so that it is more acceptable. Only a few studies have investigated how people resist influence attempts, but initial findings suggest that most of the tactics used for proactive influence attempts can also be used for resistance (O'Hair, Cody, & O'Hair, 1991; Tepper, Nehring, Nelson, & Taylor, 1997; Yukl, Fu, & McDonald, 2003). For example, when used as a resistance tactic, rational persuasion may involve explaining why the agent's proposed plan is unlikely to be successful. Collaboration may involve an offer to help accomplish the agent's objective in a different way. Legitimating may involve explaining how the agent's request is inconsistent with company rules or a formal contract.

Limitations of Research on Proactive Influence Tactics

The research on influence tactics provides some useful insights about the way managers influence people, but many questions remain unanswered. Many researchers continue to use the taxonomy of influence tactics based on the research by Kipnis and colleagues (1980), which includes only one of the four most effective tactics identified by Yukl and his colleagues. Some researchers use only broadly defined metacategories (e.g., hard vs. soft tactics) and fail to identify important differences among the specific tactics included in these metacategories. Most researchers treat each influence attempt as an isolated episode, rather than as part of a sequence of reciprocal influence processes that occur in an evolving relationship between the parties. Little effort has been made to integrate the research on proactive influence tactics with the extensive literature on other types of behavior managers use to influence people at work, such as clarifying objectives and standards, and modeling proper behavior (see Chapter 3). The influence tactics are often used together with these other forms of leader behavior and must be consistent with them. Finally, it is important to remember that any type of influence tactic can be used in a way that is deceptive and manipulative. The use of power and influence in unethical ways by leaders and the consequences of such behavior for the organization are discussed in Chapters 9 and 14.

Summary

Power is the capacity to influence the attitudes and behavior of people in the desired direction. Authority is the right to influence others in specified ways, and it is an important basis for influence in formal organizations. Potential influence derived from a manager's position in the organization is called position power, and it includes legitimate power, reward power, coercive power, information power, and ecological power.

Potential influence derived from the characteristics of the person who occupies a leadership position is called personal power, and it includes expert and referent power.

Social exchange theory describes the process by which individual leaders gain and lose power over time. Greater status and power is accorded to someone who demonstrates loyalty to the group and competence in solving task problems and making task decisions. Innovative proposals are a source of increased status and expert power when successful, but they result in lower status and expert power if failure occurs and it is attributed to poor judgment, irresponsibility, or pursuit of self-interest.

Research on the use of different forms of power by leaders suggests that effective leaders rely more on personal power than on position power. Nevertheless, position power is still important, and it interacts in complex ways with personal power to determine a leader's influence on subordinates. As Kotter (1982) suggested, effective leaders probably use a mix of different types of power.

The amount of position power necessary for leader effectiveness depends on the nature of the organization, task, and subordinates. A leader with extensive reward and coercive power is tempted to rely on them excessively, instead of using referent and expert power. This path leads to resentment and rebellion. On the other hand, a leader lacking sufficient position power to reward competent subordinates, make necessary changes, and punish chronic troublemakers will find it difficult to develop a high-performing group or organization.

The success of a manager depends greatly on the manner in which power is exercised. Effective leaders are likely to use power in a subtle, careful fashion that minimizes status differentials and avoids threats to the target person's self-esteem. In contrast, leaders who exercise power in an arrogant, manipulative, domineering manner are likely to engender resentment and resistance.

Power and influence behavior can be regarded as separate constructs, even though they are interrelated in complex ways. Three general types of influence tactics that differ in terms of their purpose include impression management tactics, political tactics, and proactive tactics. The most effective proactive tactics are rational persuasion, consultation, collaboration, and inspirational appeals. What tactics are used depends on the situation, and the choice of tactics will vary somewhat depending on whether the target person is a subordinate, peer, or superior. Any tactic can fail if it is not used in a skillful, ethical way, or it is inappropriate for the influence objective and situation.

Review and Discussion Questions

1. What sources of power stem primarily from personal attributes, and what sources of power stem primarily from the position?
2. What types of power are related most strongly to leadership effectiveness?
3. Explain how instrumental compliance, identification, and internalization differ. Can the three influence processes occur at the same time?
4. Describe how leaders gain or lose power.
5. How much position and personal power do leaders need to be effective?
6. What uses of power would be considered unethical?
7. How is power related to influence behavior?
8. Briefly define each type of influence tactic described in this chapter.
9. How does the use of influence tactics differ for downward, lateral, and upward influence attempts?

10. What tactics are used more initially, and which ones are used more after an initial influence attempt has met resistance?
11. Which influence tactics are most likely to result in commitment by the target person?

Key Terms

- agent
- apprising
- coalition
- coercive power
- collaboration
- commitment
- compliance
- consultation
- ecological power
- exchange tactics
- expert power

- information power
- ingratiation
- inspirational appeals
- instrumental compliance
- internalization
- legitimate power
- legitimating tactic
- personal appeal
- personal power
- position power
- pressure tactics

- proactive influence tactic
- rational persuasion
- referent power
- resistance
- reward power
- role modeling
- scope of authority
- simple request
- social exchange theory
- strategic contingencies theory
- target person

CASES

Restview Hospital

Mary Carter was the accounting manager at Restview Hospital, a large residential health care facility. The facility administrator, Jack Morelli, explained that he wanted to modernize Restview's system of accounts billing. He asked Mary to investigate available software packages that would be compatible with their computer system. Jack explained that he and the Restview board of directors would like to make a decision about this matter at the board meeting next month.

A week later, Jack asked Mary about her progress, and she reported that she had identified two vendors with appropriate software packages. Jack asked why her list of potential vendors did not include Standard Software Systems, the vendor from which they purchased the software currently used to process Restview's payroll. Standard had just recently developed a software package for accounts billing as a new addition to their product line, but few hospitals were using it. The preliminary information gathered by Mary suggested that Standard's software package was less appropriate for Restview than the packages offered by the other vendors. However, Mary knew that the president of Standard Software was a personal friend of Jack, and she agreed to include Standard among the vendors selected for further consideration.

During the next two weeks, sales representatives from each vendor were invited to make a presentation at Restview to demonstrate and explain their product. Mary had planned to invite the board members to these presentations, but Jack said they were too busy to attend. When the presentations were held, Mary and her office staff asked many questions, but Jack looked bored and said very little. Mary also visited some other hospitals that were already using each type of software package to get firsthand opinions about how well they worked and the difficulties experienced in installing them.

During the course of her investigation, she learned that Standard's new software package was less flexible and less user-friendly than the others. All three software packages were about the same price, but the software package from Reliable Computer was clearly the best one for Restview's needs. She prepared a short report to Jack detailing the advantages and disadvantages of each product and making her recommendation.

The next day Mary met with Jack to give him the written report and summarize her findings in person. She explained the reasons for her recommendation to purchase the software package from Reliable Computers, and she reviewed the evidence supporting it. Mary also offered to present her findings to the board of directors at their next meeting, but Jack said he could handle it himself. The board meeting was held the following week, and afterward Jack informed Mary that they decided to go with the software package from Standard. He explained that the board wanted to reward Standard for excellent customer service last year when installing their payroll software at Restview. Two years later, after thousands of dollars of unnecessary expense, the accounts billing software was still not operating smoothly for Restview. ■

SOURCE: Copyright © 1992 by Gary Yukl.

QUESTIONS

1. How would you explain the board's decision to purchase the software package from Standard?

2. How much power relative to this decision did Mary, Jack, and the president of Standard Software possess, and what type of power was it?

3. What could Mary have done to gain more influence over the decision?

Sporting Goods Store

Bill Thompson is the new manager of a retail sporting goods store in Vermont that is part of a national chain. Bill, who is 25 years old, has been working for the company for four years. Before his promotion he was the assistant manager for two years at a company store in Delaware. Last week he was briefly introduced to the employees by his boss, the regional manager.

The profit performance of this store is below average for its location and Bill is looking forward to the challenge of improving profits. When he was an assistant manager, he was given mostly minor administrative duties and paperwork, so this assignment will be his first opportunity to show he can be an effective manager. The base salaries of the 20 employees who work in Bill's store are set by the company, but appraisal ratings by the store manager influence the size of an employee's annual merit raise. These recommendations must be justified to the regional manager, especially if they are not consistent with individual and department sales. Bill can suspend or fire employees with the approval of his boss, but in practice it is difficult to do so unless the recommendation is supported by a strong case.

The store layout and most prices are set by the headquarters office. However, store performance can be affected to a limited extent by the store manager. One way is to keep the cost of employees low by making sure they are working efficiently and not taking excessive sick days. Another way is to ensure that employees are providing a high level of customer service so that customers will return to make other purchases rather than going to a different store next time. Customer service depends on knowing the products well, being polite, providing prompt service, and making sure that inventories of popular goods are maintained so that customers can find what they want. Pay is low for this type of retail selling job, turnover is high, and it takes a few months for a new employee to learn the merchandise well enough to be helpful to customers. Thus, it is also desirable to keep competent employees satisfied enough to stay with the company.

Although it is only his first week on the job, Bill believes that he has already discovered some of the problems at this store. Among the various departments in the store, the ski department has the highest potential profits during the winter, because skiing and snowboarding are popular winter sports in Vermont. At the current time the department's sales are about average for company stores in the Northeast region, with potential for considerable improvement. On several occasions Bill noticed a line of customers waiting to be served in the ski department, and he overheard some of them grumbling about how long it takes to get served. One customer said he was leaving to go to another store that didn't make him "wait all day to have the privilege of spending hundreds of dollars on ski equipment." Bill observed that Sally Jorgenson, the department manager, spends a lot of time socializing with her salespeople and with customers, including friends who drop in to visit and talk about ski conditions, resorts, fashions, equipment, racing, and so forth. Bill, who doesn't ski, cannot understand what they find so interesting to talk about. He wonders why anybody in their right mind would want to spend a small fortune and risk permanent injury to hurtle down a mountain in blizzard conditions, and then stand in long lines and ride up a freezing chairlift just to do it all over again! ∎

SOURCE: Copyright © 1987 By Gary Yukl.

QUESTIONS

1. How much of each type of power does Bill have at this time?

2. What influence tactics could be used in this situation to influence Sally? Explain what you would actually say to Sally in the process of using each tactic.

3. What should Bill do to improve store performance?

7

MANAGERIAL TRAITS AND SKILLS

Learning Objectives

After studying this chapter you should be able to:

- Understand how conceptions about the importance of traits have changed over the past 70 years.

- Understand the types of research methods that have been used to study leadership traits and skills.

- Understand what traits and skills are most relevant for effective leadership.

- Understand how traits and skills are related to leadership behavior.

- Understand how the relevance of a trait or skill depends on the situation, type of organization, and national culture.

- Understand the traits and skills that cause some people to derail in their managerial careers.

- Understand the limitations of the trait approach.

One of the earliest approaches to studying leadership was the trait approach, which assumed that some traits and skills can predict whether a person will attain positions of leadership and be effective in these positions. This chapter reviews research on the personal attributes of successful leaders. The emphasis is on traits and skills that contribute to managerial effectiveness and advancement, rather than on traits that predict who will emerge as a leader in an informal group.

Nature of Traits and Skills

The term *trait* refers to a variety of individual attributes, including aspects of personality, temperament, needs, motives, and values. Personality traits are relatively stable dispositions to behave in a particular way. Examples include self-confidence, extroversion, emotional maturity, and energy level.

A need or motive is a desire for particular types of stimuli or experiences. Psychologists usually differentiate between physiological needs (e.g., hunger, thirst) and social motives such as achievement, esteem, affiliation, power, and independence. Needs and motives are important because they influence attention to information and events, and they guide, energize, and sustain behavior.

Values are internalized attitudes about what is right and wrong, ethical and unethical, moral and immoral. Examples include fairness, justice, honesty, freedom, equality, humanitarianism, loyalty, patriotism, progress, self-fulfillment, excellence, pragmatism, courtesy, politeness, and cooperation. Values are important because they influence a person's preferences, perception of problems, and choice of behavior.

Considerable evidence shows that traits are jointly determined by learning and by an inherited capacity to gain satisfaction from particular types of stimuli or experiences (Bouchard et al., 1990). Some traits (e.g., values, social needs) are probably more influenced by learning than others (temperament, physiological needs).

The term *skill* refers to the ability to do something in an effective manner. Like traits, skills are determined jointly by learning and heredity. Skills may be defined at different levels of abstraction, ranging from general, broadly defined abilities (e.g., intelligence, interpersonal skills) to narrower, more specific abilities (verbal reasoning, persuasive ability). Of the many different taxonomies of skills, a widely accepted approach for classifying managerial skills uses the three broadly defined skill categories shown in Table 7-1. Similar versions of this taxonomy were proposed by Katz (1955) and Mann (1965). It is evident that the technical skills are primarily concerned with things, the interpersonal skills (or social skills) are primarily concerned with people, and the conceptual skills (or cognitive skills) are primarily concerned with ideas and concepts.

Some writers differentiate a fourth category of skills (called administrative skills) that are defined in terms of the ability to perform a particular type of managerial function or behavior (e.g., planning, negotiating, coaching). Administrative skills usually involve a combination of technical, cognitive, and interpersonal skills. The line between skills and behaviors becomes blurred when skills are defined in terms of ability to perform

---

TABLE 7-1 Three-Factor Taxonomy of Broadly Defined Skills

Technical Skills: Knowledge about methods, processes, procedures, and techniques for conducting a specialized activity, and the ability to use tools and equipment relevant to that activity.

Interpersonal Skills: Knowledge about human behavior and interpersonal processes, ability to understand the feelings, attitudes, and motives of others from what they say and do (empathy, social sensitivity), ability to communicate clearly and effectively (speech fluency, persuasiveness), and ability to establish effective and cooperative relationships (tact, diplomacy, listening skill, knowledge about acceptable social behavior).

Conceptual Skills: General analytical ability, logical thinking, proficiency in concept formation and conceptualization of complex and ambiguous relationships, creativity in idea generation and problem solving, ability to analyze events and perceive trends, anticipate changes, and recognize opportunities and potential problems (inductive and deductive reasoning).

managerial functions. There seems to be little difference between the two constructs when they are both measured at a low level of abstraction with items containing examples of effective behavior (Hunt, 1991). Thus, much of the research on administrative skills is discussed in relation to specific managerial behaviors in other chapters.

Research on Leader Traits and Skills

The relationship of traits to managerial success has been investigated in many ways. Some studies look for traits that predict emergence as an informal leader in groups, some studies look for traits that predict advancement to higher levels of management, and other studies look for traits related to effective performance by a manager in the current job. It is important to remember that some traits may be relevant for one criterion but not the other. For example, a manager who is highly ambitious and skilled at impression management may advance faster than other managers who have greater competence in doing the current job but are not as ambitious or adept at selling themselves. Moreover, the traits and skills required for effective performance in the current management position are not necessarily the same as those needed at a higher level of management. The most useful studies attempt to explain why a person is effective in a particular managerial position, or why the person is promoted to a higher position. Several different research programs will be described briefly.

Stogdill Reviews of the Early Research

The early leadership researchers were confident that the traits essential for leadership effectiveness could be identified by empirical research comparing leaders with nonleaders, or comparing effective leaders to ineffective leaders. The kinds of traits studied most often in the early research included physical characteristics (e.g., height, appearance), aspects of personality (e.g., self-esteem, dominance, emotional stability), and aptitudes (e.g., general intelligence, verbal fluency, creativity). Many of the studies compared leaders to nonleaders or examined the attributes of emergent leaders in newly formed groups.

Stogdill (1948) reviewed 124 trait studies conducted from 1904 to 1948 and found that the pattern of results was consistent with the conception of a leader as someone who acquires status by showing the ability to help the group in attaining its goals. Relevant traits included intelligence, alertness to the needs of others, understanding of the task, initiative and persistence in dealing with problems, self-confidence, and desire to accept responsibility and occupy a position of dominance and control. The review failed to support the basic premise of the trait approach that a person must possess a particular set of traits to become a successful leader. The importance of each trait depended on the situation, and the research did not identify any traits that were necessary or sufficient to ensure leadership success in all situations. Thus, Stogdill (1948, p. 64) concluded:

> A person does not become a leader by virtue of the possession of some combination of traits . . . the pattern of personal characteristics of the leader must bear some relevant relationship to the characteristics, activities, and goals of the followers.

TABLE 7-2 Findings in Early Research on Leader Traits and Skills	
Traits	*Skills*
Adaptable to situations	Clever (intelligent)
Alert to social environment	Conceptually skilled
Ambitious, achievement oriented	Creative
Assertive	Diplomatic and tactful
Cooperative	Fluent in speaking
Decisive	Knowledgeable about the work
Dependable	Organized (administrative ability)
Dominant (power motivation)	Persuasive
Energetic (high activity level)	Socially skilled
Persistent	
Self-confident	
Tolerant of stress	
Willing to assume responsibility	

Source: Based on R. M. Stogdill, *Handbook of Leadership: A Survey of the Literature* (New York: Free Press, 1974).

In 1974, Stogdill reviewed 163 trait studies conducted from 1949 to 1970. This body of research included more managerial selection studies, more traits and skills likely to be relevant for formal leaders, and a greater variety of measurement techniques. Many of the same traits were again related to leader effectiveness, but some additional traits and skills were found to be relevant as well (see Table 7-2). Even though the results were stronger in this second review, Stogdill (1974) made it clear that there was still no evidence of universal leadership traits. Possession of some traits and skills increases the likelihood that a leader will be effective, but they do not guarantee effectiveness. A leader with certain traits could be effective in one situation but ineffective in a different situation. Furthermore, two leaders with a different pattern of traits could be successful in the same situation.

McClelland's Research on Managerial Motivation

An extensive program of research on managerial motivation was conducted by McClelland and his associates (McClelland, 1965, 1985). In most of the research, need strength was measured with a projective technique called the Thematic Apperception Test (TAT). The test consists of a series of pictures of people in ambiguous situations. Anyone who takes the test is asked to make up a story about each picture, and the stories reveal the person's daydreams, fantasies, and aspirations. The stories are coded by the experimenter to obtain a measure of three underlying needs: power, achievement, and affiliation.

A person with a high need for achievement obtains satisfaction from experiencing success in accomplishing a difficult task, attaining a standard of excellence, developing a better way of doing something, or being the first person to accomplish a difficult feat. Such people prefer tasks in which success depends on their own effort and ability rather than on chance factors beyond their control, or on a group effort. They prefer a job in which they can exercise individual initiative in solving problems, and they desire frequent, concrete feedback about their performance.

A person with a strong need for affiliation is especially concerned about being liked and accepted and is very sensitive to cues indicating rejection or hostility from others. This type of person seeks social interaction with friends and enjoys working with other people in a friendly and cooperative team. In contrast, a person with a low need for affiliation tends to be a loner, avoids social activities, and feels uncomfortable when required to attend parties or receptions.

A person with a high need for power finds great satisfaction in exercising influence over the attitudes, emotions, and behavior of others. This type of person enjoys winning an argument, defeating an opponent, eliminating a rival or enemy, and directing the activities of a group. People with a strong power need usually seek out positions of authority (e.g., a manager, administrator, public official, police officer, lawyer, military officer) in which it is possible to exercise influence and direct the activities of others. In contrast, someone with a weak need for power is unlikely to be assertive and may sincerely believe that it is improper to tell others what to do.

McClelland and his colleagues found that people with a high need for power can be grouped into two subtypes depending on their score on another trait called activity inhibition, which is also obtained from coding TAT responses. Someone with a "socialized power orientation" has strong self-control and is motivated to satisfy the need for power in socially acceptable ways, such as influencing others to accomplish a worthy cause, or helping others to develop their skills and confidence. In contrast, someone with a "personalized power orientation" is motivated to satisfy the need for power in selfish ways by dominating others and using power to fulfill hedonistic desires. These two different power orientations are described in more detail later in the chapter.

A sizable number of studies investigated how needs are related to managerial effectiveness. In general, the results support the proposition that the optimal pattern of needs for managers in large organizations includes a strong socialized power orientation, a moderately high need for achievement, and a relatively low need for affiliation (Boyatzis, 1982; McClelland, 1975; McClelland & Boyatzis, 1982; McClelland & Burnham, 1976; Varga, 1975; Winter, 1973). Need for achievement appears to be the most important motive for predicting success for owner-managers of small businesses (Collins, Moore & Unwalla, 1964; Hundal, 1971; McClelland, 1965; McClelland & Winter, 1969; Wainer & Rubin, 1969). Of course, success in growing a new business depends on ability as well as motivation. An entrepreneurial manager needs relevant technical expertise as an inventor, product designer, promoter, financier, or marketing specialist.

The results for motives relevant for advancement in large organizations are less clear, perhaps because the relationship depends more on the type of organization and managerial position. In one study by McClelland and Boyatzis (1982), advancement of nontechnical managers to higher levels was predicted by need for power, but advancement through lower levels of management was predicted only by need for achievement. For technical managers, advancement was not predicted by either need, which is consistent with results found in an earlier study of navy officers by Winter (1979). Thus, advancement for technical managers may be more dependent on technical skills and verbal fluency than on motivation.

Miner's Research on Managerial Motivation

Miner (1965) formulated a theory of managerial role motivation to describe the type of motivational traits required for success in most management positions in large, hierarchical organizations. Managerial motivation was measured with a projective test called the Miner sentence completion scale. The test provides an overall score as well as separate scores on each of the six aspects of managerial motivation.

Miner's research includes many studies on the relationship between managerial motivation and advancement (Miner, 1978, 1985). In large bureaucratic organizations, significant correlations were found between a manager's overall score on managerial motivation and advancement to higher levels of management. The particular motivation subscales that correlated most consistently with advancement included desire to exercise power (similar to need for power), desire to compete with peers (similar to need for achievement), and a positive attitude toward authority figures. Desire to stand out from the group, perform routine administrative functions, and be actively assertive were not useful for predicting advancement.

Results from research on leaders in smaller, less bureaucratic organizations (e.g., educational administrators in small school districts) indicated that managerial motivation was not useful for predicting advancement (Miner, 1967, 1977). However, a later study found positive results even for small organizations (Berman & Miner, 1985). Top executives who had risen up through the ranks in large bureaucratic organizations had higher managerial motivation than top executives of smaller, family-owned companies, but both samples of executives had higher scores than a comparison group of managers at lower levels who were the same age. To summarize the results for Miner's research, managerial motivation predicted advancement in large organizations but the results were inconsistent for small organizations.

Critical Incident Research on Competencies

Boyatzis (1982) described a program of research conducted in a variety of different private and public sector organizations to discover competencies related to managerial effectiveness. The competencies included personality traits, motives, skills, knowledge, self-image, and some specific behaviors. The primary measure of competencies, the "behavioral event interview," was a version of the critical incident method described in Chapter 3. Effectiveness ratings were used to select samples of effective and less-effective managers at each level of management, and the managers were interviewed to collect critical incidents. Incidents were coded into competency categories, with traits and skills inferred from analysis of behavior in relation to the manager's intentions and the situation. The competencies related to managerial effectiveness included personality traits, motives, cognitive skills, and interpersonal skills.

Several personality traits differentiated between effective and ineffective managers. Effective managers had a strong efficiency orientation, which included high achievement motivation, high inner work standards, and a concern for task objectives. Effective managers also had a strong socialized power orientation, as evidenced by a high desire for power, concern for power symbols, assertive behavior, attempts to influence others, and concern about the reputation of the organization's products and services. Effective managers had high self-confidence, as evidenced by a belief in their own ideas and ability, and by behavior such as taking decisive action rather than hesitating or vacillating, and making proposals in a firm, unhesitating manner, with appropriate poise, bearing, and gestures. Finally, effective managers also demonstrated a strong belief in self-efficacy and internal locus of control, as evidenced by behavior such as initiating action (rather than waiting for things to happen), taking steps to circumvent obstacles, seeking information from a variety of sources, and accepting responsibility for success or failure.

Interpersonal skills also differentiated between effective and ineffective managers. Effective managers had strong oral presentation skills, including the ability to use symbolic, verbal, and nonverbal communication to make clear and convincing presentations to others. These managers also had interpersonal skills, including the ability to develop networks and coalitions, gain cooperation from others, resolve conflicts in a constructive manner, and use role modeling to influence others. Another type of interpersonal skill that was strong in effective managers was the ability to manage group processes and build member identification and team spirit, by behavior such as creating symbols of group identity, emphasizing common interests and need for collaboration, facilitating successful teamwork, and providing public recognition of member contributions.

Effective managers had strong conceptual skills. One conceptual skill that is sometimes called inductive reasoning includes the ability to identify patterns or relationships in information and events; the ability to convey the meaning by developing a concept, model, or theme, or by using appropriate metaphors and analogies; and the ability to develop creative solutions and new insights into problems. Another conceptual skill (sometimes called deductive reasoning) is the ability to use a concept or model to interpret events, analyze situations, distinguish between relevant and irrelevant information, and detect deviations from plans.

Longitudinal Research with Assessment Centers

Research on managerial assessment centers has yielded useful insights about traits related to managerial advancement in an organization. The term *assessment center* refers to a standardized set of procedures used to identify managerial potential. Although no two programs are exactly alike, they all utilize multiple methods of assessing traits and skills. Typical methods include interviews, projective tests, situational tests (e.g., in-basket, leaderless group discussion), written tests of personality and aptitude, a writing exercise (e.g., a short autobiographical essay) to evaluate written communication skills, and a speaking exercise to evaluate oral communication skills. The assessment process in the centers typically takes two to three days. An overall evaluation of each candidate's management potential is made by several staff members who interview the candidate, examine test scores and biographical information, observe candidate behavior in the situational exercises, and then meet to discuss their assessment and resolve any disagreements. The assessors attempt to integrate the information from these diverse sources into a coherent picture of the motives, skills, and behavioral tendencies of each candidate.

The most useful insights for leadership come from the longitudinal studies that examined the predictive power of each trait and skill for leadership advancement. A good example is the research conducted at American Telephone and Telegraph Company (AT&T) by a team of researchers (Bray, Campbell, & Grant, 1974; Howard & Bray, 1988). Years after an early group of candidates was assessed at AT&T, each candidate's progress in terms of advancement into middle management was related back to the assessment scores, which had been kept confidential so as not to affect promotion decisions. Prediction of advancement was computed after 8 years and after 20 years. The personal attributes that predicted advancement best after 20 years included desire for advancement, dominance (need for power), interpersonal skills (e.g., oral communication), cognitive skills (e.g., creativity, critical thinking), and administrative skills (e.g., organizing and planning). Some traits that predicted advancement in year 20 better when measured in year 8 were achievement orientation, self-confidence, energy level, and need for security (negative correlation).

An important discovery in the longitudinal research at AT&T was the effect of the job situation on the relevance of individual traits for managerial success. The prediction of success based on a candidate's assessed traits was more accurate if the person had a job situation favorable to individual development. A favorable situation existed when a person was encouraged to develop management skills, was given challenging assignments with increased responsibility, and had a boss who served as a role model by setting an example of how a successful, achievement-oriented manager should act. Thus, advancement was due to a combination of the relevant personal qualities and the opportunity for these qualities to be translated into competent managerial behavior.

CCL Research on Managers Who Derail

Researchers at the Center for Creative Leadership (CCL) have attempted to identify traits and behaviors associated with eventual success or failure of top executives. In the initial study (McCall & Lombardo, 1983), interviews with top executives and senior human resource managers were used to gather descriptions of 21 managers who advanced into middle or top management but subsequently failed to perform successfully. These derailed managers were dismissed or transferred, opted for early retirement, or simply plateaued without any chance of further advancement. The interviews also provided descriptions of 20 managers who made it to the top successfully. The two sets of descriptions were analyzed to identify similarities and differences between derailed and successful managers. In follow-up studies, executives and middle managers rated the extent to which various flaws are likely to derail a management career in the United States and Europe (Lombardo & McCauley, 1988; Van Velsor & Leslie, 1995).

The research did not reveal any foolproof formula for success, but it provided some important insights. Successful managers were similar in some respects to the derailed managers. Most of the managers were ambitious, they had strong technical skills, they had a string of prior successes as managers, and they were viewed as "fast risers" in their company. Every manager had both strengths and weaknesses. None of the successful executives had all of the strengths, and none of the derailed managers had all of the weaknesses. Sometimes the reason for derailing was obvious , but other times it appeared to be just a matter of bad luck involving events beyond a manager's control (e.g., unfavorable economic conditions or political battles). Sometimes the importance of a success factor seemed to depend in part on the organization culture. For example, derailment often involved weak interpersonal skills, but this factor was more important in some organizations than in others.

The researchers used a mix of traits, skills, and other competencies (e.g., ability to build and lead a team, ability to adapt to change) to describe their interpretation of the descriptive data they collected. The research results are summarized here by describing the specific traits and skills that seem to be especially relevant for predicting whether a manager advanced or derailed.

1. *Emotional stability.*   Managers who derailed were less able to handle pressure. They were more prone to moodiness, angry outbursts, and inconsistent behavior,

which undermined their interpersonal relationships with subordinates, peers, and superiors. In contrast, the successful managers were calm, confident, and predictable during crises.

2. *Defensiveness.*   Managers who derailed were more likely to be defensive about failure. They reacted by attempting to cover up mistakes or blame other people. The successful managers admitted mistakes, accepted responsibility, and then took action to fix the problem. Moreover, having dealt with the problem, they did not continue to dwell on it, but turned their attention to other things. In the more recent studies, lack of ability to learn and adapt to change was an especially important success factor, and it involves the lack of a learning orientation and defensiveness about failure.

3. *Integrity.*   The successful managers were more focused on the immediate task and the needs of subordinates than on competing with rivals or impressing superiors. In contrast, many of the derailed managers were too ambitious about advancing their career at the expense of others. These managers were more likely to betray a trust or break a promise. McCall and Lombardo (1983b, p. 28) gave the following example: "One executive didn't implement a decision as promised, causing conflicts between marketing and production that reverberated down through four levels of frustrated subordinates."

4. *Interpersonal skills.*   Managers who derailed were usually weaker in interpersonal skills. The most common reason for derailment was insensitivity, which was reflected in abrasive or intimidating behavior toward others. This flaw had been tolerated when the person was a lower-level manager, especially when the manager had outstanding technical skills, but at higher levels technical skills could not compensate for being insensitive. Some of the derailed managers could be charming when they wanted to, but over time it became evident that beneath the facade of charm and concern for others, the person was really selfish, inconsiderate, and manipulative. In contrast, the successful managers were more sensitive, tactful, and considerate. They were able to understand and get along with all types of people, and they developed a larger network of cooperative relationships. When they disagreed with someone they were direct but diplomatic, whereas the derailed managers were more likely to be outspoken and offensive. These interpersonal skills are especially relevant for building and leading a cooperative team, which was a more important success factor in the recent studies.

5. *Technical and cognitive skills.*   For most of the managers who derailed, their technical brilliance was a source of successful problem solving and technical achievement at lower levels of management, where their expertise was usually greater than that of subordinates. However, at higher levels this strength could become a weakness if it led to overconfidence and arrogance, causing the person to reject sound advice, to offend others by acting superior, and to micromanage subordinates who had more expertise. Some managers were unable to shift from a focus on technical problems to the more strategic perspective needed at a higher level of management. Some derailed managers had technical expertise only in a narrow functional area, and they advanced too quickly to learn skills needed to perform the higher-level job effectively. Successful managers usually had experience in a variety of different types of situations where they acquired a broader perspective and expertise in dealing with different types of problems.

Managerial Traits and Effectiveness

Over a period of several decades researchers examined a variety of different personality traits related to managerial effectiveness and advancement. The choice of traits and the labels used for them have varied from study to study, but the results have been fairly consistent across different research methods. This section summarizes and integrates the findings regarding the most relevant aspects of personality for effective leadership by managers and administrators in large organizations (see also Table 7-3). Whenever possible, the relevance of traits and skills is explained by linking them back to behaviors and influence processes described in earlier chapters.

Energy Level and Stress Tolerance

The trait research finds that energy level, physical stamina, and stress tolerance are associated with managerial effectiveness (Bass, 1990; Howard & Bray, 1988). High energy level and stress tolerance help managers cope with the hectic pace, long hours, and unrelenting demands of most managerial jobs. Physical vitality and emotional resilience make it easier to cope with stressful interpersonal situations, such as a punitive boss, a troubled subordinate, an uncooperative peer, or a hostile client. Managerial jobs often have a high level of stress due to the pressure to make important decisions without adequate information and the need to resolve role conflicts and satisfy incompatible demands made by different parties. Effective problem solving requires an ability to remain calm and stay focused on a problem rather than panicking, denying the problem exists, or attempting to shift responsibility to someone else. Tolerance of stress is especially important for managers confronted with difficult situations where the reputation and career of the manager, or the lives and jobs of subordinates, may hang in the balance. In addition to making better decisions, a leader with high stress tolerance and composure is more likely to stay calm and provide confident, decisive direction to subordinates in a crisis.

Self-Confidence

The term *self-confidence* is defined in a general way to include several related concepts such as self-esteem and self-efficacy. Most studies on leader self-confidence or self-efficacy found that it is related positively to effectiveness and advancement (see Bass, 1990). Self-confidence differentiated between effective and ineffective managers in the study of critical incidents by Boyatzis (1982), and self-confidence predicted subsequent

---

TABLE 7-3 Specific Traits Related to Leadership Effectiveness

- High energy level and stress tolerance
- Self-confidence
- Internal locus of control orientation
- Emotional stability and maturity
- Personal integrity
- Socialized power motivation
- Moderately high achievement orientation
- Low need for affiliation

---

advancement to higher levels of management in the assessment center research at AT&T (Howard & Bray, 1988). Other research finds that self-confidence is essential for charismatic leadership (see Chapter 9).

The relationship of self-confidence to leadership effectiveness can be understood by examining how this trait affects a leader's behavior. Without strong self-confidence, a leader is less likely to make influence attempts, and any influence attempts made are less likely to be successful. Leaders with high self-confidence are more likely to attempt difficult tasks and to set challenging objectives for themselves. Leaders with high self-efficacy take more initiative to solve problems and introduce desirable changes (Paglis & Green, 2002). Leaders who have high expectations for themselves are likely to have high expectations for subordinates as well (Kouzes & Posner, 1987). These leaders are more persistent in pursuit of difficult objectives, despite initial problems and setbacks. Their optimism and persistence in efforts to accomplish a task or mission are likely to increase commitment by subordinates, peers, and superiors to support the effort. It is especially important to act confident and be decisive in a crisis, where success often depends on the perception by subordinates that the leader has the knowledge and courage necessary to deal with the crisis effectively. Finally, self-confidence is related to an action-oriented approach for dealing with problems. Leaders with low self-confidence are more likely to put off dealing with difficult problems or to shift responsibility to someone else (Kipnis & Lane, 1962).

There are some clear advantages of having self-confidence, but if it becomes excessive some dysfunctional behaviors may occur . Excessive self-confidence may make a leader overly optimistic about the likely success of a risky venture, and it may result in rash decisions and denial of evidence that a plan is flawed. A manager with extremely high self-confidence is inclined to be arrogant, autocratic, and intolerant of dissenting viewpoints, especially if the manager is not emotionally mature. Because the manager is unresponsive to ideas and concerns expressed by others, the benefits of participative leadership are unlikely to be realized. Thus, in situations where the leader does not have much greater expertise than subordinates, a moderately high amount of self-confidence may be better than either extremely high self-confidence or low self-confidence. The arrogance and "know-it-all" attitude associated with excessive self-confidence has another negative side effect. An arrogant manager will have difficulty in developing cooperative relationships with people who are not dependent on the manager's specialized expertise. Acting arrogant towards people who have more expertise than the manager may create enemies who are able to derail the manager's career.

Internal Locus of Control

Another trait that appears to be relevant to managerial effectiveness is called the locus of control orientation, which is measured with a personality scale developed by Rotter (1966). People with a strong internal locus of control orientation (called internals) believe that events in their lives are determined more by their own actions than by chance or uncontrollable forces. In contrast, people with a strong external control orientation (called externals) believe that events are determined mostly by chance or fate and they can do little to improve their lives.

Because internals believe that they can influence their own destiny, they take more responsibility for their own actions and for the performance of their organization. Internals have a more future-oriented perspective, and they are more likely to plan proactively how to accomplish objectives. They take more initiative than externals in discovering and solving problems. They are confident in their ability to influence people and are more likely to use persuasion rather than coercive or manipulative influence tactics (Goodstadt & Hjelle, 1973). They are more flexible, adaptive, and innovative in their response to a problem and in their management strategies (Miller, Kets de Vries, & Toulouse, 1982). When setbacks or failures occur, they are more likely to learn from them rather than just dismissing them as bad luck.

Research on the relationship of this trait to managerial effectiveness is still limited, but the results suggest that a strong internal locus of control orientation is positively associated with managerial effectiveness. For example, Miller and Toulouse (1986) conducted a study of chief executive officers in 97 firms and found that internals were more effective than externals in terms of objective criteria such as profitability and sales growth. The relationship was stronger for firms in dynamic environments where it is more important to have major product innovations. Howell and Avolio (1993) conducted a study of 76 executives in a large financial institution and found that internals had better business-unit performance than externals for the year following the measurement of personality.

Emotional Stability and Maturity

The term *emotional maturity* may be defined broadly to encompass several interrelated motives, traits, and values. A person who is emotionally mature is well adjusted and does not suffer from severe psychological disorders. Emotionally mature people have a more accurate awareness of their strengths and weaknesses, and they are oriented toward self-improvement instead of denying weaknesses and fantasizing success. People with high emotional maturity are less self-centered (they care about other people), they have more self-control (are less impulsive, more able to resist hedonistic temptations), they have more stable emotions (are not prone to extreme mood swings or outbursts of anger), and they are less defensive (are more receptive to criticism, more willing to learn from mistakes). It is likely that such people are also at a high level of cognitive moral development (see Chapter 14). As a result, leaders with high emotional maturity maintain more cooperative relationships with subordinates, peers, and superiors.

Most of the empirical research on traits shows that key components of emotional maturity are associated with managerial effectiveness and advancement (Bass, 1990). A study by McCauley and Lombardo (1990) with a measure called Benchmarks found that managers with good self-awareness and a desire to improve had higher advancement. Self-objectivity and general adjustment predicted advancement in the AT&T study by Howard and Bray (1988). Other research has found that effective executives have a good understanding of their own strengths and weaknesses, and they are oriented toward self-improvement rather than being defensive (Bennis & Nanus, 1985; Tichy & Devanna, 1986). The research on socialized and personalized power orientation provides evidence about the importance of emotional maturity for effective leadership.

Research on narcissism provides additional insights into the difficulties encountered by leaders who lack emotional maturity. Narcissism refers to a personality syndrome that involves an extreme need for esteem (e.g., prestige, status, attention, admiration, adulation), a strong need for power, weak self-control, and indifference about the needs and welfare of others. This personality syndrome can be measured with a self-report scale called the Narcissistic Personality Inventory (Raskin & Hall, 1981). Narcissism includes many aspects of the personalized power orientation (House & Howell, 1992).

Researchers with a background in clinical psychology and psychoanalysis have described the origins of narcissism and the behaviors associated with it (Kets de Vries & Miller,1984, 1985; Raskin, Novacek, & Hogan, 1991). People whose parents have been emotionally unresponsive and rejecting may come to believe that they cannot depend on anyone's love or loyalty. In an effort to cope with their inner loneliness and fear, these extreme narcissists become preoccupied with establishing their power, status, and control. They have fantasies of success and power. They have a grandiose, exaggerated sense of their own self-importance and unique talents. To support this self-deception, they seek continuous attention and admiration from others. Because they are so preoccupied with their own ego needs, narcissists have little empathy or concern for the feelings and needs of others. They exploit and manipulate others to indulge their desire for self-aggrandizement without feeling any remorse. They expect special favors from others without feeling any need for reciprocity. Narcissists tend to oversimplify human relationships and motives and see everything in extreme good and bad terms. Relationships are polarized between loyal supporters and enemies. Narcissists are very defensive, and any criticism by others is interpreted as a sign of rejection and disloyalty. Although sometimes capable of being charming and helpful, they have a tendency to be aggressive and cruel toward people who oppose them or stand in their way.

Narcissists in leadership positions have a number of characteristic flaws (Kets de Vries & Miller, 1984, 1985). They surround themselves with subordinates who are loyal and uncritical. They make decisions without gathering adequate information about the environment. In the belief that they alone are sufficiently informed and talented to decide what is best, objective advice is not sought or accepted from subordinates and peers. They tend to undertake ambitious, grandiose projects to glorify themselves, but in the absence of an adequate analysis of the situation, the projects are likely to be risky and unrealistic. When a project is not going well, they tend to ignore or reject negative information, thereby missing the opportunity to correct problems in time to avert a disaster. When failure is finally evident, the narcissistic leader refuses to admit any responsibility, but instead finds scapegoats to blame. Finally, because they exploit the organization to compensate for their own sense of inadequacy, extreme narcissists are unable to plan for an orderly succession of leadership. They see themselves as indispensable and cling to power, in contrast to emotionally mature executives who are able to retire gracefully when their job is done and it is time for new leadership.

Personal Integrity

Integrity means that a person's behavior is consistent with espoused values, and the person is honest, ethical, and trustworthy. Integrity is a primary determinant of interpersonal trust. Unless one is perceived to be trustworthy, it is difficult to retain the loyalty of followers or to obtain cooperation and support from peers and superiors. Moreover, a major determinant of expert and referent power is the perception by others that a person is trustworthy.

Several types of behaviors are related to integrity. One important indicator of integrity is the extent to which one is honest and truthful rather than deceptive. Leaders lose credibility when people discover that they have lied or made claims that are grossly distorted. Another indicator of integrity is keeping promises. People are reluctant to negotiate agreements with a leader who cannot be trusted to keep promises. A third indicator of integrity is the extent to which a leader fulfills the responsibility of service and loyalty to followers. The trust of followers will be lost if they discover the leader exploited or manipulated them in pursuit of self-interest. A fourth indicator of integrity is the extent to which a leader can be trusted not to indiscriminately repeat something said in the utmost confidence. People will not pass on important but sensitive information to a leader who cannot be trusted to keep a secret. A key determinant of perceived integrity is the extent to which a leader's behavior is consistent with values articulated repeatedly to followers. A leader who hopes to inspire others to support an ideology or vision must set an example in his or her own behavior. Finally, integrity also means taking responsibility for one's actions and decisions. Leaders appear weak and undependable when they make a decision or take a position on an issue, then try to deny responsibility later if the decision is unsuccessful or the position becomes controversial.

Integrity was mentioned as an important value by most of the 45 British chief executives in a study by Cox and Cooper (1989). The CCL study described earlier in this chapter found that lack of integrity was common among the managers whose career derailed, whereas managers who succeeded were regarded as having strong integrity. The successful managers were honest and dependable, as reflected in the following precept (McCall & Lombardo, 1983b, p. 30): "I will do exactly what I say I will do when I say I will do it. If I change my mind, I will tell you well in advance so you will not be harmed by my actions."

Power Motivation

Someone with a high need for power enjoys influencing people and events and is more likely to seek positions of authority. Most studies find a strong relationship between need for power and advancement to higher levels of management in large organizations (e.g., Howard & Bray, 1988; McClelland & Boyatzis, 1982; Stahl, 1983). People with a strong need for power seek positions of authority and power, and they are likely to be more attuned to the power politics of organizations.

A strong need for power is relevant to managerial role requirements involving the use of power and influence. Managers in large organizations must exercise power to influence subordinates, peers, and superiors. People who are low in need for power usually lack the desire and assertiveness necessary to organize and direct group activities, to negotiate favorable agreements, to lobby for necessary resources, to advocate and promote desirable changes, and to impose necessary discipline. A person who finds such behavior difficult and emotionally disturbing or who believes it is wrong to exercise power over others is unlikely to satisfy the role requirements of a managerial job (Miner, 1985).

A strong need for power is desirable, but a manager's effectiveness also depends on how this need finds expression. The empirical research indicates that a socialized power orientation is more likely to result in effective leadership than a personalized power orientation (Boyatzis, 1982; House, Spangler, & Woycke, 1991; McClelland & Boyatzis, 1982; McClelland & Burnham, 1976). Only a few studies have examined the behaviors associated with each power orientation, but the results suggest that personalized power managers differ from socialized power managers in ways that have significant consequences (McClelland, 1975, 1985).

Managers with a personalized power orientation use power to aggrandize themselves and satisfy their strong need for esteem and status. They have little inhibition or self-control, and they exercise power impulsively. According to McClelland and Burnham (1976, p. 103), "They are more rude to other people, they drink too much, they try to exploit others sexually, and they collect symbols of personal prestige such as fancy cars or big offices." Personalized power leaders seek to dominate subordinates by keeping them weak and dependent. Authority for making important decisions is centralized in the leader, information is restricted, and rewards and punishments are used to manipulate and control subordinates. The leader tries to play off different individuals or factions against each other to keep them weak. Assistance and advice to a subordinate is done in a way that demonstrates personal superiority and the inferiority and dependence of the subordinate. Sometimes personalized power leaders are able to inspire subordinate loyalty and team spirit, but adverse consequences are more likely to occur. When problems are encountered in the work, subordinates are reluctant to take any initiative in solving them. Instead of acting quickly to deal with a problem, they ignore it or wait for explicit directions from the leader. Any subordinate loyalty that may occur is to the leader rather than to the organization, and when the leader departs, there is likely to bedisorder and a breakdown in team spirit.

Managers with a socialized power orientation are more emotionally mature. They exercise power more for the benefit of others, are hesitant about using power in a manipulative manner, are less egoistic and defensive, accumulate fewer material possessions, have a longer-range view, and are more willing to take advice from people with relevant expertise. Their strong need for power is expressed by using influence to build up the organization and make it successful. Because of their orientation toward building organizational commitment, this kind of leader is more likely to use a participative, coaching style of managerial behavior and is less likely to be coercive and autocratic. Such leaders "help make their subordinates feel strong and responsible, bind them less with petty rules, help produce a clear organizational structure, and create pride in belonging to the unit" (McClelland, 1975, p. 302).

Achievement Orientation

Achievement orientation includes a set of related attitudes, values, and needs: need for achievement, desire to excel, drive to succeed, willingness to assume responsibility, and concern for task objectives. Many studies have been conducted on the relationship of achievement orientation to managerial advancement and effectiveness (see Bass, 1990). However, the results have not been consistent for different criteria (e.g., advancement, effectiveness) and for different types of managerial positions (e.g., entrepreneurial managers, corporate general managers, technical managers).

The relationship of achievement motivation to managerial effectiveness is complex. Some studies find a positive relationship between achievement motivation and effectiveness (e.g., Stahl, 1983; Wainer & Rubin, 1969), but other studies find a negative relationship (House, Spangler, & Woyke, 1991) or no evidence of a strong, significant relationship (Miller & Toulouse, 1986). One possible explanation for these inconsistent findings is that the relationship of achievement motivation to managerial effectiveness is curvilinear rather than linear. In other words, managers with a moderately high amount of achievement motivation are more effective than managers with low achievement motivation, or managers with very high achievement motivation. If this explanation is correct, we would expect to find a negative correlation in studies of top-level leaders where all of the leaders probably have at least a moderately high need for achievement. An example is the study of United States presidents by House, Spangler, & Woycke, 1991.

Research on the behavioral correlates of achievement orientation is still limited, but some relationships appear likely. Compared to managers with a weak achievement orientation, managers with a strong achievement orientation are likely to have a strong concern for task objectives, they are more willing to assume responsibility for solving task-related problems, they are more likely to take the initiative in discovering these problems and acting decisively to solve them, and they prefer solutions that involve moderate levels of risk rather than solutions that are either very risky or very conservative. These managers are likely to engage in task behaviors such as setting challenging but realistic goals and deadlines, developing specific action plans, determining ways to overcome obstacles, organizing the work efficiently, and emphasizing performance when talking to others (Boyatzis, 1982). In contrast, a manager with a weak achievement orientation is not motivated to seek opportunities involving challenging objectives and moderate risks and is less willing to take the initiative to identify problems and to assume responsibility for solving them.

A strong achievement orientation may also result in behavior that undermines managerial effectiveness. If need for achievement is the dominant motive for a manager, it is likely that the manager's efforts will be directed toward his or her own individual achievement and advancement rather than toward the achievements of the team or work unit headed by the manager. The manager tries to accomplish everything alone, is reluctant to delegate, and fails to develop a strong sense of responsibility and task commitment among subordinates (McClelland & Burnham, 1976; Miller & Toulouse, 1986). It is especially difficult for this type of person to function effectively in a management team in which leadership responsibility is shared.

The way in which achievement orientation finds expression in a manager's behavior depends on the overall motive pattern of the manager. Achievement motivation enhances leadership effectiveness only if it is subordinated to a stronger need for socialized power, so that the manager's efforts are directed toward building a successful team. When combined with a personalized need for power, strong achievement motivation may be focused on career advancement at any cost. This type of manager will neglect task objectives and the development of subordinates in an effort to build a personal reputation as a fast-rising star. Task decisions will be guided by a desire to for short-term achievements, even though unit performance may suffer in the longer run. The manager is likely to take personal control over promising, highly visible projects, and will take most of the credit for their success. The manager may become so competitive that he or she refuses to cooperate with peers who are viewed as potential rivals. As found in the CCL study, the result is likely to be initial advancement but eventual derailment when a manager with overriding personal ambition and excessive competitiveness makes too many powerful enemies.

Additional insights are provided by research on the Type A personality, which appears to combine a strong achievement orientation with a strong need for control over events (Baron, 1989; Nahavandi, Mizzi, & Malekzadeh, 1992; Strube et al., 1984). Managers with this personality syndrome have high expectations for themselves and are competitive. They set high performance objectives, compare themselves with others, and want to come out ahead. Type A managers are also highly concerned about time; they feel rushed much of the time, try to do more than one thing at a time, and are impatient with delays. They prefer to maintain control over all aspects of their work, which makes them poor delegators and reluctant to work as part of a team (Miller, Lack, & Asroff, 1985). Finally, Type A managers tend to be more angry and inclined to express their hostility when unable to control events. They are demanding, intolerant of mistakes, and critical of people who are not as intensely dedicated. This behavior pattern makes it more difficult for them to maintain cooperative relationships.

Need for Affiliation

As noted earlier in this chapter, people with a strong need for affiliation receive great satisfaction from being liked and accepted by others, and they enjoy working with people who are friendly and cooperative. Most studies find a negative correlation between need for affiliation and managerial effectiveness. The ineffectiveness of managers with a high need for affiliation can be understood by examining the typical pattern of behavior for such managers. These managers are concerned primarily about interpersonal relationships rather than the task, and they are unwilling to allow the work to interfere with harmonious relationships (Litwin & Stringer, 1966; McClelland, 1975). These managers seek to avoid conflicts or smooth them over rather than confront genuine differences. They avoid making necessary but unpopular decisions. They dispense rewards in a way designed to gain approval, rather than rewarding effective performance. They show favoritism to personal friends in making assignments and allowing exceptions to rules. This pattern of behavior often leaves subordinates feeling "weak, irresponsible, and without a sense of what might happen next, of where they stand in relation to their manager, or even of what they ought to be doing" (McClelland & Burnham, 1976, p. 104).

It is clearly undesirable for a manager to have a strong need for affiliation, but a very low need for affiliation may also have undesirable consequences. A person with low need for affiliation tends to be a loner who does not like to socialize with others, except perhaps the immediate family or a few close friends. This type of person may lack the motivation to engage in the many social and public relations activities that are essential for a manager, including those involved in establishing effective interpersonal relationships with subordinates, superiors, and peers. As a result, this type of person may fail to develop effective interpersonal skills and may lack confidence in being able to influence others. Thus, it is likely that the optimal level of affiliation motivation is moderately low rather than either high or extremely low.

The Big Five Personality Traits

Describing leaders in terms of their individual profiles would be easier if there was an integrative conceptual framework with a small number of metaconstructs that encompass all of the relevant traits. The proliferation of personality traits identified over the past century has resulted in efforts to find a smaller number of broadly defined categories that would simplify the development of trait theories. One such effort that appears promising is referred to as the five-factor model of personality or the Big Five model (e.g., Digman, 1990; Hough, 1992). The five broadly defined personality traits in the taxonomy have somewhat different labels from one version to another. The traits include surgency (or extraversion), dependability (or conscientiousness), adjustment (or neuroticism), intellectance (or openness to experience), and agreeableness.

In recent years, leadership scholars have shown increasing interest in using this taxonomy to facilitate interpretation of results in the massive and confusing literature on leadership traits (e.g., Goodstein & Lanyon, 1999; Hogan, Curphy, & Hogan, 1994). Table 7-4 shows how the five broad trait categories correspond to many of the specific traits found relevant for leadership emergence, advancement, or effectiveness in the trait studies reviewed earlier in this chapter. Reviews and meta-analyses of studies on the five factors find that most of them are related to leader emergence or effectiveness (e.g., Judge, Bono, Ilies, & Gerhardt, 2002). However, results are not consistent across studies, which may reflect the use of different measures to represent the five factors, including surrogate measures that do not adequately represent a factor. Another reason for inconsistent results may be the use of different criterion variables (e.g., leadership emergence, advancement, or effectiveness; subjective or objective measures).

Not all scholars agree that the Big Five model of personality is better than taxonomies with more specific traits (cf., Block, 1995; Hough, 1992). If both relevant and irrelevant traits are included in a broadly defined factor, the accuracy of prediction will be lower. Moreover, even when the component traits are all relevant, they may not have the same relationship with different criteria of leadership effectiveness. More research is needed to determine whether the Big Five traits predict and explain leadership effectiveness better than the specific component traits. Such research should be based on a theory that clearly describes how specific leader traits are related to specific types of behavior that mediate the effects of the traits on leadership effectiveness.

TABLE 7-4 Correspondence of the Big Five Traits with Specific Traits

Big Five Personality Traits	*Specific Traits*
Surgency	Extroversion (outgoing) Energy/Activity level Need for power (assertive)
Conscientiousness	Dependability Personal integrity Need for achievement
Agreeableness	Cheerful and optimistic Nurturance (sympathetic, helpful) Need for affiliation
Adjustment	Emotional stability Self-esteem Self-control
Intellectance	Curious and inquisitive Open-minded Learning oriented

Source: Based on R. J. Hogan, G. J. Curphy, and J. Hogan, "What We Know About Personality: Leadership and Effectiveness," *American Psychologist*, 49 (1994), pp. 493–504.

Managerial Skills and Effectiveness

The early trait studies and other research described in this chapter identified a number of skills that are relevant to managerial effectiveness. The three broad skill categories defined earlier will be used to organize the findings about specific types of skills.

Technical Skills

Technical skills include knowledge about methods, processes, and equipment for conducting the specialized activities of the manager's organizational unit. Technical skills also include factual knowledge about the organization (rules, structure, management systems, employee characteristics), and knowledge about the organization's products and services (technical specifications, strengths, and limitations). This type of knowledge is acquired by a combination of formal education, training, and job experience. Acquisition of technical knowledge is facilitated by a good memory for details, and the ability to learn technical material quickly. Effective managers are able to obtain information and ideas from many sources and store it away in their memory for use when they need it.

Managers who supervise the work of others need extensive knowledge of the techniques and equipment used by subordinates to perform the work. Technical knowledge of products and processes is necessary to plan and organize work operations, to direct and train subordinates with specialized activities, and to monitor and evaluate their performance. Technical expertise is needed to deal with disruptions in the work due to equipment breakdowns, quality defects, accidents, insufficient materials, and coordination problems. Ample evidence indicates that technical skills are related to the effectiveness of civilian and military leaders, especially at lower levels of management (see Bass, 1990). The CCL study described earlier found that technical knowledge about products and work processes is related to effectiveness and advancement at lower levels of management, but it becomes relatively less important at higher levels of management (McCall & Lombardo, 1983a).

Technical knowledge is also relevant for entrepreneurial managers. The inspirational vision of a new product or service may seem to spring from out of nowhere, but it is actually the result of many years of learning and experience. Research on entrepreneurs who started successful companies or introduced important new products in established companies suggests that their technical knowledge is the fertile ground in which the seeds of inspiration take root to yield innovative products (Westley & Mintzberg, 1989). Some examples include Edwin Land, the inventor of the instant camera and founder of Polaroid Corporation, and Steve Jobs, the cofounder of Apple Computer. It is not enough to have an intimate knowledge of the products and processes for which a manager is responsible. Managers also need to have extensive knowledge of the products and services provided by competitors. Strategic planning is unlikely to be effective unless a manager can make an accurate evaluation of the organization's products (or services) in comparison to those of competitors (Peters & Austin, 1985).

Conceptual Skills

In general terms, conceptual (or cognitive) skills involve good judgment, foresight, intuition, creativity, and the ability to find meaning and order in ambiguous, uncertain events. Specific conceptual skills that can be measured with aptitude tests include analytical ability, logical thinking, concept formation, inductive reasoning, and deductive reasoning. Cognitive complexity involves a combination of these specific skills and is defined as the ability to utilize cues to make distinctions and develop categories for classifying things, as well as the ability to identify complex relationships and develop creative solutions to problems. A person with low cognitive complexity sees things in simplistic black and white terms and has difficulty in seeing how many diverse elements fit together to make a meaningful whole. A person with high cognitive complexity is able to see many shades of gray, and is able to identify complex patterns of relationships and predict future events from current trends.

Conceptual skills such as cognitive complexity are essential for effective planning, organizing, and problem solving. A major administrative responsibility is coordination of the separate, specialized parts of the organization. To accomplish effective coordination, a manager needs to understand how the various parts of the organization relate to each other and how changes in one part of the system affect the other parts. Managers must also be able to comprehend how changes in the external environment will affect the organization. Strategic planning requires considerable ability to analyze events and perceive trends, anticipate changes, and recognize opportunities and potential problems. A manager with high cognitive complexity is able to develop a better mental model of the organization to help understand the most critical factors and the relationships among them. A model is like a road map that depicts the terrain for a region, shows where things are located in relation to each other, and helps you decide how to get from one place to another. Managers with weak conceptual skills tend to develop a simplistic mental model that is not especially useful because it is unable to describe the complex processes, causal relationships, and flow of events in the organization and external environment.

Effective managers often use an appropriate mix of intuition and conscious reasoning for the type of decision situation confronting them (Agor, 1986; Lord & Maher, 1991). Intuition is not a mystical process but rather is the result of extensive experience with similar problems (Simon, 1987). The relevant knowledge gained from this experience can be tapped when needed without much conscious awareness, in the same way that a champion chess player quickly understands what move to make next without having to make a careful and detailed analysis of the chess pieces on the board.

Conceptual skills have been measured with a variety of different methods, including traditional aptitude tests, situational tests, interviews, critical incidents, and constructed response tasks. Research with traditional pencil-and-paper measures of conceptual skills finds strong evidence they are related to managerial effectiveness, especially in high-level managerial positions (Bass, 1990). Cognitive skills measured with incident interviews differentiated between effective and ineffective managers in the study by Boyatzis (1982). Cognitive skills measured in an assessment center predicted advancement to higher levels of management in the study at AT&T (Howard & Bray, 1988). In a longitudinal study of managers in four companies, cognitive complexity measured with an individual assessment interview predicted managerial advancement remarkably well 4–8 years later (Stamp, 1988). In the CCL study described previously, weak conceptual skills were one reason for managers who derailed (McCall & Lombardo, 1983b, p. 26): "The charming but not brilliant find that the job gets too big and the problems too complex to get by on interpersonal skills."

Another way to measure cognitive skills is with constructed response tasks. A manager is asked to explain how to solve representative types of problems described in a set of scenarios, and then raters determine the level of skill demonstrated by the answers. In a large sample of army officers at different ranks, complex problem-solving skills that were measured in this way were related to career achievement (Connelly et al., 2000).

Interpersonal Skills

Interpersonal (or social) skills include knowledge about human behavior and group processes, ability to understand the feelings, attitudes, and motives of others, and ability to communicate clearly and persuasively. Specific types of interpersonal skills such as empathy, social insight, charm, tact and diplomacy, persuasiveness, and oral communication ability are essential to develop and maintain cooperative relationships with subordinates, superiors, peers, and outsiders. Someone who understands people and is charming, tactful, and diplomatic will have more cooperative relationships than a person who is insensitive and offensive.

Interpersonal skills are essential for influencing people. Empathy and social insight mean the ability to understand someone's motives, values, and emotions. Understanding what people want and how they perceive things makes it easier to select an appropriate influence strategy; persuasiveness and oral communication skill enhance the success of influence attempts.

Interpersonal skills also enhance the effectiveness of relationship-oriented behaviors. Strong interpersonal skills help a manager listen in an attentive, sympathetic, and nonjudgmental way to somebody with a personal problem, complaint, or criticism. Empathy and social insight are important for understanding the feelings and perceptions of other people, and for resolving conflicts in a constructive way. Even managerial behaviors that are primarily task-oriented (e.g., making assignments and giving instructions) require considerable interpersonal skill to be enacted in a way that reflects a concern for people as well as task objectives.

Some people have a misconception that interpersonal skill is nothing more than considerate behavior to be turned on occasionally in special situations. Katz (1955, p. 34) takes a different viewpoint:

> Real skill in working with others must become a natural, continuous activity, since it involves sensitivity not only at times of decision making but also in the day-by-day behavior of the individual . . . Because everything a leader says and does (or leaves unsaid or undone) has an effect on his associates, his true self will, in time, show through. Thus, to be effective, this skill must be naturally developed and unconsciously, as well as consistently, demonstrated in the individual's every action.

The trait research described earlier in this chapter shows consistently that interpersonal skills are important for managerial effectiveness and advancement (Bass, 1990). In the AT&T study, interpersonal skills predicted advancement. In the study of leadership competencies by Boyatzis (1982), interpersonal skills differentiated between effective and ineffective managers, regardless of the situation. In the CCL study, deficiencies in interpersonal skills were a major reason for managers who eventually derailed in their management careers. McCall and Lombardo (1983, p. 28) recount the following incident involving an abrasive manager who derailed:

> The manager walked into the subordinate's office, interrupting a meeting, and said, "I need to see you." When the subordinate tried to explain that he was occupied, his boss snarled, "I don't give a goddamn. I said I wanted to see you now."

Another interpersonal skill is self-monitoring, which is the ability to use cues from others to understand one's own behavior and its effects on others. Self-monitors are able to learn from the feedback and adjust their behavior to fit the requirements of the situation. People high in self-monitoring, as measured by a scale developed by Snyder (1979), are more likely to emerge as leaders in a small group, and they resolve conflicts with others more effectively (Baron, 1989; Dobbins, Long, Dedrick, & Clemons, 1990; Zaccaro, Foti, & Kenny, 1991). However, more research is needed to determine how self-monitoring is related to leadership effectiveness.

Other Relevant Competencies

In recent years some additional leadership competencies have been identified, including emotional intelligence, social intelligence, and metacognition. Although competencies are typically regarded as skills, they usually involve a cluster of specific skills and complementary traits. The new leadership competencies identified in recent years include some of the skills and traits described earlier in this chapter but they are defined and measured in unique ways.

Emotional Intelligence

Emotional intelligence is another attribute that appears to be important for effective leadership (Goleman, 1995; Mayer & Salovey, 1995). Emotions are strong feelings that demand attention and are likely to affect cognitive processes and behavior. Some examples of emotions include anger, fear, sadness, happiness, disgust, shame, surprise, and love. Even after the intensity of an emotion fades, it is likely to linger on as a positive or negative mood, which can also affect leadership behavior (George, 1995). Emotional intelligence is the extent to which a person is attuned to his or her own feelings and to the feelings of others and is able to integrate emotions and reason such that emotions are used to facilitate cognitive processes, and emotions are cognitively managed. Although emotional intelligence is distinct from cognitive intelligence, the two types of psychological processes are interrelated (Forgas, 1995; Mayer & Salovey, 1997). Emotional intelligence, which is conceptualized primarily as a skill, also appears related to personality traits such as emotional maturity, self-monitoring, self-confidence, and achievement orientation.

Emotional intelligence includes several interrelated component skills. Self-awareness is an understanding of one's own moods and emotions, how they evolve and change over time, and their implications for task performance and interpersonal relationships. Another aspect of emotional intelligence that requires both self-awareness and communication skills is the ability to accurately express one's feelings to others with language and nonverbal communication. Empathy is the ability to recognize moods and emotions in others, to differentiate between genuine and false expression of emotions, and to understand how someone is reacting to your emotions and behavior. Self-regulation is the ability to channel emotions into behavior that is appropriate for the situation, rather than responding with impulsive behavior (e.g., lashing out at someone who made you angry, or withdrawing into a state of depression after experiencing disappointment).

Emotional intelligence is relevant for leadership effectiveness in many ways (Goleman, 1995; Goleman, Boyatzis, & McKee, 2002; Mayer & Salovey, 1995). Emotional intelligence can help leaders solve complex problems, make better decisions, plan how to use their time effectively, adapt their behavior to the situation, and manage crises. Self-awareness makes it easier to understand one's own needs and likely reactions if certain events occurred, thereby facilitating evaluation of alternative solutions. Self-regulation facilitates emotional stability and information processing in difficult, stressful situations, and it helps leaders maintain their own optimism and enthusiasm about a project or mission in the face of obstacles and setbacks. Empathy is associated with strong social skills that are needed to develop cooperative interpersonal relationships. Examples include the ability to listen attentively, communicate effectively, and express appreciation and positive regard. The ability to understand and influence emotions in others will help a leader who is attempting to arouse enthusiasm and optimism for a proposed activity or change. A leader with high emotional intelligence will have more insight about the type of rational or emotional appeal most likely to be effective in a particular situation.

As yet only a limited amount of research supports the proposed relationships between emotional intelligence and leadership effectiveness. A study by McClelland (described in Goleman, 1995) found that division managers with high emotional intelligence had significantly higher performance (in terms of earnings goals) than division managers with low emotional intelligence. Wong and Law (2002) found that emotional intelligence was related to follower job satisfaction and performance. Emotional intelligence can be learned, but not as a result of knowledge-oriented training in a classroom setting (Goleman, 1995). Any significant increase in emotional intelligence probably requires intensive individual coaching, relevant feedback, and a strong desire for significant personal development.

Social Intelligence

Social intelligence is defined as the ability to determine the requirements for leadership in a particular situation and select an appropriate response (Cantor & Kihlstrom, 1987; Ford, 1986; Zaccaro, Gilbert, Thor, & Mumford, 1991). The two primary components of social intelligence are social perceptiveness and behavioral flexibility.

Social perceptiveness is the ability to understand the functional needs, problems, and opportunities that are relevant for a group or organization, and the member characteristics, social relationships, and collective processes that will enhance or limit attempts to influence the group or organization. A leader with high social perceptiveness understands what needs to be done to make a group or organization more effective and how to do it. Social perceptiveness involves the conceptual skills and specific knowledge needed for strategic leadership, including the ability to identify threats and opportunities that are jointly determined by environmental events and the core competencies of the organization, and the ability to formulate an appropriate response (see Chapter 12). Social perceptiveness also involves interpersonal skills (e.g., empathy, social sensitivity, understanding of group processes) and knowledge of the organization (structure, culture, power relationships), which jointly determine whether it is feasible to initiate change and the best way to do it (see Chapter 10).

Behavioral flexibility is the ability and willingness to vary one's behavior to accommodate situational requirements. A leader with high behavioral flexibility knows how to use a variety of different behaviors and is able to evaluate his or her behavior and modify it as needed. High behavioral flexibility implies a mental model with fine distinctions among different types of leadership behavior rather than a simplistic taxonomy. The person must have a large repertoire of skilled behaviors from which to select, as well as knowledge about the effects and limiting conditions for each type of behavior. Behavioral flexibility is facilitated by self-monitoring, because leaders who are high on self-monitoring are more aware of their own behavior and how it affects others. Whether social intelligence is used primarily to achieve collective rather than personal objectives probably depends on the leader's emotional maturity and socialized power motivation.

Considerable overlap is apparent between social intelligence and emotional intelligence, although the latter construct seems to be more narrowly defined (Kobe, Reiter-Palmon, & Rickers, 2001; Salovey & Mayor, 1990). More research is needed to clarify how these two competencies are interrelated and to assess the relevance of their component skills for leadership effectiveness.

Systems Thinking

Understanding the complex interdependencies among organizational processes and the implications of efforts to make changes requires cognitive skills and "systems thinking" (Senge, 1990). It is important to understand that complex problems often have multiple causes, which may include actions taken earlier to solve other problems. In large systems such as organizations, actions invariably have multiple outcomes, including unintended side effects. Changes often have delayed effects that tend to obscure the real nature of the relationship. A change in one part of a system will eventually affect other parts, and reactions to the change may cancel out the effects (see Chapter 11).

When making decisions or diagnosing the cause of problems, it is essential to understand how the different parts of the organization are interrelated. Even when the immediate objective is to deal with one type of challenge, such as improving efficiency, leaders need to consider the likely consequences for other performance determinants and the possibility that any immediate benefits will be nullified by later events as the effects of a decision or change eventually ripple through the system (Yukl & Lepsinger, 2004). Although strategic thinking about these issues is clearly more important for high-level leaders than for lower-level leaders, it is relevant for leaders at all levels.

Ability to Learn

In a turbulent environment in which organizations must continually adapt, innovate, and reinvent themselves, leaders must be flexible enough to learn from mistakes, change their assumptions and beliefs, and refine their mental models. One of the most important competencies for successful leadership in changing situations is the ability to learn from experience and adapt to change (Argyris, 1991; Dechant, 1990; Marshall-Mies et al., 2000; Mumford & Connelly, 1991). This competency, sometimes called a metacognition, is distinct from other conceptual skills (e.g., verbal reasoning, creative thinking) and from social skills. It involves learning how to learn, which is the ability to introspectively analyze your own cognitive processes (e.g., the way you define and solve problems) and to find ways to improve them. It also involves self-awareness, which is an understanding of your own strengths and limitations (including both skills and emotions).

In a study of 1,800 high-level military officers, this competency predicted self-reported career achievements (Zaccaro, Mumford, Marks et al., 1997). A study of military officers by Marshall-Mies and colleagues (2000) provides additional evidence that metacognition is important for leadership effectiveness. In the recent CCL research on factors that cause civilian managers to derail, the ability to learn and adapt was considered an important success factor by both American and European executives (Van Velsor & Leslie, 1995). As research on this subject increases, we will discover more about the nature of this competency and its relation to leadership behavior and effectiveness.

The ability to learn from experience and adapt to change probably involves traits as well as skills (Spreitzer, McCall, & Mahoney, 1997). These traits appear to be the same ones associated with emotional and social intelligence. Achievement orientation, emotional stability, intellectance, self-monitoring, and an internal locus of control orientation all appear relevant for learning from success and failure experiences. Managers with these traits are motivated to achieve excellence, they are inquisitive and open-minded, they have the confidence and curiosity to experiment with new approaches, and they actively seek feedback about their strengths and weaknesses.

Situational Relevance of Skills

Managers need many types of skills to fulfill their role requirements, but the relative importance of the various skills depends on the leadership situation. Relevant situational moderator variables include managerial level, type of organization, and the nature of the external environment.

Skills Needed at Different Levels

One aspect of the situation influencing skill importance is a manager's position in the authority hierarchy of the organization (Boyatzis, 1982; Jacobs & Jaques, 1987; Katz, 1955; Mann, 1965; Mumford & Connelly, 1991; Mumford, Marks, Connelly, Zaccaro, & Reiter-Palmon, 2000). Skill priorities at different levels of management are related to the differing role requirements at each level (see Chapter 2). Figure 7-1 shows the relative importance of the three broad skill categories to leadership effectiveness for low-level managers, middle-level managers, and top executives. Managerial level affects not only the relevance of the three broad categories of skills described earlier (i.e., conceptual, interpersonal, technical), but also the relative importance of specific types of skills within each category.

In general, higher levels of management have a greater number and variety of activities to be coordinated, the complexity of relationships that need to be understood and managed is greater, and the problems that need to be solved are more unique and ill-defined (Jacobs & Jaques, 1987, 1990; Jaques, 1989; Mumford & Connelly, 1991). Whereas a department supervisor may have to coordinate the work of employees with mostly similar jobs, a CEO must coordinate the diverse activities of several organizational units, each with large numbers of people. Increasing complexity as one ascends to higher levels in an organization is reflected in increased requirements for conceptual

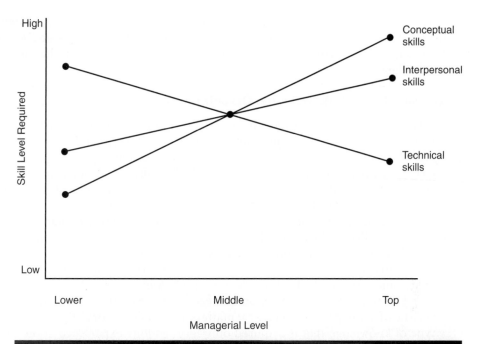

FIGURE 7-1   Relative Importance of Skills for Different Levels of Management

skills. Top executives need to analyze vast amounts of ambiguous and contradictory information about the environment in order to make strategic decisions and to interpret events for other members of the organization. Executives need to have a long-term perspective and the ability to comprehend complex relationships among variables relevant to the performance of the organization. A top executive must be able to anticipate future events and know how to plan for them. The quality of strategic decisions ultimately depends on conceptual skills, even though some technical knowledge is necessary to make these decisions, and interpersonal skills are necessary for developing relationships, obtaining information, and influencing subordinates to implement decisions (Katz & Kahn, 1978).

The role of middle-level managers is primarily one of supplementing existing structure and developing ways to implement policies and goals established at higher levels (Katz & Kahn, 1978). This role requires a roughly equal mix of technical, interpersonal, and conceptual skills. Low-level managers are mainly responsible for implementing policy and maintaining the work flow within the existing organizational structure; for these managers, technical skills are relatively more important than conceptual skills or interpersonal skills.

The skill requirements for managers at each level vary somewhat depending on the type of organization, its size, the organization structure, and the degree of centralization of authority (McLennan, 1967). For example, technical skills are more important for top executives in organizations where operating decisions are highly centralized. Likewise, more technical skill is needed by top executives who have functionally specialized roles (e.g., selling to key customers, product design) in addition to general administrative responsibilities. More conceptual skills are needed by middle- and lower-level managers who are expected to participate in strategic planning, product innovation, and leading change.

Transferability of Skills Across Organizations

An interesting question about managerial skills is the extent to which they are transferable from one type of organization to another. Writers generally agree that lower-level managers cannot easily transfer to a different functional specialty (e.g., from sales manager to engineering manager), because the technical skills needed at this level of management are so different across functions. However, less agreement is evident about the transferability of skills across organizations at the executive level.

Katz (1955) proposed that top-level managers with ample human relations and conceptual skills can be shifted from one industry to another with great ease and no loss of effectiveness. Some other writers contend that the transferability of skills for top executives is limited due to variations in ownership, traditions, organizational climate, and culture (Dale, 1960; Kotter, 1982; McLennan, 1967; Shetty & Peery, 1976). Different industries have unique economic, market, and technological characteristics. Familiarity with technical matters, products, personalities, and tradition is a type of knowledge that is acquired only through long experience in the organization. Only the general components of conceptual and technical skills can be used in a different situation; the unique knowledge component of these skills must be re-learned. Moreover, an executive who moves to a different industry must develop a new network of external contacts, whereas the old network would still be relevant for a move to another organization in the same industry. In general, it seems to be more difficult for an executive to make a successful transition to a different industry or type of organization, especially if the new position requires extensive technical expertise and an extensive network of external contacts (Kotter, 1982; Shetty & Peery, 1976).

Requisite Skills and the External Environment

Recent research and theory on how organizations evolve and adapt to a changing environment suggests that the mix of skills needed for effective leadership may change over time. The skills needed by an entrepreneurial manager to build a new organization are not identical to the skills needed by the chief executive of a large, established organization. The skills needed to lead an organization with a stable, supportive environment are not identical to the skills needed to lead an organization facing a turbulent, competitive environment (Hunt, 1991; Lord & Maher, 1991; Quinn, 1992).

As noted in Chapter 2, unprecedented changes affecting organizations are changing the nature of managerial work. To cope with these changes, most managers may need more of the new competencies as well as the skills identified in earlier research (Conger, 1993; Hunt, 1991; Van Velsor & Leslie, 1995). As the pace of globalization, technological development, and social change continues to increase, so will the premium on competencies such as cognitive complexity, emotional and social intelligence, self-awareness, cultural sensitivity, behavioral flexibility, systems thinking, and the ability to learn from experience and adapt to change.

Evaluation of the Trait Research

Considerable progress has been made in identifying traits and skills relevant for managerial effectiveness and advancement. Nevertheless, this line of research has been hindered by some methodological and conceptual limitations. The abstract nature of most traits limits their utility for understanding leadership effectiveness. It is difficult to interpret the relevance of abstract traits except by examining how they are expressed in the actual behavior of leaders. Unfortunately, most trait studies are not guided by a theory that explains how traits are related to managerial effectiveness and advancement. Relatively few trait studies include measures of leader behavior. A move in this direction can be seen in some of the current research on charismatic leadership, which is discussed in Chapter 9.

Most trait studies examined how single traits or skills are related to leadership effectiveness or advancement. When traits are examined one at a time, the results are usually weak and difficult to interpret. This approach fails to consider how the traits are interrelated and how they interact to influence leader behavior and effectiveness. For example, achievement orientation affects a leader's motivation to acquire relevant knowledge and skills (Dweck, 1986). Emotional maturity affects a leader's capacity to learn from feedback and experience, and adapt behavior to changing conditions. Self-confidence and stress tolerance increase the capacity of a leader to make use of cognitive skills in stressful situations (Mumford & Connelly, 1991). Emotional intelligence affects a leader's capacity to process information and make rational analyses. A more holistic approach is needed to examine patterns of leader traits and skills in relation to leader effectiveness. One possible remedy is to use cluster analysis to develop a typology of leaders based on distinct trait (or skill) profiles. However, there are many methodological problems in such research, and it often yields a typology with oversimplified stereotypes that fail to improve our understanding of leadership.

Another useful concept that deserves more attention from researchers is the idea of balance. In some cases balance means that the optimal amount of some trait is a moderate amount rather than either a very low or a very high amount of the trait. For example, leaders need self-confidence to be effective in influencing others to believe in them and their proposals, but excessive self-confidence makes a leader unresponsive to negative information and insensitive to dissenting views. Unfortunately, most trait studies test only for simple, linear relationships. There is a need for more theory-based studies that include analyses to test whether a curvilinear relationship is supported by the data.

Sometimes balance means tempering one trait with another, which gets back to the analysis of trait patterns. For example, effective leaders balance a high need for power with the emotional maturity required to ensure that subordinates are empowered rather than dominated. Leaders often find themselves in situations involving trade-offs between competing values (McCall, Lombardo, & Morrison, 1988; Quinn, 1988). Examples include task versus people, risk taking versus prudent caution, toughness versus compassion, control versus empowerment, continuity versus change, and efficiency versus flexibility. More research is needed to discover how effective leaders balance competing values.

The concept of balance has been described for individuals, but it applies to shared leadership as well. For example, balance may involve several different leaders in a management team who have complementary attributes that compensate for each other's weaknesses and enhance each other's strengths (Bradford & Cohen, 1984). A better understanding of leadership in an organization may be gained by examining the pattern of traits for the executive team rather than focusing on the traits of a single leader such as the chief executive officer (see Chapter 12).

Applications for Managers

The finding that particular skills and traits are positively related to managerial effectiveness and advancement has some practical implications for people in planning their own managerial careers. The following guidelines (summarized in Table 7-5) are based on research, theory, and practitioner findings about traits and skills.

- **Maintain self-awareness.**

Self-awareness includes a good understanding of one's own needs, emotions, abilities, and behavior. Awareness of your emotions and motives (an aspect of emotional intelligence) can help you solve complex problems, make better decisions, adapt your behavior to the situation, and manage crises. Awareness of your likely emotional reactions to events facilitates information processing and decision making in stressful situations and it helps you maintain optimism and enthusiasm about a project or mission in the face of obstacles and setbacks. Awareness of your behavior and its influence on others makes it easier to learn from experience and to assess your strengths and weaknesses. Understanding of strengths makes it easier to build on them and become more effective. Understanding of weaknesses makes it easier to correct them or compensate for them. Insights can be gained by monitoring your own behavior and its consequences. It is important to be receptive to feedback from others about positive and negative aspects of behavior as they perceive it. Take advantage of opportunities to gain systematic feedback about strengths and weaknesses from multisource feedback programs and assessment centers (see Chapter 13).

- **Develop relevant skills.**

Effective managers are more oriented toward continuous learning and self-development. Learn about the key traits and skills necessary for the type of managerial position you hold or aspire to occupy, and assess the extent to which you have them. After identifying skills that need to be strengthened, it is wise to seek opportunities to develop these skills. Some training may be obtained in specialized management development workshops run by one's employer or by consulting companies. Other approaches for developing new skills include challenging assignments, personal coaching, and self-development activities (see Chapter 13).

TABLE 7-5   Guidelines for Understanding
                 and Improving Relevant Competencies

- Maintain self-awareness.
- Develop relevant skills.
- Remember that a strength can become a weakness.
- Compensate for weaknesses.

- **Remember that a strength can become a weakness.**

A trait or skill that is a strength in one situation can later become a weakness when the situation changes. People tend to emphasize a skill that brings repeated success early in their careers, and later when it is no longer as relevant, the strength becomes a weakness. For example, a study conducted by CCL researchers found that staff managers who performed brilliant analytical work could not develop the action orientation necessary to implement ideas when they moved into a line position. Successful line managers had the opposite problem; they seemed incapable of the reflective analysis and cooperative teamwork that was necessary in a staff position. Any trait taken to an extreme can also become a weakness, even when the situation has not changed. Confidence can become arrogance, innovation can become recklessness, decisiveness can become rashness, integrity can become fanaticism, and global vision can become lack of focus.

- **Compensate for weaknesses.**

One way to compensate for weaknesses is to select subordinates who have complementary strengths and allow them to assume responsibility for aspects of the work they are more qualified to perform. Sometimes it is appropriate to delegate responsibilities to qualified individuals, and other times it is better to have a management team (in which you are a member) share the responsibility for a particular problem or challenge.

Summary

The early trait studies attempted to identify physical characteristics, personality traits, and abilities of people who were believed to be "natural leaders." Hundreds of trait studies were conducted, but individual traits failed to correlate in a strong and consistent manner with leadership effectiveness. The early researchers did not pay much attention to the question of how traits interact as an integrator of personality and behavior, or how the situation determines the relevance of different traits and skills for leader effectiveness. Better results were found after researchers began to include more relevant traits and skills, to use better measures, and to take into account the situation.

Some personality traits found to be especially relevant for effectiveness include energy level and stress tolerance, self-confidence, internal control orientation, emotional maturity, and integrity. Managerial motivation is also important for effective leadership. The motive pattern characteristic of many effective managers includes a socialized power orientation, a moderately strong need for achievement, and a relatively weaker need for affiliation.

To be successful, a leader also needs interpersonal, cognitive, and technical skills. The relative priority of the three types of skills and the optimal mix of specific skills probably depends on the type of organization, the level of management, and the nature of the challenges confronting a leader. Some skills such as persuasiveness, analytical ability, speaking ability, and memory for details will help a leader be successful in any situation, whereas some other skills are not easily transferred to a different type of position. Relevant competencies identified in more recent research include emotional intelligence, social intelligence, systems thinking, and the ability to learn and adapt to change.

The trait approach has important implications for improving managerial effectiveness. Information about a person's traits and skills is essential for selecting people to fill managerial positions, for identifying training needs in the current job, and for planning management development activities to prepare the person for promotion to higher-level jobs. Leadership development is discussed in Chapter 13.

Review and Discussion Questions

1. What traits are the best predictors of managerial performance and advancement?
2. Is it possible to have too much of a good thing with some traits?
3. How does consideration of trait patterns advance our understanding beyond what is learned from studying single traits by themselves?
4. How is managerial motivation related to the effectiveness and advancement of managers in large organizations?
5. What are the major reasons some managers derail in their careers?
6. How are technical, conceptual, and interpersonal skills related to managerial effectiveness?
7. Why is it important to consider the nature of the managerial job situation when trying to identify essential traits and skills?
8. Which skills are most important at lower, middle, and higher levels of management?
9. What are emotional intelligence and social intelligence, and how are they relevant for effective leadership?
10. What can be done to compensate for deficiencies in personality traits or skills that are relevant for a leader's position?
11. Are some traits and values more likely to be associated with unethical leadership behavior?

Key Terms

- assessment centers
- big five personality traits
- cognitive skills
- conceptual skills
- competencies
- derailed careers
- emotional intelligence
- emotional maturity
- emotional stability
- interpersonal skills
- locus of control orientation
- managerial motivation
- need for achievement
- need for affiliation
- need for power
- personal integrity
- personalized power orientation
- self-awareness
- self-confidence
- self-monitoring
- social intelligence
- socialized power orientation
- systems thinking
- stress tolerance
- technical skills

CASES

The Intolerable Boss

It was three o'clock on Sunday afternoon, and Bob Parker's stomach began to hurt. By dinner he wasn't hungry, and at bedtime he couldn't sleep. In the morning, the persistent buzzing of the alarm took forever to pierce his troubled dreams. As he drove to the office, with each mile he felt the spring inside him coil tighter.

It was not the challenge of the job. The adversity and risk of turning a business around or building a plant in the jungle were exhilarating, not immobilizing. Success in tough business situations marked his career, and he had numerous and rapid promotions. No, it wasn't the overwhelming responsibility of his current job that brought this 40-year-old executive to his knees; it was his boss. For the first time in his career, Bob was faced with a situation that he didn't know how to handle. Even more frustrating was the feeling that, with such an important job to be done, this situation simply should not exist.

It was evident how his boss got where he was. Extremely confident and incredibly talented in handling technical problems, he got results. But his remarkable results were achieved at a horrible cost to others. Bob's boss was completely devoid of sensitivity, kindness, and patience. He treated people as if they were no different from material or financial resources, to be bought, sold, and used up. If one of his people made a serious mistake, he'd write the person off no matter how competent and successful the person was previously. Moody and volatile, he might come down on anyone at any time. His intelligence was a club that he wielded with impunity, chewing out subordinates in front of others, mounting scathing attacks on other people's ideas, and sometimes deliberately setting up subordinates to make them look stupid. Ironically, he could be charming and pleasant when it suited his purpose, which was usually when interacting with top management.

Bob tried to cope with personal despair and frustration by playing mind games with himself. He tried to convince himself that he worked for the company not for the boss. As he watched his boss exploit and demean subordinates, he vowed never to treat anyone that way himself. As more Mondays went by, Bob had to learn skills for dealing with adversity that were not needed in previous tough assignments. He learned to maintain his composure under direct personal assault. He began to time his moves around his boss's moods, and gave up some things to get what he wanted from others. He leaned on others for support, as they did on him. He learned that even when you can't do much to change someone else, you can change your own behavior to make the best of a bad situation.

In his bleakest moments, Bob felt that top management had forgotten him and his brilliant career was at an end. Then, unexpectedly, his boss was fired and Bob was promoted to the boss's job. He found out later that the company had already written off his boss weeks ago, and it was Bob who was being judged. By keeping cool and by continuing to do his job despite the terrible circumstances, Bob had passed a test he didn't even know he was taking. He learned that he could handle this type of adversity, and he learned that his company would not tolerate behavior like that of his former boss. Ironically, while watching the dazzling brilliance of his boss in action he also learned how to be more effective in dealing with technical problems. ■

SOURCE: Adapted from unpublished material based on interviews conducted for the Lessons of Leadership study at the Center for Creative Leadership by Morgan W. McCall, Jr., Michael M. Lombardo, and Ann M. Morrison.

QUESTIONS

1. What traits and skills explain how the boss had initial career success but eventual derailment?

2. How difficult is it for someone in Bob's situation to learn useful lessons from experience?

3. What traits helped Bob survive and learn from his ordeal?

National Products

Susan Thomas is the vice president for human resources at National Products, a manufacturing company with 500 employees. The company has an opening for a general manager in one of its product divisions, and the president asked Susan to review the backgrounds of three department managers who are interested in being promoted to this position. She is expected either to recommend one of the three internal candidates or to begin recruitment of external candidates. The internal candidates are Charley Adams, Bill Stuart, and Ray Johnson. The following information about each candidate was obtained from performance records, interviews with the candidates, and discussions with the boss of each candidate.

CHARLEY ADAMS

Charley Adams has been a production manager for the past eight years. He is an easy-going person who loves to swap jokes and tell stories. Charley stresses the importance of cooperation and teamwork. He is uncomfortable with conflict, and he tries to smooth it over quickly or find an acceptable compromise.

Before becoming a manager, Charley was always willing to take on extra assignments for his boss and to provide helpful advice to less experienced coworkers in his department. Charley is proud of his reputation as a good team player and a loyal company man. It is important to Charley to be liked and appreciated by people in the organization.

Charley comes from a cultural background emphasizing the importance of close family ties. He holds frequent Sunday dinners at which the entire Adams clan gathers for an afternoon of swimming, baseball, eating, and singing. On Saturdays, Charley likes to play golf with friends, including some of the other managers in the company.

Charley wants his department to have a good performance record, but he is reluctant to jeopardize relations with subordinates by pushing them to improve their performance beyond current levels, which he believes are adequate. When Charley gives out performance bonuses to subordinates, he usually tries to give something to everyone.

BILL STUART

Bill Stuart has been the manager of an engineering department for three years. He was promoted to that position because he was the best design engineer in the company and was ambitious to further his career by going into management. At the time, Bill had little understanding of what the job would be like, but he saw it as both an opportunity and a challenge.

Bill grew up as somewhat of a loner. He still feels awkward around people he doesn't know well, and he dislikes social functions such as cocktail parties and company picnics. As a design engineer, Bill preferred assignments where he could work alone rather than team projects. He is impatient with bureaucratic authority figures and he is critical of corporate policies that he regards as too restrictive. Bill gets along well with his present boss, because he is left alone to run his engineering group in his own way.

Bill likes challenging assignments, and he tries to save the most difficult and interesting design projects for himself. Although Bill usually performs these tasks effectively, his preoccupation with them sometimes takes time away from some of his managerial responsibilities, such as developing and mentoring subordinates.

RAY JOHNSON

Ray Johnson has been a corporate marketing manager for five years. He grew up in a poor ethnic neighborhood where he learned to be tough in order to survive. He has worked hard to get where he is, but for Ray, good performance has been a way to get ahead rather than something he enjoys for its own sake.

Ray lives in a large house with a big swimming pool in the best part of town, and he likes to throw big parties at his home. He wears expensive clothes, drives a luxury car, and he belongs to the best country club. Ray is married, but fancies himself as quite a playboy and has had many affairs, including some with female employees.

Ray views the organization as a political jungle, and he is quick to defend himself against any threats to his reputation, authority, or position. He tries to undermine, isolate, or discredit anybody who criticizes or opposes him. He keeps a tight control over the operations of his department, and he insists that subordinates check with him before taking any action that is not routine. ∎

SOURCE: Copyright © 1978 by Gary Yukl.

QUESTIONS

1. What are the dominant motives for each candidate?

2. What are the implications of these traits for the success of each candidate if selected for the general manager position?

3. Should Susan recommend one of these candidates for the position, or look for external candidates?

8

EARLY CONTINGENCY THEORIES OF EFFECTIVE LEADERSHIP

Learning Objectives

After studying this chapter you should be able to:

- Understand why effective leadership depends on the situation.

- Understand how aspects of the situation enhance or diminish the influence of a leader on follower performance.

- Understand what aspects of the situation are most relevant as determinants of effective leadership.

- Understand how aspects of the situation can serve as a substitute for the influence of formal leaders.

- Understand the primary contingency theories of effective leadership.

- Understand the conceptual weaknesses of each contingency theory.

- Understand the findings from empirical research on contingency theories and the limitations of this research.

In earlier chapters we saw that aspects of the situation determine the role requirements for leaders. Comparative research on the way managerial behavior varies across situations (see Chapter 2) provides some useful insights, but it is only an indirect approach for discovering what type of leadership is optimal in a given situation. A more direct approach is to determine how leader traits or behaviors are related to indicators of leadership effectiveness in different situations. Aspects of the situation that enhance or nullify the effects of a leader's traits or behavior are called situational moderator variables. Theories that explain leadership effectiveness in terms of situational moderator variables are called *contingency theories* of leadership. This type of theory is most useful when it includes intervening variables to explain why the effect of behavior on outcomes varies across situations.

The current chapter reviews six contingency theories of leadership: path-goal theory, situational leadership theory, leader substitutes theory, the multiple-linkage model, LPC contingency theory, and cognitive resources theory. These theories were popular during the 1970s and 1980s, and some of them stimulated considerable research during that period of time. Each theory is described briefly and evaluated in terms of conceptual adequacy and empirical support. The chapter ends with some general guidelines for varying leadership behavior from situation to situation.

LPC Contingency Model

Fiedler's (1964, 1967) LPC contingency model describes how the situation moderates the relationship between leadership effectiveness and a trait measure called the least preferred coworker (LPC) score.

Leader LPC Score

The LPC score is determined by asking a leader to think of all past and present coworkers, select the one with whom the leader could work least well, and rate this person on a set of bipolar adjective scales (e.g., friendly-unfriendly, cooperative-uncooperative, efficient-inefficient). The LPC score is the sum of the ratings on these bipolar adjective scales. A leader who is generally critical in rating the least preferred coworker will obtain a low LPC score, whereas a leader who is generally lenient will obtain a high LPC score.

The interpretation of LPC scores has changed several times over the years. According to Fiedler's (1978) most recent interpretation, the LPC score indicates a leader's motive hierarchy. A high LPC leader is primarily motivated to have close, interpersonal relationships with other people, including subordinates, and will act in a considerate, supportive manner if relationships need to be improved. Achievement of task objectives is a secondary motive that will become important only if the primary affiliation motive is already satisfied by close, personal relationships with subordinates and peers. A low LPC leader is primarily motivated by achievement of task objectives and will emphasize task-oriented behavior whenever task problems arise. The secondary motive of establishing good relations with subordinates will become important only if the group is performing well and it encounters no serious task problems.

Rice (1978) reviewed 25 years of research on LPC scores and concluded that the data support a value-attitude interpretation better than a motive hierarchy interpretation; that is, low LPC leaders value task success, whereas high LPC leaders value interpersonal success. As with the motive hierarchy interpretation, the pattern of leadership behavior varies with the situation. Rice's interpretation is basically in accord with Fiedler's motive hierarchy interpretation but is more parsimonious and better supported by diverse types of research.

Situational Variables

The relationship between leader LPC score and effectiveness depends on a complex situational variable called situational favorability (or situational control), which is defined as the extent to which the situation gives a leader control over subordinates. Three aspects of the situation are considered.

1. *Leader-member relations:*   The extent to which subordinates are loyal, and relations with subordinates are friendly and cooperative.
2. *Position power:*   The extent to which the leader has authority to evaluate subordinate performance and administer rewards and punishments.
3. *Task structure:*   The extent to which standard operating procedures are in place to accomplish the task, along with a detailed description of the finished product or service and objective indicators of how well the task is being performed.

Favorability is determined by weighting and combining these three aspects of the situation. The weighting procedure assumes that leader-member relations are more important than task structure, which in turn is more important than position power. The possible combinations yield eight levels of favorability, called octants (see Table 8-1).

Propositions

According to the model, the situation is most favorable for the leader (octant 1) when relations with subordinates are good, the leader has substantial position power, and the task is highly structured. When leader-member relations are good, subordinates are more likely to comply with leader requests and directions, rather than ignoring or subverting them. When a leader has high position power, it is easier to influence subordinates. When the task is structured, it is easier for the leader to direct subordinates and monitor their performance. The situation is least favorable for the leader (octant 8) when relations with subordinates are poor, the task is unstructured, and position power is low.

The causal relationships among the variables are depicted in Figure 8-1. According to the model, when the situation is either very favorable (octants 1–3) or very unfavorable (octant 8), low LPC leaders will be more effective than high LPC leaders. When the situation is intermediate in favorability (octants 4–7), high LPC leaders will be more effective than low LPC leaders.

Research on the Theory

A large number of studies were conducted to test the LPC contingency theory. Reviews of this research by Strube and Garcia (1981) and by Peters, Hartke, and Pohlmann

TABLE 8-1   Relationships in the LPC Contingency Model

Octant	L-M Relations	Task Structure	Position Power	Effective Leader
1	Good	Structured	Strong	Low LPC
2	Good	Structured	Weak	Low LPC
3	Good	Unstructured	Strong	Low LPC
4	Good	Unstructured	Weak	Low LPC
5	Poor	Structured	Strong	High LPC
6	Poor	Structured	Weak	High LPC
7	Poor	Unstructured	Strong	High LPC
8	Poor	Unstructured	Weak	Low LPC

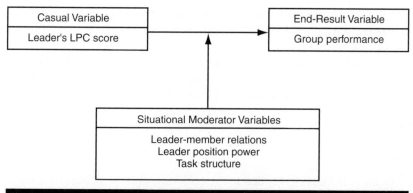

FIGURE 8-1   Causal Relationships in the LPC Contingency Model

(1985) concluded that the research tends to support the model, although not for every octant and not as strongly for field studies as for laboratory studies.

Although the results were mostly positive, the methods used to test the theory have been strongly criticized by a number of writers. One criticism is that the empirical support is based on correlational results that fail to achieve statistical significance in a majority of cases, even though correlations may be in the right direction (Graen, Alvares, Orris, & Martella, 1970; McMahon, 1972; Vecchio, 1983). Another criticism involves the process by which three different aspects of the situation are combined into a single continuum. The weights used to compute situational favorability and establish the octants seem arbitrary (Shiflett, 1973).

Conceptual Weaknesses

The LPC contingency theory has some serious conceptual weaknesses. The LPC score is a "measure in search of a meaning" (Schriesheim & Kerr, 1977, p.23). Its interpretation has been changed in an arbitrary fashion, and the current interpretation is speculative. LPC scores may not be stable over time and may be more complex than assumed (Yukl, 1970).

The model is not really a theory, because it does not explain how a leader's LPC score affects group performance (Ashour, 1973). The lack of explicit leader behaviors and intervening variables limit the utility of the model. In the absence of behavior variables, the model does not provide any guidance for training leaders how to adapt to the situation. If LPC is a relatively stable personality trait, as usually assumed, then changing it is not an option for improving leadership. Another option is to select the leader to fit the situation, but the LPC scale cannot satisfy the requirements for a valid selection tool. The final option is to change the situation to fit the leader. It may be possible to make the situation more or less favorable to fit the leader's LPC score (Fiedler & Chemers, 1982), but reducing favorability is probably counterproductive. For example, the idea that some leaders should try to make leader-member relations worse (e.g., by being much less supportive) seems unethical as well as unwise (Schriesheim & Kerr, 1977b). Likewise, any changes that are made in the task structure should be guided by concern for efficient use of people and resources, not by the desire to make task structure compatible with the leader's LPC score. Research suggests that modifying task structure has up to 10 times the effect on group performance as leader LPC scores (O'Brien & Kabanoff, 1981).

The model (and most of the research) neglects medium LPC leaders, who probably outnumber the high and low LPC leaders. Research suggests that medium LPC leaders are more effective than either high or low LPC leaders in a majority of situations (five of the eight octants), presumably because they balance affiliation and achievement concerns more successfully (Kennedy, 1982; Shiflett, 1973).

Summary

Fiedler (1973, 1977) replied to the criticisms, and the debate over the validity of the model is still continuing. However, interest in the theory has waned over the years as better leadership theories have developed. The LPC contingency model was one of the earliest contingency theories of leadership, and its major contribution may have been to encourage greater interest in situational factors.

Path-Goal Theory of Leadership

The path-goal theory of leadership was developed to explain how the behavior of a leader influences the satisfaction and performance of subordinates. Building on an early version of the theory by Evans (1970), House (1971) formulated a more elaborate version that included situational variables. The theory was further refined by various writers (e.g., Evans, 1974; House & Dessler, 1974; House & Mitchell, 1974).

According to House (1971, p. 324), "The motivational function of the leader consists of increasing personal payoffs to subordinates for work-goal attainment and making the path to these payoffs easier to travel by clarifying it, reducing roadblocks and pitfalls, and increasing the opportunities for personal satisfaction en route." Leaders also affect subordinate satisfaction, particularly satisfaction with the leader. According to House and Dessler (1974, p. 13), ". . . leader behavior will be viewed as acceptable to subordinates to the extent that the subordinates see such behavior as either an immediate source of satisfaction or as instrumental to future satisfaction." The effect of a leader's actions on subordinate satisfaction is not necessarily the same as the effect on subordinate performance. Depending on the situation, leader behavior may affect satisfaction and performance the same way, or both differently, or one but not the other.

Explanatory Processes

A motivation theory called expectancy theory (Georgopoulos, Mahoney, & Jones, 1957; Vroom, 1964) is used to explain how a leader can influence subordinate satisfaction and effort. Expectancy theory describes work motivation in terms of a rational choice process in which a person decides how much effort to devote to the job at a given point of time. In choosing between a maximal effort and a minimal (or moderate) effort, a person considers the likelihood that a given level of effort will lead to successful completion of the task and the likelihood that task completion will result in desirable outcomes (e.g., higher pay, recognition, promotion, sense of achievement) while avoiding undesirable outcomes (e.g., layoffs, accidents, reprimands, rejection by coworkers, excessive stress). The perceived probability of an outcome is called an *expectancy*, and the desirability of an outcome is called its *valence*.

How the many expectancies and valences for different outcomes and levels of effort combine to determine a person's motivation is still a matter of speculation and controversy. In general, if subordinates believe that valued outcomes can be attained only by making a serious effort and they believe such an effort will succeed, then they will make the effort. The effect of a leader's behavior is primarily to modify these perceptions and beliefs.

Leader Behaviors

The initial version of the theory contained only two broadly defined leader behaviors: supportive leadership (similar to consideration) and directive leadership (similar to initiating structure and instrumental leadership). Two other leader behaviors were added in the later version by House and Mitchell (1974). The four behaviors are defined as follows:

1. *Supportive leadership:*   Giving consideration to the needs of subordinates, displaying concern for their welfare, and creating a friendly climate in the work unit.
2. *Directive leadership:*   Letting subordinates know what they are expected to do, giving specific guidance, asking subordinates to follow rules and procedures, and scheduling and coordinating the work.
3. *Participative leadership:*   Consulting with subordinates and taking their opinions and suggestions into account.
4. *Achievement-oriented leadership:*   Setting challenging goals, seeking performance improvements, emphasizing excellence in performance, and showing confidence that subordinates will attain high standards.

Situational Variables

According to path-goal theory, the effect of leader behavior on subordinate satisfaction and effort depends on aspects of the situation, including task characteristics and subordinate characteristics. These situational moderator variables determine both the potential for increased subordinate motivation and the manner in which the leader must act to improve motivation. Situational variables also influence subordinate preferences for a particular pattern of leadership behavior, thereby influencing the impact of the leader on subordinate satisfaction. The causal relationships in the theory are illustrated in Figure 8-2.

Major Propositions

When the task is stressful, boring, tedious, or dangerous, supportive leadership leads to increased subordinate effort and satisfaction by increasing self-confidence, lowering anxiety, and minimizing unpleasant aspects of the work. In expectancy theory terminology, the leader increases both the intrinsic valence (enjoyment) of doing the task and the expectancy that it will be successfully completed. However, if a task is interesting and enjoyable, and subordinates are already confident, then supportive leadership has little, if any, effect. The hypothesized causal chain for supportive leadership is depicted in Figure 8-3.

When the task is unstructured and complex, the subordinates are inexperienced, and there is little formalization of rules and procedures to guide the work, then directive leadership will result in higher subordinate satisfaction and effort. The role ambiguity

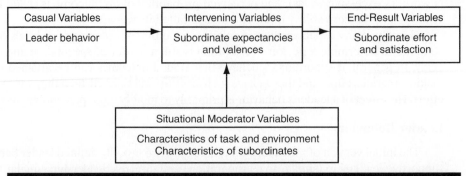

FIGURE 8-2   Causal Relationships in Path–Goal Theory of Leadership

that exists when subordinates do not understand how to do the work effectively causes them to have a low expectancy of success, even for a maximum effort. By reducing role ambiguity, the leader increases expectancies and thus effort. The theory further assumes that role ambiguity is unpleasant and reducing it will lead to greater subordinate satisfaction. When the task is structured or subordinates are highly competent, directive leadership will have no effect on effort. Moreover, in this situation, if subordinates perceive close supervision and direction to be an unnecessary imposition of leader control, satisfaction may actually decline.

The hypothesized causal chain for directive leadership is depicted in Figure 8-4. As the figure shows, directive leadership affects subordinate effort in a number of ways. Effort can be increased by finding new and larger performance rewards and making them more closely contingent upon subordinate performance. This option was included in the initial formulation of the theory by Evans (1970) and House (1971) but was neglected in most subsequent versions and in the validation research, perhaps because positive reward behavior does not fit well into the prevailing definition of directive behavior.

The propositions for participative leadership and achievement-oriented leadership are not as well developed or researched as those for supportive and directive leadership.

FIGURE 8-3   Causal Relationships for Effects of Supportive Leadership on Subordinate

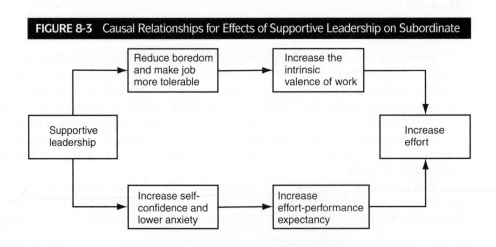

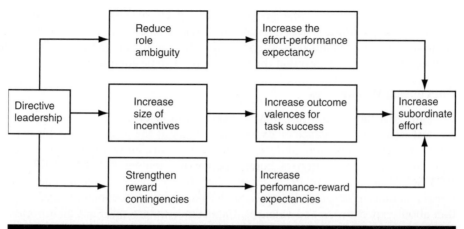

FIGURE 8-4 Causal Relationships for Effects of Directive Leadership on Subordinate

Participative leadership is hypothesized to increase subordinate effort and satisfaction when the task is unstructured by increasing role clarity. When the task is structured, this behavior has little or no effect. Participative leadership may also increase the intrinsic valence of the work and thus satisfaction for subordinates with a high need for achievement and autonomy. Achievement-oriented leadership is hypothesized to increase subordinate effort and satisfaction when the task is unstructured (i.e., complex and nonrepetitive) by increasing self-confidence and the expectation of successfully accomplishing a challenging task or goal. When the task is simple and repetitive, this behavior has little or no effect.

Research on the Theory

Research conducted to test path-goal theory has yielded mixed results. Wofford and Liska (1993) reviewed 120 survey studies on the theory and conducted a meta-analysis of the results for task and relations behavior. Podsakoff, MacKenzie, Ahearne, and Bommer (1995) also conducted an extensive review of the research on moderator variables in leadership. Despite the large number of studies that have tested the theory, the results were inconclusive. Not enough studies were available to provide an adequate test of hypotheses about situational moderators of participative and achievement-oriented leadership. Most propositions about situational moderators of directive leadership were not supported; some evidence indicated that directive behavior correlated more strongly with satisfaction for subordinates with low ability than for subordinates with high ability, but only an indirect test of the proposition was possible. There was little or no moderating effect of the situation on the relationship between leader supportive behavior and subordinate satisfaction with the leader. As in the earlier research (see Chapter 3), most studies find a positive effect of supportive leadership on satisfaction, regardless of the situation.

Methodological limitations make it difficult to interpret the results from much of the research testing the theory (Wofford & Liska, 1993; Yukl, 1989). Most studies used subordinate questionnaires to measure leader behavior and used a static correlational design. These studies have the same limitations as much of the earlier behavior research (see Chapter 3). Another limitation of the research is that most studies deal with only a few aspects of the theory while ignoring other aspects, such as the intervening motivational processes (expectancies and valences). Many studies measured surrogates instead of the situational variables actually specified by the theory. Taken together, these limitations of the research suggest that the theory has yet to be adequately tested.

Conceptual Weaknesses

Path-goal theory also has some conceptual deficiencies that limit its utility. The greatest weakness is reliance on expectancy theory as the primary basis for explaining leader influence. This rational decision model provides an overly complex and seemingly unrealistic description of human behavior (Behling & Starke, 1973; Mitchell, 1974; Schriesheim & Kerr, 1977). Expectancy theory does not take into account emotional reactions to decision dilemmas, such as denial or distortion of relevant information about expectancies and valences. Expectancy theory does not incorporate some important aspects of human motivation such as self-concepts (see Chapter 9). Expectancy theory limits the explanation of leadership influence to changes in subordinate perceptions about the likely outcomes of different actions.

Another conceptual limitation is the reliance on broad categories of leader behavior that do not correspond closely to the mediating processes. It is easier to make a link between leader behavior and subordinate motivation by using specific behaviors such as clarifying role expectations, recognizing accomplishments, giving contingent rewards, modeling appropriate behaviors for subordinates to imitate, and communicating high expectations about subordinate performance.

Some of the explanations for hypothesized relationships in path-goal theory are questionable. It is assumed that role ambiguity will cause a person to have an unrealistically low expectancy, and that leader behavior resulting in greater clarity will automatically increase expectancies. However, clarification of the subordinate's role sometimes makes it evident that successful task performance and the attainment of specific task goals are more difficult than the subordinate initially believed (Yukl, 1989). It is assumed that role ambiguity is determined primarily by task structure (defined as a characteristic of the task, not the employee), but a more appropriate moderator variable is an employee's ability and experience in relation to the task. The same, supposedly structured task may be clear to an experienced subordinate but ambiguous to an inexperienced subordinate.

Another limitation of path-goal theory is that each type of leadership behavior is considered separately. Likely interactions among the behaviors or interactions with more than one type of situational variable are not considered (Osborn, 1974). For example, the theory says that directive leadership will be beneficial when the task is unstructured, but directive leadership may not be beneficial for an unstructured task if there is another situational determinant of subordinate role clarity, such as a high level of professional training and experience.

To make path-goal theory more comprehensive, House (1996) extended it to include some behaviors from more recent theories such as charismatic and transformational leadership (see Chapter 9). However, it is doubtful that the effects of these behaviors can be explained in terms of expectancy theory. Charismatic leadership emphasizes emotional arousal and influencing followers to do things that are not consistent with rational calculations (e.g., make self-sacrifices and take risks for ideological reasons). Moreover, the extended theory is much too complicated to be useful for practitioners.

Summary

Despite its limitations, path-goal theory has made an important contribution to the study of leadership by providing a conceptual framework to guide researchers in identifying potentially relevant situational variables. The recent extension of the theory (House, 1996) makes it more comprehensive but less parsimonious. It is too early to evaluate whether the extended theory is an improvement over the earlier versions.

Situational Leadership Theory

Hersey and Blanchard (1977) proposed a contingency theory that specifies the appropriate type of leadership behavior for different levels of subordinate maturity in relation to the work. A high-maturity subordinate has both the ability and confidence to do a task, whereas a low-maturity subordinate lacks ability and self-confidence.

Major Propositions

According to the theory, the level of subordinate maturity determines the appropriate mix of task and relation behavior for the leader (see Figure 8-5). Four degrees of maturity (quadrants M1 to M4) are distinguished, even though they are merely segments of a continuum ranging from immature to mature.

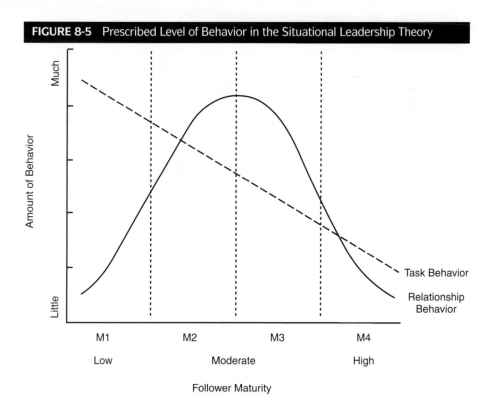

FIGURE 8-5   Prescribed Level of Behavior in the Situational Leadership Theory

When a subordinate is very immature in relation to the task (M1), the leader should use substantial task-oriented behavior and be directive in defining roles, clarifying standards and procedures, and monitoring progress on attainment of objectives. As subordinate maturity increases up to a moderate level (M2 and M3), the leader can decrease the amount of task-oriented behavior and provide more relations-oriented behavior. The leader should act supportive, consult with the subordinate, and provide praise and attention. When the subordinate is very mature (M4), the leader should use a low level of task-oriented and relations-oriented behaviors. A mature subordinate has the ability to do the work without much direction or monitoring by the leader, and the confidence to work without much supportive behavior by the leader.

According to Hersey and Blanchard, the maturity level of a subordinate can be influenced by developmental interventions. For example, the leader and subordinate may negotiate an agreement regarding the delegation of additional responsibilities and how the leader will help the subordinate accomplish the goals set for these responsibilities. This type of developmental process is similar to the role-making process described in the leader-member exchange (LMX) theory (see Chapter 5). How long it takes to increase the subordinate's maturity depends on the complexity of the task and the skill and confidence of the subordinate. There is no set formula, and it may take as little as a few days or as long as a few years to advance a subordinate from low to high maturity on a given task. Hersey and Blanchard recognized that subordinate maturity may also regress, requiring a flexible adjustment of the leader's behavior. For example, a highly motivated subordinate may become apathetic after a personal tragedy, which would require closer supervision and a developmental intervention designed to boost maturity back up to the former high level.

Evaluation of the Theory

Even though this theory has been used in many management development programs, not many studies have been conducted to directly evaluate the theory (e.g., Blank, Weitzel & Green, 1990; Fernandez & Vecchio, 1997; Goodson, McGee, & Cashman, 1989; Hambleton & Gumpert, 1982; Norris & Vecchio, 1992; Vecchio, 1987). A few studies found support for the proposition that more directive supervision is needed for subordinates who have low ability and confidence. However, there was little evidence that using the contingent pattern of task and relations behavior prescribed by the theory will make leaders more effective. The studies designed to test the theory did not examine the effect of developmental interventions. With regard to other research on task and relations behavior (see Chapter 3), it is more consistent with the leadership model proposed by Blake and Mouton, which specifies that a relatively high level of both task and relations behavior is optimal as long as the specific types of behavior are appropriate for the situation.

Conceptual weaknesses limit the utility of situational leadership theory and help to explain the lack of support for it in the research. Leadership behavior is not defined in a clear and consistent way from quadrant to quadrant, and sometimes task and relations behaviors are defined in terms of decision styles such as autocratic telling, consulting, and delegating (Graeff, 1983). The model lacks a clear explanation of the process by which leader behavior influences subordinate performance. Maturity is a composite of diverse elements (task complexity, subordinate confidence, ability, and motivation), and the procedure used to weight and combine them is highly questionable (Barrow, 1977).

For example, the assumption that a subordinate is less mature if skilled but unmotivated than if motivated but unskilled is doubtful. It is easier to explain leadership effectiveness when the components of maturity are conceptualized as distinct variables. Hersey and Blanchard acknowledge that leaders can influence some components of maturity with developmental interventions, and it is more appropriate to conceptualize subordinate ability and motivation as intervening variables that can be influenced by the leader than as exogenous situational variables. Finally, the theory fails to consider other situational variables that are important for determining the appropriate pattern of leadership behavior.

Despite its deficiencies, the theory has made some positive contributions to our understanding of dyadic leadership. One contribution was the emphasis on flexible, adaptive behavior, which has become a central tenet of some recent theory and research. Hersey and Blanchard pointed out that it is essential to treat different subordinates differently, and to vary behavior as the situation changes. Moreover, they advanced the proposition that leaders should be aware of opportunities to build the skills and confidence of subordinates rather than assuming that a subordinate with deficiencies in skill or motivation must forever remain a problem employee.

Leadership Substitutes Theory

Kerr and Jermier (1978) developed a model to identify aspects of the situation that reduce the importance of leadership by managers and other formal leaders. The theory makes a distinction between two kinds of situational variables: substitutes and neutralizers. Substitutes make leader behavior unnecessary and redundant. They include any characteristics of the subordinates, task, or organization that ensure subordinates will clearly understand their roles, know how to do the work, be highly motivated, and be satisfied with their jobs. Neutralizers are any characteristics of the task or organization that prevent a leader from acting in a specified way or that nullify the effects of the leader's actions. For example, a leader's lack of authority to reward effective performance is a situational constraint that serves as a neutralizer, whereas subordinate lack of interest in an incentive offered by the leader is a condition that makes the behavior pointless.

The theory does not explicitly identify intervening variables, but two of them (role clarity and task motivation) are implicit in the assumptions of the model. As noted by Howell and colleagues (1990, p. 23), ". . . leadership substitutes focus on whether subordinates are receiving needed task guidance and incentives to perform without taking it for granted that the formal leader is the primary supplier." In effect, substitutes are aspects of the situation that cause intervening variables to be at optimal levels, whereas neutralizers are constraints that prevent or discourage the leader from doing anything to improve existing deficiencies in intervening variables.

In the initial version of the model, Kerr and Jermier (1978) were mostly concerned with identifying substitutes and neutralizers for supportive and instrumental leadership. Supportive leadership is similar to consideration, and instrumental leadership is similar to initiating structure. A preliminary list of substitutes and neutralizers for these broad behavior categories is shown in Table 8-2. According to Kerr and Jermier, various attributes of the subordinates, the task, and the organization may serve as substitutes or neutralizers for leader behavior.

TABLE 8-2 Substitutes and Neutralizers for Supportive and Instrumental Leadership		
Substitute or Neutralizer	*Supportive Leadership*	*Instrumental Leadership*
A. Subordinate Characteristics		
1. Experience, ability, training		Substitute
2. Professional orientation	Substitute	Substitute
3. Indifference toward rewards	Neutralizer	Neutralizer
B. Task Characteristics		
1. Structured, routine task		Substitute
2. Feedback provided by task		Substitute
3. Intrinsically satisfying task	Substitute	
C. Organization Characteristics		
1. Cohesive work group	Substitute	Substitute
2. Low position power	Neutralizer	Neutralizer
3. Formalization (roles, procedures)		Substitute
4. Inflexibility (rules, policies)		Neutralizer
5. Dispersed subordinate work sites	Neutralizer	Neutralizer

Source: Based on S. Kerr and J. M. Jermier, "Substitutes for Leadership: Their Meaning and Measurement," *Organizational Behavior and Human Performance,* 22 (1978), pp. 375–403

Subordinate Characteristics

Little direction is necessary when subordinates have extensive prior experience or training, because they already possess the skills and knowledge to know what to do and how to do it. For example, medical doctors, airline pilots, accountants, electricians, and other professionals do not require much supervision and often do not want it. Likewise, professionals who are internally motivated by their values, needs, and ethics do not need to be encouraged by the leader to do high-quality work.

The attractiveness of various organizational rewards depends in part on the needs and personality of subordinates. Indifference toward rewards controlled by the manager serves as a neutralizer of both supportive and instrumental behavior by the manager. For example, subordinates who desire more time off with their family will not be motivated by the offer of more money for working extra hours.

Task Characteristics

Another substitute for instrumental leadership is a simple, repetitive task. Subordinates can quickly learn the appropriate skills for this type of task without extensive training and direction by the leader. When the task provides automatic feedback on how well the work is being performed, the leader does not need to provide much feedback. For example, one study found that workers in a company with networked computer systems and computer integrated manufacturing did not need much supervision because they were able to obtain feedback about productivity and quality directly from the information system, and they could get help in solving problems by asking other people in the network (Lawler, 1981).

If the task is interesting and enjoyable, subordinates may be sufficiently motivated by the work itself without any need for the leader to encourage and inspire them. In addition, a task that is interesting and enjoyable may serve as a substitute for supportive leadership with regard to ensuring a high level of job satisfaction.

Group and Organization Characteristics

In organizations with detailed written rules, regulations, and policies, little direction is necessary once the rules and policies have been learned by subordinates. Rules and policies can serve as a neutralizer as well as a substitute if they are so inflexible that they prevent a leader from making changes in job assignments or work procedures to facilitate subordinate effort. Supportive and instrumental leader behaviors are neutralized when subordinates are geographically dispersed and have only infrequent contact with their leader, as in the cases of many sales representatives. An automatic reward system such as commissions or gain sharing can substitute for a leader's use of rewards and punishments to motivate subordinates. Limited position power or a strong labor union tends to neutralize a manager's use of rewards and punishments to motivate subordinates.

Another substitute for supportive leadership is a highly cohesive work group in which subordinates obtain psychological support from each other when needed. Group cohesiveness may substitute for leadership efforts to motivate subordinates if social pressure exists for each member to make a significant contribution to the group task. On the other hand, cohesiveness may serve as a neutralizer if relations with management are poor, and social pressure is exerted to restrict production.

Implications for Improving Leadership

Howell and colleagues (1990) contend that some situations have so many neutralizers that it is difficult or impossible for any leader to succeed. In this event, the remedy is not to replace the leader or provide more training, but rather to change the situation. One approach is to make the situation more favorable for the leader by removing neutralizers. Another approach is to make leadership less important by increasing substitutes.

Kerr and Jermier (1978) suggest the interesting possibility that substitutes may be increased to the point where leaders are altogether superfluous. However, it is important to remember that their model was designed to deal only with substitutes for leadership behavior by a formal leader. For many substitutes, behavior by the formal leader is merely replaced by similar leadership behavior carried out by peers or other informal leaders. Early behavior research demonstrated that leadership functions may be shared among members of a group, rather than being performed entirely by a single formal leader (Bowers & Seashore, 1966; Slater, 1955). Research on self-managed teams has verified that members can assume responsibility for many of the leadership functions formerly performed by an appointed manager. However, even self-managed teams usually have an internal coordinator, and for most of these teams it is also desirable to have an external leader to perform leadership functions that involve relationships with the larger organization (see Chapter 11).

Research on the Theory

The empirical research has found support for some aspects of the theory, but other aspects have not been tested or supported (e.g., Howell & Dorfman, 1981, 1986; Pitner, 1986; Podsakoff, Niehoff, MacKenzie, & Williams, 1993). One comprehensive review (Podsakoff et al., 1995) found little evidence that situational variables moderate the relationship between leader behavior and subordinate motivation or satisfaction, but the research found considerable evidence that situational variables directly affect subordinate satisfaction or motivation. The results seem to support the conclusion reached by McIntosh (1988) that much of the evaluation research has emphasized the wrong aspects of the theory. She proposed that it is more useful to evaluate the direct effect of situational variables on criterion variables (e.g., substitutes) or on leader behavior (constraints) than to continue searching for situational moderating effects on leader behavior (e.g., enhancers and neutralizers).

Conceptual Weaknesses

The theory has several conceptual weaknesses. It does not provide a detailed rationale for each substitute and neutralizer in terms of causal processes involving explicit intervening variables. A description of explanatory processes would help differentiate between substitutes that reduce the importance of an intervening variable and substitutes that involve leadership behavior by people other than the leader. For example, the importance of subordinate ability for group performance can be reduced by technological improvements such as automation and artificial intelligence. A quite different situation is one in which ability remains important, but the task skills needed by subordinates are enhanced by someone besides the formal leader (e.g., coworkers, outside trainers).

It is difficult to identify specific substitutes and neutralizers for broadly defined behavior categories such as supportive and instrumental leadership. The theory would be improved by replacing them with more specific behaviors. Some more recent studies testing the theory have used specific behaviors such as contingent rewarding and role clarification, but the development of the theory has not kept up with this research.

Summary

The complexity and ambiguity of leadership substitutes theory makes it difficult to test. In view of the limitations in research on leadership substitutes, it is premature to assess the theory's validity. Perhaps the greatest contribution of the theory is to provide a different perspective on leadership. In the 1970s when this theory was formulated, most leadership theories emphasized the role of formal leaders as the primary determinant of subordinate motivation and satisfaction. Leader substitutes theory deemphasized the importance of formal leaders by showing how their influence can be replaced by work design, reward systems, informal peer leadership, and self-management. As such, the theory helped to encourage more of a systems perspective on leadership processes in groups and organizations.

Multiple-Linkage Model

The multiple-linkage model (Yukl, 1981, 1989) builds upon earlier models of leadership and group effectiveness. The model includes four types of variables: managerial behaviors, intervening variables, criterion variables, and situational variables. The model describes in a general way the interacting effects of managerial behavior and situational variables on the intervening variables that determine the performance of a work unit. The causal relationships among major types of variables are depicted in Figure 8-6. Situational variables in the model exert influence at three points: (1) they

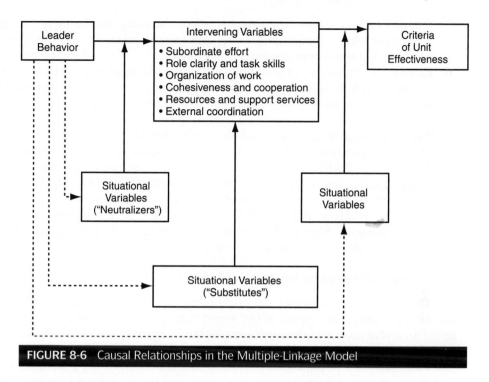

FIGURE 8-6   Causal Relationships in the Multiple-Linkage Model

constrain managerial behavior and moderate its effects; (2) they directly influence intervening variables; and (3) they determine the relative importance of the intervening variables.

Intervening Variables

To understand how a leader can influence the performance of a group or organizational subunit, it is helpful to examine intervening variables that determine group performance. The six intervening variables in the model are based on earlier research and theory on determinants of individual and group performance (e.g., Hackman, Brousseau, & Weiss, 1976; Likert, 1967; McGrath, 1984; Porter & Lawler, 1968). Unlike most other situational theories, the intervening variables are defined primarily at the group level, as in theories of team leadership (see Chapter 11).

1. *Task commitment.*   The extent to which unit members strive to attain a high level of performance and show a high degree of personal commitment to unit task objectives.
2. *Ability and role clarity.*   The extent to which unit members understand their individual job responsibilities, know what to do, and have the skills to do it.
3. *Organization of the work.*   The extent to which effective performance strategies are used to attain unit task objectives and the work is organized to ensure efficient utilization of personnel, equipment, and facilities.
4. *Cooperation and mutual trust.*   The extent to which group members trust each other, share information and ideas, help each other, and identify with the work unit.

5. *Resources and support.*   The extent to which the group has the budgetary funds, tools, equipment, supplies, personnel, and facilities needed to do the work, and necessary information or assistance from other units.

6. *External coordination.*   The extent to which activities of the work unit are synchronized with the interdependent activities in other parts of the organization and other organizations (e.g., suppliers, clients, joint venture partners).

The intervening variables interact with each other to determine the effectiveness of a group or organizational subunit. A serious deficiency in one intervening variable may lower group effectiveness, even though the other intervening variables are not deficient. The greater the relative importance of a particular intervening variable, the more group performance will be reduced by a deficiency in this variable. The relative importance of the intervening variables depends on the type of work unit and other aspects of the situation. Aspects of the situation that make an intervening variable especially important are summarized in Table 8-3.

Situational Influences on Intervening Variables

The situation can influence the intervening variables independently of anything done by the leader. This aspect of the model is similar to Kerr and Jermier's "substitutes." In a very favorable situation, some of the intervening variables may already be at their maximum short-term level, making the job of the leader much easier.

Two situational variables that influence task commitment are the formal reward system and the intrinsically motivating properties of the work itself. Member commitment to perform the task effectively will be greater if the organization has a reward system that provides attractive rewards contingent on performance, as in the case of many sales jobs. Intrinsic motivation is likely to be high for subordinates if the work requires varied skills, is interesting and challenging, and provides automatic feedback about performance.

Situational variables that affect the ability of group members include the recruitment and selection system of the organization and the prior training and experience of the members. An organization with effective recruiting and selection procedures and high salaries is more likely to attract qualified people with high ability. Ability is likely to be higher also for professionals and people in skilled trades who receive extensive training prior to joining the organization.

Role clarity is affected by task structure, prior member experience, and external dependencies. Group members are likely to have a better understanding of role requirements when the task is simple, they have considerable experience doing the work, or the organization has elaborate rules and regulations dictating how the work should be done and subordinates are familiar with them. Conditions that increase role ambiguity are as follows: (1) the task has multiple performance criteria that are somewhat incompatible with each other and priorities are unclear; (2) the task requires continuous coordination and mutual adjustment among members; (3) the nature of the work or technology is changing, requiring new skills and procedures; (4) a crisis or emergency creates confusion; and (5) work unit operations are frequently affected by changes in policies, plans, or priorities determined by higher management or clients.

TABLE 8-3 Conditions Affecting the Intervening Variables in the Multiple-Linkage Model

Intervening Variable	Conditions Where Already High	Situations Where Most Important
Subordinate Effort and Commitment	• Interesting, challenging, intrinsically motivating task. • Subordinates have strong work ethic values. • Crisis where failure would be costly for subordinates.	• Complex, labor-intensive work requiring high subordinate initiative and persistence. • High exposure task for which mistakes are very costly.
Subordinate Ability Role Clarity	• Subordinates have extensive prior training and experience. • Organization provides detailed formal rules and procedures. • Work is highly automated.	• Work unit has complex, difficult tasks with unique aspects. • Work requires a high degree of technical skill by subordinates. • High exposure task for which mistakes are very costly. • Frequent changes in priorities or schedules due to clients and users. • Work is subject to unpredictable disruptions and crises.
Cooperation and Teamwork	• Group has stable, homogeneous, compatible membership. • Members have shared goals consistent with task objectives. • Work unit has strong traditions that evoke pride of membership.	• Task roles in the work unit are highly inter-dependent. • Subordinates share scarce equipment or limited facilities. • Subordinates work together in close proximity for long time.
Organization of Work and Performance Strategies for it	• Organization specifies optimal way to structure the work. • Subordinates have extensive prior training and experience.	• Work unit has a complex and difficult mission. • Work unit has several diverse tasks (need coordination). • High exposure task for which mistakes are very costly.
Resources Needed to Do the Work	• Organization provides adequate resources as needed. • Organization has good inventory control system for materials.	• The work requires large amounts of scarce resources. • Work unit is highly dependent on unreliable sources of supply.
External Coordination	• Organization has structural mechanisms for achieving lateral coordination. • External coordination is done by higher management or other people in organization.	• Work unit has high lateral interdependence with other units in the same organization. • Frequent changes in priorities or schedules due to client demands. • Work unit is highly dependent on unreliable sources of supply.

Situational variables that affect work group organization include the type of technology used to do the work and the competitive strategy of the organization. Work roles and procedures are more likely to be imposed by top management when the task is simple and repetitive than when it is complex and variable. However, standard procedures imposed by the organization to maximize efficiency are only a substitute for leader planning and organizing when they result in optimal performance strategies, which is not always true even for highly structured tasks. There are many examples of organizations in which the operating workers find better ways to do the work than the staff experts.

Cooperation and teamwork are influenced by the size of the group, the stability of membership, the similarity among members in values and background, the reward system, and the organization of the work. More cohesiveness and cooperation are likely in small groups with a stable, homogeneous membership. Less cooperation is likely when group members have highly specialized jobs with different task objectives, or when the reward system fosters intense competition among individuals. In view of the prevalence of conflict in organizations, it is likely that the team building will continue to be an important function for most leaders.

The adequacy of resources needed to do the work is influenced by the organization's formal budgetary systems, procurement systems, and inventory control systems, as well as by economic conditions at the time. An adequate level of resources and support is more likely to be provided when the organization is prosperous and growing than when the organization is in decline and faces severe resource shortages. Because few organizations have abundant extra resources in today's competitive world, it is likely that the role of obtaining resources will continue to be important for most leaders.

External coordination is affected by the formal structure of the organization. High lateral interdependence increases the amount of coordination needed among subunits of an organization. Sometimes this coordination is facilitated by special integrating mechanisms such as integrator positions and cross-functional committees (Galbraith, 1973; Lawrence & Lorsch, 1967). Dependency on outsiders such as clients or subcontractors increases the need for external coordination, and sometimes this coordination is facilitated by people in special liaison positions. Nevertheless, structural mechanisms to facilitate external coordination are unlikely to entirely substitute the need for this leadership role.

Short-Term Actions to Correct Deficiencies

A basic proposition of the theory is that leader actions to correct any deficiencies in the intervening variables will improve group performance. A leader who fails to recognize opportunities to correct deficiencies in key intervening variables, who recognizes the opportunities but fails to act, or who acts but is not skilled will be less than optimally effective. An ineffective leader may make things worse by acting in ways that increase rather than decrease the deficiency in one or more intervening variables. For example, a leader who uses coercive influence tactics may reduce subordinate effort.

Table 8-4 summarizes possible short-term actions to deal with deficiencies in the intervening variables. Leaders may influence group members to work faster or do better quality work (e.g., by offering special incentives, by giving an inspiring talk about the importance of the work, by setting challenging goals). Leaders may increase member ability to do the work (e.g., by showing them better methods for doing the work, by clearing up confusion about who is responsible for what). Leaders may organize and coordinate

TABLE 8-4 Leader Actions to Deal with Deficiencies in Intervening Variables

Subordinates are apathetic or discouraged about the work.
- Set challenging goals and express confidence subordinates can attain them.
- Articulate an appealing vision of what the group could accomplish or become.
- Use rational persuasion and inspirational appeals to influence commitment.
- Lead by example.
- Use consultation and delegation.
- Provide recognition.
- Reward effective behavior.

Subordinates are confused about what to do or how to do their work.
- Make clear assignments.
- Set specific goals and provide feedback about performance.
- Provide more direction of ongoing activities.
- Provide instruction or coaching as needed.
- Identify skill deficiencies and arrange for necessary skill training.
- Recruit and hire skilled people to work in unit.

The group is disorganized and/or it uses weak performance strategies.
- Develop plans to accomplish objectives.
- Identify and correct coordination problems.
- Reorganize activities to make better use of people, resources, and equipment.
- Identify and eliminate inefficient and unnecessary activities.
- Provide more decisive direction of ongoing activities in a crisis.

Little cooperation and teamwork exist among members of the group.
- Emphasize common interests and encourage cooperation.
- Encourage constructive resolution of conflict and help mediate conflicts.
- Increase group incentives and reduce competition.
- Use symbols and rituals to build identification with the work unit.
- Use team-building activities.

The group has inadequate resources to do the work.
- Requisition or borrow specific resources needed immediately for the work.
- Find more reliable or alternative sources of supplies
- Ration available resources if necessary.
- Initiate improvement projects to upgrade equipment and facilities.
- Lobby with higher authorities for a larger budget.

External coordination with other subunits or outsiders is weak.
- Network with peers and outsiders to develop more cooperative relationships.
- Consult more with peers and outsiders when making plans.
- Keep peers and outsiders informed about changes.
- Monitor closely to detect coordination problems quickly.
- Meet with peers and outsiders to resolve coordination problems.
- Negotiate favorable agreements with peers and outsiders for group outputs.

activities in a more efficient way (e.g., by finding ways to reduce delays, duplication of effort, and wasted effort; by matching people to tasks better; by finding better ways to use people and resources). Leaders may obtain resources needed immediately to do the work (e.g., information, personnel, equipment, materials, supplies). Leaders may act to improve external coordination by meeting with outsiders to plan activities and resolve conflicting demands on the work unit.

The model does not imply that there is only one optimal pattern of managerial behavior in any given situation. Leaders usually have some choice among intervening variables in need of improvement and different patterns of behavior are usually possible to correct a particular deficiency. The overall pattern of leadership behavior by the designated leader and other group members is more important than any single action. In this respect, the model is similar to Stewart's (1976) choices (see Chapter 2). However, a leader whose attention is focused on intervening variables that are not deficient or not important will fail to improve unit performance.

Some aspects of the situation limit a leader's discretion in making changes and reacting to problems. These influences are similar to Stewart's (1976) constraints and Kerr and Jermier's (1978) neutralizers. The extent to which a leader is capable of doing something in the short run to improve any of the intervening variables is limited by the leader's position power, organizational policies imposed by top management, the technology used to do the work, and legal-contractual restrictions (e.g., labor-management agreements, contracts with suppliers, requirements mandated by government agencies). Constraints may prevent a leader from rewarding or punishing members, changing work assignments or procedures, and procuring supplies and equipment.

Long-Term Effects on Group Performance

Over a longer period of time, leaders can make larger improvements in group performance by modifying the situation to make it more favorable. Effective leaders act to reduce constraints, increase substitutes, and reduce the importance of intervening variables that are not amenable to improvement. In addition, effective leaders take actions that have direct but delayed effects on the intervening variables. The indirect effects, shown by the dotted lines in Figure 8-6, occur concurrently with continued efforts to make immediate improvements in the intervening variables. These indirect effects of leaders usually involve sequences of related behaviors carried out over a longer time period. The effects are slower to be felt, but they are often more important for the organization. A similar distinction between direct and indirect effects has been made by other theorists as well (e.g., Hunt, 1991; Lord & Maher, 1991), and it reflects the systems perspective of leadership that seems to be gaining favor.

More research has been conducted on short-term, reactive behaviors by leaders than on long-term, proactive behaviors by leaders, and the latter are still difficult to classify in any meaningful way. Useful insights are provided by some of the descriptive research reviewed in Chapter 2. Stewart (1976) described how managers exploit different opportunities to improve conditions, Mintzberg (1973) described how managers initiate improvement projects, Kanter (1982) described how middle managers get innovations accepted, Kotter (1982) described how managers get long-term aspects of their agenda implemented, and Gabarro (1985) described how CEOs turn around failing organizations. The literature describing how leaders change the mission or basic strategy of an organization and influence the culture of the organization is reviewed in more detail in Chapters 10 and 12.

Some examples of possible actions a leader may take to improve the situation are as follows (see also Table 8-4):

- Gain more control over acquisition of resources necessary to do the work by cultivating better relationships with suppliers, finding alternative sources, and reducing dependence on unreliable sources.
- Gain more control over the demand for the unit's products and services by finding new customers, opening new markets, advertising more, and modifying the products or services to be more acceptable to clients and customers.
- Initiate new, more profitable activities for the work unit that will make better use of personnel, equipment, and facilities.
- Initiate long-term improvement programs to upgrade personnel, equipment, and facilities in the work unit, such as by replacing old equipment, establishing training programs, and reconstructing facilities.
- Modify the formal structure of the work unit to solve chronic problems and reduce demands on the leader for short-term troubleshooting, such as by redefining authority relationships, centralizing (or decentralizing) some decision making, creating (or eliminating) positions, modifying information systems, and simplifying (or eliminating) rules and standard procedures.
- Alter the culture of the organization to emphasize values, beliefs, and norms that are internalized sources of motivation to excel, learn, and cooperate.

Evaluation of the Multiple-Linkage Model

The multiple-linkage model is more complex and comprehensive than earlier theories, because it includes more of the relevant intervening variables, a wider range of leader behaviors, and more situational variables. It was one of the first contingency theories to emphasize leadership processes at the group level rather than the dyadic level.

The model has several conceptual weaknesses. It does not specify how different types of leader behavior interact with each other in their effects on intervening variables. The long-term actions of managers are described only in general terms, and specific hypotheses about these behaviors are needed. The interaction among situational variables has not been specified explicitly, and the theory fails to identify common configurations of them. Thus, the multiple-linkage model is still more a general conceptual framework than a refined theory.

The complexity of the model makes it difficult to test in a single study. Indirect support for some aspects of the model is provided by relevant research on other leadership theories that include similar aspects of leadership behavior. However, relatively few studies on leader behavior included intervening variables, and as already noted the studies on situational variables yielded weak, inconsistent results. The best prospects for testing the model may be the growing interest in team leadership, which has stimulated research on models similar to the multiple-linkage model (see Chapter 11).

Cognitive Resources Theory

A more recent situational model developed by Fiedler and his colleagues (Fiedler, 1986; Fiedler & Garcia, 1987) deals with the cognitive abilities of leaders. This theory examines the conditions under which cognitive resources such as intelligence and experience are related to group performance. It is an important research question, because organizations use measures of prior experience and intelligence for selecting managers. According to cognitive resources theory, the performance of a leader's group is determined by a complex interaction among two leader traits (intelligence and experience), one type of leader behavior (directive leadership), and two aspects of the leadership situation (interpersonal stress and the nature of the group's task).

Propositions

The primary causal relationships in cognitive resources theory are depicted in Figure 8-7. According to the theory, interpersonal stress for the leader moderates the relation between leader intelligence and subordinate performance. Stress may be due to a boss who creates role conflict or demands miracles without providing necessary resources and support. Other sources of stress include frequent work crises and serious conflicts with subordinates. Under low stress, high intelligence results in good plans and decisions. In this situation, a highly intelligent leader relies on intellectual ability to analyze the problem and find the best solution. In contrast, under high stress, there is no relationship (or a negative relationship) between leader intelligence and decision quality. The theory provides several possible explanations why highly intelligent leaders sometimes make terrible task decisions when under stress. The most plausible explanation is that stress interferes with information processing and decision making. Under high stress, a leader is more likely to be distracted and unable to focus on the task. Intelligence provides no advantage, because it cannot be applied. The leader may withdraw and let the group drift, or the leader may display nonproductive behavior that disrupts the group processes.

Interpersonal stress for the leader also moderates the relationship between leader experience and subordinate performance. Experience is usually measured in terms of time on the job, and it is assumed to result in habitual behavior patterns for effectively dealing with task problems. It is also assumed that people under stress tend to deal with task problems by reverting to previously learned behavior rather than by treating them as new problems. Experience will be positively related to the quality of leader decisions under high interpersonal stress, but it is not related to decision quality under low stress. Presumably, experienced leaders rely mostly on intelligence under low stress, and they rely mostly on experience under high stress. Leaders with little experience rely on intelligence in both situations.

The theory also describes one aspect of leader behavior that mediates the relationship between a leader's cognitive resources and group performance. This part of the

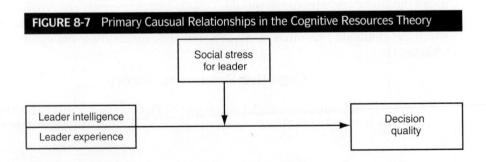

FIGURE 8-7 Primary Causual Relationships in the Cognitive Resources Theory

theory is similar to some parts of the Vroom-Yetton (1973) normative decision model (see Chapter 4). Leader intelligence and expertise contribute to group performance only when the leader is directive and subordinates require guidance to perform the task effectively. The theory assumes that intelligent leaders devise better plans and action strategies for doing the work than nonintelligent leaders, especially when the task is complex. The theory also assumes that a leader's plans and decisions are communicated to subordinates through directive behavior. If the leader has low ability but group members have high ability and also share the leader's task objectives, then a nondirective (participative) leader is more effective than a directive (autocratic) leader for a complex task. For a simple, routine task that subordinates already know how to perform, no relationship is likely to occur between leader intelligence and group performance, even for directive leaders.

Fiedler has attempted to link cognitive resource theory to the least preferred coworker (LPC) contingency model by proposing that leader LPC scores may be the primary determinant of directive behavior in high and low stress situations. However, little research has been conducted to explore this possibility.

Research on Cognitive Resources Theory

Evidence supporting the proposition that stress moderates the effect of intelligence and experience was found in a study of Coast Guard officers (Potter & Fiedler, 1981) and a study of fire department officers (Frost, 1983). However, only one study examined possible reasons why stress moderates the relation of leader intelligence and experience to effectiveness. Gibson, Fiedler, and Barrett (1993) reanalyzed data from an earlier study on three-person groups of ROTC cadets with a creative task. Under low stress conditions, intelligence was positively related to the production of creative ideas by leaders and followers alike, and the more intelligent leaders had more productive groups. Under high stress conditions, leader intelligence was not related to the production of creative ideas by the leader, and it was negatively related to the production of creative ideas by followers. Intelligent leaders talked more, but they tended to ramble and contributed few useful ideas. By dominating the discussion, these leaders prevented members from contributing more. The net effect was that under high stress, the more intelligent leaders had less productive groups.

The proposition that intellectual ability is related more to performance for directive leaders than for nondirective leaders was generally supported in five earlier studies reported by Fiedler and Garcia (1987, p. 161) and in three subsequent studies (Blyth, 1987; Murphy, Blyth, & Fiedler, 1992; Vecchio, 1990). This proposition from cognitive resource theory also is also supported by some studies conducted to evaluate the Vroom-Yetton model (see Chapter 4).

Limitations of the Research

It is too early to reach any conclusions about the utility of the theory. Results from the validation research are inconsistent across studies, methodological problems make it difficult to interpret some of the results, and some aspects of the theory have not been adequately tested (Fiedler, 1992; Gibson, 1992; Vecchio, 1990). Several methodological weaknesses have been identified.

Most of the studies cited by Fiedler and Garcia (1987) were conducted to test the LPC contingency model and only later reanalyzed to test cognitive resource theory. These correlational studies do not provide a complete test of the propositions in the theory (Vecchio, 1990). A better research design would be an experiment comparing outcomes for various combinations of intelligence and experience under stress and nonstress conditions.

The most controversial aspect of the theory is the idea that leader effectiveness is predicted by intelligence in low stress conditions and by experience in high stress conditions. The theory provides some possible reasons for poor-quality decisions under stress, but the explanations have not been verified. More studies with measures of mediating processes are needed.

Most of the validation studies relied on surrogate measures of experience, such as time on the job, rather than using a direct measure of relevant job expertise. Bettin and Kennedy (1990) found that the leadership performance of Army officers was predicted by the amount of relevant prior experience, but not by time in present position, time in the service, or number of previous positions. Similar results were found by Avery and colleagues (2003) for head coaches in the National Basketball Association. Another problem with the use of time in position as a measure of experience is that this measure may be contaminated by extraneous factors related to stress. One alternative explanation for Fiedler's results is that experienced leaders have more stress tolerance, because leaders who could not handle the stress already quit or were dismissed. Another rival explanation is that experienced leaders have had more time to develop a network of support relationships that will help them under stressful conditions.

Conceptual Weaknesses

The cognitive resources theory also has some conceptual weaknesses that limit its utility for explaining effective leadership. A major trait variable in the theory is general intelligence. No explicit rationale is provided for use of general intelligence rather than specific cognitive skills. It is likely that the theory would be improved by identifying specific aspects of intellectual ability relevant to the task (Vecchio, 1990).

There is only one leadership behavior in the theory, and it is too general to capture the complexities found in earlier research on participative leadership. The Vroom-Yetton model described in Chapter 4 provides a much better explanation of the effects of participative decision procedures under different conditions. Cognitive resources theory would be improved by a more precise explanation of the influence of cognitive resources on leader behavior and effectiveness.

General Evaluation of Contingency Theories

Table 8-5 lists the major features of the contingency theories described in this chapter and the Vroom and Yetton (1973) normative decision model described in Chapter 4. The table makes it easier to compare the theories with respect to content and validation. All seven theories contain situational moderator variables, but the variety of situational variables is greater in some theories than in others. It seems desirable for a contingency theory to include many relevant aspects of the situation, but to do so makes a theory difficult to test. Intervening variables are helpful to explain how leaders influence subordinate performance, but only three of the theories have explicit intervening variables.

TABLE 8-5	Comparison of Contingency Theories				
Contingency Theory	**Leader Traits**	**Leader Behavior**	**Situational Variables**	**Intervening Variables**	**Validation Results**
LPC Contingency Model	LPC	None	Task structure, L-M relations	None	Many studies, some support
Path-Goal Theory	None	Instrumental, supportive, participative, achievement	Many aspects	Expectancies, valences, role ambiguity	Many studies, some support
Situational Leadership Theory	None	Task and relations	Subordinate maturity	None	Few studies, little support
Leadership Substitutes Theory	None	Instrumental, supportive	Many aspects	None	Few studies, inconclusive
Multiple-Linkage Model	None	Many aspects	Many aspects	Effort, ability, organization, teamwork, resources, external coordination	Few studies, inconclusive
Cognitive Resource Theory	Intelligence and experience	Directive	Stress, group ability	None	Few studies, some support
Normative Decision Theory	None	Decision procedures	Many aspects	Decision quality and acceptance	Many studies, good support

A contingency theory is supported by a pattern of results that is consistent with the propositions of the theory. If the theory postulates a causal chain of sequential effects from leader behavior to intervening variable to outcomes, the results must be consistent with this explanation. Unfortunately, most of the contingency theories are stated so ambiguously that it is difficult to derive specific, testable propositions. Most of the research provides only a partial test of the theories. In general, the research suffers from lack of accurate measures and reliance on weak research designs that do not permit strong inferences about direction of causality (Korman & Tanofsky, 1975; Schriesheim & Kerr, 1977).

Some behavioral scientists have questioned whether contingency theories such as those reviewed in this chapter have any utility for showing managers how to become more effective. For example, McCall (1977) contends that the hectic pace of managerial work and the relative lack of control over it by managers make it impossible to apply complex theories that specify the optimal behavior for every type of situation. Managers are so busy dealing with problems that they don't have time to stop and analyze the situation with a complicated model. McCall also questions the implicit assumption of most contingency theories that there is a single best way for the manager to act within a given situation. Leaders face an immense variety of rapidly changing situations, and several different patterns of behavior may be equally effective in the same situation. The contingency theories do not provide sufficient guidance in the form of general principles to help managers recognize the underlying leadership requirements and choices in the myriad of fragmented activities and problems confronting them. What may be needed is a theory with both universal elements (e.g., general principles) and situational elements (e.g., guidelines to help identify desirable behaviors for a particular type of situation).

Applications for Managers

Despite their deficiencies, the contingency theories and related research provide insights about effective leadership in different situations. The following guidelines, which are summarized in Table 8-6, describe conditions where specific leadership behaviors are likely to increase subordinate satisfaction and performance. Additional situational propositions can be found in other chapters of the book.

- **Maintain situational awareness.**

Situational awareness means understanding aspects of the situation that are relevant for the effectiveness of a manager. It is important to understand the external events and trends that will impact performance and require adjustments in strategy and work processes. It is also important to understand the processes and people within the organization. It is difficult to resolve a problem, initiate a change, or inspire commitment without a clear understanding of the shared values and beliefs that make up the organization culture, the prior events and decisions that determine how the organization got to where it is now, the impact proposed changes could have on work processes and customers, and the political processes that affect major decisions. To become more situationally aware, it is necessary to actively probe beneath surface appearances to learn about prior events, power relationships, interpersonal relationships, informal processes, hidden agendas, and the attitudes and feelings of the people who will be involved in a decision or affected by it. Procedures for obtaining and analyzing information about the situation are described in Chapters 4, 10, and 12.

- **Use more planning for a long, complex task.**

A long, complex task is one that involves many interrelated activities performed by a large group of people over a considerable period of time (e.g., weeks or months).

TABLE 8-6   Guidelines for Leaders

- Maintain situational awareness.
- Use more planning for a long, complex task.
- Consult more with people who have relevant knowledge.
- Provide more direction to people with interdependent roles.
- Provide more direction and briefings when a crisis occurs.
- Monitor a critical task or unreliable person more closely.
- Provide more coaching to an inexperienced subordinate.
- Be more supportive to someone with a highly stressful task.

Completing the task successfully, on time, with expenditure of minimum resources requires careful planning of the activities. Planning is most useful when the steps necessary to carry out the task are known in advance, and the environment is relatively predictable. Some examples of such activities include a construction project, installation of new equipment, introduction of new information systems, and the design and execution of a training program. The leader should identify the list of necessary activities, determine the optimal sequence for them, estimate when each activity should begin and end, determine who should be responsible for performing each activity, and identify the resources needed for it. When the leader is responsible for managing a simple, routine task that will not take long to complete, a detailed plan is unnecessary.

- **Consult more with people who have relevant knowledge.**

A major prescription of the Vroom-Yetton (1973) model (see Chapter 4) was the need for more participative leadership when the task is complex and unstructured, and subordinates (or team members) have relevant knowledge and creative ideas about how to perform the task. An additional condition for effective use of consultation is goal congruence. The quality of decisions is likely to be improved when the leader consults with people who have both relevant expertise and strong commitment to achieve task objectives. Sometimes it is appropriate to hold meetings to jointly solve problems, and other times it is more appropriate to consult with one or two individuals before making a decision.

- **Provide more direction to people with interdependent roles.**

Role interdependence among group members increases role ambiguity, because it requires frequent mutual adjustments in behavior. A team will not achieve high performance unless the actions of its members are closely coordinated. Even when the individual tasks seem relatively structured, members may be confused about how to make mutual adjustments to coordinate their actions. Confusion is greater when team members lack prior experience in performing a particular task together. Some examples include a newly formed team, an established team that experiences a significant change in membership, or an established team that must perform a new type of task. Such a situation requires ongoing direction to coordinate the interdependent actions of different team members. The amount of direction needed by the leader can be reduced by asking the team to practice its response to a simulated crisis, so that members become accustomed to working together closely and can anticipate each other's behavior. Examples include sports teams (e.g., basketball, ice hockey), rescue teams, combat teams, and teams that operate complex equipment (e.g., airplanes, submarines).

- **Provide more direction and briefings when a crisis occurs.**

The need for more direction is especially great for a team that must react quickly in a coordinated way to cope with a serious crisis or emergency for which it is unprepared. Knowing how to remain calm and deal with a crisis in a systematic but decisive manner requires a leader with considerable skill and confidence. It is essential for the leader to make a quick but systematic analysis of the situation, organize an appropriate response, direct the actions of group members, and keep subordinates informed about the nature of the crisis and what is being done to deal with it (Torrance, 1954; Yukl & Van Fleet, 1982). In the absence of timely and accurate information, harmful rumors are likely to occur, and people may become discouraged and afraid. A manager can help prevent unnecessary stress for subordinates by interpreting threatening events and emphasizing positive elements rather than leaving people to focus on negatives. When feasible, it is helpful to provide short, periodic briefings about progress in efforts to deal with the crisis.

- **Monitor a critical task or unreliable person more closely.**

Monitoring provides information needed to detect and correct performance problems. More frequent and intensive monitoring is appropriate for a critical task that involves high exposure, so that problems can be detected before they get so bad that they will be costly and difficult to correct. However, the appropriate amount of monitoring depends also on the reliability of the subordinates who are doing the task. The less dependable and competent a subordinate is, the more monitoring is needed. An appropriate form of monitoring in this situation is the use of observation and specific questions about the work. A probing but nonevaluative style of questioning is better than a threatening, critical tone. Questions usually elicit better information if worded in an open-ended way rather than asking for a simple yes-no answer. For example, ask the subordinate to explain what has been done, rather than asking if there are any problems. Subordinates are often afraid to inform their boss about problems, mistakes, and delays, especially when the response is likely to be an angry outburst from the boss. Thus, it is essential to react to information about problems in a constructive, nonpunitive way.

- **Provide more coaching to an inexperienced subordinate.**

When the work is complex and a subordinate is inexperienced at doing it, more instruction and coaching by the leader is needed. Lack of experience is likely for subordinates who are new to the job, but it also occurs when there is a major change in how the work is done (e.g., new technology, reconfigured jobs). A leader with strong expertise can help a person discover the reasons for weak performance. One diagnostic approach is to jointly review step by step how the person carries out the task to determine whether any essential steps are omitted, unnecessary steps are included, or key steps are performed incorrectly. To increase self-reliance and problem solving, it is better to encourage the person to suggest ways to improve performance rather than dictating what needs to be done. Help the person evaluate ideas for improving performance by asking probing questions about them. When appropriate suggest additional things the person should consider to improve performance. If it becomes evident that additional instruction is necessary for a specific aspect of the task, take the person aside to show him or her how to do the work correctly, or ask an experienced coworker to provide this instruction.

- **Be more supportive to someone with a highly stressful task.**

A person who becomes emotionally upset will have more difficulty performing a task successfully, especially if it requires reasoning and problem solving. Stress is increased by unreasonable demands, uncontrollable problems, difficult interpersonal relations (e.g., critical, abusive customers), dangerous conditions (e.g., firefighting, combat, police work), and the risk of costly errors (surgery, financial advisor, aircraft maintenance). People in such situations have more need for emotional support, which may be provided by a leader, coworkers, and other people outside the organization. It is especially important for the leader to reduce rather than increase stress on a subordinate. Stress is reduced by showing appreciation, listening to problems and complaints, providing assistance when necessary, doing things to make the work environment more enjoyable, and buffering the person from unnecessary demands by outsiders. Stress is increased by being critical, making unreasonable demands, pressuring the person to work faster, and insisting on compliance with unnecessary bureaucratic requirements.

Summary

The managerial job is too complex and unpredictable to rely on a set of standardized responses to events. Effective leaders are continuously reading the situation and determining how to adapt their behavior to it. They seek to understand the task requirements, situational constraints, and interpersonal processes that determine which course of action is most likely to be successful. This chapter examined six early contingency theories that prescribe different patterns of leader behavior (or traits) for different situations.

The LPC contingency model deals with the moderating influence of three situational variables on the relationship between a leader trait (LPC) and subordinate performance. According to the model, leaders with high LPC scores are more effective in moderately favorable situations, whereas leaders with low LPC scores are more favorable in situations that are either very favorable or very unfavorable.

The path-goal theory of leadership examines how aspects of leader behavior influence subordinate satisfaction and motivation. In general, leaders motivate subordinates by influencing their perceptions of the likely consequences of different levels of effort. If subordinates believe that valued outcomes can be attained only by making a serious effort and that such an effort will be successful, then they are likely to make the effort. Aspects of the situation such as the nature of the task, the work environment, and subordinate characteristics determine the optimal level of each type of leadership behavior for improving subordinate satisfaction and effort.

In the situational leadership theory, the appropriate mix of task and relations behavior for the leader depends on the confidence and skill of a subordinate in relation to the task. Over time the leader may be able to increase subordinate maturity with a developmental intervention.

Leadership substitutes theory identifies aspects of the situation that make leadership behavior redundant or irrelevant. Various characteristics of the subordinates, task, and organization serve as substitutes for leadership and/or neutralizers of its effects. Substitutes make some types of behavior by the leader unnecessary and redundant, whereas neutralizers are constraints that prevent the leader from doing anything to improve conditions.

The multiple-linkage model describes how a leader can influence intervening variables to improve group effectiveness. The performance of a group or organizational subunit is highest when members have high task skill and motivation, they are efficiently organized, the level of member cooperation is high, adequate resources are available, and unit activities are coordinated with those of interdependent units. These intervening variables are affected by a variety of situational variables in addition to the actions of the leader. In the short run, a leader can improve group performance by taking direct action to correct any deficiencies in the intervening variables. In the longer run, the leader can improve group performance by taking action to make the situation more favorable. These actions may involve reducing constraints, enhancing substitutes, altering the relative importance of the intervening variables, or making changes to indirectly improve intervening variables.

Cognitive resources theory examines the conditions under which cognitive resources such as intelligence and experience are related to group performance. Situational variables, such as interpersonal stress, group support, and task complexity, determine whether a leader's intelligence and experience enhance group performance. Directive leader behavior is an intervening variable used to explain how a leader's cognitive resources affect group performance.

The contingency theories reviewed in this chapter are complex and difficult to test. Although they provide insights about reasons for leadership effectiveness, a major limitation of the contingency theories is a lack of sufficient attention to leadership processes that transform the way followers view themselves and their work. A better description of these processes is provided by the theories of transformational and charismatic leadership discussed in the next chapter.

Review and Discussion Questions

1. What is a situational moderator variable?
2. Briefly explain the path-goal theory.
3. Briefly explain the leadership substitutes theory.
4. Briefly explain the multiple-linkage model.
5. Briefly explain Fiedler's LPC contingency model.
6. Briefly explain Fiedler's cognitive resource theory.
7. Briefly explain Hersey and Blanchard's situational leadership theory.
8. Compare and contrast the contingency theories in this chapter with regard to level of analysis, leader characteristics, explanatory processes, and the number and type of situational variables.
9. Which theory do you think would be most useful for helping managers become more effective?
10. How well is each theory supported by the empirical research?
11. In what situations are planning, clarifying, and monitoring most likely to be effective?
12. In what situations are supporting, coaching, and consulting most likely to be effective?
13. Can you think of a situation where a group could perform effectively without any leadership (either by a designated leader or by the various group members)?

Key Terms

- cognitive resources model
- developmental intervention
- directive leadership
- intervening variable
- instrumental leadership
- least preferred coworker
- LPC contingency model
- moderator variable
- multiple-linkage model
- neutralizer
- path-goal theory
- substitute for leadership

CASE

Foreign Auto Shop

Part 1

Alan has been the owner and manager of a small auto repair shop for seven years. The auto shop has a steady and loyal clientele who appreciate the fact that they receive quick, reliable service at a fair price. Alan employs seven mechanics and two office workers.

Gil and Hans are the two oldest mechanics, and they are the easiest to supervise. When Alan assigns work to them (mostly high-precision, specialist jobs), they do it quickly and hardly ever make a mistake. Bart and Herbie are also skilled mechanics. Bart specializes in repairing motorcycles, and Herbie is a whiz at troubleshooting engine problems. Three younger workers do the jobs that call for lower-level skills, under Alan's more careful guidance. Kirk has a degree in Industrial Arts, but he couldn't get a job in his specialty without moving to another city, and he seems to have resigned himself to auto repair work. LaMont enjoys working on sports cars and is getting to be quite an expert at operating the electronic diagnostic machines. Joanie does general mechanical work and does it well.

Alan takes care of customers when they drop off their cars in the morning, then he plans the work schedule and assigns the mechanics to work on particular cars. Most of the work is done by individual mechanics, but occasionally a job requires two mechanics to work together. The work of repairing cars and conducting routine maintenance on them is well-defined; there are standard procedures and standard times to perform each type of repair task. Mechanics receive feedback about the quality of their work from testing the car and from customers (who will complain if something is not fixed properly). Alan does not spend much time actually directing or supervising the repair work. He leaves the mechanics alone unless they are having a problem and need technical advice. He almost never tells someone to do something in a directive way. Instead, he suggests various ways to deal with a problem, or he shows them how he would have handled it. When not busy with administrative responsibilities, Alan enjoys working alongside his mechanics, where he is available to answer any questions about the work. Alan's style of leadership suits his easy-going personality.

Alan also encourages his employees to participate in making decisions such as what new equipment to purchase or how to improve quality. They know that Alan is sincere in asking for their opinions and is not just doing it as a manipulative strategy to minimize their opposition to decisions that have already been made. Alan's fairness and openness have earned him the continuing respect and trust of his employees. ∎

SOURCE: Adapted from William J. Wasmuth and Leonard Greenhalgh, *Effective Supervision: Developing Your Skills Through Critical Incidents.* Prentice Hall, Copyright © 1979.

QUESTIONS

1. What is the usual leadership situation in the auto repair shop (consider the nature of the task, subordinates, and environment)?

2. Describe Alan's typical leadership style and evaluate whether it is appropriate for the leadership situation.

Part 2

Alan looked anxiously out of his office window. The sky was very dark over the nearby hills, and the storm seemed to be advancing rapidly toward the valley where his auto repair shop was located. Just to be on the safe side, Alan went out and rolled up the windows of the customer's cars in the parking lot. He noticed the creek was already running high, the result of melting snow during the warm spring days. Before he could get back into the shop, a sudden downpour of huge drops of rain soaked his clothing. Some of the mechanics laughingly teased him for "not having enough sense to come in out of the rain."

After 15 minutes of the pelting rain, Alan realized that this was no ordinary rainstorm. He went out to look at the creek again and found that it had already risen to almost the height of its banks. Alan figured it wouldn't be long before the muddy water would flood the parking lot and come swirling around the shop doors. He ran back into the shop and announced in a loud voice that the creek was going to flood. He told three of his mechanics to drop everything and start moving cars. The cars that were parked next to the creek needed to be driven, pushed, or towed up to the high ground across the road. Alan told the other mechanics to put the tools away and help move all the boxes of parts and supplies off the floor and into the storage racks in the storeroom and the office. Alan had everybody's attention, but nobody seemed to be moving. If anything the mechanics seemed to be amused.

Kirk strolled over to Alan with a tolerant smile on his face. "Come on, Alan," he said. "There's no sweat. The water's never been more than an inch deep in the parking lot. We've never had any inside . . ."

Alan interrupted him, looking him right in the eye, and said in an assertive way, "Listen Kirk, and listen good! You and the rest of the crew are going to do what I say, and you're going to do it now! We can talk later about whether it was a good idea."

This time, the mechanics dropped everything and began preparing for a flash flood. Alan barked instructions as he helped them move everything that could be damaged by water. All of the boxes were off the floor before the first trickle of water came under the door. By the time the water was ankle-deep, all the cars inside the shop had been jacked up and were sitting on cement blocks.

At its peak, the water was 10 inches deep in the shop, but by then the rain had stopped and the sun was already shining. The water level began to recede slowly, but it didn't drop below shop-floor level until after 9 p.m.. At 10 p.m. the mechanics voluntarily returned to the shop to help with the cleanup, which was not completed until 3 a.m. Alan personally thanked each one and gave them all the next morning off.

The next afternoon, Alan gave an informal speech during the coffee break. He gave the mechanics all the credit for avoiding thousands of dollars of property damage. He even went to the trouble of pointing out particular contributions each of them had made. For instance, he thanked LaMont for his quick thinking in throwing the master switch before the water reached the electric outlets. He thanked Kirk for the idea of jacking up all the disabled cars inside the shop. And so on until everyone's contribution, no matter how minor, had been recognized.

At 5 o'clock, everyone left but Gil, the oldest mechanic. He decided to stay and chat with Alan.

"You really surprised us yesterday!" Gil told Alan. "We could hardly believe it was you."

"Whaddaya mean?" Alan asked, pretending to be offended.

"You sounded like my old drill sergeant!" Gil chuckled. "Usually, you're so mild mannered we forget you're the boss!"

"Maybe I'm a little too mild mannered," Alan replied. "When I told you guys to prepare for the flood you all laughed at me." ∎

QUESTIONS

1. Describe Alan's leadership style during the flood, and evaluate how appropriate it was for the leadership situation.

2. Identify effective behaviors by Alan after the flood subsided.

3. How should Alan behave toward his employees in the future?

9

CHARISMATIC AND TRANSFORMATIONAL LEADERSHIP

Learning Objectives

After studying this chapter you should be able to:

- Understand how the theories of charismatic and transformational leadership differ from earlier leadership theories.

- Understand similarities and differences among the major theories of charismatic and transformational leadership.

- Understand why attributions of charisma are jointly determined by the leader, the followers, and the situation.

- Understand what traits, behaviors, and influence processes are involved in charismatic and transformational leadership.

- Understand why charismatic leadership can result in undesirable consequences for followers and the organization.

- Understand what research methods have been used to evaluate theories of transformational and charismatic leadership.

- Understand the major findings in empirical research on the effects of charismatic and transformational leadership.

- Understand how to apply the theories to become more effective as a leader.

In the 1980s, management researchers became very interested in the emotional and symbolic aspects of leadership. These processes help us to understand how leaders influence followers to make self-sacrifices and put the needs of the mission or organization above their materialistic self-interests. The theories of charismatic and transformational leadership describe this important aspect of leadership.

The terms *transformational* and *charismatic* are used interchangeably by many writers, but despite the similarities there are some important distinctions. This chapter describes the major theories, examines relevant empirical research, compares charismatic and transformational leadership, evaluates the theories, and provides some practical guidelines for leaders. The chapter begins by briefly reviewing two early theories that have influenced current conceptions of charismatic and transformational leadership.

Two Early Theories

Charisma

The current theories of charismatic leadership were strongly influenced by the ideas of an early sociologist named Max Weber. *Charisma* is a Greek word that means "divinely inspired gift," such as the ability to perform miracles or predict future events. Weber (1947) used the term to describe a form of influence based not on tradition or formal authority but rather on follower perceptions that the leader is endowed with exceptional qualities. According to Weber, charisma occurs during a social crisis, when a leader emerges with a radical vision that offers a solution to the crisis and attracts followers who believe in the vision. The followers experience some successes that make the vision appear attainable, and they come to perceive the leader as extraordinary.

In the past two decades, several social scientists formulated newer versions of the theory to describe charismatic leadership in organizations (e.g., Conger & Kanungo, 1987, 1998; House, 1977; Shamir, House, & Arthur, 1993). These "neocharismatic" theories incorporate some of Weber's ideas, but in other respects they depart from his initial conception about charismatic leadership (Beyer, 1999; Conger, 1989). The neocharismatic theories describe the motives and behaviors of charismatic leaders, and psychological processes that explain how these leaders influence followers (Jacobsen & House, 2001).

Transforming Leadership

The theories of transformational leadership were strongly influenced by James McGregor Burns (1978), who wrote a bestselling book on political leadership. Burns contrasted transforming leadership with transactional leadership. Transforming leadership appeals to the moral values of followers in an attempt to raise their consciousness about ethical issues and to mobilize their energy and resources to reform institutions. Transactional leadership motivates followers by appealing to their self-interest and exchanging benefits. For a political leader, these activities include providing jobs, subsidies, lucrative government contracts, and support for desired legislation in return for campaign contributions and votes to reelect the leader. For corporate leaders, transactional leadership means providing pay and other benefits in return for work effort. Transactional leadership may involve values, but they are values relevant to the exchange process, such as honesty, fairness, responsibility, and reciprocity. Finally, Burns also identified a third form of leadership influence based on legitimate authority and respect for rules and tradition. Bureaucratic organizations emphasize this form of influence more than influence based on exchange or inspiration.

The process by which leaders appeal to followers' values and emotions is a central feature in current theories of transformational and visionary leadership in organizations (e.g., Bass, 1985; 1996; Bennis & Nanus, 1985; Sashkin, 1988; Tichy & Devanna, 1986, 1990). In contrast to Burns, however, the newer theories of transformational leadership are more concerned with attainment of pragmatic task objectives than with the moral elevation of followers or social reform. The views of Burns on ethical leadership are discussed in Chapter 14.

Attribution Theory of Charismatic Leadership

Conger and Kanungo (1987) proposed a theory of charismatic leadership based on the assumption that charisma is an attributional phenomenon. Subsequently, a refined version of the theory was presented by Conger (1989) and by Conger and Kanungo (1998). According to the theory, follower attribution of charismatic qualities to a leader is jointly determined by the leader's behavior, expertise, and aspects of the situation.

Leader Traits and Behaviors

Follower attributions of charisma depend on several types of leader behavior. These behaviors are not assumed to be present in every charismatic leader to the same extent, and the relative importance of each type of behavior for attribution of charisma depends to some extent on the leadership situation.

Charisma is more likely to be attributed to leaders who advocate a vision that is highly discrepant from the status quo, but still within the latitude of acceptance by followers. That is, followers will not accept a vision that is too radical, and they are likely to view a leader who espouses such a vision as incompetent or crazy. Noncharismatic leaders typically support the status quo, or advocate only small, incremental changes.

Charisma is more likely to be attributed to leaders who act in unconventional ways to achieve the vision. The leader's methods for attaining the idealized goal must differ from conventional ways of doing things in order to impress followers that the leader is extraordinary. The use of innovative strategies that appear successful results in attribution of superior expertise to the leader by followers.

Leaders are more likely to be viewed as charismatic if they make self-sacrifices, take personal risks, and incur high costs to achieve the vision they espouse. Trust appears to be an important component of charisma, and followers have more trust in a leader who seems less motivated by self-interest than by concern for followers. Most impressive is a leader who actually risks substantial personal loss in terms of status, money, leadership position, or membership in the organization.

Leaders who appear confident about their proposals are more likely to be viewed as charismatic than are leaders who appear doubtful and confused. Unless the leader communicates self-confidence, the success of an innovative strategy may be attributed more to luck than to expertise. A leader's confidence and enthusiasm can be contagious. Followers who believe the leader knows how to attain the shared objective will work harder, thereby increasing the actual probability of success.

Followers are more likely to attribute charisma to leaders who inspire them with emotional appeals than to leaders who use authority or a participative decision process. Leaders who use authority to implement an innovative strategy for attaining important objectives may gain more expert power if the strategy is successful, but unless they articulate an ideological vision to justify the strategy, they are unlikely to appear charismatic. Likewise, followers who meet with the leader to develop a consensus strategy may be satisfied and highly motivated, but the leader will not appear to be extraordinary.

The ability to see opportunities that others fail to recognize is another reason for a leader to be viewed as extraordinary. Charismatic leaders influence people to collectively accomplish great things that initially seemed impossible. The risks inherent in the use of novel strategies make it important for the leader to have the skills and expertise to make a realistic assessment of environmental constraints and opportunities for implementing the strategies. Timing is critical; the same strategy may succeed at one time but fail completely if implemented earlier or later. Leaders need to be sensitive to the needs and values of followers as well as to the environment in order to identify a vision that is innovative, relevant, timely, and appealing.

Influence Processes

The initial version of the theory did not explain the influence processes involved in charismatic leadership, but interviews conducted by Conger (1989) provided more insight about the reasons why followers of charismatic leaders become so strongly committed to the task or mission.

The primary influence process is personal identification, which is influence derived from a follower's desire to please and imitate the leader. Charismatic leaders appear so extraordinary, due to their strategic insight, strong convictions, self-confidence, unconventional behavior, and dynamic energy, that subordinates idolize these leaders and want to become like them. Leader approval becomes a measure of the subordinate's own self-worth. This approval is expressed by praise and recognition of subordinate behavior and accomplishments, which builds self-confidence and a deeper sense of obligation to live up to the leader's expectations in the future. Charismatic leaders create a sense of urgency that requires greater effort by subordinates to meet high expectations. Many subordinates of charismatic leaders reported that desire for leader approval was their primary source of motivation. At the same time, it was evident that followers were also motivated by fear of disappointing the leader and being rejected.

The influence of a charismatic leader is also due to internalization of new values and beliefs by followers. Conger (1989) emphasized that it is more important for followers to adopt the leader's attitudes and beliefs about desirable objectives and effective strategies than merely to imitate superficial aspects of the leader's behavior such as mannerisms, gestures, speech patterns. A charismatic leader who articulates an inspirational vision can influence followers to internalize attitudes and beliefs that will subsequently serve as a source of intrinsic motivation to carry out the mission of the organization.

Facilitating Conditions

Contextual variables are especially important for charismatic leadership, because attributions of exceptional ability for a leader seem to be rare and may be highly dependent upon characteristics of the situation. One important situational variable is follower disenchantment. Charismatic leaders are more likely to emerge in crisis situations. However, unlike Weber (1947), Conger and Kanungo do not consider an objective crisis to be a necessary condition for charismatic leadership. Even in the absence of a genuine crisis, a leader may be able to create dissatisfaction with current conditions and simultaneously provide a vision of a more promising future. The leader may precipitate a crisis where none existed previously, setting the stage for demonstration of superior expertise in dealing with the problem in unconventional ways. Likewise, the leader may be able to discredit the old, accepted ways of doing things to set the stage for proposing new ways. The impact of unconventional strategies is greater when followers perceive that conventional approaches are no longer effective.

Self-Concept Theory of Charismatic Leadership

House (1977) proposed a theory to explain charismatic leadership in terms of a set of testable propositions involving observable processes rather than folklore and mystique. The theory identifies how charismatic leaders behave, their traits and skills, and the conditions in which they are most likely to emerge. One limitation of the initial theory was ambiguity about the influence processes. Shamir, House, and Arthur (1993) revised and extended the theory by incorporating new developments in thinking about human motivation and a more detailed description of the underlying influence processes. The following assumptions were made about human motivation: (1) behavior is expressive of a person's feelings, values, and self-concept as well as being pragmatic and goal oriented; (2) a person's self-concept is composed of a hierarchy of social identities and values; (3) people are intrinsically motivated to enhance and defend their self-esteem and self-worth; and (4) people are intrinsically motivated to maintain consistency among the various components of their self-concept, and between their self-concept and behavior.

Indicators of Charisma

Evidence of charismatic leadership is provided by the leader-follower relationship. As in the earlier theory by House (1977), a charismatic leader has profound and unusual effects on followers. Followers perceive that the leader's beliefs are correct, they willingly obey the leader, they feel affection toward the leader, they are emotionally involved in the mission of the group or organization, they have high performance goals, and they believe that they can contribute to the success of the mission. Attribution of extraordinary ability to the leader is likely, but in contrast to the theory by Conger and Kanungo (1987), it is not considered a necessary condition for charismatic leadership.

Leader Traits and Behaviors

Leader traits and behaviors are key determinants of charismatic leadership. Charismatic leaders are likely to have a strong need for power, high self-confidence, and a strong conviction in their own beliefs and ideals. The leadership behaviors that explain how a charismatic leader influences the attitudes and behavior of followers include the following: (1) articulating an appealing vision, (2) using strong, expressive forms of communication when articulating the vision, (3) taking personal risks and making self-sacrifices to attain the vision, (4) communicating high expectations, (5) expressing confidence in followers, (6) modeling behaviors consistent with the vision, (7) managing follower impressions of the leader, (8) building identification with the group or organization, and (9) empowering followers.

Influence Processes

Shamir and his colleagues recognize that personal identification is one type of influence process that may occur for some followers of a charismatic leader. When strong personal identification occurs, followers will imitate the leader's behavior, carry out the leader's requests, and make an extra effort to please the leader. Personal identification and follower attributions of charisma to a leader are more likely when the leader articulates an appealing vision, demonstrates courage and conviction, and makes self-sacrifices for followers or the mission (e.g., Choi & Dalton, 1999; DeCremer, 2002; Halverson, Holladay, Kazama, & Quinones, 2004; Yorges, Weiss, & Strickland, 1999). However, unlike the attribution theory of charismatic leadership, the self-concept theory does not emphasize personal identification. More important as sources of leader influence over followers are social identification, internalization, and augmentation of individual and collective self-efficacy.

Strong social identification occurs when people take pride in being part of the group or organization and regard membership as one of their most important social identities (Ashforth & Mael, 1989). They see how their efforts and work roles are related to a larger entity, making their work more meaningful and important. They are more willing to place the needs of the group above individual needs and make self-sacrifices for the sake of the group. Moreover, social identification results in strengthening of shared values, beliefs, and behavior norms among members of the group.

Charismatic leaders can increase social identification by articulating a vision that relates a follower's self-concept to shared values and role identities associated with the group (see Conger, Kanungo, & Menon, 2000). By emphasizing the ideological importance of the mission and the group's unique qualifications to perform it, the leader can imbue the group with a unique collective identity. Social identification can also be increased by the skillful use of slogans, symbols (e.g., flags, emblems, uniforms), rituals (singing the organization's song or anthem, saluting the flag, reciting the creed), and ceremonies (e.g., initiation of new members). Other relevant leadership behaviors include telling stories about past successes, heroic deeds by members, and symbolic actions by the founder or former leaders.

Internalization occurs when attainment of task objectives becomes a way for followers to express their values and social identities. Sometimes charismatic leaders influence followers to embrace new values, but it is much more common for charismatic leaders to increase the salience of existing follower values and link them to task objectives. Charismatic leaders articulate a vision describing task objectives in ideological terms that reflect follower values. By emphasizing the symbolic and ideological aspects of the work, the leader makes it seem more meaningful, noble, heroic, and morally correct. The ultimate form of internalization occurs when followers come to view their work role as inseparably linked to their self-concept and self-worth. They carry out the role because it is a part of their essential nature and destiny.

Task motivation also depends on individual self-efficacy and collective efficacy. Individual self-efficacy is the belief that one is competent and capable of attaining difficult task objectives. People with high self-efficacy are willing to expend more effort and persist longer in overcoming obstacles to the attainment of task objectives (Bandura, 1986). Collective efficacy refers to the perception of group members that they can accomplish exceptional feats by working together. When collective efficacy is high, people are more willing to cooperate with members of their group in a joint effort to carry out their mission. A leader can enhance the self-efficacy and collective efficacy of followers by articulating an inspiring vision, expressing confidence that they can accomplish their collective task objectives, providing intellectual stimulation, and providing necessary coaching and assistance (see Kark, Shamir, & Chen, 2003).

Facilitating Conditions

The motivational effects of charismatic leaders are more likely to occur when the leader's vision is congruent with existing follower values and identities. Thus, charismatic leaders must be able to understand the needs and values of followers. In addition, it must be possible to define task roles in ideological terms that will appeal to followers. High-technology industries can be linked to values such as scientific progress, economic development, and national pride, but it is more difficult to develop an appealing ideology in industries with controversial products such as alcoholic beverages, tobacco, or firearms. Work roles that have low potential for ideological appeals include simple, repetitive work with little inherent meaning or social significance. However, the story of the two bricklayers illustrates the possibility of making even routine work more meaningful. When asked what he was doing, one bricklayer replied that he was making a wall; the second bricklayer replied that he was building a cathedral.

According to Shamir and his colleagues, a crisis condition is not necessary for the effectiveness of charismatic leadership. Nevertheless, charismatic leadership is more likely to occur when a group or organization is in serious trouble, it is not clear what must be done to ensure survival and prosperity, and there is considerable anxiety or even panic among the members (e.g., Bligh, Kohles, & Meindl, 2004; Halverson et al., 2004; House et al., 1991; Pillai, 1996; Pillai & Meindl, 1998). Such conditions favor the emergence of a leader who is able to interpret the crisis and offer credible strategies for coping with it successfully. However, the charismatic effects of such a leader will be temporary unless the vision continues to be relevant after the immediate crisis is resolved (Boal & Bryson, 1988; Hunt, Boal, & Dodge, 1999).

Other Conceptions of Charisma

This section reviews some other conceptions of charisma that provide useful insights into the nature of this complex form of leadership. Two alternative perspectives on charismatic influence processes (psychodynamic and social contagion) are examined first. These two theories and the two described earlier are compared in Table 9-1. The section ends with a discussion of close versus distant charismatics and routinization of charisma.

Psychodynamic Processes

A few theorists have attempted to explain charisma in terms of Freudian psychodynamic processes in followers (Kets de Vries, 1988; Lindholm, 1988). These theorists attempt to explain the unusual and seemingly irrational influence of some charismatic leaders who are idolized as a superhuman hero or worshiped as a spiritual figure. The intense personal identification of followers with such leaders is explained in terms of psychodynamic processes such as regression, transference, and projection. Regression involves a return to feelings and behaviors that were typical of a younger age. Transference

TABLE 9-1 Comparison of Four Charismatic Theories				
Attribute of Theory	**Attributed Charisma**	**Self-Concept Theory**	**Psycho-dynamic**	**Social Contagion**
Influence Processes				
1. Personal identification	Yes	Yes	Yes	No
2. Value internalization	Yes	Yes	No	No
3. Social identification	No	Yes	No	No
4. Social contagion	No	No	No	Yes
5. Enhanced self-efficacy	No	Yes	No	No
Leader Behaviors				
1. Innovative visioning	Yes	Yes	No	No
2. Unconventional behavior	Yes	Yes	No	Yes
3. Impression management	Yes	Yes	Yes	No
4. Self-sacrifice and personal risk	Yes	Yes	No	No
5. Role modeling exemplary behavior	Yes	Yes	Yes	Yes
6. Showing confidence in followers	Yes	Yes	Yes	No
7. Enhancing team identity	No	Yes	No	No
8. Sharing power for key decisions	No	Yes	No	No
9. Analyzing the environment	Yes	No	No	No
Facilitating Conditions				
1. Crisis or disenchantment	Yes	Yes	Yes	Yes
2. Complex, significant task	No	Yes	No	No
3. Weak, dependent followers	No	Yes	Yes	No

occurs when feelings toward an important figure from the past (e.g., a parent) are shifted to someone in the present. Projection involves a process of attributing undesirable feelings and motives to someone else, thereby shifting the blame for things about which one feels guilty.

According to one psychoanalytic explanation, followers suffering from fear, guilt, or alienation may experience a feeling of euphoric empowerment and transcendence by submerging their identity in that of a seemingly superhuman leader. For example, a young man has a severe identity crisis because he is unable to develop a clear conception of an ideal self due to weak or abusive parents. He develops a strong emotional attachment and dependence on a charismatic gang leader who serves as the ideal to emulate. In another example, a person who has caused great injury to others suffers from overwhelming guilt. By identifying with a charismatic religious leader who is perceived to exemplify moral values, the person vicariously experiences the leader's moral superiority and is able to overcome the guilt. Followers of a charismatic leader may regress to childhood feelings of dependence on a parent who seemed to have magical powers, they may identify with the leader as an idealized self who exemplifies their wishes and fantasies, and they may be encouraged to project their feelings of guilt and hostility to an external figure or group.

Attributions of charisma are especially likely by people who have feelings of inadequacy, guilt, fear, and alienation, and who share beliefs and fantasies that will serve as the basis for emotional and rational appeals by the leader. For example, the combination of a severe economic depression and the collective shame of defeat in World War I left a fertile ground in Germany for the rise of Hitler. In another example, hero worship and personal identification with charismatic entertainers or cult leaders is more likely to occur among adolescents who have low self-esteem and a weak social identity.

Social Contagion and Charisma

The theories reviewed up to now describe leader influence on follower attitudes and behavior, and most of the influence processes assume considerable interaction between the leader and followers. According to Meindl (1990), these theories do not explain why charismatic attributions are made by people who do not interact directly with the leader, and in some cases do not even have an opportunity to observe the leader at a distance or on television. Such people can be found in a social movement, new religion, or revolutionary political faction. Meindl offered an explanation of attributed charisma that focuses on influence processes among the followers themselves more than on how the leader directly influences individual followers.

The process used to explain how followers influence each other is social contagion, which involves the spontaneous spread of emotional and behavioral reactions among a group of people. This process occurs when inhibitions on latent tendencies to behave in a particular way are released by observing someone else display the behavior openly. According to Meindl, many people have a heroic social identity in their self-concept. In other words, these people have a positive image of themselves as emotionally involved in a righteous cause for which they are willing to make self-sacrifices and exert extra effort. This social identity is usually inhibited by other, more central social identities, by social norms about appropriate behavior, and by the desire for material benefits. However, these people are waiting for a leader and a cause to activate the heroic social identity. Activation is most likely to occur in a social crisis where the self-esteem or survival of people is threatened. In contrast to the other theories of charisma, it does not matter much who actually becomes the symbolic leader of a new cause (and the focus of follower adulation) as long as it is someone sufficiently attractive and exceptional to qualify for the role. Thus, loyalty may abruptly shift to another idol or leader if the initial one is no longer available or a more attractive one appears on the scene.

Meindl speculated that the process of social contagion may involve a typical sequence of events. It is likely to begin with a few insecure, marginal members who do not have strong social identification with an organization and are more inclined to deviate from its norms. The heroic behavior syndrome is activated in these people by an emergent leader who articulates an appealing ideology or symbolizes it (e.g., the person is a descendant of a famous religious or political leader). Although not specifically mentioned by Meindl, the influence process for these initial disciples is probably personal identification. They imitate nontraditional behavior by the leader and do things that symbolize allegiance to the new cause (e.g., wear special clothing or insignias, use ritualized salutes or gestures, recite special oaths or slogans). Other members may initially view the behavior of the new disciples as bizarre and inappropriate. However, as the inhibitions of more people are released, some initial doubters will become converts and the process of social contagion can spread rapidly.

Attribution of charisma to the leader occurs as part of the attempt by followers to understand and rationalize their new feelings and behavior. The need for this type of rationalization may be especially strong when social contagion results in behavior that is inconsistent with the usual social identities and espoused beliefs of the followers. The qualities attributed to a leader may become highly exaggerated as rumors and stories circulate among people who have no direct contact with the leader. For example, stories about a leader's heroic deeds and exceptional feats may spread among members of a political movement; stories about miracles performed by the leader may spread among members of a religious cult.

Close and Distant Charisma

Shamir (1995) proposed that attributions of charisma for followers who have close contact with the leader differ in some important ways from attributions made by followers who only view the leader from a distance. An exploratory study was conducted in Israel to see whether the proposed differences could be verified. Students were interviewed and asked to describe a charismatic leader with whom they had a direct relationship and one with whom they did not have a direct relationship. Responses were content analyzed to identify leader traits, skills, behaviors, and effects.

The results support Shamir's proposition that the amount of direct interaction between a leader and followers affects attributions of charisma. Distant charismatics were described more often in terms of their substantive achievements and effects on follower political attitudes. Close charismatics were more often described in terms of their effects on follower motivation, task behavior, and identification with the leader. The findings suggest that attributions of greatness for distant leaders are affected more by performance cues and shared stereotypes, whereas attributions of greatness for close leaders are affected more by leader behavior and interpersonal skills. However, this exploratory study was subject to several limitations. A subsequent study by Yagil (1998) in the Israeli army did not find support for the proposition that interpersonal qualities are more important in determining attributions of charisma for close rather than distant leaders. More research is needed to clarify how distance affects attributions of charisma. Antonakis and Atwater (2002) pointed out the need to make a careful distinction between vertical social distance (proximity in the authority hierarchy of an organization) and physical distance. Moreover, the frequency and nature of interactions with followers also determine how each social and physical distance will moderate the influence of a leader on followers.

Routinization of Charisma

Charisma is a transitory phenomenon when it is dependent on personal identification with an individual leader who is perceived to be extraordinary. When the leader departs or dies, a succession crisis is likely. Many organizations founded by an autocratic charismatic leader fail to survive this succession crisis (Bryman, 1992; Mintzberg, 1983). Charismatic leaders can do several things in an effort to perpetuate their influence on the organization after they depart (Bryman, 1992; Trice & Beyer, 1986). The three approaches for routinization of charisma are not mutually exclusive, and they all may occur to some degree in the same organization.

One approach is to transfer charisma to a designated successor through rites and ceremonies. However, it is seldom possible to find a successor for an extraordinary leader. In addition, there are many reasons why a charismatic leader may be unwilling to identify a strong successor early enough to ensure a smooth transition. The possible reasons include defense mechanisms (e.g., the leader avoids thinking about death or retirement), preoccupation with the mission, and fear of potential rivals.

A second approach is to create an administrative structure that will continue to implement the leader's vision with rational-legal authority (Weber, 1947). This "routinization of charisma" can reduce the effectiveness of the organization. It is difficult to maintain the enthusiastic commitment of organization members when a charismatic leader with whom they identified is succeeded by bland bureaucrats who emphasize obedience to formal rules. Even when not actively encouraged by the leader, a formal administrative structure usually evolves in a new organization as it grows larger and more successful. Conflicts are likely to occur between bureaucratic administrators and the charismatic leader. Sometimes the administrators are able to wrest control of the organization away from the leader. A case study by Weed (1993) provides a vivid example.

> Candy Lightner is the charismatic founder of Mothers Against Drunk Driving (MADD). In 1980, after her daughter was killed by a drunk driver who was a repeat offender, she created MADD to lobby for stricter penalties for drunk driving in California. By 1985 she had successfully built MADD into a large national organization with 360 local chapters in the United States and a budget of $13 million. As MADD grew its central administrative structure became more formalized. The size of the Board of Directors was increased, and its composition changed from local chapter directors who were very loyal to Lightner to professionals with a background in law, public relations, social services, and nonprofit advocacy organizations. The central staff evolved from a small circle of close friends to a larger staff of professional administrators whose primary loyalty was to the organization rather than to Lightner. By 1983 there were increasing conflicts between Lightner and other members of the central staff, who resented her autocratic style, her inconsistency about assignments, and her defensiveness about criticism or dissent. Turnover increased, and disputes erupted about her use of funds. Finally when her contract lapsed in 1985, the Board ousted Lightner from her position as president of MADD.

A third approach to perpetuate the leader's vision is to embed it in the culture of the organization by influencing followers to internalize it and empowering them to implement it. How leaders can modify organization culture is described in Chapter 10.

Consequences of Charismatic Leadership

The study of historical leaders reveals examples of both positive and negative charismatics. Franklin D. Roosevelt lifted the United States out of the Great Depression, implemented major social programs such as social security, and mobilized the nation for World War II. In the same historical period, Adolph Hitler transformed Germany in a manner resulting in paranoid aggression, persecution, destruction, and the death of millions of people. This section discusses the positive and negative consequences of charismatic leadership for followers and the organization.

Positive and Negative Charismatics

How to differentiate between positive and negative charismatic leaders has been a problem for leadership theory. It is not always clear whether a particular leader should be classified as a positive or negative charismatic. One approach is to examine the consequences for followers. However, most charismatic leaders have both positive and negative effects on followers, and disagreement about their relative importance is likely. Sometimes observers even disagree about whether a particular outcome is beneficial or detrimental.

A better approach for differentiating between positive and negative charismatics is in terms of their values and personality (House & Howell, 1992; Howell, 1988; Musser, 1987). Negative charismatics have a personalized power orientation. They emphasize personal identification rather than internalization. They intentionally seek to instill devotion to themselves more than to ideals. They may use ideological appeals, but merely as a means to gain power, after which the ideology is ignored or arbitrarily changed to serve the leader's personal objectives. They seek to dominate and subjugate followers by keeping them weak and dependent on the leader. Authority for making important decisions is centralized in the leader, rewards and punishments are used to manipulate and control followers, and information is restricted and used to maintain an image of leader infallibility or to exaggerate external threats to the organization. Decisions of these leaders reflect a greater concern for self-glorification and maintaining power than for the welfare of followers.

In contrast, positive charismatics have a socialized power orientation. These leaders emphasize internalization of values rather than personal identification. They seek to instill devotion to ideology more than devotion to themselves. In terms of influence processes, they emphasize internalization rather than personal identification. Authority is delegated to a considerable extent, information is shared openly, participation in decisions is encouraged, and rewards are used to reinforce behavior consistent with the mission and objectives of the organization. As a result, their leadership is more likely to be beneficial to followers, although it is not inevitable if the strategies encouraged by the leader are inappropriate.

The Dark Side of Charisma

The major theories of charismatic leadership emphasize positive consequences, but a number of social scientists have also considered the dark side of charisma (Bass & Steidlmeier, 1999; Conger, 1989; Conger & Kanungo, 1998; Hogan, Raskin, & Fazzini, 1990; House & Howell, 1992; Kets de Vries & Miller, 1985; Mumford et al., 1993; O'Connor et al., 1995; Sandowsky, 1995). Negative consequences that are likely to occur in organizations led by charismatics are summarized in Table 9-2. Two interrelated sets of consequences combine to increase the likelihood that the leader's career will be cut short. Charismatic leaders tend to make more risky decisions that can result in a serious failure, and they tend to make more determined enemies who will use such a failure as an opportunity to remove the leader from office.

Leader optimism and self-confidence are essential to influence others to support the leader's vision, but excessive optimism makes it more difficult for the leader to recognize flaws in the vision. Identifying too closely with a vision undermines the capacity to evaluate it objectively. The experience of early success and the adulation of subordinates may cause the leader to believe that his or her judgment is infallible. In a persistent quest to attain the vision, a charismatic leader may ignore or reject evidence that it is unrealistic and doomed to fail. Followers who believe in the leader will be inhibited from pointing out flaws or suggesting improvements, which makes a bad decision all the more likely

---

TABLE 9-2   Some Negative Consequences of Charismatic Leaders

- Being in awe of the leader reduces good suggestions by followers.
- Desire for leader acceptance inhibits criticism by followers.
- Adoration by followers creates delusions of leader infallibility.
- Excessive confidence and optimism blind the leader to real dangers.
- Denial of problems and failures reduces organizational learning.
- Risky, grandiose projects are more likely to fail.
- Taking complete credit for successes alienates some key followers.
- Impulsive, nontraditional behavior creates enemies as well as believers.
- Dependence on the leader inhibits development of competent successors.
- Failure to develop successors creates an eventual leadership crisis.

(see Finkelstein, 2003). The negative consequences of overconfidence are evident in this example about Edwin Land, the inventor of the Polaroid camera (Conger, 1989).

> Land had been correct in his earlier perception that people wanted cameras that would make instant photographs, but in 1970 he decided to develop a radical new camera (the SX-70) that would make the earlier versions obsolete. Ignoring evidence that the market demand would be very limited, Land invested a half billion dollars to develop and produce the perfect instant camera. This strategy proved to be unsuccessful. Sales for the first year were far below estimated levels, and several years of design changes and price cuts were necessary to gain market acceptance for the camera.

The same impulsive, unconventional behavior that causes some people to view a leader as charismatic will offend and antagonize other people who view the behavior as disruptive and inappropriate. Likewise, the leader's strong conviction to untraditional ideologies alienates people who remain committed to the traditional ways of doing things. Even some of the initial supporters may become disillusioned if the leader fails to acknowledge their significant contributions to major achievements by the group or organization. Bass (1985) noted that the response of people to a charismatic leader is likely to be polarized; the same leader arouses extreme admiration by some people and extreme hatred by others. Thus, the advantage of having some dedicated followers who identify with the leader is offset by having some determined enemies, possibly including powerful members of the organization who can undermine the leader's programs or conspire to remove the leader from office.

Despite all of the adverse consequences, not even a negative charismatic leader is doomed to failure. There are many examples of narcissistic charismatics who established political empires, founded prosperous companies, or initiated new religious sects and retained control of them throughout their lifetimes. Continued success is possible for a leader who has the expertise to make good decisions, the political skill to maintain power, and the good luck to be in a favorable situation.

Effects of Positive Charismatics

Followers are likely to be much better off with a positive charismatic leader than with a negative charismatic. They are more likely to experience psychological growth and development of their abilities, and the organization is more likely to adapt to an environment that is dynamic, hostile, and competitive. A positive charismatic leader usually creates an "achievement-oriented" culture (Harrison, 1987), "high-performing system" (Vaill, 1978), or "hands-on, value-driven" organization (Peters & Waterman, 1982). The organization has a clearly understood mission that embodies social values beyond mere profit or growth, members at all levels are empowered to make important decisions about how to implement strategies and do their work, communication is open and information shared, and organization structures and systems support the mission. Such an organization has obvious advantages, but Harrison (1987, p. 12) contends that proponents also overlook some potential costs:

> In their single-minded pursuit of noble goals and an absorbing task, people lose their sense of balance and perspective; the end can come to justify the means. The group or organization exploits its environment, and its members—to the detriment of their health and quality of life—willingly exploit themselves in the service of the organization's purpose.

If prolonged as a normal operating mode, a single-minded achievement culture creates excessive stress, and members who are unable to tolerate this stress experience psychological disorders. An achievement culture created within one subunit of a larger organization may result in elitism, isolation, and lack of necessary cooperation with other subunits. Harrison concludes that subordinating member needs to the mission can be justified in a severe crisis, the moral equivalent of war, but under less demanding conditions a better balance between task concerns and people concerns is appropriate.

Practical Implications for Organizations

Some writers (Bryman, 1992; Schein, 1992; Trice & Beyer, 1993) have criticized the idea that charismatic leadership is a panacea for solving the problems of large organizations. The critics point out several reasons why it is not always feasible or desirable to have charismatic leaders occupy important positions in private and public sector organizations.

Charismatic leadership is risky. It is impossible to predict the result when people give too much power to an individual leader in the often irrational hope that he or she will actually be able to deliver on a vision of a better future. The power is often misused while the vision remains an empty dream. History is full of charismatic leaders who caused untold death, destruction, and misery in the process of building an empire, leading a revolution, or founding a new religion.

Charismatic leadership implies radical change in the strategy and culture of an organization, which may not be necessary or appropriate for organizations that are currently prosperous and successful. It is difficult to make radical change in an organization if no obvious crisis exists and many members see no need for change. If there is more than one charismatic leader in the organization and they have incompatible visions, the organization may be torn apart by disruptive conflict. Historical accounts suggest that many charismatic leaders find it too difficult to implement their radical vision within an existing organization, and they leave to establish a new one (e.g., a new business, religious order, political party, or social movement).

Charisma is a rare and complex phenomenon that is difficult to manipulate (Trice & Beyer, 1993). People who advocate training of leaders to be charismatic underestimate the difficulty of achieving the right mix of conditions necessary for the attribution of charisma to occur. Even when charisma can be achieved, it is a transitory phenomenon. Unless institutionalized, the changes made by a charismatic leader (or the new organization established by the leader) may not survive the leader's departure.

Finally, most of the descriptive research (e.g., Bennis & Nanus, 1985; Collins, 2001; Kouzes & Posner, 1987; Peters & Austin, 1985; Tichy & Devanna, 1986) suggests that a charismatic leader is not necessary to achieve major changes in an organization. The research found that chief executives of successful organizations used transformational behaviors, but these leaders were seldom viewed as charismatic by members of the organization.

Transformational Leadership

As noted at the beginning of the chapter, several theories of transformational or inspirational leadership were strongly influenced by the ideas of Burns (1978), but there has been more empirical research on the version of the theory formulated by Bass (1985, 1996) than on any of the others. The essence of the theory is the distinction between transformational and transactional leadership. The two types of leadership were defined in terms of the component behaviors used to influence followers and the effects of the leader on followers.

With transformational leadership, the followers feel trust, admiration, loyalty, and respect toward the leader, and they are motivated to do more than they originally expected to do. According to Bass, the leader transforms and motivates followers by (1) making them more aware of the importance of task outcomes, (2) inducing them to transcend their own self-interest for the sake of the organization or team, and (3) activating their higher-order needs. In contrast, transactional leadership involves an exchange process that may result in follower compliance with leader requests but is not likely to generate enthusiasm and commitment to task objectives.

For Bass (1985), transformational and transactional leadership are distinct but not mutually exclusive processes. Transformational leadership increases follower motivation and performance more than transactional leadership, but effective leaders use a combination of both types of leadership.

Leader Behaviors

Transformational and transactional leadership behaviors are described in terms of two broad categories of behavior, each with specific subcategories (see Table 9-3). The taxonomy was identified primarily by factor analysis of a behavior description questionnaire called the Multifactor Leadership Questionnaire (MLQ). The original formulation of the theory (Bass, 1985) included three types of transformational behavior: idealized influence, intellectual stimulation, and individualized consideration. Idealized influence is behavior that arouses strong follower emotions and identification with the leader. Intellectual stimulation is behavior that increases follower awareness of problems and influences followers to view problems from a new perspective. Individualized consideration includes providing support, encouragement, and coaching to followers. A revision of the theory added another transformational behavior called

TABLE 9-3 Transformational and Transactional Behaviors

Transformational Behaviors

  Idealized influence

  Individualized consideration

  Inspirational motivation

  Intellectual stimulation

Transactional Behaviors

  Contingent reward

  Active management by exception

  Passive management by exception

Source: Based on B. M. Bass, *A New Paradigm of Leadership: An Inquiry into Tranformational Leadership* (Alexandria, VA: U.S. Army Research Institute for the Behavioral and Social Sciences, 1996).

inspirational motivation which includes communicating an appealing vision, using symbols to focus subordinate effort, and modeling appropriate behaviors (Bass & Avolio, 1990a). The most recent revision (Bass & Avolio, 1997) made separate scales for idealized influence behavior and idealized influence attributions, although it is not clear why the latter was retained in a questionnaire designed to measure observable behavior.

The original formulation of the theory included two types of transactional behavior: contingent reward and passive management by exception. Contingent reward behavior includes clarification of the work required to obtain rewards and the use of incentives and contingent rewards to influence motivation. Passive management by exception includes use of contingent punishments and other corrective action in response to obvious deviations from acceptable performance standards. Another transactional behavior called active management by exception was added in more recent versions of the theory (Bass & Avolio, 1990a). This behavior is defined in terms of looking for mistakes and enforcing rules to avoid mistakes.

Newer versions of the theory also include laissez-faire leadership as a third metacategory. This type of leader shows passive indifference about the task and subordinates (e.g., ignoring problems, ignoring subordinate needs). It is best described as the absence of effective leadership rather than as an example of transactional leadership. The revised version of the theory (Avolio, 1999) is sometimes called the Full Range Leadership Model. As noted in Chapter 3, this label is inappropriate because some important leadership behaviors are not included in the model (Antonakis & House, 2002; Yukl, 1999a).

Several studies have used factor analysis to assess the construct validity of the MLQ (e.g., Antonakis, Avolio, & Sivasubramaniam, 2003; Avolio, Bass, & Jung, 1999; Bycio, Hackett, & Allen, 1995; Carless, 1998; Den Hartog, Van Muijen, & Koopman, 1997; Tejeda, Scandura, & Pillai, 2001; Tepper & Percy, 1994; Yammarino, Spangler & Dubinsky, 1998). Most of these studies found support for the distinction between transformational and transactional leadership as broad metacategories, but in some cases only after eliminating many weak items or entire subscales. Results for the component behaviors were not consistent from study to study. Sometimes idealized influence combined with inspirational motivation. Sometimes passive management by exception combined with laissez-faire leadership. Contingent reward usually correlated more highly with the transformational behaviors than with other transactional behaviors. Even when the factor analysis supports the distinctiveness of the transformational behaviors, they are so highly intercorrelated that it is not possible to clearly determine their separate effects. Consequently, many studies on the antecedents or consequences of transformational leadership use only a composite score for it rather than the component behaviors.

Successive revisions of the MLQ have added types of transformational behavior not represented in the initial version. Moreover, when effective leadership behaviors not explicitly measured by the MLQ are included in the factor analysis research, some of them are confounded with the transformational behaviors (Hinkin & Tracey, 1999; Yukl, 1999a). The expanding scope of the transformational metacategory and the likelihood that composite scores for it are influenced by unmeasured behaviors creates ambiguity about what the MLQ actually measures and complicates interpretation of results from research using the questionnaire. There is need for research to show that the component behaviors for transformational leadership can be manipulated independently in experiments, that they have different antecedents and outcomes, and that they can be clearly differentiated when measured in other ways, such as with observation, incident diaries, or interviews.

Influence Processes

The underlying influence processes for transactional and transformational leadership are not clearly explained, but they can be inferred from the description of the behaviors and effects on follower motivation. The primary influence process for transactional leadership is probably instrumental compliance (see Chapter 6). Transformational leadership probably involves internalization, because inspirational motivation includes efforts to link the task to follower values and ideals with behavior such as articulating an inspirational vision. A leader can increase intrinsic motivation by increasing the perception of followers that task objectives are consistent with their authentic interests and values (see Bono & Judge, 2003; Charbonneau, Barling & Kelloway, 2003).

Transformational leadership also appears to involve personal identification, because idealized influence results in follower attributions of charisma to the leader. According to Bass (1985, p. 31), "Charisma is a necessary ingredient of transformational leadership, but by itself it is not sufficient to account for the transformational process." Other processes that may mediate the effects of transformational leadership on follower performance have been identified in research on the theory. Transformational behaviors such as inspirational motivation (e.g., optimistic visioning) and individualized consideration (e.g., coaching) may increase the self-efficacy of individual subordinates (McColl-Kennedy & Anderson, 2002) and the collective efficacy of teams (see Chapter 11). Intellectual stimulation may increase the creativity of individual followers and teams (Howell & Avolio, 1993; Keller, 1992; Sosik, Kahai, & Avolio, 1998).

Facilitating Conditions

According to Bass (1996, 1997), transformational leadership is considered effective in any situation or culture. The theory does not specify any conditions under which authentic transformational leadership is irrelevant or ineffective. In support of this position, the positive relationship between transformational leadership and effectiveness has been replicated for many leaders at different levels of authority, in different types of organizations, and in several different countries (Bass, 1997, 1998). The criterion of leadership effectiveness has included a variety of different types of measures. The evidence supports the conclusion that in most if not all situations, some aspects of transformational leadership are relevant. However, universal relevance does not mean that transformational leadership is equally effective in all situations or equally likely to occur.

A number of situational variables may increase the likelihood that transformational leadership will occur, or may enhance the effect of such leadership on followers (Bass, 1985, 1996; Hinkin & Tracey, 1999; Howell & Avolio, 1993; Pawar & Eastman, 1997; Pettigrew, 1987; Waldman, Ramirez, House, & Puranam, 2001). Transformational leadership is likely to be more important in a dynamic, unstable environment that increases the need for change, and such leadership is more likely when leaders are encouraged and empowered to be flexible and innovative (e.g., a decentralized organization with an entrepreneurial culture). Finally, there is growing evidence that follower traits and values may determine how they respond to transformational or charismatic behaviors by a leader (e.g., de Vries, Roe, & Tharsi, 2002; Ehrhart & Klein, 2001).

Research Methods for Assessing the Theories

A wide variety of different research methods have been employed in the research on charismatic and transformational leadership. Most of the research has been focused on leader behavior and how it affects follower motivation, satisfaction, and performance. Much of the research was designed only to test one particular theory of charismatic or transformational leadership, but the findings are usually relevant for evaluating more than one of the theories. This section of the chapter describes examples of the different approaches used to study the effects of charismatic and transformational leadership.

Survey Research

Field survey studies have been used more often than any other method for research on transformational and charismatic leadership. Several different questionnaires have been developed (Bass & Avolio, 1990a; Conger & Kanungo, 1994, 1998; Podsakoff, MacKenzie, Moorman, & Fetter, 1990; Shamir, Zakey, & Popper, 1998), but most survey studies have used the MLQ or a modified version of it. Like the early behavior questionnaires (see Chapter 3), the newer ones have many of the same limitations, including response biases and effects of stereotypes and attributions.

Lowe, Kroeck, and Sivasubramaniam (1996) conducted a meta-analysis of results from 39 of the studies using the MLQ. The newest scales (inspiration, active monitoring) were not included in this analysis, because they were not used in many of the studies. The meta-analysis found that transformational leadership was significantly related to measures of leadership effectiveness. Typical of survey research on leadership behavior, the relationship was stronger for subordinate self-rated effort than for an independent criterion of leadership effectiveness (e.g., ratings of the leader by superiors, objective performance of the leader's organizational unit). The transformational leadership behaviors correlated more strongly and consistently with leadership effectiveness than did the transactional leadership behaviors. Contingent rewarding, a transactional behavior, correlated with leadership effectiveness in some studies but not others. As noted earlier, the high correlation among transformational behaviors makes it difficult to determine their independent effects.

Laboratory Experiments

Experiments allow stronger inferences about causality than descriptive studies or survey research, but only a small number of laboratory experiments have been conducted on charismatic and transformational leadership (Awamleh & Gardner, 1999; Choi & Mai-Dalton, 1999; Howell & Frost, 1989; Hunt, Boal, & Dodge, 1999; Jaussi & Dionne, 2003; Jung & Avolio, 1999; Kirkpatrick & Locke, 1996; Shea & Howell, 1999; Yorges et al., 1999). An example of this type of research is described briefly.

Kirkpatrick and Locke (1996) conducted a laboratory experiment to investigate the separate effects of three leadership behaviors: visioning, using a highly expressive style of communication, and providing advice to followers in how to do the work better. Actors served as the leaders, and they displayed different patterns of leadership behavior toward students who worked in small groups at an assembly task. This study was the first one to map the complex causal effects of different types of leader behavior through intervening variables to performance.

Followers in the vision condition perceived the task to be more interesting, challenging, and important, and they set higher performance goals, had higher trust in the leader, and perceived the leader to be higher in charisma, inspiration, and intellectual stimulation. Visioning had a positive effect on quality of follower performance (mediated by higher goals for quality and more self-efficacy) but did not affect quantity of follower performance (probably because the vision was not relevant for quantity). Clarifying appropriate work procedures had a positive effect on follower role clarity, job satisfaction, perceived leader intellectual stimulation, and both the quality and quantity of follower performance (the latter effect was mediated by higher goals for quantity). Style of communication affected ratings of leader charisma but did not affect follower attitudes or performance. The study provided some evidence for the effect of visioning, but stronger effects were found for clarifying work procedures, which is a traditional task-oriented behavior for supervisors (see Chapter 3).

Field Experiments

Field experiments are conducted with real leaders in an organizational setting, rather than in temporary groups of students. As noted in Chapter 3, the usual approach in field experiments is to manipulate leader behavior and observe the effects on subordinate attitudes, behavior, and performance. Only a few field experiments have been conducted on transformational and charismatic leadership, and in each case leader behavior was manipulated with a training intervention (e.g., Barling, Weber, & Kelloway, 1996; Dvir, Eden, Avolio, & Shamir, 2002). The experimental condition in each case involved an attempt to increase a leader's overall use of transformational and charismatic behaviors.

The study by Dvir and colleagues (2002) provides an example of this type of research. The researchers studied transformational leadership by infantry officers in the Israeli Defense Force. The researchers used a special three-day workshop on transformational leadership as a substitute for the regular leadership training in the six-month course required for all infantry squad officers (who are usually lieutenants). When the course was completed, the participants became infantry squad leaders in a field setting, where officers in the experimental condition were subsequently compared to officers who had attended the regular leadership training (the control group). In the field setting subordinates rated a squad leader's use of transformational behavior. The subordinates also rated themselves on variables expected to mediate the effects of leadership on squad performance, including motivation (self-efficacy, extra effort), critical/independent thinking, and internalized values. The subordinates included the soldiers in a squad and the noncommissioned officers (NCOs) who serve as intermediate leaders between the officers and their regular squad members.

The experimental manipulation of behavior was moderately successful. In the field training exercises, platoons in the experimental condition performed better than platoons in the control condition. Ratings by the NCOs indicated that they perceived more use of transformational behavior by squad leaders in the experimental condition than by squad leaders in the control condition. However, this difference was not found in the leader behavior ratings provided by regular squad members. The NCOs in the experimental condition rated themselves higher on motivation and independent thinking than NCOs in the control condition, but here again a significant difference was not found for the data from regular squad members. The inconsistent results for the two types of subordinates make it difficult to explain why transformational leaders had higher squad performance or how the NCOs contributed to this performance. The effects of leadership on squad performance may have been easier to understand if the researchers had included measures of other types of leadership behavior likely to be relevant (e.g., task-oriented behaviors), measures of NCO behavior, and mediating variables involving group processes as well as individual motivation.

Descriptive and Comparative Studies

Some descriptive studies look for common attributes among leaders identified as charismatic or transformational. Other descriptive studies have compared leaders identified beforehand as either charismatic or noncharismatic, or they have compared charismatic leaders in different situations (e.g., close vs. distant relationships). The source of behavior descriptions varies somewhat from study to study. Most researchers use interviews with the leaders and some of the followers, and sometimes the interviews are supplemented by observation. A content analysis is usually conducted to identify characteristic behaviors, traits, and influence processes (e.g., Bennis & Nanus, 1985; Conger, 1989; Fiol, Harris, & House, 1999; Howell & Higgins, 1990; Jacobsen & House, 2001; Kouzes & Posner, 1987; Levinson & Rosenthal, 1984; Peters & Austin, 1985; Shamir, 1995; Tichy & Devanna, 1986). Biographies, case studies, and articles about the leader are another source of behavior descriptions, and they may include speeches and writings by the leader (e.g., Bligh, Kohles, & Meindl, 2004; Deluga, 1998; House, Spangler, & Woycke, 1991; Mumford & Van Doorn, 2001; O'Connor et al., 1995; Strange & Mumford, 2002; Van Fleet & Yukl, 1986a; Westley & Mintzberg, 1989; Willner, 1984). Still another source of behavior descriptions in the descriptive research is the use of critical incidents (e.g., Bryman, Stephens, & Campo, 1996; Kirby, King, & Paradise, 1992; Yukl & Van Fleet, 1982). Following are two examples of descriptive, comparative studies.

House, Spangler, and Woycke (1991) conducted a comparative study on charismatic leadership in U.S. presidents. The first step was to ask several historians to classify as charismatic or noncharismatic each of 31 former presidents who were elected to office and served at least two years of their first term. Then the motive pattern of each president was measured by content analysis of his first inaugural address. The biographies of two or more cabinet members were content analyzed to measure a president's use of charismatic behaviors. Leadership effectiveness was measured in several ways, including ratings of presidential greatness made by a sample of historians, and analysis of biographical information about the outcomes of each president's decisions and actions during the first term of office. The results were mostly consistent with the theory. Presidents with a socialized power orientation exhibited more of the charismatic leadership behaviors and were more likely to be viewed as charismatic by others. Moreover, the charismatic presidents used more direct action to deal with problems and were rated higher in performance.

Bennis and Nanus (1985) conducted a five-year descriptive study of dynamic, innovative leaders, including 60 top-level corporate leaders and 30 leaders of public sector organizations. The researchers collected data with unstructured interviews lasting 3–4 hours, sometimes supplemented with observation. The leaders were diverse, and few fit the common stereotype of a charismatic leader. The researchers did not find larger-than-life individuals who make emotional speeches, display unconventional behavior, and polarize people into devoted followers and relentless critics. Instead, most of the leaders were ordinary in appearance, personality, and general behavior. The researchers identified some common themes in the interview protocols that provide insights about transformational leadership. The leaders all had a vision of a desirable and possible future for their organization. It was sometimes just a vague dream, and at other times it was as concrete as a written mission statement. The leaders demonstrated commitment to the vision by their decisions and behavior. Follower commitment to the vision depended on their trust in the leader, which was more likely when the leader's statements and actions were consistent. The leaders channeled the collective energies of organizational members in pursuit of the common vision.

Intensive Case Studies

Another type of descriptive research consists of intensive case studies of individual charismatic leaders (e.g., Beyer & Browning, 1999; Roberts, 1985; Roberts & Bradley, 1988; Trice & Beyer, 1986; Weed, 1993). Longitudinal case studies follow a leader's career over a period of time and examine the interaction between leader and followers, the leadership context, and outcomes of the leader's influence attempts. A good example is the study by Roberts (1985) of the same leader in two successive positions.

The study began when the leader was the superintendent of a public school district. Data were collected by archival searches, analysis of newspaper articles, participant observation of formal and informal meetings, and interviews with the superintendent, other administrators, board members, staff, teachers, parents, and students. The leader was deemed to be effective, because she was able to implement large, mandated budget cuts in a way that satisfied diverse stakeholders and still allowed progress on implementing desirable educational innovations. Her budget was approved unanimously by the school board after only a brief discussion. The teachers gave her a standing ovation for her efforts, even though the plan required program cuts and elimination of jobs. She was described as a "visionary" who had almost a "cultlike following" in the district.

The actions taken by the leader to achieve this successful outcome were the following: (1) a mission statement was formulated and referred to frequently during the change process; (2) a strategic vision was developed during a series of meetings and workshops involving district personnel; (3) several personnel in key positions were replaced with more competent, dynamic people to support the change effort; (4) performance objectives and action plans were developed for immediate subordinates (the school principals), progress was monitored by reports and meetings, and extensive participation by subordinates was encouraged during this process; (5) temporary task forces were created to involve all stakeholders in recommending where to make the budget cuts and how to deal with other budget and educational issues; and (6) staff members were trained in how to run structured public meetings in which task forces made presentations and solicited suggestions about budget cuts.

Roberts characterized the process as more a matter of creating and managing energy than of shaping culture or managing meaning. The leader was energetic, created enthusiasm, channeled emotions aroused by the budget crisis, and galvanized people into action. The leader helped people recognize that they could make a difference by working together toward common objectives. The following episode provides an example of the leader's influence (Roberts, 1985, p. 1035):

> After a scheduled 40-minute presentation to district staff, teachers besieged the stage to ask for more of her time to discuss the various initiatives the district was pursuing. Their requests turned into a four-hour dialogue with 800 people, in which the superintendent shared her hopes, her dreams, her past, her disappointments. Many people were moved to tears, including the superintendent. A critical point in the exchange came in answer to a question of how people could be certain that what she and the School Board promised would indeed occur. The superintendent's response was, "Well I guess you just have to trust us. I trust you." Dead silence followed as people drew in their breaths and held them for a moment or two. Upon being asked what this silence meant, people responded that the superintendent had proven her point. That was what the dialogue and the honesty were all about. She had trusted them with her thoughts, hopes, and feelings, and they in turn would trust her. Mutual trust had created a bond between the superintendent and her audience.

When the superintendent was appointed to her position, she was not initially perceived as a charismatic leader; this attribution occurred only after she had been in the position for two years and the change process was well underway. Roberts concluded that charisma was attributed to the leader because of the way the leader resolved the budget crisis, and not as an inevitable result of the leader's personal qualities. This conclusion is consistent with the findings of a follow-up study made after the same individual was appointed the commissioner of education for the state in 1983 (Roberts & Bradley, 1988).

Data for the follow-up study were obtained from a variety of sources. Interviews were conducted with the new commissioner during the four years from 1983 to 1987, and interviews were also conducted with state legislators, representatives from the governor's office, the board of education, school boards, and teacher unions. The commissioner was observed during speaking engagements, meetings with her staff, press conferences, formal and informal presentations to teachers and superintendents, and informal meetings with members of the state department of education. Additional information was obtained from analysis of official documents, newspaper articles, and reports made by special interest groups.

The new commissioner's approach for implementing change at the state level was similar to the one she used as superintendent. She formulated a mission statement and vision for change, and she moved quickly to replace several assistant commissioners with people from outside the education department who would support her programs. Enthusiasm and support were generated by conducting visits to nearly all of the school districts in the state. A survey was conducted to assess public opinion on school issues, and meetings were held with community groups throughout the state to identify public concerns and hopes for the schools.

At the end of her four-year term, the commissioner was evaluated as an effective administrator by the governor, and she was reappointed for another term. People usually described her as innovative and committed, but some peers and subordinates were critical rather than supportive. The commissioner's initiatives had some positive benefits, but they did not generate any widespread support for major change in the education system. Overall, there was no evidence that she was perceived as extraordinary or charismatic in her new position.

Roberts and Bradley (1988) suggested several reasons why the same person was seen as charismatic in one position and not in the other. First, at the district level, a serious crisis justified the need for innovative solutions, whereas at the state level there was no crisis to focus attention and provide a rationale for radical change. Second, as a district superintendent she had much more autonomy and authority than as a commissioner. The latter position was more political and involved a larger and more complex web of stakeholder relationships that served to constrain her actions and make change difficult (e.g., the governor, the legislature, members of the education department, interest groups, teachers unions, school officials). Third, the large size of the state agency and the complexity of the job as commissioner made it essential to delegate more responsibility, but strong political opposition and bureaucratic resistance undermined her efforts to restructure the education department and build a cooperative team of executives to help implement new initiatives effectively. Finally, as superintendent she was able to inspire strong trust and affection in meetings with constituents, whereas as commissioner a close relationship with constituents did not develop. Speaking to large audiences with intrusive television coverage, her speeches lacked the enthusiasm and vivid, emotional language that often occurred in her earlier speeches as superintendent to smaller, more informal groups of teachers, principals, and parents.

Transformational vs. Charismatic Leadership

One of the most important issues for leadership scholars is the extent to which transformational leadership and charismatic leadership are similar and compatible. Some theorists treat the two types of leadership as essentially equivalent, whereas other theorists view them as distinct but overlapping processes. Even among theorists who view the two types of leadership as distinct processes, there remains disagreement about whether it is possible to be both transformational and charismatic at the same time (Yukl, 1999b).

Conceptual ambiguity and a lack of consistency in definitions make it difficult to compare transformational and charismatic leadership, or even to compare theories of the same general type. In recent years, the major charismatic theories have been revised in ways that appear to move them closer to the transformational theories. The major transformational theories have been revised to incorporate additional forms of effective leadership behavior. The term *transformational* has been broadly defined by many writers to include almost any type of effective leadership, regardless of the underlying influence processes. The label may refer to the transformation of individual followers or to the transformation of entire organizations.

One source of apparent differences in the two types of theories is the emphasis on attributed charisma and personal identification. The essence of charisma is being perceived as extraordinary by followers who are dependent on the leader for guidance and inspiration. Attributed charisma and personal identification are more central for the theory by Conger and Kanungo (1998) than for the theory by Shamir and colleagues (1993). Bass (1985) proposed that charisma is a necessary component of transformational leadership, but he also noted that a leader can be charismatic but not transformational. The essence of transformational leadership appears to be inspiring follower commitment to shared objectives, increasing social identification, and developing follower skills and collective efficacy. Thus, the essential influence processes for transformational leadership may not be entirely compatible with the essential influence process for charismatic leadership, which involves dependence on an extraordinary leader. Some support for this distinction is provided in a study by Kark, Shamir, and Chen (2003); they found that personal identification mediates the effect of the leader on follower dependence and social identification mediates the effect of the leader on follower self-efficacy and collective efficacy.

Many of the leadership behaviors in the theories of charismatic and transformational leadership appear to be the same, but some important differences are evident as well. Transformational leaders probably do more things that will empower followers and make them less dependent on the leader, such as delegating significant authority to individuals, developing follower skills and self-confidence, creating self-managed teams, providing direct access to sensitive information, eliminating unnecessary controls, and building a strong culture to support empowerment. Charismatic leaders probably do more things that foster an image of extraordinary competence for the leader, such as impression management, information restriction, unconventional behavior, and personal risk taking.

Some other likely differences between transformational and charismatic leadership include how common it is, the facilitating conditions for it, and typical reactions of people. According to Bass, transformational leaders can be found in any organization at any level, and this type of leadership is universally relevant for all types of situations (Bass, 1996, 1997). In contrast, charismatic leaders are rare, and their emergence appears to be more dependent on favorable conditions (Bass, 1985; Beyer, 1999; Shamir & Howell, 1999). They are most likely to be visionary entrepreneurs who establish a new organization, or reformers who emerge in an established organization when formal authority has failed to deal with a severe crisis and traditional values and beliefs are questioned. The reactions of people to charismatics are usually more extreme and diverse than reactions to transformational leaders (Bass, 1985). The affective reaction they arouse often polarizes people into opposing camps of loyal supporters and hostile opponents. The intense negative reaction by some people to charismatic leaders helps to explain why these leaders are often targets for assassination or political tactics to remove them from office.

The empirical research on transformational and charismatic leadership was not designed to examine issues of comparability and compatibility among different theories. Few studies examine underlying influence processes or go beyond the superficial and often ambiguous data provided by behavior description questionnaires. Resolution of this interesting and important question will require additional research and greater use of intensive methods.

Evaluation of the Theories

The available evidence supports many of the key propositions of the major theories of charismatic and transformational leadership. Collectively, the theories appear to make an important contribution to our understanding of leadership processes. They provide an explanation for the exceptional influence some leaders have on subordinates, a level of influence not adequately explained by earlier theories of instrumental leadership or situational leadership. The new theories emphasize the importance of emotional reactions by followers to leaders, whereas the earlier theories emphasized rational-cognitive aspects of leader-follower interactions. The new theories also acknowledge the importance of symbolic behavior and the role of the leader in making events meaningful for followers. The earlier theories did not recognize that symbolic processes and management of meaning are as important as management of things. Finally, the new theories include a more comprehensive set of variables (e.g., traits, behaviors, mediating processes, situation) and integrate them better in explanations of effective leadership.

Efforts to evaluate what is really unique are complicated by the hype found in some descriptions of transformational and charismatic leadership. Although clothed in different jargon, some of the new wisdom reflects themes that can be found in earlier theories of leadership and motivation. For example, the underlying explanation for the distinction between transformational and transactional leadership is similar to the distinction between intrinsic and extrinsic motivation. The importance of developing and empowering subordinates echoes the emphasis on power sharing, mutual trust, teamwork, participation, and supportive relationships by writers such as Argyris (1964), McGregor (1960), and Likert (1967). Some leadership behaviors in the new theories are similar to behaviors identified as important in research that preceded it in the 1970s.

Despite their positive features, the new theories also have some conceptual weaknesses (Beyer, 1999; Bryman, 1993; Yukl, 1999b). Examples include ambiguous constructs, insufficient description of explanatory processes, a narrow focus on dyadic processes, omission of some relevant behaviors, insufficient specification of situational variables, and a bias toward heroic conceptions of leadership. Some of these limitations will be explained in more detail.

Most theories of transformational and charismatic leadership lack sufficient specification of underlying influence processes. The self-concept theory of charismatic leadership provides the most detailed explanation of leader influence on followers, but even this theory needs more clarification of how the various types of influence processes interact, their relative importance, and whether they are mutually compatible. Most of the theories are still leader-centered, and they emphasize the influence of the leader on followers. More attention needs to be focused on reciprocal influence processes, shared leadership, and mutual influence among the followers themselves.

Most of the theories focus too narrowly on dyadic processes. Although leader influence on individual followers is important, it is not sufficient to explain how leaders build exceptional teams (see Chapter 10). The theories would be strengthened by a better explanation of how leaders enhance mutual trust and cooperation, empowerment, collective identification, collective efficacy, and collective learning. The theories do not explain the task-oriented functions of leaders that are essential for the effective performance of a team. As noted in Chapter 3, transactional leadership is defined in a mostly negative way, and the MLQ does not explicitly measure effective forms of task-oriented behavior such as planning activities, clarifying roles and objectives, and solving operational problems. To fill this conceptual gap, some scholars have imputed additional meaning to transactional leadership, such as assuming that it includes these other types of task-oriented behavior. However, it is inappropriate for researchers to make inferences about unmeasured behaviors, and the underlying influence process for transactional leadership (i.e., exchange and instrumental compliance) is not sufficient to explain how task-oriented behaviors affect individual or collective performance. Finally, the theories fail to explain the leader's external roles, such as monitoring the environment to identify threats and opportunities, building networks of contacts who can provide information and assistance, serving as a spokesperson for the team or organization, negotiating agreements with outsiders, and helping to obtain resources, political support, and new members with appropriate skills (see Chapter 2).

The charismatic and transformational theories describe how a leader can influence the motivation and loyalty of organization members, which is relevant for understanding effective leadership. However, these theories are primarily extensions of motivation theory, and much more is needed to explain how leaders influence the financial performance and survival of an organization (Beyer, 1999; Yukl & Lepsinger, 2004). A leader may influence followers to be more motivated, creative, and cooperative, but what the followers are motivated to do and how appropriate it is for the situation are also important factors. Having highly motivated and loyal followers will not prevent disaster if the leader pursues unrealistic objectives or misguided strategies (cf. Finkelstein, 2003). The theories do not provide a good explanation for a strong effect of CEO behavior on the financial performance of a company. When a significant correlation is found in a survey field study (e.g., Jung, Chow & Wu, 2003; Tosi et al., 2003; Waldman et al., 2001), a likely alternative explanation is that the leaders of successful companies are perceived as more transformational or charismatic than leaders of unsuccessful companies (regardless of their behavior), and this attribution will be stronger when the environment is turbulent. Some efforts have been made to overcome the limitations of the theories by examining explanatory processes at multiple levels (e.g., Waldman & Yammarino, 1999). However, rather than trying to stretch dyadic theories to explain organizational processes, it is better to develop theories of strategic leadership that include explanatory processes at the appropriate level of conceptualization and take into account other important determinants of organizational performance. Theories of strategic leadership are discussed in Chapters 10 and 12.

A final limitation in the theories is the overemphasis on universal leader attributes that are relevant for all situations. More attention is needed to situational variables that determine whether transformational or charismatic leadership will occur and how effective it will be (Beyer, 1999; Bryman, 1992; Yukl, 1999b). Some progress has been made in developing theory about situational variables that may enhance charismatic or transformational leadership (e.g., Antonakis & Atwater, 2002; Conger & Kanungo, 1989; Klein & House, 1995; Pawar & Eastman, 1997; Shamir & Howell, 1999; Trice & Beyer, 1986). However, the number of empirical studies on contextual variables is still small, and the results are inconsistent (e.g., Bass, 1996; House et al., 1991; Howell & Avolio, 1993; Pillai, 1996; Pillai & Meindl, 1998; Podsakoff, MacKenzie, & Bommer, 1996; Roberts & Bradley, 1988; Tosi et al., 2004; Waldman, Javidan, & Varella, 2004; Waldman et al., 2001).

Applications: Guidelines for Leaders

Although much remains to be learned about transformational leadership, the convergence in findings from different types of research suggests some tentative guidelines for leaders who seek to inspire followers and enhance their self-confidence and commitment to the mission. The guidelines (see Table 9-4 for summary) are based on the theories and research findings reviewed in this chapter. Additional guidelines on change-oriented leadership can be found in Chapter 10.

- **Articulate a clear and appealing vision.**

Transformational leaders strengthen the existing vision or build commitment to a new vision. A clear vision of what the organization could accomplish or become helps people understand the purpose, objectives, and priorities of the organization. It gives the work meaning, serves as a source of self-esteem, and fosters a sense of common purpose. Finally, the vision helps guide the actions and decisions of each member of the organization, which is especially important when individuals or groups are allowed considerable autonomy and discretion in their work decisions (Hackman, 1986; Raelin, 1989). Procedures for developing a vision with appealing content are described in Chapter 10.

The success of a vision depends on how well it is communicated to people (Awamleh & Gardner, 1999; Holladay & Coombs, 1993, 1994). The vision should be communicated at every opportunity and in a variety of ways. Meeting with people directly to explain the vision and answer questions about it is probably more effective than less interactive forms of communication (e.g., letters or e-mail messages to followers, newsletter articles, televised news conferences, videotaped speeches). If a noninteractive form of communication is used to present the vision, then it is helpful to provide opportunities

TABLE 9-4 Guidelines for Transformational Leadership

- Articulate a clear and appealing vision.
- Explain how the vision can be attained.
- Act confident and optimistic.
- Express confidence in followers.
- Use dramatic, symbolic actions to emphasize key values.
- Lead by example.

for followers to ask questions afterward (e.g., use e-mail, a hotline, open meetings, or visits by the leader to department meetings).

The ideological aspects of a vision can be communicated more clearly and persuasively with colorful, emotional language that includes vivid imagery, metaphors, anecdotes, stories, symbols, and slogans. Metaphors and analogies are especially effective when they excite the imagination and engage the listener in trying to make sense out of them. Anecdotes and stories are more effective if they invoke symbols with deep cultural roots, such as legendary heroes, sacred figures, and historical ordeals and triumphs. A dramatic, expressive style of speaking augments the use of colorful language in making an emotional appeal. Conviction and intensity of feeling are communicated by a speaker's voice (tone, inflection, pauses), facial expressions, gestures, and body movement. Use of rhyme, rhythm, and repetition of key words or phrases can make a vision more colorful and compelling.

- **Explain how the vision can be attained.**

It is not enough to articulate an appealing vision; the leader must also convince followers that the vision is feasible. It is important to make a clear link between the vision and a credible strategy for attaining it. This link is easier to establish if the strategy has a few clear themes that are relevant to shared values of organization members (Nadler, 1988). Themes provide labels to help people understand issues and problems. The number of themes should be large enough to focus attention on key issues, but not so large as to cause confusion and dissipate energy. It is seldom necessary to present an elaborate plan with detailed action steps. The leader should not pretend to know all the answers about how to achieve the vision, but instead should inform followers that they will have a vital role in discovering what specific actions are necessary.

The strategy for attaining the vision is most likely to be persuasive when it is unconventional yet straightforward. If it is either simplistic or conventional, the strategy will not elicit confidence in the leader, especially when there is a crisis. Consider the example of a company that was losing market share in the face of intense competition.

> The CEO proposed to make the company's product the best in the world by improving product design and quality (the old strategy was to keep price low by cutting costs). The product would be designed to be reliable (few moving parts, durable materials, extensive product testing, quality control by every worker) as well as user friendly (simple operating procedures, easy-to-read displays, clear instructions). This strategy contributed to the successful turnaround of the company.

- **Act confident and optimistic.**

Followers are not going to have faith in a vision unless the leader demonstrates self-confidence and conviction. It is important to remain optimistic about the likely success of the group in attaining its vision, especially in the face of temporary roadblocks and setbacks. A manager's confidence and optimism can be highly contagious. It is best to emphasize what has been accomplished so far rather than how much more is yet to be done. It is best to emphasize the positive aspects of the vision rather than the obstacles and dangers that lie ahead. Confidence is expressed in both words and actions. Lack of self-confidence is reflected in tentative, faltering language (e.g., "I guess," "maybe," "hopefully") and some nonverbal cues (e.g., frowns, lack of eye contact, nervous gestures, weak posture).

- **Express confidence in followers.**

The motivating effect of a vision also depends on the extent to which subordinates are confident about their ability to achieve it. Research on the *Pygmalion effect* found that people perform better when a leader has high expectations for them and shows confidence in them (Eden, 1984, 1990; Eden & Shani, 1982; Field, 1989; Sutton & Woodman, 1989). It is especially important to foster confidence and optimism when the task is difficult or dangerous, or when team members lack confidence in themselves. If appropriate, the leader should remind followers how they overcame obstacles to achieve an earlier triumph. If they have never been successful, the leader may be able to make an analogy between the present situation and success by a similar team or organizational unit. Review the specific strengths, assets, and resources that they can draw on to carry out the strategy. List the advantages they have relative to opponents or competitors. Tell them that they are as good as or better than an earlier team that was successful in performing the same type of activity.

- **Use dramatic, symbolic actions to emphasize key values.**

A vision is reinforced by leadership behavior that is consistent with it. Concern for a value or objective is demonstrated by the way a manager spends time, by resource allocation decisions made when trade-offs are necessary between objectives, by the questions the manager asks, and by what actions the manager rewards. Dramatic, highly visible actions are an effective way to emphasize key values, as in the following example:

> The division manager had a vision that included relationships in which people were open, creative, cooperative, and oriented toward learning. Past meetings of the management team had been overly formal, with detailed agendas, elaborate presentations, and excessive criticism. He began a three-day meeting to communicate his vision for the division by inviting people to a beachfront ceremony where they burned a pile of agendas, handouts, and evaluation forms.

Symbolic actions to achieve an important objective or defend an important value are likely to be more influential when the manager risks substantial personal loss, makes a self-sacrifice, or does things that are unconventional. The effect of symbolic actions is increased when they become the subject of stories and myths that circulate among members of the organization and are retold time and again over the years to new employees. In one example recounted by Peters and Austin (1985), the CEO personally destroyed some low-quality versions of the company's product that had been sold previously as seconds. This widely publicized action demonstrated his commitment to the new policy that, henceforth, the company would make and sell only products of the highest quality.

- **Lead by example.**

According to an old saying, actions speak louder than words. One way a leader can influence subordinate commitment is by setting an example of exemplary behavior in day-to-day interactions with subordinates. Leading by example is sometimes called role modeling. It is especially important for actions that are unpleasant, dangerous, unconventional, or controversial. A manager who asks subordinates to observe a particular standard should also observe the same standard. A manager who asks subordinates to make special sacrifices should set an example by doing the same. Some of the most inspirational military leaders have been ones who led their troops into battle and shared the dangers and hardships rather than staying behind in relative safety and comfort (Van Fleet & Yukl, 1986b). A negative example is provided by the executives in a large company that was experiencing financial difficulties. After asking employees to defer their expected pay increases, the executives awarded themselves large bonuses. This action created resentment among employees and undermined employee loyalty to the organization and commitment to its mission. A more effective approach would have been to set an example by cutting bonuses for top management before asking for sacrifices from other employees.

The values espoused by a leader should be demonstrated in his or her daily behavior, and it must be done consistently, not just when convenient. Top-level leaders are always in the spotlight, and their actions are carefully examined by followers in a search for hidden meanings that may not be intended by the leader. Ambiguous remarks may be misinterpreted and innocent actions may be misrepresented. To avoid sending the wrong message, it is important to consider in advance how one's comments and actions are likely to be interpreted.

Summary

Attributions of charisma are the result of an interactive process between leader, followers, and the situation. Charismatic leaders arouse enthusiasm and commitment in followers by articulating a compelling vision and increasing follower confidence about achieving it. Attribution of charisma to the leader is more likely if the vision and strategy for attaining it are innovative, the leader takes personal risks to promote it, and the strategy appears to be succeeding. Other relevant behaviors have also been identified, but they vary somewhat across the different theories. Some leader traits and skills such as self-confidence, strong convictions, poise, speaking ability, and a dramatic flair increase the likelihood of attributed charisma, but more important is a context that makes the leader's vision especially relevant to follower needs.

Charismatic leaders can have a tremendous influence on an organization, but the consequences are not always beneficial. Many entrepreneurs who establish a prosperous company are tyrants and egomaniacs whose actions may cause the eventual downfall of their company. The personalized power orientation of these charismatics makes them insensitive, manipulative, domineering, impulsive, and defensive. They emphasize devotion to themselves rather than to ideological goals, which are used only as a means to manipulate followers. Positive charismatics seek to instill devotion to ideological goals and are more likely to have a beneficial influence on the organization. However, the achievement culture fostered by positive charismatics may also produce some undesirable consequences if the needs of individual followers are ignored. More research is needed to discover whether it is possible to achieve the positive outcomes of charismatic leadership without the negative consequences.

Transformational leaders make followers more aware of the importance and value of the work and induce followers to transcend self-interest for the sake of the organization. The leaders develop follower skills and confidence to prepare them to assume more responsibility in an empowered organization. The leaders provide support and encouragement when necessary to maintain enthusiasm and effort in the face of obstacles, difficulties, and fatigue. As a result of this influence, followers feel trust and respect toward the leader, and they are motivated to do more than they originally expected to do.

The empirical research relevant for the theories of transformational leadership has generally been supportive, but few studies have examined the underlying influence processes that account for the positive relationship found between leader behavior and follower performance. More research is needed to determine the conditions in which different types of transformational behavior are most relevant and the underlying influence processes that explain why the behaviors are relevant.

The theories of transformational and charismatic leadership emphasize that emotional processes are as important as rational processes, and symbolic actions are as important as instrumental behavior. These theories provide new insights into the reasons for the success or failure of leaders, but the underlying explanatory processes in these theories do not provide a sufficient basis for a theory of strategic leadership in organizations. To understand how leaders can influence an organization's financial performance and survival, it is also necessary to examine organizational processes and aspects of strategic management not explicitly described in most charismatic and transformational theories. These subjects are discussed in Chapters 10 and 12.

Review and Discussion Questions

1. Briefly describe the attribution theory of charismatic leadership.
2. Briefly describe the self-concept theory of charismatic leadership.
3. Briefly describe the psychoanalytic and social contagion theories.
4. What influence processes are emphasized by each charismatic theory?
5. What behaviors are generally associated with charismatic leadership?
6. What is routinization of charisma, and how is it accomplished?
7. What problems are charismatic leaders likely to create for an organization?
8. In what type of situation is a charismatic leader most likely to be beneficial?
9. Briefly describe the theory of transformational leadership proposed by Bass.
10. What are some similarities and differences between charismatic and transformational leadership?
11. What new insights are provided by the theories of transformational and charismatic leadership?
12. What can leaders do to become more transformational?

Key Terms

- charisma
- charismatic leadership
- empowering
- idealized influence
- inspirational motivation
- intellectual stimulation
- internalization

- personal identification
- role modeling
- routinization of charisma
- self-concept
- self-efficacy
- social contagion
- social identification

- symbolic action
- transactional leadership
- transforming leadership
- transformational leadership
- vision

CASES

Metro Bank

Marsha Brown was the new manager of a suburban office of Metro Bank. The branch office was experiencing low morale and lower productivity than expected. One of the difficulties was that the office served as an informal training center for young managers. New hires who needed experience as loan officers or assistant branch managers were assigned here for training. When they reached a certain level of competence, they were promoted out of the branch office. This practice was demoralizing to the less mobile tellers and other assistants, who felt exploited and saw no personal reward in training their boss. After some checking with her boss and other people at corporate headquarters, Marsha concluded that it would be impossible to change this program. Her branch was one of those considered to be essential for executive development in Metro Bank.

During her first few months on the job, Marsha got to know her employees quite well. She reviewed performance records and met with each employee in the branch to talk about the person's career aspirations. She learned that many of her employees were quite capable and could do much more than they were presently doing. However, they had never seen themselves as going anywhere in the organization. Marsha searched for a unique vision for the branch office that would integrate the needs of her employees with the objectives of the executive development program, and in the process better serve the bank's customers. She formulated the following strategic objective: "To be the branch that best develops managerial talent while still offering quality customer service."

From this decision flowed a series of actions. First, Marsha declared that development opportunities for growth would be open to all, and she initiated a career development program for her employees. For those who wanted career advancement, she negotiated with the central training department for spaces in some of its programs. She persuaded the personnel department to inform her regularly about job openings that might interest her employees, including those not involved in the executive development program. Next, she built rewards into the appraisal system for employees who helped others learn, so that even those who did not aspire to advance would get some benefit from contributing to the new objective. To provide adequate backup in service functions, she instituted cross-training. Not only did this training provide a reserve of assistance when one function was experiencing peak workloads, it also contributed to a better understanding of the policies and procedures in other functions. Marsha also used developmental assignments with her own subordinate managers. She frequently had the assistant managers run staff meetings, represent the branch office at corporate meetings, or carry out some of her other managerial responsibilities.

The changes made by Marsha resulted in major gains. By repeatedly stressing the strategic objectives in her words and actions, she gave the branch office a distinctive character. Employees felt increased pride and morale improved. Some of the old-timers acquired new aspirations and, after developing their skills, advanced into higher positions in the bank. Even those who remained at the branch office felt good about the advancement of others, because now they saw their role as crucial for individual and organizational success rather than as a thankless task. The new spirit carried over to the treatment of customers, and together with the increased competence provided by cross-training, it resulted in faster and better service to customers. ■

SOURCE: Adapted from Bradford and Cohen, *Managing For Excellence* (New York: Wiley and Sons, 1984), pp. 106–107. Copyright © 1984 by John Wiley & Sons, Inc.

QUESTIONS

1. What leadership behaviors did Marsha use to change the branch office and motivate employees?

2. Describe Marsha's vision for her branch office of the bank.

3. Do you think Marsha should be classified as a charismatic leader, a transformational leader, or both?

Astro Airlines

Part 1

Arthur Burton established Astro Airlines in 1980, two years after the airlines were deregulated. Burton's vision for the new airline has two key elements. First, the airline would provide low-cost, no-frills service to people who formerly could not afford to travel by air. Second, the airline would have a novel type of organization that provided a better way for people to work together, thereby unleashing their creativity and improving productivity. Burton was a dynamic, emotionally stirring speaker with a kind of evangelical fervor, and he took advantage of every opportunity to teach and affirm his vision. He was regarded by many employees as an inspirational leader who made you believe that you could do anything. The climate at Astro Airlines in the initial years was one of enthusiasm, excitement, and optimism.

Instead of the typical bureaucratic organization, the new company had only three levels of management and few support staff. The emphasis was on equality, informality, participative leadership, and self-management. Employees were organized into teams with shared responsibility for determining how to do their work. The teams elected members to represent them in advisory and coordinating councils that met with top management, thereby enabling them to participate in making important decisions. Managers were expected to provide direction but not to dictate methods or police efforts. Employees were expected to perform multiple jobs and to learn new skills. Even the managers were expected to spend some time doing regular line jobs to keep informed about problems and customer needs. The status perks found in most large organizations were eliminated. For example, executives answered their own telephones and typed their own letters. New employees were carefully screened, because Burton sought to hire young, enthusiastic employees who were willing to learn new jobs and who could function as part of a cooperative team. All permanent employees were required to share in the ownership of the company, and they could purchase shares of stock at a reduced price.

Burton believed that a strategy of discount fares and convenient schedules with frequent flights would attract new passengers who would normally travel by car, train, or bus, or who would otherwise not travel. By keeping operating costs low, Astro Airlines was able to offer fares that were much lower than those of competitors. The salaries of managers and employees were lower than normal for the airline industry, although employees also received generous fringe benefits, profit sharing, and stock dividends. Costs were also reduced by purchasing surplus aircraft at bargain rates, by reconfiguring aircraft to carry more passengers (e.g., converting first class into coach seats), and by innovative scheduling that allowed the planes to fly more hours each day. Customers were charged for some frills such as meals and baggage handling that other airlines included in the price of the ticket. To reduce space normally needed for ticket counters at terminals, the ticketing for flights was done either in advance by travel agents or on the plane itself with innovative ticketing machines.

The new company was an immediate success, and passenger volume expanded rapidly. In less than three years the company grew from a few hundred employees with three planes to more than 3,000 employees with 22 planes servicing 20 cities. This success occurred despite dismal conditions that caused widespread operating losses in the airline industry, including a severe economic recession, a crippling national strike of air traffic controllers, and brutal price wars. The flexibility of the company and the commitment and creativity of its employees aided its early growth and facilitated rapid adaptation to crises such as the strike of air traffic controllers.

SOURCE: Copyright © 1993 by Gary Yukl.

QUESTIONS

1. Describe Burton's leadership behavior.

2. Was Burton a charismatic leader in the company at this time? Explain your answer.

Part 2

Despite the early successes, the rapid growth of the company was also creating some serious organizational problems. Employees believed that after the initial chaos of starting up the company, things would settle down and the intensely heavy workload would be alleviated. They were wrong; communication problems increased, the workload remained overwhelming, decisions were taking too long to be made, and too many decisions had to be resolved by top management. These problems were due in part to the informality and absence of structure. As the number of routes, facilities, and flights increased, operational problems became more complex, but formal structures were not developed to deal with them effectively. The number of managers did not increase nearly as fast as the number of nonsupervisory employees. Burton refused to recruit experienced managers from outside the company, preferring to promote current employees into positions for which they initially lacked sufficient expertise. Overburdened managers lacked adequate support personnel to which they could delegate routine responsibilities. Managers complained about the pressure and stress. They spent too much time in meetings, they could not get issues resolved and implemented, and they could not provide adequate training for the rapidly increasing number of new service employees. The new employees were not getting the extensive training and socialization necessary to prepare them to provide quality service, rotate among different service jobs, and use team management practices. Operating problems (e.g., canceled flights) and declining customer service (e.g., rude attendants) alienated customers and eroded the company's reputation.

Adding to the confusion was the worsening conflict between Burton, who as CEO was responsible for strategic planning, and the company president who was responsible for operational management. In 1982 the president resigned, and Burton assumed his responsibilities rather than finding an immediate replacement. At this time Burton finally decided to appoint a task force composed of executives to develop ideas for improving the organization. The task force presented some initial proposals for new managerial roles and structures. Employees were subsequently promoted to these roles, and management training activities were initiated for them. Burton was heavily involved in this training; he conducted some of it himself, and he faithfully attended sessions taught by others, thereby indicating the importance he placed on it. However, other necessary changes in management processes were not implemented, and the position of president was still not filled. In short, Burton seemed unwilling to take the steps necessary to transform Astro Airlines from an entrepreneurial start-up to an established organization. Indeed, his remedy for the firm's problems was to set out on a new growth path rather than to concentrate on consolidation. He believed that what the company needed was an even bigger vision to get people excited again. Thus, he began yet another period of rapid expansion. The airline added new routes, purchased new and larger aircraft, and hired more new employees.

By 1984, Burton no longer seemed content to run a successful regional airline. He continued to make changes designed to transform Astro into an international airline that would compete with the major carriers. He decided to acquire some other regional and commuter airlines that were financially weak. His strategy of rapid expansion was overly optimistic, and it ignored some important changes that were occurring in the external environment. Burton failed to anticipate the likely reactions of major airlines that were stronger financially and prepared to conduct a long price-cutting war to protect their market position. New passenger traffic did not increase enough to justify the cost of the added flights, and Astro was unsuccessful in attracting many business travelers accustomed to frills and better service. The company began to experience losses instead of profits.

Internal problems also worsened in 1985. There was an attempt to unionize the pilots, and a substantial number of pilots quit, complaining that they were exploited and mistreated. Other employees began questioning Burton's sincerity and accused him of being a manipulator. The perception among many employees was that he was now acting like a dictator, and no one dared to cross him. When asked about the absence of independent outsiders on the board of directors, Burton replied that he was the founder and largest shareholder, and he could determine what was best for the company. He fired a key managing officer who had been with the company since it was formed, presumably for challenging him and asking questions he no longer wanted to hear. Another founding executive whom Burton had appointed as president resigned and took several other employees with him to establish a new airline.

In 1986, as financial performance continued to deteriorate, Burton abruptly abandoned the distinctive strategy of discount fares and no-frills service and began offering full service with higher fares to lure business travelers. However, operating losses continued to mount, and in a last desperate move,

Burton changed back to his original strategy. It was all to no avail. By the summer of 1986, the losses increased and the company entered bankruptcy proceedings. ∎

SOURCE: Copyright © 1993 by Gary Yukl.

QUESTION

1. What dysfunctional aspects of charismatic leadership were displayed by Burton?

CHAPTER

10 LEADING CHANGE IN ORGANIZATIONS

Learning Objectives

After studying this chapter you should be able to:

- Understand the different reasons for resisting change.

- Understand the different types of organizational change.

- Understand the psychological processes involved in making major changes.

- Understand the different ways that leaders can influence the culture of an organization.

- Understand the characteristics of an effective vision.

- Understand how to develop an appealing vision for the organization.

- Understand the characteristics of a learning organization.

- Understand how leaders can increase learning and innovation in organizations.

Leading change is one of the most important and difficult leadership responsibilities. For some theorists, it is the essence of leadership and everything else is secondary. Effective leadership is needed to revitalize an organization and facilitate adaptation to a changing environment. This subject became especially relevant in the 1980s when many private and public sector organizations were confronted with the need to change the way things are done in order to survive. This chapter builds on the previous one and provides a practitioner-oriented perspective on strategic, change-oriented leadership.

Major change in an organization is usually guided by the top management team, but any member of the organization can initiate change or contribute to its success. The chapter describes how leaders can influence the organization culture, develop a vision, implement change, and encourage learning and innovation. The chapter begins by describing different change processes and approaches.

Change Processes in Organizations

Efforts to implement change in an organization are more likely to be successful if a leader understands the reasons for resistance to change, sequential phases in the change process, different types of change, and the importance of using appropriate models for understanding organizational problems. Each topic will be examined more closely.

Resistance to Change

Resistance to change is a common phenomenon for individuals and organizations. There are a number of different reasons why people resist major changes in organizations (Connor, 1995), and they are not mutually exclusive.

1. *Lack of trust.*   A basic reason for resistance to change is distrust of the people who propose it. Distrust can magnify the effect of other sources of resistance. Even without an obvious threat, a change may be resisted if people imagine hidden, ominous implications that will only become obvious at a later time. Mutual mistrust may encourage a leader to be secretive about the reasons for change, thereby further increasing suspicion and resistance.

2. *Belief that change is unnecessary.*   Resistance is more likely if the current way of doing things has been successful in the past and there is no clear evidence of serious problems that require major change. The signs of a developing problem are usually ambiguous at the early stage, and it is easy for people to ignore or discount them. If top management has been able to exaggerate how well the organization is performing, then convincing people of the need for change will be even more difficult. Even when a problem is finally recognized, the usual response is to make incremental adjustments in the present strategy, to do more of the same, rather than to do something different.

3. *Belief that the change is not feasible.*   Even when problems are acknowledged, a proposed change may be resisted because it seems unlikely to succeed. Making a change that is radically different from anything done previously will appear difficult if not impossible to most people. Failure of earlier change programs creates cynicism and makes people doubtful the next one will be any better.

4. *Economic threats.*   Even if a change would benefit the organization, it may be resisted by people who would suffer personal loss of income, benefits, or job security. The latter concern is especially relevant when change involves replacing people with technology or improving processes to make them more efficient. Prior downsizing and layoffs raise anxiety and increase resistance to new proposals, regardless of the actual threat.

5. *Relative high cost.*   Even when a change has obvious benefits for the organization, it always entails some costs and they may be higher than the benefits. Familiar routines must be changed, causing inconvenience and requiring more effort. Resources are necessary to implement change, and resources already invested in doing things the traditional way will be lost. Performance invariably suffers during the transition period as the new ways are learned and new procedures debugged. Concern about costs in relation to benefits will be more difficult to allay when it is not possible to estimate them with any accuracy.

6. *Fear of personal failure.*   Change makes some expertise obsolete and requires learning new ways of doing the work. People who lack self-confidence will be reluctant to trade procedures they have mastered for new ones that may prove too difficult to master. A proposed change will be more acceptable if it includes ample provision for helping people learn new ways of doing things.

7. *Loss of status and power.*   Major changes in organizations invariably result in some shift in relative power and status for individuals and subunits. New strategies often require expertise not possessed by some of the people currently enjoying high status as problem solvers. People responsible for activities that will be cut back or eliminated will lose status and power, making them more likely to oppose a change.

8. *Threat to values and ideals.*   Change that appears to be inconsistent with strong values and ideals will be resisted. Threat to a person's values arouses strong emotions that fuel resistance to change. If the values are embedded in a strong organization culture, resistance will be widespread rather than isolated.

9. *Resentment of interference.*   Some people resist change because they do not want to be controlled by others. Attempts to manipulate them or force change will elicit resentment and hostility. Unless people acknowledge the need for change and perceive they have a choice in determining how to change, they will resist it.

Resistance to change is not merely the result of ignorance or inflexibility, it is a natural reaction by people who want to protect their self-interests and sense of self-determination. Rather than seeing resistance as just another obstacle to batter down or circumvent, it is helpful to view it as energy that can be redirected to improve change (Jick, 1993; Maurer, 1996). Active resistance indicates the presence of strong values and emotions that could serve as a source of commitment for opponents who are converted to supporters.

Understanding resistance to change requires going beyond an examination of individual reasons for resisting. Resistance at the individual level is compounded by system dynamics at the group and organization level. Changes in one part of a system may elicit a reaction from other parts that nullifies the effect of the change. The interlocking nature of social systems creates tremendous inertia. Just as it takes miles to turn a supertanker at sea, it often takes years to implement significant change in a large organization.

Stages in the Change Process

Change process theories describe a typical pattern of events that occur from the beginning of a change to the end. One of the earliest process theories was Lewin's (1951) force-field model. He proposed that the change process can be divided into three phases: unfreezing, changing, and refreezing. In the unfreezing phase, people come to realize that the old ways of doing things are no longer adequate. This recognition may occur as a result of an obvious crisis, or it may result from an effort to describe threats or opportunities not evident to most people in the organization. In the changing phase, people look for new ways of doing things and select a promising approach. In the refreezing phase, the new approach is implemented and it becomes established. All three phases are important for successful change. An attempt to move directly to the changing phase without first unfreezing attitudes is likely to meet with apathy or strong resistance. Lack of systematic diagnosis and problem solving in the changing phase will result in a weak change plan. Lack of attention to consensus building and declining enthusiasm in the third stage may result in the change being reversed soon after it is implemented.

According to Lewin, change may be achieved by two types of actions. One approach is to increase the driving forces toward change (e.g., increase incentives, use position power to force change), the other is to reduce restraining forces that create resistance to change (e.g., reduce fear of failure or economic loss, co-opt or remove opponents). If the restraining forces are weak, it may be sufficient merely to increase driving forces. However, when restraining forces are strong, a dual approach is advisable. Unless restraining forces can be reduced, an increase in driving forces will create an intense conflict over the change, and continuing resistance will make it more difficult to complete the refreezing phase.

Stages in Reaction to Change

Another process theory describes how people in organizations react to changes imposed upon them (Gebert, Boerner, & Lanwehr, 2003; Krause, 2004; Jick, 1993; Woodward & Bucholz, 1987). The theory builds on observations about the typical sequence of reactions by people to sudden, traumatic events such as the death of a loved one, the breakup of a marriage, or a natural disaster that destroys one's home (Lazarus, 1991). A similar pattern of reactions is assumed to occur during organizational change. The reaction pattern has four stages: denial, anger, mourning, and adaptation. The initial reaction is to deny that change will be necessary ("This isn't happening" or "It's just a temporary setback"). The next stage is to get angry and look for someone to blame. At the same time, people stubbornly resist giving up accustomed ways of doing things. In the third stage, people stop denying that change is inevitable, acknowledge what has been lost, and mourn it. The final stage is to accept the need to change and go on with one's life. The duration and severity of each type of reaction can vary greatly, and some people get stuck in an intermediate stage. Understanding these stages is important for change leaders, who must learn to be patient and helpful. Many people need help to overcome denial, channel their anger constructively, mourn without becoming severely depressed, and have optimism about adjusting successfully.

A related topic is how psychological reactions to change are affected by experiencing repeated, traumatic change. Competing hypotheses can be made (Jick, 1993). One hypothesis is that repeated change leaves people less resilient and more vulnerable to adverse effects from subsequent change. The explanation for this effect involves prolonged stress and the failure to completely resolve the emotional trauma of an earlier change. For example, after losing two jobs in five years as a result of downsizing, Linda cannot deal with the threat of losing another job and seeks early retirement. The alternative hypothesis is that experiencing traumatic events will inoculate people and leave them better prepared to change again without such an intense or prolonged period of adjustment. For example, having experienced and survived the loss of two jobs in five years, Sally is confident about taking more risky, less secure jobs in the future. Another possibility is that repeated change makes some people more resilient and others less resilient. We do not have any good answers yet about the effects of repeated change on individuals, but the accelerating pace of change in organizations makes it a relevant question to investigate.

Different Types of Organizational Change

The success of a major change depends in part on what is changed. Many attempts to introduce change in an organization emphasize changing either attitudes or roles but not both (Beer, Eisenstat, & Spector, 1990). The attitude-centered approach involves changing attitudes and values with persuasive appeals, training programs, team-building activities, or a culture change program. In addition, technical or interpersonal skills may be increased with a training program. The underlying assumption is that new attitudes and skills will cause behavior to change in a beneficial way. It is hoped that converts become change agents themselves and transmit the vision to other people in the organization.

The role-centered approach involves changing work roles by reorganizing the workflow, redesigning jobs to include different activities and responsibilities, modifying authority relationships, changing the criteria and procedures for evaluation of work, and changing the reward system. The assumption is that when work roles require people to act in a different way, they will change their attitudes to be consistent with the new behavior. Effective behavior is induced by the new role requirements and reinforced by the evaluation and reward system.

An example will clarify the difference between the two approaches to organizational change. A company is having difficulty getting people in different functionally specialized departments to cooperate in developing new products rapidly and getting them into the marketplace. One approach is to talk about the importance of cooperation and to use a process analysis intervention or team-building activity to increase understanding and mutual respect among people from different functions. This approach assumes that increased trust and understanding will increase cooperation back in the workplace. Another approach is to create cross-functional teams that are responsible for the development of a new product, and then reward people for contributions to the success of the team. This approach assumes that people who cooperate to achieve a common goal will come to understand and trust each other.

Over the years, there has been controversy about which approach is the most effective. Either approach can succeed or fail depending on how well it is implemented. Beer and his colleagues (1990) argue that a role-centered program is more likely to be successful than an attitude-centered program. However, the two approaches are not incompatible, and the best strategy is to use them together in a mutually supportive way. Efforts to change attitudes and skills to support new roles reduce the chance that the role change will be subverted by opponents before it has a chance to succeed.

Not all change efforts are focused on attitudes or roles. Another type of change is in the technology used to do the work. Many organizations have attempted to improve performance by implementing new information and decision support systems. Examples include networked workstations, human resource information systems, inventory and order processing systems, sales tracking systems, or an intranet with groupware for communication and idea sharing among employees. Such changes often fail to yield the desired benefits, because without consistent changes in work roles, attitudes, and skills, the new technology will not be accepted and used in an effective way.

Still another major type of change is in the competitive strategy of the organization. Examples of this strategy-centered approach include introduction of new products or services, entering new markets, use of new forms of marketing, initiation of Internet sales in addition to direct selling, forming alliances or joint ventures with other organizations, modifying relationships with suppliers (e.g., partnering with a few reliable suppliers). To be successful, changes in competitive strategy often require consistent changes in people, work roles, organization structure, and technology. For example, the decision to begin providing a more intensive type of customer service may require service personnel with additional skills and better technology for communicating with customers.

Internal changes in an organization may emphasize either economic factors or human factors (Beer & Nohria, 2000). The economic approach seeks to improve financial performance with changes such as downsizing, restructuring, and adjustments in compensation and incentives. The organizational approach seeks to improve human capability, commitment, and creativity by increasing individual and organizational learning, strengthening cultural values that support flexibility and innovation, and empowering people to initiate improvements. Attempts to make large-scale change in an organization often involve some aspects of both approaches, but incompatible elements can undermine the change effort if not carefully managed. For example, making drastic layoffs to reduce costs can undermine the trust and loyalty needed to improve collective learning and innovation. It is difficult to improve organizational performance unless a leader can find ways to deal with the trade-offs and competing values involved in making major change, and this subject is discussed in more detail in Chapter 12.

Many organizations implement improvement programs that are popular at the time, even if there is little or no empirical evidence to indicate that they are effective. Some examples of widely used programs during the past two decades include downsizing, delayering, reorganization (e.g., into small product divisions), total quality management, reengineering, self-managed teams, outsourcing, and partnering (e.g., with suppliers). A common mistake is to implement a new program without first making a careful diagnosis of the problems confronting the organization. Management programs and structural changes often fail to solve organizational problems and sometimes make them worse (Beer et al., 1990). The benefits obtained from changes made in one part of the organization often fail to improve the overall performance of the organization and may cause new problems for other subunits (Goodman & Rousseau, 2004). Before initiating major changes, leaders need to be clear about the nature of the problem and the objectives of the program.

Systems Models for Organizational Diagnosis

Just as in the treatment of a physical illness, the first step is a careful diagnosis to determine what is wrong with the patient. The organizational diagnosis can be conducted by the top management team, by outside consultants, or by a task force composed of representatives of the various key stakeholders in the organization. To understand the reasons for a problem and how to deal with it requires a good understanding of the complex relationships and systems dynamics that occur in organizations. Systems models that acknowledge complex relationships and cyclical causality can be used to improve organizational diagnosis (Gharajedaghi, 1999; Goodman & Rousseau, 2004; Senge, 1990).

In a systems model, problems have multiple causes, which may include actions taken earlier to solve other problems. Actions have multiple outcomes, including unintended side effects. Changes often have delayed effects that tend to obscure the real nature of the relationship. Sometimes actions that appear to offer quick relief may actually make things worse in the long run, whereas the best solution may offer no immediate benefits. A person who is impatient for quick results may keep repeating inappropriate remedies, rather than pursuing better remedies that require patience and short-term sacrifice.

A change in one part of a system often elicits reactions from other parts to maintain system equilibrium. The reactions tend to dampen or cancel out the effects of the initial change. An example is when a manager downsizes the workforce to reduce costs, but pressure to maintain the same output requires expensive overtime and use of consultants (including some of the same people who were downsized), thereby negating most or all of the cost savings.

Another common phenomenon is a reinforcing cycle wherein small changes grow into much bigger changes that may or may not be desirable. A positive example is when a change made to improve processes in one subunit is successful, and other subunits are encouraged to imitate it, resulting in more benefits for the organization than initially expected. A negative example is when rationing is introduced to conserve a resource and people rush to get more of it than they currently need, thereby causing greater shortages.

Influencing Organization Culture

Large-scale change in an organization usually requires some change in the organization culture as well as direct influence over individual subordinates. By changing the culture of an organization, top management can indirectly influence the motivation and behavior of organization members. Research on organizational culture provides further insight into the dynamics of transformational leadership and the processes by which a leader's charisma may become institutionalized (see Chapter 9).

Nature of Organization Culture

Schein (1992) defines the culture of a group or organization as shared assumptions and beliefs about the world and their place in it, the nature of time and space, human nature, and human relationships. Schein distinguishes between underlying beliefs (which may be unconscious) and espoused values, which may or may not be consistent with these beliefs. Espoused values do not accurately reflect the culture when they are inconsistent with underlying beliefs. For example, a company may espouse open communication, but the underlying belief may be that any criticism or disagreement is detrimental and should be avoided. It is difficult to dig beneath the superficial layer of espoused values to discover the underlying beliefs and assumptions, some of which may be unconscious.

The underlying beliefs representing the culture of a group or organization are learned responses to problems of survival in the external environment and problems of internal integration. The primary external problems are the core mission or reason for existence of the organization, concrete objectives based on this mission, strategies for attaining these objectives, and ways to measure success in attaining objectives. Most organizations have multiple objectives, and some of them may not be as obvious as others. Agreement on a general mission does not imply agreement about specific objectives or their relative priority. Schein (1992, p. 56) provides an example of a company with consensus about having a line of winning products but disagreement about how to allocate resources among different product groups and how to market the products:

> One group thought that marketing meant better image advertising in national magazines so that more people would recognize the name of the company, one group was convinced that marketing meant better advertising in technical journals, one group thought it meant developing the next generation of products, while yet another group emphasized merchandising and sales support as the key element in marketing. Senior management could not define clear goals because of a lack of consensus on the meaning of key functions and how those functions reflect the core mission of the organization.

All organizations need to solve problems of internal integration as well as problems of external adaptation. Objectives and strategies cannot be achieved effectively without cooperative effort and reasonable stability of membership in the organization. Internal problems include the criteria for determining membership in the organization, the basis for determining status and power, criteria and procedures for allocating rewards and punishments, an ideology to explain unpredictable and uncontrollable events, rules or customs about how to handle aggression and intimacy, and a shared consensus about the meaning of words and symbols. The beliefs that develop about these issues serve as the basis for role expectations to guide behavior, let people know what is proper and improper, and help people maintain comfortable relationships with each other.

A major function of culture is to help us understand the environment and determine how to respond to it, thereby reducing anxiety, uncertainty, and confusion. The internal and external problems are closely interconnected, and organizations must deal with them simultaneously. As solutions are developed through experience, they become shared assumptions that are passed on to new members. Over time, the assumptions may become so familiar that members are no longer consciously aware of them.

Primary Ways to Influence Culture

Leaders can influence the culture of an organization in a variety of ways. According to Schein (1992), five primary mechanisms offer the greatest potential for embedding and reinforcing aspects of culture (see Table 10-1).

1. *Attention.*   Leaders communicate their priorities, values, and concerns by their choice of things to ask about, measure, comment on, praise, and criticize. Much of this communication occurs when the leader is planning activities and monitoring operations. Emotional outbursts by leaders have an especially strong effect in communicating values and concerns. In contrast, by not paying attention to something, a leader sends the message that it is not important.

2. *Reactions to crises.*   Because of the emotionality surrounding crises, a leader's response to them can send a strong message about values and assumptions. A leader who faithfully supports espoused values even when under pressure to take expedient actions inconsistent with them communicates clearly that the values are really important. For example, one company with lower sales avoided layoffs by having all employees (including managers) work fewer hours and take a pay cut; the decision communicated a strong concern for preserving employee jobs.

TABLE 10-1   How Leaders Shape Culture

Primary Mechanisms

    What things are attended to by the leader

    Ways of reacting to crises

    Role modeling

    Criteria for allocating rewards

    Criteria for selection and dismissal

Secondary Mechanisms

    Design of management systems and procedures

    Design of organization structure

    Design of facilities

    Stories, legends, and myths

    Formal statements

Source: Based on E. H, Schein, *Organizational Culture and Leadership*, 2nd ed. (San Francisco, Jossey-Bass, 1992).

3. *Role modeling.*   Leaders can communicate values and expectations by their own actions, especially actions showing loyalty, self-sacrifice, and service beyond the call of duty. A leader who institutes a policy or procedure but fails to act in accordance with it is communicating the message that it is not really important or necessary.

4. *Allocation of rewards.*   The criteria used as the basis for allocating rewards signal what is valued by the organization. Formal recognition in ceremonies and informal praise communicate a leader's concerns and priorities. Failure to recognize contributions and achievements sends a message that they are not important. Finally, differential allocation of rewards and status symbols affirms the relative importance of some members compared to others. For example, in comparison to companies in the United States, Japanese companies use far fewer status symbols and privileges of rank such as large offices, special dining rooms, and private parking spaces.

5. *Criteria for selection and dismissal.*   Leaders can influence culture by their choice of criteria for recruiting, selecting, promoting, and dismissing people. Leaders also communicate their values and concerns by providing realistic information about the criteria and requirements for success in the organization.

Secondary Ways to Influence Culture

In addition to the five primary mechanisms, Schein described five secondary mechanisms that are useful for embedding and reinforcing culture when they are consistent with the primary mechanisms.

1. *Design of systems and procedures.* Formal budgets, planning sessions, reports, performance reviews, and management development programs can be used to emphasize some activities and criteria, while also helping to reduce role ambiguity. A preference for formality reflects strong values about control and order.

2. *Design of organization structure.* The design of structure is often influenced more by assumptions about internal relationships or implicit theories of management than by actual requirements for effective adaptation to the environment. A centralized structure reflects the belief that only the leader can determine what is best, whereas a decentralized structure or the use of self-managed teams reflects a belief in individual initiative and shared responsibility.

3. *Design of facilities.*   Although seldom done as an intentional strategy, leaders can design facilities to reflect basic values. For example, an open office layout is consistent with a value for open communication. Having similar offices and the same dining facilities for all employees is consistent with egalitarian values.

4. *Stories, legends, and myths.*   Stories about important events and people in the organization help transmit values and assumptions. However, stories and myths are more a reflection of culture than a determinant of it. The potential use of this mechanism by leaders to influence culture is limited in any organization or society where open communication makes it possible to detect a false story. To be useful the story must convey a clear message about values, and it must describe a real event.

5. *Formal statements.*   Public statements of values by the leader and written value statements, charters, and philosophies can be useful as a supplement to other mechanisms. However, formal statements usually describe only a small portion of an organization's cultural assumptions and beliefs, and they have no credibility unless the words are supported by leader actions and decisions.

Cultural Forms

Another way to influence the culture is to change cultural forms such as symbols, slogans, and rituals (Trice & Beyer, 1993). A number of different changes are possible, including elimination of existing cultural forms that symbolize the old ideology, modification of existing cultural forms to express the new ideology, and creation of new cultural forms. The following description of changes in the U.S. Postal Service provides some examples (Biggart, 1977).

> When Winton Blount became the new Postmaster General in 1972, he initiated a number of changes to signal a new ideology which emphasized efficiency, competitiveness, and self-sufficiency rather than service at any cost and dependence on Congress. Changes in symbols included a new name for the post office, a new logo (an eagle poised for flight rather than Paul Revere riding a horse), new postal colors, and a new typeface for publications. The employee newsletter was drastically changed from a media for disseminating trivial information to a vehicle for advocating the new ideology and celebrating the success of local post offices that achieved the new efficiency standards. An advertising office was created to promote a new image for the postal service, and a training institute was established to train thousands of postal supervisors each year in management procedures consistent with the new ideology.

Rituals, ceremonies, and rites of passage can be used to strengthen identification with the organization as well as to emphasize core values. In many organizations new members are required to make a public oath of allegiance, to demonstrate knowledge of the ideology, or to undergo an ordeal to demonstrate loyalty. Also common are ceremonies to celebrate a member's advancement in rank, to inaugurate a new leader, and to acknowledge the retirement of a member. Formal orientation programs can be used to socialize new employees and teach them about the culture of an organization. Formal training programs designed to increase job skills can also be used to teach participants about the ideology of the organization. Other approaches for socialization of new members include use of formal mentors who are selected because they are able to model and teach key values, and the use of internships, apprenticeships, or special assignments to work in subunits of the organization where the culture is strong (Fisher, 1986).

Culture and Growth Stages of Organizations

The influence of a leader on the culture of an organization varies depending on the developmental stage of the organization. The founder of a new organization has a strong influence on its culture. The founder typically has a vision of a new enterprise and proposes ways of doing things that, if successful in accomplishing objectives and reducing anxiety, will gradually become embedded in the culture. However, creating culture in a new organization is not necessarily a smooth process; it may involve considerable conflict if the founder's ideas are not successful or other powerful members of the organization have competing ideas. To succeed, the founder needs an appropriate vision and the ability and persistence to influence others to accept it. If the founder does not articulate a consistent vision and act consistently to reinforce it, the organization may develop a dysfunctional culture reflecting the inner conflicts of the founder (Kets de Vries & Miller, 1984).

One of the most important elements of culture in new organizations is the set of beliefs about the distinctive competence of the organization that differentiates it from other organizations. The beliefs are likely to include the reason why the organization's products or services are unique or superior and the internal processes that account for continued ability to provide these products and services. Implications for the relative status of different functions in the organization and the strategies for solving crises differ depending on the source of distinctive competence. For example, in a company that is successful due to its development of innovative products, the research and development function is likely to have higher status than other functions, and the likely response to a recent decline in sales is to introduce some new products. In a company that has been able to provide a common product at the lowest price, manufacturing will have higher status, and the response to a decline in sales is likely to involve the search for ways to reduce costs below those of competitors.

The culture in young, successful organizations is likely to be strong because it is instrumental to the success of the organization, the assumptions have been internalized by current members and transmitted to new members, and the founder is still present to symbolize and reinforce the culture. In such an organization, the culture will evolve slowly over the years as experience reveals that some assumptions need to be modified. Eventually, as the organization matures and people other than the founder or family members occupy key leadership positions, the culture will become more unconscious and less uniform. As different subcultures develop in different subunits, conflicts and power struggles may increase. Segments of the culture that were initially functional may become dysfunctional, hindering the organization from adapting to a changing environment.

In general, it is much more difficult to change culture in a mature organization than to create it in a new organization. One reason is that many of the underlying beliefs and assumptions shared by people in an organization are implicit and unconscious. Cultural assumptions are also difficult to change when they justify the past and are a matter of pride. Moreover, cultural values influence the selection of leaders and the role expectations for them. In a mature, relatively prosperous organization, culture influences leaders more than leaders influence culture. Drastic changes are unlikely unless a major crisis threatens the welfare and survival of the organization. Even with a crisis, it takes considerable insight and skill for a leader to understand the current culture in an organization and implement changes successfully.

Developing a Vision

The research on charismatic and transformational leadership indicates that a clear and compelling vision is useful to guide change in an organization (see Chapter 9). Before people will support radical change, they need to have a vision of a better future that is attractive enough to justify the sacrifices and hardships the change will require. The vision can provide a sense of continuity for followers by linking past events and present strategies to a vivid image of a better future for the organization. The vision provides hope for a better future and the faith that it will be attained someday. During the hectic and confusing process of implementing major change, a clear vision helps to guide and coordinate the decisions and actions of thousands of people working in widely dispersed locations.

Desirable Characteristics for a Vision

A number of writers have attempted to describe the essential qualities of a successful vision (Bennis & Nanus, 1985; Kotter, 1996; Kouzes & Posner, 1995; Nanus, 1992; Tichy & Devanna, 1986). A vision should be simple and idealistic, a picture of a desirable future, not a complex plan with quantitative objectives and detailed action steps. The vision should appeal to the values, hopes, and ideals of organization members and other stakeholders whose support is needed. The vision should emphasize distant ideological objectives rather than immediate tangible benefits. The vision should be challenging but realistic. To be meaningful and credible, it should not be a wishful fantasy, but rather an attainable future grounded in the present reality. The vision should address basic assumptions about what is important for the organization, how it should relate to the environment, and how people should be treated. The vision should be focused enough to guide decisions and actions, but general enough to allow initiative and creativity in the strategies for attaining it. Finally, a successful vision should be simple enough to be communicated clearly in five minutes or less.

Elements of a Vision

Vision is a term with many different meanings, which creates widespread confusion. It is unclear whether a mission statement, strategic objective, value statement, or slogan constitutes an effective vision. In the absence of direct research on this question, one way to answer it is to examine each construct in relation to the desirable characteristics for a vision.

The mission statement usually describes the purpose of the organization in terms of the type of activities to be performed for constituents or customers. In contrast, an effective vision tells us what these activities mean to people. The core of the vision is the organization's mission, but different aspects of it may be emphasized. A successful vision tells you not only what the organization does, but why it is worthwhile and exciting to do it. A successful vision makes the typical dull, abstract mission statement come alive, infusing it with excitement, arousing emotions, and stimulating creativity to achieve it. For example, consider an automobile company with the mission to make and sell cars at a profit. A possible vision might be the following:

> We will create an empowered organization to unleash our creativity and focus our energies in cooperative effort; it will enable us to develop and build the best personal vehicles in the world, vehicles that people will treasure owning because they are fun to use, they are reliable, they keep people comfortable and safe, and they enable people to have freedom of movement in their environment without harming it.

This vision conveys an image of what can be achieved, why it is worthwhile, and how it can be done. Note that the vision is flexible enough to encourage the possibility of finding alternative power sources in the future and developing other types of vehicles besides conventional ground cars (e.g., fusion-powered air cars, as in the movie *Back to the Future*).

A value statement is a list of the key values or ideological themes considered important for an organization. The values usually pertain to treatment of customers, treatment of organization members, core competencies, and standards of excellence. Common themes include satisfying customers, achieving excellence in products or services, providing an innovative product or service, developing and empowering employees, and making important contributions to society. A value statement provides a good beginning for developing a more complete vision. However, just listing values does not clearly explain their relative priority, how they are interrelated, or how they will be expressed and achieved. An effective vision statement provides a glimpse of a possible future in which all the key values are realized at the same time.

Slogans are used to summarize and communicate values in simple terms. However, a slogan is limited in how many values can be expressed. Consider the following examples: technology is our business, quality is job one, we feel good when you feel good, all the news people want to read, and partners in making dreams come true. Only the last slogan has more than one value; it describes the ideal service provided to customers and the ideal relationship among the providers. Slogans can be useful as part of a larger vision, but overemphasis on a simplistic slogan can trivialize the vision and diminish important values not included in the slogan (Richards & Engle, 1986).

Strategic objectives are tangible outcomes or results to be achieved, sometimes by a specific deadline. A performance objective may be stated in terms of the absolute level of performance (e.g., profits, sales, return on investment), or the relative level of performance (e.g., becoming number one in the industry or region, outperforming a traditional rival). Neither type of objective is likely to involve enduring, ideological themes. Performance objectives are useful to guide planning and facilitate evaluation of progress, but the focus of a vision should be on values and ideological themes, not on improvement of economic outcomes or outperforming rivals. If performance objectives are included in a vision, they should be regarded as milestones along the way toward achieving ideological objectives.

Project objectives are defined in terms of the successful completion of a complex activity (e.g., developing a new type of product, implementing a new MBA program, establishing a subsidiary in China). These objectives can emphasize economic outcomes, ideological outcomes, or both. For example, a pharmaceutical company has a project to develop a new vaccine that will prevent a disease; successful completion of the project will improve profits, provide health benefits to society, and enhance scientific knowledge. A limitation of most project objectives is their relatively short time perspective. When the project is completed, the vision is ended. Project objectives can be included in the long-term vision for an organization, or a supplementary vision can be built around an especially important project. However, no single project should be allowed to eclipse the fuller, more enduring vision for the organization.

To understand what an effective project vision looks like, it is helpful to examine a specific example. When Walt Disney conceived the idea of Disneyland, it was an entirely new type of activity for his company, and it was unlike any earlier amusement park. It would be expensive to build, and it was uncertain whether enough visitors would be attracted to yield a profit. At the time it was not obvious that Disneyland would become such a phenomenal success, and people were skeptical about the risky project. An inspiring vision was needed to gain support from other key members of top management and outside investors. Disney's vision for the park was described in the following way:

> The idea of Disneyland is a simple one. It will be a place for people to find happiness and knowledge. It will be a place for parents and children to spend pleasant times in one another's company: a place for teachers and pupils to discover greater ways of understanding and education. Here the older generation can recapture the nostalgia of days gone by, and the younger generation can savor the challenge of the future. Here will be the wonders of Nature and Man for all to see and understand. Disneyland will be based upon and dedicated to the ideals, the dreams and hard facts that have created America. And it will be uniquely equipped to dramatize these dreams and facts and send them forth as a source of courage and inspiration to all the world. Disneyland will be something of a fair, an exhibition, a playground, a community center, a museum of living facts, and a showplace of beauty and magic. It will be filled with the accomplishments, the joys and hopes of the world we live in. And it will remind us and show us how to make those wonders part of our own lives. (Thomas, 1976, p. 246)

Most of the evidence about the importance of a vision for successful change in organizations comes from leadership research that is focused more on the process of envisioning than on the content of the vision. As noted in Chapter 9, the visions articulated by effective leaders were sometimes elaborate and sometimes simple. A descriptive study on the content of organizational visions found that most of them were expressed in the form of a performance objective or value statement that was very brief, strategic, and future oriented (Larwood, Falbe, Kriger, & Miesing, 1995). A study by Berson, Shamir, Avolio, and Popper (2001) found that leaders who were rated as highly transformational were more likely to develop visions that were future oriented and reflected a high level of optimism and confidence. A study of small entrepreneurial firms by Baum, Locke, and Kirkpatrick (1998) found that the CEO of the fastest growing firms was more likely to communicate a vision that emphasized future growth. The results from these studies seem to suggest that few organizations actually have a well-developed vision with significant ideological content. In recent years some scholars have begun to question whether the importance of a vision for organization change has been overstated. More research is needed to determine what type of vision is sufficient to guide and inspire change in organizations, and the conditions where an ideological vision is most important.

Procedures for Developing a Vision

It is extremely difficult to develop a vision that will elicit commitment for major change from the many diverse stakeholders whose support is needed. Such a vision cannot be generated by a mechanical formula. Judgment and analytical ability are needed to synthesize the vision, but intuition and creativity are important as well. To develop an appealing vision, it is essential to have a good understanding of the organization (its operations, products, services, markets, competitors, and social-political environment), its culture (shared beliefs and assumptions about the world and the organization's place in it), and the underlying needs and values of employees and other stakeholders. In most cases a successful vision is not the creation of a single, heroic leader working alone, but instead it reflects the contributions of many, diverse people in the organization (Tichy & Devanna, 1986). The vision is seldom created in a single moment of revelation, but instead it takes shape during a lengthy process of exploration, discussion, and refinement of ideas.

Some tentative guidelines to help leaders develop a vision are summarized in Table 10-2. The guidelines are based on leadership theories, empirical research, and practitioner insights (e.g., Conger, 1989; Kotter, 1996; Kouzes & Posner, 1987; Nadler, Shaw, Walton, & Associates, 1995; Nanus, 1992; Peters, 1987; Peters & Austin, 1985; Tichy & Devanna, 1986; Trice & Beyer, 1993).

- **Involve key stakeholders.**

A single leader is unlikely to have the knowledge needed to develop a vision that will appeal to all the stakeholders whose support is necessary to accomplish major organizational change. Even when the initial ideas for a vision originate with the leader, it is desirable to involve key stakeholders in refining these ideas into a vision with widespread appeal. Key stakeholders may include owners, executives, other members of the organization, customers, investors, joint venture partners, and labor unions.

TABLE 10-2   Guidelines for Formulating a Vision

- Involve key stakeholders.
- Identify strategic objectives with wide appeal.
- Identify relevant elements in the old ideology.
- Link the vision to core competencies.
- Evaluate the credibility of the vision.
- Continually assess and refine the vision.

Often the best place to begin is with senior executives, the group most likely to have the broad perspective and knowledge necessary to understand the need for change. Insights about their ideals, values, and attitudes about change can be explored in strategic planning sessions (see Chapter 12). Another approach is to ask executives to develop a personal vision statement describing what they see as their ideal future role in the organization. The personal vision statements can be examined to identify shared values and appealing images of how the organization should be transformed. Discovery of shared values often requires considerable time and effort, and there is no guarantee of success. If serious disagreement exists about the ideal qualities for an ideal organization, then it will be difficult to find a vision that transcends these differences.

Tichy and Devanna (1986) suggested some techniques that are useful for helping executives develop a shared vision of what the organization should be like. One technique is to ask them to write a magazine article in journalistic style describing the organization as they would like it to be at a specified time in the future. A variation of this technique is a role play in which half of the executives (the "reporters") interview the remaining executives and ask them to describe how they would like the organization to be in 10 years. Still another technique is to have people describe a fictitious organization that would be able to compete effectively with the leading companies in a specified market. The group then determines how the current organization differs from the fictitious one and looks for ways to close the gaps.

Executives are not the only stakeholders to consult in formulating a vision. Understanding the values, hopes, and aspirations of other people in the organization is essential to finding a vision that will engage them. Gaining this insight can be difficult, because people may be unable or unwilling to explain what is really important to them. Kouzes and Posner (1987, p. 115) offered the following description of how leaders learn about follower needs and values:

> Leaders find the common thread that weaves together the fabric of human needs into a colorful tapestry. They seek out the brewing consensus among those they would lead. In order to do this, they develop a deep understanding of the collective yearnings. They listen carefully for quiet whisperings in dark corners. They attend to the subtle cues. They sniff the air to get the scent. They watch the faces. They get a sense of what people want, what they value, what they dream about.

- **Identify strategic objectives with wide appeal.**

It is easier to get agreement on strategic objectives than on a more elaborate vision. A group discussion of strategic objectives can provide insights about values and ideals. The first step is to ask people to identify specific performance objectives that are challenging and relevant to the mission of the organization. Then ask people to discuss the relative importance of the various objectives and the reasons why an objective is important. Look for shared values and ideals that can become the basis for a vision with wide appeal.

- **Identify relevant elements in the old ideology.**

Even when radical change is necessary in an organization, some elements in the current ideology may be worthy of preservation. Look for values and ideals that will continue to be relevant for the organization in the foreseeable future. Sometimes traditional values that were subverted or ignored can serve as the basis for a new vision, as in the following example.

> A manufacturing company that once had a reputation for making the best products in the industry decided to pursue a strategy of cost reduction to compete with the inexpensive products of foreign competitors. The strategy was not successful. After several years of declining sales the company lost its dominant position in the market and its products were perceived to be of inferior quality. Major changes were made to implement a new strategy that emphasized quality and innovation rather than low price. The strategy was justified as a return to key values from the glorious early years of the firm.

- **Link the vision to core competencies.**

A successful vision must be credible as well as appealing. People will be skeptical about a vision that promises too much and seems impossible to attain. Leaders face a difficult task in crafting a vision that is both challenging and believable. Lofty visions often require innovative strategies, and untested strategies are risky and difficult to assess. In the absence of a tested strategy, people need a basis for believing the vision is attainable. One basis is confidence in their ability to collectively solve problems and overcome obstacles (collective efficacy). A vision that entails new and difficult types of activities is more credible if the core competencies of the organization and the skills of its members are relevant for these activities, as in the following example.

> When President Kennedy first articulated his visionary objective to land a man on the moon by the end of the decade, only about 15 percent of the necessary technology and procedures had been developed, and it was not evident that so many difficult things could be done successfully in such a short time. However, the availability of scientists and engineers with the necessary expertise and confidence to tackle these formidable problems made the vision more credible.

- **Continually assess and refine the vision.**

A successful vision is likely to evolve over time. As strategies to achieve the vision are implemented, people can learn more about what is feasible and what is not. As progress is made toward achieving the vision, new possibilities may be discovered, and objectives that seemed unrealistic may suddenly become attainable. Although some continuity in the vision is desirable, the leader should keep looking for ways to make the vision more appealing and credible (e.g., new metaphors, slogans, and symbols that capture the essence of the vision). The development of a vision is an interactive, circular process, not a simple, linear progression from vision to strategy to action. Indeed, an intensive review of strategy may provide the ideas for a new vision, rather than the other way around.

Implementing Change

Organization scholars have been interested in determining how the approach used to implement change affects the success of the effort. It is likely that the success of efforts to transform an organization depend in part on when, where, and how various aspects of the change are implemented, and who participates in the process in what ways.

Responsibility for Implementing Major Change

Large-scale change in an organization is unlikely to be successful without the support of top management. However, contrary to common assumptions, major changes are not always initiated by top management, and they may not become involved until the process is well underway (Beer, 1988; Belgard, Fisher, & Rayner, 1988). Major changes suggested by lower levels may be resisted by top managers who are strongly committed to traditional approaches and do not understand that the old ways of doing things are no longer appropriate. As noted in Chapter 12, the major transformation of an organization often requires the replacement of top management by new leaders with a mandate for radical change.

The essential role of top management in implementing change is to formulate an integrating vision and general strategy, build a coalition of supporters who endorse the strategy, then guide and coordinate the process by which the strategy will be implemented. Complex changes usually involve a process of experimentation and learning, because it is impossible to anticipate all the problems or to prepare detailed plans for how to carry out all aspects of the change. Instead of specifying detailed guidelines for change at all levels of the organization, it is much better to encourage middle and lower-level managers to transform their own units in a way that is consistent with the vision and strategy. Top management should provide encouragement, support, and necessary resources to facilitate change, but should not try to dictate the details of how to do it.

The Pace and Sequencing of Changes

A debate continues among change scholars about the optimal pace and sequencing of desired changes. Some scholars have advocated rapid introduction of changes throughout the organization to prevent the buildup of resistance, whereas other scholars favor a more gradual introduction of change to different parts of the organization at different times. The limited amount of longitudinal research does not yet provide clear answers to these questions, but some evidence favors the latter approach (e.g., Beer, 1988; Hinings & Greenwood, 1988; Pettigrew, Ferlie, & McKee, 1992). In a 12-year study of 36 national sports organizations in Canada, Amis, Slack and Hinings (2004) found evidence that major change was more successful when it was implemented slowly, beginning in highly visible, important ways that convey the message that the change is a serious, long-lasting effort. Controversial changes occurred in a nonlinear way, with delays and reversals as aspects of the change were modified to deal with opponent concerns or postponed until a time when opponents would be more receptive to them. This process provided opportunities for the change agents to establish trust and use a process of collaborative problem solving for contentious issues.

Whenever feasible it seems beneficial to change interdependent subunits of the organization simultaneously so that the effects will be mutually supporting. However, in a large organization with semi-autonomous subunits (e.g., separate product divisions) simultaneous change is not essential, and it may not be feasible to implement change in all subunits at the same time. One way to demonstrate the success of a new strategy is to implement it on a small scale in one subunit or facility on an experimental basis. A successful change that is carried out in one part of an organization can help to stimulate similar changes throughout the organization. However, it is unwise merely to assume that the same changes will be appropriate in all subunits, especially when they are very diverse. This type of mistake is more likely to be avoided when middle managers are allowed to have a major voice in determining how to implement a strategy in their own organizational subunits (Beer, Eisenstat, & Spector, 1990).

Successful implementation of a major new strategy usually requires changes in the organization structure to make it consistent with the strategy. However, when structural change is likely to be resisted, it may be easier to create an informal structure to support the new strategy and postpone changes in the formal structure until people realize that they are needed. Informal teams can be created to facilitate the transition, without any expectation that these temporary structures will become permanent. For example, one company created temporary task forces to plan and coordinate changes; they eventually evolved into permanent cross-functional committees with formal authority to plan and monitor continuing improvements in product quality and operational procedures.

Applications: Guidelines for Leading Change

Successful implementation of change requires a wide range of leadership behaviors. These behaviors can be grouped into two distinct but overlapping categories called political/organizational actions and people-oriented actions (see Table 10-3). The two aspects of leadership are discussed separately.

Political/Organizational Actions

The following guidelines describe current thinking about the best way to deal with political and structural issues when implementing major change in an organization. The guidelines are based on theory, research findings, and practitioner insights (Beer, 1988; Connor, 1995; Kotter, 1996; Nadler et al., 1995; Pettigrew & Whipp, 1991; Tichy & Devanna, 1986). Although the guidelines describe actions a chief executive can take, most of them also apply to other leaders who want to make major changes.

- **Determine who can oppose or facilitate change.**

To evaluate the feasibility of various strategies for accomplishing major change in the organization, a leader must understand the political processes, the distribution of power, and the identity of people whose support is necessary to make the change happen. Before beginning a major change effort, it is useful to identify likely supporters and opponents. Time should be set aside to explore each of the following questions. Which key people will determine whether a proposal will be successfully implemented? Who is likely to support the proposal? How much resistance is likely and from whom? What would be necessary to overcome the resistance? How could skeptics be

TABLE 10-3   Guidelines for Implementing Change

Guidelines for Political/Organizational Actions:

- Determine who can oppose or facilitate change.
- Build a broad coalition to support the change.
- Fill key positions with competent change agents.
- Use task forces to guide implementation.
- Make dramatic, symbolic changes that affect the work.
- Monitor the progress of change.

Guidelines for People-Oriented Actions:

- Create a sense of urgency about the need for change.
- Prepare people to adjust to change.
- Help people deal with the pain of change.
- Provide opportunities for early successes.
- Keep people informed about the progress of change.
- Demonstrate continued commitment to the change.
- Empower people to implement the change.

converted into supporters? How long will it take to get approval from all of the key parties?

- **Build a broad coalition to support the change.**

The task of persuading people to support major change is not easy, and it is too big a job for a single leader to do alone. Successful change in an organization requires cooperative effort by people who have the power to facilitate or block change. It is essential to build a coalition of supporters, both inside and outside the organization. A supportive coalition may be even more important in pluralistic organizations that have collective leadership (e.g., hospitals, universities, professional associations) than in hierarchical business organizations where the top management team may have sufficient power to authorize major change (Denis, Lamothe, & Langley, 2001). The first step is to ensure that the executive team is prepared to undertake the difficult task of implementing major change in the organization, and some changes in the team may be necessary. Supporters are needed not only within the top executive team, but also among middle and lower levels of management. In a study by Beer (1988) of six companies undergoing a major change effort, the companies with a successful transformation had more middle managers who supported the changes and possessed relevant skills to facilitate it. The external members of the coalition may be consultants, labor union leaders, important clients, executives in financial institutions, or officials in government agencies.

- **Fill key positions with competent change agents.**

It is especially important to get the commitment of people directly responsible for implementing the change, the people in key positions who will make it happen. These change agents must support the change with their actions as well as their words. They should be people who are committed to the vision and have the ability to communicate it clearly. Whenever possible, people in key positions who cannot be won over to the new vision and strategy should be replaced. If left in place, opponents may go beyond passive resistance and use political tactics in an effort to block additional change. Pockets of resistance can develop and grow strong enough to prevent the new strategy from being implemented successfully. Acting quickly to remove opponents who symbolize the old order not only removes people who will resist change, it also signals that you are serious about the change.

- **Use task forces to guide implementation.**

Temporary task forces are often useful to guide the implementation of major change in an organization, especially when it involves modification of the formal structure and the relationships among subunits. Examples of typical responsibilities for a task force include exploring how key values in the vision can be expressed more fully; developing action plans for implementing a new strategy that cuts across subunits; designing procedures for performing new types of activities; and studying how the appraisal and reward structure can be modified to make it more consistent with the new vision and strategy. The composition of each task force should be appropriate for its responsibilities. For example, a task force to improve customer service should include people from all the functions that affect the quality of this service, and the task force should actually meet with some important customers. The leader of each task force should be someone who understands and supports the new vision and has skills in how to conduct meetings, manage conflict, and involve people in constructive problem solving.

- **Make dramatic, symbolic changes that affect the work.**

An effort to implement major change in the organization should begin with dramatic, symbolic changes that demonstrate commitment to the new vision and affect the everyday lives of organization members in significant ways. One type of symbolic change involves how the work is done and the authority of various parties over the work. For example, in a manufacturing company that adopted a new strategy of total product quality, the position of quality inspector was eliminated, production employees were given the responsibility for checking quality and correcting any quality problems, quality circles were established to identify ways to improve quality, and employees were empowered to stop the production line to correct quality problems. Another type of symbolic change involves where the work is done. In a large insurance company that reorganized from a functionally specialized hierarchy into 14 small, semi-autonomous divisions, the CEO sold the old high-rise office building and relocated each division into its own, separate, low-rise facility. The move emphasized to employees the new strategy of empowering each division to find its own ways to improve customer service. Symbolic changes may also involve cultural forms such as symbols, ceremonies, and rituals.

- **Monitor the progress of change.**

Innovative changes are by nature ventures into uncharted waters, and it is impossible to predict all of the obstacles and difficulties that will be encountered. Many things must be learned by doing, and monitoring is essential for this learning. Feedback about the effects of change should be collected and analyzed to evaluate progress and refine mental models about the relationship among key variables that affect the performance of the organization. Monitoring is also important to coordinate different aspects of the change. Accurate, timely information is needed about the effect of the changes on people, processes, and performance. This information can be gathered in a variety of ways, one of which is to hold frequent progress review meetings with people in key positions.

People-Oriented Actions

An important part of the process of implementing change involves motivating, supporting, and guiding people. Even the people who initially endorse a change will need support and assistance to sustain their enthusiasm and optimism as the inevitable difficulties and setbacks occur. Major change is always stressful and painful for people, especially when it involves a prolonged transition period of adjustment, disruption, and dislocation. The following guidelines are based on theory, research, and practitioner insights (Connor, 1995; Jick, 1993; Kotter, 1996; Nadler et al., 1995).

- **Create a sense of urgency about the need for change.**

When changes in the environment are gradual and no obvious crisis has occurred, many people fail to recognize emerging threats (or opportunities). An important role of the leader is to persuade other key people in the organization of the need for major changes rather than incremental adjustments. To mobilize support for proposed changes, it is essential to explain why they are necessary and to create a sense of urgency about them. Explain why not changing will eventually be more costly than making the proposed changes now. If people have little sense of the problems, it is important for the leader to provide relevant information and help people understand what it means. For example, distribute a summary of customer complaints each week with selective quotes from irate customers. Arrange for people to meet with dissatisfied customers. Prepare analyses of costs involved in correcting quality problems. Compare the performance of the organizational unit to the performance of key competitors as well as to unit performance in prior years.

- **Prepare people to adjust to change.**

Even when a change is necessary and beneficial, it will require difficult adjustments by the people who are most affected. If people are unable to handle the stress and trauma of change, they will become depressed or rebellious. Even enthusiastic change agents are not immune from the difficulties experienced in a long-term change effort. Alternating successes and setbacks may leave change agents feeling as if they are on an emotional rollercoaster ride. Ambiguity about progress and the recurring discovery of new obstacles increase fatigue and frustration. These negative aspects of change are easier to deal with if people expect them and know how to cope with them. Rather than presenting change as a panacea without any costs or problems, it is better to help people understand what adjustments will be necessary. One approach is to provide a realistic preview of some typical types of problems and difficulties people can expect. For example, ask people who have experienced a similar change to speak about their experiences and what they did to get through the change successfully. Make available training on how to manage stress, anxiety, and depression. Form support groups to help people cope with the disruptions caused by a major change. Use electronic networks to enable members of the organization to get advice and support from each other more easily.

- **Help people deal with the pain of change.**

    When radical changes are made, many people experience personal pain at the loss of familiar things to which they had become attached. The trauma of change may be experienced regardless of whether the change involves new strategies and programs, new equipment and procedures for doing the work, new facilities, and new management practices, or new leaders. It is difficult for people to accept the failure of past decisions and policies, and it may be necessary to help them accept the need for change without feeling personally responsible for the failure. Ceremonies and rituals may be used to help people express their grief and anger over the loss of sentimental elements of the old organization. An example is provided by the following description of a special management conference held in a large electronics company that had recently undergone many changes (Deal, 1985, p. 321).

    > The conference opened with a general discussion of culture and then continued with three successive small-group sessions of thirty participants each. When asked for metaphors to capture the essence of the company, the group overwhelmingly came up with transitive images: afloat in a stormy sea without an anchor, a two-headed animal, and so on. Each group specifically addressed the issue of loss. In the last session, the CEO was present; the word had spread that the discussions were yielding some significant perceptions. The tension in the room was obvious. At one point, the participants were asked to name what they had lost, and these were written on a flip chart. The list included values, symbols, rituals, ceremonies, priests, and heroes. As people contributed specific losses, someone got up and dimmed the lights. The emotion was obviously high. The group then launched into a discussion of the positive features of the company in its new incarnation. The CEO incorporated much of the preceding discussion into an excellent closing speech, and the company moved ahead.

- **Provide opportunities for early successes.**

    The confidence of an individual or team can be increased by making sure people experience successful progress in the early phases of a new project or major change. Some skeptics will only become supporters after they see evidence of progress in initial efforts to do things a new way. Kouzes and Posner (1987) recommend breaking up a challenging task into initial small steps or short-term goals that do not appear too difficult. People are more willing to undertake an activity if they perceive that their efforts are likely to be successful and that the costs of failure would not be great. As the initial steps or goals are accomplished, people experience success and gain more self-confidence. Then they are willing to try for larger wins and to invest more resources in the effort.

- **Keep people informed about the progress of change.**

    A major change, like any other crisis, creates anxiety and stress in people who are affected by it. When a new strategy does not require many visible changes in the early stages of implementation, people will begin to wonder whether the effort has died and things are going back to the way they were. People will be more enthusiastic and optimistic if they know that the change program is progressing successfully.

One way to convey a sense of progress is to communicate what steps have been initiated, what changes have been completed, and what improvements have occurred in performance indicators. Hold ceremonies to announce the inauguration of major activities, to celebrate significant progress or success, and to give people recognition for their contributions and achievements. These celebrations provide an opportunity to increase optimism, build commitment, and strengthen identification with the organizational unit. Recognizing the contributions and accomplishments of individuals makes the importance of each person's role in the collective effort more evident.

When obstacles are encountered, explain what they are and what is being done about them. If the implementation plan must be revised, explain why it was necessary. Otherwise, people may interpret any revisions in the plan or schedule as a sign of faltering commitment.

- **Demonstrate continued commitment to the change.**

Responsibility for guiding various aspects of the change can be delegated to other change agents, but the leader who is identified as the primary proponent and sponsor of the change must continue to provide the attention and endorsement that signal commitment to see it through to the end. Initial enthusiasm and support for a major change may decline as problems are encountered, setbacks occur, and people come to understand the necessary costs and sacrifices. People look to their leaders for signs of continued commitment to the change objectives and vision. Any indication that the change is no longer viewed as important or feasible may have ripple effects that undermine the change effort. Supporters will be lost and opponents encouraged to increase overt resistance. Continued attention and endorsement signal a leader's commitment to see the change program through to a successful conclusion. The leader should persistently promote the vision guiding the change process and display optimism that the inevitable setbacks and difficulties will be overcome. The leader must reject easy solutions for dealing with immediate problems when these solutions are inconsistent with the underlying objectives of the change effort. Demonstrating commitment is more than just talking about the importance of the change. The leader must invest time, effort, and resources in resolving problems and overcoming obstacles. When appropriate, the leader should participate in activities related to the change. For example, attendance at a special meeting or ceremony relevant to the change effort has a clear symbolic meaning for other people in the organization that the change must be important.

- **Empower people to implement the change.**

A major change is less likely to be successful if top management tries to dictate in detail how it will be implemented in each part of the organization. Whenever feasible, the authority to make decisions and deal with problems should be delegated to the individuals or teams responsible for implementing change. Competent supporters in key positions should be empowered to determine the best way to implement a new strategy or support a new program, rather than telling them in detail what to do. Empowering people also means reducing bureaucratic constraints that will impede their efforts and providing the resources necessary for them to implement change successfully.

Innovation and Organizational Learning

The environment of most organizations is becoming increasingly dynamic and competitive. Competition is becoming more intense, customer expectations are rising, less time is available to develop and market new products and services, and they become obsolete sooner. To succeed in this turbulent environment, organizations need to have people at every level who are oriented toward learning and continuous improvement.

Organizational learning involves acquiring and using new knowledge. The new knowledge can be created internally or acquired from outside the organization (Nevis, Dibella, & Gould, 1995). After new knowledge and information is acquired, it must be conveyed to the people who need it and applied to improve the organization's products, services, and work processes (Crossan, Lane, & White, 1999). The processes involved in acquiring, disseminating, and applying new knowledge are described in this section of the chapter.

Internal Creation of New Knowledge

Many organizations have formal subunits with primary responsibility for research and development of new products and services, and some organizations also have subunits with responsibility for continually assessing and improving work processes. These dedicated subunits can be an important source of innovation in organizations, but they are not the only internal source; many important innovations are developed informally by employees apart from their regular job activities. Efforts to help employees find better ways to do the work or to make improvements in products usually require only a small investment of resources in the developmental stage.

Many good ideas die before having a chance to be tested, because it is not possible to gain approval for them in an organization where traditional ways of doing things are favored. To facilitate the development and approval of innovations, it is helpful to have sponsors or champions who will shepherd new ideas through the long and tedious review and approval process in organizations. Also important is an impartial but systematic process for reviewing and assessing new ideas suggested by individual employees or teams. Examples include venture boards or innovation teams to identify high potential ideas and determine which ideas will receive additional funding and development (Pryor & Shays, 1993).

One way to assess the feasibility of new ideas is to test them on a small scale. In recent years, the trend has been for more organizations to use small experiments and controlled tests to facilitate learning. A well-known example of an organization with an experimental orientation is Wal-Mart, which regularly conducts hundreds of tests in its stores on sales promotions, displays, and improving customer service. Small-scale experiments provide an opportunity to try out new ideas without the risks entailed by major change programs. People who like the traditional ways of doing something may be more willing to try a new approach if they do not have to be concerned about appearing foolish or incompetent. People who are skeptical about a controversial new approach may be willing to conduct an experiment on a small scale to evaluate it. People will be more objective in evaluating the outcome of a change when they do not have to make it appear successful to protect their reputation (Nystrom & Starbuck, 1984). The amount of learning that results from an experiment depends on how well it is designed and executed. Even a simple experiment can provide useful information.

However, experiments do not always produce useful knowledge, and the results may even be misleading. Careful planning is needed to ensure that a controlled test yields clear, meaningful results.

External Acquisition of New Knowledge

New ideas and knowledge can be acquired also from outside of the organization. One way to counteract the "not invented here" syndrome is to identify relevant best practices used in successful organizations. This process is sometimes called benchmarking (Camp, 1989). An example is provided by Main (1992).

> The benchmarking manager for Xerox read an article about the success of L.L.Bean, the catalog retailer, in filling customer orders quickly and accurately. He organized a fact-finding visit to the headquarters office of L.L.Bean in Freeport, Maine. The team found that good planning and software support helped to make Bean three times faster than Xerox in filling small orders. The team used this knowledge to help redesign the procedures used at Xerox warehouses, resulting in significant improvements.

Another example is provided by Peters and Austin (1985).

> The owner of a chain of successful dairy stores conducts regular visits to competing stores accompanied by several of his employees. They look for things the competitor does better, and everyone is challenged to find at least one good idea that can be used. Nobody is allowed to discuss things done better by their store, which would bias the visitors to look for negative rather than positive things. During the return trip in the van, the discussion of ideas and how to implement them provides a unique opportunity for each employee to become an empowered member of a team of retailing experts.

Imitating the best practices of others can be a useful source of innovation, but you should be careful to evaluate the relevance of these practices before adopting them. Moreover, it is important to remember that imitation alone seldom provides much of a competitive advantage. It is also necessary to improve upon the best practices of others, and to invent new approaches not yet discovered by competitors.

Studying what other organizations do is not the only way to acquire knowledge from outsiders. Other ways include purchasing the right to use specific knowledge from an organization, hiring outsiders with special expertise to fill key positions, using external consultants to provide training in new processes, and entering joint ventures that will provide learning opportunities. For example, General Motors gained valuable insights about Japanese production methods from the automobile plant jointly operated with Toyota. More recently, IBM has made an alliance with Motorola to design a new generation of microprocessors and with Apple Computers to create operating systems.

Knowledge Diffusion and Application

New knowledge is of little value unless it is made available to people who need it and is used by them. Some organizations are successful at discovering knowledge, but fail to apply it effectively. One example is provided by a multinational company that established a center of marketing excellence in its Australian operations (Ulrich,

Jick, & Von Glinow, 1993). Successful pilot programs increased market share by 25 percent, but the lessons learned never reached the European and U.S. divisions, where the benefits would have been even greater. Similar examples can be found in many organizations.

Secrecy is the enemy of learning, and easy access to information about the organization's operations, including problems and failures, facilitates learning. There are several different approaches to encourage and facilitate knowledge sharing in organizations (Earl, 2001). An increasing number of companies have sophisticated information systems to facilitate easy access by employees to relevant information. An employee with a difficult task can discover how other people in the organization handled a similar task in the past, and employees can interact with each other to get advice and support about common problems.

A more formalized mechanism for translating learning into practice is to describe best practices and effective procedures in written or electronic manuals. For example, when the U.S. Army discovers an effective way to conduct some type of operation, it is translated into doctrine to guide others who will be performing the same operation. Formal doctrine can be useful, but it is not as flexible or easily updated as posting best practices and lessons learned on an interactive network. Moreover, formal doctrine often ends up being used in a way that discourages subsequent learning and innovation.

Another approach for diffusing new knowledge in an organization is a special purpose conference to facilitate sharing of new knowledge and ideas among the subunits of an organization. General Electric conducts best practice workshops to encourage sharing of ideas among managers. A large government agency holds a conference each year to enable participants from different facilities to present new ideas and informally discuss how to improve service quality.

Seminars and workshops can be used to teach people how to perform new activities or use new technology. When it is not feasible for people to attend a conference or workshop, a team of experts can be dispatched to different work sites to show people how to use new procedures. An alternative approach is to transfer individuals with new knowledge to other units, or assign them on a temporary basis to teach others. A person who has participated in a successful change can serve as a catalyst and consultant for change in another unit.

Learning Organizations

All organizations learn things, but some do it much better than others. The term *learning organization* has been used to describe organizations that learn rapidly and use the knowledge to become more effective (e.g., Crossan et al., 1999; Fiol & Lyles, 1985; Huber, 1991; Levitt & March, 1988). In these organizations, the values of learning, innovation, experimentation, flexibility, and initiative are firmly embedded in the culture of the organization (Baer & Frese, 2003; James, 2002; Kotter & Heskett, 1992; Miron, Erez, & Naveh, 2004; Popper & Lipshitz, 1998). The leaders develop and refine shared conceptual tools and mental models for understanding how things work, how to adapt to the environment, and how to achieve the organization's objectives. People at all levels are empowered to deal with problems and find better ways of doing the work. Knowledge is diffused or made easily available to anyone who needs it, and people are encouraged to apply it to their work. Top management creates and sustains processes to nurture ideas and support changes initiated by people at lower levels in the organization. Resources are invested in promoting learning and funding entrepreneurial activities.

The formal appraisal and compensation system provides equitable rewards for knowledge creation, sharing, and application (Bartol, & Srivastava, 2002). The advantage of a learning culture is shown by Meyer's (1982) study of how hospitals responded to a physicians strike.

> The hospital that adapted most successfully had a culture in which innovation, professional autonomy, and entrepreneurial activity were strong values. The administrator anticipated the strike and encouraged a task force to develop scenarios describing how it would affect the hospital. Supervisors were asked to read the scenarios and develop contingency plans. When the strike actually occurred, the hospital was able to adapt quickly and continue making profits, despite a drastic drop in the number of patients. When the strike ended, the hospital was able to readapt quickly. In the process the hospital even discovered some new ways to cut operating costs.

Applications: Guidelines for Increasing Learning and Innovation

Leaders at all levels can help to create conditions favorable to learning and innovation (Vera & Crossan, 2004; Yukl & Lepsinger, 2004). The following guidelines (see Table 10-4) are based on theory, research findings, and practitioner insights (e.g., Cavaleri & Fearon, 1996; Chaston, Badger, & Mangles, 2001; Garvin, 1993; James, 2002; McGill, Slocum, & Lei, 1993; Nadler et al., 1995; Senge, 1990; Schein, 1993a; Ulrich, Jick, & Von Glinow, 1993; Yeung, Ulrich, Nason, & Von Glinow, 1999).

- **Encourage appreciation for flexibility and innovation.**

Major change will be more acceptable and less disruptive if people develop pride and confidence in their capacity to adapt and learn. Confident people are more likely to view change as an exciting challenge rather than an unpleasant burden. To develop an appreciation for flexibility and adaptation, encourage people to view all practices as temporary. Each activity should be examined periodically to determine whether it is still needed and how it can be improved or eliminated. Encourage subordinates and peers to question traditional assumptions about the work and to think outside the box when solving problems. Encourage people to apply creative ideas for improving work processes. Encourage and support relevant learning practices and quality improvement programs (e.g., after-activity reviews, benchmarking, Six Sigma, TQM, quality circles).

TABLE 10-4   Guidelines for Increasing Learning and Innovation

- Encourage appreciation for flexibility and innovation.
- Encourage and facilitate learning by individuals and teams.
- Help people improve their mental models.
- Leverage learning from surprises and failures.
- Encourage and facilitate sharing of knowledge and ideas.
- Set innovation goals.
- Reward entrepreneurial behavior.

- **Encourage and facilitate learning by individuals and teams.**

  Organizations can only learn when individual members of the organization are learning (Senge, 1990). More individual learning will occur if the organization has strong cultural values for personal development and lifelong education, and it provides training and development programs to help individuals learn new skills (see Chapter 13). However, providing learning opportunities is not enough to guarantee actual learning will occur. Leaders should keep subordinates informed about relevant learning opportunities (e.g., workshops, training programs, college courses) and make it easier for them to pursue these opportunities (e.g., allowing time, providing education subsidies). Leaders can also encourage and facilitate collective learning by teams (see Chapter 11). Finally, leaders can provide tangible rewards to encourage individuals to acquire new knowledge and apply it to improve their job performance.

- **Help people improve their mental models.**

  In addition to conscious beliefs about the causes of performance and the source of problems, people have implicit assumptions of which they are unaware, and these assumptions bias how they interpret events. Obtaining more information about a complex problem will not help a person solve it without a good mental model to interpret the information. As noted earlier in this chapter, to develop a better understanding of complex problems often requires systems thinking. Leaders should help people understand and improve their mental models about the way things work in organizations and the reasons for success or failure. By helping people to understand complex systems, a leader can increase their ability to learn and solve problems (Senge, 1990). In this way the leader also helps people understand that they are not powerless and can collectively influence events in the organization.

- **Leverage learning from surprises and failures.**

  Surprises and failures usually provide more opportunity for learning than expected events and outcomes. Things that turn out just as expected confirm existing theories or assumptions, but do not provide new insights. Unfortunately, many people tend to discount or ignore unexpected information that does not fit their theories or assumptions about how things work. Some of the most important scientific discoveries resulted from investigating unexpected accidents or anomalies that would be overlooked by people only interested in confirming prior beliefs. It is helpful to specify in advance what results are expected from an activity or change and the underlying assumptions on which the prediction is based. Otherwise, instead of using unexpected results to reevaluate the model, people are more likely to overlook them or assume that they could have been predicted in advance. Make specific predictions and reasons for them a regular part of the planning process, and make evaluation of outcomes in relation to predictions a regular part of the after-activity review process.

- **Encourage and facilitate sharing of knowledge and ideas.**

  Leaders at all levels should encourage and facilitate the effective dissemination of knowledge in the organization. Attend meetings with people from different subunits of the organization (or send a representative) to discuss ideas for solving common problems. Encourage subordinates to sharing relevant ideas and knowledge with other people in the organization who can use it to improve their own performance. Encourage subordinates to support and make use of knowledge management programs (e.g., a resource directory, data bases, groupware, etc.). Invite experts or outside consultants to inform members of the unit or team about relevant discoveries, new technology, and improved practices.

- **Set innovation goals.**

The pressure of meeting normal task deadlines tends to leave little time for reflective thinking about ways to make things better. A leader should encourage entrepreneurial activity and help employees find the time to pursue their ideas for new or improved products and processes. One way to increase the number of creative ideas is to set innovation goals for individuals or teams. A special meeting is scheduled on a monthly or quarterly basis to discuss these ideas and review progress. Goals can also be set for the application of ideas to improve products and work processes. For example, some companies set a goal to have new products or services (e.g., those introduced within the last three years) account for a substantial percentage of sales each year.

- **Reward entrepreneurial behavior.**

Employees who invent new products for the company or suggest ways to improve existing products and processes should receive appropriate recognition and equitable rewards. The support and cooperation of many people are needed to get new ideas accepted and implemented effectively in an organization. Therefore, it is essential to ensure that recognition and equitable rewards are provided not only to the individuals or teams who contribute creative ideas, but also to the individuals who serve as sponsors, advocates, and champions for innovations.

Summary

One of the most important and difficult leadership responsibilities is to guide and facilitate the process of making a major change in an organization. People tend to resist major change for many reasons, including distrust, doubts about the need for change, doubts about the feasibility of change, doubts that the benefits from change would justify the costs, fear of economic loss, fear of losing status and power, fear of personal failure, perception the change is inconsistent with values, and resentment about interference from above. Resistance should be viewed as a normal defensive response, not as a character weakness or a sign of ignorance.

The change process can be described as having different stages, such as unfreezing, changing, and refreezing. Moving too quickly through the stages can endanger the success of a change effort. People typically transit through a series of emotional stages as they adjust to the need for a drastic change in their lives. Understanding each of these change processes helps leaders guide and facilitate change. It is also helpful for leaders to realize that changing attitudes and roles at the same time is more effective than using either approach alone.

Organizational culture involves assumptions, beliefs, and values that are shared by members of a group or organization. It is much easier to embed culture in new organizations than to change the culture of mature organizations. Culture can be influenced by several aspects of a leader's behavior, including examples set by the leader, what the leader attends to, how the leader reacts to crises, how the leader allocates rewards, and how the leader makes selection, promotion, and dismissal decisions. Supplementary mechanisms for shaping culture include the design of organization structure, management systems, facilities, formal statements of ideology, and informal stories, myths, and legends.

Before people will support radical change, they need to have a vision of a better future that is attractive enough to justify the sacrifices and hardships the change will require. To be inspiring the vision must include strong ideological content that appeals to organization members' shared values and ideals concerning customers, employees, and the mission of the organization. The vision is usually created in a progressive, interactive process involving key stakeholders.

A leader can do many things to facilitate the successful implementation of change. Political actions include identifying likely supporters and opponents, creating a coalition to approve changes, forming teams to guide the implementation of changes, filling key positions with competent change agents, making symbolic changes that affect the work, and monitoring the progress of change to detect problems that require attention. People-oriented actions include creating a sense of urgency, preparing people for change, helping them cope with change, providing opportunities for early successes, keeping people informed, demonstrating continued commitment to the change program, and empowering people to implement change.

As workforce knowledge becomes more important as a source of competitive advantage, the capacity to learn is becoming even more important to an organization. New knowledge and innovative ideas can be discovered through reflection, research, and systematic learning activities, or acquired externally by imitation, purchase of expertise, or participation in joint ventures. The discovery of new knowledge is of little use to the organization if it is not disseminated to people who need it and used to improve products, services, and processes. Individual leaders can do many things to encourage and facilitate learning and innovation in the organization.

Review and Discussion Questions

1. What are major reasons for resistance to change?
2. What are process theories of change and how are they useful?
3. What is organization culture and how can it be influenced by a leader?
4. What are the desirable characteristics for a vision?
5. Discuss the utility of developing a mission statement, strategic objectives, values lists, and catchy slogans.
6. What are some guidelines for formulating a compelling vision?
7. What are some reasons why efforts to change organizations often fail?
8. What are some guidelines to help leaders implement change?
9. What is a learning organization and what kind of learning occurs?
10. How much influence do leaders have on learning and innovation in organizations?
11. How can leaders increase collective learning and innovation?

Key Terms

- adaptation to environment
- benchmarking
- change agent
- core competencies
- cultural forms
- culture change mechanisms
- diffusion of knowledge
- innovation
- learning organization
- mental models
- mission statement
- organizational culture
- organizational diagnosis
- organization growth stages
- resistance to change
- stakeholders
- symbolic changes
- systems thinking
- value statement
- vision

CASES

Falcon Computer Company

Falcon Computer was a small but rapidly growing company located in the Silicon Valley area of California. The CEO thought it would be timely for a young company still in the start-up phase to create and instill an appropriate culture. The CEO and a small group of top executives met regularly on Wednesday mornings to develop a statement capturing what they considered to be the ideal Falcon Culture. After several weeks of brainstorming, debating, and revising, they eventually produced a two-page document called Falcon Values that covered such topics as treatment of customers, relations among work colleagues, interpersonal communication, decision-making processes, and the nature of the working environment. The values document was posted in prominent places and distributed to all company employees. Department heads were asked to explain the document to employees in their department meetings.

Peter Richards read the Falcon Values statement shortly after he was hired as a software trainer. After observing managerial and employee behavior at Falcon for a few weeks, he was struck by the wide discrepancy between the values expressed in the document and what he observed as actual practice within the company. For example, the Falcon Values document contained the following statement about quality: "Attention to detail is our trademark; our goal is to do it right the first time. We intend to deliver defect-free products and services to our customers on the date promised." However, Peter learned that design flaws caused many defects during the manufacturing process, slowing production. Moreover, some of the defective computers were being shipped to customers without being repaired. When Peter inquired

about this problem, he learned that employees were pressured to "get the product out the door quickly" so the company could generate more sales. People were afraid to incur the wrath of the production manager by pointing out the quality defects. Peter experienced the quality problems himself when he borrowed four brand-new Falcon computers for use in a training class and found that only two of them started correctly without additional technical work on his part.

Another example of a discrepancy between the Falcon Values document and actual practice concerned interpersonal communication. The document contained the following statement: "Managing by personal communication is part of the Falcon way. We value and encourage open, direct, person-to-person communication as part of our daily routine." Peter had heard the open communication buzzword a lot since coming to Falcon, but he hadn't seen much evidence of it. Peter believed that the real organizational culture at Falcon was characterized more by secrecy than openness. Contrary to the ideal of open, two-way communication, all of the meetings he observed used a formal arrangement, with an executive at the front of the room who did most of the talking. Employees were not encouraged to suggest ideas or express concerns about the decisions reached by top management. Even the Falcon Values statement had been created in secret without input from anyone not in the top management group.

Peter learned that most employees did not take the values document seriously, and he soon became disillusioned himself. Employees understood what was really emphasized in the organization, namely hierarchy, secrecy, and expediency. For some employees, the disparity between the values statement and the actual culture was so obvious it was a subject of cynical humor. Meanwhile, customers were becoming dissatisfied with the poor quality and late delivery of Falcon computers. Sales begin to decline, and before long the company was losing $2 million a month. Despite his frustration, Peter stayed with Falcon Computers until it filed for bankruptcy two years later. As he cleaned out his desk, he reflected about the failure of top management to create the culture depicted in the values statement. ■

SOURCE: Adapted from J. Newstrom and K. Davis, *Organizational Behavior: Human Behavior at Work* (New York: McGraw-Hill, 1993), pp. 504–505. Reproduced with permission from the McGraw-Hill Companies.

QUESTIONS

1. Why was the actual culture so discrepant from the written values document?

2. What mistakes were made by top management in their effort to change the culture?

3. What could have been done to make the culture more consistent with the values statement?

Ultimate Office Products

Ultimate Office Products was an old, established manufacturing company in the turbulent office products industry. Discount merchandisers and office product superstores were spreading rapidly around the country, altering the traditional distribution channels once dominated by wholesalers and smaller retail stores. The growing power of the new superstores was forcing manufacturers to improve customer service. The traditional manufacturers were being challenged by new companies more willing to cut prices and use technologies favored by the superstores, such as electronic orders and billing. Ultimate Office Products was losing market share and profits were declining.

Richard Kelly was the director of information systems, a newly created position in the company. When the CEO met with Richard to discuss his new responsibilities and objectives, she explained that it was essential to speed up order processing and improve customer service. Richard knew that the order processing system used by the company was obsolete. He prepared a plan to automate the system and got approval from the CEO for it. Then he purchased new computer workstations and a software package to support them. The software would enable customers to make electronic orders, and it would improve order processing, billing, and inventory control. However, months after the equipment and software arrived, it was still waiting to be used. The managers from sales, production, accounting, shipping, and customer service could not agree about the requirements of the new system, which was necessary to get it operating. These managers were Richard's peers, and he had no direct authority over them. Even though he encouraged cooperation, meetings among the managers usually ended with heated accusations about who was responsible for the company's problems. Most of the managers disagreed about the reason for the delays in filling orders, and some questioned the need for an expensive new system. Meanwhile, the CEO was becoming impatient about the lack of progress. She made it clear that, after spending a small fortune on new technology, she expected

Richard to find a way to resolve the problem. Richard decided it was time to take a different approach.

His first step was to gather more information about the reasons for delays in processing and filling orders. He began by having his staff map the workflow from the time orders were received until the filled orders were shipped. As he suspected, many unnecessary activities created bottlenecks that could be eliminated to speed up the process. The problems extended across functional boundaries and required changes in all departments. The preliminary results were presented to the CEO, who agreed on the need for dramatic improvements and authorized Richard to begin reengineering the process. Despite having the support of the CEO, Richard knew that widespread commitment would be needed for major changes to be successful. Richard met with the department managers to get their assistance in forming some cross-functional task forces. Although he knew that one task force would probably be enough to determine what changes were needed, he wanted to involve more people in the change process so that they would understand and support it. An outside consultant was secured to advise the task forces in their work.

Each task force examined a different aspect of the problem. They analyzed processes, met with key customers to learn what they wanted, and visited other companies to learn how they processed orders more efficiently. As people began working together to understand the system, they began to realize how serious the problems were. The participants were able to put aside their functional biases and cooperate in finding ways to improve efficiency and customer service. Each team made recommendations to the steering committee, composed of Richard and the department managers. The CEO also attended these meetings to emphasize their importance. When one of the department managers opposed a change, everyone in the meeting looked at the CEO, who made it clear that she supported the task force recommendation. Within a year, the company eliminated many of the steps formerly required to process an order, and the average number of days to fill an order was reduced by nearly half. Many more orders were being made electronically, and most mistakes in the billing process were eliminated. As people discovered that they could actually change things for the better, many of them volunteered to serve on teams that would continue to look for ways to improve quality and customer service. ■

SOURCE: Copyright © 1996 by Gary Yukl.

QUESTIONS

1. Why did Richard fail in his first attempt to implement change?

2. Identify subsequent actions by Richard that were more effective for implementing change in the organization.

3. Evaluate the change leadership provided by the CEO.

11

LEADERSHIP IN TEAMS AND DECISION GROUPS

Learning Objectives

After studying this chapter you should be able to:

- Understand the processes that determine how well a group performs an operational task.

- Understand how leaders can influence team processes and improve performance.

- Understand the different types of teams that are commonly used in organizations and the implications for team leadership.

- Understand how leadership is shared in self-managed teams and the conditions that make these teams more effective.

- Understand the advantages of cross-functional teams and the difficulties confronting leaders of these teams.

- Understand procedures to facilitate team learning and build trust and cooperation.

- Understand why some groups make better decisions than others.

- Understand the primary leadership functions in decision groups.

- Understand procedures for leading successful meetings.

A growing trend in organizations is to give more responsibility for important activities to teams. In many cases, the teams are empowered to make decisions that were formerly made by individual managers. As the use of teams increases, so does the amount of research on leadership in teams. This chapter examines what has been learned about leadership in various types of teams, including cross-functional teams and self-managed teams. Top executive teams are discussed in Chapter 12.

A related topic is leadership in the context of group meetings. As we saw in Chapter 4, meetings are commonly used to make decisions in organizations. Behavioral scientists have been studying leadership processes in such meetings for more than four decades, and practitioners have also contributed to our knowledge about the subject. The last section of this chapter examines what has been learned about effective leadership in meetings held to solve a problem or make a decision.

The Nature of Teams

Most organizations have small subunits (departments, sections) that perform a functional task (e.g., production, operations, sales, accounting, research) under the supervision of an appointed manager. In many of these subunits the members work alone at jobs that are highly independent. They may perform the same type of work, but they do not depend on each other and need little coordination (e.g., sales representatives, professors, tax accountants, machine operators). This type of work unit is sometimes called a coacting group because there is little role interdependence among the members.

The word *team* usually refers to a small task group in which the members have a common purpose, interdependent roles, and complementary skills. To clarify the distinction, interacting teams are found in basketball and soccer, whereas in bowling or wrestling the teams are actually coacting groups. Dyadic leadership theories are useful for describing leadership in coacting groups, but in interacting teams some additional leadership processes are needed to explain team performance. These processes are especially complex when an extensive amount of shared leadership occurs among team members.

Several distinct types of teams can be found in organizations, including functional operating teams, cross-functional teams, self-managed teams, and executive teams. Table 11-1 shows how these four types of teams differ with regard to autonomy to determine the team's mission, autonomy to determine work processes, authority of the internal leader, duration of the team's existence, stability of team membership over time, and the functional diversity of members. The extent to which members are co-located or

TABLE 11-1   Common Characteristics of Four Types of Teams

Defining Characteristic	Functional Operating Team	Cross-Functional Team	Self-Management Operating Team	Top Executive Team
Autonomy to determine mission and objectives	Low	Low to Moderate	Low to Moderate	High
Autonomy to determine work procedures	Low to Moderate	High	High	High
Authority of the internal leader	High	Moderate to High	Low	High
Duration of existence for the team	High	Low to Moderate	High	High
Stability of the membership	High	Low to Moderate	High	High
Diversity of members in functional background	Low	High	Low	High

geographically dispersed (virtual teams) is another basis for describing teams, but functional, cross-functional, self-managed, and executive teams can also have some degree of virtuality.

Functional Teams

In a functional operating team, the members are likely to have jobs that are somewhat specialized but still part of the same basic function (e.g., equipment operating crew, maintenance crew, combat squad, submarine crew, SWAT team). The teams typically continue operating for a long duration of time, and the membership is relatively stable. There is usually an appointed leader who has considerable authority for internal operations and managing external relationships with other parts of the organization. In a functional work team, leadership responsibilities are usually concentrated in a formal leader, although other group members may assist in performing specific leadership functions.

Cross-Functional Teams

Cross-functional teams are being used increasingly in organizations to improve coordination of interdependent activities among specialized subunits (Ford & Randolph, 1992). The team usually includes representatives from each of the functional subunits involved in a project, and it may include representatives from outside organizations such as suppliers, clients, and joint venture partners. The team is given responsibility for planning and conducting a complex activity that requires considerable coordination, cooperation, and joint problem solving among the parties. Examples of these activities include developing a new product and bringing it into production, implementing a new information system, identifying ways to improve product quality, planning an ad campaign for the client of an advertising agency, carrying out a consulting project, developing a new health care program in a hospital, and developing a new MBA program in a university.

Separate cross-functional teams may be formed in an organization for different activities, projects, or clients. Some cross-functional teams may be permanent additions to the formal structure of the organization, but most are temporary and only exist until they complete their task or mission. The membership may be stable over the life of the team, or it may change as some functions become more important and others decline in importance (e.g., product development teams). The members may work for the team either on a part-time or full-time basis. In most cases the members of a cross-functional team are also members of a functional subunit of the organization (a matrix structure). In some organizations people are members of more than one cross-functional team.

Cross-functional teams offer many potential benefits to an organization (Ford & Randolph, 1992; Manz & Sims, 1993). The teams allow flexible, efficient deployment of personnel and resources to solve problems as they are discovered. Functional expertise is preserved because team members maintain close contact with their respective functional areas. When the right people are selected for the team, it is likely to have more expertise than individual managers to make important design and operating decisions. Coordination is improved and many problems are avoided when people from different functions come together to work on a project at the same time, rather than working on it sequentially. The diversity of member backgrounds fosters communication with external sources of ideas and information, and it increases creativity in the generation of ideas and problem solutions (Keller, 2001). Working on a cross-functional team helps members learn to view a problem or challenge from different perspectives, rather than from only a narrow functional viewpoint. Members can learn new skills that will be carried back to their functional jobs and to subsequent teams.

Many organizations have reported great success with cross-functional teams. For example, a cross-functional team at Chrysler developed an innovative new subcompact (the Neon) in a record time of only 42 months and at a fraction of the cost of developing new models at other car companies (Woodruff, 1993). At Hallmark Cards, the use of teams drastically reduced the time needed to bring new holiday and greeting cards to market from more than 3 years to less than 1 year, while also improving quality and responsiveness to changing customer preferences (George & Jones, 1996). However, cross-functional teams are not always successful, and effective leadership is required to meet the challenges inherent in the use of these teams.

The same conditions that create potential advantages for a cross-functional team also create difficulties for the team leader (Denison, Hart, & Kahn, 1996; Ford & Randolph, 1992). Meetings are time consuming, and it can be difficult to get sufficient participation from team members who also have responsibilities in a functional department and may be on more than one team. The functional diversity of the members increases communication barriers. Each function usually has its own jargon and ways of thinking about things. The functional subunits represented by team members often have different objectives, time orientation, and priorities. These differences tend to create conflicts, as the following example shows (Stern, 1993).

> A team was formed in a large petrochemicals company to develop a better plastic resin. Members from research and development wanted to spend several months developing a new resin, whereas the members from production and marketing wanted to alter the existing product and quickly get it into production. The project was stalled because the different factions could not agree about a strategy.

Members whose primary loyalty is to their functional units may be more concerned about protecting their functional turf than about accomplishing team objectives. Decisions can become difficult and time consuming if members need to get approval from their functional superiors before agreeing to a major change. The team usually has a tight deadline to meet for completing its work, which puts additional pressure on the leader to resolve disagreements and maintain steady progress.

Self-Managed Teams

In self-managed work teams (or semi-autonomous work groups), much of the responsibility and authority usually vested in a manager's position is turned over to the team members (Cohen, 1991; Katzenbach & Smith, 1993; Orsburn, Moran, Musselwhite, & Zenger, 1990; Wellins, Byham, & Wilson, 1991). Most self-managed work teams are responsible for producing a distinct product or service. Any type of team can be self-managed, but this form of team governance is typically used for teams that perform the same type of operational task repeatedly and have a relatively stable membership over time. Unlike cross-functional project teams composed of different specialists, the members of these self-managed work teams typically have similar functional backgrounds (e.g., maintenance technicians, production operators). The members often take turns performing the various tasks for which the team is responsible. When members learn to perform multiple tasks, it increases team flexibility, makes the work more interesting, and provides an opportunity to learn new skills.

Self-managed work teams are used most often for manufacturing work or process production, but they are also finding increasing application to service work. Examples of companies that have used self-managed teams include AT&T, Colgate-Palmolive Company, Cummins Engine Company, Digital Equipment Corporation, General Electric, General Foods, Goodyear Tire and Rubber, Motorola, Procter and Gamble, TRW, Volvo, Xerox, and the Saturn division of General Motors.

The parent organization usually determines the mission, scope of operations, and the budget for self-managed teams. The amount of authority for other types of decisions varies greatly from one organization to another. Each team is usually given authority and responsibility for operating decisions such as setting performance goals and quality standards, assigning work, determining work schedules, determining work procedures, making purchases of necessary supplies and materials, dealing with customers and suppliers, evaluating team member performance, and handling performance problems of individual members. The teams are usually allowed to make small expenditures for supplies and equipment without prior approval, but in most organizations any recommendations for large purchases must be approved by management. Sometimes self-managed teams are also given the primary responsibility for personnel decisions such as selecting, hiring, and firing team members, and determining pay rates (within specified limits). Table 11-2 shows results from one survey of the different forms of authority delegated to self-managed teams.

Self-managed work teams offer a number of potential advantages, including stronger commitment of team members to the work, more effective management of work-related problems, improved efficiency, more job satisfaction, less turnover, and less absenteeism. Having team members cross-trained to do different jobs makes the work more interesting for members and increases the flexibility of the team in dealing with personnel shortages resulting from illness or turnover. Their extensive knowledge of work processes helps team members solve problems and suggest improvements. Finally, the changeover to self-managed groups typically reduces the number of managers and staff specialists in an organization, which lowers costs.

TABLE 11-2 Percentage of Companies That Delegate Responsibility to Self-Managed Teams	
Set work schedules	69%
Deal directly with external customers	59
Set performance targets	57
Conduct training	55
Purchase equipment or services	47
Deal with vendors or suppliers	46
Prepare budgets	35
Hire team members	29
Fire team members	21

Source: Based on J. Gordon, "Work Teams: How Far Have They Come?" *Training* (October 1992), pp. 59–65.

How many of these potential advantages are realized depends greatly on how the teams are implemented in an organization. The potential advantages depend in part on the amount of autonomy that is provided to the team, and member feelings of collective empowerment (Kirkman & Rosen, 1999; Tesluk & Matthieu, 1999). As in the case of psychological empowerment for individuals (see Chapter 4), giving authority to a self-managed team rather than to an individual leader does not necessarily result in collective feelings of empowerment. The team may replace an autocratic supervisor with social pressure on members to conform to strict group norms and established procedures (Barker, 1993; Sinclair, 1992).

Reviews of the literature on self-managed teams (Cohen & Bailey, 1997; Goodman, Devadas, & Hughson, 1988; Kirkman & Rosen, 1999; Pearce & Ravlin, 1987) suggest that this form of employee empowerment can improve job satisfaction and team performance. However, much of the evidence favoring self-managed teams is based on weak research methods or anecdotal reports published in business periodicals. Only a small number of experimental or quasi-experimental field studies have been conducted to evaluate self-managed teams (e.g., Banker, Field, Schroeder, & Sinha, 1996; Cohen & Ledford, 1994; Cordery, Mueller, & Smith, 1991; Pasmore, 1978; Pearson, 1992; Wall, Kemp, Jackson, & Klegg, 1986). These studies found some favorable outcomes for self-managed teams, but the results were not consistent from study to study and did not substantiate the large performance improvements reported in the anecdotal reports.

Self-managed teams are difficult to implement, and they can be a dismal failure when used in inappropriate situations or without competent leadership and support (Hackman, 1986; Lawler, 1986). The research on these teams suggests several conditions under which the potential advantages are likely to be realized, and they are listed in Table 11-3 (Cohen & Bailey, 1997; Goodman, Devadas, & Hughson, 1988; Hackman, 1986; Kirkman & Rosen, 1999; Pearce & Ravlin, 1987; Sundstrom, DeMeuse, & Futrell, 1990).

Virtual Teams

In virtual teams, the members are geographically separated and they seldom if ever meet face-to-face (Bell & Kozlowski, 2002). Most of the communication among members relies on computer and telecommunications technology (e.g., e-mail, videoconferencing, groupware, cellular phones). There has been a rapid increase in the use of virtual teams in organizations, and some writers have predicted that they will revolutionize the workplace of the future (Townsend, DeMarie, & Hendrickson, 1998). There are several reasons for increased use of virtual teams, including the rapid pace of globalization,

TABLE 11-3 Facilitating Conditions for Self-Managed Teams

- Clearly defined objectives
- Complex and meaningful task
- Small size and stable membership
- Substantial discretion over work processes
- Access to relevant information
- Appropriate recognition and rewards
- Strong support by top management
- Competent external leader
- Members have strong interpersonal skills

increased interorganization cooperation (e.g., joint ventures, partnering), employee desire for more flexibility in work arrangements (e.g., telecommuting, independent contractors), growing emphasis on service and knowledge management activities, and need for more flexibility and innovation in product development and delivery of customized services. Virtual teams can provide potential benefits in relation to each of these reasons for using them.

Any type of team can be virtual, but the most common form is similar to a cross-functional team. A virtual team may be either a temporary arrangement to carry out a specific task, or a more durable arrangement to carry out ongoing responsibilities such as solving technical problems, planning recurring events, coordinating activities among dispersed units of an organization, and maintaining external coordination with suppliers and clients. With virtual teams it is possible to involve the most qualified persons who are available to work on a project or make a decision, regardless of where they are located. For example, in a two-year project to develop a new type of refrigerator, Whirlpool used a virtual team with experts from the United States, Italy, and Brazil (Geber, 1995). The membership of virtual teams is often fluid, because the technology makes it easy for people to participate in different ways only when they are needed. As compared to teams with members who work together in the same location (co-located teams), a virtual team is more likely to have members from different cultures, times zones, and organizations. However, a diverse, fluid membership creates additional problems that may prevent the team from realizing the potential benefits. These problems are described later in the chapter.

Determinants of Team Performance

In order to understand leadership in teams, it is helpful to examine the collective processes that determine team performance. Leaders can improve team performance by influencing these processes in a positive way. Several theorists have proposed models of team performance (Gladstein, 1984; Hackman, Brousseau, & Weiss, 1976; Hewett, O'Brien, & Hornik, 1974; McGrath, 1984; O'Brien & Kabanoff, 1981; Pearce & Ravlin, 1987; Shiflett, 1979; Wofford, 1982; Zaccaro, Rittman, & Marks, 2001). A similar model was used for the multiple linkage theory described in Chapter 8. Table 11-4 lists key performance determinants and ways for leaders to influence them.

Commitment to Shared Objectives

Group performance will be higher when its members are highly motivated to attain shared objectives (e.g., Podsakoff, MacKenzie, & Ahearne, 1997). Task commitment is higher when the team considers the objectives worthwhile and the strategy for attaining them appropriate. A shared understanding about what needs to be done and why it is important increases member commitment to carry out the strategy. A shared understanding by team members about the nature and cause of a problem and likely solutions is sometimes called a shared mental model (Cannon-Bowers, Salas, & Converse, 1993).

Leadership behaviors that are especially relevant for increasing member commitment to shared objectives include articulating an appealing vision of what can be accomplished by the team, describing the task in a way that links it to member values and ideals, explaining why a project or task is important, involving members in planning strategies

TABLE 11-4 Mediating Variables for Effect of Leader Behaviors on Team Performance	
Leadership Behavior	*Mediating Variable*
Visioning, expressing confidence, celebrating progress	Task commitment, collective efficacy
Involving members in making decisions, leading meetings to make decisions	Task commitment, quality of performance strategies
Recruiting and selecting competent team members	Member skills, collective efficacy
Coaching, training, and clarifying role expectations and priorities	Member skills and role clarity, individual and collective efficacy
Planning and organizing team activities and projects	Efficiency and internal coordination, collective efficacy
Facilitating team learning	Adaptation to change, quality of performance strategies, collective efficacy
Team building and constructive resolution of conflict	Mutual trust and cooperation, member identification with the team
Networking, monitoring/scanning of the external environment	Adaptation to change, external coordination, quality of performance strategies
Representing, promoting, lobbying, negotiating	Resources and political support, external coordination

for attaining the objectives, and empowering members to find creative solutions to problems (see Chapters 4 and 9).

Member Skills and Role Clarity

Team performance will be higher when members have the knowledge and skills necessary to do the work and they understand what to do, how to do it, and when it must be done. Member skills and clear role expectations are more important when the task is complex and difficult to learn. A leader can do several things to improve the level of member skills. When the team is being formed, or replacements are needed for departing members, the leader can influence the selection of new members and ensure an appropriate mix of complementary skills (Klimoski & Jones, 1995). In a newly formed team, or when the team has a new type of task to perform, the leader can clearly explain member responsibilities and relevant procedures for performing specific types of activities (Marks, Zaccaro, & Mathieu, 2000). At appropriate times in the performance cycle, leaders can assess the skills of current members to identify training needs, provide constructive feedback and coaching, and arrange for members to receive necessary instruction in other ways (e.g., from more experienced members, or in workshops and courses).

Internal Organization and Coordination

The performance of a team depends not only on the motivation and skills of members, but also on how members are organized to use their skills. The design of work roles and the assignment of people to them determine how efficiently the team carries out its work. Performance will suffer if a team has talented people but they are given tasks for which their skills are irrelevant, or if the team uses a performance strategy that is not consistent with member skills. Team performance also depends on the extent to which the interdependent activities of different members are mutually consistent and synchronized. A high level of coordination is especially important when the team performs a complex task under rapidly changing conditions. Coordination is determined by decisions made during the planning phase prior to the start of a new task, and by adjustments made during the team's performance of the task. A team will usually perform a new task better if it takes some time to plan an explicit strategy before beginning to work on the task (Hackman & Morris, 1975), and the planning takes into account potential obstacles and problems that could limit performance (Tesluk & Mathieu, 1999).

There are several things a leader can do to ensure that necessary activities are well organized and carried out in a timely, efficient way. Relevant leadership behaviors include planning how to make efficient use of personnel and resources, making contingency plans to deal with possible obstacles and emergencies, involving members with relevant expertise in planning operations for the team, and leading meetings to collectively solve problems and plan activities. Leaders can improve coordination by planning how to schedule and sequence activities to avoid unnecessary delays and wasted time, and by actively monitoring the team's performance and using this information to direct and synchronize member activities.

When the team performs a complex task under rapidly changing conditions, it may be necessary for members to share some of the responsibility for internal coordination. The leader can help members learn to anticipate each other's reactions to changing conditions and quickly adjust their own behavior as needed. Developing member skills about how to work together as a team is facilitated by frequent rehearsal of complex activities. Training together under realistic conditions is especially important for teams that have difficult, dangerous activities to perform (e.g., combat teams, disaster relief teams, emergency medical teams, SWAT teams, firefighting teams).

External Coordination

The performance of a team also depends upon adjusting their activities to be consistent with the activities of interdependent units inside or outside the organization (including suppliers), and the needs of clients who must be accommodated (Ancona, 1990; Ancona & Caldwell, 1992; Galbraith, 1973; Sundstrom, DeMeuse, & Futrell, 1990). External coordination requires timely and accurate information about client needs and outside events that affect the work of the team. The ability of a team to identify an effective strategy for dealing with the external environment depends in part on member agreement about the implications of external events and the requirements for effectively responding to them (Marks, Zaccaro, & Mathieu, 2000).

Many specific types of leadership behaviors are relevant for improving external coordination and adaptation. Examples include maintaining a network of contacts who can provide relevant information, monitoring external events to identify threats and opportunities for the team, meeting with clients or users to learn more about their needs, consulting with other units of the organization about plans and decisions that affect them, and facilitating shared mental models that accurately describe the relationship between the team and its environment.

Resources and Political Support

Group performance also depends on getting information, resources, and political support needed to do the work (Druskat & Wheeler, 2003; Peters, O'Connor, & Rudolf, 1980; Peters, O'Connor, & Eulberg, 1985; Tesluk & Mathieu, 1999). Relevant resources may include budgetary funds, tools and equipment, supplies and materials, and facilities. A production team cannot maintain a high level of output without a dependable supply of materials. An air force crew will be rendered ineffective if they have no jet fuel to fly their plane. Maintaining a dependable supply of resources is especially important when the work cannot be done without them and no substitutes can be found. Resource acquisition is less important for a group that needs few resources to do the work or has its own ample supply of resources.

Leadership behaviors that are relevant for obtaining necessary resources from outsiders include planning the resources required for a special project or activity; preparing budgets and making briefings to superiors to justify requests; lobbying with superiors to provide additional resources; influencing superiors to authorize use of unusual equipment, supplies, or materials; promoting and defending the reputation of the team with superiors; establishing cooperative relationships with outsiders who are a potential source of necessary resources and assistance; and negotiating favorable agreements with suppliers and vendors.

Mutual Trust and Cooperation

Even a talented, well-organized team may fail in carrying out its mission unless there is a high level of cooperation and mutual trust among the members. Cooperation is especially important when the mission requires members to share information and resources, help each other, and work together in close proximity for long periods of time under stressful conditions (e.g., crew of a submarine). Lack of trust and cohesiveness is more likely to be a problem in newly formed teams, in teams with frequent changes in membership, in teams with members who are culturally diverse, and in teams with emotionally immature members (Barrick, Stewart, Neubert, & Mount, 1998; Watson, Kumar, & Michaelsen, 1993).

Cooperation is more likely when members identify with the team, value their membership in it, and are intrinsically motivated to support it. Cooperation is also facilitated by a high level of mutual trust. There are many ways a leader can increase mutual trust and collective identification with the team. Different aspects of team building and guidelines about how to do it are described later in this chapter. Activities used by consultants to increase mutual trust are described in Chapter 13.

Collective Efficacy and Potency

Member commitment depends in part on the shared belief of members that the team is capable of successfully carrying out its mission and achieving specific task objectives (Bandura, 2000; Guzzo, Yost, Campbell, & Shea, 1993; Pearce, Gallagher, & Ensley, 2002). This shared belief is called collective efficacy or potency. A highly confident team is also likely to have a more positive mood (Pirola-Merlo, Hartel, Mann, & Hirst, 2002). Collective efficacy is likely to be higher for a team with strong member skills, a high level of mutual trust and cooperation, ample resources, and a relevant performance strategy. Prior success can increase collective efficacy, which in turn can enhance a team's subsequent performance. A downward spiral can also occur for a team, with failure resulting in lower collective efficacy, negative affect, and declining performance.

Several studies provide evidence that collective efficacy (or potency) is related to team performance, (e.g., Campion, Papper, & Medsker, 1996; Chen & Bliese, 2002; Gibson, 2001; Gibson, Randel, & Earley, 2000; Gully, Incalcaterra, Joshi, & Beaubien, 2002; Mulvey & Klein, 1998; Pearce, Gallagher, & Ensley, 2002). Recent evidence shows that a leader can influence collective efficacy with types of behavior usually associated with transformational or charismatic leadership (e.g., Bass, Avolio, Jung, & Berson, 2003; Lester, Meglino, & Korsgaard, 2002; Sosik, Kahai, & Avolio, 1998; Sivasubramaniam, Murry, Avolio, & Jung, 2002). To build member confidence in the team a leader can display optimism and a positive mood, express confidence in the team, set realistic goals or subtask targets that will provide an opportunity to experience early success, help the team find ways to overcome obstacles, and celebrate progress and important achievements (Eden, 1990; Pescosolido, 2002; Sutton & Woodman, 1989; Kouzes & Posner, 1987).

Leadership in Different Types of Teams

Leadership roles in different types of teams are similar in many ways, but each type of team also has some unique challenges for leaders. This section will review the limited research on what type of skills and behavior are needed for effective leadership in cross-functional teams, self-managed teams, and virtual teams.

Cross-Functional Teams

The difficulties in gaining commitment from members with other duties and conflicting loyalties increase the need in cross-functional teams for a designated leader with significant position power and good interpersonal skills. Most cross-functional teams have a formal leader who is selected by higher management. When a cross-functional project team is self-managed, an excessive amount of time may be consumed by process problems and unresolved conflicts, leaving less time to perform the primary mission of the team. Research on cross-functional project teams indicates that they are less likely to be successful when self-managed (Cohen & Bailey, 1997).

Despite the extensive use of cross-functional project teams during the past 20 years, research on the skills required for effective leadership in these teams is still limited. Because the tasks of many cross-functional teams require innovation, research on leading creative people is also relevant for understanding effective leadership in these teams. Reviews of the relevant research (Ford & Randolph, 1992; Mumford, Scott, Gaddis, & Strange, 2002) suggest that leaders of cross-functional project teams need technical expertise, cognitive skills interpersonal skills, project management skills, and political skills (see Table 11-5).

In their review of research on leading creative teams Mumford and colleagues (2002) found three themes that described essential processes: (1) idea generation, (2) idea structuring, and (3) idea promotion. With regard to idea generation, it is essential for the leader to stimulate and facilitate creativity by members. With regard to idea structuring, it is important for the leader to provide clear objectives for the project and explain how it is relevant for the organization, but also to allow ample autonomy

TABLE 11-5   Skills Required for Leading Cross-Functional Project Teams

1. **Technical expertise:** The leader must be able to communicate about technical matters with team members from diverse functional backgrounds.
2. **Cognitive skills:** The leader must be able to solve complex problems that require creativity and systems thinking, and must understand how the different functions are relevant to the success of the project.
3. **Interpersonal skills:** The leader must be able to understand the needs and values of team members, to influence them, resolve conflicts, and build cohesiveness.
4. **Project management skills:** The leader must be able to plan and organize the project activities, select qualified members of the team, and handle budgeting and financial responsibilities.
5. **Political skills:** The leader must be able to develop coalitions and gain resources, assistance, and approvals from top management and other relevant parties.

with regard to how the project objectives will be attained. With regard to idea promotion, necessary resources and support for the project must be obtained from the parent organization. These themes indicate specific roles or types of leadership behavior that are relevant for each process.

From interviews and observations of teams, Barry (1991) identified four leadership roles that appear to be essential for teams that solve problems, manage projects, or develop policy. The roles include (1) envisioning, (2) organizing, (3) social integrating, and (4) external spanning. Envisioning provides a shared objective, organizing helps the team decide how to attain it, social integrating helps to maintain internal cohesiveness, and external spanning helps to keep group decisions compatible with the needs of stakeholders outside the team. The four roles also provide a parsimonious way to describe the specific leadership behaviors used in cross-functional groups to build task commitment, develop effective performance strategies, ensure member trust and cooperation, obtain necessary resources, and maintain external coordination. Table 11-6 shows a modified version of the four-role taxonomy that incorporates other findings in team leadership.

The relative importance of the different leadership roles varies somewhat depending on the stage of group development. For example, envisioning is especially important when the group is forming, whereas organizing is more important after the group has agreed on an objective. Even when the capacity to provide each type of leadership is present, the team will not be successful unless the leader and members understand that different patterns of leadership are needed at different times. Research on cross-functional teams indicates that the leader must be flexible and adaptive as conditions change (e.g., Lewis, Welsh, Dehler, & Green, 2002).

The difficulties and obstacles facing many cross-functional teams are so great that the formal leader may be unable to carry out all of the relevant leadership roles alone. The different lines of research on leadership in cross-functional teams all indicate that success requires the efforts of multiple leaders (Barry, 1991; Cohen & Bailey, 1997; Mumford et al., 2002). Some of the internal leadership responsibilities may be shared at times with individual members of the team who have special expertise about a particular aspect of the project. With regard to idea promotion and external spanning, it may be necessary to enlist the aid of one or more project champions who are not members of the team. Finally, it is important for higher management to provide a clear mission, necessary resources, and political support for the implementation of ideas developed by the team.

TABLE 11-6 Leadership Behaviors Needed in Cross-Functional Teams

Envisioning

- Articulating strategic objectives or a vision that inspires commitment by team members.
- Helping the team understand and improve their assumptions and mental models regarding the relationships among task variables.
- Suggesting creative ideas and encouraging the team to consider innovative performance strategies.

Organizing

- Planning and scheduling team activities to achieve coordination and meet project deadlines.
- Helping the team establish standards and methods for assessing progress and performance.
- Arranging and conducting meetings to solve problems and make decisions in a systematic way.

Social Integrating

- Encouraging mutual trust, acceptance, and cooperation among team members.
- Facilitating open communication, equal participation, and tolerance of dissenting views.
- Mediating conflicts among members and helping them find integrative solutions.

External Spanning

- Monitoring the external environment of the team to identify client needs, emerging problems, and political processes that will affect the team.
- Promoting a favorable image of the team among outsiders.
- Influencing people outside the team to provide adequate resources, approvals, assistance, and cooperation.

Self-Managed Work Teams

When describing leadership in self-managed teams, it is helpful to differentiate between internal and external leadership roles. The internal leadership role involves management responsibilities assigned to the team and shared by group members. It is typical for self-managed teams to have an internal team leader who is elected by the members, and the position may be rotated among different members on a regular basis (e.g., quarterly or annually). Whether elected or appointed, the team leader does not simply replace the former first-line manager. In self-managed teams, most important responsibilities are shared by group members, not concentrated in the team leader. The primary responsibility of the internal leader is to coordinate and facilitate the process of making and implementing team decisions (e.g., conduct meetings, prepare work schedules and administrative paperwork).

Shared leadership in self-managed teams can take many different forms besides rotation of the team leader position among members. The members usually meet to discuss important matters and make a group decision. At various times, a different member may assume responsibility for providing coordination and direction on specific team activities, depending on who has the most expertise. Routine administrative tasks may be assigned to individual members, or someone with a strong interest in a task may take the initiative to do it without being asked. However, difficult supervisory functions such as enforcing group norms may be performed collectively, as in the following example described by Barker (1993).

A small manufacturing company changed from traditionally managed work groups to self-managed teams. The team members collectively formulated standards of appropriate behavior. The new standards were more demanding than the earlier work rules, and compared to the supervisors of the traditionally managed work groups, the team was less tolerant of unacceptable behavior. Members first confronted an offender with a reminder of the standards or a warning to improve, then they used their coercive power to dismiss anyone who was not willing to do what was expected.

The role of an external leader involves managerial responsibilities not delegated to the team. The external leaders may be middle managers, special facilitators, or some of the previous first-line supervisors. Each external leader usually works with several teams. One leadership role that is especially important when the team is formed is to serve as a coach, facilitator, and consultant to the team. Considerable coaching and encouragement are usually necessary to get a new team off to a successful start. The coaching role includes helping members learn task skills necessary to plan and organize the work. The external leader also helps team members acquire the interpersonal skills necessary to function effectively as a team. Most of these skills are difficult to learn, and it may take a year or more for the team to become proficient in managing its own task and interpersonal processes. During this learning period, an important function of the external leader is to build the self-confidence of team members. As the group evolves, members can gradually assume more responsibility for coaching new members and improving their own working relationships.

Another important role is to obtain necessary information, resources, and political support from the organization. Because external leaders serve as a linking pin between the team and organization, it is essential to build and maintain cooperative relationships and an effective exchange of information. The external leader must be able to influence team members to think and behave in ways that increase team effectiveness, and to influence other people in the organization to do what is necessary to facilitate team effectiveness. As compared to leaders of traditional functional teams, effective external leaders of self-managed teams are less likely to use their legitimate power in directive ways to influence the team; instead they are more likely to ask questions and use influence based on their expert and referent power (Druskat & Wheeler, 2003).

Some writers have assumed that once a team is formed, most of the leadership functions will be carried out by team members, making an external leader redundant. This position is challenged by other writers (e.g., Druskat & Wheeler, 2003; Hackman, 1986) who contend that the external leader is important for the success of self-managed teams, not only in the early stages but later as well. As the team continues to develop, the external leader should communicate clear expectations about new responsibilities of members for regulating their own behavior. To improve external coordination in a dynamic environment, the external leader should clearly communicate new objectives and changing priorities. Finally, the external leader should continue to serve as a champion and advocate for the team, helping it to obtain necessary resources and political support from the organization. This representative role is especially important when other managers fear that the use of self-managed groups will cause major shifts of power and authority in the organization.

Virtual Teams

In comparison to traditional, co-located teams, virtual teams present some unique challenges for leaders. The lack of face-to-face contact makes it more difficult to monitor the performance of members, to influence members, and to develop mutual trust and collective identification. As in cross-functional teams, it is difficult to gain commitment from diverse members who are doing many other things and may have different objectives or priorities. The leadership challenges are increased when members represent different organizations and are located in different time zones and cultures. Virtual teams also face greater coordination problems when the task is complex, members have highly interdependent roles, and the environment is dynamic and volatile.

Researchers have begun to examine the possible differences between co-located and geographically dispersed teams (see Bell & Kozlowski, 2002; Bordia, 1997; Duarte & Snyder, 1999). There has been considerable speculation about the implications for effective leadership in virtual teams, but much more research is needed to clarify these issues. It is likely that the same leadership roles relevant for co-located teams are also relevant for virtual teams, but the relative importance of these roles and how they are carried out may differ somewhat for virtual teams.

Procedures for Facilitating Team Learning

The extent to which a team can learn how to work more effectively and adapt its performance strategies to changes in the nature of the task and environment is probably an important determinant of long-term team effectiveness. Team leaders (and members) can encourage and facilitate the use of team learning. Two procedures that are appear useful for facilitating team learning are after-activity reviews and dialogue sessions.

After-Activity Reviews

Learning from experience is more likely when a systematic analysis is made after an important activity is finished to discover the reasons for success or failure. The after-activity review (also called an after-action review or postmortem) is a procedure for collectively analyzing the processes and resulting outcomes of a team activity. Members of a team meet to examine what was done well in the activity and what can be improved the next time a similar activity is conducted. They review their initial plans and objectives for the activity, the procedures used to carry out the activity, problems or obstacles encountered in doing the activity, key decisions that were made, and the outcomes. Then the group plans how to use what they learned to improve performance in the future. For long projects or training simulations, it is also useful to conduct progress review sessions at convenient intermediate points. The use of after-activity reviews for evaluating activities and planning improvements is pervasive now in the U.S. Army, and it is slowly gaining acceptance in civilian organizations as well (see Baird, Holland, & Deacon, 1999).

A review meeting may be conducted by the team leader or an outside facilitator. The role of the leader or facilitator is to guide the review process and keep it focused on constructive problem solving. The team is encouraged to objectively analyze what happened and find ways to improve group performance in the future, not to criticize individuals for what they did or failed to do. Use of an outside facilitator is common when the group is participating in a training activity or simulation, but for regular work activities it is seldom feasible to have an outside facilitator.

In after-activity reviews, task decisions and work processes usually get much more attention than interpersonal relationships or leadership issues. In groups with a formal leader, subordinates may be afraid to point out mistakes made by the leader or to suggest ways the leader could be more effective in the future. Most leaders are reluctant to have their actions and decisions critiqued by subordinates in an open meeting. Feedback about leadership and interpersonal processes is most likely when the leader and team members are emotionally mature and there is a high level of mutual trust (Bradford, 1976). An outside facilitator can encourage the team to discuss leadership processes and may provide personal feedback to the leader in private, much like an executive coach (see Chapter 13).

There has been little research to evaluate the benefits of after-activity reviews, the facilitating conditions, or the best procedures. Tannenbaum, Smith-Jentsch, and Behson (1998) conducted a study to evaluate the effect of training team leaders to increase their skills in conducting after-activity reviews. Five-member teams carried out a series of realistic exercises in a simulated combat information center for a navy ship. Teams with leaders trained to conduct reviews were compared with untrained leaders. In the training, team leaders learned the importance of reviewing and analyzing team activities and processes, and they practiced specific behaviors for facilitating the discussion. The trained leaders subsequently displayed more of the effective behaviors than untrained leaders, and their teams had greater improvement in performance. This study and the literature on feedback suggest several leadership behaviors that can improve the effectiveness of after-activity reviews. Table 11-7 lists guidelines for these leadership behaviors.

Dialogue Sessions

An important prerequisite for team learning is for members to understand each other. Members who understand each other's perceptions and role expectations are able to coordinate their actions more easily (Cannon-Bowers, Salas, & Converse, 1993). Mutual understanding is also important for implicit assumptions about task issues. Problem solving is more difficult when team members have different assumptions

---

TABLE 11-7 Guidelines for Conducting an After-Activity Review

1. Near the beginning, make a self-critique that acknowledges shortcomings.
2. Encourage feedback from others and model nondefensive acceptance of it.
3. Ask members to identify effective and ineffective aspects of team performance.
4. Encourage members to examine how group processes affected team performance.
5. Keep the discussion focused on behaviors rather than on individuals.
6. If necessary, provide your own assessment of team performance.
7. Recognize improvements in team performance.
8. Ask members for suggestions on how to improve team performance.
9. Propose improvements not already included in the team's suggestions.

Source: Based on S. I. Tannenbaum, K. Smith-Jentsch, and S. J. Behson, "Training Team Leaders to Facilitate Team Learning and Performance," in J. A. Cannon-Bowers and E. Salas (Eds.), *Making Decisions Under Stress: Implications for Individual and Team Training* (Washington, DC: American Psychological Assoication, 1998), pp. 247–270.

about the cause of the problem, and these assumptions are not openly examined and evaluated. The discussion is likely to become a debate about competing proposals, with little consideration of implicit assumptions. Unless the group examines these assumptions and reaches an agreement about the cause of the problem, a good solution is unlikely to be found.

Team learning also depends on accurate interpretation of feedback about the consequences of an action (Senge, 1990). How feedback is interpreted depends on one's assumptions about the causal relationship among task variables and the timing of effects. A poor mental model about causal relationships is likely to result in an inaccurate conclusion. For example, a team that does not understand how long it will take for a new quality improvement program to improve sales may judge the program a failure if sales do not show an immediate improvement. A team with a more accurate mental model would understand when it is appropriate to evaluate sales, and it would measure mediating variables that are affected earlier to assess how well the program is being implemented. Team members with different mental models are likely to disagree about the meaning of feedback. Unless their implicit mental models are directly discussed, the team members will not even understand why they cannot agree.

Implicit assumptions are unlikely to be examined closely when there is excessive advocacy by team members. Excessive advocacy means they act as if the group discussion is a debate to be won. They make exaggerated claims, present inferences as facts, make assertions or forecasts unsupported by any evidence, and try to deflect or refute dissent rather than considering it seriously. Little effort is made to understand the feelings and assumptions of people who take a different position on an issue. Excessive advocacy makes it difficult to find an integrative solution that would satisfy all the parties to a dispute and get their commitment. Integrative problem solving requires open disclosure of assumptions, preferences, and exclusive information about a problem (Walton, 1987).

To facilitate mutual understanding, improve problem solving, and increase team learning, advocacy should be balanced with inquiry (Senge, Roberts, Ross, Smith, & Kleiner, 1993). Inquiry occurs when assumptions are openly discussed, evidence is carefully examined, and risks are identified along with benefits. Any team member can encourage greater use of inquiry, but it is helpful to have an outside process facilitator conduct a dialogue session to help team members become less defensive, more open, and more tolerant of dissent (Schein, 1993b; Senge, 1990). The facilitator encourages team members to identify implicit assumptions, inquire into the reasons for them, and explore alternative ways of looking at an issue. Members are encouraged to view each other as colleagues in a mutual quest for insight, not as antagonists seeking converts to their own viewpoint. People try to build on each other's ideas and improve them rather than just ignoring or attacking them. Members of the team identify the points of agreement and disagreement in their respective mental models of how the task variables are interrelated. Possibilities for an integrated consensus model are explored, and members plan ways to obtain information useful for refining the models and resolving disagreements (e.g., experiments, better data).

Applications: Guidelines for Team Building

The purpose of team building is to increase cohesiveness, mutual cooperation, and identification with the group (Dyer, 1977). Results from research on the effects of team

TABLE 11-8 Team-Building Behaviors and Procedures
• Emphasize common interests and values.
• Use ceremonies and rituals.
• Use symbols to develop identification with the group.
• Encourage and facilitate social interaction.
• Tell people about group activities and achievements.
• Conduct process analysis sessions.
• Conduct alignment sessions.
• Increase incentives for mutual cooperation.

building are mixed, but they suggest that team-building activities can be beneficial under some conditions (Sundstrom et al., 1990; Tannenbaum, Beard, & Salas, 1992). Most of the team-building literature describes large-scale interventions that are conducted by an external facilitator. However, a team leader can also do things to improve member cohesiveness and cooperation, two common objectives of team-building interventions. The following guidelines based on research, theory, and practitioner insights describe team-building procedures that can be used alone or in various combinations that are relevant for the current situation (see also Table 11-8).

- **Emphasize common interests and values.**

    Members are more likely to identify with a group in which there is agreement about objectives, strategies for attaining them, and the need for cooperation. The leader should emphasize mutual interests , identify shared objectives, and explain why cooperation is necessary to attain them. An example of an appeal to shared values and objectives is provided by the following critical incident from the Korean War (Yukl, 1989, p. 328).

> The commanding officer of a squadron (a lieutenant colonel) learned that interracial trouble had arisen among airmen in his squadron, and he was determined to stop it before it got out of hand. He called together the officers and airmen in his outfit and gave them an inspiring speech about democracy and discrimination. He pointed out that they were over there to preserve democracy and democratic principles, and discrimination among themselves was no way to attain this purpose. He put the challenge directly to the men and had the two racial groups appoint representatives that could hold meetings to iron out any difficulties that might arise in the future. Not only did this help defuse the conflict, but working conditions and squadron morale were improved also.

- **Use ceremonies and rituals.**

    Ceremonies and rituals can be used to increase identification with a group and make membership appear special. Initiation rituals are used to induct new members into a group, and retirement rituals are used to celebrate the departure of old members. Ceremonies are used to celebrate special achievements or mark the anniversary of special events in the history of the group. Rituals and ceremonies are most effective when they emphasize the group's values and traditions.

- **Use symbols to develop identification with the group.**

Symbols of group identity such as a team name, slogan, logo, insignia, or emblem may be displayed on flags, banners, clothing, or jewelry. Even a particular type or color of clothing may indicate group membership, as in the case of many urban gangs. Symbols can be effective for helping to create a separate identity for a team. Group identification is strengthened when members agree to wear or display the symbols of membership.

- **Encourage and facilitate social interaction.**

Development of a cohesive group is more likely if the members get to know each other on a personal basis and find it satisfying to interact socially. One way to facilitate pleasant social interaction is to hold periodic social activities such as dinners, lunches, and parties. Various types of outings can be used to facilitate social interaction (e.g., go to a sports event or concert together, or on a camping or rafting trip). When group members work in the same facility, social interaction can be promoted by designating a room for the group to use for meetings and coffee breaks. The room can be decorated with symbols of the group's accomplishments, statements of its values, and charts showing progress in accomplishing group objectives.

- **Tell people about group activities and achievements.**

People tend to feel alienated and unappreciated when they receive little information about the plans, activities, and achievements of their team or department. It is important to keep members informed about these things and to explain how their work contributes to the success of the mission. An example is provided by Admiral Elmo Zumwalt's description of an early command assignment in which he attempted to keep every person on the ship informed about the reason for each tactical exercise and maneuver.

> We made frequent announcements over the loudspeaker about the specific event that was going on. At the beginning and the end of each day, I discussed with the officers who, in turn, discussed with their men what was about to happen and what had just happened, what the competition was doing and what we should do to meet it. We published written notes on the plan of the day that would give the crew some of the color or human interest of what the ship was doing. I had bull sessions in the chief petty officers' quarters, where I often stopped for a cup of coffee. More important than any of the details, of course, was the basic effort to communicate a sense of excitement, fun and zest in all that we were doing. (Zumwalt, 1976, p. 186)

Within 18 months of initiating these practices, his ship moved from last to first place in the squadron with regard to efficiency ratings.

- **Conduct process analysis sessions.**

Process analysis sessions involve frank and open discussion of interpersonal relationships and group processes in an effort to improve them. One approach is to ask each person to suggest ways to make the group more effective. These suggestions should focus on how members communicate, work together, make decisions, and resolve disagreements rather than on the technical aspects of the work. A similar approach is to ask each member to describe what other members could do to make his or her role in the group easier. The discussion should result in a list of concrete suggestions for improving working relationships. Follow-up meetings can be used to chart progress in implementing the suggestions.

It is usually better to have a trained facilitator conduct the process analysis session instead of the team leader. Discussing interpersonal relationships is more difficult than discussing work procedures, and it takes considerable skill to conduct this type of session. A team leader without training in process consultation may make team relationships worse rather than better. An outside facilitator is likely to be more objective and impartial, which is especially important if the leader is contributing to the difficulties the group has in working together.

- **Conduct alignment sessions.**

There is less mutual trust and acceptance among people who view each other in terms of negative stereotypes and attributions. Negative stereotypes are common in teams with very diverse members, and negative attributions are common when members disagree about task issues. For example, someone who takes the opposing side on a controversial issue is considered unreasonable, selfish, devious, insensitive, or unintelligent. Personal attributions tend to persist, even when incorrect, and they can become self-fulfilling prophecies. People usually notice confirming evidence about stereotypes and attributions more than disconfirming evidence. Actions based on a false attribution about a person can elicit a reaction that appears to confirm the attribution. For example, a person treated as an enemy is likely to become one. Defensive routines used to avoid embarrassment make it difficult for people to examine personal attributions (Argyris, 1985). In an effort to appear rational and tolerant of team members, most people avoid expressing suspicions about personal intentions or displeasure about behavior that is irritating or disruptive. If people talk about these things at all, it is with someone else such as another coworker or a friend who is not a member of the team.

The purpose of an alignment session is to increase mutual understanding among team members (Mitchell, 1986). Prior to the session, each member is given an open-ended questionnaire about values, concerns, and personal objectives. Examples of questions include what you want to accomplish in your career, how you want to be remembered, what about you is most often misunderstood, what work experiences are most satisfying, what work experiences are most frustrating, and how you would like to change your work role. Members are asked to prepare responses that will help others understand and appreciate them. At the session itself, each member spends some time describing and explaining these answers. A facilitator keeps the session focused on increasing mutual understanding. The intervention was tested in an experiment with teams of MBA students working on field projects (Mitchell, 1986). Relations among team members two months after the intervention improved in the alignment condition but not in a control group or a feedback workshop (the feedback was ratings of each member's traits by the other members).

- **Increase incentives for mutual cooperation.**

Incentives based on individual performance encourage team members to compete with each other, whereas incentives based on group performance encourage cooperation. One way to increase cohesiveness and team identification is to emphasize formal incentives such as a bonus based on improvements in team performance. Another way is to use spontaneous, informal rewards to emphasize the importance of service to the team. For example, give the members extra days off after the team completes a difficult project, especially one that involved working overtime or on weekends. Hold a special celebration party for team members and their families after the team achieves an important objective.

Decision Making in Groups

Groups are used frequently to solve problems and make decisions in organizations. As noted in Chapter 4, using a group to make a decision has several potential advantages over decisions made by an individual leader. Groups have more relevant knowledge and ideas that can be pooled to improve decision quality, and active participation will increase member understanding of decisions and member commitment to implement them. On the negative side, group decisions usually take longer, the members may be unable to reach agreement if they have incompatible objectives, and process problems may undermine the quality of decisions.

The process by which a group arrives at a decision is a major determinant of decision quality. Many things can prevent a group from effectively utilizing the information and achieving its full potential. The quality of a group decision depends on the contribution of information and ideas by group members, the clarity of communication, the accuracy of prediction and judgments, the extent to which the discussion is focused on the problem, and the manner in which disagreement is resolved. Common process problems that reduce decision quality include member inhibition, groupthink, false consensus, hasty decisions, polarization, and lack of action planning for implementation.

Determinants of Group Processes

Group processes are influenced by several characteristics of the group or team (Guzzo & Shea, 1992; Hackman, 1992). Each characteristic will be described briefly.

1. **Group size.**   Large groups may have more information and a wider variety of perspective about a problem, as well as more opportunity to involve all parties who will be affected by a decision. However, as the number of members increases, communication becomes more difficult, less time is available for each person to speak, factions are more likely to form, and it is more difficult to reach a consensus (Hill, 1982; Shull, Delbecq, & Cummings, 1970).

2. **Status differentials.**   Large differences in member status can inhibit information exchange and accurate evaluation of ideas. Low-status members are usually reluctant to criticize or disagree with high-status members. Moreover, the ideas and opinions of high-status members have more influence and tend to be evaluated more favorably, even when the basis of their status is irrelevant to the decision problem (Berger, Cohen, & Zelditch, 1972; Harvey, 1953).

3. **Cohesiveness.**   The amount of mutual affection among members and attraction to the group is an important determinant of group processes, but high cohesiveness can be a mixed blessing. A cohesive group of people with similar values and attitudes is more likely to agree on a decision, but members tend to agree too quickly without a complete, objective evaluation of the alternatives. Members of a cohesive

group are less willing to risk social rejection for questioning a majority viewpoint or presenting a dissenting opinion. Consequently, the critical evaluation of ideas is inhibited during decision making, and creativity is reduced during problem solving. Highly cohesive groups sometimes foster a phenomenon called groupthink that undermines effective decision making (Janis, 1972). The group strives to maintain the illusion of internal harmony by avoiding open expression of disagreement. Members develop an illusion of invulnerability, and the group is likely to overestimate the probability of success for a risky course of action. Moreover, the group's illusion of moral superiority makes it easy to justify a course of action that would normally be considered unethical by individual members.

4. **Member diversity.**   The extent to which members vary with regard to personality, demographic attributes (e.g., age, gender, ethnic identity, education), and functional specialization has implications for group processes and outcomes (Triandis, Kurowski, & Gelfand, 1994; Watson, Kumar, & Michaelsen, 1993). Groups with diverse membership are likely to be less cohesive, because people tend to be less accepting of others who have different beliefs, values, and traditions. As noted earlier, diversity can also impede communication when members use different language, jargon, measures, or criteria. On the positive side, having members with different perspectives, experiences, and knowledge can result in more creative solutions to problems. It is easier to convert diversity into cooperative problem solving when members are highly interdependent for attainment of important shared objectives, but making it happen is a major leadership challenge.

5. **Emotional maturity.**   Groups with members who are low on emotional maturity tend to have more disruptive self-oriented behavior (e.g., making provocative comments, clowning, bragging, showing off) and aggressive behavior (e.g., interrupting or shouting down other members, making threats or personal insults). This kind of member behavior can reduce group cohesiveness and mutual trust (Bradford, 1976; Fouriezos, Hutt, & Guetzkow, 1950).

6. **Physical environment.**   Meetings are held in a physical environment that can also affect group processes (Bradford, 1976; Golde, 1972; Jay, 1976). For face-to-face meetings, the seating arrangement can create psychological separation between the leader and other members, resulting in a climate of stiff formality. A long rectangular table may emphasize status differentials and inhibit conversation, whereas a round table or a circular arrangement of chairs is more conducive to open communication and informality.

7. **Communication technology.**   The communication technology available to the group can affect group processes and the resulting decisions (Nunamaker, Briggs, & Mittleman, 1995). Advances in communication technology offer benefits not only for virtual groups but also for groups with face-to-face meetings. Networked computers can be used as a decision support system for meetings among people who are in the same room or thousands of miles apart. Some types of groupware allow members to anonymously suggest or evaluate ideas, and the collective ideas and ratings provided by group members can be compiled and displayed in the form of lists, charts, or graphs without the source being identified. This technology can reduce inhibition about expressing attitudes and domination of the discussion by assertive or high-status individuals.

Leadership Functions in Meetings

Quality of leadership is one of the most important determinants of a group's success in making decisions. Leadership is important to facilitate the use of effective processes and avoid process problems (Basadur, 2004). The leadership role can be shared to some extent, but members of decision groups often prefer to have one designated discussion leader who has primary responsibility for conducting the meeting (Berkowitz, 1953; Schlesinger, Jackson, & Butman, 1960). An effective leader ensures that the group uses a systematic decision process (process control), but does not dominate the discussion (content control). The job of conducting a meeting is a difficult one, because the group is likely to be ineffective if the leader is either too passive or too domineering. A considerable amount of skill is needed to achieve a delicate balance between these two extremes. The behaviors and procedures used to achieve this balance are discussed in the remaining sections of this chapter.

We saw in Chapter 3 that leadership behavior can be classified as task-oriented or relationship-oriented, and a similar distinction can be made for leadership behavior in group meetings. Of course, specific aspects of leadership behavior often involve both task and relationship concerns simultaneously, but the distinction helps to remind group leaders how important it is to balance task and relationship concerns in leading meetings. Several writers have proposed two-factor taxonomies of group leader behavior (Bales, 1950; Benne & Sheats, 1948; Bradford, 1976; Lord, 1977; Schein, 1969). Table 11-9 shows a simplified, composite taxonomy of task-oriented and group maintenance functions and their primary objectives.

Task and Group Maintenance Functions

Task-oriented behavior in a group meeting facilitates the systematic communication, evaluation, and analysis of information and ideas, and it aids problem solving and decision making. Some examples of task-oriented behavior include developing an agenda for the meeting, presenting a problem to the group, asking members for specific information or ideas, asking a member to explain an ambiguous statement, helping the

TABLE 11-9 Major Types of Leadership Behavior in Decision Groups

Task Function	Specific Objective
1. Process structuring	Guide and sequence discussion
2. Stimulating communication	Increase information exchange
3. Clarifying communication	Increase comprehension
4. Summarizing	Check on understanding and assess progress
5. Consensus testing	Check on agreement

Group Maintenance Function	Specific Objective
1. Gatekeeping	Increase and equalize participation
2. Harmonizing	Reduce tension and hostility
3. Supporting	Prevent withdrawal, reduce tension
4. Standard setting	Regulate behavior
5. Process analyzing	Discover and resolve process problems

group understand the relevance of ideas, explaining how different ideas are related, keeping the discussion on track, reviewing and summarizing what has been said or done, checking on the amount of agreement among members, suggesting procedures for making a decision, assigning responsibility for follow-up action, and recessing or ending a meeting.

It is not sufficient for a leader simply to carry out the behaviors, a sense of proper timing is also essential (Bradford, 1976). Any task-oriented behavior can be useless or even detrimental if it is premature or overdone. For example, summarizing too soon may discourage contribution of additional ideas on a subject. A discussion may be excessively prolonged if the leader keeps on stimulating communication instead of testing for a consensus. It is also important for the leader to have considerable skill in the use of each kind of task-oriented behavior. For example, an unskilled leader who tries to clarify a member's statement may succeed only in creating more confusion. A leader who is unskilled in summarizing may make a summary that leaves out key points and fails to organize contributions in a meaningful way.

Group maintenance behavior in a group meeting increases cohesiveness, improves interpersonal relations, aids resolution of conflict, and satisfies the personal needs of members for acceptance, respect, and involvement. Some examples of group maintenance behavior include encouraging participation by quiet members, preventing dominant members from monopolizing the discussion, smoothing over conflict, suggesting compromises, asking members to resolve differences in a constructive way, using humor to reduce tension, expressing appreciation for suggestions and ideas, suggesting norms and standards of behavior, reminding the group of norms agreed upon earlier, asking members for their perception of group processes, and pointing out process problems to the group.

Just as machines need periodic maintenance to keep them running smoothly, so also do human relationships in a group. As with machines, preventive maintenance should be carried out frequently rather than waiting to do corrective maintenance after a serious breakdown. Group maintenance should be an ongoing activity designed to build teamwork and prevent the development of chronic apathy, withdrawal, interpersonal conflict, and status struggles. If allowed to develop, these problems will disrupt the task-oriented activity in a group and reduce the effectiveness of the group.

Some group maintenance behavior occurs in any meeting, but it is neglected by many leaders who are unaware of its importance. Standard setting and process analyzing are the aspects of behavior least likely to occur, perhaps because they require an explicit recognition of maintenance needs. As in the case of task-oriented behaviors, the group maintenance behaviors require skill and a sense of proper timing to be performed effectively.

Who Should Perform the Leadership Functions

Behavioral scientists generally agree that task-oriented behavior and group maintenance behavior are both essential for the effectiveness of decision groups, but they disagree about who should perform these functions and about their relative priority. One part of the controversy began when some behavioral scientists proposed that the two functions are basically incompatible and should be performed by separate task and maintenance leaders in each group (e.g., Slater, 1955). Other behavioral scientists took the position that it is best for the designated leader in a group to perform both

TABLE 11-10   Comparison of Two Viewpoints on Leadership in Decision Groups

Basis for Comparison	Leader Centered	Group Centered
1. Responsibility for group	Leader responsible	Shared by leader and group
2. Control over final choice	Held by leader	Vested in group
3. Leader position power	Emphasized and guarded	Deemphasized
4. Leader perception of group	As a set of individuals	As a collective entity
5. Task-oriented functions	Carried out by leader	Shared by leader and group
6. Group maintenance	Not done systematically	Emphasized, shared with group
7. Socioemotional processes	Mostly ignored by leader	Observed closely by leader
8. Expression of needs/feelings	Discouraged	Encouraged and discussed

Source: Based on L. P. Bradford, *Making Meetings Work* (La Jolla, CA: University Associates, 1976).

roles if capable of doing so (Borgotta, Crouch, & Bales, 1954). This early controversy has been largely superseded by a debate over whether leaders should perform both kinds of functions alone or encourage group members to share responsibility for performing them. Table 11-10 summarizes the two major viewpoints identified by Bradford (1976).

The traditional view is that the formal leader should direct and control the activities of the group. According to this leader-centered view, the group leader should keep discussion focused on the task, discourage expression of feelings, retain control over the final decision (i.e., use consultation rather than group decision), and protect his or her authority in the group. According to Bradford, this kind of group leadership produces some favorable results but at an unacceptable price. Meetings are orderly and decisions get made, but members become apathetic and resentful, which leads to a loss of potential contributions and a reduction in quality of decisions. Acceptance of decisions by group members may also be reduced if members feel manipulated and unable to influence the decisions significantly.

With group-centered leadership, the role of the leader is to serve as a consultant, advisor, teacher, and facilitator, rather than as a director or manager of the group. The group maintenance functions are considered to be as important as the task-oriented functions, because feelings and interactions profoundly affect the problem-solving and decision-making processes in a group. Responsibility for both kinds of functions is shared by group members, because no one person can be sensitive to all of the process problems and needs of the group. The leader should encourage expression of feelings as well as ideas, model appropriate leadership behaviors, and encourage members to learn to perform these behaviors themselves. According to Bradford, sharing responsibility for leadership functions will improve the quality of the decisions and make members more satisfied with the group.

Bradford (1976) recognized some difficulties in implementing group-centered leadership. He noted that this kind of leadership requires considerable interpersonal skill, maturity, and trust in both the leader and group members. Some leaders are afraid to risk sharing control with group members or dealing openly with emotional behavior. Such leaders may also be concerned that the new approach will make them appear weak or incompetent. Some members may be unwilling to deal openly with emotions or may prefer to avoid assuming more responsibility for leadership functions in the group. Many decision groups are only temporary and do not meet over a long enough time to develop the necessary trust, skills, and member commitment. Some committees have unwilling members who prefer to meet as seldom as possible and to assume as little responsibility as possible for committee activities. The traditional approach is often reinforced by ritual and established procedures, which represent additional obstacles to the introduction of group-centered leadership. For example, some decision groups are legally required by their charter or bylaws to follow cumbersome procedural rules (e.g., Robert's rules of order) that are more appropriate for large, formal groups. Despite these many obstacles, Bradford is optimistic about the prospects for successful implementation of group-centered leadership.

Applications: Guidelines for Leading Meetings

This section describes specific procedures that leaders can use to improve group effectiveness in solving problems and making decisions. The guidelines for leading meetings (see Table 11-11) are based on ideas proposed by various scholars over the years (e.g., Basadur, 2004; Janis & Mann, 1977; Jay, 1976; Maier, 1963; Tropman, 1996).

- **Inform people about necessary preparations for a meeting.**

A problem-solving meeting will be more effective if people know how to prepare for it. To ensure that people plan to attend the meeting, they should be informed in advance about the time, place, and important subjects on the agenda. People who are expected to present briefings, provide technical information, or evaluate a proposal should be given clear guidance and ample time to prepare. Any reports or proposals to be studied in preparation for the meeting should be provided in advance with the agenda.

- **Share essential information with group members.**

When the problem is presented, essential facts known to the leader should be reviewed briefly, including how long the problem has been evident, the nature of the problem symptoms, and what, if anything, has been done about it up to that time. The amount of information that should be presented depends on the nature of the problem and the group's prior information. The information may be provided prior to the meeting, at the

---

TABLE 11-11 Guidelines for Leading Decision Group Meetings

- Inform people about necessary preparations for a meeting.
- Share essential information with group members.
- Describe the problem without implying the cause or solution.
- Allow ample time for idea generation and evaluation.
- Separate idea generation from idea evaluation.
- Encourage and facilitate participation.
- Encourage positive restatement and idea building.
- Use systematic procedures for solution evaluation.
- Encourage members to look for an integrative solution.
- Encourage efforts to reach consensus when feasible.
- Clarify responsibilities for implementation.

beginning of the meeting, or as the problem diagnosis is made. The leader should be careful to present facts with as little interpretation as possible. For example, if the problem is how to increase sales, it is better simply to review sales figures for each district than to make judgments such as "sales are terrible in the central district."

- **Describe the problem without implying the cause or solution.**

The problem should be stated objectively in a way that does not assign blame for it to some or all of the group members. Implying blame will make members defensive and reduce their willingness to help in solving a mutual problem. The problem statement should not suggest the reasons for the problem or possible solutions to it. This kind of statement would limit the consideration of different problem diagnoses by the group. Instead, the problem statement should encourage exploration of a variety of causes and a variety of possible solutions.

- **Allow ample time for idea generation and evaluation.**

The leader should plan meetings so that enough time is available to diagnose the problem, develop alternative solutions, and explore the implications and consequences of each alternative. Even when a group has members who are not inhibited, a strong majority coalition may propose a favored decision and ram it through before the critics have an opportunity to explain their concerns and gather support. The pressure of time is another reason for hasty decisions, and they often occur when a meeting is about to end and members desire to resolve matters quickly to avoid another meeting. When an important decision is being considered but time is not sufficient to evaluate solutions, the leader should try to postpone the decision until another meeting. If an immediate decision is not necessary and it is obvious that more information is needed, the leader may want to adjourn the meeting and arrange for additional information to be obtained.

- **Separate idea generation from idea evaluation.**

Research has found that idea generation is less inhibited when it is separated from idea evaluation (Maier, 1963). Procedures have been developed to reduce inhibition and facilitate idea generation in groups. With brainstorming, members are encouraged to suggest any idea about the problem that comes to mind, the ideas are written on a blackboard or flip chart, and no positive or negative evaluation of ideas is permitted (including scowls, groans, sighs, or gestures). The rationale is that inhibition would be reduced by deferring evaluation of ideas, domination would be reduced by making contributions brief and spontaneous, and creativity would be increased by mutual facilitation of ideas and a climate of acceptance for strange and novel ideas. Brainstorming improves idea generation in comparison with a regular interacting group, but some inhibition may still occur (White, Dittrich, & Lang, 1980).

The nominal group technique was developed to correct the deficiencies of brainstorming (Delbecq, Van de Ven, & Gustafson, 1975). Members are asked to write their ideas on a slip of paper without discussing them; then the leader posts the ideas for everyone to see. Group members are invited to build on ideas already listed or add new ideas stimulated by seeing the list. Then the leader reviews the list to see if there are any questions about the meaning of an idea or its relevance to the problem.

In a recent improvement of this procedure (called brain writing), the evaluation of ideas is postponed until a later meeting and participants are encouraged to continue thinking about the problem and writing new ideas in the interim (Paulus & Yang, 2000). The rationale for a follow-up meeting is that members do not have adequate time to reflect upon each other's ideas when they are busy writing ideas of their own, and an incubation period is necessary to realize the potential for mutual stimulation of ideas.

- **Encourage and facilitate participation.**

When some members loudly advocate a particular solution and other members remain silent or fail to take a position, the silent ones are usually assumed to be in agreement. In fact, silence may indicate dissent rather than agreement. The leader can do much to facilitate complete participation by engaging in appropriate gatekeeping behavior. Each member should be encouraged to contribute ideas and concerns, and members should be discouraged from dominating the discussion and using social-pressure tactics (e.g., threats, derogatory comments) to intimidate people who disagree with them. When computer-based groupware is available, it can be used to facilitate anonymous interaction during the posting and evaluation of ideas. Members generate ideas on their individual computers, and the composite list of ideas can be displayed on each member's computer screen. Display of the initial lists can be delayed for several minutes to ensure they are generated independently (as in the nominal group technique), or ideas can be displayed immediately after they are generated (as in brainstorming). Any member can add new ideas stimulated by seeing the list, request more information from the (anonymous) source of an idea, or suggest ways to improve an idea. Duplicate ideas can be combined if desired, and a rating procedure can be used to determine which ideas are most acceptable.

- **Encourage positive restatement and idea building.**

Two procedures that are especially useful to create a more supportive climate for idea generation are positive restatement and idea building. One of the most useful techniques for nurturing new ideas is to ask group members to restate another member's idea and find something worthwhile about it before saying anything critical. The procedure works even better when a member who points out a deficiency or limitation of another's idea is required to suggest a way to correct the deficiency or overcome the limitation. This approach also emphasizes careful listening and constructive, helpful behavior.

- **Use systematic procedures for solution evaluation.**

Procedures have been developed to help decision groups evaluate and compare potential solutions. These procedures are especially useful when members appear to be divided into opposing factions (polarization) that each strongly supports a different alternative. With the two-column procedure, members mutually identify and post the advantages and disadvantages of each alternative (Maier, 1963). Members then discuss the advantages and disadvantages and try to agree on an overall ranking of alternatives. A similar but more detailed procedure is cost-benefit analysis. This procedure can be used when the consequences of each solution are fairly certain and it is possible to make reasonably accurate estimates of the benefits and costs in monetary terms. The analysis should be conducted in a systematic manner, and care should be taken to avoid biasing estimates of costs and benefits to support a preferred solution. After the alternatives have all been analyzed, the group selects the best one by using whatever economic criterion seems most appropriate (e.g., maximize net benefit, maximize return on investment).

- **Encourage members to look for an integrative solution.**

When a group is sharply divided in support of competing alternatives, it is sometimes feasible to develop an integrative solution that involves the best features of the rival solutions. One way to begin this procedure is to examine both alternatives closely to identify what features they have in common as well as how they differ. This comparison develops a better understanding and appreciation of the opposing alternative, especially if all group members become actively involved in the discussion. The leader should encourage participation, keep the discussion analytical rather than critical, and post the results of the comparison to provide a visual summary of the similarities and differences. It is also useful to list the essential qualities of each solution and the relative priorities of different criteria or objectives. Even when it is not possible to develop a hybrid solution, the process may help the group identify an entirely different solution that is superior to the others.

- **Encourage efforts to reach consensus when feasible.**

Voting is a common procedure for making a decision, but whenever feasible, the leader should encourage the group to try to reach a consensus rather than deciding on the basis of a simple majority. A consensus occurs when all members of the group agree that a particular alternative is acceptable, even though it is not necessarily the first choice of every member. A consensus decision usually generates more commitment than a majority decision, but more time is typically needed to make the decision and a group consensus is not always possible. When the group has a large majority in support of one alternative, but a few dissenters still remain, the leader should carefully weigh the possible benefits of winning them over against the cost of additional discussion time. If adequate time has already been devoted to discussion of alternatives, it is usually not worthwhile to prolong the discussion merely to persuade one or two stubborn members. In this situation, the leader should take the initiative and declare that a group decision has been reached.

- **Clarify responsibilities for implementation.**

Before the meeting ends, the leader should make some provisions for implementing the decision. Necessary action steps should be specified and responsibility for each action step assigned to individuals. Many good decisions made by groups are unsuccessful simply because nobody bothers to ensure that they are implemented. If a follow-up meeting is needed, the preparations required for that meeting should be determined and responsibilities assigned. Also, the date and time should be determined, if possible, when everyone is present. After the meeting, the leader should distribute a summary of what was discussed and decided, and what responsibilities were assigned to whom.

Summary

Organizations increasingly rely on teams to improve quality, efficiency, and adaptive change. Cross-functional teams help to improve coordination among the different parties involved in carrying out a joint project. Self-managed teams are delegated most of the responsibility and authority traditionally vested in first-line supervisors. Virtual teams involve the people who are most qualified to carry out a project or solve a problem.

The potential advantages of teams include greater employee satisfaction and commitment, better quality of products and services, and greater efficiency and productivity. However, the benefits do not occur automatically, and successful implementation depends on a variety of facilitating conditions, including the quality of leadership. Some essential leadership processes in teams include building commitment for shared objectives, identifying effective performance strategies and organizing team activities, enhancing member skills and role clarity, building mutual trust and cooperation, identifying and procuring needed resources, maintaining confidence and optimism, and facilitating external coordination. In a self-managed team, many of the leadership roles are carried out informally and shared among the members. However, even in teams that have a formal leader, it is often beneficial for other members to share responsibility for some of the leadership roles.

The success of a team also depends in part on its capacity to learn from experience. Two types of group processes that can facilitate team learning are after-activity reviews and dialogue sessions. An after-activity review is a meeting held to determine what worked well and what did not. A dialogue session is a problem-solving meeting in which team members examine their implicit assumptions, emphasize inquiry rather than advocacy, and try to agree on appropriate mental models.

Team-building activities are used to increase cohesiveness, group identification, and cooperation. Some examples include emphasizing common interests and values, using ceremonies and rituals, using symbols to develop group identification, facilitating social interaction among members, informing members about group activities and achievements, conducting process analysis sessions, conducting alignment sessions, fostering appreciation and tolerance for diversity, and creating incentives for mutual cooperation.

A group decision is potentially superior to a decision made by a single individual such as the leader, but many things can prevent a group from realizing its potential. A major determinant of group effectiveness is the quality of leadership. Leadership functions in the context of group meetings can be divided into task-oriented functions and group maintenance functions. Both leadership functions appear essential for the success of a decision group, and they require skill and a sense of proper timing to be effective.

The leadership role is difficult, because the decision process will be adversely affected if the leader is either too passive or too domineering. To improve group problem solving and avoid common process problems, a leader should present the problem in an unbiased manner, encourage the group to consider alternative conceptions of the problem, separate idea generation from idea evaluation, and use systematic procedures for solution evaluation.

Research on leadership in teams has increased in recent years, but it continues to lag behind the pace of change in the way teams are used in organizations. A case in point is the increasing use of virtual teams in organizations. The extent to which effective leadership is different in virtual teams has yet to be determined, and rapid advances in technology make it difficult to predict whether the results from ongoing research will still be relevant in the future.

Review and Discussion Questions

1. What factors determine the performance of a team?
2. What leadership processes are important for cross-functional teams?
3. Why is leadership more difficult in cross-functional teams than in traditional functional teams?
4. What leadership roles and processes are important for self-managed teams?
5. Under what conditions are self-managed work teams most likely to be successful?
6. Explain how after-activity reviews and dialogue sessions can improve team learning.
7. What can be done to improve group cohesiveness and collective identification?
8. What factors determine the quality of group decisions?
9. What are the major types of task-oriented and group maintenance leadership functions in decision groups?
10. What can a leader do to improve decision-making processes in a group meeting?
11. Compare the leadership processes in functional work groups, cross-functional teams, and self-managed teams.
12. What are some implications of the new telecommunications and computer technologies for leadership in teams, now and in the future?

Key Terms

- action planning
- after-activity reviews
- brainstorming
- cohesiveness
- collective efficacy
- collective identification
- consensus
- cross-functional teams
- decision support systems
- dialogue sessions
- external coordination
- functional teams
- group maintenance behaviors
- member diversity
- nominal group technique
- performance strategies
- potency
- self-managed teams
- shared mental models
- task-oriented behaviors
- team building
- team learning
- virtual teams

CASES

Southwest Engineering Services

Donna Burke was a systems engineer at Southwest Engineering Services for five years when she was invited to participate in a project to develop a new type of software for the company. The project director was Ron Morrison, who had a reputation as a software whiz and rising star in the company. Donna was not sure why she was invited to work on this project, but she was very excited about it. She understood that the work would be important, and she knew that a successful project would also provide a big boost for her career in the company.

Ron called a meeting the first day for the 12 people invited to be part of the project team. After introducing himself, Ron gave a short welcoming speech to the group. "All of you are here today because you have special skills that are essential for the success of this project. Each of you was recommended by your boss, and only the most qualified people in the company were invited to participate. As you know, the volume of business handled by Southwest Engineering has been growing steadily. The company needs a better type of decision support system for managing engineering projects in a way that will guarantee quality while keeping costs low. Southwest Engineering faces an increasingly competitive market, and this decision support system is essential for the company to remain profitable. Our objective is to develop a new and innovative system that is better than anything else currently available. It is an extremely challenging assignment, but I believe we can pull it off if we have total commitment by every member of the team. If you are going to be part of this team, the project must take priority over everything else in your life for the next nine months. We will be working long days and even many weekends. If anyone has reservations about making a total commitment, there is still time to withdraw from the team. Please let me know your decision by 9:00 a.m. tomorrow." The next day, Donna and 10 other employees joined the team. The one person who declined to join had family health problems that would prevent him from working extra hours on the project.

As the team plunged into the project, the work was even more intense than Donna had expected. On weekdays it was common to order in food and work late into the evening. Working Saturday mornings was taken for granted, and the team would often go to lunch together after finishing work on Saturdays. Ron had an attitude of enthusiasm and optimism that was contagious, and before long even the most cynical and unemotional member of the team was caught up in the excitement. Despite the long hours, the work was exhilarating because everyone knew that they were part of something that would change the way things are done in the company.

Ron provided a clear picture of the specifications necessary for the new system, and this picture was important for guiding the work of team members and keeping them focused on the same objective. However, Ron did not dictate how the work should be done. Team members were expected to use their expertise to determine how to do the work. Ron was available to provide guidance if asked, but he was careful not to impose himself when not needed. When someone was experiencing difficulties in doing a task, Ron was supportive and helpful. Nevertheless, it was clear that he would not tolerate less than a maximum effort. During the first two weeks of the project, one member of the team failed to do the normal check procedure that would have enabled him to find and correct a mistake in a programming document. The person was required to explain what happened to the team and apologize for the problems he caused them. It was the last careless mistake he would make.

Ron pushed relentlessly for continued progress in the work. The team met regularly to evaluate progress and determine how to deal with obstacles and problems. Every member of the team had an opportunity to influence important decisions about the design of the software system, and the actual influence for a particular issue depended on one's expertise and quality of ideas rather than on status in the company or years of experience.

An important part of Ron's job as project director was to make sure the team got the resources and assistance it needed from the company. Ron spent considerable time traveling to various company facilities to meet with key people whose support and cooperation were needed to design and implement the new system. Before leaving on these trips, Ron would ask a member of the team to carry out his internal leadership responsibilities. When it was her turn, Donna was at first apprehensive, but she found it to be an interesting and satisfying experience. As Ron debriefed her afterward, he encouraged her to consider a managerial position at Southwest Engineering in her career plans.

At one point during the fourth month, the team became discouraged over a series of setbacks involving some persistent technical problems. Ron called a meeting to give them a pep talk. He said to them, "I know you are discouraged about these setbacks, but it happens in any project that is breaking new ground. We have made tremendous progress, and I am really proud of what you have accomplished so far. I am confident we can overcome this latest obstacle and make the project a success. Let's take the rest of the day off to give ourselves a little rest and meet again tomorrow to discuss some new ideas for integrating the system components."

The following week the team figured out an innovative way to deal with the obstacle.

They celebrated this breakthrough with a party at Ron's house. The project was completed three months later, which was several weeks earlier than the original deadline. The project was a great success, and they felt tremendous pride in what they accomplished. A final celebration party was held before people dispersed back to their regular units or to new projects. Afterward, Donna and another team member reminisced about their experiences. Donna gave Ron much credit for being a fantastic coach and facilitator, and she hoped to have the opportunity to work with him again on another project. However, she also realized that their success was a team effort that could not have been accomplished without the significant contributions of all the team members and their willingness to cooperate and put the needs of the project above individual self-interests. ■

SOURCE: Copyright © 1991 by Gary Yukl.

QUESTIONS

1. Describe the leadership behaviors Ron used and their influence on the attitudes and behavior of the team members.

2. Compare this cross-functional project team to a self-managed operations team by identifying similarities and differences in the leadership roles.

Building Maintenance Inc.

Building Maintenance is a company with 325 employees who provide cleaning and maintenance services for office buildings and shopping centers. The company occupies an old office building that is scheduled for demolition. Bud Crandon, the founder and president of the company, sent a memo to the executive group announcing a meeting two days later to decide where to relocate the company offices. The executives include Karen, Marty, Liz, and Nick. The morning of the meeting, Bud came into the conference room 10 minutes late to find that the others were already seated.

> BUD: Sorry to be a few minutes late. I got tied up at the bank talking to a loan officer. The reason I called this meeting is to decide where to locate our new offices. I assume you have given some thought to this matter already. Let me go over the alternatives. We can

either relocate to some decent space in one of the newly refurbished downtown buildings, or we can get slightly better space in a suburban park. Karen, as our financial officer, you must have some relevant facts and figures about these two options.

KAREN: Bud, I have looked into a variety of possibilities as you requested a few weeks ago. We can get adequate downtown space for about $21 per square foot, or we could get first-rate accommodations in a suburban park for about $22 dollars per square foot. Relocation costs would be approximately the same for each location.

BUD: Marty, from your vantage point as a sales manager, where do you think we should relocate?

MARTY: That's what I like to see, a business owner who puts the customers first. Customers are influenced by image, and as long as we have a good image, I think they will be satisfied. Modern offices in a suburban park would give us a better image with customers. By the way, our image is being undermined by order clerks who are rude to customers on the phone. Remember, all we sell is service. Lots of other companies have good power-cleaning equipment, and our only edge is the service we offer customers.

BUD: Liz, what implications does the relocation decision have for human relations management?

LIZ: I agree with Marty that customer service should get top priority in any relocation decision. Customer service is a direct result of having an efficient crew of maintenance employees. A suburban park may sound glamorous, but it could be a disaster in terms of

recruiting employees. Most of our maintenance workers live in the city and are dependent on mass transportation to get to work. They don't own cars and have no affordable way to get to a suburban office. If we relocate to a suburban office park, we would still have to rent a small office downtown to recruit workers and handle personnel matters that require face-to-face interaction.

BUD: What are you saying, Liz? Are you recommending that we should open an employment office downtown and move the executive office to a suburban office park?

LIZ: I agree with part of your reasoning, Bud, but I am not suggesting that we need two offices. I'm less concerned about where we put the executive office than about finding a location that makes it possible to hire the employees we need.

KAREN: I don't think we can afford to have two offices. It would be a major increase in our overhead costs. By the way, who was supposed to bring the coffee and pastries to this meeting? How can we make such a big decision without refreshments?

BUD: Nick, what do you think? Which location would be best for you as director of maintenance operations?

NICK: I'm not in the office very much. I spend most of my time in the field overseeing our supervisors and their crews. Most of our workers never see the office after they are hired, unless they have a major problem. They report directly to their work sites. Other things are more important than the location of the offices. One of the important things we should be considering is whether to hold a big holiday party again this year. It's a real morale booster, and I think it is very cost effective in terms of reducing turnover. Some of the cleaning workers stay on for a couple of extra months just to attend the party.

KAREN: Nick, do you have any figures to prove that a holiday party is cost effective? It would cost at least $20 per person, and most of the workers would bring guests.

NICK: So what? You can't put a dollar figure on morale.

MARTY: It looks like you folks have got the major issues out on the table.

I really don't care where we relocate as long as the needs of the customer come first. In a few minutes I have to leave for a lunch meeting that could mean a big shopping plaza contract for us.

NICK: Bud, where do you think we should relocate? We'll go along with any sensible decision.

BUD: Well, it seems that it may be premature for us to reach a decision on this important matter today. Maybe we should call in a relocation consultant to help us decide what to do. In the meantime, let's talk some more about the office party. I kind of like that idea. ■

SOURCE: Adapted from Andrew J. DuBrin, *Contemporary Applied Management* (New York: McGraw-Hill, 1989), pp. 136–138. Copyright © 1989 by Business Publications Inc. Reproduced with permission of McGraw-Hill.

QUESTIONS

1. Identify effective and ineffective actions by Bud in conducting the meeting.

2. What could have been done to make the meeting more successful?

STRATEGIC LEADERSHIP BY EXECUTIVES

Learning Objectives

After studying this chapter you should be able to:

- Understand the findings in research about the importance of strategic leadership.

- Understand the conditions that determine how difficult it is for a chief executive to make changes in an organization.

- Understand how tenure in office is related to a chief executive's leadership behavior.

- Understand the potential advantages of executive teams and the conditions that increase their effectiveness.

- Understand how leaders can influence different performance determinants to improve organizational effectiveness.

- Understand the leadership challenges posed by trade-offs, competing demands, and changing situations.

- Understand some procedures commonly used to monitor the environment and formulate a good competitive strategy.

Much of the early leadership literature was concerned with supervisors and middle managers in organizations. In recent years the attention of many leadership theorists has shifted to strategic leadership by executives and the top management team (Cannella & Monroe, 1997). The shift in focus reflects an increased interest in understanding how corporate executives must transform their companies to cope with growing international competition. This chapter examines relevant theories and research on strategic leadership in organizations, and it draws upon the literature in related areas such as organization theory, strategic management, and decision making.

One controversial issue examined in the chapter is the importance of executives for the performance of large organizations. Some writers argue that leaders have a major influence on organizational performance (e.g., Finkelstein & Hambrick, 1996; Katz & Kahn, 1978; Peters & Waterman, 1982), whereas other writers contend that leaders have little influence on performance (e.g., Hannan & Freeman, 1984; Meindl, Ehrlich, & Dukerich, 1985; Pfeffer, 1977b). The doubters provide several related arguments against the importance of an individual leader such as the chief executive officer (CEO). One argument is that the performance of an organization is largely determined by factors beyond the leader's control, including economic conditions, market conditions, governmental policies, and technological change. A second argument is that the discretion of an individual executive is limited by internal and external constraints, so that only political coalitions have enough influence to make major changes in organizations. A third argument is that people exaggerate the influence of individual leaders on organizations, and they are given more credit for successes and more blame for failures than they actually deserve.

This chapter examines the arguments in more detail and reviews relevant research on leadership importance. Key topics include constraints on executive action, attributions about leadership importance, conditions in which change-oriented leadership is most important, the political processes that affect the amount of change, the consequences of leadership succession for organizational performance, the relation of executive tenure to change-oriented leadership, and the processes by which a CEO can influence the financial performance and survival of an organization. An alternative to leadership by a single heroic leader is shared leadership by an executive team, and the chapter examines conditions in which top management teams are likely to be effective. The last section of the chapter provides guidelines for two important types of strategic leadership behavior, namely external monitoring and strategy formulation.

Constraints on Executives

The power and discretion to make major changes is an important determinant of a leader's potential influence on organization performance. In Chapter 2 we saw that managers face many strong constraints on their action. This section of the chapter examines the situational constraints on the discretion of executives and aspects of the situation that determine how much influence top executives can have on the performance of their organization.

Internal Constraints

The CEO's discretion can be limited by a variety of internal organizational factors (Hambrick & Finkelstein, 1987). One type of constraint involves powerful inside forces or coalitions in the organization. There is less discretion when the CEO must operate in the shadow of the company founder, satisfy a dominant owner (e.g., the organization is a family-owned firm or the subsidiary of another firm), or answer to a strong board of directors with rigid ideas about the appropriate way to do things. Power and discretion are greater when the CEO is a major owner or shareholder of the firm or when the board of directors is easily influenced to support the CEO. Discretion is limited when internal factions and coalitions have sufficient counterpower to block changes a leader wants to make (e.g., labor unions, other executives with a strong power base). Discretion is increased when surplus financial reserves are available to fund new ventures, or the firm's prosperity makes it easy to finance innovations by borrowing funds.

Another type of internal constraint is a strong organization culture that is resistant to change. Large organizations with a strong bureaucracy and standardized ways of doing things have an inertia that is difficult to overcome. People resist change that threatens their status and power, contradicts their values and beliefs, or requires learning new ways of doing things.

External Constraints

External constraints on the discretion of a CEO include the nature of the organization's primary products and services, and the type of markets in which the organization operates. Managerial discretion is greater if the organization is in a growth industry that has rapidly increasing demand rather than flat or declining demand, if the organization's products or services can be differentiated from those of competitors (not a standardized commodity such as gasoline or cement), and if the organization dominates its markets and faces little or no direct competition (e.g., it is a monopoly or has a dominant share of the market).

Discretion is also constrained by powerful external stakeholders who can dictate conditions, as when a few major clients account for most of the company's sales, or when the company is dependent on a single source of key materials. Other external constraints include political-legal limitations (e.g., environmental regulations, safety requirements, legal obligations). Even when the organization is a monopoly, discretion in key areas such as pricing, technology, and product changes may be severely limited by government regulation.

The discretion of an executive to make major changes depends in part on how internal and external stakeholders perceive the performance of the organization. In a crisis situation where organization performance is declining and the survival of the organization is in doubt, leaders are expected to take more decisive, innovative actions to deal with the crisis. Innovative changes are less likely to occur in periods of relative stability and prosperity for the organization. When people do not perceive any crisis, attempts by the leader to make major changes are likely to be viewed as inappropriate, disruptive, and irresponsible.

Constraints and Executive Traits As Joint Determinants

Internal and external constraints interact with each other and with the leader's personality and skills to influence the leader's behavior. Over time pressures arise that favor a match between the type of leadership situation and the type of person filling it. The most restrictive situation is one in which internal and external constraints are so severe that the CEO is merely a figurehead who cannot implement any significant strategy changes or innovations. This type of position is unlikely to be filled by an ambitious, innovative leader, in part because such a person would not normally seek (or remain in) a figurehead position, and in part because the organization selection process will favor a conservative, risk-averse, compliant person.

The opposite extreme is the situation with few internal and external constraints and ample discretion. Ambitious, dynamic leaders will be attracted to this type of position.

Ample discretion provides opportunities for innovative leadership but does not guarantee it. Even in a situation with few constraints, some leaders lack the cognitive skill to perceive innovative options or the motivation to pursue them.

Biased Attributions About Chief Executives

The day-to-day behavior of most low-level leaders can be observed by subordinates, peers, and superiors, and the leader's actions often have immediate consequences for the performance of the team or group. In contrast, few members of the organization have an opportunity to directly observe the actions of the top executive. Many of these actions only indirectly affect performance, and the effect may be delayed by months or years, making it difficult to see the connection between leader actions and consequences. In the absence of relevant information, people are biased to attribute more responsibility for an organization's performance to the CEO (Meindl et al., 1985).

Determinants of Attributions

As we saw in earlier chapters, attributions about leader effectiveness are influenced by a number of interrelated factors. A leader who takes decisive action to deal with a crisis is likely to be viewed as exceptional if organization performance improves soon afterward. In contrast, a leader who fails to take decisive action in a crisis, or who takes action that fails to resolve the crisis quickly, is likely to be viewed as incompetent. Leaders of profitable organizations who maintain existing strategies or make incremental improvements rather than innovative changes are likely to be viewed as competent but not exceptional.

Follower perception of leader competence is influenced more by highly visible actions to deal with an immediate crisis than by actions to improve conditions and avoid a future crisis (Lord & Maher, 1991). Thus, a leader who makes slow, deliberate changes to avoid potential problems gets less credit than a leader who allows problems to develop and then acts directly to solve them in a very visible way. How visible, dramatic actions influence attributions about executive competence can be seen by comparing two automobile executives: Lee Iacocca and Philip Caldwell (Lord & Maher, 1991; Trice & Beyer, 1991).

> By the time Lee Iacocca took over as CEO in 1979, Chrysler had experienced major losses for several years, and few people believed it could survive. He carried out a series of dramatic, highly visible actions such as persuading the U.S. government to guarantee bank loans of $1.5 billion to the company, negotiating more than $1 billion in reduced wages and benefits with the labor unions, promoting his vision and the company's products by appearing in television commercials, and publishing a best-selling autobiography (Iacocca, 1984) that extolled his own leadership. Dramatic strategic decisions included the acquisition of American Motors, the introduction of extended warranties on vehicles, reintroduction of convertibles (none had been built in the U.S. for years), and production of the innovative, highly popular minivan. Symbolic actions included slashing his own salary to $1 in 1979, replacing the glossy, full-color annual report with a plain document printed on recycled paper, and getting the president of the United Auto Worker's union appointed to the board of directors. He also made major changes in the internal management processes of the company to improve production planning, product development, and quality. Many of his decisions

and leadership actions were viewed as bold and radical (O'Toole, 1985). By 1983, Chrysler was making profits again and had paid back the government-backed loans before they were due.

Philip Caldwell, the CEO of Ford Motors from 1980 to 1985, also assumed leadership of a company in financial distress. Although he took some direct leadership actions such as extensive cost cutting and the decision to bet the company on the Taurus program (Doody & Bingaman, 1988), he mostly concentrated on less dramatic actions to change the corporate culture, strategic orientation, and decision processes (Lord & Maher, 1991). He created a new externally oriented approach to product design with more emphasis on consumers (e.g., information from market research was used in making design decisions). He emphasized quality, teamwork, and worker participation in decisions to improve quality and productivity. He modified the reward system to support the new culture by establishing a profit sharing program for hourly workers. After three years of losses (1980–1982), the company became profitable again. Ford earned record profits for the auto industry in 1986 and 1987, and it was the only U.S. auto company to increase market share at that time. Several of Ford's products became the best sellers in their vehicle class and they continued to sell well into the early 1990s.

Caldwell's accomplishments were at least as great as those of Iacocca, yet he never attained Iacocca's public reputation for successful leadership. Many people viewed Iacocca as the heroic savior of Chrysler, whereas Caldwell was unknown to most people outside the auto industry. One explanation for this difference in leadership attributions is that Caldwell's actions were less visible or dramatic and the turnaround in company performance less evident (performance improved but did not become exceptional until after he had already left office).

Attributions and Executive Discretion

Attributions about a leader's competence and perceptions about the need for change have implications for the leader's capacity to influence the future performance of the organization. Lord and Maher (1991) proposed that the effectiveness of top-level leaders depends on their discretion to make innovative, major changes in key areas of organization strategy that will affect the performance of the organization 5 to 20 years in the future. As explained in Chapter 6, the amount of legitimate power and discretion allowed a leader depends on the perception by followers and other stakeholders (e.g., board of directors, banks, government agencies, stockholders) that the leader has the expertise to solve important problems facing the organization. This perception depends in large part on how the past actions of the leader are interpreted.

Research on Effects of Leadership Succession

Research on the consequences of changing the chief executive of an organization is especially relevant to the issue of leadership importance. These succession studies attempt to assess how a change in top leadership affects organization performance. The implicit assumption in this research is that if leadership is important, and the external factors remain relatively constant over the time period of the study, then new leadership should be associated with large changes in the performance of the organization.

The succession studies demonstrate the difficulty of doing research on leadership importance. The selection of an appropriate criterion of organizational performance has been a particular problem. Day and Lord (1988) found that some results from succession research have been understated due to methodological problems such as failure to correct for the effects of organization size, failure to correct dollar-denominated criteria for effects of inflation, and failure to allow enough time for new leaders to influence quantitative performance outcomes. For example, Lieberson and O'Connor (1972) examined the relative effects of year, industry, and company CEO on the earnings of 167 companies in 13 industries. Leadership succession accounted for only 7.5 percent of the variance in net income with no lag time or correction for size. In contrast, leadership succession explained 32 percent of the profit margin (i.e., net income corrected for size of organization) for a three-year lagged effect. In another example, Salancik and Pfeffer (1977b) examined the relative effects of city, year, and mayor on budget variables for 30 U.S. cities. Mayor effects accounted for only 10 percent of budget outcomes when results were not corrected for city size, but when city size was controlled, mayor effects accounted for over 24 percent of budget outcomes. Day and Lord (1988) pointed out that writers such as Pfeffer (1977b), Brown (1982), and Meindl, Ehrlich, and Dukerich (1985) erroneously interpreted these studies as demonstrating that leadership is not important.

The substantial effect of leadership on appropriate criteria in the studies by Lieberson and O'Connor (1972) and Salancik and Pfeffer (1977b) is consistent with results in subsequent research. Weiner and Mahoney (1981) examined 193 manufacturing companies over a 19-year period and found that leadership explained 44 percent of the variance in profits as a percentage of assets. Thomas (1988) studied the performance of 12 retailing companies in England over a 20-year period and found that leadership explained 51 percent of the variance in profit margins after controlling for some nonleadership variables. Additional evidence for the influence of top executives on organization performance was found in a study by Barrick, Day, Lord, and Alexander (1991). Support for the importance of top leadership is provided even in studies that found a negative mean effect of succession on performance (e.g., Alexander & Lee, 1996; Miller, 1993).

New leaders are unlikely to have much effect on organizational performance unless they differ considerably in skill from the leader they replace. If the successor is more skilled, performance is likely to improve, whereas if the successor is less skilled, performance is likely to decline. The influence of successor ability on organizational effectiveness was examined in two studies, one on church ministers (Smith, Carson, & Alexander, 1984) and the other on basketball coaches in the NBA (Pfeffer & Davis-Blake, 1986). In both studies, leadership succession resulted in improved performance only for leaders with a previous record of effectiveness. However, even for these leaders, the effects on performance were small. A plausible explanation for the weak results in these two studies is that they involved middle-level administrators rather than top executives (Day & Lord, 1988). Unlike owners and general managers, the athletic managers and coaches for NBA teams do not have much influence on important determinants of team performance such as player salaries, the scouting staff, and the farm system. Moreover, the potential to influence performance may be less for leaders in churches and professional athletic teams than for CEOs of companies.

In summary, the succession research is still limited, and the results are not conclusive due to the many methodological problems in measuring leader effects. The research seems to indicate that top-level leadership can have a substantial effect on organization performance, but most of the succession studies do not explain how a leader actually influences performance, nor do they measure the conditions that determine how much influence a particular leader will have (Day & Lord, 1988; House & Singh, 1987).

Evolutionary Change and Strategic Leadership

The opportunity of top executives to exert strong influence on the performance of an organization depends in part on historical factors such as the evolutionary stage of the organization (Lord & Maher, 1991; Miller & Friesen, 1984; Tushman & Romanelli, 1985; Tushman, Newman, & Romanelli, 1986). Tushman and Romanelli (1985) formulated a punctuated equilibrium model to describe how organizations evolve over time and the role of top executives in this evolutionary process. The evolution of an organization was described in terms of alternating periods of reorientation and convergence that typically occur over the lifetime of an organization.

Periods of Reorientation

A performance decline may occur at any point, and eventually it will trigger a period of reorientation, which, if successful, will renew and revitalize the organization. Reorientation occurs as a relatively short period of intense activity during which top-level leaders make major changes in the organization's strategy, structure, and work processes. Reorientation may be initiated in response to a variety of environmental changes, including new competition, major changes in technology, declining demand for the organization's products and services, or a different political-regulatory climate. For example, in the automobile industry, the emergence of strong foreign competition combined with changing consumer preferences and new government regulations (safety, gas mileage, pollution controls) created the need for major changes in strategy. Changing technology in the computer industry created major upheavals, making products rapidly obsolete and allowing the emergence of new competitors. In the financial services industry (banks, insurance, stocks and bonds) deregulation created a sudden need for major changes after many years of stable conditions.

A major shift in strategy will cause ripples of change throughout the organization. Changes will be necessary in the distribution of power (some will gain at the expense of others), structuring of subunits and reporting relationships, allocation of resources to various activities, patterns of required interaction and communication, operational procedures, norms and values about how things are done, assignment of formal and informal roles, and the staffing of key positions. To succeed, reorientation requires concurrent changes in interrelated aspects of strategy, structure, work processes, and people. It is essential to overcome inevitable pockets of resistance that will emerge as some people attempt to protect their advantages and maintain the old, familiar ways of doing things. Top-level executives should guide and coordinate the change effort and provide the vision, energy, and guidance needed to make it succeed.

Periods of Convergence

The periods of upheaval and revolutionary change are typically followed by much longer periods of convergence. During periods of convergence, only small, incremental changes are made to solidify and reinforce the new strategy and increase the consistency between strategy, organization structure, culture, and people. Examples of this type of fine tuning include refining policies and procedures, creating specialized units and linking mechanisms, clarifying roles and relationships, modifying reward systems to be compatible with the strategy, selecting and developing personnel suited to the strategy, and building commitment to the strategy. The convergence period also includes minor changes in strategy to adapt to the environment. However, these incremental changes do not add up to produce fundamental transformation in an organization (Romanelli & Tushman, 1994).

The incremental changes made during a convergence period have both advantages and disadvantages. The advantage is that they help the organization execute its strategy successfully. Mutually reinforcing patterns of strong cultural values, clearly understood work procedures, and clearly defined relationships make it easier for members of the organization to carry out operations without much confusion, conflict, and politics. The disadvantage is that internal forces for stability are strengthened, making it harder for executives to make major changes when they are eventually required due to changes in the environment. Furthermore, some top executives pursue a winning strategy to extremes, which can weaken an organization and make it more vulnerable to competition (Miller, 1990).

Influence of Top Management

Top-level executives are viewed by Tushman and Romanelli (1985) as the mechanism for mediating between forces for stability and forces for change. The forces for stability increase during periods of convergence as the culture becomes stronger and the organization develops standardized, familiar ways of doing things. The forces for reorientation occur when the organization becomes so misaligned with the environment that incremental changes are no longer able to prevent a crisis of declining performance. How executives perceive these forces and deal with them has major implications for the performance of their organization (Tushman & O'Reilly, 1996; Yukl & Lepsinger, 2004).

The effect of a CEO on the performance of an organization depends on where it is in the evolutionary cycle. The CEO has less potential impact when the environment is stable and the fit between the organization and environment is still good and likely to remain so. Managing incremental changes during convergence requires considerable expertise, but much of the responsibility can be delegated to managers at lower levels. The potential influence of a CEO on organization performance is much larger when major changes in the environment threaten to undermine the effectiveness of the existing strategy, or they provide unusual opportunities to pursue a new strategy. A CEO who foresees the need for change and takes bold steps to deal with threats and capitalize on opportunities can have a dramatic effect on the long-term survival and effectiveness of the organization. Organizations that are the early pioneers in the use of new technologies or development of new markets can gain an advantage over competitors who decide much later to pursue a similar strategy (Tushman & Anderson, 1986).

Unfortunately, an entrenched management is likely to continue making incremental changes rather than initiate a major strategy reorientation. Executives are strongly influenced by the implicit beliefs, assumptions, and values underlying the current culture and strategy. Many executives persist too long in the belief that a previously successful strategy is still relevant despite changes in the external environment (Audia, Locke, & Smith, 2000; Lant, Milliken, & Batra, 1992; Miller & Chen, 1994). Faced with declining performance or new competition, most executives attempt to improve implementation of the existing strategy rather than questioning it. Efforts to strengthen the current strategy by cutting costs and tightening controls often results in a temporary improvement in performance, making top management appear to be successful (Johnson, 1992). However, even when such efforts fail to yield improvements, some CEOs will continue to invest more resources in a strategy rather than admit failure (Staw & Ross, 1987).

It is difficult for a CEO to get support for major changes when the need for them is not obvious. In the absence of a crisis, powerful members of the organization will question the need for changing things and they may succeed in blocking the changes or removing the CEO. Major changes usually cause a temporary decline in performance, as resources are diverted to implement them and people learn new ways of doing things (Lord & Maher, 1991). It usually takes considerable time to verify the success of a major change (3–5 years), and the delay is an additional risk that many executives may prefer to avoid. Thus, to lead an organization through a successful reorientation in the absence of a crisis requires unusual talent, energy, and power. Even when a crisis is finally evident, the current top management may not be able to formulate a new strategy that is credible. By then attributional biases will work against the current leadership, making it easier for a coalition of powerful stakeholders to replace the CEO.

Consistent with the risks and difficulties, visionary executives who foresee the need for major change and take bold steps to deal with it are rare. Tushman, Newman, and Romanelli (1986) found that reorientation was initiated by the current CEO in only 15 percent of the 40 companies they studied, and in each of these six cases the CEO replaced some of the executive team with new people who had different skills and a fresh perspective. Thus, most reorientations were initiated by new leadership, and the new CEO was often an outside successor with a mandate for major change. A different pattern of CEO turnover is typical during periods of convergence. Consistent with the emphasis on continuity of the existing strategy, CEO turnover during convergence periods is due more often to retirement or voluntary resignation than to forced succession, outside successors are seldom selected, and successors are unlikely to have a mandate for major change.

The tendency for major changes in strategy to be initiated by new leadership is supported by other research as well (e.g., Lauterback, Vu, & Weisberg, 1999; Samuelson, Galbraith, & McGuire, 1985; Schwartz & Menon, 1985; Virany, Tushman, & Romanelli, 1992). In a study of 28 large and medium-sized British companies that went from declining performance to sharply improving performance, the turnaround was led by a new CEO in 55 percent of the companies, and significant changes in the executive team occurred in 85 percent of the companies (Grinyer, Mayes, & McKiernan, 1990). The sharp turnaround in these companies was attributed to a new vision, high energy, and a positive, action-oriented approach taken by the new executive team. The successful executive teams focused on improving the core business and exploiting opportunities related to it.

Political Power and Strategic Leadership

The amount of change that occurs in an organization is also determined by power struggles among different factions or coalitions. As noted in Chapter 6, strategic contingencies theory attempts to explain how changes in the environment of the organization affect the relative power of different subunits (Hickson et al., 1971). According to the theory, subunits with unique expertise in solving critical problems gain more power to influence the organization's strategic decisions. The most powerful subunit is often able to get one of its members selected as the CEO of the organization, and the representatives of this subunit have more influence in groups responsible for strategic planning (e.g., executive committee, board of directors). Thus, according to the theory, there is a process of natural selection wherein the people who are most qualified to help the organization adapt to the environment gain the most influence in strategic decisions, thereby facilitating successful adaptation.

Some support for the theory was found in several studies (Brass, 1984, 1985; Hambrick, 1981; Hinings, Hickson, Pennings, & Schneck, 1974; Hills & Mahoney, 1978; Pfeffer & Moore, 1980; Pfeffer & Salancik, 1974). However, the theory is not able to explain how a subunit sometimes retains power even after changes in the environment make its expertise less critical. This explanation is provided by extending the theory to include political processes in organizations (Pfeffer, 1981; Salancik & Pfeffer, 1977a).

The process by which powerful individuals or subunits use political tactics to increase their power or protect existing power sources is called *institutionalization*. Salancik and Pfeffer (1977a) proposed that a coalition of top executives (including leaders of the dominant subunit) can use political processes to maintain power even after their expertise is no longer critical to the organization. Ambiguity about the nature of the environment and how it is changing provides an opportunity for top executives to interpret events in a biased manner, to magnify the importance of their expertise, and to justify their policies. Control over distribution of information about how well the organization is performing allows top executives to exaggerate the success of past decisions and cover up mistakes. The power of top management can also be used to deny others the resources and opportunity needed to demonstrate their superior expertise. Critics and potential rivals can be silenced, co-opted, or expelled from the organization (Pfeffer, 1981).

The evolutionary shift in power described by strategic contingencies theory can be delayed by the use of these political tactics, but the reprieve for top management is not unlimited. When major changes occur in the environment and top management lacks the expertise to develop an appropriate strategy, the performance of the organization will decline. This process will occur much faster when the organization has strong competition for its products and services, and competitors are able to adapt more rapidly to changes in the environment. Unless the organization replaces top management, it will eventually go bankrupt or be taken over by outsiders who desire its assets.

Executive Tenure and Strategic Leadership

A CEO's strategic leadership behavior is also affected by time in office. Hambrick and Fukutomi (1991) presented a life cycle model to explain the pattern of changing behavior observed in many CEOs over a period of several years. The changing patterns of behavior have important implications for the effectiveness of a CEO, and the model helps to explain why a major reorientation is seldom initiated by a CEO who has been in office for many years.

Behavior in the initial stage is greatly influenced by the implicit mandate given the CEO by the board of directors or the owner of the firm (e.g., an individual, family, or another corporation). The mandate may be to make major changes or to keep things the same. Outside successors tend to make more immediate changes than inside successors, probably because they are usually brought in with a mandate to do so. The new CEO will attempt to demonstrate early successes in order to gain more discretion later. Initial changes are usually made in the functional areas where the executive has the most experience (Gabarro, 1985). For example, a CEO who was formerly a production executive is likely to make changes in manufacturing processes, a marketing executive is likely to make changes in marketing and advertising, and a finance executive is likely to make changes in financial arrangements. The initial changes will also reflect the prior experience of the new CEO in earlier executive positions, especially if the relevance of this experience was a major reason for selecting the person. If the CEO assumed office in the midst of a crisis, initial changes will be made to seek some immediate relief and buy time for longer-term solutions. However, if initial changes are costly to implement and disruptive to operations, the net effect may be a further decline in organizational performance until the benefits of the change finally begin to materialize (Gabarro, 1987; Haveman, 1992).

After trying to satisfy the initial mandate and get a political foothold, the executive is likely to experiment with various approaches. The early period typically involves intense information gathering from internal and external sources to identify problems and opportunities. The CEO also tries to evaluate the effects of initial changes before making additional ones. Eventually (usually in the second or third year), the executive may gain enough knowledge and influence to select an enduring theme or strategy and begin to implement it. Subsequent behavior consists mostly of incremental steps to bolster the new theme or strategy. If the mandate was to maintain continuity or the executive is conservative and risk averse, then the new theme may be much like that of the former CEO.

Once a theme or strategy is selected, commitment to it tends to increase over time. The CEO becomes increasingly narrow-minded and inflexible about considering other alternatives. The task becomes less exciting, and the behavior of the executive becomes more habitual and routine. Less search for external information occurs, negative information tends to be discounted or ignored, and the CEO puts forth less effort to learn and improve. Early successes tend to make the CEO complacent about the effectiveness of the strategy. The longer a CEO is in office, the more power will be institutionalized in the ways described earlier. This power makes it more difficult for others to question the CEO's strategy. Thus, when the external environment is dynamic and strategic changes are needed more often, it may be dysfunctional for the organization to have a CEO with extended tenure.

Hambrick and Fukutomi (1991) remind us that this pattern is not inevitable. Various aspects of the environment, organization, and individual interact to decrease the likelihood that a CEO will become complacent and inflexible. For example, in a dynamic, hostile environment, a CEO who is oriented toward achievement, has a high tolerance of ambiguity, seeks information from a diversity of sources (including negative feedback), and learns from experience is likely to remain vigilant and flexible. However, a CEO with a low tolerance of ambiguity and less ambition is likely to take refuge in a single-minded theme as a way to cope with the ambiguity and threat of an uncertain environment. More flexibility and vigilance are facilitated also by strong internal stakeholders (e.g., owners, board of directors, unions, and employee associations) who demand continued high performance from the CEO as a condition of remaining in office. Thus, one approach to help avoid the dysfunctions of long tenure is to avoid concentrating power in the hands of a single, dominant CEO. It is better to have a diverse team of empowered executives who will provide different perspectives and insist on continuous improvement. It is also beneficial to have a strong, independent board of directors who are mostly outsiders rather than executives of the firm.

Although the life cycle model was developed to describe the effects of CEO succession, aspects of the model may also apply to succession in leadership positions at lower levels and in some types of teams. Several studies suggest that stagnation effects are likely when a leader has been in office for a considerable period of time (e.g., Gabarro, 1987; Giambatista, 2004; Katz, 1982). The life cycle model of leader tenure has some empirical support, but longitudinal studies on leadership are still rare, and more research is needed to examine and explain the processes that occur during a leader's tenure in office.

Executive Teams

All organizations have a top management group that includes the CEO and other top executives, but organizations differ greatly in the way this group operates. The traditional approach is to have a clear hierarchy of authority with a chief executive officer (usually the chairman of the board, but sometimes the president of the organization), a chief operating officer (usually the president of the organization), and several subordinate executives (e.g., vice presidents) who head various subunits of the organization. This structure is still prominent, but an increasingly popular alternative is to share power within the top management team (Ancona & Nadler, 1989). Executives in the team collectively assume the responsibilities of the chief operating officer in managing the internal operations of the organization, and they assist the CEO in formulating strategy. Another, less common variation is the "office of the chairperson" structure in which the responsibilities of the CEO are shared, even though one executive (the chairperson) usually has more power than the others (the vice chairpersons). Executive teams are becoming more acceptable due to their effective use in other countries (such as Japan) and a growing awareness that the stereotype of the heroic, individual leader is unrealistic for complex organizations in a turbulent environment. An example of a company that has long used executive teams is Nordstrom Inc., a department store chain (Yang, 1992).

> During the 1980s the executive team consisted of three of the founder's grandsons, Bruce, John, and James. The title of President rotated among the three executives. Later in the 1990s, when Nordstroms encountered sluggish sales and lower profits, the executive team was modified. The three co-presidents and one other relative were elevated to co-chairmen. They focus on strategy issues, such as expansion plans and selection of store sites. Four non-family members were promoted to the positions of co-president. They are jointly responsible for making operating decisions on how to

conduct the day-to-day affairs of the company. Each co-president is responsible for a different type of merchandise. Although they have considerable autonomy in their own domain of responsibility, they operate as a unified team. They hold weekly meetings and communicate frequently with each other. Despite lively debates, they cooperate in finding solutions that will be best for the customer, their common goal.

Regardless of the formal structure of an organization, differences will occur in the extent to which strategic leadership is actually shared among the top executives. Even an organization with an executive team may have an autocratic CEO who allows other executives little influence over strategic decisions. And even an organization with a traditional hierarchymay have a CEO who empowers other top executives to share responsibility for making strategic decisions. As noted earlier in this chapter, it is much easier to exercise control over key decisions when the CEO has substantial ownership power, when the board of directors is weak or submissive, or when the CEO is given a mandate by a powerful board of directors to make major changes in the strategies and structure of the organization (Finkelstein, 1992; Hambrick & Finkelstein, 1987).

Potential Advantages of Executive Teams

Executive teams offer a number of potential advantages for an organization (Ancona & Nadler, 1989; Bradford & Cohen, 1984; Eisenstat & Cohen, 1990; Hambrick, 1987; Nadler, 1998). An executive team has the potential to make better strategic decisions when members have relevant skills and knowledge that the CEO lacks. Team members can compensate for weaknesses in the skills of the CEO. The decisions made by a team are more likely to represent the diverse interests of organization members. Important tasks are less likely to be neglected if several people are available to share the burden of leadership. Communication and cooperation among executives from different subunits is improved by meeting regularly as a team. The participation of team members in making strategic decisions will improve their understanding and commitment to implement these decisions. A recent study found that when the CEO allowed other members of a top executive team to influence a strategic decision, the decision quality was better, the decision was perceived as more fair, team members were more committed to implement the decision, their trust in the leader increased, and they identified more with the team (Korsgaard, Schweiger, & Sapienze, 1995).

The potential advantages of having an executive team depend in part on the situation (Ancona & Nadler, 1989). Teams are more important in a complex, rapidly changing environment that places many external demands on the CEO. Growing turbulence in the environment of organizations due to rapid technological changes and emergence of an interdependent world economy has made the responsibility for developing successful strategy even more difficult than before. Teams are also more important when the organization has diverse but highly interdependent business units that require close coordination across units. In an organization with several diverse business units, a single leader is unlikely to have the broad expertise necessary to direct and coordinate the activities of these units.

The team approach is also a way to facilitate succession of leadership in large, diverse organizations. The development of leadership skills is likely to be greater for executives who have experience in dealing with the major issues and decisions facing the organization. Moreover, when several executives share responsibility for strategic leadership of the organization, it is easier for the current CEO and the board of directors to determine which executive in the team is most qualified to become the next CEO.

There is no guarantee that the potential advantages of an executive team will be realized. As Bradford and Cohen (1984) point out, new teams typically progress through a series of developmental stages before the members come to trust and respect each other and are able to resolve conflicts in a constructive way. This difficult developmental process causes some chief executives to abandon the effort in an early stage and revert to autocratic leadership. Whether a CEO is able to develop an effective executive team depends in part on his or her attitudes and skills. Team success also depends on aspects of the situation. It is more difficult to develop mutual trust and cooperation when team members represent subunits with different objectives or members are competing to become the successor to the current CEO.

Research by Eisenstat and Cohen (1990) with top management teams found that they are more likely to be successful when the CEO selects team members with relevant skills and experience, clearly defines objectives consistent with shared values, gives the team considerable discretion but clearly specifies the limits of team authority in relation to CEO authority, helps the team establish norms that will facilitate group processes, facilitates learning of skills in working together effectively, and encourages openness and mutual trust among team members. The CEO should avoid actions that encourage competition or distrust, such as overtly making comparative evaluations among team members and meeting with individual executives to deal with issues that should be addressed by the entire team. It is also essential for the CEO to help the team avoid process problems that may prevent them from making good decisions (see Chapter 11).

Executive Teams and Organizational Effectiveness

In an executive team, strategic decision making is affected not only by the attributes of the CEO, but also by those of other members. A number of studies have investigated how characteristics of executive teams are related to organizational effectiveness (e.g., Bantel & Jackson, 1989; Edmondson, Roberto, & Watkins, 2003; Hambrick, 1987; Hambrick & Mason, 1984; Hitt & Tyler, 1991; Keck & Tushman, 1993). Most of the early research examined how the composition of the team and the mix of member attributes (e.g., age, education, functional area, and tenure as a board member) affect the type of decisions made and the performance of the organization.

One characteristic that appears to be important is the functional background or specialized field of the team members. Executives with a different functional background usually develop different values and attitudes that affect their interpretation of the environment, preference for particular types of strategy, and capacity to generate innovative solutions to problems. For example, an executive team dominated by marketing executives is likely to pursue a different strategy than one dominated by finance executives or production executives. The cognitive skills of team members and their knowledge of the industry also determine the capacity of the team to analyze environmental information and develop an innovative, adaptive strategy. Team members with relevant skills and knowledge can offset the CEO's biases and improve flexibility of decision making (Nutt, 1993). For example, Pascale (1990) found that the CEOs of successful companies such as Ford, Honda, and Hewlett-Packard included executives with complementary strengths in their top management team.

Results from research on the composition of top management teams have not been consistent from study to study, and scholars have identified some serious limitations in the research (Edmondson et al., 2003; Pettigrew, 1992; Priem, Lyon, & Dess, 1999). Demographic attributes such as functional background, age, or tenure in office are only proxies for other constructs such as attitudes and behavior, and the research seldom examined these other constructs or the processes by which team composition affects outcomes. Moreover, most of the research makes the unrealistic assumption that conditions are consistent over time and the relation of team composition to performance is the same, regardless of the situation. The optimal mix of executive characteristics depends not only on the diversity of team members, but also on the nature of the environment, the organizational context in which the team must operate, and the decision style and leadership skills of the CEO.

A diversity of backgrounds and perspectives can improve the quality of the strategic decisions made by a team if the knowledge and skills of members are relevant for understanding the threats and opportunities in a turbulent, uncertain environment (Bantel & Jackson, 1989; Murray, 1989). However, as found in the research on decision groups (see Chapter 11), the potential benefits of diversity will not be achieved unless the team can process information and make decisions in a way that utilizes the relevant knowledge and ideas of members. Highly divergent interests and knowledge also make it more difficult to achieve mutual understanding. The implicit assumptions and inconsistent mental models among members can impede communication and undermine problem solving. It is more difficult to determine when relevant information needs to be shared (they assume it is widely known), and an adequate discussion of relevant options and potential risks is less likely to occur (Edmondson et al., 2003).

The quality of a strategic decision is likely to be better if influence over the decision is greater for individuals with the most expertise for that type of decision, especially if the environment is turbulent and uncertain. If the CEO dominates decisions, the potential benefits of diverse members with relevant knowledge may not be realized. Haleblian and Finkelstein (1993) found that computer firms with the best performance had larger top management teams and less concentration of power in the CEO. In the more stable natural gas industry, team size and CEO dominance of the team were not related to a firm's performance.

It is not enough to make good strategic decisions; they must be implemented effectively to be successful. Member commitment is important for effective implementation of strategic decisions made by executive teams (Schweiger & Sandberg, 1991). It is not necessary for every member to agree on all aspects of a strategic decision, but some degree of consensus is necessary (Bourgeois, 1980; Eisenhardt, 1989; Priem, 1990). If the decision process involves affective conflict (i.e., accusations, name calling, blaming), it will be difficult to achieve a cooperative effort to implement the decision (Amason, 1996). Although it is desirable to confront disagreements openly in order to make use of the team's collective knowledge, the discussion of differences must be done in a way that does not cause personal hostility and resentment among team members. The discussion should be focused on cognitive differences relevant to the decision, and criticism or blaming of individuals should be avoided.

In a dynamic, turbulent environment, it is important to make decisions in a timely way. Eisenhardt (1989) conducted a study of eight minicomputer firms to investigate how the speed and quality of strategic decisions were affected by the decision processes in these firms. The study found that strategic decisions were both faster and better when the executive team conducted a simultaneous evaluation of several alternatives rather than using the common "satisficing" procedure of examining alternatives sequentially until a satisfactory one is found. An intensive decision process helped the team evaluate the strengths and weaknesses of each alternative, avoid premature commitment to a particular alternative, and identify a fallback position to use if attempts to implement the chosen alternative encountered unexpected obstacles. The study also found that a team was more effective when it considered how a decision was related to other strategic decisions, and when it considered tactical plans (e.g., action steps, budgets, schedules) for implementing a strategic decision as part of the process for evaluating its feasibility. This integrative approach appears to provide a better understanding of the alternatives and their implications, and it tends to reduce anxiety about possible adverse consequences, thereby increasing confidence in the team's evaluation and willingness to move forward with a decision. Decisions were made faster when the CEO sought advice widely but relied more on a few executives who had the most relevant expertise and experience. Finally, decisions were made faster when the CEO emphasized the need for consensus among the executives most affected by a decision, rather than prolonging the process in an effort to achieve consensus among everyone in the top management group.

In summary, research findings on top management teams are generally consistent with findings in research on small decision groups, but the complexities are much greater for executive teams. The strategic decision processes in executive teams is a research topic with rich potential for understanding organization effectiveness, and researchers are making progress in improving our understanding of it.

How Leaders Influence Organizational Performance

One of the most important research questions in strategic leadership is how leaders actually influence the overall effectiveness of large organizations. The Flexible Leadership Theory , was formulated to answer this question (Yukl & Lepsinger, 2004). It incorporates ideas from earlier leadership theories and related areas of study, including organization theory, strategic management, and change management (e.g., Beer & Nohria, 2000; Katz & Kahn, 1978; Lawrence & Lorsch, 1969; Miller, & Friesen, 1984; Mott, 1972; Quinn, 1988; Tushman & Romanelli, 1985; Zajac, Kraatz, & Bresser, 1999). The four types of constructs in the theory include organizational performance (or effectiveness), performance determinants, leadership processes, and situational variables.

Organizational effectiveness is the long-term prosperity and survival of the organization. It depends on three types of performance determinants: (1) efficiency and process reliability, (2) human relations and resources, and (3) innovation and adaptation to the environment. The relative importance of these performance determinants will differ across organizations and over time for the same organization. Aspects of the situation that determine the relative importance of the performance determinants include the type of organization or unit, and the amount of volatility and uncertainty in the external environment. Complex interdependencies among the performance determinants mean that efforts by leaders to influence one can affect the others in a positive or negative way. The three types of performance determinants and the conditions that increase their importance will be described in more detail before looking more closely at the leadership processes.

Efficiency and Process Reliability

Efficiency involves using people and resources to carry out essential operations in a way that minimizes costs. Efficiency is especially important when the competitive strategy of the organization is to offer its products and services at a lower price than competitors, or when a financial crisis occurs and there are insufficient funds to support essential operations. This performance determinant is less important when an organization is able to pass along cost increases to customers, or the organization is highly subsidized by the government. Efficiency can be increased by redesigning work processes, using new technology, and coordinating unit activities to avoid unnecessary activities and wasted resources.

Process reliability means avoiding unnecessary delays, errors, quality defects, or accidents. This performance determinant is especially important when defective products or unreliable processes can affect the health and safety of employees (e.g., injury or death from accidents or exposure to harmful substances), result in financial loss (e.g., mistakes in contracts, stolen or misappropriated funds, costly lawsuits), or cause damage to expensive equipment. Process reliability can be improved by using extra resources to ensure that quality standards are maintained, products or services are delivered on time, and accidents are avoided, but this approach may also reduce efficiency. However, sometimes it is possible to improve process reliability without reducing efficiency, or to improve both at the same time. For example, by simplifying workflows, work processes can be redesigned to reduce costs as well as errors and delays.

Innovation and Adaptation

The effectiveness of an organization also depends on responding in appropriate ways to external threats and opportunities. When changes in the external environment affect the capacity of the organization to carry out its mission, successful adaptation requires recognition of threats and opportunities, and the willingness to make changes in the processes, products, services, or the competitive strategy of the organization.

Innovative change is more important when the external environment is volatile and uncertain, which is likely in situations of rapid technological change, political and economic turmoil, or new threats from competitors or external enemies. Innovation is especially important for an organization with a competitive strategy that emphasizes unique, leading-edge products or services designed to satisfy the changing needs of customers and clients. For the strategy to be effective, it is necessary to make innovative changes and respond rapidly to threats and opportunities.

Adaptation is enhanced by accurate interpretation of information about the environment; collective learning by members (understanding of processes and causal relationships); effective knowledge management (retention and diffusion of new knowledge within the organization); flexibility of work processes (capacity to change them quickly as needed); innovations in products, services, or processes; and availability of discretionary resources (to support new initiatives and crisis management). A company is more likely to adapt successfully to its environment if it has a relevant competitive strategy that specifies the types of products or services to offer and how to influence potential customers or clients. The strategy may also specify methods for acquiring new competencies or expanding into new markets (e.g., acquisitions, mergers, joint ventures), and methods for obtaining necessary financial resources (e.g., stocks, bonds, loans, donations). Because the performance determinants are so closely interwoven, the competitive strategy must be compatible with them. For example, a competitive strategy that involves providing more complex products or services may fail unless the company has employees with the required skills and motivation. A strategy to compete on the basis of low prices may fail if the company has high costs.

Human Resources and Relations

Human resources include the task-relevant skills and experience of unit members. The term *human capital* is sometimes used to describe the quality of an organization's human resources. Performance will be better when members understand what must be done and how to do it. Human relations include cooperation, mutual trust, and organizational commitment. The term *social capital* is sometimes used to describe the quality of the human relationships in an organization. Collective work is performed more effectively when members are strongly committed to task objectives, they have a high level of mutual trust, and they develop cooperative relationships with people who can provide essential information and assistance. Human relations and resources also affect the other performance determinants. For example, it is difficult to improve efficiency and innovation if employees lack the motivation and skills necessary to achieve these objectives.

Human resources and relations are more important when the work is complex and difficult to learn, new members require extensive training, successful performance requires a high level of skill and motivation, and it is difficult to recruit and train competent replacements for people who leave (e.g., hospitals, consulting firms, legal firms, advertising agencies, research universities). The importance of human relations and resources is increased by a competitive strategy that relies on services delivered by unique experts who, if dissatisfied, can find jobs in competing companies or start their own competing company. Human resources and relations are relatively less important for an organization with highly automated processes and few employees, for a virtual organization that has outsourced nearly all functions, and for an organization that has an ample supply of people willing to work for low wages in jobs that require little skill or cooperation.

Leader Influence on Performance Determinants

Leaders can improve organization effectiveness by enhancing the performance determinants. As noted in Chapter 3, most forms of direct leadership behavior can be classified into three general types or *metacategories* that are differentiated by their primary objective. The task-oriented behaviors are used primarily to improve efficiency and process reliability. The change-oriented behaviors are used primarily to improve adaptation to the external environment. The relations-oriented behaviors are used primarily to improve human relations and human resources. Specific types of behavior in each metacategory were described in Chapter 3, and some behaviors will be more useful than others in a particular situation or for a particular type of leader. For example, most of the change-oriented behaviors are more relevant in a rapidly changing environment than in a relatively stable environment, and they are used more by top executives than by low-level supervisors.

Another way for leaders to influence the performance determinants is by implementing or modifying formal programs, management systems, and aspects of formal

TABLE 12-1   Management Systems, Programs, and Structural Forms for Improving
Performance Determinants

Efficiency and Process Reliability

- Performance management and goal setting programs (e.g., MBO, zero defects)
- Process and quality improvement programs (quality circles, TQM, Six Sigma)
- Cost reduction programs (downsizing, outsourcing, just-in-time inventory)
- Structural forms (functional specialization, formalization, standardization)
- Appraisal, recognition, and reward systems focused on efficiency and process reliability

Human Resources and Relations

- Quality of worklife programs (flextime, job sharing, child care, fitness center)
- Employee benefit programs (health care, vacations, retirement, sabbaticals)
- Socialization and team building (orientation programs, ceremonies and rituals, social events and celebrations)
- Employee development programs (training, mentoring, 360 feedback, education subsidies)
- Human resource planning (succession planning, assessment centers, recruiting programs)
- Empowerment programs (self-managed teams, employee ownership, industrial democracy)
- Recognition and reward programs focused on loyalty, service, or skill acquisition

Innovation and Adaptation

- Competitor and market analysis programs (market surveys, focus groups, consumer panels, comparative product testing, benchmarking competitor products and processes)
- Innovation programs (intrapreneurship, quality circles, innovation goals)
- Knowledge acquisition (consultants, joint ventures, import best practices from outside)
- Organizational learning (knowledge management systems, postmortems, joint ventures)
- Temporary structural forms for implementing change (steering committee, task forces)
- Growth and diversification programs (mergers and acquisitions, franchises, joint ventures)
- Structural forms (research departments, small product divisions, product managers cross-functional product development teams, facilities designed to encourage innovation)
- Appraisal, recognition, and reward systems focused on innovation and customer satisfaction

structure. As noted in Chapter 1, this type of influence is sometimes called *indirect leadership* (Hunt, 1980; Lord & Maher, 1991), because no direct interaction with followers is necessary to influence their attitudes and behavior. Table 12-1 lists examples of improvement programs, management systems, and structural forms used in many organizations.

The two different approaches for influencing performance determinants are complementary rather than mutually exclusive. The direct behaviors can be used to facilitate the implementation of new programs or systems and their successful use. A major change is more likely to be accepted when top management explains why it is needed, and how it will benefit the organization. A new knowledge management system is more likely to be successful when managers encourage subordinates to input relevant information and use the system in appropriate ways. A new training program is more likely to be successful when managers encourage subordinates to attend the program and provide them with opportunities to use newly learned skills on the job.

Management programs and systems can enhance the effects of direct leadership behaviors. For example, encouraging innovative thinking is much more likely to increase actual innovation when an organization has a well-designed intrapreneurship program. Without such a program, employees may doubt that their creative ideas about products or processes will be supported and eventually adopted by the organization. As noted in Chapter 8, programs and structures can also limit the use of leadership behaviors or nullify their effects. For example, it is difficult to empower subordinates when there are elaborate rules and standard procedures.

Management programs and systems can also serve as substitutes for some types of direct behaviors (see Chapter 8). For example, company-wide training programs can reduce the amount of training that managers need to provide to their immediate subordinates. Management programs and systems provide a way to ensure that common activities are carried out in an efficient and uniform way across subunits. A company-wide bonus system with clear guidelines is likely to be more equitable than having each subunit manager determine the size and frequency of bonuses and the criteria for allocating them. Training of generic skills that are relevant for all employees is likely to be more efficient and consistent if provided by expert trainers as part of a company training program rather than by many individual managers in the company.

Flexible, Adaptive Leadership

A behavior, program, system, or structural form that is intended to improve one performance determinant often has implications for the other performance determinants as well. Sometimes the unintended consequences are beneficial, but they can also be detrimental. A leader who puts too much emphasis on influencing one performance determinant may have an adverse effect on another performance determinant, and the result may be lower organizational performance. The following example of events at Home Depot shows how attempts to improve efficiency can adversely affect both human relations and adaptation (Foust, 2003; Mathews, 2003).

> The company had always encouraged its store managers to view their stores as their own and to manage them as they saw fit. While this approach motivated employees to be entrepreneurial and customer-focused, it increased the cost of operations. When Bob Nardelli became chairman and CEO, he decided to cut costs by centralizing purchasing decisions, reducing inventory, and establishing clearer performance standards. However, less freedom to make their own decisions was upsetting to the store managers, and many chose to leave rather than surrender their autonomy to headquarters. Reductions in inventory meant that customers could no longer be sure of finding what they needed. Hiring more part-time people (up to half of the workforce) as a cost-cutting measure led to more complaints by customers that they could no longer get advice from knowledgeable, experienced salespeople. In the first few years of Nardelli's tenure, sales slowed dramatically and the stock fell by 51%.

> Nardelli soon realized that the changes created new problems, and he acted quickly to find a better balance among efficiency, human relations, and adaptation. The changes included an increase in the number of full-time employees, exciting new incentives for achieving quarterly sales goals (including Disney cruise vacations), an increase in store inventories to provide customers more choice, and a major remodeling program to make the stores more attractive to customers. After these changes were implemented, sales and profits at Home Depot turned around and began to increase.

When there are difficult trade-offs, it is essential for a leader to find an appropriate balance that reflects the relative priorities of the performance determinants and the potential for improving each one (Beer, 2001; Quinn, 1988; Yukl & Lepsinger, 2004). Whenever possible, the leader should find ways to enhance more than one performance determinant at the same time.

The task of balancing trade-offs among the performance determinants is further complicated by changes in conditions affecting the relative importance of the performance determinants. A leader may achieve a good balance only to find that changing conditions have upset it again. It is essential to continually assess the situation and determine what types of behavior, programs, management systems, and structural forms are relevant and mutually compatible. Using a particular type of behavior, program, or strategy because it proved successful in the past or for other leaders may not yield the desired results. Considerable skill is required to monitor and diagnose the situation accurately and integrate diverse leadership activities in a way that is relevant for changing conditions (Boal & Hooijberg, 2001; Hooijberg, Hunt, & Dodge, 1997).

The findings in some of the recent research on leader traits and skills (see Chapter 7) is consistent with the idea that flexible, adaptive leadership is essential to deal successfully with the difficult challenges posed by trade-offs, competing objectives, and changing situations. Relevant competencies include strategic thinking skills (systems thinking and social intelligence), interpersonal skills (social and emotional intelligence), a learning orientation (openness to feedback and new ideas), and knowledge of the organization (e.g., culture, processes, products or services). These competencies are relevant for leaders at all levels, but they are especially important for top executives.

The leadership challenge is greatest when all three performance determinants are highly important and there are difficult trade-offs among them. To enhance adaptation, efficiency, and human relations simultaneously requires commitment, cooperation, and coordination among all leaders in the organization. The fates of different leaders are closely intertwined in complex ways, and decisions made by different leaders must be compatible with each other and with the overall strategy of the organization. Even though top management has primary responsibility for deciding which programs and systems are appropriate, ensuring they are effectively implemented is a challenge for all leaders in an organization.

Monitoring the Environment

One of the most important activities of executives is to monitor the external environment and identify threats and opportunities for the organization. Most leaders need to be sensitive to a wide range of events and trends that are likely to affect their organization (Ginter & Duncan, 1990). Some representative questions likely to be important for a business organization are shown in Table 12-2. It is essential to learn about the concerns of customers and clients, the availability of suppliers and vendors, the actions of competitors, market trends, economic conditions, government policies, and technological developments. The information may be gathered in a variety of ways (e.g., reading government reports and industry publications, attending professional and trade meetings, talking to customers and suppliers, examining the products and reports of competitors, conducting market research).

TABLE 12-2   Questions for External Monitoring

1. What do clients and customers need and want?
2. What is the reaction of clients and customers to the organization's current products and services?
3. Who are the primary competitors?
4. What strategies are they pursuing (e.g., pricing, advertising and promotions, new products, customer service, etc.)?
5. How do competitors' products and services compare to those of the manager's organization?
6. What events affect the acquisition of materials, energy, information, and other inputs used by the organization to conduct its operations?
7. How will the organization be affected by new legislation and by government agencies that regulate its activities (e.g., labor laws, environmental regulations, safety standards, tax policies, etc.)?
8. How will new technologies affect the organization's products, services, and operations?
9. How will the organization be affected by changes in the economy (employment level, interest rates, growth rates)?
10. How will the organization be affected by changing population demographics (e.g., aging, diversity)?
11. How will the organization be affected by international events (e.g., trade agreements, import restrictions, currency changes, wars and revolutions)?

External monitoring (also called environmental scanning) provides the information needed for strategic planning and crisis management. Bourgeois (1985) studied 20 nondiversified companies and found that profitability was greater when executives had an accurate perception of the amount of industry volatility in markets and technology. Grinyer, Mayes, and McKiernan (1990) studied 28 British companies that experienced a sharp improvement in performance and a matched sample of firms with only average performance; the top management of the high-performing companies did more external monitoring (e.g., environmental scanning, consultation with key customers) and were quicker to recognize and exploit opportunities. The amount of change and turbulence in the environment will determine how much external monitoring is necessary. More external monitoring is needed when the organization is highly dependent on outsiders (e.g., clients, customers, suppliers, subcontractors, joint venture partners), when the environment is rapidly changing, and when the organization faces severe competition or serious threats from outside enemies (Ginter & Duncan, 1990).

Monitoring of the external environment is usually considered more important for upper-level managers than for lower-level managers (Kraut, Pedigo, McKenna, & Dunnette, 1989; Pavett & Lau, 1983). However, the difficulties involved in scanning and interpreting information about environmental changes make this responsibility one that should be shared by managers in an organization. One study found that most middle and upper-level managers did some external monitoring, regardless of their area of functional specialization, and this monitoring was usually not limited to the environmental sector that corresponded to their area of specialization (Aguilar, 1967; Hambrick, 1981b; Kefalas & Schoderbek, 1973). For example, production executives examined market conditions as well as developments in production technology and procedures. Other studies show that more active participation in external monitoring improves accuracy of perception about the environment (Sutcliffe, 1994; Thomas & McDaniel, 1990).

TABLE 12-3 Guidelines for External Monitoring

- Identify relevant information to gather.
- Use multiple sources of relevant information.
- Learn what clients and customers need and want.
- Learn about the products and activities of competitors.
- Relate environmental information to strategic plans.

Guidelines for External Monitoring

The following guidelines describe what leaders can do to learn about events and changes in the external environment that are relevant for the organization (see summary in Table 12-3).

- **Identify relevant information to gather.**

A broad focus can overwhelm an executive with information, and collecting too much information is costly. On the other hand, a narrow focus on the environment is likely to overlook important trends and developments. How to deal with this trade-off is a dilemma for executives. One of the most important choices is to determine what information deserves their attention. Top management needs relevant, timely information about the specific sectors of the environment upon which the organization is highly dependent. Top management also needs information about the performance of the organization in relation to competitors, progress in attaining objectives, and the organization's current capabilities. A useful approach for identifying relevant information is to develop a causal model that specifies the environmental variables that affect the organization (Bates, 1985; Narchal, Kittappa, & Bhattacharya, 1987). Another useful approach is to begin each scanning cycle (e.g., once a year) with a broad perspective that examines all potentially relevant sectors, identifies the issues in each sector most likely to have an important impact on the organization, and then monitors and analyzes these issues more closely during the remainder of the cycle (Bates, 1985).

- **Use multiple sources of relevant information.**

As in the case of internal monitoring, it is unwise to rely on a single source of information about something important. All individuals are biased in their selection and interpretation of information, and they may discount or distort information about important developments and trends (Milliken & Vollrath, 1991). Moreover, an individual who provides information may deliberately bias it to influence a strategic decision. Independent sources of information should be used whenever feasible. A leader should be continually alert about finding new sources of relevant information about the external environment. In addition to informal network contacts, useful information can be obtained from a variety of printed publications, such as journals and newsletters published by professional and trade organizations; reports and databases prepared by information services; and documents and reports published by government agencies (Jain, 1984). Just as it is useful to have multiple sources of information, it is also useful to have several people interpret information about the external environment. Interpretations are likely to be more accurate, and the experience is likely to facilitate the development of strategic management skills among participants.

- **Learn what clients and customers need and want.**

It is essential to learn as much as possible about the specific needs and requirements of customers and what they think about the organization's products and services. It is useful to discover what they like, what they dislike, and how the products or services could be improved. Market surveys are one common source of information about clients and customers, but more personal contacts are also desirable. Some manufacturing organizations have teams of production, engineering, and sales employees from different levels of the organization visit with major clients to learn more about their needs and get ideas for product improvements (Peters & Austin, 1985). Clients and suppliers are also invited to visit the organization's facilities, meet with production and engineering personnel, and attend meetings on how to improve quality, product design, or customer service.

- **Learn about the products and activities of competitors.**

Knowledge about the products and services of competitors is essential for making strategic decisions. Studying the products and activities of competitors is a good way to assess what they are doing. This information provides a basis for evaluating your own products and processes (a process called *benchmarking*), and it provides a source of good ideas on how to improve them (see Chapter 10). Detailed information about the products and services of competitors is sometimes difficult to obtain but worth the effort. Learning about competitors' products can be accomplished in a variety of ways: use them yourself, conduct comparative product testing, read evaluations conducted by product testing companies or governmental agencies, have customers directly compare the organization's products and services to those of competitors, visit the facilities of competitors, read competitors' advertising literature, and attend trade shows where competitors display and demonstrate their wares.

- **Relate environmental information to strategic plans.**

Information about the external environment should be used to evaluate and revise strategic plans (Hambrick, 1982). Discovery of emerging threats and opportunities is of little consequence unless the manager plans how to deal with them. Relating environmental information to the organization's current strategies is also helpful for evaluating the relevance of the various types of measures and indicators that are being used.

Formulating Strategy

Strategy is a plan or blueprint for carrying out the mission and attaining strategic objectives. For business organizations, a major part of the strategy is how to compete effectively in the marketplace and remain profitable (Porter, 1980). Some examples of possible competitive strategies include the following: selling a product or service at the lowest price; having superior quality, customer service, or the most innovative products and services; providing a unique product or service in a segment of the market ignored by competing organizations (niche strategies); and being the most flexible about customizing products or services to meet each client's needs. Sometimes it is feasible to pursue a mix of strategies at the same time (e.g., have the least expensive standard product or service as well as the best customized versions of the product or service).

Strategy may also involve the way the product or service is produced, delivered, marketed, financed, and guaranteed.

A meta-analytical review of research on strategic planning found support for the proposition that strategic planning by top executives improves an organization's performance (Miller & Cardinal, 1994). They also found that strategic planning was more important as the complexity and ambiguity of the environment increased. However, a limitation of most studies on effects of strategic planning is the lack of attention to strategy content and implementation. Strategy formulation will not improve organization performance unless the strategies are relevant and feasible, they are communicated to middle and lower-level managers, and these managers become committed to implement the strategies.

A relevant strategy takes into account changes in the external environment, and it is realistic in terms of the organization's strengths and weaknesses. The strategy should reflect the core mission and high-priority objectives of the organization. Beer (1988) found that organizations were less successful if they were focused on means rather than ends. Although strategy may include changing structure or management processes, such changes should be clearly relevant to strategic objectives. For example, it is not enough to propose downsizing, elimination of management layers, or reorganization into separate product divisions without providing a clear purpose for such changes. Unfortunately, many executives under extreme pressure to improve weak short-term performance succumb to the appeal of faddish remedies.

Guidelines for Formulating Strategy

One of the most difficult responsibilities for executives is to develop a competitive strategy for the organization, and there are no simple answers on how to do it effectively. The following guidelines (see Table 12-4), which are based on relevant theory, research, and practitioner insights, provide a brief overview of the process (Bennis & Nanus, 1985; Kotter, 1996; Nanus, 1992; Wall & Wall, 1995; Worley, Hitchin, & Ross, 1996). The guidelines do not depict a rigid sequence of steps, but rather a set of overlapping, cyclical activities that must be interwoven in a meaningful way.

- **Determine long-term objectives and priorities.**

It is difficult to make strategic plans without knowing the objectives to be attained and their relative priority. Long-term objectives and priorities should be based on the stated mission and vision for the organization. Strategic objectives for a business organization may involve such things as maintaining a specified profit margin or return on

---

TABLE 12-4   Guidelines for Formulating Strategy

- Determine long-term objectives and priorities.
- Assess current strengths and weaknesses.
- Identify core competencies.
- Evaluate the need for a major change in strategy.
- Identify promising strategies.
- Evaluate the likely outcomes of a strategy.
- Involve other executives in selecting a strategy.

investment, improving market share, and providing the best products or service in the industry. Strategic objectives for an organization with a humanitarian mission may include such things as finding a way to cure or prevent a disease, eliminating illiteracy in a specified population, and ending deaths from drunk driving. Strategic objectives for an educational institution may include improving the learning of essential skills, preparing students for specific careers, and increasing the number of students who graduate.

- **Assess current strengths and weaknesses.**

Strategic planning is facilitated by a comprehensive, objective evaluation of current performance in relation to strategic objectives and compared to the performance of competitors. Much of the information needed for this evaluation is provided by internal and external monitoring. Several types of analysis are useful. Review indicators of organizational performance for the past several years and progress toward achieving strategic objectives. Examine performance (e.g., sales, market share, costs, profits) for each product, service, and market. Identify products or services that are successful and those that are not meeting expectations. Compare the organization's products or services to those of competitors to identify strengths and weaknesses. Compare the efficiency of the organization's processes to that of similar organizations. Identify tangible resources that currently provide an advantage over competitors, such as financial assets, unique equipment and facilities, and patents on products or technology used to do the work. Identify conditions that provide an advantage, such as low operating costs, employees with relevant skills, a special relationship with suppliers, and an outstanding reputation for quality or customer service. Identify weaknesses as well as strengths.

Estimate how long current strengths and weaknesses are likely to continue. The competitive advantage to be gained from current strengths depends on how long they will last and how difficult they are for competitors to overcome or duplicate. For example, a pharmaceutical company with a patented new drug that is better and cheaper than any alternatives has a strong competitive advantage that will likely continue for several years. In contrast, a service company that devises a new and attractive promotion (e.g., special discounts) may only enjoy its competitive advantage for a few weeks or months (as long as it takes competitors to imitate it). An organization that is first into a new market has an advantage, but only if it is difficult for competitors to follow quickly. A product or service that is costly to develop but easy and cheap to duplicate offers little advantage. Capabilities should be evaluated together, not in isolation. A unique resource (e.g., an improved product or process) may offer no competitive advantage if organizational weaknesses or external constraints prevent it from being used effectively. A weakness may not be so serious if it can be corrected quickly or offset by other strengths.

- **Identify core competencies.**

A core competency is the knowledge and capability to carry out a particular type of activity (Barney, 1991). Unlike tangible resources, which are depleted when used, core competencies increase as they are used (Prahalad & Hamel, 1990). A core competency usually involves a combination of technical expertise and application skills. For example, a core competency for W. L. Gore is their expertise about a special type of material (GORE-TEX) and their capability to discover and exploit new uses for this material. Core competencies provide a potential source of continuing competitive advantage if they are used to provide innovative, high-quality products and services that cannot easily be copied or duplicated by competitors. Core competencies can help an organization remain competitive in its current businesses and diversify into new businesses. Canon's core competencies in optics, acquired as a producer of quality cameras, enabled the company to become a successful producer of copiers, fax machines, semiconductor lithographic equipment, and specialized video systems, while continuing to be a successful producer of cameras and the first to develop a microprocessor-controlled camera. Competence in display systems, which involves knowledge of microprocessor design, ultrathin precision casing, material science, and miniaturization enabled Casio to be successful in such diverse businesses as calculators, miniature television sets, digital watches, monitors for laptop computers, and automotive dashboards (Prahalad & Hamel, 1990).

- **Evaluate the need for a major change in strategy.**

One of the most important responsibilities of executives is to help interpret events and determine whether the organization needs a different strategy or just incremental improvements in the existing strategy. A new strategy may be needed when there is a performance crisis for the organization and established practices are not sufficient to deal with it. When a serious crisis is imminent, it is appropriate to be pragmatic and flexible rather than defensive and tradition bound in deciding how to respond. In this situation, a leader who attempts to defend the old, obsolete strategy rather than proposing necessary changes is likely to be replaced. However, proposing a different strategy when the current strategy can be easily fixed is also dangerous, both for the organization and the leader. A new strategy may not be needed if disappointing performance seems to be caused by a temporary worsening of conditions or by problems in implementing the current strategy.

- **Identify promising strategies.**

If a major change in strategy is necessary, it is better to begin by exploring a range of possible strategies. Focusing attention too quickly on one strategy will preclude finding better ones that are less obvious. Success in finding a new strategy will be greater if the quest is guided by a clear, meaningful conception of the organization's mission, long-term strategic objectives, core competencies, and current performance. Sometimes it is necessary to redefine the mission of the organization to include new activities that are relevant for the environment and the organization's core competencies. For example, Williams Company was making pipelines for transporting oil and gas, but it was losing business to larger competitors with lower costs. Recognizing that it was unlikely to find a way to compete successfully in the pipeline business, top management looked around for other opportunities to use the company's core competencies. They discovered that their piping was perfect for housing fiber optic cable, a newly emerging market, and they could market it to cable television and telecommunications companies at a lower price than other suppliers in that industry (Worley, Hetchin, & Ross, 1996).

- **Evaluate the likely outcomes of a strategy.**

A strategy should be evaluated in terms of the likely consequences for the attainment of key objectives. Relevant consequences include benefits and costs for the various stakeholders in the organization. The costs include the extra resources and lost productivity associated with any organizational changes necessary to support the strategy.

It is difficult to forecast the consequences of a strategic change, especially when competitors can adjust their own strategies to cope with your changes. A number of procedures have been developed to assess likely customer response to a new product or service (market surveys, focus groups, product trials in selected locations or markets). Scenarios provide another way to improve the evaluation of likely consequences for a proposed change (Van der Heijden, 1996). A scenario is a detailed description of what the future will be like if a proposed change or strategy is pursued. Scenarios can be developed to describe what would happen under the most and least favorable conditions, as well as under the most likely conditions. The process of developing the scenarios often provides insights about unexpected consequences of a strategy and implicit assumptions that were not realistic.

- **Involve other executives in selecting a strategy.**

A key responsibility of executives is to make strategic decisions that will improve the organization. However, few leaders are so brilliant that they can make such decisions alone. The strategy should be developed with the full participation of other members of the top management team. In the event of considerable uncertainty and disagreement about the best strategy, it is wise to select one that is flexible enough to permit later modification after more knowledge about its effectiveness can be obtained. Systematic procedures have been developed by scholars and consultants to facilitate the process of strategy formulation by a group of executives. One example is the scenario development procedure called *Quest* (Bennis & Nanus, 1985), which is a two-day exercise held with executives and relevant outsiders to discuss long-range opportunities and risks, and possible reactions by the organization.

Summary

A major controversy in the leadership literature is whether chief executives have much impact on the effectiveness of an organization. Critics argue that a CEO has little influence on organization performance due to constraints such as powerful stakeholders, internal coalitions, a strong culture, scarce resources, strong competitors, and unfavorable economic conditions. According to the critics, the importance of top executives is often exaggerated because people with biased attributions discount the importance of other explanations such as industry performance and economic conditions. The attribution research demonstrates that leaders have less influence over organizational events than is often assumed, but the research does not support the conclusion that leaders are unimportant. Moreover, when artifacts are eliminated, succession studies demonstrate a moderately strong influence of top executives on organizational performance. Despite all the constraints, individual executives and executive teams can still have a substantial influence on the effectiveness of an organization.

A CEO has the most potential impact on the performance of the organization when there is a crisis and the strategy of the organization is no longer aligned with its environment. A major change is more likely to be successful if initiated early before a crisis becomes serious and the organization no longer has any slack resources to finance it. However, it is more difficult to initiate major change when no need for it is apparent and resistance is strong.

The amount of change is also affected by power struggles among different subunits or coalitions. According to strategic contingencies theory, the evolutionary process of power acquisition and loss will ensure that strategic decisions are made by the most qualified people. However, this evolutionary process may not occur if the dominant faction's power is institutionalized through political processes. Major strategic change is less likely to be initiated by a chief executive who has been in office for a long period of time, or by an internal successor.

An executive team is more important in a complex, rapidly changing environment that places many external demands on the CEO. Teams are also more important in an organization with diverse but highly interdependent business units, because a single leader is unlikely to have the broad expertise necessary to direct and integrate the activities of these units. The executive characteristics necessary for team effectiveness depend on the organizational context in which the team must operate, on the nature of the environment, and on the leadership behavior of the CEO. Diversity of backgrounds and perspectives improves the quality of the strategic decisions made by a team facing a turbulent, uncertain environment, but diversity also makes it more difficult to reach consensus.

The flexible leadership theory explains how CEOs and other executives can influence the prosperity and survival of the organization by improving efficiency and process reliability, human relations and resources, and innovation and adaptation. The relative importance of these organizational processes and the potential trade-offs among them are determined by aspects of the situation such as the type of organization and the amount of change in the external environment. It is a difficult challenge to balance these trade-offs, adapt to changing conditions, and coordinate the efforts of multiple leaders in the organization.

External monitoring provides information needed for strategic planning and crisis management. To detect threats and discover opportunities in a timely way, top management must actively monitor relevant sectors of the environment, sources of dependency for the organization, and current performance. A strategy for adapting to the environment is more likely to be effective if it builds on core competencies, is relevant to long-term objectives, and is feasible in terms of current capabilities.

Review and Discussion Questions

1. Briefly summarize major research findings on attributions about leadership as a determinant of organizational effectiveness.
2. What conditions limit the discretion of a CEO?
3. How is CEO discretion and potential effectiveness related to the evolutionary cycle of the organization?
4. How important is executive leadership in organizations? Defend your position.
5. How is organizational change affected by political processes and the relative influence of different factions over strategic decisions?
6. How is CEO behavior related to tenure in office?
7. What are the potential benefits and problems with executive teams?
8. What conditions determine the effectiveness of an executive team?
9. What are some guidelines for external monitoring?
10. What are some guidelines for strategy formulation?
11. What are the major performance determinants for organizations, and what trade-offs occur among them?
12. How can leaders influence each type of performance determinant?

Key Terms

- adaptation
- attributions
- chief executive officer (CEO)
- competitive strategy
- convergence
- core competencies
- external and internal constraints

- external monitoring
- executive team
- executive tenure
- flexible leadership
- impression management
- leadership succession
- performance determinants
- reorientation

- scenarios
- strategy formulation
- strategic leadership
- strategic planning
- trade-offs among determinants

CASES

Columbia Corporation

Columbia Corp. is a young, rapidly growing company that manufactures computer accessories and specialized components for networked computer workstations. It has some unique products and a strong reputation for quality. However, the market is very competitive, and continued success requires innovation and high-quality products. The company currently employs 500 people, a number that has doubled in the past three years. Sales have nearly tripled in the same period, and a recent contract with a large computer company will increase sales even more. However, along with this success the company is also experiencing some problems. Quality rejects have begun to increase, and in recent months the company failed repeatedly to meet delivery schedules.

The top executives include Matt Walsh, CEO and founder of the company, and the vice presidents of production, engineering, sales, and accounting. Walsh is a forceful manager who tightly controls important decisions in the company. The other executives are required to get his approval before making any significant changes in operations. Walsh's style has been to deal with each VP separately, rather than meeting as a group to address problems. Relationships between departments

have been deteriorating for the past two years. Distrust, competition, and political maneuvering have increased, and Walsh intervenes frequently to resolve conflicts between executives. The distrust and hostility has spilled over to relationships among lower-level employees of the departments.

The production VP believes that the rash of quality problems is the result of frequent changes in product design by the engineering department. The production supervisors have little warning of these changes and insufficient time to determine how to make necessary adjustments in production methods. As for the delivery problems, the production VP believes that the sales department makes unrealistic promises to win new customers. Production capacity has not increased fast enough to meet the growing volume of orders, and additional delays are caused by product modifications designed for customers by engineering. The sales VP blames the late deliveries on manufacturing delays. She believes the production people spend so much time trying to correct quality problems that they can't get the product out the door. The sales VP and the engineering VP both believe the production VP is set in his ways and unwilling to adapt to the special needs of important customers.

The sales VP is upset with the accounting VP for tightening customer credit requirements without prior notice. She only discovered the new policy when a key customer complained after credit was denied on a large order. The sales VP believes the new policy will reduce sales, and the reduction will be blamed on her. She complained to Walsh, who apparently approved the decision without understanding the implications. The accounting VP also upset the production VP by abruptly canceling all overtime for production employees for the remainder of this month. This action appears unwarranted, and it put production even farther behind schedule. The production VP has asked Walsh to reverse this decision.

Concerned about the growing problems, Walsh asked a management consultant for advice on what to do. The consultant told Walsh that he needs an effective top management team that will work together smoothly to guide the company through this period of rapid, turbulent growth. The executive team needs to become more adept at understanding and resolving key problems such as insufficient production capacity and declining quality. Walsh asked the consultant for advice on how to create an effective top management team that would take responsibility for shaping the future direction of the company. This change would be consistent with his desire to become less involved in the day-to-day management of the company so that he can spend more time in outside pursuits. The company has made him a millionaire, and he wants to begin enjoying some of the benefits from his success as an entrepreneur. He finds dealing with the day-to-day problems of managing an established company much less fulfilling than it was to create a new company. ∎

SOURCE: Copyright © 1997 by Gary Yukl.

QUESTIONS

1. What issues must be resolved to create an effective executive team?

2. What types of changes should be considered?

3. To what extent is Matt Walsh part of the problem?

4. If Walsh decided to retire, and you were hired from the outside to be the new CEO, explain briefly what you would do during your first year on the job.

Turnaround at Nissan

In 1999, Nissan was in a state of serious decline and had lost money in all but one of the previous eight years. Only Renault's willingness to assume part of Nissan's debt saved the Japanese company from going bankrupt. As part of the deal, the French auto maker appointed Carlos Ghosn to become Nissan's chief operating officer. However, there was widespread skepticism that the alliance between Renault and Nissan could succeed, or that someone who was not Japanese could provide effective leadership at Nissan.

During the three months prior to assuming the position of COO at Nissan, Ghosn met with hundreds of people, including employees, union officials, suppliers, and customers, to learn more about the company and its strengths and weaknesses. From these meetings and earlier experiences with turn-around assignments, Ghosn understood that major changes would not be successful if they were dictated by him and the experts he brought with him from Renault. Soon after assuming his new position at Nissan in June 1999, Ghosn created nine cross-functional teams and gave them responsibility for determining what needed to be done to revive the company. Such teams had never been used before at Nissan, and it was unusual in a Japanese company to involve a broad cross-section of managers in determining major changes.

The cross-functional teams examined different aspects of company operations to identify problems and recommend solutions to Ghosn and the executive committee. Several interrelated problems were identified, and they were mostly consistent with Ghosn's initial impressions. The poor financial performance at Nissan was a joint result of declining sales and excessive costs, and weak management was the primary reason for the failure to resolve these problems. Management lacked a coherent strategy, a strong profit orientation, and a clear focus on customers. There was little cooperation across functions, and there was no urgency about the need for major change.

One reason for excessive costs at Nissan was that only half of the available capacity in the company's factories was being used; production capacity was sufficient to build almost a million more cars a year than the company could sell. To reduce costs, Ghosn decided to close five factories in Japan and eliminate more than 21,000 jobs, which was 14 percent of Nissan's global workforce. To simplify production operations at the remaining factories and make them more efficient, Ghosn planned to reduce the number of car platforms by half and the number of powertrain combinations by a third. Plant closings can undermine relations with employees, and Ghosn took steps to ensure that employees knew why they were necessary and who would be affected.

In general, he understood that most employees prefer to learn what would happen to them and prepare for it, rather than remaining in a state of uncertainty and anxiety. Ghosn attempted to minimize adverse effects on employees by selling subsidiaries and using natural attrition, early retirements, and opportunities for part-time work at other company facilities.

Purchasing costs represent 60 percent of the operating costs for an automaker, and Nissan was paying much more than necessary for the parts and supplies used to build its cars. After comparing expenses at Nissan and Renault, Ghosn discovered that Nissan's purchasing costs were 25 percent higher. One reason was the practice of purchasing small orders from many suppliers instead of larger orders from a smaller number of global sources. It would be necessary to reduce the number of suppliers, even though this action was unprecedented in a country where supplier relationships were considered sacrosanct. Higher purchasing costs were also a result of overly exacting specifications imposed on suppliers by Nissan engineers. The engineers who worked with the cross-functional team on purchasing initially defended their specifications, but when they finally realized that they were wrong, the team was able to achieve greater savings than expected. Excessive purchasing costs are not the type of problem that can be solved quickly, but after three years of persistent effort it was possible to achieve Ghosn's goal of a 20 percent reduction.

Years of declining sales at Nissan were caused by a lack of customer appeal for most of the company's cars. When Ghosn made a detailed analysis of sales data he discovered that only 4 of the 43 different Nissan models had sufficient sales to be profitable. Final decisions about the design of new models were made by the head of engineering. Designers were taking orders from engineers who focused completely on performance, and there was little effort to determine what types of cars customers really wanted. To increase the customer appeal of Nissan vehicles, Ghosn hired the innovative designer Shiro Nakamura, who became another key leader in the turnaround effort. The designers would now have more authority over design decisions, and Ghosn encouraged them to be innovative rather than merely copying competitors. For the first time in more than a decade, Nissan began coming up with cars that excited customers both in Japan and abroad. Ghosn planned to introduce 12 new models over a three-year period, but the time necessary to bring a new model into production meant that few would be available until 2002.

Another reason for declining sales was Nissan's weak distribution network. In Japan strong brand loyalty is reinforced by efforts to maintain close relationships with customers, and it is essential for the dealerships to be managed by people who can build customer loyalty and convert it into repeat sales. In 1999, many Nissan dealerships in Japan were subsidiaries managed by Nissan executives nearing retirement, and they viewed their role more in social terms than as an entrepreneur responsible for helping the company to increase market share and profits. Ghosn reduced the number of company-owned dealerships (10 percent were closed or sold), and he took steps to improve management at the remaining dealerships.

Saving Nissan would also require major changes in human resource practices, such as guaranteed lifetime employment and pay and promotion based on seniority. Transforming these strongly embedded aspects of the company culture without engendering resentment and demoralizing employees was perhaps the most difficult challenge. The changes would primarily affect nonunionized employees at Nissan, including the managers. A merit pay plan was established, and instead of being rewarded for seniority, employees were now expected to earn their promotions and salary increases through effective performance. Areas of accountability were sharply defined so that performance could be measured in relation to specific goals. New bonuses provided employees an opportunity to earn up to a third of their annual salary for effective performance, and hundreds of upper-level managers could also earn stock options. These and other changes in human resource practices would make it possible for Ghosn to gradually replace weak middle and upper level managers with more competent successors.

In October 1999, Ghosn announced the plan for revitalizing Nissan. He had been careful to avoid any earlier leaks about individual changes that would be criticized without understanding why they were necessary and how they fit into the overall plan. The announcement included a pledge that Ghosn and the executive committee would resign if Nissan failed to show a profit by the end of 2000. It was an impressive demonstration of his sincerity and commitment, and it made what he was asking of others seem more acceptable. Fortunately, the primary objectives of the change were all achieved on schedule, and by 2001 earnings were at a record high for the company. That year Ghosn was appointed as the chief executive officer at Nissan, and in 2005, he would become the CEO of Renault as well. ■

SOURCES: This case is based on information in C. Ghosn and P. Ries, *Shift: Inside Nissan's Historic Revival* (New York: Currency-Doubleday, 2005); and A. Taylor III, "Nissan's turnaround artist: Carlos Ghosn is giving Japan a lesson in how to compete," *Fortune International*, February 18, 2002, p. 34.

QUESTIONS

1. What was done to improve efficiency, adaptation, and human relations, and how were the potential trade-offs among these performance determinants handled?

2. What effective change management practices were used at Nissan (see Chapter 10)?

13

DEVELOPING
LEADERSHIP SKILLS

Learning Objectives

After studying this chapter you should be able to:

- Understand the importance of leadership training and development in organizations.

- Understand how coaching, mentoring, action learning, special assignments, simulations, and 360-degree feedback are used for management development.

- Understand the benefits and limitations of the primary methods for leadership training and development.

- Understand the findings in research conducted to evaluate the methods.

- Understand the organizational conditions that facilitate leadership training and development.

- Understand what leaders can do to encourage and facilitate the leadership development of their subordinates.

- Understand what leaders can do to develop their own skills.

- Understand why leader development should be integrated with human resource management and strategic planning.

The increasing rate of change in the external environment of organizations, and the many new challenges facing leaders suggest that success as a leader in the twenty-first century will require a higher level of skill and some new competencies as well. As the need for leadership competencies increases, new techniques for developing them are being invented and old techniques are being refined. Leadership development is now a multibillion dollar business in the United States (Fulmer & Vicere, 1996).

Leadership competencies can be developed in a number of ways, including (1) formal training, (2) developmental activities, and (3) self-help activities. Most formal training occurs during a defined time period, and it is usually conducted away from the manager's immediate work site by training professionals (e.g., a short workshop at a training center, a management course at a university). Developmental activities are usually embedded within operational job assignments or conducted in conjunction with those assignments. The developmental activities can take many forms, including coaching by the boss or an outside consultant, mentoring by someone at a higher level in the organization, and special assignments that provide new challenges and opportunities to learn relevant skills. Self-help activities are carried out by individuals on their own. Examples include reading books, viewing videos, listening to audiotapes, and using interactive computer programs for skill building.

The effectiveness of training programs, developmental experiences, and self-help activities depends in part on organizational conditions that facilitate or inhibit learning of leadership skills and the application of this learning by managers. Facilitating conditions include things such as support for skill development from top management, reward systems that encourage skill development, and cultural values that support continuous learning. This chapter examines various approaches for leadership development and the key facilitating conditions.

Leadership Training Programs

Formal training programs are widely used to improve leadership in organizations. Most large organizations have management training programs of one kind or another, and many organizations send their managers to outside seminars and workshops (Saari, Johnson, McLaughlin, & Zimmerle, 1988). Most leadership training programs are designed to increase generic skills and behaviors relevant for managerial effectiveness and advancement. The training is usually designed more for lower- and middle-level managers than for top management, and there is usually more emphasis on skills needed by managers in their current position than on skills needed to prepare for promotion to a higher position (Rothwell & Kazanas, 1994). However, the old pattern of selecting mostly fast track managers for leadership training and providing it only once or twice during a manager's career is gradually being replaced by a series of leadership training opportunities that are available to any manager in the organization at appropriate points in his or her career (Vicere & Fulmer, 1997).

Leadership training can take many forms, from short workshops that last only a few hours and focus on a narrow set of skills, to programs that last for a year or more and cover a wide range of skills. Many consulting companies conduct short leadership workshops that are open to managers from different organizations. Other consulting companies design leadership training programs tailored to the needs of a particular organization. Most universities offer management development programs (e.g., Executive MBA) that take 1–3 years to complete on a part-time basis. Many organizations compensate employees for the cost of attending outside workshops and courses. Many large organizations (e.g., General Electric, Motorola, Toyota, Unilever) operate a management training center or corporate university for employees (Fulmer, 1997; Meister, 1994).

A number of training programs are based on the application of a particular leadership theory. Some examples include training programs based on least preferred coworker (LPC) contingency theory (Fiedler & Chemers, 1982), the normative decision model (Vroom & Jago, 1988), transformational leadership (Bass, 1996; Bass & Avolio, 1990b), situational leadership theory (Hersey & Blanchard, 1984), and managerial motivation (Miner, 1986). Reviews of research on these theory-based training programs find evidence that they sometimes improve managerial effectiveness (Bass, 1990; Latham, 1988; Tetrault, Schriesheim, & Neider, 1988). However, it is important to note that most of the studies fail to establish whether improved effectiveness is the result of actually applying the theory, or is merely the result of gaining more interpersonal and administrative skill.

Designing Effective Training

The effectiveness of formal training programs depends greatly on how well they are designed. The design of training should take into account learning theory, the specific learning objectives, characteristics of the trainees, and practical considerations such as constraints and costs in relation to benefits. Leader training is more likely to be successful if designed and conducted in a way that is consistent with findings in research on learning processes and training techniques (see reviews by Baldwin & Padgett, 1993; Campbell, 1988; Howell & Cooke, 1989; Noe & Ford, 1992; Salas & Cannon Bowers, 2000; Tannenbaum & Yukl, 1992). Key findings are summarized briefly in this section (see also Table 13-1).

Clear Learning Objectives

Learning objectives describe the behaviors, skills, or knowledge trainees are expected to acquire from the training. Specific learning objectives help to clarify the purpose of the training and its relevance for trainees. In most cases it is useful to explain not only what will be learned, but also why the training is worthwhile for trainees. Thus, at the beginning of a training program, the trainer should identify clear learning objectives and explain why the training will help people improve their leadership effectiveness.

Clear, Meaningful Content

The training content should be clear and meaningful. It should build on a trainee's prior knowledge, and it should focus attention on important things. The training should include lots of examples that are concrete and relevant. Periodic summaries and restatements of key points should be used to facilitate comprehension and memorization of material. Conceptual learning can be increased by providing relevant category systems, diagrams, analogies, and models. The models and theories should be simple enough to be remembered and relevant enough to help trainees interpret their experiences.

TABLE 13-1   Conditions for Successful Training

- Clear learning objectives
- Clear, meaningful content
- Appropriate sequencing of content
- Appropriate mix of training methods
- Opportunity for active practice
- Relevant, timely feedback
- High trainee self-confidence
- Appropriate follow-up activities

Appropriate Sequencing of Content

The training activities should be organized and sequenced in a way that will facilitate learning. For example, it is better to learn prerequisite concepts, symbols, rules, and procedures before doing activities that require this knowledge. Training should progress from simple to more complex ideas. Complex material should be broken into components or modules that are easier to learn separately. Appropriate intervals between training sessions provide opportunities for repeated practice, and rest breaks help to avoid fatigue during long training sessions.

Appropriate Mix of Training Methods

The choice of training methods should take into account the trainee's current skill level, motivation, and capacity to understand and remember complex information. The methods should be appropriate for the knowledge, skills, attitudes, or behavior to be learned. For example, it is usually better to demonstrate a procedure than to describe it in abstract terms. The methods should be appropriate for the training conditions and setting. For example, role plays are difficult to use in a very large class. Training methods should be varied as needed to maintain trainee interest. Lectures longer than 30 minutes may lose the interest and attention of trainees, so it is desirable to shift periodically from lecturing to discussions and exercises.

Opportunity for Active Practice

Trainees should actively practice the skills to be learned (e.g., practice behaviors, recall information from memory, apply principles in doing a task). Retention and transfer are greater when a trainee must restate principles (rather than just recognizing or recalling them) and must apply the principles to varying situations and adapt them accordingly (rather than just learning one way to deal with one type of situation). Practice should occur both during the training sessions and shortly afterward in the job situation. Skills involving team activities should be practiced by the team under realistic conditions.

Relevant, Timely Feedback

Trainees should receive relevant feedback from a variety of available sources, and feedback should be accurate, timely, and constructive. Learning of tasks that require analytical processing is facilitated by helping trainees to monitor their own progress and evaluate what they know and do not know. Feedback may be of little value if the learner is using an inappropriate mental model and the feedback does not help the trainee develop a better one. Learning can be facilitated by showing people how to seek and use relevant feedback about their strategy for doing a task (e.g., what strategy was used, what was done correctly and what mistakes were made, what might have been done instead.). Diagnostic questions, analytical procedures, and clues about the meaning of various patterns of results help people analyze and interpret performance feedback.

Enhancement of Trainee Self-Confidence

The instructional processes should enhance trainee self-efficacy and expectations that the training will be successful. The trainer should communicate expectations of success and be patient and supportive with trainees who experience learning difficulties. Trainees should have ample opportunities to experience progress and success in mastering the material and learning the skills. For example, training should begin with simple behaviors that can be mastered easily, then progress to more complex behaviors as trainees become more confident. Praise and encouragement should be used whenever appropriate to bolster the confidence of trainees.

Appropriate Follow-Up Activities

Complex skills are difficult to learn in a short training course with limited opportunities for practice and feedback. Learning of such skills can be enhanced by appropriate follow-up activities. One useful approach is to hold a follow-up session at an appropriate interval after the training program is completed to review progress in the application of learned skills, discuss successes and problems, and provide additional coaching and support. Another useful approach is to have trainees carry out specific projects that require the use of skills learned in the training. Meetings are held periodically with the trainees to review progress, discuss what was learned, and provide additional support and coaching. Other types of follow-up activities include short refresher courses and periodic coaching sessions with individuals.

Special Techniques for Leadership Training

A large variety of methods have been used successfully for leadership training (Bass, 1990; Burke & Day, 1986; Latham, 1988; Tetrault, Schriesheim, & Neider, 1988). Lectures, demonstrations, procedural manuals, videotapes, equipment simulators, and interactive computer tutorials are used to learn technical skills. Cases, exercises, business games, simulations, and videotapes are used to learn conceptual and administrative skills. Lectures, case discussion, videotapes, role playing, and group exercises are used to learn interpersonal skills. Three techniques widely used for leadership training are behavioral role modeling, cases, and large-scale simulations. These techniques will be examined in more detail.

Behavior Role Modeling

Behavior role modeling uses a combination of two older methods (demonstration and role playing) to enhance interpersonal skills. The theoretical basis for behavioral role modeling is Bandura's (1986) social learning theory. Early proponents of behavior role modeling (Goldstein & Sorcher, 1974) argued that merely presenting and demonstrating behavior guidelines is not sufficient to ensure people will learn and use behavior that is awkward, difficult, or contrary to typical ways of dealing with a tense interpersonal situation. Such behavior is unlikely to be learned unless trainees actually practice it and receive encouragement and feedback in a nonthreatening learning environment.

In behavior role modeling training, small groups of trainees observe someone demonstrate how to handle a particular type of interpersonal problem (e.g., provide corrective feedback, provide coaching), then they practice the behavior in a role play and get nonthreatening feedback. The effective behaviors are usually shown on a short videotape. An alternative approach is for the trainer to model the appropriate behaviors in a role play conducted in front of the class with a trainee or another trainer. Sometimes both positive and negative behaviors are modeled to show the difference, but research on the benefits of including negative behaviors is still inconclusive (Baldwin, 1991, 1992; Trimble, Nathan, & Decker, 1991). In most programs the trainer explains the learning points prior to the modeling demonstration, then trainees observe them enacted in the video. Sometimes learning points also appear on the video as the behaviors occur.

The next step is for trainees to participate in a role play to practice applying the learning points. These role plays can be conducted in front of the class or in small groups. The latter approach gives several trainees the opportunity to practice at the same time and is less threatening to them. Feedback can be obtained from a variety of sources, including the trainer, other trainees who serve as observers, or a videotape of behavior in the role play. In most programs trainees are asked to develop specific action plans for implementing the behavior guidelines back on the job. After writing these action plans, trainees can discuss them in dyads, in small groups, or with the trainer privately to do some reality testing and obtain guidance and encouragement.

Burke and Day (1986) conducted a meta-analysis of studies evaluating behavior modeling and concluded that it was one of the most effective training methods for managers. Subsequent studies and reviews also support the utility of this training method (e.g., Latham, 1989; Mayer & Russell, 1987; Robertson, 1990; Smith-Jentsch, Salas, & Baker, 1996), but the reviewers also expressed concerns about the limitations of the research. Most studies found evidence of learning, but few studies measured actual behavior change back on the job or improvement in managerial effectiveness. Few studies investigated issues such as when, why, and for whom behavioral role modeling training method is effective.

Another major question is the type of skills for which this training method is appropriate. Behavior role modeling seems useful for concrete behaviors that are known to be effective in a particular type of leadership situation, but there is little evidence that the method is effective for teaching flexible adaptive behaviors or cognitive knowledge. Behavior modeling programs that emphasize rigid, arbitrary learning points are unlikely to promote flexible, adaptive behavior (Parry & Reich, 1984; Robertson, 1990). Unless trainees are encouraged to understand the general principles upon which the learning points are based, they are not prepared to deal with situations where some of the learning points are inappropriate. A possible remedy is to explain general principles, then encourage trainees to devise alternative ways for applying them in varying situations. More research is needed to resolve these questions and determine the most effective procedures for behavior modeling programs.

Case Discussion

Cases are descriptions of events in an organization. There are many types of cases, ranging from detailed descriptions of events that occurred over a period of several years to brief descriptions of incidents lasting only a few minutes. Cases are used in a variety of ways in courses to develop management skills. Long cases about an organization's competitive strategy and financial performance are used to practice analytical and decision-making skills. Trainees analyze a detailed description of a business situation and use management principles and quantitative decision techniques to determine how to deal with it. The case may be discussed in the class as a whole or in small groups that report back on their findings and recommendations. Use of small groups requires more time, but it increases the level of active participation. After recommendations are presented, they are evaluated and compared to what was actually done by the organization.

One potential benefit of a case is to increase understanding about situations managers encounter. A case can be used to show how a problem or event may appear different to people who do not have the same values, interests, and assumptions. For example, a conflict or controversial decision may be described from the perspective of different parties. Most cases are still in written form, but dramatized cases on videotape are increasingly being used to help people vicariously experience some of the more stressful and difficult situations they may encounter.

Another use of cases is to increase understanding about effective managerial behavior. Trainees analyze a detailed description of a manager's actions to identify appropriate and inappropriate behavior and make recommendations about what the manager should have done or should do next. This type of case is usually short, and it emphasizes human relations aspects of management. Such cases may be used also to assess a person's ability to analyze the reason for human relations problems and identify effective ways of handling interpersonal situations.

Research on the effectiveness of using cases for leadership training is still limited. The following guidelines for trainers summarize prevailing opinions about conditions likely to facilitate learning.

- Clarify expectations for trainees. Explain the purpose of the case, how it will be used, and what trainees are expected to do.
- Ask questions to encourage and facilitate participation in the discussion. Be receptive to alternative viewpoints, and avoid dominating the discussion.
- Emphasize the complexity of problems and the desirability of identifying alternative remedies.
- Use different diagnoses as an opportunity to demonstrate how people approach a problem with different assumptions, biases, and priorities.
- Ask trainees to relate the case to their work experience. Discussing prior experiences reduces dependence on the case to provide insight and provoke thought.
- Vary the composition of discussion groups to expose trainees to different points of view.

Business Games and Simulations

Business games and simulations have been used for many years for management training. As with cases, simulations require trainees to analyze complex problems and make decisions. However, unlike cases, trainees must deal with the consequences of their decisions. After decisions are made, trainees usually receive feedback about what happened as a result of their decisions. Most business games emphasize quantitative financial information and are used to practice analytical and decision skills taught in a formal training program. Games can be used also to assess training needs, the success of prior training, or the validity of a manager's mental model for a particular decision situation. The most sophisticated simulations are based on a systems model of the complex causal relationships among important variables for a particular type of company and industry. Participants work individually or in small groups to make managerial decisions about product pricing, advertising, production output, product development, and capital investment. Following is an example of one participant's experience in a computerized simulation of a start-up airline company:

> Sally stared blankly off into space. What had started out so well had turned into a nightmare. She had taken over an airline company that had three planes and gross revenues of $32 million a year, and in just four years she had grown the company to a half-billion-dollar firm with a fleet of 100 aircraft. She had sweated over decisions in the areas of human resources, aircraft acquisition, marketing, pricing, and service scope, and in each case, her airline had triumphed. But then she had reached a turning point. Her market had collapsed, Her service quality had eroded. Losses had piled up so fast that the ability of her company to absorb them was in doubt. It would all turn around though, it had to. All she needed was one more quarter. . . . But instead of the next quarter's financial reports she received notification that her creditors were forcing her into bankruptcy. Time had run out. . . . What did I do wrong, she thought. All her decisions had seemed to make sense at the time. She reached over and pressed the save button. She would have to analyze her decisions to see what went wrong later. Right now she had another strategy she wanted to try. She hit the restart button to begin the simulation. She was back to having three planes and gross revenues of $32 million. (Kreutzer, 1994, p. 536)

Large-scale simulations evolved from business games, but they combine many of the features of other training methods such as human relations cases, role playing, the in-basket exercise, and group problem-solving exercises. Large-scale simulations emphasize interpersonal skills as much as cognitive skills and decision making. A large-scale simulation typically involves a single hypothetical organization with multiple divisions (e.g., bank, plastics company). Participants are assigned to different positions in the organization and carry out the managerial responsibilities for a period of one or two days. Prior to the simulation, each participant is provided extensive background information, such as a description of the organization's products and services, financial reports, industry and market conditions, an organization chart, and the duties and responsibilities of the position. Each participant is also given copies of recent correspondence (e.g., memos, reports) with other members of the organization and outsiders. Participants have separate work spaces, but they are allowed to communicate by various media (e.g., memos, e-mail) and to schedule meetings. Participants make strategic and operational decisions just as they would in a real organization. They react to each other's decisions, but unlike business games, they usually do not receive information about the financial consequences of their decisions during the simulation itself.

After the simulation is completed, participants receive feedback about group processes and their individual skills and behaviors. Feedback is usually provided by observers who track the behavior and decisions of the participants. Additional feedback can be provided by videotaping participant conversations and meetings. The facilitators help the participants understand how well they functioned as executives in collecting and processing information, analyzing and solving problems, communicating with others, influencing others, and planning strategy and operations. The best known of large-scale simulation(called Looking Glass)was developed by the Center for Creative Leadership (Kaplan, Lombardo, & Mazique, 1985; Van Velsor, Ruderman, & Phillips, 1989). It is a simulation of a glass manufacturing company. Other large-scale simulations have been developed to depict specific types of organizations such as banks, insurance companies, chemical-plastics companies, and public school systems.

What participants learn from a large-scale simulation depends in part on who participates. If participants are strangers from a variety of different organizations, most of the learning will be at the level of individual self-awareness of strengths and weaknesses. However, if the participants are a family group of managers from the same organization, their behavior in the simulation will reflect the prevailing culture and relationships in that organization. The feedback to participants in family groups can be used to help them understand and improve their decision-making and conflict resolution processes. For example, most of the managers from one company that participated in the Looking Glass simulation made hasty decisions and looked for information to justify them, rather than carefully gathering information to determine the nature of the problem and available opportunities. During the debrief, participants became aware of their ineffective behavior and realized that it was consistent with the culture of their company.

The research on business games and simulations is still limited, but there is increasing evidence they can be very useful for leadership development (Keys & Wolfe, 1990; Thornton & Cleveland, 1990; Wolf & Roberts, 1993). Nevertheless, more research is needed to determine what types of learning occur and the conditions that facilitate learning. It was once assumed that interpersonal skills and problem-solving skills would be learned automatically by participants in a simulation. Now it is obvious that the potential benefits are unlikely to be achieved without extensive preparation, planned interventions with specific feedback and coaching during the simulation, and intensive debriefing with discussion of lessons learned after the simulation.

Some serious limitations in most large-scale simulations need to be addressed. The short time period for the simulation makes it difficult for participants to make effective use of behaviors that necessarily involve a series of related actions over time, such as inspirational leadership, networking, team building, developing subordinates, and delegation. A possible remedy is to spread out the simulation sessions over several weeks, which also provides more opportunity for facilitators to provide feedback and coaching after each session. Improved communication technology makes it easier to use virtual meetings among team members who normally work in widely dispersed locations, which can solve some of the logistical problems of holding repeated meetings for team members over a longer period of time. There is a continuing effort to design more flexible and realistic simulations that incorporate more challenging developmental activities and provide more feedback about participant behavior and its consequences for the organization.

Learning from Experience

Much of the skill essential for effective leadership is learned from experience rather than from formal training programs (Davies & Easterby-Smith, 1984; Kelleher, Finestone, & Lowy, 1986; Lindsey, Homes, & McCall, 1987; McCall, Lombardo, & Morrison, 1988). Special assignments provide an opportunity to develop and refine leadership skills during the performance of regular job duties. Coaching and mentoring can be used to help managers interpret their experiences and learn new skills. Managers can emulate the effective behaviors modeled by competent bosses (McCall et al., 1988; Manz & Sims, 1981). Managers can also learn what not to do from superiors who are ineffective (Lindsey et al., 1987; McCall et al., 1988).

The extent to which leadership skills and values are developed during operational assignments depends on the type of experiences afforded by these assignments. Researchers at the Center for Creative Leadership have studied the relationship between specific types of job experiences and leadership development (Lindsey et al., 1987; McCall et al., 1988; McCauley, 1986; McCauley, Lombardo, & Usher, 1989). A more recent study by Mumford and his associates (Mumford et al., 2000) examined the relationship between experience and development of leadership skills for officers in the U.S. Army. These studies indicate that learning from experience is affected by amount of challenge, variety of tasks or assignments, and quality of feedback.

Amount of Challenge

A challenging situation is one that involves unusual problems to solve, difficult obstacles to overcome, and risky decisions to make. The research at CCL found that challenge was greatest in jobs that required a manager to deal with change, take responsibility for high-visibility problems, influence people without authority, handle external pressure, and work without much guidance or support from superiors. Some examples of challenging situations include dealing with a merger or reorganization, leading a cross-functional team or task force, implementing a major change, coping with unfavorable business conditions, turning around a weak organizational unit, making the transition to a different type of managerial position (e.g., from a functional line position to a general manager or staff position), and managing in a country with a different culture. These situations required managers to seek new information, view problems in new ways, build new relationships, try out new behaviors, learn new skills, and develop a better understanding of themselves. Researchers at CCL developed an instrument called the Developmental Challenge Profile to measure the amount and types of challenge in a managerial position or assignment (McCauley, Ruderman, Ohlott, & Morrow, 1994).

Experiencing success in handling difficult challenges is essential for leadership development. In the process, managers learn new skills and gain self-confidence. Learning from experience involves failure as well as success. The research at CCL also found that managers who experienced adversity and failure earlier in their career were more likely to develop and advance to a higher level than managers who experienced only a series of early successes. Types of hardship experiences found to be significant for development included failure in business decisions, mistakes in dealing with important people, career setbacks, and personal trauma (e.g., divorce, serious injury or illness). However, experiencing failure may not result in beneficial learning and change unless a person accepts some responsibility for it, acknowledges personal limitations, and finds ways to overcome them (Kaplan, Kofodimos, & Drath, 1987; Kovach, 1989; McCall & Lombardo, 1983). Moreover, when the amount of stress and challenge is excessive, support and coaching may be needed to prevent people from giving up and withdrawing from the situation before development occurs.

Variety of Tasks or Assignments

Growth and learning are greater when job experiences are diverse as well as challenging. Diverse job experiences require managers to adapt to new situations and deal with new types of problems. Repeated success in handling one type of problem reinforces the tendency of a person to interpret and handle new problems in the same way, even when a different approach may be more effective. Thus, it is beneficial for managers to have early experience with a wide variety of problems that require different leadership behavior and skills. Some ways to provide a variety of job challenges include making special assignments within a manager's current position, rotating managers among positions in different functional subunits of the organization, providing assignments in both line and staff positions, and making foreign as well as domestic assignments.

Relevant Feedback

More learning occurs during operational assignments when people get accurate feedback about their behavior and its consequences and use this feedback to analyze their experiences and learn from them. Unfortunately, useful feedback about a manager's behavior is seldom provided within operational assignments, and even when available it may not result in learning. The hectic pace and unrelenting demands make introspection and self-analysis difficult in any management job. The extent to which a person is willing to accept feedback depends on some of the same traits that are related to managerial effectiveness (Bunker & Webb, 1992; Kaplan, 1990; Kelleher, Finestone & Lowy, 1986). People who are defensive and insecure tend to avoid or ignore information about their weaknesses. People who believe that most events are predetermined by uncontrollable external forces (i.e., people who do not have a high internal locus of control orientation) are less likely to accept responsibility for failure or to view feedback as a way to improve their skills and future performance. Hard-driving, achievement-oriented managers are more likely to be successful early in their careers, but these traits may also interfere with their capacity to learn how to adapt to changing situations.

The obstacles to learning from experience are greatest at higher levels of management (Kaplan, Kofodimas, & Drath, 1987). Executives tend to become isolated from all but a small number of people with whom they interact regularly in the organization, and these people are mostly other executives who are also isolated. Success in attaining such a high position of power and prestige tends to give executives self-confidence about their style of management. This confidence may even progress to a feeling of superiority that causes the executive to ignore or discount criticism from others who are not so successful. Moreover, as executives become more powerful, people become more reluctant to risk offending them by providing criticism.

Developmental Activities

A number of activities can be used to facilitate learning of relevant skills from experience on the job (see Table 13-2). These developmental activities can be used to supplement informal coaching by the boss or coworkers, and most of them can be used in conjunction with formal training programs. For example, multisource feedback from the workplace is provided to participants in some leadership training programs. Each type of activity or technique will be reviewed and evaluated briefly.

Multisource Feedback

Providing behavioral feedback from multiple sources has become a popular method for management development, and it is widely used in large organizations (London &

TABLE 13-2 Activities for Facilitating Leadership Development

- Multisource feedback
- Developmental assessment centers
- Developmental assignments
- Job rotation programs
- Action learning
- Mentoring
- Executive coaching
- Outdoor challenge programs
- Personal growth programs

Smither, 1995). This approach is called by various names, including 360-degree feedback and multirater feedback. Multisource feedback programs can be used for a variety of purposes, but the primary purpose is to assess the strengths and developmental needs for individual managers. The design and use of 360-degree feedback programs is described in several books (e.g., Lepsinger & Lucia, 1997; Tornow & London, 1998).

In a feedback program, managers receive information about their skills or behavior from standardized questionnaires filled out by other people such as subordinates, peers,

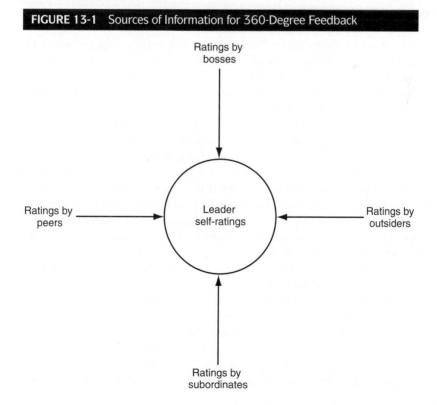

FIGURE 13-1 Sources of Information for 360-Degree Feedback

Ratings by bosses

Ratings by peers

Leader self-ratings

Ratings by outsiders

Ratings by subordinates

superiors, and sometimes outsiders such as clients (see Figure 13-1). The questionnaires used to provide feedback may be customized for a particular organization, but most feedback workshops still utilize standardized questionnaires. Sixteen survey instruments commonly used in feedback workshops are described by Van Velsor, Leslie, and Fleenor (1997), who also reviewed the empirical evidence about the strengths and limitations of each instrument. Each participating manager receives a report that compares ratings made by others to self-ratings by the manager and to norms for other managers. Sometimes managers receive a feedback report with built-in aids for interpreting the results, but in most programs, managers attend a workshop conducted by an experienced facilitator who provides assistance in interpreting the feedback and identifying developmental needs.

Feedback is likely to be more accurate when the rating questionnaire tracks behaviors that are meaningful and easy to observe. Accurate feedback also depends on gaining the cooperation of a representative set of respondents who interacted frequently with the manager over a period of time and had adequate opportunity to observe the behaviors in the questionnaire. Respondents are more likely to provide accurate ratings if they understand the purpose of the survey, how the results will be used, and the procedures to ensure confidentiality of answers. Ratings are more likely to be accurate if the feedback is used only for developmental purposes and is not part of the formal performance appraisal process (London, Wohlers, & Gallagher, 1990).

Behavioral feedback can be presented in a number of different ways, and the format of the feedback report helps to determine how clear and useful the feedback is to the recipients. Providing feedback separately for each direction (e.g., subordinates, peers, superiors) makes it more informative and easier to interpret. It is a common practice to highlight large discrepancies between what others say about a manager's behavior and self-ratings by the manager. Self-ratings that are much higher than ratings by others indicate a possible developmental need. Interpretation of feedback is facilitated by norms (e.g., percentile scores) based on a large sample of managers. Ratings of the manager's behavior that are well below normal provide another indicator of a possible developmental need.

There has been much discussion but little research on the advantages of different types and forms of feedback. Some writers have questioned the value of providing feedback based on quantitative ratings for abstract traits and vaguely defined behaviors that are difficult to observe and remember. Moses, Hollenbeck, and Sorcher (1993) suggested providing feedback on what the rater expects the manager would do in a well-defined, representative situation. Kaplan (1993) suggested supplementing numerical feedback with concrete examples of effective and ineffective behavior by the manager. The examples would be obtained by interviewing respondents or including open-ended questions on the survey questionnaire. An example of an open-ended question is to ask respondents what they think the manager should start doing, stop doing, or continue doing (Bracken, 1994). Quantitative feedback about a manager's current behavior can be supplemented with respondent recommendations about desirable changes in the manager's behavior.

The effectiveness of multisource feedback programs depends not only on the type and form of feedback, but also on how it is presented to managers (Kaplan, 1993; Yukl & Lepsinger, 1995). Three common variations are the following: (1) managers just receive a feedback report and are left to interpret it alone; (2) managers receive a feedback report followed by a one-on-one meeting with a facilitator; and (3) managers attend a group workshop with a facilitator to help interpret their feedback reports. A facilitator can explain the rating categories and their relevance for leadership effectiveness, prepare participants to be receptive to behavioral feedback, encourage participants to interpret the feedback in light of their leadership situation, stress the positive aspects of feedback as well as negatives, help participants work through feelings about adverse feedback, and encourage participants to plan how to use the feedback to improve their leadership effectiveness. A field experiment by Seifert, Yukl, and McDonald (2003) found that a feedback workshop with a facilitator was more effective for enhancing the influence behavior of bank managers than merely giving them a feedback report to read. Individual meetings can be used following a group workshop to provide an opportunity for participants to meet with a facilitator to discuss their feedback data privately (Chappelow, 1998).

Despite the widespread use of multisource feedback in recent years, its effectiveness has not been adequately determined (Waldman, Atwater, & Antonioni, 1998). Several studies examined the effects of upward feedback to leaders from subordinates (e.g., Atwater, Roush, & Fischtal, 1995; Hegarty, 1974; Nemeroff & Cosentino, 1979; Reilly, Smither, & Vasilopoulos, 1996; Smither et al., 1995; Wilson, O'Hare, & Shipper, 1990). A much smaller number of studies evaluated the effects of multisource feedback (e.g., Bernardin, Hagan, Kane, 1995; Hazucha, Hezlett, & Schneider, 1993; Seifert, Yukl, & McDonald, 2003). Evidence of positive change in leader behavior was found in some studies but not others.

With so few studies that are directly relevant for evaluating multisource feedback to managers, it is worthwhile to also consider results from research on feedback in other contexts. A meta-analysis of 131 quasi-experimental studies and experiments (many conducted in the laboratory) found a weak positive effect of feedback on performance (Kluger & DeNisi, 1996). The results varied greatly across studies, and a negative effect was found in one third of the studies. Taken together, the different types of empirical research suggest that behavioral feedback can be useful in some situations, but the evidence fails to support for the widespread assumption that it is a potent method of leadership development (Waldman et al., 1998).

Feedback from other people can help a manager identify strengths and weaknesses, but the manager may not be willing or able to apply the feedback. When multisource feedback is used only for development, managers are usually not required to share the feedback with their boss or to discuss it with the raters. Some participants may dismiss negative feedback or distort its meaning (Conger, 1992). Even when a participant acknowledges a skill deficiency and wants to improve, how to improve may not be evident.

The extent to which the feedback results in improvement of skills may also depend on what training and follow-up activities occur afterward. A study by Walker and Smither (1999) found that managers were more likely to improve if they held a meeting with the raters (who were subordinates) to discuss the feedback received from them. Such a meeting provides an opportunity to gain a better understanding of the reason for discrepancies in self and other ratings, and it may increase the manager's sense of accountability to make use of the feedback. Other types of follow-up activities that may facilitate behavior change include skill training, coaching, and linking the manager's developmental action plan to subsequent appraisal and reward decisions (London & Smither, 1995).

In summary, there is insufficient evidence to reach any firm conclusions about the utility of multisource feedback for improving leadership skills. More research is needed to determine what form of feedback is most useful, the conditions under which feedback is likely to result in beneficial change, the types of skills or behavior likely to be improved, and the types of managers likely to benefit from multisource feedback.

Developmental Assessment Centers

As noted in Chapter 7, traditional assessment centers utilize multiple methods to measure managerial competencies and potential for advancement. These methods may include interviews, aptitude tests, personality tests, situational tests, a short autobiographical essay, a speaking exercise, and a writing exercise. Information from these diverse sources is integrated and used to develop an overall evaluation of each participant's management potential. The assessment center process typically takes two to three days, but some data collection may occur beforehand. In the past, most assessment centers were used only for selection and promotion decisions, but in recent years assessment centers have increasingly been used for developing managers (Boehm, 1985; Goodge, 1991; Munchus & McArthur, 1991; Rayner & Goodge, 1988).

Compared to feedback workshops, developmental assessment centers use more intensive measurement procedures and a more comprehensive set of measures to increase self-understanding, identify strengths and weaknesses, and assess developmental needs. Information about a manager's behavior may be obtained from people who interact with the manager regularly and from observation of the manager in simulations and exercises. The facilitators also collect information about the manager's prior experience, motives, personality traits, skills, interests, and aspirations. Information about behavior and skills is integrated with information about motives, background, experience, and career aspirations to provide a more complete picture of the person's strengths, weaknesses, and potential. The rationale is that behavioral feedback alone is insufficient to change ineffective behavior supported by strong motives, values, and self-concepts. Helping the person to confront weaknesses and develop a better self-understanding increases the likelihood of behavior change. Participants also receive counseling about developmental needs and career choices. To avoid the inherent dangers in this enhanced feedback, Kaplan and Palus (1994) emphasize the need for careful selection of participants to screen out people who would not benefit from it (or who may not be able to handle the stress).

Studies on participant perceptions of the benefits from developmental assessment centers and similar feedback intensive programs suggest that they can enhance self-awareness, help to identify training needs, and facilitate subsequent development of leadership skills (e.g., Fletcher, 1990; Guthrie & Kelly-Radford, 1998; Young & Dixon, 1996). Two studies found evidence that developmental assessment centers can improve the later performance of managers (Engelbracht & Fischer, 1995; Papa & Graham, 1991), but the results are difficult to interpret because other developmental activities were involved (e.g., skill training, special assignments, additional coaching). As with feedback workshops, developmental assessment workshops are likely to be more successful when followed by relevant training or developmental activities. We still do not know much about the underlying psychological processes that occur in developmental assessment centers, and more research on this subject is needed. Finally, the benefits of a developmental assessment center may not be limited to participants; managers who serve on the staff of these centers may also experience an increase in their managerial skills (Boehm, 1985).

Developmental Assignments

Some developmental assignments can be carried out concurrently with regular job responsibilities, whereas others require taking a temporary leave from one's regular job. Lombardo and Eichinger (1989) cataloged types of special assignments that can be used to develop managerial skills in the current job. Some examples of these assignments include managing a new project or start-up operation, serving as the department representative on a cross-functional team, chairing a special task force to plan a major change or deal with a serious operational problem, developing and conducting a training program for the organizational unit, and assuming responsibility for some administrative activities previously handled by the boss (e.g., preparing a budget, developing a strategic plan, conducting a meeting). Some examples of developmental assignments away from one's regular job include working in an assessment center, serving as an understudy or staff member for an exceptional leader in another part of the organization, serving in a temporary liaison position in another organization (e.g., a client or supplier), and serving in a visiting assignment to another organization (e.g., a manager is loaned to a government agency to help implement a major change).

An example of a systematic use of developmental assignments is provided by Citibank in the 1990s (Clark & Lyness, 1991). The development of interpersonal and strategic skills was considered important to prepare managers for advancement to senior executive positions. High potential managers were given two types of special assignments, each lasting from 3 to 4 years. One assignment involved a major strategic challenge and the other involved difficult people-management challenges.

Research on the effectiveness of developmental assignments is still limited. The longitudinal research at AT&T (see Chapter 7) provided evidence that diverse, challenging assignments early in one's career facilitated career advancement. The research at CCL and elsewhere suggests that different skills are learned from different types of challenges and hardship experiences (Lindsey et al., 1987; McCall et al., 1988; McCauley et al., 1994; McCauley, Eastman, & Ohlott, 1995; Valerio, 1990). However, this research relied on the managers' retrospective reports of their own development, not on a systematic comparison among different types of assignments using measures of competencies taken before and after the assignment. We still have much to learn about what types of assignments are effective for what type of skills and what type of people.

An important research question is the amount of time required to optimize learning in developmental assignments. A person who is moved too quickly may not find an opportunity to complete the assignment, to see the consequences of one's actions and decisions, or to reflect on one's experiences and comprehend what was learned (Ohlott, 1998). On the other hand, staying in the assignment too long can result in boredom and lost opportunities for more meaningful experiences.

McCauley, Eastman, and Ohlott (1995) suggested some ways to improve the planning and use of developmental assignments. The challenges and learning opportunities provided by each type of assignment should be matched to the manager's developmental needs and career aspirations. Managers need to become more aware of the importance of developmental assignments, and they should share in the responsibility for planning them. The challenges and benefits provided by special assignments should be tracked, and this information should be related to career counseling and succession planning. After a developmental assignment is completed, it is important for a manager to reflect on the experience and identify the lessons that were learned. This process of retrospective analysis is likely to increase learning from experience, and it can be facilitated by the boss, a mentor, or a training and development professional (Ohlott, 1998).

Dechant (1994) suggested that learning from special assignments can be facilitated by preparation of a concrete learning plan. The person who has the assignment analyzes the task objectives, context, and job requirements for everyone who will be involved in the task. Skill requirements are compared with available skill resources, any gaps in necessary skills or knowledge are identified, and plans are made to acquire the skills or knowledge needed to carry out the assignment successfully. This process should increase the likelihood that a person will recognize and take advantage of learning opportunities in a special assignment. Learning needs for others are also identified and incorporated into the action plan for the assignment, which fosters a systems perspective.

The effectiveness of developmental assignments is reduced when bias and discrimination are widespread in the organization. A variety of studies suggest that women are less likely than men to be given challenging, high-visibility assignments (e.g., Ruderman & Ohlott, 1994; Van Velsor & Hughes, 1990). Despite the existence of laws prohibiting it, discrimination based on gender, race, or age still occurs in making assignments and awarding promotions (see Chapter 14).

Job Rotation Programs

In most job rotation programs, managers are assigned to work in a variety of different functional subunits of the organization for periods of time varying from six months to three years. Individuals change jobs for developmental reasons, not as the result of a promotion decision. In most formal job rotation programs, the pattern of assignments is similar for each participant and is not based on an analysis of each individual's current skills or deficiencies. Job rotation programs with substantive assignments in different subunits of an organization offer a number of developmental opportunities. Managers face the challenge of quickly learning how to establish cooperative relationships and deal with new types of technical problems for which they lack adequate preparation. Managers can learn about the unique problems and processes in different (functional or product) subunits and the interdependencies among different parts of the organization. Job rotation also provides managers the opportunity to develop a large network of contacts in different parts of the organization.

Despite the widespread use of job rotation in industry, only a few studies actually evaluated this developmental activity. A study on scientists and engineers found that they benefited in several ways from participating in a job rotation program (London, 1989). Participants reported developing higher mutual respect for other functions, a greater appreciation of the need for collaboration, and a stronger belief in the value of viewing problems from different perspectives.

A study by Campion, Cheraskin, and Stevens (1994) surveyed employees in a variety of organizations to examine the costs and benefits of job rotation. Participants reported that job rotation resulted in increased managerial, technical, and business skill and knowledge. The amount of job rotation was positively correlated with the participants' rate of advancement, but the direction of causality was not clear. One interpretation is that rotation increases skills and subsequently facilitates promotion. An alternative interpretation is that managers viewed as highly skilled and promotable are more likely to be selected for job rotation programs. To clarify the relationship of job rotation to skill acquisition and advancement, we need longitudinal research with repeated measurement of key variables at appropriate intervals.

The study by Campion and colleagues (1994) showed that job rotation also has some costs. One cost is lower productivity for the rotated individuals, which is due to the normal learning curve for a new type of job. When the rotated individuals occupy managerial positions, their lack of technical expertise is likely to adversely affect the productivity of subordinates as well. Another cost is lower satisfaction for people in the functional units who are required to accommodate and assist the managers. These people often resent having to do extra work to help fast trackers move on to an eventual promotion for which they are not eligible.

In the absence of more information about the costs and benefits of job rotation, it is difficult to determine how much rotation is desirable or how long managers should remain in each position. Little is known about how long it takes for the desired learning to occur, or about the necessary facilitating conditions.

The feasibility of job rotation programs may be limited by some of the current trends in organizations. For example, downsizing leaves fewer available positions to support job rotation programs. Furthermore, managers in a downsized organization will be more reluctant to lose an experienced subordinate in exchange for an inexperienced, temporary substitute (Hall & Foulkes, 1991). A question that deserves more attention is whether the benefits of job rotation can be achieved with other types of special assignments that are less costly.

Action Learning

Action learning is an approach that is often used for combining formal training with learning from experience (Dotlich, & Noel, 1998; Margerison, 1988; Revans, 1982). Individuals or teams conduct field projects on complex organizational problems and develop solutions that are often applied by the organization. The projects are usually selected to facilitate the development of cognitive and interpersonal skills rather than technical knowledge. The types of project that can be used are very diverse, and they may take from several weeks to several months. The participants meet periodically with a skilled facilitator to discuss, analyze, and learn from their experiences. When multiple teams are involved, they may meet periodically in a seminar to share their experiences and learn from each other.

Many action learning projects are linked to formal training, but an alternative approach is to link the projects to a process of mutual coaching and mentoring (Smith, 1990). An individual manager identifies an important organizational problem that cannot be solved alone and also identifies some people who can contribute to the problem solving. The project participants identify learning objectives for themselves and each other. The group meets periodically to devise solutions to the problem, evaluate progress, and discuss what was learned.

The effectiveness of action learning for developing leadership skills depends on the type of project, the composition of the team, and the type of coaching provided. If the scope of the project is narrow, managers may learn specific skills that do not apply to other types of situations (Baldwin & Padgett, 1993). Unless the project involves considerable challenge, it is unlikely to provide much learning of leadership skills. More learning is likely when projects are assigned to teams rather than to individual managers. Marsick (1990) found that action learning works best when teams are composed of people with diverse backgrounds so that participants are exposed to different viewpoints and perspectives.

Only a few studies have been conducted to evaluate the effects of action learning, and the results were inconclusive (Marson & Bruff, 1992; McCauley & Hughes-James, 1994; Prideaux & Ford, 1988). A limitation of these studies was reliance on self-reported benefits rather than objective indicators of behavior change and performance improvement. Research is needed with experimental designs to determine the unique benefits from developmental projects and to identify the project characteristics likely to embody sufficient challenge and opportunity for learning leadership skills.

Mentoring

Formal mentoring programs are used to facilitate management development in many organizations (Giber, Carter, & Goldsmith, 1999; Noe, 1991). Mentoring is a relationship in which a more experienced manager helps a less experienced protégé; the mentor is usually at a higher managerial level and is not the protégé's immediate boss (McCauley & Douglas, 1998). Research on mentors (Kram, 1985; Noe, 1988) finds that they provide two distinct types of functions for the protégé: a psychosocial function (acceptance, encouragement, coaching, counseling) and a career-facilitation function (sponsorship, protection, challenging assignments, exposure and visibility). Mentors can facilitate adjustment, learning, and stress reduction during difficult job transitions, such as promotion to one's first managerial position, a transfer or promotion to a different functional unit in the organization, an assignment in a foreign country, or assignments in an organization that has been merged, reorganized, or downsized (Kram & Hall, 1989; Zey, 1988). Several studies show that mentoring results in more career advancement and success for the protégé (Chao, Walz, & Gardner, 1992; Dreher & Ash, 1990; Fagenson, 1989; Scandura, 1992; Turban & Dougherty, 1994; Whitely & Coetsier, 1993). Mentors may also benefit from the mentoring experience, because it is likely to increase their job satisfaction and help them develop their own leadership skills. A study by Wilbur (1987) found that career advancement in a service company was predicted both by mentoring given and mentoring received.

Despite the potential benefits from mentoring, it is not always successful. Research on conditions likely to increase the effectiveness of mentoring suggests that informal mentoring is more successful than formal mentoring programs. For example, Noe (1988) found that personality conflicts and lack of mentor commitment were more likely to occur with assigned mentors. The difference between formal and informal mentoring may be due primarily to the way a formal program is conducted, including the selection and training of the mentors. The success of a formal mentoring program is probably increased by making participation voluntary, by providing mentors some choice of a protégé, by explaining the benefits and pitfalls, and by clarifying the expected roles and processes for both mentor and protégé (Chao et al., 1992; Hunt & Michael, 1983). Protégés can be proactive in initiating mentoring relationships rather than waiting for a mentor to select them, especially in an organization that supports this type of developmental activity. Turban and Dougherty (1994) found that protégés were more likely to initiate mentoring relationships and get more mentoring if they had high emotional stability, self-monitoring, and internal locus of control orientation.

Mentoring is also affected by some demographic factors such as age, gender, and race. Women and minorities have more difficulty finding successful mentoring relationships (Ilgen & Youtz, 1986; Ohlott, Ruderman, & McCauley, 1994; Noe, 1988; Ragins & Cotton, 1991, 1993; Ragins & McFarlin, 1990; Thomas, 1990). Common difficulties for women include stereotypes about appropriate behavior, concern about intimacy with men, awkwardness about discussing some subjects, lack of appropriate role models, resentment by peers, and exclusion from male networks. Some of these difficulties remain even when women mentor women. Despite the difficulties, empirical studies found no evidence that gender affects the success of mentoring (e.g., Dreher & Ash, 1990; Turban & Dougherty, 1994).

In general, the research suggests that mentoring can be a useful technique for facilitating career advancement, adjustment to change, and job satisfaction of a protégé. However, there is little research yet on the ways a mentor actually facilitates development of leadership competencies in a protégé. Little is known about the skills, values, and behaviors most likely to be acquired or enhanced in a mentoring relationship, the learning processes, and the conditions facilitating development.

Executive Coaching

In recent years individual coaching has become popular as another type of developmental intervention for leaders in business organizations (Hall, Otazo, & Hollenbeck, 1999; Kilburg, 1996; Peterson, 1966). The type of leader who receives coaching is usually a high-level executive. The person who provides the coaching may be an external or internal consultant. The coach is usually either a successful former executive or a behavioral scientist with extensive experience as a management consultant. Use of an external coach provides some advantages such as wider experience, greater objectivity, and more confidentiality. An internal coach offers other advantages, such as easy availability, more knowledge of the culture and politics, and a better understanding of the strategic challenges and core competencies.

The primary purpose of executive coaching is to facilitate learning of relevant skills. Coaches also provide advice about how to handle specific challenges, such as implementing a major change, dealing with a difficult boss, or working with people from a different culture. Having a coach provides the unusual opportunity to discuss issues and try out ideas with someone who can understand them and provide helpful, objective feedback and suggestions, while maintaining strict confidentiality. Executive coaching is especially useful in conjunction with techniques that provide information about developmental needs but do not directly improve skills (e.g., multisource feedback, developmental assessment center).

An executive coach is not a permanent mentor, and the coach is usually employed for a limited period of time ranging from a few months to a few years. Coaching may be provided on a weekly or biweekly basis, and in extreme cases, the coach may be on call to provide advice whenever needed. Sometimes the decision to obtain coaching is made by the executive, and other times it is made by higher management to help prepare an executive for advancement, or to prevent derailment.

Executive coaching offers several advantages over formal training courses, including convenience, confidentiality, flexibility, and more personal attention. One obvious disadvantage is the high expense of one-on-one coaching, even when used for a limited time. The high cost is one reason why personal coaching is used primarily for executives. Another limitation is the shortage of competent coaches. It is important to find a coach who is able to establish a good working relationship with the executive while also remaining objective and professional. The coach should not have a personal agenda such as excessive bias for a particular theory, the desire to sell more consulting time (for an external consultant), or the desire for more power (for an internal consultant). Organizations need clear guidelines regarding the selection and use of executive coaches to avoid the potential problems with this developmental technique (Hall et al., 1999).

The executives who are being coached usually value honest, accurate feedback about strengths and weaknesses, as well as clear, relevant advice about ways to become more effective. Examples of the types of behaviors and skills that can be enhanced by a coach include listening, communicating, influencing people, building relationships, handling conflicts, team building, initiating change, conducting meetings, and developing subordinates. The coach can also provide advice about other things the executive can do to acquire relevant knowledge and skills. Guidelines for effective coaching of executives can be found in recent books on the subject (e.g., Dotlich & Cairo, 1999).

Research on the effects of executive coaching on personal development and leadership effectiveness is limited, but the evidence so far is favorable. Hall and colleagues (1999) interviewed a sample of 75 executives from six companies who had experienced executive coaching. Most of the respondents evaluated the coaching as very satisfactory. The executives reported that it helped them acquire new skills, attitudes, or perspectives. As a result of the coaching, they were able to solve problems better and accomplish things they could not do previously.

A quasi-experimental study by Olivero, Bane, and Kopelman (1999) assessed the effects of executive coaching in a public agency. Managers in the agency received a three-day training workshop, followed by eight weeks of coaching related to individual action learning projects. The training resulted in higher productivity for the managers, and personal coaching augmented this increase. The coaching had a stronger effect than the training. A limitation of the study was the lack of information about changes in the managers' attitudes, skills, or behaviors, which could explain why productivity increased.

Outdoor Challenge Programs

Outdoor challenge programs involve physical activities performed by a group of people in an outdoor setting (Galagan, 1987). The typical program involves a sequence of increasingly challenging physical activities that require mutual trust and cooperation among group members. An experienced facilitator conducts the activities, provides coaching and encouragement, and helps participants understand the link between their experiences in an activity and organizational life. One type of activity commonly used early in the program is to have each group member fall backward off a wall into the hands of waiting teammates. An example of a more difficult activity is the pole climb; each participant must climb a 25 foot pole to a small platform at the top, then jump to a trapeze hanging 12 feet away. The exercise is actually quite safe, but participants perceive it to be very risky. Despite wearing a helmet and a harness with a safety line held by teammates, most participants experience fear when standing at the top of a swaying pole that seems much higher than it actually is. Teammates below watch the person on the pole with rapt attention, provide continuous encouragement, and share in the feeling of accomplishment after a successful jump. In some outdoor challenge programs, groups travel to a real wilderness area to perform activities such as rappelling down a cliff or whitewater rafting.

The purpose of outdoor adventure programs is personal growth and team building (Conger, 1992). Personal growth comes from increased awareness of one's own feelings, and the possibility that feelings can be discrepant from cognitions (e.g., despite knowing an activity is safe, you are still scared). The developmental activities are designed to increase self-confidence, self-control, risk taking, and willingness to give and receive trust. Team building is facilitated by exercises that help participants learn the importance of mutual trust and cooperation. A series of such exercises by the same group over a period of two or more days provides a bonding experience that usually results in strong group identification and cohesiveness. When the group is an intact management team from an organization, the hope is that increased trust and cohesiveness will transfer back to the workplace.

Only a few studies have investigated the effectiveness of outdoor challenge programs as a developmental technique for improving leadership. Gall (1987) found that turnover dropped 10 percent for a group of managers who were in an outdoor challenge program but remained constant for a group of managers not in the program. Marsh, Richards, and Barnes (1986) found long-term improvements in the self-concept of managers who participated in an outward bound program. Baldwin, Wagner, and Roland (1991) compared the attitudes of program participants to nonparticipants three months after an outdoor challenge program and found no significant difference in positive self-concept or trust. However, they found that perceptions of teamwork and individual problem solving increased for participants, especially when intact groups were used. In summary, the results are somewhat inconsistent, and more research is needed with objective indicators of improvement in leadership effectiveness.

Personal Growth Programs

Personal growth programs are designed to improve self-awareness and overcome inner barriers to psychological growth and development of leadership competencies. These programs evolved from the humanistic psychology movement in the 1960s, and many of the founders had prior experience in programs emphasizing development of human potential, such as the Peace Corps and the National Training Laboratories in Bethel, Maine (Conger, 1993).

Personal growth workshops are based on a series of interrelated assumptions about people and leadership. One key assumption is that many people have lost touch with their inner feelings and values. Inner fears and conflicts, which are often unconscious, limit creativity and risk taking. Before one can become a successful leader, it is necessary to reconnect with one's feelings, confront the latent fears, and resolve the underlying conflicts. Another key assumption is that successful leadership requires a high level of emotional and moral development. A person with high emotional maturity and integrity is more likely to put devotion to a worthwhile cause above self-interest and become a supportive, inspiring, and empowering leader. Understanding your own values, needs, and feelings is necessary to determine whether you are able to provide this type of leadership, and indeed, whether it is really what you want to do.

Personal growth programs are usually conducted at a conference center, and the program may last from two days to a week. Participants are usually managers who do not work together, but sometimes a personal growth program is conducted for an intact management group. The programs typically include a series of psychological exercises in which participants attempt to understand their purpose for living and working and share this understanding with each other. Sometimes outdoor challenge activities are incorporated into the program to increase the experience of shared risk taking. An experienced facilitator presents conceptual models and conducts the exercises. The models usually describe how human development occurs, how organizations change over time, and the role of leadership in organizational change.

The process of developing self-understanding begins when participants are asked to explain their reasons for attending the program. In another, more intensive exercise, participants are told to imagine their company has been acquired and only the three best leaders will be retained in the newly merged organization. Each person has five minutes to prepare a two-minute appeal describing his or her positive leadership qualities and reasons to be retained (a variation of this exercise is to imagine that you are at sea in a sinking boat with a small life raft that will only allow three people to be saved). Participants discuss each appeal and vote to determine the three people who have made the most convincing case.

An important exercise near the end of most programs is for each participant to develop a personal vision for the future and present it to the rest of the group. To facilitate development of a vision, participants are encouraged to imagine they are at the end of their lives and have achieved a sense of completion and gratitude; now they must consider what they have done and how they have lived to reach that state. After each presentation, the audience provides feedback on whether they perceive the vision to be sincere and right for the person.

Personal growth programs usually involve strong emotional experiences and are more likely than most training programs to have a lasting effect on participants. The changes may include an increase in interpersonal skills relevant for leadership. However, it is also possible that some participants will change in ways that reduce leadership effectiveness (Conger, 1993). Successful leadership often involves a passionate pursuit of a vision or cause, which sometimes requires sacrificing aspects of one's personal and family life. The net effect of personal growth programs that encourage people to find a better balance between their work and personal life may be to reduce commitment to the organization. Moreover, increased awareness of unconscious needs and conflicts does not necessarily result in their resolution, and the experience is sometimes more detrimental than helpful to the person. As yet, there are few studies on the consequences of personal growth programs for leaders, followers, or the organization.

Self-Help Activities

The focus of this chapter was on what organizations can do to develop the leadership skills of their members, not on what an individual can do to develop his or her own skills. Nevertheless, as noted in the introduction to the chapter, self-help activities provide another approach to enhance leadership skills. Many self-help techniques are available for improving leadership, including practitioner books, instructional videotapes or compact disks, and interactive computer programs. Some of these techniques are intended to be a

---

TABLE 13-3 Guidelines for Self-Development of Leadership Skills

- Develop a personal vision of career objectives.
- Seek appropriate mentors.
- Seek challenging assignments.
- Improve self-monitoring.
- Seek relevant feedback.
- Learn from mistakes.
- Learn to view events from multiple perspectives.
- Be skeptical of easy answers.

---

substitute for formal training programs, some are used to supplement training, and others are intended to facilitate learning from experience. Unfortunately, there is almost no empirical research on the effectiveness of self-learning techniques (Baldwin & Padgett, 1993). We know little about the benefits derived from them or the extent to which they can substitute for formal instruction. Research is needed to evaluate how much self-help activities contribute to the development of leadership competencies, and the conditions under which these activities are most effective. Table 13-3 provides a list of tentative recommendations for self-development of leadership skills.

Facilitating Conditions for Development

Regardless of the developmental methods that are used (formal training, experiential learning, self-learning activities), the acquisition of leadership skills can be facilitated or inhibited by conditions within an organization. These conditions help to determine how much training is provided, how much job challenge people experience, how much feedback is provided, how much people are encouraged to learn new skills, how much people are motivated to help others learn, and how people interpret mistakes and failure. A few of the facilitating conditions will be examined briefly.

Support by the Boss

The immediate boss can facilitate development of leadership skills in subordinates (Hillman, Schwandt, & Bartz, 1990; London & Mone, 1987; Valerio, 1990). However, a manager who does not understand the importance of coaching and mentoring is unlikely to provide much of it to subordinates. Managers who are preoccupied with immediate crises or their own career advancement are unlikely to spend much time developing subordinates as leaders. Managers who are insecure are unlikely to develop subordinates who could become potential competitors. Development will also be impeded by managers who treat mistakes by subordinates as personal failures rather than learning experiences. Even for managers who want to develop subordinates, it is difficult to find the right balance between providing necessary guidance and encouraging them to solve problems independently. A manager who is overly protective of subordinates and fails to provide enough challenge and honest feedback to them is unlikely to be successful in developing their leadership skills.

Motivation to learn leadership skills and apply them at work is also influenced by the extent to which a person's boss promotes and supports training activities (Facteau,

---

TABLE 13-4   Ways to Support Leadership Training of Subordinates

Before the Training

- Inform subordinates about opportunities to get training.
- Explain why the training is important and beneficial.
- Ask others who received the training to explain how it was useful.
- Change the work schedule to make it easier to attend training.
- Give a subordinate time off if necessary to prepare for the training.
- Support preparation activities such as distribution of questionnaires.
- Tell subordinates they will be asked to report on what was learned.

After the Training

- Meet with the person to discuss what was learned how it can be applied.
- Jointly set specific objectives and action plans to use what was learned.
- Make assignments that require use of newly learned skills.
- Hold periodic review sessions to monitor progress in applying learning.
- Provide praise for applying the skills.
- Provide encouragement and coaching when difficulties are encountered.
- Include application of new skills in performance appraisals.
- Set an example for trainees by using the skills yourself.

Dobbins, Russell, Ladd, & Kudisch, 1995; Ford, Quinones, Sego & Sorra, 1992; Hand, Richards, & Slocum, 1973; Huczynski & Lewis, 1980; Kozlowski & Hults, 1987; Noe & Schmitt, 1986; Rouiller & Goldstein, 1993; Tracey, Tannenbaum, & Kavanagh, 1995). Some things that can enhance learning and its subsequent application are listed in Table 13-4.

Learning Climate

The amount of management training and development that occurs in an organization depends in part on prevailing attitudes and values about development, sometimes referred to as the learning climate (Ford & Weissbein, 1997). These general conditions augment the influence of a manager's immediate boss. More leadership development is likely when individual learning is regarded as highly important for organizational effectiveness. In such an organization, more resources will be devoted to training, and more effort will be made to explicitly measure and reward learning. Managers will provide more coaching and mentoring when these activities are explicitly measured and rewarded. More members of the organization will be encouraged to seek opportunities for personal growth and skill acquisition. For example, a person is more likely to accept a difficult, high-risk assignment if performance in the assignment will be evaluated in terms of skill development as well as task success. A supportive organizational climate and culture also encourages managers to apply the skills they have learned in training or developmental experiences.

Many things can be done to create and maintain a supportive climate for continuous learning and development. Some examples include the following: (1) make job assignments that allow people to pursue their interests and learn new skills; (2) establish work schedules that allow enough free time to experiment with new methods; (3) provide financial support for continuing education by employees; (4) arrange special speakers and skills workshops for employees; (5) establish a sabbatical program to allow employees to renew themselves; (6) establish a career counseling program to help employees develop self-awareness and find ways to achieve their full potential; (7) establish voluntary skill assessment and feedback programs; (8) make pay increases partly dependent on skill development; (9) provide awards for innovations and improvements; and (10) use symbols and slogans that embody values such as experimentation, flexibility, adaptation, self-development, continuous learning, and innovation.

Developmental Criteria for Placement Decisions

At present, most organizations do not make job assignments that explicitly provide adequate developmental opportunities and a logical progression of learning (Baldwin & Padgett, 1993). The idea of using job assignments for leadership development is somewhat at odds with the traditional approach to selection and placement in an organization, which seeks a good match between manager skills and job requirements (Ruderman, Ohlott, & McCauley, 1990). It is common practice to label someone as a specialist in a particular type of activity or problem and assign the same types of activities or tasks repeatedly to the person. Most organizations promote individuals to higher positions within the same functional specialty rather than moving them to management positions in a different functional specialty.

Assigning a challenging job to someone who does not already possess all of the necessary skills is likely to increase development, but it entails a risk of serious mistakes and failure. Even if the person is successful, it will require a longer learning period to master the job. Thus, it is not surprising that most organizations try to select the person with the best skills for a managerial position. More leadership development is likely to occur when executives are aware of the developmental opportunities in operational assignments and value development enough to risk giving important jobs to people who have not already demonstrated experience in performing them (Hall & Foulkes, 1991). Evidence from one study shows that consideration of developmental needs when making succession planning decisions is likely to result in better performance for the organization (Friedman, 1986). Developmental objectives are more likely to be incorporated into placement decisions when top executives have a systems perspective on leadership development.

A Systems Perspective on Leadership Development

The distinction among formal training programs, developmental activities, and self-help activities is useful up to a point, but it implies that the categories are mutually exclusive. In fact, the different categories overlap and are interrelated in complex ways (see Figure 13-2).

Relationships Among Approaches

Learning acquired from one approach can facilitate or enhance learning from the other approaches. For example, a self-help activity such as using a computer interactive program may be useful to prepare for a developmental assignment. Short courses or workshops are useful to prepare someone for a special operational assignment, or to strengthen skills identified as deficient in a developmental assessment center or 360-degree feedback.

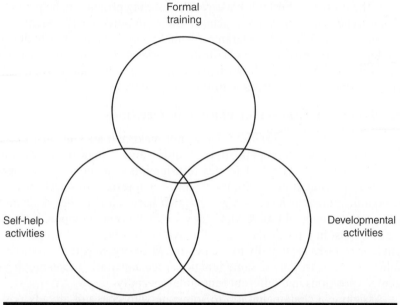

FIGURE 13-2   Three Ways to Acquire Leadership Competencies

Sometimes the approaches are used in conjunction with each other. Action learning projects often combine formal training with learning from experience, and participants are encouraged to use self-help activities and peer coaching to acquire additional knowledge as needed for the project. Realistic simulations can be used as a self-contained developmental experience or as part of a formal training course. Some formal leadership development courses now include 360-degree feedback for participants from their coworkers. Personal growth activities are also included now in some leadership courses. Special mentors can be assigned to people who have developmental assignments, or designated resource people may be available on the Internet to provide advice and coaching as needed.

There has been little research on the relative advantage of training, development, and self-help activities for different types of leadership skills. Likewise, little is known about the best way to combine training, development, and self-help activities to maximize their mutual effects. There is clearly need for a more systematic approach to the study of leadership development activities.

Integrating Developmental Activities

In most organizations there is little integration of leadership training and development activities with each other or with related human resources practices such as performance appraisal, career counseling, and succession planning. Decisions about what types of training and development to provide are often influenced by current fads and vendor hype rather than by a systematic analysis of essential competencies that need to be enhanced. Promotion decisions are often influenced more by a person's prior performance than by rigorous assessment of competencies needed to perform effectively in the next position. As a consequence of poor selection and development, many top executives end up derailing for weaknesses that could have been predicted in advance (McCall, 1998).

Planning of developmental experiences for individual managers is often haphazard and unsystematic when it is determined independently by each manager's current boss and is passed on to the next boss. Few organizations have a specialized position with primary responsibility for planning and coordinating the overall process of leadership development for the organization. McCall (1992) recommended using a developmental facilitator or committee to identify essential competencies for the organization, design tracking systems to assess current skills and developmental needs of individual managers, identify assignments with high developmental potential, sponsor special training programs when needed, find ways to strengthen rewards for managers who develop subordinates, and promote greater use of developmental activities such as mentors, special assignments, and feedback workshops.

To be optimally effective, leadership development must be consistent with an organization's competitive strategy as well as with other human resource activities (Day, 2000; McCall, 1998; McCauley, 2001; Vicere & Fulmer, 1996). Unfortunately, the developmental activities in most organizations are not based on strategic business objectives, and there is seldom any effort to determine if the activities are relevant to these objectives. The disconnect between developmental activities and strategic objectives probably reflects a lack of understanding about the interdependencies between them. We are only beginning to learn how developmental activities affect the acquisition of leadership competencies and how the competencies are related to organizational effectiveness. In a time of rapid change, it is not easy to predict the extent to which specific competencies will continue to be relevant in the future. Thus, even when top executives realize leadership development should be guided by strategic objectives, it is difficult to design developmental systems that will meet the needs of an organization in a turbulent environment. Some suggestions on how to do it can be found in recent books (e.g., London, 2002; McCall, 1998; Moxley & O'Connor-Wilson, 1998; Vicere & Fulmer, 1996).

Summary

Training of leadership skills is conducted by universities, consulting companies, and organization training centers. Despite the massive volume of formal leadership training that occurs, there isrelatively little research to assesses its effectiveness. Training methods such as behavior role modeling, cases, and simulations appear promising, but we need to learn more about how to use these techniques for enhancing leadership skills.

The importance of learning from experience on the job is now widely acknowledged, and researchers are now mapping the relationships between specific experiences and specific leadership competencies. In general, more development occurs for managers who experience challenges that require adaptation to new situations and provide opportunity to learn to deal with a variety of different types of problems and hardships. More learning also occurs when people get accurate feedback about their behavior and its consequences and use this feedback to analyze their experiences and learn from them.

Developmental techniques with the potential to increase learning from experience include multisource feedback workshops, developmental assessment centers, special assignments, job rotation, action learning, mentoring, personal growth programs, executive coaching, and outdoor challenge programs. Although most of these developmental techniques are widely used, the amount of research to evaluate their effectiveness is still limited. We are just beginning to learn what types of leadership competencies are enhanced by each technique, the optimal conditions for using a technique, and the type of people most likely to benefit from it.

The extent to which leadership competencies are acquired and used depends on the type of developmental activities that occur (e.g., training, experiential learning, self-learning), facilitating conditions (e.g., boss support, learning environment), and qualities of the individual managers (flexible, pragmatic, learning-oriented). Training and development are more effective when they are coordinated with each other, supported by a strong learning culture, and integrated with other human resource activities such as career counseling, staffing decisions, performance appraisal, and succession planning. It is essential to integrate these different elements to create and sustain favorable conditions for leadership development. It is also imperative for leadership development to be consistent with an organization's strategic objectives. A systems approach to leadership development will become more common as more organizations realize that this activity is as strategically important for long-term organizational effectiveness as product development, marketing, and customer service (Hall & Seibert, 1992; McCall, 1992).

Review and Discussion Questions

1. How useful are cases, behavioral role modeling, and large-scale simulations for leadership training?
2. What features of a training program are likely to make it more effective?
3. What conditions facilitate learning from experience by managers, and what obstacles impede learning?
4. How are special assignments and job rotation programs relevant for development of leadership skills?
5. What are the likely benefits of mentoring for developing leaders?
6. What are the similarities and differences between multisource feedback workshops and developmental assessment centers?
7. What is action learning, and how is it relevant for leadership development?
8. What are the objectives and common assumptions of outdoor challenge programs and personal growth programs?
9. What conditions in an organization enhance leadership development?
10. What can be done to integrate the leadership training, development, and self-help activities?
11. Why is it important for the leadership development programs in an organization to be consistent with the human resource management practices and the competitive strategy?

Key Terms

- action learning
- behavior role modeling
- case discussion
- developmental assessment centers
- developmental assignments
- executive coaching
- job rotation programs
- leadership development
- learning climate
- learning from experience
- mentoring
- multisource feedback
- outdoor challenge programs
- personal growth programs
- self-help activities
- simulations

CASE

Federated Industries

Patricia Paterson is the new vice president for human resources at Federated Industries, a conglomerate with several diverse subsidiaries. Her primary responsibility is to provide support and advice to each subsidiary and monitor their personnel practices to ensure they are consistent with corporate policy and strategy. She reports directly to the CEO of Federated. The CEO is concerned that not enough capable leaders are coming up through the ranks. The subsidiaries have complete responsibility for their own internal management development, but the CEO wonders whether it is time for a more uniform approach. The CEO asked Patricia to find out what each subsidiary is doing to develop leadership skills, then report back with recommendations for improving leadership development overall at Federated Industries. Patricia arranged to meet with the personnel directors of the three major subsidiaries and asked each director to prepare a short briefing.

The first director to speak was Peter Proskin, from an engineering company. He explained that his company provides only technical training, because they lack the staff to provide management training. All management training is done outside the company. A manager (or an employee who wants to become a manager) can look at the listing of available training and request any seminar or workshop that appears relevant. If the employee's boss approves the request, the manager is sent to the training at company expense. Some employees are enrolled in the evening MBA degree program at the local university, and they are reimbursed for half of the tuition cost. Peter said they do not pay complete tuition for degree programs, because it is too costly. After some employees finish their MBA, they leave for higher-paying jobs at

other companies eager to get people who have managerial as well as technical skills.

The second director to report was Alice Alston, from a company that makes consumer products. She explained that the company provides a program to develop leadership skills in high-potential managers. Managers at each level are encouraged to identify a promising subordinate to mentor. The protégé gets lots of personal coaching and is given special, developmental assignments. For example, a couple of junior managers are put on each executive committee to learn about strategic issues and observe how the senior managers work. Other assignments include serving on cross-functional project teams and carrying out improvement projects such as studying work processes and recommending ways to make them more efficient. Alice said that most of the mentors and protégés like the program. However, people not in the program (roughly two-thirds of the employees) sometimes complain about the lack of developmental opportunity in the company.

The last director to speak was Hal Harwick, from an electronics company. Hal explained that they concentrate their training on managers who previously demonstrated their executive capacity. The six most promising managers below the top executive level are selected to participate in a series of seminars held once a month. Each seminar is conducted by one of the top executives, who talks about company activities in his or her area of expertise. Three or four times a year, Hal arranges for an outside consultant to conduct a training workshop on a specific topic such as project management, budgeting, or delegation. The participating managers know they are fast-trackers in line for promotion to top management. They like the program and have told him it is very worthwhile. When one of them is promoted, another promising manager is selected for the program by the top management team. The only drawback is the political infighting that sometimes occurs when executives try to get their protégés selected for the program. ■

SOURCE: Copyright © 1996 by Gary Yukl.

QUESTIONS

1. Identify strengths and weaknesses in leadership development at Federated Industries.

2. What types of changes are most likely to improve leadership development at Federated Industries?

3. What additional information is needed to make a good report to the CEO?

14

ETHICAL LEADERSHIP AND DIVERSITY

Learning Objectives

After studying this chapter you should be able to:

- Understand the difficulties in defining and assessing ethical leadership.

- Understand the major conceptions of ethical leadership and how they relate to current leadership theories.

- Understand how gender issues have been studied and the limitations of this research.

- Understand the findings in research on gender differences in leadership.

- Understand how leadership processes can be affected by national culture.

- Understand the difficulties of studying cross-cultural leadership and the limitations of research on this subject.

- Understand why it is important to manage diversity and provide equal opportunity to all members of an organization.

The purpose of this book is to provide a broad overview of the field, with an emphasis on the theories and research that offer important insights and practical knowledge about effective leadership in organizations. Several interesting and controversial subjects mentioned only briefly until now include ethical leadership, cross-cultural differences in leadership, how gender affects leadership, and the role of leaders in managing diversity. These distinct but interrelated subjects will be examined more closely in the present chapter.

Ethical Leadership

Influence is the essence of leadership, and powerful leaders can have a substantial impact on the lives of followers and the fate of an organization. As Gini (1998) reminds us, the primary issue is not whether leaders will use power, but whether they will use it wisely and well. Powerful leaders can use their authority to advance their own careers and economic gain at the expense of organization members and the public. Moreover, by making unethical practices appear to be legitimate, a leader can influence other members of the organization to engage in crimes of obedience (Beu & Buckley, 2004). The great potential for misuse of power is one reason so many people are interested in the ethical aspects of leadership. Another reason is the declining public trust in business and public leaders, which has been fueled by repeated scandals publicized in the news media, in books, and in movies (Kouzes & Posner, 1993).

Despite the growing interest in ethical leadership, there is considerable disagreement about the appropriate way to define and assess it. In a scientific discipline that values objectivity, even to discuss this subject causes some people to feel uneasy. However, as Heifetz (1994) pointed out, there is no ethically neutral ground for theories of leadership, because they always involve values and implicit assumptions about proper forms of influence. This section of the chapter will examine some different conceptions of ethical leadership, describe some ethical dilemmas commonly faced by leaders, and identify some things leaders can do to promote ethical behavior in organizations.

General Conceptions of Ethical Leadership

Ethical leadership is an ambiguous construct that appears to include a variety of diverse elements. It is useful to make a distinction between the ethics of an individual leader and the ethics of specific types of leadership behavior (Bass & Steidlmeier, 1999). Both types of ethics are difficult to evaluate.

Several criteria are relevant for judging individual leaders, including the person's values, stage of moral development, conscious intentions, freedom of choice, use of ethical and unethical behavior, and types of influence used. Famous leaders usually have a mix of strengths and weaknesses with regard to these criteria. One difficulty in evaluating the morality of individual leaders is the subjectivity inherent in determining which criteria to use and their relative importance. The final evaluation can be influenced as much by the qualities of the judge as by the qualities of the leader.

Judgments about the ethics of a particular decision or action usually take into account the purpose (ends), the extent to which behavior is consistent with moral standards (means), and the consequences for self and others (outcomes). The three criteria are usually considered in relation to each other, and a common issue is the extent to which the ends justify the means. For example, is deception justified when the purpose is to help another person avoid serious personal harm?

Moral standards used to evaluate means include the extent to which leader behavior violates basic laws of society, denies others their rights, endangers the health and lives of other people, or involves attempts to deceive and exploit others for personal benefit. Examples of behavior that is usually considered unethical in Western nations include falsifying information, stealing assets for personal use, blaming others for one's own mistakes, provoking unnecessary hostility and distrust among others, selling secrets to competitors, showing favoritism in return for a bribe, and engaging in reckless behaviors that are likely to injure others. Judgments about ethical leadership vary somewhat across cultures, but researchers find that some types of leader behavior (e.g., exploiting followers) are considered improper regardless of national culture (Den Hartog, House, Hanges, Ruiz-Quintanilla, Dorfman, & Associates, 1999).

Diverse Perspectives on Ethical Leadership

Much of the current thinking about ethical leadership was influenced by a few scholars who viewed leadership from a broader perspective than most of the theories reviewed in this book. The examples used by these scholars often involve political leaders in national or local government, leaders of social movements, leaders of religious groups, community leaders, and leaders in not-for-profit organizations. How each scholar described ethical leadership is briefly reviewed.

Burns.   As noted in Chapter 9, Burns (1978) formulated a theory of transforming leadership from descriptive research on political leaders. For Burns, a primary leadership role or function is to increase awareness about ethical issues and help people resolve conflicting values. Burns (1978, p. 20) described transforming leadership as a process in which "leaders and followers raise one another to higher levels of morality and motivation." These leaders seek to raise the consciousness of followers by appealing to ideals and moral values such as liberty, justice, equality, peace, and humanitarianism, not to baser emotions such as fear, greed, jealousy, or hatred. Followers are elevated from their everyday selves to their better selves. For Burns, transforming leadership may be exhibited by anyone in the organization in any type of position. It may involve influencing peers and superiors as well as subordinates. It can occur in the day-to-day acts of ordinary people, but it is not ordinary or common.

Burns described leadership as a process, not a set of discrete acts. It is a process in which leaders and followers influence each other as the relationships evolve over time. Transforming leadership is an influence process between individuals, but it is also a process of mobilizing power to change social systems and reform institutions. The leader seeks to shape, express, and mediate conflict among groups of people, because this conflict can be useful for mobilizing and channeling energy to achieve shared ideological objectives. Thus, transforming leadership involves not only the moral elevation of individual followers, but also collective efforts to accomplish social reforms. In the process, both the leader and followers will be changed. They will begin to consider not only what is good for themselves, but also what will benefit larger collectivities such as their organization, community, and nation.

Heifetz.   In his book entitled *Leadership without Easy Answers*, Ronald Heifetz (1994) proposed that the primary role of leaders is to help followers confront conflict and find productive ways to deal with it. The leader must engage people in facing challenges, changing perspectives, and learning new ways to work together effectively. Like Burns, Heifetz described leadership as both a dyadic and collective process. Leaders influence individuals, and they also mobilize collective efforts to accomplish adaptive work. The type of influence used by leaders includes not only use of rationality and appeal to values, but also formal authority. Leaders can use their authority to direct attention to problems, frame issues, structure decision processes, mediate conflicts, allocate resources to support problem solving, and delegate specific responsibilities to individuals or groups. However, formal authority is not necessary to provide ethical leadership. Emergent leaders can acquire informal authority by taking responsibility for exercising leadership in situations where it is needed. Heifetz emphasizes that meaningful change requires shared leadership, and it cannot be accomplished by a single, heroic individual.

Leaders can do many things to help people collectively solve problems in an effective way. One important leadership function is to influence people to acknowledge an important problem, rather than denying it, discounting the seriousness of the problem, procrastinating about corrective action, or providing fake remedies and stress-reducing diversions. Another important function is to help frame problems by clarifying key issues, encouraging dissenting views, distinguishing causes from symptoms, and identifying complex interdependencies. Leaders can facilitate problem solving by helping people get information, by identifying points of agreement and disagreement, and by encouraging people to find integrative solutions to conflicts.

It is important to set the pace of collective work at a rate people can tolerate. If pushed too fast, people may resort to defensive avoidance mechanisms, such as concluding that temporary relief or limited progress is a complete solution. Leaders must educate people about the difficulties that will be encountered and the self-sacrifices that will be necessary to succeed. At the same time, it is important to build hope and optimism about finding a solution. Finding the right balance is a difficult challenge for leaders. Heifetz's ideas seem especially relevant for evaluating political candidates who deny or oversimplify problems, promise unrealistic solutions, and pander to short-term individual interests rather than collective needs.

Greenleaf.   In 1970, Robert Greenleaf proposed the concept of servant leadership and it became the title of a book published in 1977. For Greenleaf, service to followers is the primary responsibility of leaders and the essence of ethical leadership. Service includes nurturing, defending, and empowering followers. A servant leader must attend to the needs of followers and help them become healthier, wiser, and more willing to accept their responsibilities. It is only by understanding followers that the leader can determine how best to serve their needs. Servant leaders must listen to followers, learn about their needs and aspirations, and be willing to share in their pain and frustration.

The servant leader must stand for what is good and right, even when it is not in the financial interest of the organization. Social injustice and inequality should be opposed whenever possible. Even the weak and marginal members of society must be treated with respect and appreciation. Greenleaf proposed that providing meaningful work for employees is as important as providing a quality product or service for the customer. He advocated that business organizations should consider social responsibility as one of the major objectives, and the board of directors should take primary responsibility for evaluating and facilitating progress on this objective.

The servant leader must empower followers instead of using power to dominate them. Trust is established by being completely honest and open, keeping actions consistent with values, and showing trust in followers. Greenleaf believed that followers of such leaders are inspired to become servant leaders themselves. People should prepare themselves to lead and accept the opportunity when offered. The result will be more people who serve as moral agents in society.

Personal Integrity and Ethical Leadership

Discussions of ethical leadership invariably involve the concept of personal integrity. As noted in Chapter 7, personal integrity is an attribute that helps to explain leadership effectiveness. In cross-cultural research on the essential traits for effective leadership, integrity is near the top of the list in all cultures that have been studied (see discussion of the GLOBE project later in this chapter). Most scholars consider integrity to be a requirement for ethical leadership. However, integrity has been defined in a variety of ways, and the appropriate definition is still a subject of debate (Barry & Stephens, 1998; Locke & Becker, 1998).

The most basic definition emphasizes honesty and consistency between a person's values and behavior. What the leader values and how the person acts are not part of this definition. Critics contend that this definition is insufficient, because the values must be moral and the behavior must be ethical (e.g., Becker, 1998). For these critics, integrity means that a person's behavior is consistent with a set of justifiable moral principles. Consistency between actions and immoral principles does not qualify. Thus, a thief who believes it is morally acceptable to steal from corrupt organizations would not be classified as high in integrity. A limitation of this more rigorous definition is the difficulty of getting agreement about justifiable moral principles. It is especially a problem for values and principles that differ across cultures, and for principles that involve competing values (e.g., the abortion controversy or mercy killing).

Some examples of behaviors usually regarded as morally justifiable include following the same rules and standards applied to others, being honest and candid when providing information or answering questions, keeping promises and commitments, and acknowledging responsibility for mistakes while also seeking to correct them. However, a leader may have ulterior motives for using behaviors that appear morally justifiable. For example, a leader may use kindness to gain the trust of people who will later be exploited. For this reason, it is necessary to consider the leader's intentions and values as well as behaviors when evaluating ethical leadership. To be ethical, the leader must intend no harm and respect the rights of all affected parties (Gini, 1998).

Dilemmas in Evaluating Ethical Leadership

Influencing follower commitment and optimism are central aspects of most theories of effective leadership. Leaders are usually expected to influence follower commitment to an existing task or a new activity. However, this influence is also the source of ethical concerns. The problem for evaluating ethical leadership is to determine when such influence is proper.

The ethics of influencing followers is of primary concern for theories of transformational and charismatic leadership, because most of these theories involve substantial leader influence over follower attitudes and behavior. Opponents question the ethics of some practices endorsed by these theories (e.g., Stephens, D'Intino & Victor, 1995; White & Wooten, 1986). In response, proponents of the theories have attempted to clarify the criteria for determining when this type of leadership is ethical (e.g., Bass & Steidlmeier, 1999; Howell & Avolio, 1992). Examples of these criteria are shown in Table 14-1. The criteria appear plausible, but they may not take into account all of the complexities and dilemmas in evaluating ethical leadership. How the various criteria can be applied remains a question of discussion and debate.

It is easier to evaluate ethical leadership when the interests of the leader, the followers, and the organization are congruent and can be attained by actions that do not involve much risk or cost to any of the parties. However, in many situations the influence process may involve (1) creating enthusiasm for a risky strategy or project, (2) inducing followers to change their underlying beliefs and values, and (3) influencing

TABLE 14-1   Suggested Criteria for Evaluating Ethical Leadership

Criterion	Ethical Leadership	Unethical Leadership
Use of leader power and influence	• Serves followers and the organization	• Satisfies personal needs and career objectives
Handling diverse interests of the multiple stakeholders	• Attempts to balance and integrate them	• Favors coalition partners who offer the most benefits
Development of a vision for the organization	• Develops a vision based on follower input about their needs, values, and ideas	• Attempts to sell a personal vision as the only way for the organization to succeed
Integrity of leader behavior	• Acts consistent with espoused values	• Does what is expedient to attain personal objectives
Risk taking in leader decisions and actions	• Is willing to take personal risks and make necessary decisions	• Avoids necessary decisions or actions that involve personal risk to the leader
Communication of relevant information operations	• Makes a complete and timely disclosure of information about events, problems, and actions	• Uses deception and distortion to bias follower perceptions about problems and progress
Response to criticism and dissent by followers	• Encourages critical evaluation to find better solutions	• Discourages and suppresses any criticism or dissent
Development of follower skills and self-confidence	• Uses coaching, mentoring, and training to develop followers	• Deemphasizes development to keep followers weak and dependent on the leader

decisions that will benefit some people at the expense of others. Each type of influence involves some ethical dilemmas.

Influencing Expectations.   An important leadership responsibility is to interpret confusing events and build consensus around strategies for dealing with threats and opportunities. Sometimes success requires a strategy or project that is bold and innovative. A risky venture may result in great benefits for followers if completed successfully, but the costs can also be high, especially if the project fails or takes much longer than expected. How the leader influences follower perception of the risks and prospects for success is relevant for evaluating ethical leadership.

Most people would agree that it is unethical to deliberately manipulate followers to do something contrary to their self-interest by making false promises or deceiving them about likely outcomes. One proposed standard for ethical leadership in the case of risky ventures is for the leader to fully inform followers about the likely costs and benefits and ask followers to make a conscious decision about whether the effort is worthwhile. However, it is often difficult for the leader (or anyone else) to find any objective basis for predicting the likely outcomes of an innovative strategy and project. If an obvious crisis already exists for the group or organization, expressing doubts and sharing complete information can create panic and ensure failure. As Heifetz (1994) proposed, it is important to help people understand a problem without demoralizing them. Effective leaders do not dwell too much upon the risks or obstacles, but instead emphasize what can be accomplished with a concerted, shared effort. Hope and optimism can eventually become a self-fulfilling prophecy if combined with effective problem solving. Thus, in situations where sharing information and interpreting events involves competing values, there are complex ethical issues to be resolved. This aspect of ethical leadership deserves more attention in the future.

Influencing Values and Beliefs.   Even more controversial is an attempt to change the underlying values and beliefs of individual followers. Some writers contend that this type of leader influence is clearly unethical, even when the intended outcome is to benefit followers as well as the organization (e.g., Stephens, D'Intino, & Victor, 1995; White & Wooten, 1986). These writers question the implicit assumption that the leader knows what is best for followers, and there is concern about the misuse of power and control over information to bias follower perceptions about problems and events. A special concern is the influence of charismatic leaders on followers who are weak and insecure.

A contrary view is that framing the issue in terms of leader indoctrination and manipulation of followers may be appropriate for religious cults, but it obscures the complexity of leadership processes in most large organizations. It is an important responsibility of leaders to help an organization reinvent itself when necessary to ensure its survival and effectiveness. A large-scale organizational change will not be successful without some changes in member beliefs and perceptions. Effective leaders engage members and other stakeholders in a dialogue to determine what types of changes are necessary and morally right for the organization. The process may (or may not) result in the emergence of a new set of shared beliefs and values. However, as noted in Chapter 10, the chief executive cannot dictate changes in the organization culture. The change, if it occurs, will reflect the influence of many leaders throughout the organization. How much influence the CEO or any other individual should try to exert on this process, and the form of the influence, are ethical questions that are yet to be resolved.

Multiple Stakeholders.   The difficulties in evaluating leadership effectiveness (see Chapter 1) include multiple criteria with complex trade-offs and stakeholders with partially conflicting interests. The diverse consequences of a leader's decisions and actions complicate the evaluation of ethical leadership. The same actions that benefit followers in some ways may also harm followers in other ways or at a later time. The same actions that serve the interests of some followers may be contrary to the interests of other followers. Doing what is best for owners may not be what is best for employees, customers, the community, the national economy, or the environment. Efforts to balance competing values and interests involve subjective judgments about rights, accountability, due process, and social responsibilities. When stakeholder interests are incompatible, it is more difficult to evaluate ethical leadership.

The traditional perspective is that managers in business organizations are agents who represent the interest of the owners in achieving economic success for the organization. From this perspective, ethical leadership is satisfied by maximizing economic outcomes that benefit owners while not doing anything strictly prohibited by laws and moral standards. For example, the decision to move a manufacturing plant from Kansas to Mexico would be considered ethical if it would significantly improve profits, regardless of the effects on plant employees or the local economy. The pursuit of short-term profits is often used as the excuse for making strategic decisions that are harmful to stakeholders other than shareholders looking for a quick increase in the value of their stock.

A very different perspective is that managers should serve multiple stakeholders inside and outside the organization (Block, 1993; Gini, 1998; Greenleaf, 1977; O'Toole, 1995; Sharp-Paine, 1994). From this perspective, judgments about ethical leadership must take into account the extent to which a leader balances and integrates the interests of different stakeholders within the constraints imposed by legal and contractual obligations. An integrative orientation appears more ethical than supporting the faction that will provide the highest personal gain for the leader, playing stakeholders off against each other (e.g., by encouraging negative stereotyping and mutual distrust), or trying to ignore substantive conflicts of interest. The following incident described by Nielsen (1989) provides an example of the integrative approach.

> The division manager for a paper products company was confronted with a difficult problem. Top management decided to close some paper mills unless operational costs for them could be reduced. The manager was concerned that cutting costs would prevent the mills from meeting government pollution control requirements. However, unless costs were reduced, the mills would close, seriously hurting the economy of the local community. The manager decided to look for an integrative win-win solution. He asked the research and engineering people in his division to look for ways to make the mills more efficient and also reduce pollution. He asked the operations and financial people in his division to estimate how much it would cost to build better mills, and when the operations would achieve a breakeven payback. When a good solution was found, he negotiated an agreement with top management to implement the plan.

The conception of leadership as a servant or steward is appealing, but it is often difficult to apply. When different stakeholders have incompatible objectives, an integrative solution may not be possible. Further difficulties occur when stakeholders desire objectives that are immoral or contrary to their own best interests, and when stakeholders expect a leader to use whatever methods are necessary to attain their desired objectives. Even when followers agree about the objectives and regard the methods as justified, the effect may be to harm people not considered legitimate stakeholders. History is full of examples of leaders who caused much suffering and misery in their dedicated pursuit of virtuous objectives (Price, 2003).

Promoting Ethics vs. Opposing Unethical Practices

Some writers make a distinction between doing things to encourage and promote ethical practices and doing things to oppose unethical activities or decisions (e.g., Nielsen, 1989). Examples of each approach are shown in Table 14-2. The two approaches are not mutually exclusive, and both can be used at the same time.

Leaders can do many things to promote ethical practices in organizations. The leader's own actions provide an example of ethical behavior to be imitated by people who admire and identify with the leader. Leaders can set clear standards and guidelines for dealing with ethical issues (e.g., help to establish an ethical code of conduct), provide opportunities for people to get advice about dealing with ethical issues (e.g., ethics hotline), and initiate discussions about ethical issues to make them more salient. Leaders can reinforce ethical behavior by including it in the criteria used to evaluate and reward follower performance. The leader can help to mediate conflicts in a way

TABLE 14-2 Two Aspects of Ethical Leadership

Promoting an Ethical Climate
- Set an example of ethical behavior in your own actions.
- Facilitate the development and dissemination of a code of ethical conduct.
- Initiate discussions with followers or colleagues about ethics and integrity.
- Recognize and reward ethical behavior by others.
- Take personal risks to advocate moral solutions to problems.
- Help others find fair and ethical solutions to conflicts.
- Initiate support services (e.g., ethics hotline, online advisory group).

Opposing Unethical Practices
- Refuse to share in the benefits provided by unethical activities.
- Refuse to accept assignments that involve unethical activities.
- Try to discourage unethical actions by others.
- Speak out publicly against unethical or unfair policies in the organization.
- Oppose unethical decisions and seek to get them reversed.
- Inform proper authorities about dangerous products or harmful practices.
- Provide assistance to others who oppose unethical decisions or practices.

that is consistent with ethical standards and procedural justice. It is appropriate to look for an integrative solution, but even if one cannot be found, it is still desirable to promote trust, fairness, and mutual respect among the factions.

Opposition to unethical practices can also take many different forms (Nielsen, 1989). Examples include refusing to comply with unethical assignments or rules, threatening to complain to higher management, making actual complaints to higher management, threatening to publicize unethical practices to outsiders, and actually revealing unethical practices to outsiders or a regulatory agency. Opposition to unethical practices is usually a difficult and risky course of action. Speaking out against injustices and opposing unethical practices may put one in danger of retaliation by powerful people in the organization. Many whistle-blowers discover that their actions result in loss of their job or derailment of their career. To successfully oppose unethical practices may require the use of ethically questionable tactics, such as coercion, deception, and manipulation. The use of such tactics for ethical purposes may unintentionally increase the legitimacy of using the same types of tactics for unethical purposes. Thus, deciding whether the means justify the ends can become a difficult dilemma for leaders who want to stop unethical practices.

Determinants of Ethical Leadership

An interesting research question is the reason for differences in ethical behavior among leaders. One explanation is provided by theories of cognitive moral development. Kohlberg (1984) proposed a model to describe how people progress through six sequential stages of moral development as they grow from a child to an adult. With each successive stage, the person develops a broader understanding of the principles of justice, social responsibility, and human rights. At the lowest level of moral development the primary motivation is self-interest and the satisfaction of personal needs. At a middle level of moral development, the primary motivation is to satisfy role expectations and social norms determined by groups, organizations, and society. At the highest level of moral development, the primary motivation is to fulfill internalized values and moral principles. A person at this level may deviate from norms and risk social rejection, economic loss, and physical punishment in order to achieve an important ethical objective.

Unlike physical maturation, moral development is not inevitable, and some people become fixated at a particular stage. As noted earlier, stage of moral development is one basis for evaluating individual leaders. A leader who is at a higher level of development is usually regarded as more ethical than one at a lower level of development. Some research indicates that cognitive moral development is related to ethical decisions in business organizations (e.g., Trevino, 1986; Trevino & Youngboood, 1990). Specific training based on the model can be used to help people move to a higher level of cognitive moral development.

Ethical leadership is also related to the individual needs and personality traits of leaders (Mumford, Gessner, Connelly, O'Connor, & Clifton, 1993; O'Connor, Mumford, Clifton, Gessner, & Connelly, 1995). Destructive, self-oriented behavior is more likely for leaders with personality traits such as high narcissism, low emotional maturity, an external locus of control orientation, and a personalized power orientation. This type of leader is more likely to perceive that other people are untrustworthy and to view them as objects to be manipulated for personal gain. The leader uses power to exploit others and advance his or her own career, rather than to achieve organizational objectives.

Ethical behavior occurs in a social context and it can be strongly influenced by aspects of the situation (Trevino, 1986; Trevino, Butterfield, & McCabe, 1998). Unethical behavior is more likely in organizations with high pressure for increased productivity, intense competition for rewards and advancement, strong emphasis on obedience to authority, strong position power for leaders, and a lack of strong cultural values and norms about ethical conduct and individual responsibility.

Leader personality and cognitive moral development interact with aspects of the situation in the determination of ethical and unethical behavior. That is, ethical behavior can be explained better by consideration of both the individual and the situation than by either variable alone. Emotionally mature leaders with a high level of cognitive moral development are more likely to resist social pressure to use destructive or unethical practices.

Future Research on Ethical Leadership

Empirical research on ethical issues in leadership is a relatively new topic, and much still needs to be learned about it. Kahn (1990) proposed an agenda of research questions that would help to bridge the apparent gap between normative concepts (defining ethical behavior) and contextual concepts (the conditions influencing ethical behavior). The objective is to produce knowledge that strengthens both the theory and practice of ethical conduct in organizations. Examples of relevant research questions include the language used to frame and communicate ethical issues, the conditions under which conversations about ethics are likely to occur, the process by which ethical dilemmas and disagreements are resolved, the process by which ethical principles are adapted to changing conditions, and the ways that leaders influence ethical awareness, dialogue, and consensus. It is also important to study how leader influence on ethical values in the culture of an organization may affect important outcomes such as the commitment and loyalty of members (Dickson, Smith, Grojean, & Ehrhart, 2001).

Gender and Leadership

A topic of great interest among practitioners as well as scholars is the possible difference between men and women in leadership behavior and effectiveness. A related topic of great importance is the reason for continued discrimination against women in leadership selection. This section of the chapter will briefly discuss both topics and review what has been learned about gender and leadership.

Sex-Based Discrimination

Widespread discrimination is clearly evident in the low number of women who hold important, high-level leadership positions in most types of organizations. The strong tendency to favor men over women in filling high-level leadership positions has been referred to as the glass ceiling. According to Adler (1996), in 1995, about 5 percent of nations had a female head of state (e.g., prime minister, president). The number of women in top executive positions in large business organizations is also very small (3%), although it is gradually increasing (Ragins, Townsend, & Mattis, 1998). In the complete absence of sex-based discrimination, the number of women in chief executive positions in business and government should be close to 50 percent.

Throughout the twentieth century, gender-based discrimination was supported by age-old beliefs that men are more qualified than women for leadership roles. These beliefs involved assumptions about the traits and skills required for effective leadership in organizations (implicit theories), assumptions about inherent differences between men and women (gender stereotypes), and assumptions about appropriate behavior for men and women (role expectations). There is no empirical support for these beliefs, and laws now exist in the United States to stop sex-based discrimination in the selection of leaders. The antidiscrimination laws are based on the premise that men and women are equally qualified to hold leadership positions in business organizations. Nevertheless, the belief that men are more qualified to be leaders persists in a segment of the population.

Implicit Theories.   Biased beliefs about the skills and behaviors necessary for effective leadership are one reason for sex-based discrimination. For a long time it was assumed that effective leaders must be confident, task-oriented, competitive, objective, decisive, and assertive, all of which were traditionally viewed as masculine attributes (Schein, 1975; Stogdill, 1974). As shown in earlier chapters, effective leadership also requires strong interpersonal skills, concern for building cooperative, trusting relationships, and use of behaviors traditionally viewed as feminine (e.g., supporting, developing, empowering). These values, skills, and behaviors were always relevant for effective leadership, but now they are more important than in earlier times because of changing conditions in work organizations (see Chapters 2 and 7). As popular conceptions of effective leadership become more accurate and comprehensive, role expectations for leaders will become less gender biased. The rapidly growing number of practitioner-oriented books on leadership in recent years may help to create a more accurate popular conception of the relevant traits, skills, and behaviors.

Stereotypes and Role Expectations.   Sex-based discrimination in leadership selection also reflects the influence of popular stereotypes and role expectations for men and women. For a long time, women were assumed to be unable or unwilling to use the masculine behaviors considered essential for effective leadership. Some laboratory studies found that even when women leaders use masculine behaviors, they are evaluated less favorably than men who use them (e.g., Eagly, Makhijani, & Klonsky, 1992; Rojahn & Willemsen, 1994). However, the effects of gender stereotypes on evaluation of female managers may be overstated in laboratory studies with students. The experience of working for men and women leaders over a period of time can reduce the effects of gender stereotypes on evaluation of the leaders (Powell, 1990). As gender stereotypes change over time in the general population, they will probably become less important as a source of biased role expectations for leaders. Unfortunately, gender stereotypes may be changing more slowly than we would prefer, and especially among male managers (Brenner, Tomkiewicz, & Schein, 1989; Powell, Butterfield, & Parent, 2002).

Other Explanations.   Other possible reasons for the glass ceiling have been suggested (Ragins et al., 1998: Tharenou, Latimer, & Conroy, 1994), including: (1) a lack of opportunity to gain experience and visibility in types of positions that would facilitate advancement, (2) higher standards of performance for women than for men, (3) exclusion of women from informal networks that aid advancement, (4) lack of encouragement and opportunity for developmental activities, (5) lack of opportunity for effective mentoring, (6) difficulties created by competing family demands, (7) a lack of strong action by top management to ensure equal opportunity, and (8) intentional efforts by some men to retain control of the most powerful positions for themselves. The explanations are not mutually exclusive, and they may combine to create an inhospitable corporate climate for female managers. To date, sufficient research is not available to determine the relative importance of the different factors and how they interact in creating barriers to advancement for women.

Feminine Advantage.   A more recent controversy is fueled by claims that women are more likely than men to possess the values and skills necessary for effective leadership in modern organizations (Book, 2000; Carr-Ruffino, 1993; Grant, 1988; Hegelsen, 1990; Rosener, 1990). Proponents of the feminine advantage theory contend that women are more concerned with consensus building, inclusiveness, and interpersonal relations; they are more willing to develop and nurture subordinates and share power with them. Like the earlier claim that men are more qualified as leaders, the claims about a feminine advantage appear to be based on weak assumptions and exaggerated gender stereotypes. Evaluation of assertions about gender superiority in leadership requires a careful consideration of the findings in the empirical research.

Research on Gender Differences

Many studies compared men and women leaders with regard to their leadership behavior. Reviews of this research on gender and leadership disagree about the results (e.g., Bass, 1990; Dobbins & Platz, 1986; Eagly, Darau, & Makhijani, 1995; Eagly & Johnson, 1990; Powell, 1993). Some reviewers concluded that there is no evidence of important gender differences in leadership behaviors or skills. Other reviewers concluded that there are gender-related differences for some behaviors or skills in some situations. A recent debate published in *Leadership Quarterly* shows the complexity of the issues and the extent to which scholars disagree (Eagly & Carli, 2003a, 2003b; Vecchio, 2002, 2003).

Many of the early studies on gender differences in leadership behavior involved task and relationship behavior. Eagly and Johnson (1990) conducted a meta-analysis of the gender studies with actual managers and found no gender differences in the use of task-oriented behavior or supportive behavior. However, the study did find that participative leadership was used slightly more by women than by men. In a more recent meta-analysis (Eagly, Johannesen-Schmidt, & Van Engen, 2003), women used slightly more transformational leadership behavior than men, and the primary difference was for individualized consideration, which includes supportive behavior and efforts to develop subordinates skills and confidence. Results for transactional leadership were mixed. Women also used slightly more contingent reward behavior, and men used slightly more passive management by exception.

Results from studies on gender differences in leadership effectiveness are also mixed. A meta-analysis by Eagly and colleagues (1995) found no overall difference in effectiveness for men and women managers. However, when role requirements for different types of managerial positions were identified, male managers were more effective than women managers in positions that required strong task skills, and women managers were more effective in positions that required strong interpersonal skills. Because most leadership positions require both types of skills, gender is unlikely to be useful as a predictor of leadership effectiveness for these positions.

Serious limitations in much of the research on gender differences complicate interpretation of the results (Lefkowitz, 1994). As noted in Chapter 2, comparative studies are prone to contamination from extraneous variables. Gender is often correlated with other variables known to affect leader behavior (e.g., level, function, time in position, type of organization). If these other variables are not measured and their effects controlled, any differences in behavior will be attributed to gender. Unfortunately, most studies reporting male-female differences do not control for this type of contamination.

Results in studies on gender differences in leadership are also distorted by exaggeration of trivial differences. In comparative studies a statistically significant difference is of little interest if the magnitude of the difference is quite small, because the differences among women themselves (and among men themselves) are much greater than the mean difference between women and men. Knowing the sex of a leader is of no practical help for predicting the person's behavior when gender differences are small. Unfortunately, it is common practice to report tests of statistical differences without reporting effect sizes. Studies that fail to provide evidence of practical significance as well as statistical significance perpetuate exaggerated stereotypes about men and women.

The utility of meta-analyses for summarizing research is limited when the results in the published literature are not representative. Assessment of gender differences is seldom the primary purpose for conducting a field study on leadership, and gender is usually just one of several demographic variables that are measured. Because gender differences are a popular topic, significant relationships will be reported more often than nonsignificant relationships. Thus, a significant but small gender difference in a meta-analysis may result from unrepresentative sampling as well as confounding.

It is essential to discover the reasons for any difference found between men and women in their leadership behavior or effectiveness. One possible explanation is that biologically based differences reinforced by differential treatment during childhood cause men and women to have different values, traits, skills, and ways of dealing with situations. Another possible explanation is that differential stereotypes about men and women result in different role expectations, which influence leadership behavior as well as the perception and evaluation of that behavior by others. Although not mutually exclusive, the two explanations lead to different implications for the selection and training of leaders. Unfortunately, most studies on gender differences in leadership fail to investigate possible reasons for them. In the absence of such evidence, people are more likely to attribute gender differences to inherent biological factors than to stereotypes and biases that could be changed.

Taking into account both the findings and limitations of the research on gender differences in leadership, the conclusions reached by Powell (1990, pg. 74) still seem appropriate:

> There is little reason to believe that either women or men make superior managers, or that women and men are different types of managers. Instead, there are likely to be excellent, average, and poor managerial performers within each sex. Success in today's highly competitive marketplace calls for organizations to make best use of the talent available to them. To do this, they need to identify, develop, encourage, and promote the most effective managers, regardless of sex.

Leadership in Different Cultures

Most of the research on leadership during the past half century was conducted in the United States, Canada, and Western Europe. However, interest in cross-cultural leadership and research on leadership in non-Western cultures has increased rapidly during the past decade (Dickson, Den Hartog, & Michelson, 2003; Dorfman, 2003). A major issue is the extent to which leadership theories developed and tested in one culture can be generalized to different cultures. A related issue is identification of similarities and differences in managerial practices across countries. This section of the chapter discusses several aspects of cross-cultural leadership, including the importance of cross-cultural research, the process by which culture influences leadership perceptions and behavior, types of cross-cultural research on leadership, problems in conducting the research, examples of the research, and some of the findings.

Importance of Cross-Cultural Research

Cross-cultural research on leadership is important for several reasons (Dorfman, 1996; House, Wright, & Aditya, 1997). Increasing globalization of organizations makes it more important to learn about effective leadership in different cultures. Leaders are increasingly confronted with the need to influence people from other cultures, and successful influence requires a good understanding of these cultures. Leaders must also be able to understand how people from different cultures view them and interpret their actions. To understand these issues, it is essential to validate a theory of leadership in cultures that differ from the one in which the theory was developed. Some aspects of a leadership theory may be relevant for all cultures, but other aspects may apply only to a particular type of culture.

Cross-cultural research also requires researchers to consider a broader than usual range of variables and processes, which can provide new insights and improve leadership theories. Research to develop or validate taxonomies of leadership behavior in different cultures can reveal new aspects of behavior that are relevant for effective leadership. Examination of cross-cultural differences may cause researchers to pay more attention to possible effects of situational variables not usually included in current theories of leadership (e.g., religion, language, history, laws, political systems, ethnic subcultures). Finally, cross-cultural research poses some unique methodological challenges that may result in improved procedures for data collection and analysis.

Cultural Influences on Leadership Behavior

Cultural values and traditions can influence the attitudes and behavior of managers in a number of different ways (Adler, 1997; Fu & Yukl, 2000; House et al., 1997; Lord & Maher, 1991). The values are likely to be internalized by managers who grow up in a particular culture, and these values will influence their attitudes and behavior in ways that may not be conscious. In addition, cultural values are reflected in societal norms about the way people relate to each other. Cultural norms specify acceptable forms of leadership behavior and in some cases may be formalized as societal laws limiting the use of power to influence the decisions and actions of others. Regardless of whether they internalize cultural values about influence behavior, most managers will conform to social norms about this behavior. One reason is that deviation from societal norms may result in diminished respect and social pressure from other members of the organization. Another reason for conformity with social norms is that use of unacceptable behavior is likely to undermine the effectiveness of the behavior.

Leadership behavior is influenced by other situational variables besides national culture (Bass, 1990; House et al., 1997). Some examples include characteristics of the organization (e.g., type of organization, size, organization culture and climate) and characteristics of the managerial position (e.g., level and function of the manager, position power, and authority). The cultural and noncultural determinants of behavior are not always congruent. Some situational variables may have parallel effects across national cultures, but other situational variables may interact with national culture in complex ways.

Even when some types of leadership behaviors are not clearly supported by the prevailing cultural values and traditions in a country, it does not necessarily mean that these behaviors would be ineffective if used more often. Managers who have little experience with a particular type of leadership behavior may not understand how effective it could be (House et al., 1997). Finally, it is important to remember that the values and traditions in a national culture can change over time, just as they do in an organization culture. For example, countries in which the traditional autocratic political systems are replaced by democratic systems are likely to become more accepting of participative leadership and empowerment in organizations. Countries in which strong gender differentiation is replaced by gender equality can be expected to become more accepting of leadership practices that reflect traditional feminine attributes (e.g., nurturing, developing, building cooperative relationships). As values change, beliefs about the skills and behaviors necessary for effective leadership are likely to change in consistent ways.

Types of Research and Difficulties

As in the case of the leadership research conducted within a single culture, much of the cross-cultural research on leadership involves leader behavior. The growing body of cross-cultural research has examined 4 types of research questions(Brett, Tinsley, Janssens, Barsness, & Lytle, 1997) : (1) differences in the conceptualization of leadership behavior, as defined by factor structures or leadership prototypes; (2) differences in beliefs about effective leadership behavior; (3) differences in the actual pattern of leadership behavior in each country; and (4) differences in the relationship of leadership behavior to outcomes such as subordinate satisfaction, motivation, and performance. For this latter issue, culture is treated as a moderator variable rather than as a direct determinant of leadership behavior.

Several methodological problems make cross-cultural research especially difficult: (1) lack of equivalence of meaning for measures developed in one country and then used in other countries; (2) confounding effects of demographic and situational variables that are not controlled by sampling or by covariance analysis; (3) response biases that differ across cultures (e.g., more central tendency in some Asian countries); (4) statistically significant differences that are too weak to have any practical significance; and (5) lack of representative samples from which to generalize about countries with large regional differences. The utility of many cross-cultural studies is limited by their failure to acknowledge these problems and deal with them in an adequate way.

Even for well-designed studies, the interpretation of results is often difficult. Many studies fail to include variables that will explain the reason for cross-cultural differences in leadership. For example, it is useful to learn that a particular type of leadership behavior has stronger effects in a particular culture, but it is even better to learn why. Interpretation of results is also complicated by cultural differences in underlying values and assumptions about human nature and about organizations (Boyacigiller & Adler, 1991). To minimize this type of problem it is advisable to have a research team with qualified representatives from the different cultures included in the study.

Finally, the conceptual frameworks used to describe cultural dimensions affect interpretation of results from cross-cultural research on leadership. The identification of appropriate value dimensions is itself a difficult challenge. Different sets of dimensions have been proposed (e.g., Hofstede, 1980, 1993; House et al., 1997; Schwartz, 1992; Trompenaars, 1993), but scholars do not yet agree about their relative merits. Hofstede's taxonomy has been used most often in the cross-cultural research on leadership (see Table 14-3). All of the current taxonomies have limitations, and researchers continue to seek a more comprehensive and useful way to describe cultural dimensions.

Cross-Cultural Differences in Leadership

The cross-cultural research finds both similarities and differences among countries with regard to beliefs about effective leadership, patterns of leadership behavior, and use of specific managerial practices (Dickson et al., 2003; Dorfman, 2003; Hofstede, 2001; Trompenaars, 1993). Some cross-cultural differences involve quantitative analyses of ratings on behavior questionnaires to determine whether a type of behavior is used more in one culture or country than another. For example, Dorfman and colleagues

TABLE 14-3 Examples of Cultural Dimensions

Power Distance: The extent to which people accept differences in power and status among themselves. In a high power distance culture, leaders have more authority, they are entitled to special rights and privileges, they are less accessible, and they are not expected to share power with subordinates.

High: Russia, China, Philippines, Mexico, Venezuela, India
Medium: Netherlands, Italy, Pakistan, Japan, Spain, Greece
Low: Israel, Austria, Denmark, England, New Zealand, United States

Individualism: The extent to which the needs and autonomy of individuals are more important than the collective needs of the work unit or society. In individualistic cultures, people are identified more by their own achievements than by their group memberships or contributions to collective success, and individual rights are more important than social responsibilities.

High: United States, Netherlands, England, Australia, Canada, Belgium
Medium: Russia, Japan, Austria, Israel, Spain, India
Low: China, Indonesia, Thailand, Pakistan, Hong Kong, Venezuela

Uncertainty Avoidance: The extent to which people feel comfortable with ambiguous situations and inability to predict future events. In cultures with high avoidance of uncertainty, there is more fear of the unknown, security and stability are more important, conflict is avoided, plans and forecasts are more valued, and there is more emphasis on formal rules and regulations.

High: Japan, France, Russia, Argentina, Spain, Belgium
Medium: China, Netherlands, Switzerland, Pakistan, Taiwan, Finland
Low: Singapore, Hong Kong, Denmark, England, Sweden, United States

Gender Egalitarianism: The extent to which men and women receive equal treatment, and both masculine and feminine attributes are considered important and desirable. In cultures with high gender egalitarianism, sex roles are not clearly differentiated, jobs are not segregated by gender, and attributes such as compassion, empathy, and intuition are as important as assertiveness, competitiveness, and objective rationality.

High: Denmark, Norway, Finland, Sweden, Netherlands, Chile
Medium: Canada, Indonesia, Israel, France, India, China
Low: Japan, Austria, Italy, Mexico, Venezuela, Switzerland

Note: Selection of countries is based primarily on findings in research by Hofstede (1980). Note that gender egalitarianism is the reverse of Hofstede's masculinity/feminity dimension.

(1997) found that American managers used more participative leadership than managers in Mexico or Korea. However, a quantitative comparison of scale means from behavior description questionnaires is complicated by methodological problems such as confounding and lack of equivalence (Peng, Peterson, & Shyi, 1991). For example, lower scores may be obtained in one country because the behavior items have a different meaning there, or because respondents in that culture typically use extreme ratings on a questionnaire.

Other cross-cultural studies attempt to identify qualitative differences in the way a specific type of behavior is enacted in each country. For example, one study (Podsakoff, Dorfman, Howell, & Todor, 1986) found that positive reward behavior was important for leadership effectiveness in different cultures, but the types of behavior rewarded and the way rewards were used differed across cultures. Another study (Smith, Misumi, Tayeb, Peterson, & Bond, 1989) found differences in the way managers communicated directions and feedback to subordinates. American managers were more likely to use a face-to-face meeting to provide directions to subordinates and to give negative feedback (criticism), whereas Japanese managers were more likely to use written memos for directions and to channel negative feedback through peers.

Some cross-cultural studies examined differences in the relationship of leadership behavior to outcomes such as subordinate satisfaction and performance. For example, Scandura, Von Glinow, and Lowe (1999) found that supportive behavior by leaders was significantly related to subordinate satisfaction and leadership effectiveness in the United States but not in two Middle Eastern countries (Jordan and Saudi Arabia). In contrast, structuring behavior by leaders was significantly related to both criterion variables in the Middle Eastern countries but not in the United States.

Another study (Dorfman et al., 1997) found that directive leadership was related to organizational commitment in Mexico and Taiwan, but not in the United States, South Korea, or Japan. Supportive leadership was related to satisfaction with the manager in all five countries, but cross-cultural differences were found for the relation of supportive leadership to subordinate performance and organizational commitment. Leader use of contingent rewards was related to subordinate organizational commitment in the United States, Mexico, and Japan, but not in Korea or Taiwan. Participative leadership was related to subordinate performance in the United States but not in Mexico or South Korea.

The GLOBE Project

The GLOBE project is a cross-cultural study of leadership in 62 different cultures representing all major regions of the world (House et al., 2004). The project includes 180 researchers in different countries working together in a coordinated, long-term effort. The objective of the project is to develop an empirically based theory that describes the relationships between societal culture, organizational processes, and leadership. Multiple methods of data collection are being used, including survey questionnaires, interviews, media analysis, archival records, and unobtrusive measures. The strategy for sampling and analysis is designed to control for the influence of industry, management level, and organizational culture.

One specific research question is the extent to which different cultures have similar beliefs about effective leader attributes and behaviors. Preliminary results indicate that the following attributes (traits, skills, behaviors) are rated highly relevant for effective leadership in all of the cultures: integrity (honest, trustworthy, just), visionary (shows foresight, plans ahead), inspirational (positive, dynamic, encourages, motivates, builds confidence), decisive, diplomatic (effective bargainer, looks for win-win solutions), achievement-oriented, team integrator, and administrative skills. Some attributes found to vary widely in relevance across cultures were the following: ambitious, cautious, compassionate, domineering, formal, independent, indirect, intuitive, logical, orderly, risk taker, self-effacing, self-sacrificing, sensitive, status conscious, and willful.

The researchers also examined the relationship between leader attributes and cultural value dimensions. For example, being team oriented (collaborative, diplomatic, team integrator) was considered more relevant for leadership effectiveness in cultures that are collectivistic rather than individualistic. Being participative was considered more relevant for leadership effectiveness in cultures with low power distance and low avoidance of uncertainty. Being charismatic (visionary, inspirational, decisive, and self-sacrificing) was considered more relevant in cultures with a high performance orientation.

The GLOBE project is also examining the relationship among societal culture, other situational variables (organizational strategy, culture, technology, size, environmental uncertainty), leadership processes, and organizational effectiveness. The research includes an in-depth, qualitative description of each culture as well as analyses of quantitative variables. The researchers hope to use laboratory and field experiments to verify causal relationships and moderating effects of national culture.

Managing Diversity

Diversity can take many forms, including differences in race, ethnic identity, age, gender, education, socioeconomic level, and sexual orientation. The amount of diversity in the workforce is increasing in the United States (Milliken & Martins, 1996). More women are entering traditionally male jobs, the number of older workers is increasing, and there is more diversity with regard to ethnic, religious, and racial backgrounds. The increasing number of joint ventures, mergers, and strategic alliances is bringing together people from different types of organizations and national cultures.

As noted in earlier chapters, diversity offers potential benefits and costs for a group or organization (Cox & Blake, 1991; Milliken & Martins, 1996; Triandis et al., 1994). A greater variety of perspectives increases creativity, and full utilization of a diverse workforce will increase the amount of available talent for filling important jobs. However, diversity can also result in more distrust and conflict, lower satisfaction, and higher turnover. Thus, managing diversity is an important responsibility of leaders in the twenty-first century. A major difficulty is to find an appropriate balance between promoting diversity and building a strong organization culture. An organization is less likely to have shared values and strong member commitment when it has many diverse members who identify primarily with their own subgroup. How well the two competing objectives can be integrated is still a matter of debate and continuing research.

Foster Appreciation and Tolerance of Diversity

Leaders can do many things to foster appreciation and tolerance for diversity. Some recommended action steps for individual leaders are listed in Table 14-4. These actions can be divided into two categories that are similar to the distinction made earlier for ethical leadership behavior. Some actions seek to encourage tolerance and appreciation, whereas other actions challenge discrimination and intolerance.

Diversity training programs provide a formal approach to encourage tolerance, understanding, and appreciation (Cox & Blake, 1991). One type of training seeks to create a better understanding of diversity problems and the need for self-awareness about stereotyping and intolerance. Another type of diversity training seeks to educate employees about cultural differences and how to respond to them in the workplace. The specific aspects of diversity that are included vary depending on the program (e.g., ethnic background, religion, national culture, age differences, employee sex, sexual orientation, physical disabilities). The two types of diversity training can be used either alone or together. Avon, Hewlett-Packard, Mobil Oil, Procter & Gamble, and Xerox are just a few examples of companies that have used such programs.

A problem with some diversity training programs is their emphasis on placing blame for discrimination rather than on increasing self-awareness and mutual understanding

TABLE 14-4 Guidelines for Managing Diversity

- Set an example in your own behavior of appreciation for diversity.
- Encourage respect for individual differences.
- Promote understanding of different values, beliefs, and traditions.
- Explain the benefits of diversity for the team or organization.
- Encourage and support others who promote tolerance of diversity.
- Discourage use of stereotypes to describe people.
- Identify biased beliefs and role expectations for women or minorities.
- Challenge people who make prejudiced comments.
- Speak out to protest against unfair treatment based on prejudice.
- Take disciplinary action to stop harassment of women or minorities.

(Nemetz & Christensen, 1996). Leaders who implement diversity training should ensure that the content of the program remains consistent with an appealing vision of what appreciation of diversity can mean for all members of the organization.

Structural mechanisms to uncover discrimination and reward tolerance are also helpful. Examples include (1) appraisal criteria that include diversity issues, (2) task forces or advisory committees to help identify discrimination or intolerance and develop remedies, (3) measures that allow systematic monitoring of progress, and (4) hotlines or other special mechanisms that make it easier for employees to report discrimination and intolerance. Efforts to change attitudes are more likely to be successful when diversity training is directed at people who have not already formed strong prejudices, and the organization has a culture that supports appreciation for diversity (Nemetz & Christensen, 1996).

Provide Equal Opportunity

To make full use of the talent represented by the diverse members of the organization, it is essential to eliminate constraints that prevent qualified people from selection for important positions. Many things can be done to facilitate equal opportunity and reduce discrimination in personnel decisions (Cox, 1991). Some examples include (1) recruitment practices that encourage affirmative action without imposing reverse discrimination; (2) selection criteria based on relevant skills rather than biased conceptions; (3) mentorship programs that provide adequate advice, encouragement, and assistance to women and minorities; and (4) management development programs that provide adequate opportunities for every employee to learn relevant skills and gain valuable experience. The success of these mechanisms depends not only on top management, but also on the support of leaders at middle and lower levels of the organization. All leaders in the organization share the responsibility for ensuring equal opportunity.

Summary

The amount of discussion and research on ethical leadership is increasing as people become more cynical about the motives, competence, and integrity of business and political leaders. Conceptions of ethical leadership include nurturing followers, empowering them, and promoting social justice. Ethical leadership includes efforts to encourage ethical behavior as well as efforts to stop unethical practices. Ethical leaders seek to build mutual trust and respect among diverse followers and to find integrative solutions to conflicts among stakeholders with competing interests. Such leaders do not foster distrust or play favorites to gain more power or achieve personal objectives. Determinants of ethical behavior by a leader include situational influences and aspects of leader personality such as level of cognitive moral development. The criteria for evaluating ethical leadership include leader values, intentions, and the extent to which leader behavior is morally justifiable. Evaluation of morality for individual leaders is complicated by multiple stakeholders, the diverse consequences of a leader's actions, and disagreements about the extent to which ends justify means.

Sex-based discrimination in the selection and promotion of leaders continues to be a serious problem in large organizations. There are several different reasons for such discrimination, but more research is needed to understand the problem better and find ways to deal with it. Many studies have examined gender-based differences in leadership behavior and effectiveness, but the findings are weak and inconsistent. Future studies need to control for effects of likely contaminating variables, report the magnitude of any significant differences that are found, and measure processes that provide insight into the reasons for the differences.

With the rapid pace of globalization and economic development, cross-cultural leadership has become an important topic for research. The amount of cross-cultural research is increasing, but it is still too early to draw any firm conclusions about the universal and unique aspects of leadership. The methodological difficulties in conducting this type of research are substantial. In many of the studies, equivalence of meaning is not assured, the sampling procedures are inadequate, controls for contaminating factors are absent, explanatory variables are not included, and interpretation of results is questionable. Faster progress may require greater use of large-scale research projects such as GLOBE.

An important responsibility for leaders in this new century is the management of diversity. Leaders play an essential role in helping to bring about equal opportunity and elimination of unfair discrimination in selection and promotion decisions. Leaders can do many things to encourage tolerance and appreciation of diversity in organizations. However, it will be a challenge for leaders to foster diversity while also attempting to build a strong organizational culture with shared values and collective identification.

Review and Discussion Questions

1. Why is it so difficult to evaluate the ethics and morality of individual leaders?
2. What are some examples of ethical and unethical leadership behavior?
3. Can unethical behavior occur for a leader who has proper values and intentions?
4. What are some likely reasons for the glass ceiling for women in large organizations?
5. What can be done to reduce the barriers and create a level playing field for women?
6. Summarize the findings in research comparing male and female leaders in terms of behavior and effectiveness.
7. What are the major research questions in studies of cross-cultural leadership?
8. What are some of the difficulties encountered in conducting cross-cultural research on leadership?
9. What does the cross-cultural research on leadership reveal?
10. What can leaders do to manage diversity in organizations?

Key Terms

- cross-cultural differences
- cultural sensitivity
- cultural value dimensions
- discrimination in personnel decisions
- diversity training

- ethical dilemmas
- ethical leadership
- equal opportunity programs
- glass ceiling
- GLOBE project
- integrity

- multiple stakeholders
- servant leadership
- sex-role stereotypes
- stages of cognitive moral development

CASE

Madison, Jones, and Conklin

After graduating from a prestigious business school, Laura Kravitz accepted a job at Madison, Jones, and Conklin, a medium-sized firm that did accounting and consulting projects for corporate clients. After a series of successful assignments working as a member of a project team, Laura was promoted to a team manager position with broader responsibilities. Laura felt confident about her qualifications. The other team managers seemed to respect her, and clients were happy with the projects she managed. With this record of success, Laura hoped to eventually become a partner in the company. However, as the only woman manager in a male-dominated company, she knew that there would be some obstacles to overcome.

Laura felt that some of the senior managers were very conservative and did not accept her as an equal. In the quarterly planning meetings, these managers were often inattentive when she spoke and seemed unreceptive to her suggestions for improvements. Several times she proposed an idea that was ignored, and the same idea was later suggested by someone else who received the credit for it.

Laura did not have a mentor in the company to tell people about her skills and help to advance her career. Moreover, she did not feel accepted into the informal network of relationships that provided opportunities to interact with senior managers. She did not like to play golf and was not a member of the exclusive golf club to which many of the male managers belonged. She was not invited to most of the social activities hosted by senior managers for friends and select members of the company.

Laura also felt that the assignment of projects was biased. The high-profile projects were always given to the male managers. When Laura asked her boss for more challenging projects, she was told that the older clients usually preferred to deal with men. Because she was not given the more profitable accounts, her performance numbers did not look as good as the numbers for some of the male managers. Two male managers who had joined the company around the same time she was hired were promoted ahead of her.

Frustrated by the apparent glass ceiling at the company, Laura asked to meet with the president to talk about her career. The president was surprised to hear that Laura was unhappy about her advancement in the company. He assured her that she was a valuable employee and should be patient about a promotion. However, after another year with little improvement in how she was treated, Laura resigned from the company. With two friends from graduate school who also felt unappreciated, she formed a new company and served as the chief executive officer. In a relatively short time, this company became highly successful. ∎

SOURCE: Copyright © 1999 by Gary Yukl.

QUESTIONS

1. What forms of gender discrimination did Laura experience?

2. What could Laura have done to overcome the obstacles she encountered?

3. What could the president have done to create equal opportunity in this company?

15

OVERVIEW AND INTEGRATION

Learning Objectives

After studying this chapter you should be able to:

- Summarize major findings about leadership traits, skills, behavior, influence processes, and situational variables.

- Understand key points of convergence in findings from these different approaches for studying leadership.

- Understand what progress has been made in integrating the findings in different approaches for studying leadership.

- Understand how biases in the conceptualization of leadership affect theory and research.

- Understand how the methods used for studying leadership affect what is learned about it.

- Understand the advantages offered by multimethod research on leadership.

- Understand what has been learned about the essence of effective leadership.

This final chapter summarizes the major findings from earlier chapters and examines convergence across different approaches for studying leadership. An integrating conceptual framework is presented, and some essential leadership qualities are identified. The chapter also reexamines some conceptual and methodological biases that limit progress in theory development and empirical research on leadership. The chapter begins with a summary of what researchers learned about leadership in the past half-century.

Major Findings in Leadership Research

The field of leadership was in a state of ferment and confusion for decades. The field rushed from one fad to the next, but the actual pace of theory development was quite slow. Several thousand empirical studies were conducted on leadership effectiveness, but the results are often inconsistent and inconclusive. The confused state of the field can be attributed in large part to the sheer volume of publications, the disparity of approaches, the proliferation of confusing terms, the narrow focus of most research, the preference for simplistic explanations, the high percentage of studies on trivial questions, and the scarcity of studies using strong research methods. As the old adage goes, it is difficult to see the forest for the trees. Nevertheless, the preceding chapters of this book demonstrate that substantial progress has been made in learning about effective leadership. The major findings from different lines of leadership research are summarized briefly.

The Leadership Situation

People in leadership positions face relentless and conflicting demands on their time. There is a constant stream of requests, problems, inquiries, and reports from the many different people who interact with a leader. The pattern of necessary interactions with subordinates, peers, superiors, and outsiders is determined by aspects of the situation such as the nature of the work (e.g., repetitive or variable, uncertain or predictable) and dependencies involving the different parties. The people who interact with a leader communicate role expectations about appropriate behavior, and competing demands from different people (insiders vs. outsiders, subordinates vs. bosses) create role conflicts. Role expectations and activity patterns are also affected by the nature of the position (e.g., level, function, type of unit or team), the type of organization, the culture of the organization, and the national culture. The decisions and actions of leaders are limited by many internal and external constraints, such as policies, rules, standard procedures, budgetary requirements, and labor laws.

Aspects of the situation also determine the importance of leadership and what type of leadership is needed. A group with members who are confused and discouraged needs more leadership than a cohesive, well-organized group with committed members. An organization in a highly turbulent environment needs more strategic leadership to survive and prosper than an organization that is already operating efficiently in a more stable environment. Despite all the situational demands and constraints on leaders, they still have choices about what aspects of the job to emphasize, how to allocate their time, and with whom to interact. Effective leaders seek to understand demands and constraints, and they adapt their behavior accordingly. They are able to reconcile the role conflicts, and they take advantage of role ambiguity as an opportunity for discretionary action. They seek to exploit opportunities, expand their range of choices, and shape the impressions formed by others about their competence and expertise.

Leadership Behavior

More research has been conducted on leader activities and behavior than on any other aspect of leadership. The descriptive research found that effective leaders develop a mental agenda of short-term and long-term objectives and strategies. The agenda is used to guide their actions, manage their time, and help them become more proactive. Effective leaders identify problems that are both important and solvable, and they take responsibility for dealing with the problems in a systematic and timely way. By relating problems to each other and to informal objectives, they find opportunities to solve more than one problem at the same time.

Effective leaders find task, relations, and change-oriented behavior that are appropriate for the current situation. Task-oriented behaviors are used to improve or maintain internal efficiency and coordination in a team or organization. Effective leaders plan and schedule activities in a way that will make better use of people, resources, information, and equipment. They assign tasks, determine resource requirements, and coordinate interrelated activities. They encourage and facilitate efforts to improve quality, productivity, and utilization of resources. They help to clarify objectives, priorities, and standards for evaluating results. They monitor the internal operations of a group or organization to assess performance and detect problems to be resolved.

Relations-oriented behaviors are used to build commitment to work objectives, mutual trust and cooperation, and identification with the team or organization. Effective leaders use a variety of different relations-oriented behaviors. They are supportive toward people (show trust and respect) and provide recognition for accomplishments and contributions. They provide coaching and mentoring to build follower skills and self-efficacy. They consult with people before making decisions that will affect those individuals in important ways. They empower people to resolve operational problems in their work and provide better service to customers and clients. They use team-building behaviors to increase identification with the group and build member trust and cooperation. Finally, these leaders build and maintain a network of cooperative relationships with outsiders who are a valuable source of information, assistance, and political support.

Effective leaders use change-oriented behaviors to modify objectives, strategies, and work processes and facilitate adaptation to the external environment. A major responsibility for leaders at the executive level is to formulate an adaptive strategy that is relevant for the external environment and consistent with the organization's core competencies and ideology. Effective leaders monitor the external environment to obtain information about trends and events that require adaptive changes. The leaders interpret external events, focus attention on threats and opportunities, and relate proposed changes to a clear, appealing vision that is relevant to follower values, ideals, and core competencies. The leaders encourage and facilitate innovative thinking and the creation, acquisition, diffusion, and application of new knowledge to improve products, services, and work processes. To gain approval and support for major change, it is usually necessary to forge a coalition of internal and external supporters. Effective leaders also empower competent change agents to facilitate effective implementation of strategic decisions throughout the organization. Symbolic actions and role modeling are used by leaders at all levels to show continued personal commitment to a new strategy or major change. Providing opportunities to experience progress and repeated small wins gives followers more confidence in themselves, the vision, and the leadership.

Power and Influence

Influence is the essence of leadership, and much of the activity of formal leaders involves attempts to influence the attitudes and behavior of people, including subordinates, peers, superiors, and outsiders. How much power and influence a leader needs depends on the situation. More influence is needed to make major changes in strategy when strong resistance to change is encountered. Less influence is needed when people have the same objectives and are intrinsically motivated to do what is needed. Influence derived from position power is especially important when it is necessary to control rebels who try to disrupt the activities of the organization or criminals who want to steal its resources. Inspirational influence and confidence building are important for successful performance of a difficult task that frustrates and discourages people, or a dangerous task that makes them fearful. Upward and lateral influence are important for the leader to provide satisfactory benefits, obtain adequate resources, facilitate the work of the team, buffer subordinates from unreasonable demands, and represent their interests effectively.

Position power is derived from aspects of the situation such as the amount of formal authority, control over distribution of rewards and punishments, control over information, and access to important people. Exclusive access to information about internal and external events provides an opportunity to interpret reality for people and influence their decisions. Influence over subordinates is enhanced by having a moderate amount of authority to make necessary changes and dispense tangible rewards and benefits. However, too much position power entails the risk that the leader will be tempted to rely on it and neglect more effective forms of influence for building commitment. Effective leaders develop referent and expert power to supplement their position power and use it to make nonroutine requests and motivate commitment to tasks that require high effort, initiative, and persistence. Referent power is developed by being supportive, caring, fair, and accepting. Expert power is acquired by successfully handling external threats and internal problems.

The manner in which a leader exercises power largely determines whether it results in enthusiastic commitment, passive compliance, or stubborn resistance. Effective leaders exert both position power and personal power in a subtle, easy fashion that minimizes status differentials and avoids threatening the self-esteem of others. These leaders use power in ethical ways and seek to integrate the competing interest of different stakeholders. Effective leaders attempt to empower followers in ways that are appropriate for the situation.

A variety of social influence techniques can be used for developing commitment to task objectives and compliance with requests. Effective leaders use proactive influence tactics that are appropriate for the objectives, context, and relationship. These leaders also use indirect ways of influencing people, such as management systems, reward systems, improvement programs, structural forms, and facilities. Political tactics are used to influence strategic decisions, especially in situations characterized by strong disagreement about organizational objectives and priorities.

The distribution and sharing of power over decisions has important implications for leadership effectiveness in groups and organizations, especially in cultures that value democracy. Extensive participation can result in better decisions when relevant information and ideas are distributed among people, they are willing to cooperate in finding a good solution, and ample time is available to use a participative process. Participants are more likely to understand and accept the decision if the decision process allows sufficient opportunity to present ideas and influence the outcome. The quality of group decisions depends to a considerable extent on whether essential leadership functions are carried out and the group is able to avoid common process problems such as hasty decisions, polarization, and groupthink. Successful empowerment of individuals or groups requires substantial agreement about objectives and priorities, a willingness to assume responsibility for making decisions, and a high degree of mutual trust.

Traits and Skills

Technical, conceptual, and interpersonal skills are needed for most leadership roles and functions. Cognitive skills are necessary to analyze problems, develop creative solutions, identify patterns and trends, differentiate between relevant and irrelevant information, understand complex relationships, and develop effective mental models. Interpersonal skills are needed to influence people, develop cooperative relationships, establish and maintain networks, understand individuals, facilitate teamwork, and resolve conflicts constructively. Technical skills are needed to understand activities, operational processes, products and services, technology, and legal/contractual requirements. The relative importance of different skills varies greatly from situation to situation, but some specific skills are probably useful in all leadership positions.

Personality traits seem less important than skills for effective leadership. Nevertheless, individual needs, core values, and temperament are clearly relevant to effective leadership. Traits affect a person's willingness and ability to assume leadership responsibilities and tolerate the stress and relentless pressures of the job. Traits also help to determine a leader's desire to accumulate power, influence people, develop relevant skills, and learn from feedback.

Some traits and skills seem especially relevant to the accumulation and use of power. Leaders with a personalized power orientation seek to accumulate more power, and they exercise it in a manipulative, impulsive, domineering manner intended to aggrandize themselves and gain personal loyalty from subordinates. In contrast, leaders with a socialized power orientation and a high level of cognitive moral development use their influence to build commitment to idealized goals, and they seek to empower subordinates by sharing information and using more consultation, delegation, and development of subordinate skills and confidence. Leaders with an internal control orientation, high need for power, and high self-confidence make more influence attempts. Self-confidence, persuasive ability, expertise, and political insight facilitate the effectiveness of the influence attempts.

Some traits and skills appear to be especially relevant for effective task-oriented leadership. People with high self-confidence, internal control orientation, and achievement orientation are more likely to take the initiative to identify and resolve task-related problems. Cognitive and technical skills are needed for planning projects, coordinating complex relationships, directing unit activities, and analyzing operational problems. Cognitive and interpersonal skills are needed to conduct effective problem-solving meetings.

Some traits and skills appear to be especially relevant for effective relations-oriented leadership. Communications skills (listening and presentation), emotional maturity, and emotional intelligence facilitate development of cooperative relationships and make influence attempts more effective. Personal integrity is essential for maintaining mutual trust and credibility. A leader with a socialized power orientation is more likely to support, develop, and empower subordinates. An appreciation for individual and cultural differences can help a leader influence people in diverse groups and facilitate cooperation and teamwork.

Some traits and skills appear to be especially relevant for effective change-oriented leadership. A strong achievement orientation can be a source of motivation to strive for excellence and pursue innovative improvements. Strong cognitive skills and relevant technical knowledge help a leader to recognize threats and opportunities in the external environment and formulate an appropriate strategy based on the organization's core competencies. A socialized power orientation, strong integrity, and a high level of moral development are found in leaders whose primary concern is the welfare of followers and the organization, not their own career advancement or personal gain. Social and emotional intelligence help a leader determine who needs to be influenced to support change and how to do it. Communication skills help a leader articulate an appealing vision and persuade people of the need for change.

The willingness and ability to learn and adapt are important requirements for effective leadership in today's uncertain and turbulent world. Effective leaders are flexible enough to adjust their behavior as conditions change, and they find ways to balance competing values and resolve role conflicts. Relevant skills and knowledge can be acquired through a combination of formal training, developmental activities, and self-learning activities. However, a person's motivation and personality also influence the desire to learn new skills, the willingness to take risks in trying new approaches, and the readiness to accept feedback about deficiencies. Thus, the effectiveness of a leadership development program will depend in part on the personality traits of the individual participants.

Toward an Integrating Conceptual Framework

Leadership research has a narrow focus, and there has been little integration of findings from the different approaches. Most of the early trait research did not include measures of leadership behavior, even though it is evident that the effects of leader traits on criteria of leadership success are mediated by this behavior. Most of the early behavior research did not include leader traits or power, even though they influence a leader's behavior, or intervening variables that would explain how leader behavior affects success criteria. The power-influence approach includes some research on influence tactics, but other types of leadership behavior were not included. Until recently little research was conducted on the relationship of leader and follower traits to influence behavior. Finally, most situational theories examine how the situation enhances or nullifies the effects of selected leader behaviors or traits, rather than taking a broader view of the way traits, power, behavior, and situation interact to jointly determine leadership effectiveness.

Despite the prevailing pattern of segmentation in research on leadership over the past 50 years, the number of studies that straddle more than one approach is increasing, and the different lines of research are gradually converging. Most of the findings from different lines of research are consistent and mutually supportive. Table 15-1 shows examples of convergence in key concepts from different perspectives on leadership.

When the different approaches are viewed as part of a larger network of interacting variables, they appear to be interrelated in a meaningful way. Figure 15-1 provides an integrating conceptual framework that encompasses each set of variables. The proposed conceptual framework is based on the assumption that a core set of intervening variables determines performance for individuals, groups, and the overall organization. Intervening variables such as follower motivation, skills, role clarity, and self-efficacy mediate the effects of leadership behavior on the performance of individual followers. Intervening variables such as cooperation and mutual trust, coordination, collective efficacy, and collective identification mediate the effects of leader behavior on team performance. Intervening variables such as process efficiency, human and social capital, collective learning, product and process innovation, and relevant competitive strategies

TABLE 15-1   Approximate Correspondence Among Concepts in Different Approaches

Behavior	Power	Influence Process	Influence Tactic	Leader Trait	Leader Skill
Planning operations	Expert & Legitimate	Modify expectancies	Persuasion	Achievement orientation	Cognitive
Clarifying roles/goals	Expert & Legitimate	Modify expectancies	Persuasion	Achievement orientation	Technical
Monitoring performance	Legitimate	Instrumental compliance	Pressure	Achievement orientation	Technical
Contingent rewarding	Reward	Instrumental compliance	Exchange	Personalized power motivat.	Technical
Contingent punishing	Coercive	Instrumental compliance	Pressure	Personalized power motivat.	Technical
Supporting	Referent	Increase pers. identification	Collaboration	Socialized self-efficacy	Interpersonal power mot.
Recognizing	Expert	Increase self-efficacy	Ingratiation	Socialized power motivat.	Technical & Interpersonal
Coaching & Mentoring	Expert & Referent	Increase efficacy	Persuasion, Apprising	Socialized power motivat.	Technical & Interpersonal
Role modeling & self-sacrifice	Referent	Personal identification	Inspirational appeals	Self-confidence	Interpersonal
Team building	Referent & Legitimate	Collective identification	Inspirational appeals	Socialized power motivat.	Interpersonal
Visioning	Expert	Internalization, Increase potency	Inspirational appeals	Achievement orientation	Cognitive & Interpersonal
Explain need for change	Expert	Modify expectancies	Persuasion	Achieve. orient. self-confidence	Cognitive
Encouraging innovation	Referent & Legitimate	Increase potency and self-efficacy	Persuasion, Insp. appeals	Socialized power motivat.	Interpersonal
Participative leadership	Referent & Legitimate	Empowering & Internalization	Consultation, Coalition	Socialized power motivat.	Interpersonal

mediate the effects of leaders on organizational performance. Leaders can directly and indirectly influence the intervening variables in a variety of ways, and these effects are described in many of the leadership theories reviewed in this book.

The arrow from situational variables to the intervening variables is similar to substitutes for leadership that reduce the importance of leaders or make their job easier when the situational effects are favorable. Over a longer period of time the leader may be able to influence some of these situational variables, and this effect is shown by the arrow from leader behavior to situational variables. By taking actions to make the situation more favorable, leaders can indirectly influence the intervening variables and the overall performance of the organization. The arrow from situational variables to the success criteria reflects the direct effect of external conditions that are usually beyond

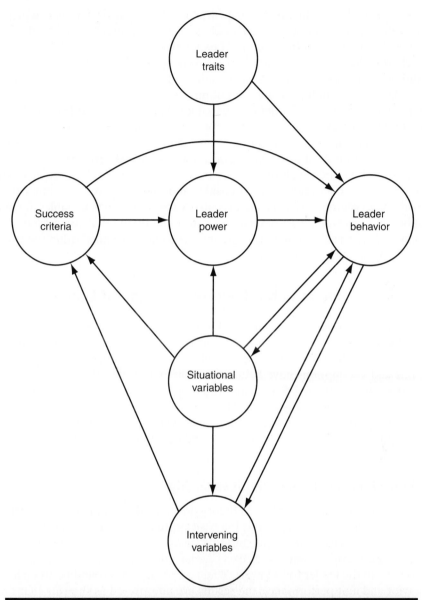

FIGURE 15-1   An Integrating Conceptual Framework

the influence of the leader (e.g., the economy, market conditions, government regulations). These other determinants of organizational effectiveness are sometimes strong
enough to overwhelm the efforts of leaders to save an organization from financial ruin.

The model allows for reciprocal influence processes. Leader behavior is both an
independent and dependent variable at the same time. Leader behavior is influenced
by a variety of factors, including leader traits, leader power, situational demands and
constraints, feedback about the success criteria, and feedback about the results of prior

attempts to change the intervening variables. The reciprocal influence processes occur in the causal links between leader behavior and the intervening variables and are depicted by arrows in both directions. Leader power is determined jointly by leader traits such as technical expertise and persuasiveness, aspects of the situation such as formal authority and control over rewards, and by the feedback effects of success or failure.

The model applies to any level of management in a large organization, but the intervening variables and situational variables change somewhat from level to level. Indirect effects are especially important for top management. Aspects of the situation that top-level leaders can usually influence over a longer period of time include the core ideology and cultural values of the organization, the formal structure and management systems, the skills and capabilities of organization members, the competitive strategy, and the network of cooperative relationships and joint ventures with other organizations. Some intervening variables for executives are situational variables for managers of subunits. For example, top executives determine the overall structure of the organization, whereas a subunit manager organizes subunit activities within the constraints imposed by the larger structure.

Biases in the Conceptualization of Leadership

Efforts to reconcile findings and develop an integrating framework are limited by the biases, narrow focus, and superficiality of most leadership theory and research. In Chapter 1, different ways to conceptualize leadership were introduced. Some conceptions and assumptions have been more dominant than others in the development of theories about effective leadership. The way leadership is portrayed in most of the theories reveals some strong biases. They include the often implicit assumption that leadership is primarily about heroic individuals who possess essential traits and skills and use appropriate behaviors to motivate and develop effective dyadic relationships with subordinates.

Heroic Individuals vs. Shared Leadership

Much previous research and theory on leadership emphasized the primary importance of a single, heroic leader. It is a basic postulate of most recent theories of transformational or charismatic leadership that an effective leader will influence followers to make self-sacrifices and exert exceptional effort. Influence is unidirectional, and it flows from the leader to followers. When a correlation is found between leadership behavior and unit performance, the results are interpreted as showing that the leader influenced followers to perform better.

The emphasis on individual leaders as the perceived cause of organizational performance can be explained in terms of human cognition. Organizations are complex social systems of patterned interactions among people. In their effort to understand the causes, dynamics, and outcomes of organizational processes, people interpret events in simple, human terms. Stereotypes, implicit theories, and simplified assumptions about causality help people to make sense out of events that would otherwise be incomprehensible. One especially strong and prevalent explanation of organizational events is to attribute causality to the influence of individual leaders (Calder, 1977; Pfeffer, 1977b).

Calder (1977) argued that people exaggerate the importance of leaders in order to explain events in a way that fits their assumptions and implicit theories. Leaders are pictured as heroic figures who are capable of determining the fate of their organizations. The mystical, romantic quality associated with leadership is similar to the common stereotype for other heroes in our culture, such as the lone cowboy who single-handedly vanquishes the bad guys, and the secret agent who acts alone to save the world from nuclear destruction by terrorists. The emphasis on leadership as a cause of organizational events reflects a cultural bias in Western nations toward explaining experience primarily in terms of the rational actions of people, as opposed to uncontrollable natural forces, actions by supernatural beings, or random events not susceptible to human comprehension.

Beliefs about heroic leadership may help to justify large salaries for chief executives, but they also foster unrealistic expectations. The heroic leader is expected to be wiser and more courageous than anyone else in the organization and to know everything that is happening in it. Leaders are seldom able to live up to these expectations. Just as they are given too much credit for success, they are also blamed for failure. According to Bradford and Cohen (1984), shared responsibility for leadership functions and empowerment of subordinates is more effective than heroic leadership, but it is unlikely to occur as long as people expect an individual leader to take full responsibility for the fate of the organization.

An alternative perspective that is slowly gaining more adherents is to define leadership as a shared process of enhancing the capability of people to accomplish collective work effectively (Heifetz, 1994). According to this perspective, leadership processes cannot be understood apart from the dynamics of the social system in which they are embedded (Dachler, 1984; Drath, 2001; Gronn, 2002). Instead of a heroic leader who can perform all essential leadership functions, they are distributed among different members of the team or organization. Some leadership functions (e.g., making important decisions) may be shared by all members of a group, and some leadership functions may be allocated to individual members (e.g., whoever is most qualified). Different people may perform a particular leadership function at different times. The leadership actions of any individual leader are much less important than the collective leadership provided by the members of the organization. To be effective the collective leadership must be coordinated and complementary, not working at cross purposes.

The heroic bias strongly influenced theory development and research on effective leadership, and as a result, some important aspects of leadership did not receive as much attention as they deserve. The extent to which leadership can be shared, the conditions facilitating the success of shared leadership, and the implications for design of organizations are all important and interesting questions that leadership scholars only recently began to investigate. The initial attempts to develop models of shared leadership are promising (e.g., Gronn, 2002; Pearce & Sims, 2000), but more theory development is necessary to integrate the diverse literatures relevant to this important subject.

The feasibility of research on shared leadership was demonstrated for self-managed teams (see Chapter 11), executive teams (see Chapter 12), and democratic organizations (see Chapter 4). Aspects of shared and distributed leadership also appeared in the theory and research on followership (see Chapter 5) and organizational change (see Chapter 10). Several researchers examined leadership as a shared process embedded within social systems (e.g., Brown & Gioia, 2002; Brown & Hosking, 1986; Crouch &

Yetton, 1988; Dachler, 1984; Denis, Lamothe, & Langley, 2001; Hunt & Ropo, 1995; Jacobs & Jaques, 1987; Lawler, 1986; Semler, 1989). Despite these efforts, more research is needed to examine shared and distributed leadership in teams, networks, and hierarchies. Viewing leadership in terms of reciprocal, recursive influence processes among multiple parties in a systems context is different from studying unidirectional effects of a single leader on subordinates, and new research methods may be needed to describe and analyze the complex nature of leadership processes in social systems over time.

Dyadic vs. Collective Focus

Most theory and research on leadership effectiveness takes a dyadic perspective that emphasizes the influence processes between a leader and a single follower. Key questions include the motivational effects of the leader, attributions made by each party about the other, and how the leader-follower relationship develops over time. Much of the research on these issues has been done on lower-level supervisors of coacting groups. Although the research investigated worthwhile questions, the dyadic perspective does not take into account some of the most important aspects of leadership. The success of teams and organizations is not determined primarily by dyadic processes. In retrospect, the dominance of the dyadic perspective appears to have limited the scope of leadership theory and research.

Many writers advocate the need for a broader perspective that relates leadership to an open-systems theory of organizations. This theoretical perspective recognizes that teams and organizations are created to perform work that cannot be accomplished by individuals working alone. Survival and prosperity depend on favorable exchanges with outside parties (getting resources, satisfying customers) and efficient internal processes (making products and services). Leadership involves influencing collective processes that will ensure the survival and effectiveness of a team or organization. Important leadership decisions include determining the purpose (mission, strategic objectives), determining how to attain the purpose and adapt to environmental changes (formulating strategies, organizing, planning, coordinating), and establishing the boundaries and determining membership criteria (who is in and who is not). The influence processes include getting and maintaining member commitment to objectives and strategies, and gaining acceptance and political support from other stakeholders who have a vested interest in the activities and performance of the group or organization (e.g., owners, shareholders, lenders, customers, governments). The processes that determine survival and prosperity create competing values for the organization, because increasing one determinant (e.g., efficiency) can reduce another (e.g., adaptation). How the leadership functions are performed in an organization is itself strongly influenced by the priorities of different stakeholders and by cultural norms and societal laws.

Conceptualizing leadership as an essential process for the survival and effectiveness of teams and organizations is a broader perspective that appears to offer a more promising path to the eventual development of a general theory. Compared to a dyadic perspective, this alternative perspective encourages researchers to pay more attention to external leadership roles, lateral and upward influence processes, power and politics, organization culture, organization structure, and the external environment. Focusing on leadership processes in organizations is also more compatible with the growing interest in shared and distributed leadership. It is rarely possible to understand why an organization is effective by studying only a single, heroic leader.

Some progress has been made in learning about leadership in teams and organizations, but this type of research is limited in comparison to the many studies on dyadic leadership. More research is clearly needed on collective processes and contextual factors that determine leadership effectiveness in teams, organizations, and interorganizational joint ventures (House & Aditya, 1997; Osborn, Hunt, & Jauch, 2002).

Importance of Explanatory Processes

Most theories developed to explain effective leadership involve a prediction model that changed little in more than a half-century. The theories usually involve one or more predictor variables (e.g., leader traits or behaviors) and one or two criterion variables (e.g., subordinate satisfaction or performance). Sometimes the theories include situational moderator variables as well. The weakest link in most leadership theories is the absence of mediating variables that are necessary to explain leadership influence on individuals, group processes, and organizational effectiveness.

Most dyadic theories of leadership rely on a theory of individual motivation or performance as the primary explanation of leader influence. For example, path-goal theory is based on the expectancy theory of motivation, LMX theory is based on exchange theory, and theories of charismatic or transformational leadership are based on self-concept theory, goal setting theory, and social learning theory. Even when underlying motivational processes are identified, the explanation of how they mediate the effects of leader behavior is usually too narrow. There is seldom a clear description of the causal paths from specific types of leader behavior through mediating processes to outcomes.

Biases in the theories are reflected in research based on them. The studies seldom include measures of mediating variables, even when the theory includes such variables. When predictor-criterion correlations are found, they are often interpreted as showing causality that reflects the underlying motivational processes assumed by the theory. Examples of assumed influence and motivational processes include aroused needs, increased self-efficacy, altered path-goal expectancies, increased goal acceptance, new self-identities, internalized beliefs and values, increased identification with the leader or group, and altered perceptions of equity and justice. Unless the mediating variables are measured in a comprehensive way the interpretation of predictor-criterion correlations can be biased. The researchers seldom assess alternative explanations for the hypothesized effects of the focal leader, such as reciprocal influence, reverse causality, follower self-management, intrinsic motivation derived from the work itself, peer leadership, or the direct and indirect influence of other leaders in the organization.

Summary

How leadership is conceptualized has important implications for theory and research. The assumption that effective leadership can be explained in terms of dyadic influence by a heroic leader limits the scope of research and theory and discourages exploration of shared leadership, collective processes, and reciprocal influence. A more balanced perspective is desirable in the future. Most leadership theories are also limited by a lack of adequate attention to explanatory processes. The theories often propose relationships or causal effects without explaining why they occur. Future theories must do more to explain as well as predict the effects of leaders on individuals, groups, and organizations.

Issues About Research Methods

The choice of research methods can also affect the rate of progress in learning about effective leadership. Beliefs about the most useful research methods and the type of information needed to understand leadership processes are related to biases in the conceptualization of leadership. Major issues include (1) the utility of quantitative, hypothesis-testing methods versus descriptive, qualitative methods, (2) the utility of survey versus experimental studies, and (3) the appropriate level of analyses for quantitative and qualitative data. This section of the chapter provides a brief review of the issues and implications for theory and research. It also includes a brief description of common methodological limitations that undermine the potential contributions of leadership studies.

Qualitative vs. Quantitative Methods

More research is conducted on leader behavior than on any other aspect of leadership, and most of the studies use questionnaires that ask subordinates or peers to retrospectively rate how often or how much a leader exhibited some behavior over a period of several months or years. As noted in Chapter 3, leader behavior descriptions are biased by attributions, stereotypes, and implicit theories about leadership. The evidence of rater bias, high intercorrelation among aspects of behavior widely viewed as effective, low correspondence among people rating the same leader, and the lack of evidence that behavior ratings are consistent with other measures of leader behavior (such as observations, interviews, and diary incidents) all raise serious doubts about what the questionnaires actually measure. Critics of this type of research contend that it has an inherent bias toward exaggerating the importance of individual leaders, and this bias is consistent with the emphasis on heroic leadership. Another criticism is that survey questionnaires are poorly suited for studying leadership as a dynamic, shared process embedded in complex social systems.

One alternative approach advocated by some scholars is to make greater use of qualitative methods such as intensive single case studies and comparative case studies (e.g., Bryman, Bresnen, Beardworth, & Keil, 1988; Luthans, Rosenkrantz, & Hennessey, 1985; Morgan & Smircich, 1980; Strong, 1984). The qualitative methods offer some advantages for studying leadership from a systems perspective, but these research methods also have limitations (House, 1988a; Martinko & Gardner, 1985). Standards for the application and evaluation of qualitative methods are not as explicit as those for traditional quantitative methods, and interpretations based on qualitative methods are sometimes very subjective. Descriptions of past events may be biased by selective memory for aspects of behavior consistent with the respondent's stereotypes and implicit theories about effective leadership. Direct observation is also susceptible to selective attention and biased interpretation of events. Attribution errors may occur if an observer or interviewer has information about unit performance. When observers immerse themselves in an organization for long periods of time in an effort to understand the context and meaning of what they see, they are likely to become involved in the very processes under observation, thereby risking objectivity.

The limitations and advantages of quantitative and qualitative methods make it appropriate in many leadership studies to use a complementary combination of both methods. For example, in survey questionnaire studies researchers could interview some of the respondents to verify that the questionnaire answers are accurately measuring the intended construct and to discover the underlying reasons for some of the quantitative results. An obstacle to more frequent use of dual methods may be the strong bias of some researchers who favor one method and fail to appreciate the comparative advantages of the other method, or who lack sufficient expertise to use the other method.

Survey vs. Experimental Studies

Another issue in the design of leadership research is the relative advantage of survey studies and experiments. Survey studies are easier to conduct, but as noted earlier, they have many limitations when used for research on leadership processes. Controlled experiments in laboratory and field settings are appropriate for many types of leadership research (Brown & Lord, 1999; Dipboye, 1990; Wofford, 1999). Some examples of laboratory and field experiments on the effects of leadership behavior can be found in Chapters 3 and 9. Unfortunately, lab and field experiments constitute only a small proportion (less than 5%) of the thousands of studies conducted on leadership over the past half-century.

The most important advantage of an experiment is the opportunity to determine causality. Researchers can manipulate leader behavior or situational variables and assess their independent and joint effects. Moreover, with laboratory experiments it is easier to measure mediating processes, control for extraneous variables, and examine the effects of conditions seldom found in actual organizations. However, many laboratory experiments have limitations, such as the use of weak manipulations, the use of tasks that do not accurately simulate realistic conditions, the use of convenience samples of students who have little work experience, and the use of brief interactions among strangers to study processes that in most organizations would involve people with established relationships. Unless it is possible to design a laboratory experiment to avoid these limitations, the potential benefits are unlikely to be realized.

Field experiments are even more difficult to conduct than laboratory experiments but offer some unique advantages. Most field experiments involve realistic working conditions and people with experience working together. Field experiments can be used to assess the effects of different patterns of leadership behavior, and they also allow a good way to assess the utility of interventions made to improve leadership (e.g., training, feedback, executive coaching). Common limitations of field experiments on leadership are weak manipulations of independent variables, failure to ensure random assignment to experimental treatments, failure to control for confounding due to extraneous variables, weak assessment of outcome variables, and failure to measure mediating processes. A field experiment on leadership is likely to be more useful if it is based on a well-specified model, it is conducted over an appropriate time period, and it includes multiple measures of relevant variables. It is easier to gain approval for having a control group if the researcher is willing to provide an opportunity for members of the control group to participate in the same intervention (e.g., training) at a later time.

Level of Analysis

Most survey research on leadership behavior uses an individual, dyadic, or group level of analysis. Analysis at the individual level usually involves correlations between variables that are measured within individuals. For example, a subordinate's ratings of leader behavior are correlated with the subordinate's ratings of task commitment across all subordinates in the sample. Dyadic analyses usually involve data obtained from both members of a leader-subordinate dyad, such as correlating subordinate ratings of leader behavior with the leader's ratings of subordinate performance across all dyads in the sample. Group-level analyses often involve individual data that are aggregated to the group level. For example, the leader behavior ratings provided by several subordinates are averaged; then the composite scores are correlated with another variable (e.g., group performance, collective efficacy) across all groups in the sample.

The appropriate type of analysis for quantitative data from survey studies depends on the underlying theory of leadership processes and the level of measurement for the variables. The level of data analysis should correspond to the level of measurement and the proposed relationships in the theory (Klein, Dansereau, & Hall, 1994). Unless an appropriate level of analysis is used, the results from a study may be misinterpreted. The analysis is more complex for a multilevel theory, which includes relationships among variables conceptualized at different levels or at more than one level. Different methods for multilevel analysis are described and compared in a special issue of *Leadership Quarterly* (see Bliese, Halverson, & Schriesheim, 2002).

One method for analyzing results at different levels simultaneously is called "within and between analysis," or WABA (Dansereau, Alutto, & Yammarino, 1984). Use of this method in several studies indicates that the data may support different conclusions about leadership depending on the level of analysis (e.g., Dansereau, Yammarino, & Markham, 1995; Yammarino, 1990; Yammarino & Bass, 1990). The WABA method provides some unique insights, but it also has limitations. The results are strongly dependent on the size of the groups selected for the study, and it is not feasible even to do the analysis when some of the data are collected only at the group level. Furthermore, deficiencies in the measures can make it difficult to understand the reasons for inconsistent results at different levels of analysis.

The major contribution of recent research on levels of analysis may have been to focus more attention on finding the appropriate levels of conceptualization and measurement when formulating and testing leadership theories (Klein et al., 1994; Rousseau, 1985). In the past, many leadership theories were not clear about the level of conceptualization for each variable (Yammarino, Dionne, & Chun, 2002). When proposed relationships involve variables at different levels of conceptualization or effects that occur at more than one level (e.g., the leader's vision affects both individual self-efficacy and collective efficacy for the team), then it may be necessary to include more than one level of analysis.

The new approaches for analyzing multilevel data can be helpful, but they do not solve some difficult problems inherent in efforts to measure qualities of a team or organization (e.g., climate, culture, potency) by aggregating the subjective perceptions of individual members. One promising approach to improve such measures is to have a group meet to discuss and reach consensus on their ratings (Kirkman & Rosen, 1999; Tesluk, Zaccaro, Marks, & Mathieu, 1997). In other words, instead of averaging the separate ratings of 10 members, the members try to reach a consensus on one rating for the group.

Other Methodological Issues

The samples used in many leadership studies are far from ideal. The common approach is to use a convenience sample, one that is easy to get, rather than to plan the type of sample that is appropriate for the research objectives and design. In comparative studies the use of convenience samples makes it difficult to identify the effects of extraneous variables that are confounded with the samples. The use of convenience samples consisting of undergraduate students with little practical experience in organizations complicates the interpretation of findings.

Most leadership studies only examine events that occur during a brief time interval. Longitudinal studies are needed to examine leadership processes that evolve over time, and to assess the delayed effects of leaders on followers. Processes such as developing dyadic relationships, building effective teams, and leading change often require months or years of study. Unfortunately, few researchers are willing to invest that much time in a study. What usually passes for longitudinal research in leadership is a survey study with measures taken a few months apart, rather than an intensive examination of evolving relationships, emerging problems, protracted decisions, sequential changes, and reciprocal influence processes.

The leadership research seems to be biased toward easy methods and faddish topics. Too many studies are merely replications of earlier studies on a popular topic. One researcher publishes a study that is interesting and easy to conduct, and others imitate it with only minor variations (a different sample, a different criterion measure). Too many studies simply correlate one questionnaire with another, even though there is no underlying theory and little reason to expect that important relationships exist. The questionnaires are often filled out by the same respondents, and interpretation of results is difficult. Finally, too many studies attempt to prove a theory, which usually yields only inconclusive results. It is better to design research that will improve a theory by testing alternative explanations, examining possible confounds, identifying limiting conditions, and assessing practical significance.

Table 15-2 provides an overview of the methodological biases discussed in this section of the chapter. Common features of leadership studies are contrasted with alternative but less common features. The primary message is the need for better balance in the design of leadership research. Greater use of the uncommon features would make leadership research more productive. Lowe and Gardner (2001) reviewed the research methods used in a decade of leadership studies published in *Leadership Quarterly* and reached similar conclusions.

TABLE 15-2 Common and Uncommon Features in Leadership Studies

Feature	Common	Uncommon
Research method	Survey study	Experiment
Research objective	Replication	Explore new issues
Level of processes	Individual/Dyadic	Group/Organizational
Time frame	Short-term	Longitudinal
Causality	Unidirectional	Reciprocal
Criterion variables	One or two	Several
Mediating variables	Few or none	Several
Data sources	Single	Multiple
Sample	Convenience	Systematic selection
Level of leader	Supervisor	Executive

Summary

Past research on leadership relied too much on weak research methods. It is important to select methods that are appropriate for the type of knowledge sought, rather than merely using the most convenient methods. The research question should dictate the methodology and choice of samples, not the other way around. Given the limitations of each type of methodology, it is desirable to use multiple methods whenever feasible for research on leadership (Jick, 1979; Yukl & Van Fleet, 1982). It is also important to consider the appropriate level of analysis for the theoretical constructs and measures. Multilevel analysis can provide new insights about leadership processes and help to determine whether parallel processes occur at different levels.

Concluding Thoughts

This final section presents my observations about the essence of leadership and some final thoughts about the state of the field.

The Essence of Effective Leadership

The book takes a broad perspective and examines many different aspects of leadership. The multitude of different theories and the lack of consistent findings make it difficult to identify the essence of effective leadership. This section presents what I think are the 10 most important leadership functions for enhancing collective work in teams and organizations. In a large organization, the conditions that create a need for these leadership acts are played out at every level of management and in every subunit. The functions can be performed by any member of the organization, but they are especially relevant for designated leaders.

1. **Help interpret the meaning of events.**   Helping people to find meaning in complex events is important, especially when the pace of change is accelerating and touching every part of our lives. Effective leaders help people to interpret events, understand why they are relevant, and identify emerging threats and opportunities.
2. **Create alignment on objectives and strategies.**   Effective performance of a collective task requires considerable agreement about what to do and how to do it. Helping to build a consensus about these choices is especially important in newly formed groups, and in organizations that have lost their way. Effective leaders help to create agreement about objectives, priorities, and strategies.
3. **Build task commitment and optimism.**   The performance of a difficult, stressful task requires commitment and persistence in the face of obstacles and setbacks. Effective leaders increase enthusiasm for the work, commitment to task objectives, and confidence that the effort will be successful.
4. **Build mutual trust and cooperation.**   Effective performance of a collective task requires cooperation and mutual trust, which are more likely when people understand each other, appreciate diversity, and are able to confront and resolve differences in a constructive way. Effective leaders foster mutual respect, trust, and cooperation.
5. **Strengthen collective identity.**   The effectiveness of a group or organization requires at least a moderate degree of collective identification. In this era of fluid teams, virtual organizations, and joint ventures, boundaries are often unclear and

loyalties are divided. Effective leaders help to create a unique identity for a group or organization, and they resolve issues of membership in a way that is consistent with this identity.

6. **Organize and coordinate activities.**   Successful performance of a complex task requires the capacity to coordinate many different but interrelated activities in a way that makes efficient use of people and resources. Effective leaders help people get organized to perform collective activities efficiently, and they help to coordinate these activities as they occur.

7. **Encourage and facilitate collective learning.**   In a highly competitive and turbulent environment, continuous learning and innovation are essential for the survival and prosperity of an organization. Members must collectively learn better ways to work together towards common objectives. Effective leaders encourage and facilitate collective learning and innovation.

8. **Obtain necessary resources and support.**   For most groups and organizations, survival and prosperity require favorable exchanges with external parties. Resources, approvals, assistance, and political support must be obtained from superiors and people outside of the unit. Effective leaders promote and defend unit interests and help to obtain necessary resources and support.

9. **Develop and empower people.**   The performance of a group or organization is likely to be better if competent members are actively involved in solving problems and making decisions. Relevant skills must be developed to prepare people for leadership roles, new responsibilities, and major change. Effective leaders help people develop their skills and empower people to become change agents and leaders themselves.

10. **Promote social justice and morality.**   Member satisfaction and commitment are increased by a climate of fairness, compassion, and social responsibility. To maintain such a climate requires active efforts to protect individual rights, encourage social responsibility, and oppose unethical practices. Effective leaders set an example of moral behavior, and they take necessary actions to promote social justice.

The State of the Field

People have been interested in leadership since the beginning of recorded history, and the study of leadership as a scientific discipline started more than half a century ago. The massive literature produced by this effort is beset with confusion and ambiguity, but the selective review of theory and research in this book shows that we are making substantial progress in learning about leadership. Nevertheless, much remains to be learned. It becomes clearer every year that effective leadership at all levels of society and in all of our organizations is essential for coping with the growing social and economic problems confronting the world. Learning to cope with these problems is not a luxury but a necessity.

Progress in understanding leadership has been slower than would be expected from the large volume of publications and the immense amount of effort expended on leadership research. Fortunately, the last decade witnessed an increase in the richness of research questions and the variety of approaches used to study them, and the field appears to be undergoing an accelerating pace of discovery. With such a vital subject, it is imperative that we continue to upgrade the quality of leadership research and theory. Faster progress will require the efforts of dedicated researchers who value discovery of useful knowledge more than publishing trivial studies.

Review and Discussion Questions

1. What are some major points of convergence among the research on traits and skills, behaviors, influence processes, and situational variables?
2. What are some of the most important findings about effective leadership in organizations?
3. How does the conceptualization of heroic versus shared leadership influence the design and interpretation of research?
4. What are the limitations of conceptualizing leadership in terms of the influence of a single leader over a single subordinate?
5. How can qualitative methods advance our understanding of leadership processes?
6. What are some common limitations of the methods used most often in leadership research? What improvements could be made in the way leadership is studied?
7. Taking into account what was learned from the thousands of studies conducted during the past half-century, how would you evaluate the rate of progress? Can we do any better? Explain your answer.

Key Terms

- distributed leadership
- dyadic perspective
- essence of leadership
- heroic leader
- integrating conceptual framework
- levels of analysis
- methodological weaknesses
- multimethod research
- shared leadership

References

Ackoff, R. L. (1994). *The democratic corporation: A radical prescription for recreating corporate America and rediscovering success*. New York: Oxford University Press.

Adler, N. J. (1996). Global women political leaders: An invisible history, and increasingly important future. *Leadership Quarterly, 7,* 133–161.

Adler, N. J. (1997). *International dimensions of organizational behavior*. Cincinnati, OH: South-Western College Publishing.

Agor, W. H. (1986). The logic of intuition: How top executives make important decisions. *Organizational Dynamics, 14* (3), 5–18.

Aguilar, F. J. (1967). *Scanning the business environment.* New York: Macmillan.

Aldag, R. J., & Brief, A. P. (1979). *Task design and employee motivation.* Glenview, IL: Scott Foresman.

Alexander, L. D. (1985). Successfully implementing strategic decisions. *Long-Range Planning, 18,* 91–97.

Allan, P. (1981). Managers at work: A large-scale study of the managerial job in New York City government. *Academy of Management Journal, 24,* 613–619.

Alexander, J. A., & Lee, S. Y. D. (1996). The effects of CEO succession and tenure on failure of rural community hospitals. *Journal of Applied Behavioral Science, 32,* 70–88.

Alvesson, M., & Sveningsson, S. (2003). The great disappearing act: Difficulties in doing "leadership." *Leadership Quarterly, 14,* 359–381.

Amabile, T. M., Schatzel, E. A., Moneta, G. B., & Kramer, S. J. (2004). Leader behaviors and the work environment for creativity: Perceived leader support. *Leadership Quarterly, 15* (1), 5–32.

Amason, A. C. (1996). Distinguishing the effects of functional and dysfunctional conflict on strategic decision making: Resolving a paradox for top management teams. *Academy of Management Journal, 39,* 123–148.

Amis, J., Slack, T., & Hinings, C. R. (2004). The pace, sequence, and linearity of radical change. *Academy of Management Journal, 47,* 15–39.

Ammeter, A. P., Douglas, C., Gardner, W. L., Hochwarter, W. A., & Ferris, G. R. (2002). Toward a political theory of leadership. *Leadership Quarterly, 13,* 751–796.

Ancona, D. G. (1990). Outward bound: Strategies for team survival in an organization. *Academy of Management Journal, 33,* 334–365.

Ancona, D. G., & Caldwell, D. F. (1992). Bridging the boundary: External activity and performance in organizational teams. *Administrative Science Quarterly, 37,* 634–665.

Ancona, D. G., & Nadler, D. A. (1989). Top hats and executive tales: Designing the senior team. *Sloan Management Review,* Fall, 19–28.

Anderson, B., & Nilsson, S. (1964). Studies in the reliability and validity of the critical incident technique. *Journal of Applied Psychology*, 48, 398–413.

Ansari, M. A., & Kapoor, A. (1987). Organizational context and upward influence tactics. *Organizational Behavior and Human Decision Processes*, 40, 39–49.

Anthony, W. P. (1978). *Participative management*. Reading, MA: Addison-Wesley.

Antonakis, J., & House, R. J. (2002). An analysis of the full-range leadership theory: The way forward. In B. J. Avolio & F. J. Yammarino (Eds.), *Transformational and charismatic leadership: The road ahead*. Amsterdam: JAI Press, pp. 3–34.

Antonakis, J., & Atwater, L. (2002). Leader distance: A review and proposed theory. *Leadership Quarterly*, 13 (6), 673–704.

Antonakis, J., Avolio, B. J., & Sivasubramaniam, N. (2003). Context and leadership: An examination of the nine-factor full-range leadership theory using the multifactor leadership questionnaire. *Leadership Quarterly*, 14, 261–295.

Argyris, C. (1964). *Integrating the individual and the organization*. New York: John Wiley.

Argyris, C. (1985). *Strategy, change, and defensive routines*. Boston: Pitman.

Argyris, C. (1991). Teaching smart people how to learn. *Harvard Business Review*, 69 (3), 99–109.

Argyris, C. (1998). Empowerment: The emperor's new clothes. *Harvard Business Review*, May–June, 98–105.

Arvey, R. D., & Ivancevich, J. M. (1980). Punishment in organizations: A review, propositions, and research suggestions. *Academy of Management Review*, 5, 123–132.

Ashforth, B. E., & Mael, F. (1989). Social identity theory and the organization. *Academy of Management Review*, 14, 20–39.

Ashkanasy, N. M., & Gallois, C. (1994). Leader attributions and evaluations: Effects of locus of control, supervisory control, and task control. *Organizational Behavior and Human Decision Processes*, 59, 27–50.

Ashour, A. S. (1973). The contingency model of leadership effectiveness: An evaluation. *Organizational Behavior and Human Performance*, 9, 339–355.

Ashour, A. S., & England, G. (1972). Subordinate's assigned level of discretion as a function of leader's personality and situational variables. *Journal of Applied Psychology*, 56, 120–123.

Atwater, L., Roush, P., & Fischtal, A. (1995). The influence of upward feedback on self and follower ratings of leadership. *Personnel Psychology*, 48, 35–59.

Audia, P. G., Locke, E. A., & Smith, K. G. (2000). The paradox of success: An archival and a laboratory study of strategic persistence following radical environmental change. *Academy of Management Journal*, 43 (5), 837–853.

Avery, D. R., Tonidandel, S., Griffith, Kl H., & Quinones, M. G. (2003). The impact of multiple measures of experience on leader effectiveness: New insights for leader selection. *Journal of Business Research*, 56, 673–679.

Avolio, B. J. (1999). *Full leadership development: Building the vital forces in organizations*. Thousand Oaks, CA: Sage.

Avolio, B. J., Bass, B. M., & Jung, D. I. (1999). Re-examining the components of transformational and transactional leadership using the multifactor leadership questionnaire. *Journal of Occupational and Organizational Psychology*, 72, 441–462.

Awamleh, R., & Gardner, W. L. (1999). Perceptions of leader charisma and effectiveness: The effects of vision content, delivery, and organizational performance. *Leadership Quarterly*, 10, 345–373.

Bachman, J. G., Smith, C. G., & Slesinger, J. A. (1966). Control, performance, and satisfaction: An analysis of structural and individual effects. *Journal of Personality and Social Psychology*, 4, 127–136.

Baer, M., & Frese, M. (2003). Innovation is not enough: Climates for initiative and psychological safety, process innovations, and firm performance. *Journal of Organizational Behavior*, 24 (1), 45–68.

Baird, L., Holland, P., & Deacon, S. (1999). Learning from action: Imbedding more learning into the performance fast enough to make a difference. *Organizational Dynamics*, 27 (4), 19–32.

Baldwin, T. T. (1991). Effects of alternative modeling strategies on outcomes of interpersonal skills training. *Journal of Applied Psychology*, 77, 147–154.

Baldwin, T. T., & Ford, J. K. (1988). Transfer of training: A review and directions for future research. *Personnel Psychology*, 41, 63–105.

Baldwin, T. T., & Padgett, M. Y. (1993). Management development: A review and commentary. In C. L. Cooper and I. T. Robertson (Eds.), *International review of industrial-organizational psychology*, vol. 8. New York: Wiley, pp. 35–85.

Baldwin, T. T., Wagner, R. J., & Roland, C. C. (1991). *Effects of outdoor challenge training on group and individual outcomes.* Paper presented at Society for Industrial and Organizational Psychology Conference, St. Louis, Missouri.

Baldwin, T. T. (1992). Effects of alternative modeling strategies on outcomes of interpersonal-skills training. *Journal of Applied Psychology*, 77, 147–154.

Bales, R. F. (1950). A set of categories for the analysis of small group interaction. *American Sociological Review*, 15, 257–263.

Bales, R. F., Cohen, S. P., & Williamson, S. A. (1979). *SYMLOG: A system for the multiple-level observation of groups*. New York: Free Press.

Baliga, B. R., & Hunt, J. G. (1988). An organizational life cycle approach to leadership. In J. G. Hunt, B. R. Baliga, H. P. Dachler, and C. A. Schriesheim (Eds.), *Emerging leadership vistas*. Lexington, MA: Lexington Books.

Baloff, N., & Doherty, E. M. (1989). Potential pitfalls in employee participation. *Organizational Dynamics*, 18 (2), 51–62.

Bandura, A. (1986). *Social foundations of thought and action: A social cognitive theory.* Englewood Cliffs, NJ: Prentice Hall.

Bandura, A. (2000). Exercise of human agency through collective efficacy. *Current Directions in Psychological Science*, 9, 75–78.

Banker, R. D., Field, J. M., Schroeder, R. G., & Sinha, K. K. (1996). Impact of work teams on manufacturing performance: A longitudinal field study. *Academy of Management Journal*, 39, 867–890.

Bantel, K. A., & Jackson, S. E. (1989). Top management and innovations in banking: Does the composition of the top team make a difference? *Strategic Management Journal*, 10, 107–112.

Barker, J. R. (1993). Tightening the iron cage: Concertive control in self-managing teams. *Administrative Science Quarterly*, 38, 408–437.

Barling, J., Weber, T., & Kelloway, E. K. (1996). Effects of transformational leadership training on attitudinal and financial outcomes: A field experiment. *Journal of Applied Psychology*, 81, 827–832.

Barnard, C. I. (1952). A definition of authority. In R. K. Merton, A. P. Gray, B. Hockey, and H. C. Selven (Eds.), *Reader in bureaucracy*. New York: Free Press.

Barnes, L. B., & Kriger, M. P. (1986). The hidden side of organizational leadership. *Sloan Management Review*, Fall, 15–25.

Barney, J. B. (1991). Firm resources and sustained competitive advantage. *Journal of Management*, 17, 99-129.

Baron, R. A. (1989). Personality and organizational conflict: Effects of the Type A behavior pattern and self-monitoring. *Organizational Behavior and Human Decision Processes*, 44, 281–296.

Barrick, M. R., Day, D. V., Lord, R. G., & Alexander, R. A. (1991). Assessing the utility of executive leadership. *Leadership Quarterly*, 2, 9–22.

Barrick, M. R., Stewart, G. L., Neubert, M. J., & Mount, M. K. (1998). Relating member abiity and personality to work-team processes and team effectiveness. *Journal of Applied Psychology*, 83, 377–391.

Barrow, J. C. (1977). The variables of leadership: A review and conceptual framework. *Academy of Management Review*, 2, 231–251.

Barry, B., & Shapiro, D. L. (1992). Influence tactics in combination: The interactive effects of soft versus hard tactics and rational exchange. *Journal of Applied Social Psychology*, 22, 1429–1441.

Barry, B. & Stephens, C. U. (1998). Objections to an objectivist approach to integrity. *Academy of Management Review*, 23, 162–169.

Barry, D. (1991). Managing the bossless team: Lessons in distributed leadership. *Organizational Dynamics*, Summer, 31–47.

Bartol, K. M., & Srivastava, A. (2002). Encouraging knowledge sharing: The role of organizational reward systems. *Journal of Leadership and Organizational Studies*, 9 (1),64–76.

Basadur, M. (2004). Leading others to think innovatively together: Creative leadership. *Leadership Quarterly*, 15 (1), 103–121.

Bass, B. M. (1960). *Leadership, psychology, and organizational behavior*. New York: Harper.

Bass, B. M. (1985). *Leadership and performance beyond expectations.* New York: Free Press.

Bass, B. M. (1990). *Handbook of leadership: A survey of theory and research.* New York: Free Press.

Bass, B. M. (1996). *A new paradigm of leadership: An inquiry into transformational leadership.* Alexandria, VA: U.S. Army Research Institute for the Behavioral and Social Sciences.

Bass, B. M. (1997). Does the transactional-transformational paradigm transcend organizational and national boundaries? *American Psychologist*, 52, 130–139.

Bass, B. M., & Avolio, B. J. (1990a). Developing transformational leadership: 1992 and beyond. *Journal of European Industrial Training*, 14, 21–27.

Bass, B. M., & Avolio, B. J. (1990b). The implications of transactional and transformational leadership for individual, team, and organizational development. In W. Pasmore and R. W. Woodman (Eds.), *Research in organizational change and development*, vol. 4, pp. 231–272. Greenwich, CT: JAI Press.

Bass, B. M., & Avolio, B. J. (1990c). *Multifactor leadership questionnaire*. Palo Alto, CA: Consulting Psychologists Press.

Bass, B. M., & Avolio, B. J. (1997). *Full range leadership development manual for the multifactor leadership questionnaire*. Palo Alto, CA: Mindgarden.

Bass, B. M., Avolio, B. J., Jung, D. I., & Berson, Y. (2003). Predicting unit performance by assessing transformational and transactional leadership. *Journal of Applied Psychology*, 88, 207–218.

Bass, B. M., & Steidlmeier, P. (1999). Ethics, character, and authentic transformational leadership. *Leadership Quarterly*, 10, 181–217.

Bass, B. M., Waldman, D. A., Avolio, B. J., & Bebb, M. (1987). Transformational leadership and the falling dominoes effect. *Group & Organization Studies*, 12 (1), 73–87.

Bates, C. S. (1985). Mapping the environment: An operational environmental analysis model. *Long-Range Planning*, 18 (5), 97–107.

Bauer, R. (1968). The study of policy formation: An introduction. In R. Bauer and K. Gergen (Eds.), *The study of policy formation*. New York: Free Press.

Bauer, T. N., & Green, S. G., (1996). The development of leader-member exchange: A longitudinal test. *Academy of Management Journal*, 39, 1538–1567.

Bauer, T., & Green, S. G. (1998). Testing the combined effects of newcomer information seeking and manager behavior on socialization. *Journal of Applied Psychology*, 83, 72–83.

Baum, R. J., Locke, E. A., & Kirkpatrick, S. (1998). A longitudinal study of the relation of vision and vision communication to venture growth in entrepreneurial firms. *Journal of Applied Psychology*, 83, 43–54.

Becker, T. E. (1998). Integrity in organizations: Beyond honesty and conscientiousness. *Academy of Management Review*, 23, 154–161.

Beer, M. (1988). The critical path for change: Keys to success and failure in six companies. In R. H. Kilmann and T. J. Covin (Eds.), *Corporate transformation: Revitalizing organizations for a competitive world*. San Francisco: Jossey-Bass, pp. 17–45.

Beer, M. (2001). How to develop an organization capable of sustained high performance: Embrace the drive for results-capability development paradox. *Organizational Dynamics*, 29, 233–247.

Beer, M., Eisenstat, R. A., & Spector, B. (1990). Why change programs don't produce change. *Harvard Business Review*, November–December, 158–166.

Beer, M., & Nohria, N. (2000). Cracking the code of change. *Harvard Business Review*, May–June, 133–141.

Behling, D., & Starke, F. A. (1973). The postulates of expectancy theory. *Academy of Management Journal*, 16, 373–388.

Belgard, W. P., Fisher, K. K., & Rayner, S. R. (1988). Vision, opportunity, and tenacity: Three informal processes that influence formal transformation. In R. H. Kilmann and T. J. Covin (Eds.), *Corporate transformation: Revitalizing organizations for a competitive world*. San Francisco: Jossey-Bass, pp. 131–151.

Bell, B. S., & Kozlowski, S. W. (2002). A typology of virtual teams. *Group & Organization Management*, 27 (1), 14–49.

Benne, K. D., & Sheats, P. (1948). Functional roles of group members. *Journal of Social Issues*, 2, 42–47.

Bennis, W. G. (1959). Leadership theory and administrative behavior: The problem of authority. *Administrative Science Quarterly*, 4, 259–260.

Bennis, W. G., & Nanus, B. (1985). *Leaders: The strategies for taking charge*. New York: Harper & Row.

Berger, J., Cohen, B. P., & Zelditch, M. (1972). Status characteristics and social interaction. *American Sociological Review*, 37, 241–255.

Berkowitz, L. (1953). Sharing leadership in small decision-making groups. *Journal of Abnormal and Social Psychology*, 48, 231–238.

Berlew, D. E. (1974). Leadership and organizational excitement. In D. A. Kolb, I. M. Rubin, and J. M. McIntyre (Eds.), *Organizational psychology: A book of readings*. Englewood Cliffs, NJ: Prentice Hall.

Berman, F. E., & Miner, J. B. (1985). Motivation to manage at the top executive level: A test of the hierarchic role-motivation theory. *Personnel Psychology*, 38, 377–391.

Bernardin, H. J., Hagan, C., & Kane, J. S. (1995). *The effects of a 360-degree appraisal system on managerial performance: No matter how cynical I get, I can't keep up*. Paper presented at the Annual Conference of the Society for Industrial and Organizational Psychology, Orlando, May.

Berson, Y., Shamir, B., Avolio, B. J., & Popper, M. (2001). The relationship between vision strength, leadership style, and context. *Leadership Quarterly*, 12, 53–73.

Bettenhausen, K. L. (1991). Five years of group research: What we have learned and what needs to be addressed. *Journal of Management*, 17, 345–381.

Bettin, P. J., & Kennedy, J. K., Jr. (1990). Leadership experience and leader performance: Some empirical support at last. *Leadership Quarterly*, 1, 219–228.

Bettman, J. R., & Weitz, B. A. (1983). Attributions in the board room: Causal reasoning in corporate annual reports. *Administrative Science Quarterly*, 28, 165–183.

Beu, D. S., & Buckley, M. R. (2004). This is war: How the politically astute achieve crimes of obedience through the use of moral disengagement. *Leadership Quarterly*, 14, 551–568.

Beyer, J. M. (1999). Taming and promoting charisma to change organizations. *Leadership Quarterly*, 10, 307–330.

Beyer, J. M., & Browning, L. D. (1999). Transforming an industry in crisis: Charisma, routinization, and supportive cultural leadership. *Leadership Quarterly*, 10, 483–520.

Biggart, N. W. (1977). The creative-destructive process of organizational change: The case of the post office. *Administrative Science Quarterly*, 22, 410–426.

Biggart, N. W. (1989). *Charismatic capitalism*. Chicago: University of Chicago Press.

Biggart, N. W., & Hamilton, G. G. (1984). The power of obedience. *Administrative Science Quarterly*, 29, 540–549.

Blake, R. R., & Mouton, J. S. (1964). *The managerial grid*. Houston: Gulf Publishing.

Blake, R. R., & Mouton, J. S. (1982). Management by grid principles or situationalism: Which? *Group and Organization Studies*, 7, 207–210.

Blake, R. R., & Mouton, J. S. (1984). *Solving costly organizational conflict: Achieving intergroup trust, cooperation, and teamwork*. San Francisco: Jossey-Bass.

Blake, R. R., Shepard, H. A., & Mouton, J. S. (1964). *Managing intergroup conflict in industry*. Houston: Gulf Publishing.

Blank, W., Weitzel, J. R., & Green, S. G. (1990). A test of situational leadership theory. *Personnel Psychology*, 43, 579–597.

Blankenship, L. V., & Miles, R. E. (1968). Organizational structure and managerial decision making. *Administrative Science Quarterly*, 13, 106–120.

Blau, P. M. (1956). *Bureaucracy in modern society*. New York: Random House.

Blau, P. M. (1974). *Exchange and power in social life*. New York: John Wiley.

Bliese, P. D., Halverson, R. R., & Schriesheim, C. A. (2002). Special Issue: Benchmarking multi-level methods in leadership. *Leadership Quarterly*, 13 (1).

Bligh, M. C., Kohles, J. C., & Meindl, J. R. (2004). Charisma under crisis: Presidential leadership, rhetoric, and media responses before and after the September 11 terrorist attacks. *Leadership Quarterly*, 15 (2), 211–240.

Block, P. (1987). *The empowered manager*. San Francisco: Jossey Bass.

Block, P. (1993). *Stewardship: Choosing service over self-interest*. San Francisco: Barrett Koehler Publishers.

Block, J. (1995). A contrarian view of the five-factor approach to personality description. *Journal of Personality and Social Psychology*, 117, 187–215.

Blyth, D. E. (1987). *Leader and subordinate expertise as moderators of the relationship between directive leader behavior and performance*. Unpublished doctoral dissertation, University of Washington, Seattle.

Boal, K. B., & Bryson, J. M. (1988). Charismatic leadership: A phenomenological and structural approach. In J. G. Hunt, B. R. Baliga, H. P. Dachler, and C. A. Schriesheim (Eds.), *Emerging leadership vistas*. Lexington, MA: Lexington Books, pp. 11–28.

Boal, K. B., & Hooijberg, R. (2001). Strategic leadership research: Moving on. *Leadership Quarterly*, 11 (4), 515–549.

Boehm, V. R. (1985). Using assessment centers for management development—Five applications. *Journal of Management Development*, 4 (4), 40–51.

Bono, J. E., & Judge, T. A. (2003). Self-concordance at work: Toward understanding the motivational effects of transformational leaders. *Academy of Management Journal*, 46, 554–571.

Book, E. W. (2000). *Why the best man for the job is a woman: The unique female qualities of leadership*. New York: Harper Business.

Bordia, P. (1997). Face-to-face versus computer-mediated communication: A synthesis of the experimental literature. *Journal of Business Communication*, 34, 99–121.

Borgotta, E. G., Rouch, A. S., & Bales, R. F. (1954). Some findings relevant to the great man theory of leadership. *American Sociological Review*, 19, 755–759.

Bouchard, T. J. (1971). Whatever happened to brainstorming? *Journal of Creative Behavior*, 5, 182–189.

Bouchard, T., Lykken, D. T., McGue, A., Segal, N. L., & Tellegen, A. (1990). Sources of human psychological differences: The Minnesota study of twins reared apart. *Science*, 250, 223–228.

Bourgeois, L. J. (1980). Performance and consensus. *Strategic Management Journal*, 1, 227–248.

Bourgeois, L. J. (1985). Strategic goals, perceived uncertainty, and economic performance in volatile environments. *Academy of Management Journal*, 3, 548–573.

Bowen, D. E., & Lawler, E. E. III. (1992). The empowerment of service workers: What, why, how, and when. *Sloan Management Review*, 33 (Spring), 31–39.

Bowers, D. G. (1975). Hierarchy, function, and the generalizability of leadership practices. In J. G. Hunt and L. L. Larson (Eds.), *Leadership frontiers*. Kent, OH: Kent State University Press.

Bowers, D. G., & Seashore, S. E. (1966). Predicting organizational effectiveness with a four-factor theory of leadership. *Administrative Science Quarterly*, 11, 238–263.

Boyacigiller, N., & Adler, N. (1991). The parochial dinosaur: Organizational science in a global context. *Academy of Management Review*, 16, 262–290.

Boyatzis, R. E. (1982). *The competent manager.* New York: John Wiley.

Bracken, D. W. (1994). Straight talk about multirater feedback. *Training and Development*, September, 44–51.

Bradford, D. L., & Cohen, A. R. (1984). *Managing for excellence: The guide to developing high performance organizations.* New York: John Wiley.

Bradford, L. P. (1976). *Making meetings work.* La Jolla, CA: University Associates.

Bragg, J., & Andrews, I. R. (1973). Participative decision making: An experimental study in a hospital. *Journal of Applied Behavioral Science*, 9, 727–735.

Brass, D. J. (1984). Being in the right place: A structural analysis of individual differences in an organization. *Administrative Science Quarterly*, 29, 518–539.

Brass, D. J. (1985). Technology and the structuring of jobs: Employee satisfaction, performance, and influence. *Organizational Behavior and Human Decision Processes*, 35, 216–240.

Bray, D. W., Campbell, R. J., & Grant, D. L. (1974). *Formative years in business: A long-term AT&T study of managerial lives.* New York: John Wiley.

Brenner, O. C., Tomkiewicz, J., & Schein, V. E. (1989). The relationship between sex role stereotypes and requisite management characteristics revisited. *Academy of Management Journal*, 32, 662–669.

Brett, J. M., Tinsley, C. H., Janssens, M., Barsness, Z. I., & Lytle, A. L. (1997). New approaches to the study of culture in industrial/organizational psychology. In P. C. Earley and M. Erez (Eds.), *New perspectives on industrial/organizational psychology*. San Francisco: New Lexington Press, pp. 75–127.

Brief, A. P., Schuler, R. S., & Van Sell, M. (1981). *Managing job stress.* Boston: Little Brown.

Broadwell, M. M. (1988). *The supervisor and on-the-job training,* 3rd. ed. Reading, MA: Addison-Wesley.

Brown, D. J., & Lord, R. G. (1999). The utility of experimental research in the study of transformational and charismatic leadership. *Leadership Quarterly*, 10, 531–539.

Brown, L. D. (1983). *Managing conflict at organizational interfaces.* Reading, MA: Addison-Wesley.

Brown, M. C. (1982). Administrative succession and organizational performance: The succession effect. *Administrative Science Quarterly*, 29, 245–273.

Brown, M. H., & Hosking, D. M. (1986). Distributed leadership and skilled performance as successful organization in social movements. *Human Relations*, 39, 65–79.

Brown, M. W., & Gioia, D. A. (2002). Making things click: Distributive leadership in an online division of an offline organization. *Leadership Quarterly*, 13, 397–419.

Bryman, A. (1992). *Charisma and leadership in organizations*. London: Sage.

Bryman, A. (1993). Charismatic leadership in business organizations: Some neglected issues. *Leadership Quarterly*, 4, 289–304.

Bryman, A., Bresnen, M., Beardworth, A., & Keil, T. (1988). Qualitative research and the study of leadership. *Human Relations*, 41, 13–30.

Bryman, A., Stephens, M., & Campo, C. (1996). The importance of context: Qualitative research and the study of leadership. *Leadership Quarterly*, 7, 353–370.

Bunker, K. W., & Webb, A. D. (1992). *Learning how to learn from experience: Impact of stress and coping*. Technical Report #154. Greensboro, NC: Center for Creative Leadership.

Burgoyne, J. G., & Hodgson, V. E. (1988). An experiential approach to understanding managerial action. In J. G. Hunt, D. M. Hosking, C. A. Schriesheim, and R. Stewart (Eds.), *Leaders and managers: An international perspective on managerial behavior and leadership*. New York: Pergamon Press, pp. 163–178.

Burke, M. J., & Day, R. R. (1986). A cumulative study of the effectiveness of managerial training. *Journal of Applied Psychology*, 71, 232–246.

Burke, R. J., Wier, T., & Duncan, G. (1976). Informal helping relationships in work organizations. *Academy of Management Journal*, 19, 370–377.

Burns, J. M. (1978). *Leadership*. New York: Harper & Row.

Bycio, P., Hackett, R. D., & Allen, J. S. (1995). Further assessments of the Bass (1985) conceptualization of transactional and transformational leadership. *Journal of Applied Psychology*, 80, 468–478.

Calder, B. J. (1977). An attribution theory of leadership. In B. M. Staw and G. R. Salancik (Eds.), *New direction in organizational behavior*. Chicago: St. Clair.

Camp, R. C. (1989). *Benchmarking: The search for industry best practices that lead to superior performance*. Milwaukee: ASQC Quality Press.

Campbell, J. P. (1977). The cutting edge of leadership: An overview. In J. G. Hunt and L. L. Larson (Eds.), *Leadership: The cutting edge*. Carbondale, IL: Southern Illinois University Press.

Campbell, J. P. (1988). Training design for performance improvement. In J. P. Campbell, R. J. Campbell, and Associates (Eds.), *Productivity in organizations*. San Francisco: Jossey Bass, pp. 177–216.

Campbell, J. P., Dunnette, M. D., Arvey, R. D., & Hellervik, L. W. (1973). The development and evaluation of behaviorally based rating scales. *Journal of Applied Psychology*, 57, 15–22.

Campion, M. A., Cheraskin, L., & Stevens, M. J. (1994). Career-related antecedents and outcomes of job rotation. *Academy of Management Journal*, 37, 1518–1542.

Campion, M. A., Medsker, G. J., & Higgs, A. C. (1993). Relations between work group characteristics and effectiveness: Implications for designing effective work groups. *Personnel Psychology*, 46, 823–850.

Campion, M. A., Papper, E. M., & Medsker, G. J. (1996). Relations between work team characteristics and effectiveness: A replication and extension. *Personnel Psychology*, 49, 429–452.

Cannella, A. A. Jr., & Monroe, M. J. (1997). Contrasting perspectives on strategic leaders: Toward a more realistic view of top managers. *Journal of Management*, 23 (3), 213–237.

Cannon-Bowers, J. A., Salas, E., & Converse, S. A. (1993). Shared mental models in expert team decision making. In N. J. Caltellan Jr. (Ed.), *Current issues in individual and group decision making*, pp. 221–246. Hillsdale, NJ: Lawrence Erlbaum.

Cantor, N., & Kihlstrom, J. F. (1987). *Personality and social intelligence*. Englewood Cliffs, NJ: Prentice Hall.

Carless, S. A. (1998). Assessing the discriminant validity of transformational leader behavior as measured by the MLQ. *Journal of Occupational and Organizational Psychology*, 71, 353–358.

Carlson, S. (1951). *Executive behavior: A study of the work load and working methods of managing directors*. Stockholm: Strombergs.

Carroll, S. J. Jr., & Gillen, D. J. (1987). Are the classical management functions useful in describing managerial work? *Academy of Management Review*, 12, 38–51.

Carr-Ruffino, N. (1993). *The promotable woman: Advancing through leadership skills*. Belmont, CA: Wadsworth.

Cartwright, D. (1965). Leadership, influence, and control. In J. G. March (Ed.), *Handbook of organizations*. Chicago: Rand McNally.

Case, T., Dosier, L., Murkinson, G., & Keys, B. (1988). How managers influence superiors: A study of upward influence tactics. *Leadership and Organizational Development Journal*, 9 (4), 25–31.

Cashman, J., Dansereau, F. Jr., Graen, G., & Haga, W. J. (1976). Organizational understructure and leadership: A longitudinal investigation of the managerial role-making process. *Organizational Behavior and Human Performance*, 15, 278–296.

Cavaleri, S., & Fearon, D. (1996). *Managing in organizations that learn*. Cambridge, MA: Blackwell Publishers.

Chaleff, I. (1995). *The courageous follower: Standing up to and for our leaders*. San Francisco: Berrett-Koehler Publishers.

Chappelow, C. T. (1998). 360-degree feedback. In In C. D. McCauley, R. S. Moxley, and E. Van Velsor (Eds.), *Center for Creative Leadership handbook of leadership development*. San Francisco: Jossey-Bass, pp. 29–65.

Chao, G. T., Walz, P. M., & Gardner, P. D. (1992). Formal and informal mentorships: A comparison on mentoring functions contrasted with nonmentored counterparts. *Personnel Psychology*, 45, 619–636.

Chappel, E., & Sayles, L. (1961). *The measure of management*. New York: MacMillan.

Charbonneau, D., Barling, J., & Kelloway, K. E. (2001). Transformational leadership and sports performance: The mediating role of intrinsic motivation. *Journal of Applied Social Psychology*, 31 (7), 1521–1534.

Chaston, I., Badger, B., Mangles, T., & Sadler-Smith, E. (2001). Organizational learning style, competencies, and learning systems in small, UK manufacturing firms. *International Journal of Operations and Production Management*, 21, 1417–1432.

Chen, G., & Bliese, P. D. (2002). The role of different levels of leadership in predicting self and collective efficacy: Evidence for discontinuity. *Journal of Applied Psychology*, 87 (3), 549–556.

Cho, Y. & Mai-Dalton, R. R. (1999). The model of followers' responses to self-sacrificial leadership: An empirical test. *Leadership Quarterly*, 10, 397–421.

Clark, L. A., & Lyness, K. S. (1991). Succession planning as a strategic activity at Citicorp. In L. W. Foster (Eds.), *Advances in applied business strategy*, vol. 2. Greenwich, CN: JAI Press.

Coch, L., & French, J. R. P. Jr. (1948). Overcoming resistance to change. *Human Relations*, 1, 512–532.

Cohen, A., & Bradford, D. (1989). Influence without authority: The use of alliances, reciprocity, and exchange to accomplish work. *Organizational Dynamics*, 17, 5–17.

Cohen, M. D., & March, J. G. (1974). *Leadership and ambiguity*. New York: McGraw-Hill.

Cohen, S. G. (1991). *Teams and teamwork: Future directions*. Los Angeles, CA: Center for Effective Organizations, University of Southern California.

Cohen, S. G., & Bailey, D. E. (1997). What makes teams work: Group effectiveness research from the shop floor to the executive suite. *Journal of Management*, 23, 239–290.

Cohen, S. G., & Ledford, G. E. Jr. (1994). The effectiveness of self-managing teams: A field experiment. *Human Relations*, 47, 13–43.

Collins, J. (2001). *Good to great*. New York: Harper Collins.

Collins, O. F., Moore, D. G., & Unwalla, D. B. (1964). *The enterprising man.* East Lansing, MI: Bureau of Business and Economic Research, Michigan State University.

Conger, J. A. (1989). *The charismatic leader: Behind the mystique of exceptional leadership*. San Francisco, CA: Jossey-Bass.

Conger, J. A. (1992). *Learning to lead: The art of transforming managers into leaders*. San Francisco, CA: Jossey-Bass.

Conger, J. A. (1993). The brave new world of leadership training. *Organizational Dynamics*, Winter, 46–58.

Conger, J. A. & Kanungo, R. (1987). Toward a behavioral theory of charismatic leadership in organizational settings. *Academy of Management Review*, 12, 637–647.

Conger, J. A., & Kanungo, R. N. (1988). The empowerment process: Integrating theory and practice. *Academy of Management Review*, 13, 471–482.

Conger, J. A., & Kanungo, R. N. (1990). *A behavioral attribute measure of charismatic leadership in organizations*. Paper presented at the Academy of Management Meetings, San Francisco.

Conger, J. A., & Kanungo, R. N. (1994). Charismatic leadership in organizations: Perceived behavioral attributes and their measurement. *Journal of Organizational Behavior*, 15, 439–452.

Conger, J. A., & Kanungo, R. (1998). *Charismatic leadership in organizations.* Thousand Oaks, CA: Sage Publications.

Conger, J. A., Kanungo, R. N., & Menon, S. T. (2000). Charismatic leadership and follower effects. *Journal of Organizational Behavior*, 21, 747–767.

Connelly, M. S., Gilbert, J. A., Zaccaro, S. J., Marks, M. A., & Mumford, M. D. (2000). Exploring the relationship of leadership skills and knowledge to leader performance. *Leadership Quarterly*, 11 (1), 65–86.

Connor, D. R. (1995). *Managing at the speed of change: How resilient managers succeed and prosper where others fail.* New York: Villard Books.

Cooper, M. R., & Wood, M. T. (1974). Effects of member participation and commitment in group decision making on influence, satisfaction, and decision riskiness. *Journal of Applied Psychology*, 59, 127–134.

Cordery, J. L., Mueller, W. S., & Smith, L. M. (1991). Attitudinal and behavioral effects of autonomous group working: A longitudinal field study. *Academy of Management Journal*, 34, 464–476.

Cosier, R. A. (1978). The effects of three potential aids for making strategic decisions on prediction accuracy. *Organizational Behavior and Human Performance*, 22, 295–306.

Cosier, R. A. (1982). Methods for improving the strategic decision: Dialectic versus the devil's advocate. *Strategic Management Journal*, 3, 373–374.

Cotton, J. L. (1993). *Employee involvement: Methods for improving performance and work attitudes*. Newbury Park, CA: Sage.

Cotton, J. L., Vollrath, D. A., Froggatt, K. L., Lengnick-Hall, M. L., & Jennings, K. R. (1988). Employee participation: Diverse forms and different outcomes. *Academy of Management Review*, 13, 8–22.

Cotton, J. L., Vollrath, D. A., Lengnick-Hall, M. L., & Froggatt, K. L. (1990). Fact: The form of participation does matter—A rebuttal to Leana, Locke, and Schweiger. *Academy of Management Review*, 15, 147–153.

Cox, T. H. (1991). The multi-cultural organization. *Academy of Management Executive*, 5 (2), 34–47.

Cox, T. H., & Blake, S. (1991). Managing cultural diversity: Implications for organizational competitiveness. *Academy of Management Executive*, 5 (3), 45–56.

Cox, C. J., & Cooper, C. L. (1989). *High Flyers: An anatomy of managerial success*. Oxford: Basil Blackwell.

Crant, J. M., & Bateman, T. S. (1993). Assignment of credit and blame for performance outcomes. *Academy of Management Journal*, 36, 7–27.

Crossan, M., Lane, H., & White, R. (1999). An organizational learning framework: From intuition to institution. *Academy of Management Review*, 24, 522–538.

Crouch, A., & Yetton, P. (1987). Manager behavior, leadership style, and subordinate performance: An empirical extension of the Vroom-Yetton conflict rule. *Organizational Behavior and Human Decision Processes*, 39, 384–396.

Crouch, A., & Yetton, P. (1988). The management team: An equilibrium model of management performance and behavior. In J. G. Hunt, B. R. Baliga, H. P. Dachler, & C. A. Schriesheim (Eds.), *Emerging Leadership Vistas*. Lexington, MA: Lexington Books, pp. 107–128.

Dachler, H. P. (1984). Commentary on refocusing leadership from a social systems perspective. In J. G. Hunt, D. Hosking, C. A. Schriesheim, & R. Stewart (Eds.), *Leaders and managers: International perspectives on managerial behavior and leadership*. New York: Pergamon Press, pp. 100–108.

Dahl, R. A. (1957). The concept of power. *Behavioral Science*, 2, 201–218.

Dale, E. (1960). Management must be made accountable. *Harvard Business Review*, 38, March–April, 49–59.

Dansereau, F., Alutto, J. A., & Yammarino, F. J. (1984). *Theory testing in organizational behavior: The varient approach*. Englewood Cliffs, NJ: Prentice Hall.

Dansereau, F., Jr., Graen, G., & Haga, W. J. (1975). A vertical dyad linkage approach to leadership within formal organizations: A longitudinal investigation of the role making process. *Organizational Behavior and Human Performance*, 13, 46–78.

Dansereau, F., Yammarino, F. J., & Markham, S. E. (1995). Leadership: The multiple level approaches. *Leadership Quarterly*, 6 , 251–263.

Dasborouigh, M. T., & Ashkanasy, N. M. (2002). Emotion and attribution of intentionality in leader-member relations. *Leadership Quarterly*, 13, 615–634.

Davies, J., & Easterby-Smith, M. (1984). Learning and developing from managerial work experiences. *Journal of Management Studies*, 2, 169–183.

Davis, K. (1968). Attitudes toward the legitimacy of management efforts to influence employees. *Academy of Management Journal*, 11, 153–162.

Day, D. V. (2000). Leadership development: A review in context. *Leadership Quarterly*, 11 (4), 581–613.

Day, D. V., & Lord, R. G. (1988). Executive leadership and organizational performance: Suggestions for a new theory and methodology. *Journal of Management*, 14 (3), 453–464.

Day, R. C. (1971). Some effects of combining close, punitive, and supportive styles of supervision. *Sociometry*, 34, 303–327.

Day, R. C., & Hamblin, R. L. (1964). Some effects of close and punitive styles of supervision. *American Journal of Sociology*, 69, 499–510.

Deal, T. (1985). Culture change: Opportunity, silent killer, or metamorphosis? In R. Kilmann, R. H., Saxton, M. J., & Serpa, R. (Eds.), *Gaining control of the corporate culture*. San Francisco: Jossey-Bass, pp. 292–330.

Dechant, K. (1990). Knowing how to learn: The neglected management ability. *Journal of Management Development*, 9 (4), 40–49.

Dechant, K. (1994). Making the most of job assignments: An exercise in planning for learning. *Journal of Management Education*, 18, 198–211.

DeCremer, D. (2002). Charismatic leadership and cooperation in social dilemmas: A matter of transforming motives? *Journal of Applied Social Psychology*, 32, 997–1016.

De Jong, G., & Van Witteloostuijn, A. (2004). Success for corporate democracy: Sustainable cooperation of capital and labor in the Dutch Breman Group. *Academy of Management Executive*, 18 (3), 54–66.

Delbecq, A. L., Van de Ven, A. H., & Gustafson, D. H. (1975). *Group techniques for program planning: A guide to nominal and delphi processes.* Glenview, IL: Scott Foresman.

Deluga, R. J. (1998). American presidential proactivity, charismatic leadership, and rated performance. *Leadership Quarterly*, 9, 265–291.

Deluga, R. J., & Perry, T. J. (1994). The role of subordinate performance and ingratiation in leader-member exchanges. *Group and Organization Management*, 19, 67–86.

Den Hartog, D. N., House, R. J., Hanges, P. J., Ruiz-Quintanilla, S. A., Dorfman, P. W., & Associates. (1999). Culture specific and cross-culturally generalizable implicit leadership theories: Are the attributes of charismatic/transformational leadership universally endorsed? *Leadership Quarterly*, 10, 219–256.

Den Hartog, D. N., Van Muijen, J. J., & Koopman, P. L. (1997). Transactional versus transformational leadership: An analysis of the MLQ. *Journal of Occupational and Organizational Psychology*, 70, 19–34.

Denis, J. L., Lamothe, L., & Langley, A. (2001). The dynamics of collective leadership and strategic change in pluralistic organizations. *Academy of Management Journal*, 44, 809–837.

Denison, D. R., Hart, S. L., & Kahn, J. A. (1996). From chimneys to cross-functional teams: Developing and validating a diagnostic model. *Academy of Management Journal*, 39, 1005–1023.

Dess, G. G., & Picken, J. C. (2000). Changing roles: Leadership in the 21st century. *Organizational Dynamics*, 28 (3), 18–33.

De Vries, R. E., Roe, R. A., & Taillieu, T. C. B. (2002). Need for leadership as a moderator of the relationships between leadership and individual outcomes. *Leadership Quarterly*, 13 (2), 121–137.

Dickson, M. W., Den Hartog, D. N., & Michelson, J. K. (2003). Research on leadership in a cross-cultural context: Making progress and raising new questions. *Leadership Quarterly*, 14, 729–768.

Dickson, M. W., Smith, D. B., Grojean, M., & Ehrhart, M. G. (2001). An organizational climate regarding ethics: The outcome of leader values and the practices that reflect them. *Leadership Quarterly*, 12, 197–217.

Dienesh, R. M., & Liden, R. C. (1986). Leader-member exchange model of leadership: A critique and further development. *Academy of Management Review*, 11, 618–634.

Digman, J. M. (1990). Personality structure: Emergence of the five-factor model. *Annual Review of Psychology*, 4, 417–440. Palo Alto, CA: Annual Reviews.

Dipboye, R. L. (1990). Laboratory vs. field research in industrial-organizational psychology. *International Review of Industrial and Organizational Psychology*, 5, 1–34.

Dobbins, G. H., Long, W. S., Dedrick, E. J., & Clemons, T. C. (1990). The role of self-monitoring and gender on leader emergence: A laboratory and field study. *Journal of Management*, 16, 609–618.

Dobbins, G. H., & Platz, S. J. (1986). Sex differences in leadership: How real are they? *Academy of Management Review*, 11, 118–127.

Doody, A. F., & Bingaman, R. (1988). *Reinventing the wheels: Ford's spectacular comeback.* Cambridge, MA: Ballinger.

Dorfman, P. (1996). International and cross-cultural leadership research. In B. J. Punnet and O. Shenkar (Eds.), *Handbook for international management research.* Oxford: Blackwell, pp. 267–349.

Dorfman, P. W. (2003). International and cross-cultural leadership research. In B. J. Punnett and O. Shenkar (Eds.), *Handbook for international management research*, 2nd ed. Ann Arbor, MI: University of Michigan.

Dorfman, P. W., Howell, J. P., Hibino, S., Lee, J. K., Tate, U., & Bautista, A. (1997). Leadership in Western and Asian countries: Commonalities and differences in effective leadership processes across cultures. *Leadership Quarterly*, 8 (3), 233–274.

Dorfman, P. W., & Ronen, S. (1991). *The universality of leadership theories: Challenges and paradoxes.* Paper presented at the Academy of Management Meetings, Miami, August.

Dotlich, D. L., & Cairo, P. C. (1999). *Action coaching: How to leverage individual performance for company success.* San Francisco: Jossey-Bass.

Dotlich, D. L., & Noel, J. L. (1998). *Action learning: How the world's top companies are recreating their leaders and themselves.* San Francisco: Jossey-Bass.

Douglas, C. A., & Schoorman, F. D. (1988). *The impact of career and psychosocial mentoring by supervisors and peers.* Paper presented at the 48th Annual Meeting of the Academy of Management, Anaheim, California.

Drath, W. H. (2001). *The deep blue sea: Rethinking the source of leadership.* San Francisco: Jossey-Bass.

Drath, W. H., & Palus, C. J. (1994). *Making common sense: Leadership as meaning-making in a community of practice.* Greensboro, NC: Center for Creative Leadership.

Dreher, G. F., & Ash, R. A. (1990). A comparative study of mentoring among men and women in managerial, professional, and technical positions. *Journal of Applied Psychology*, 75, 539–546.

Drucker, P. F. (1974). *Management: Tasks, responsibilities, practices.* New York: Harper & Row.

Druskat, V. U., & Wheeler, J. V. (2003). Managing from the boundary: The effective leadership of self-managing work teams. *Academy of Management Journal*, 46 (4), 435–457.

Duarte, N. T., Goodson, J. R., & Klich, N. R. (1994). Effects of dyadic quality and duration on performance appraisal. *Academy of Management Journal*, 37, 499–521.

Duarte, D. L., & Snyder, N. T. (1999). *Mastering virtual teams: Strategies, tools, and techniques that succeed.* San Francisco: Jossey-Bass.

Dubin, A. J. (1978). *Human relations: A job-oriented approach.* Reston, VA: Reston.

Duchon, D., Green, S. G., & Taber, T. D. (1986). Vertical dyad linkage: A longitudinal assessment of antecedents, measures, and consequences. *Journal of Applied Psychology*, 71, 56–60.

Dugan, K. W. (1989). Ability and effort attributions: Do they affect how managers communicate performance feedback information? *Academy of Management Journal*, 32, 87–114.

Dunbar, R., & Goldberg, W. H. (1978). Crisis development and strategic response in European corporations. In C. F. Smart and W. T. Stanbury (Eds.), *Studies on crisis management.* Toronto: Butterworth.

Dvir, T., Eden, D., Avolio, B., & Shamir, B. (2002). Impact of transformational leadership on follower development and performance: A field experiment. *Academy of Management Journal*, 45, 735–744.

Dweck, C. S. (1986). Motivational processes affecting learning. *American Psychologist*, 41, 1040–1048.

Dyer, W. G. (1977). *Team building: Issues and alternatives.* Reading, MA: Addison-Wesley.

Eagly, A. H., & Carli, L. L. (2003a). The female leadership advantage: An evaluation of the evidence. *Leadership Quarterly*, 14, 807–834.

Eagly, A. H., & Carli, L. L. (2003b). Finding gender advantage and disadvantage: Systematic research integration is the solution. *Leadership Quarterly*, 14, 851–859.

Eagly, A. H., Darau, S. J., & Makhijani, M. G. (1995). Gender and the effectiveness of leaders: A meta-analysis. *Psychological Bulletin*, 117, 125–145.

Eagly, A. H., Johannesen-Schmidt, M. C., & Van Engen, M. (2003). Transformational, transactional, and laissez-faire leadership styles: A meta-analysis comparing men and women. *Psychological Bulletin*, 95, 569–591.

Eagly, A. H., & Johnson, B. T. (1990). Gender and leadership style: A meta-analysis. *Psychological Bulletin*, 108, 233–256.

Eagly, A. H., Makhijani, M. G., & Klonsky, B. G. (1992). Gender and the evaluation of leaders. *Psychological Bulletin*, 111, 3–22.

Earl, M. (2001). Knowledge management strategies: Toward a taxonomy. *Journal of Management Information Systems*, 18, 215–233.

Earley, P. C., & Lind, E. A. (1987). Procedural justice and participation in task selection: The role of control in mediating justice judgments. *Journal of Personality and Social Psychology*, 52, 1148–1160.

Earley, P. C., Wojnaroski, P., & Prest, W. (1987). Task planning and energy expended: Exploration of how goals influence performance. *Journal of Applied Psychology*, 72, 107–114.

Eccles, T. (1993). The deceptive allure of empowerment. *Long Range Planning*, 26 (6), 13–21.

Eden, D. (1984). Self-fulfilling prophecy as a management tool: Harnessing pygmalion. *Academy of Management Review*, 9, 64–73.

Eden, D. (1990). *Pygmalion in management: Productivity as a self-fulfilling prophecy*. Lexington, MA: Lexington Books.

Eden, D., & Leviatan, U. (1975). Implicit leadership theory as a determinant of the factor structure underlying supervisory behavior scales. *Journal of Applied Psychology*, 60, 736–741.

Eden, D., & Shani, A. B. (1982). Pygmalion goes to boot camp: Expectancy, leadership and trainee performance. *Journal of Applied Psychology*, 67, 194–199.

Edmondson, A. C., Roberto, M. A., & Watkins, M. D. (2003). A dynamic model of top management team effectiveness: Managing unstructured task streams. *Leadership Quarterly*, 14 (3), 297–325.

Ehrhart, M. G., & Klein, K. J. (2001). Predicting followers' preferences for charismatic leadership: The influence of follower values and personality. *Leadership Quarterly*, 12 (2), 153–179.

Eisenhardt, K. M. (1989). Making fast strategic decisions in high-velocity environments. *Academy of Management Journal*, 32, 543–576.

Eisenstat, R. A., & Cohen, S. G. (1990). Summary: Top management groups. In J. R. Hackman (ed.), *Groups that work (and those that don't)*. San Francisco: Jossey-Bass, pp. 78–88.

Ekvall, G., & Arvonen, J. (1991). Change-centered leadership: An extension of the two-dimensional model. *Scandinavian Journal of Management*, 7, 17–26.

Emans, B., Klaver, E., Munduate, L., & Van de Vliert, E. (1999). *Constructive consequences of hard power use by leaders in organizations*. Paper presented to the European Congress on Work and Organizational Psychology, May, Espoo-Helsinki, Finland.

Engelbracht, A. S., & Fischer, A. H. (1995). The managerial performance implications of a developmental assessment center process. *Human Relations*, 48, 1–18.

Erdogan, B., & Liden, R. C. (2002). Social exchanges in the workplace: A review of recent developments and future research directions in leader-member exchange theory. In L. L. Neider and C. A. Schriesheim (Eds.), *Leadership*. Greenwich, CT: Information Age Publishing, pp. 65–114.

Erez, M.. Rim, Y., & Keider, I. (1986). The two sides of the tactics of influence: Agent vs. target. *Journal of Occupational Psychology*, 59, 25–39.

Ettling, J. T., & Jago, A. G. (1988). Participation under conditions of conflict: More on the validity of the Vroom-Yetton model. *Journal of Management Studies*, 25, 73–83.

Etzioni, A. (1991). *A comparative analysis of complex organizations*. New York: Free Press.

Evans, M. G. (1970). The effects of supervisory behavior on the path-goal relationship. *Organizational Behavior and Human Performance*, 5, 277–298.

Evans, M. G. (1974). Extensions of a path-goal theory of motivation. *Journal of Applied Psychology*, 59, 172–178.

Evans, W. M., & Zelditch, M. (1961). A laboratory experiment on bureaucratic authority. *American Sociological Review*, 26, 883–893.

Facteau, J. D., Dobbins, G. H., Russell, J. E. A., Ladd, R. T., & Kudisch, J. D. (1995). The influence of general perceptions of the training environment on pretraining motivation and perceived training transfer. *Journal of Management*, 21, 1–25.

Fagenson, E. A. (1989). The mentor advantage: Perceived career/job experiences of proteges versus non-proteges. *Journal of Organizational Behavior*, 10, 309–320.

Fairhurst, G. T. (1993). The leader-member exchange patterns of women leaders in industry: A discourse analysis. *Communication Monographs*, 60, 321–351.

Fairhurst, G. T. (In Press). The leader-follower communication. In F. Jablin and L. Putnam (Eds.), *Handbook of organizational communication*, 2nd ed. Newbury Park, CA: Sage.

Falbe, C. M., & Yukl, G. (1992). Consequences for managers of using single influence tactics and combinations of tactics. *Academy of Management Journal*, 35, 638–653.

Farh, J. L., Podsakoff, P. M., & Cheng, B. S. (1987). Culture-free leadership effectiveness versus moderators of leadership behavior: An extension and test of Ker and Jermier's substitute for leadership model in Taiwan. *Journal of International Business Studies*, 18, 43–60.

Farris, G. F., & Lim, F. G., Jr. (1969). Effects of performance on leadership, cohesiveness, satisfaction, and subsequent performance. *Journal of Applied Psychology*, 53, 490–497.

Fayol, H. (1949). *General and industrial management.* London: Pitman.

Feild, H., & Harris, S. G. (1991). Entry-level, fast-track management development programs: Developmental tactics and perceived program effectiveness. *Human Resource Planning*, 14, 261–273.

Fernandez, C. F., & Vecchio, R. P. (1997). Situational leadership theory revisited: A test of an across-jobs perspective. *Leadership Quarterly*, 8, 67–84.

Ferris, G. R., Bhawuk, D. P. S., Fedor, D. F., & Judge, T. A. (1995). Organizational politics and citizenship: Attributions of intentionality and construct definition. In M. J. Martinko (Ed.), *Advances in attribution theory: An organizational perspective*. Delray Beach, FL: St. Lucie Press, pp. 231–252.

Ferris, G. R., Judge, T. A., Rowland, K. M., & Fitzgibbons, D. E. (1994). Subordinate influence and the performance evaluation process: Test of a model. *Organizational Behavior and Human Decision Processes*, 58, 101–135.

Fiedler, F. E. (1964). A contingency model of leadership effectiveness. In L. Berkowitz (Ed.), *Advances in experimental social psychology*. New York: Academic Press.

Fiedler, F. E. (1967). *A theory of leadership effectiveness*. New York: McGraw-Hill.

Fiedler, F. E. (1970). Leadership experience and leader performance—Another hypothesis shot to hell. *Organizational Behavior and Human Performance*, 5, 1–14.

Fiedler, F. E. (1973). The contingency model: A reply to Ashour. *Organizational Behavior and Human Performance*, 9, 356–368.

Fiedler, F. E. (1977). A rejoinder to Schriesheim and Kerr's premature obituary of the contingency model. In J. G. Hunt and L. L. Larson (Eds.), *Leadership: The cutting edge.* Carbondale, IL: Southern Illinois University Press.

Fiedler, F. E. (1978). The contingency model and the dynamics of the leadership process. In L. Berkowitz (Ed.), *Advances in experimental social psychology*. New York: Academic Press.

Fiedler, F. E. (1986). The contribution of cognitive resources to leadership performance. *Journal of Applied Social Psychology*, 16, 532–548.

Fiedler, F. E. (1992). Time-based measures of leadership experience and organizational performance: A review of research and a preliminary model. *Leadership Quarterly*, 3, 5–23.

Fiedler, F. E., & Chemers, M. M. (1982). *Improving leadership effectiveness: The leader match concept,* 2nd ed. New York: John Wiley, 1982.

Fiedler, F. E., & Garcia, J. E. (1987). *New approaches to leadership: Cognitive resources and organizational performance.* New York: John Wiley.

Fiedler, F. E., & Mahar, L. (1979). The effectiveness of contingency model training: A review of the validation of leader match. *Personnel Psychology,* 32, 45–62.

Field, R. H. G. (1979). A critique of the Vroom-Yetton contingency model of leadership behavior. *Academy of Management Review,* 4, 249–257.

Field, R. H. G. (1982). A test of the Vroom-Yetton normative model of leadership. *Journal of Applied Psychology,* 67, 523–532.

Field, R. H. G. (1989). The self-fulfilling prophecy leader: Achieving the Metharme effect. *Journal of Management Studies,* 26, 151–175.

Field, R. H. G., & House, R. J. (1990). A test of the Vroom-Yetton model using manager and subordinate reports. *Journal of Applied Psychology,* 75, 362–366.

Field, R. H. G., Read, P. C., & Louviere, J. J. (1990). The effect of situation attributes on decision making choice in the Vroom-Jago model of participation in decision making. *Leadership Quarterly,* 1, 165–176.

Filley, A. C. (1970), Committee management: Guidelines from social science research. *California Management Review,* 13 (1), 13–21.

Finkelstein, S. (1992). Power in top management teams: Dimensions, measurement, and validation. *Academy of Management Journal,* 35, 505–538.

Finkelstein, S. (2003). *Why smart executives fail.* New York: Portfolio.

Finkelstein, S., & Hambrick, D. C. (1996). *Strategic leadership: Top executives and their effects on organizations.* St. Paul, MN: West.

Fiol, C. M., Harris, D., & House, R. (1999). Charismatic leadership: Strategies for effecting social change. *Leadership Quarterly,* 10, 449–482.

Fiol, C. M., & Lyles, M. A. (1985). Organizational learning. *Academy of Management Review,* 10, 803–813.

Fisher, B. M., & Edwards, J. E. (1988). Consideration and initiating structure and their relationships with leader effectiveness: A meta-analysis. *Proceedings of the Academy of Management,* August, 201–205.

Fisher, C. D. (1986). Organizational socialization: An integrative review. In K. M. Rowland and G. R. Ferris (Eds.), *Research in Personnel and Human Resources Management,* vol. 4, pp. 101–145. Greenwich, CT: JAI Press.

Flanagan, J. C. (1951). Defining the requirements of an executive's job. *Personnel,* 28, 28–35.

Fleishman, E. A. (1953). The description of supervisory behavior. *Personnel Psychology,* 37, 1–6.

Fleishman, E. A., & Harris, E. F. (1962). Patterns of leadership behavior related to employee grievances and turnover. *Personnel Psychology,* 15, 43–56.

Fleishman, E. A., Mumford, M. D., Zaccaro, S. J., Levin, K. Y., Korotkin, A. L., & Hein, M. B. (1991). Taxonomic efforts in the description of leader behavior: A synthesis and functional interpretation. *Leadership Quarterly,* 2, 245–287.

Fletcher, C. (1990). Candidates' reactions to assessment centres and their outcomes: A longitudinal study. *Journal of Occupational Psychology,* 63, 117–127.

Ford, J. D. (1981). Departmental context and formal structure as constraints on leader behavior. *Academy of Management Journal,* 24, 274–288.

Ford, J. K., Quinones, M. A., Sego D. J., & Sorra, J. S. (1992). Factors affecting the opportunity to perform trained tasks on the job. *Personnel Psychology,* 45, 511–527.

Ford, J. K., & Weissbein, D. A. (1997). Transfer of training: An updated review and analysis. *Performance Improvement Quarterly*, 10, 22–41.

Ford, M. E. (1986). A living systems conceptualization of social intelligence: Outcomes, processes, and developmental change. In R. J. Sternberg (Ed.), *Advances in the psychology of human intelligence*. Hillsdale, NJ: Erlbaum.

Ford, R. C., & Randolph, W. A. (1992). Cross-functional structures: A review and integration of matrix organization and project management. *Journal of Management*, 18, 267–294.

Forgas, J. P. (1995). Mood and judgment: The affect infusion model. *Psychological Bulletin*, 117, 39–66.

Forrester, R. (2000). Empowerment: Rejuvenating a potent idea. *Academy of Management Executive*, 14 (3), 67–80.

Fouriezos, N. T., Hutt, M. L., & Guetzkow, H. (1950). Measurement of self-oriented needs in discussion groups. *Journal of Abnormal and Social Psychology*, 45, 682–690.

Foust, D. (2003). The GE way isn't working at Home Depot. *Business Week Online*, January 17. Available at www.businessweek.com/ bwdaily/dnflash/jan2003/nf20030117_1446.htm.

French, J., & Raven, B. H. (1959). The bases of social power. In D. Cartwright (Ed.), *Studies of social power*. Ann Arbor, MI: Institute for Social Research, pp.150–167.

Fried, Y., & Ferris, G. R. (1987). The validity of the job characteristics model: A review and meta-analysis. *Personnel Psychology*, 40, 287–322.

Friedman, S. D. (1986). Succession systems in large corporations: Characteristics and correlates of performance. *Human Resource Management*, 25, 191–213.

Frost, D. C. (1983). Role perceptions and behaviors of the immediate superior moderating effects on the prediction of leadership effectiveness. *Organizational Behavior and Human Performance,* 31, 123–142.

Fu, P. P., & Yukl, G. (2000). Perceived effectiveness of influence tactics in the United States and China. *Leadership Quarterly*, 11, 251–266.

Fulmer, R. M. (1997). The evolving paradigm of leadership development. *Organizational Dynamics*, Spring, 59–72.

Fulmer, R. M., & Vicere, A. (1996). *Strategic leadership development: Crafting competitiveness.* Oxford: Capstone Publishers.

Gabarro, J. J. (1985). When a new manager takes charge. *Harvard Business Review*, May–June, 110–123.

Gabarro, J. J. (1987). *The dynamics of taking charge*. Boston: Harvard Business School Press.

Galagan, P. (1987). Between two trapezes. *Training and Development Journal*, 41 (3), 40–53.

Galbraith, J. R. (1973). *Designing complex organizations*. Menlo Park, CA: Addison-Wesley.

Gall, A. L. (1987). You can take the manager out of the woods, but . . . *Training and Development Journal*, 41 (3), 54–61.

Gallupe, R. B., Bastianutti, L. M., & Cooper, W. H. (1991). Unblocking brainstorms. *Journal of Applied Psychology*, 76, 137–142.

Ganster, D. C., Fusilier, M. R., & Mayes, B. T. (1986). Role of social support in the experience of stress at work. *Journal of Applied Psychology*, 71, 102–110.

Garvin, D. A. (1993). Building a learning organization. *Harvard Business Review*, July–August, 78–91.

Geber, B. (1995). Virtual teams. *Training*, 32, 36–40.

Gebert, D., Boerner, S., & Lanwehr, R. (2003). The risks of autonomy: Empirical evidence for the necessity of balance in promoting organizational innnovativeness. *Creativity and Innovation Management*, 12 (1), 41–49.

Gellerman, S. W. (1976). Supervision: Substance and style. *Harvard Business Review*, March–April, 89–99.

George, J. M. (1995). Leader positive mood and group performance: The case of customer service. *Journal of Applied Social Psychology*, 25, 778–794.

George, J. M., & Jones, G. R. (1996). *Understanding and managing organizational behavior*. Reading, MA: Addison-Wesley.

Georgopoulos, B. S., Mahoney, G. M., & Jones, N. W., Jr. (1957). A path-goal approach to productivity. *Journal of Applied Psychology*, 41, 345–353.

Gerstner, C. R., & Day, D. V. (1997). Meta-analytic review of leader-member exchange theory: Correlates and construct issues. *Journal of Applied Psychology*, 82, 827–844.

Gharajedaghi, J. (1999). *Systems thinking: Managing chaos and complexity*. Boston: Butterworth Heinemann.

Giber, D., Carter, L., & Goldsmith, M., Eds. (1999). *Linkage Inc.'s best practices in leadership development handbook*. Lexington, MA: Linkage Press.

Gibson, C. B. (2001). Me and us: Differential relationships among goal setting, training, efficacy, and effectiveness at the individual and team level. *Journal of Organizational Behavior*, 22, 789–808.

Gibson, C. B., Randel, A. E., & Earley, P. C. (2000). Understanding group efficacy: An empirical test of multiple assessment methods. *Group & Organization Management*, 25 (1), 67–97.

Gibson, F. W. (1992). Leader abilities and group performance as a function of stress. In K. Clark, M. B. Clark, and D. P. Campbell (Eds.), *Impact of Leadership*. Greensboro, NC: Center for Creative Leadership, pp. 333–343.

Gibson, F. W., Fiedler, F. E., & Barrett, K. M. (1993). Stress, babble, and the utilization of the leader's intellectual abilities. *Leadership Quarterly*, 4, 189–208.

Gilmore, D. C., Beehr, T. A., & Richter, D. J. (1979). Effects of leader behaviors on subordinate performance and satisfaction: A laboratory experiment with student employees. *Journal of Applied Psychology*, 64, 166–172.

Gini, A. (1998). Moral leadership and business ethics. In J. B. Ciulla (Ed.), *Ethics, the heart of leadership*. Westport, CT: Greenwood Publishing.

Ginter, P. M., & Duncan, W. J. (1990). Macroenvironmental analysis for strategic managment. *Long Range Planning*, 23, 91–100.

Gioia, D. A., & Sims, H. P., Jr. (1985). On avoiding the influence of implicit leadership theories in leader behavior descriptions. *Journal of Educational and Psychological Measurement*, 45, 217–237.

Gioia, D. A., & Sims, H. P. (1986). Cognitive-behavior connections: Attribution and verbal behavior in leader-subordinate interactions. *Organizational Behavior and Human Decision Processes*, 37, 197–229.

Gladstean, D. L. (1984). Groups in context: A model of task group effectiveness. *Administrative Science Quarterly*, 29, 499–517.

Godfrey, D. K., Jones, E. E., & Lord, C. G. (1986). Self-promotion is not ingratiating. *Journal of Personality and Social Psychology*, 50, 106–115.

Golde, R. A. (1972). Are your meetings like this one? *Harvard Business Review*, January–February, 68–77.

Goldner, F. H. (1970). The division of labor: Processes and power. In M. N. Zald (Ed.), *Power in organizations*. Nashville, TN: Vanderbilt University Press.

Goldstein, A. P., & Sorcher, M. (1974). *Changing supervisory behavior*. New York: Pergamon Press.

Goldstein, I. L. (1992). *Training and development in organizations*. Monterey, CA: Brooks-Cole.

Goleman, D. (1995). *Emotional intelligence: Why it can matter more than IQ*. New York: Bantam Books.

Goleman, D., Boyatzis, R., & McKee, A. (2002). *Primal leadership: Realizing the power of emotional intelligence.* Boston: Harvard Business School Press.

Goodge, P. (1991). Development centers: Guidelines for decision makers. *Journal of Management Development*, 10 (3), 4–12.

Goodman, P. S. (1979). *Assessing organizational change: The Rushton quality of work experiment.* New York: Wiley-Interscience.

Goodman, P. S., Devadas, R., & Hughson, T. G. (1988). Groups and productivity: Analyzing the effectiveness of self-managing teams. In J. P. Campbell and R. J. Campbell (Eds.), *Productivity in organizations.* San Francisco, CA: Jossey-Bass, pp. 295–327.

Goodman, P. S., & Rousseau, D. M. (2004). Organizational change that produces results: The linkage approach. *Academy of Management Executive*, 18 (3), 7–19.

Goodson, J. R., McGee, G. W., & Cashman, J. F. (1989). Situational leadership theory: A test of leadership prescriptions. *Group and Organization Studies*, 14, 446–461.

Goodstadt, B. E., & Hjelle, L. A. (1973). Power to the powerless: Locus of control and the use of power. *Journal of Personality and Social Psychology*, 27, 190–196.

Goodstadt, B. E., & Kipnis, D. (1970). Situational influences on the use of power. *Journal of Applied Psychology*, 54, 201–207.

Goodstein, L. D., & Lanyon, R. I. (1999). Applications of personality assessment to the workplace: A review. *Journal of Business and Psychology*, 13, 291–322.

Gordon, J. (1992). Work teams: How far have they come? *Training*, October, 59–65.

Gordon, W. J. (1961). *Synectics.* New York: Collier Books.

Graef, C. L. (1983). The situational leadership theory: A critical review. *Academy of Management Review*, 8, 285–296.

Graen, G., Alvares, K. M., Orris, J. B., & Martella, J. A. (1970). Contingency model of leadership effectiveness: Antecedent and evidential results. *Psychological Bulletin*, 74, 285–296.

Graen, G., & Cashman, J. F. (1975). A role making model of leadership in formal organizations: A developmental approach. In J. G. Hunt and L. L. Larson (Eds.), *Leadership frontiers.* Kent, OH: Kent State University Press.

Graen, G. B., Cashman, J. F., Ginsburgh, S., & Schiemann, W. (1977). Effects of linking-pin quality on the quality of working life of lower participants. *Administrative Science Quarterly*, 22, 491–504.

Graen, G., Novak, M., & Sommerkamp, P. (1982). The effects of leader-member exchange and job design on productivity and satisfaction: Testing a dual attachment model. *Organizational Behavior and Human Performance*, 30, 109–131.

Graen, G. B., & Scandura, T. (1987). Toward a psychology of dyadic organizing. *Research in Organizational Behavior*, 9, 175–208.

Graen, G. B., & Uhl-Bien, M. (1991). The transformation of work group professionals into self-managing and partially self-designing contributors: Toward a theory of leadership-making. *Journal of Management Systems,* 3 (3), 33–48.

Graen, G. B., & Uhl-Bien, M. (1995). Relationship-based approach to leadership: Development of leader-member exchange (LMX) theory of leadership over 25 years: Applying a multi-level multi-domain approach. *Leadership Quarterly*, 6, 219–247.

Grant, J. (1988). Women as managers: What they can offer to organizations. *Organizational Dynamics*, Winter, 56–63.

Gratton, L. (2004). *The democratic enterprise.* London: Financial Times Prentice Hall.

Gravenhorst, K. M. B., & Boonstra, J. J. (1998). The use of influence tactics in constructive change processes. *European Journal of Work and Organizational Psychology*, 7, 179–196.

Green, S. G., Anderson, S. E., and Shivers, S. L. (1996). Demographic and organizational influences on leader-member exchange and related work attitudes. *Organizational Behavior and Human Decision Processes*, 66, 203–214.

Green, S. G., & Liden, R. C. (1980). Contextual and attributional influences on control decisions. *Journal of Applied Psychology*, 65, 453–458.

Green, S. G., & Mitchell, T. R. (1979). Attributional processes of leaders in leader-member exchanges. *Organizational Behavior and Human Performance*, 23, 429–458.

Green, W. A., & Lazarus, H. (1988). Corporate campuses: A growing phenomenon. *Journal of Management Development*, 7 (3), 56–67.

Greene, C. N. (1975). The reciprocal nature of influence between leader and subordinate. *Journal of Applied Psychology*, 60, 187–193.

Greenleaf, R. K. (1977). *Servant leadership: A journey into the nature of legitimate power and greatness.* Mahwah, NJ: Paulist Press.

Grinyer, P. H., Mayes, D., & McKiernan, P. (1990). The sharpbenders: Achieving a sustained improvement in performance. *Long Range Planning*, 23, 116–125.

Gronn, P. (2002). Distributed leadership as a unit of analysis. *Leadership Quarterly*, 13, 423–451.

Gully, S. M., Incalcaterra, K. A., Joshi, A., & Beaubien, J. M. (2002). A meta-analysis of team-efficacy. *Journal of Applied Psychology*, 87, 819–832.

Guthrie, V. A., & Kelly-Radford, L. (1998). Feedback-intensive programs. In C. D. McCauley, R. S. Moxley, and E. Van Velsor (Eds.), *Center for Creative Leadership handbook of leadership development.* San Francisco: Jossey-Bass, pp. 66–105.

Guzzo, R. A., & Shea, G. P. (1992). Group performance and intergroup relations in organizations. In M. D. Dunnette and L. M. Hough (Eds.), *Handbook of industrial and organizational psychology*, vol. 3. Palo Alto: Consulting Psychologists Press, pp. 269–313.

Guzzo, R. A., Yost, P. R., Campbell, R. J., & Shea, G. P. (1993). Potency in groups: Articulating a construct. *British Journal of Social Psychology*, 3, 87–106.

Haas, R. N. (1994). *The power to persuade: How to be effective in an unruly organization.* Boston: Houghton-Miflin.

Hackman, J. R. (1986). The psychology of self-management in organizations. In M. S. Pollack and R. O. Perloff (Eds.), *Psychology and work: Productivity, change, and employment.* Washington, DC: American Psychological Association, p. 89–136.

Hackman, J. R. (1987). The design of work teams. In J. W. Lorsch (Ed.), *Handbook of organizational behavior.* Englewood Cliffs, NJ: Prentice Hall, pp. 315–342.

Hackman, J. R. (1990). *Groups that work (and those that don't).* San Francisco: Jossey-Bass.

Hackman, J. R. (1992). Group influences on individuals in organizations. In M. D. Dunnette and L. M. Hough (Eds.), *Handbook of industrial and organizational psychology*, vol. 3. Palo Alto: Consulting Psychologists Press, pp. 199–267.

Hackman, J. R., Brousseau, K. R., & Weiss, J. A. (1976). The interaction of task design and group performance strategies in determining group effectiveness. *Organizational Behavior and Human Performance*, 16, 350–365.

Hackman, J. R., & Morris, C. G. (1975). Group tasks, group interaction process, and group performance effectiveness: A review and proposed integration. In L. Berkowitz (Ed.), *Advances in experimental social psychology.* New York: Academic Press.

Hackman, J. R., & Oldham, G. R. (1976). Motivation through the design of work: Test of a theory. *Organizational Behavior and Human Performance*, 16, 250–279.

Hackman, J. R., & Oldham, G. R. (1980). *Work redesign.* Reading, MA: Addison-Wesley.

Haleblian, J., & Finkelstein, S. (1993). Top management team size, CEO dominance, and firm performance: The moderating roles of environmental turbulence and discretion. *Academy of Management Journal*, 36, 844–863.

Hales, C. P. (1986). What do managers do: A critical review of the evidence. *Journal of Management Studies*, 23, 88–115.

Hall, D. T., & Foulkes, F. K. (1991). Senior executive development as a competitive advantage. *Advances in Applied Business Strategy*, vol. 2. Greenwich, CT: JAI Press, pp. 183-203.

Hall, D. T., Otazo, K. L., & Hollenbeck, G. P. (1999). Behind closed doors: What really happens in executive coaching. *Organizational Dynamics*, 29 (Winter), 39–53.

Hall, D. T., & Seibert, K. W. (1992). Strategic management development: Linking organizational strategy, succession planning, and managerial learning. In D. H. Montross and C. J. Shinkman (Eds.), *Career development: Theory and practice*. Springfield, IL: Charles C. Thomas, pp. 255–275.

Halpin, A. W., & Winer, B. J. (1957). A factorial study of the leader behavior descriptions. In R. M. Stogdill and A. E. Coons (Eds.), *Leader behavior: Its description and measurement*. Columbus, OH: Bureau of Business Research, Ohio State University.

Halverson, S. K., Holladay, C. L., Kazama, S. M., & Quinones, M. A. (2004). Self-sacrificial behavior in crisis situations: The competing roles of behavioral and situational factors. *Leadership Quarterly*, 15 (2), 263–275.

Hambleton, R. K., & Gumpert, R. (1982). The validity of Hersey and Blanchard's theory of leader effectiveness. *Group and Organization Studies*, 7, 225–276.

Hambrick, D. C. (1981a). Environment, strategy, and power within top management teams. *Administrative Science Quarterly*, 26, 253–276.

Hambrick, D. C. (1981b). Specialization of environmental scanning activities among upper level executives. *Journal of Management Studies*, 18 (3), 299–320.

Hambrick, D. C. (1982). Environmental scanning and organizational strategy. *Strategic Management Journal*, 3, 159–174.

Hambrick, D. C. (1987). The top management team: Key to strategic success. *California Management Review*, 30 (1), 1–20.

Hambrick, D. C., & Finkelstein, S. (1987). Managerial discretion: A bridge between polar views of organizational outcomes. In L. L. Cummings and B. M. Staw (Eds.), *Research in Organizational Behavior*, vol. 9. Greenwich, CT: JAI Press, pp. 369–406.

Hambrick, D. C., & Fukutomi, G. D. S. (1991). The seasons of a CEO's tenure. *Academy of Management Review*, 16, 719–742.

Hambrick, D. C., & Mason, P. A. (1984). Upper echelons: The organization as a reflection of its top managers. *Academy of Management Review*, 9, 193–206.

Hammer, T. H., & Turk, J. M. (1987). Organizational determinants of leader behavior and authority. *Journal of Applied Psychology*, 72, 647–682.

Hamner, W. C., & Organ, D. W. (1978). *Organizational behavior: An applied approach*. Dallas: Business Publications Inc.

Hand, H. H., Richards, M. D., & Slocum, J. W. Jr. (1973). Organizational climate and the effectiveness of a human relations program. *Academy of Management Journal*, 16, 185–195.

Hand, H. H., & Slocum, J. (1972). A longitudinal study of the effect of a human relations training program on managerial effectiveness. *Journal of Applied Psychology*, 56, 412–418.

Hannan, M., & Freeman, J. (1984). Structural inertia and organizational change. *American Sociological Review*, 49, 149–164.

Harrison, R. (1987). Harnessing personal energy: How companies can inspire employees. *Organizational Dynamics*, Autumn, 4–21.

Harvey, O. J. (1953). An experimental approach to the study of status relationships in informal groups. *American Sociological Review*, 18, 357–367.

Haveman, H. A. (1992). Between a rock and a hard place: Organizational change and performance under conditions of fundamental environmental transformation. *Administrative Science Quarterly*, 37, 48–75.

Hazucha, J. F., Hezlett, S. A., & Schneider, R. J. (1993). The impact of 360-degree feedback on management skills development. *Human Resource Management*, 32, 325–351.

Hegarty, W. H. (1974). Using subordinate ratings to elicit behavior change in supervisors. *Journal of Applied Psychology*, 59, 764–766.

Hegelsen, S. (1990). *The female advantage: Women's way of leadership*. New York: Doubleday/Currency.

Heifetz, R. (1994). *Leadership without easy answers*. Cambridge, MA: Belnap Press of Harvard University Press.

Heilman, M. E., Hornstein, H. A., Cage, J. H., & Herschlag, J. K. (1984). Reactions to prescribed leader behavior as a function of role perspective: The case of the Vroom-Yetton Model. *Journal of Applied Psychology*, 69, 50–60.

Heizer, J. H. (1972). Manager action. *Personnel Psychology*, 25, 511–521.

Heller, F., & Yukl, G. (1969). Participation, managerial decision making, and situational variables. *Organizational Behavior and Human Performance*, 4, 227–241.

Hemphill, J. K. (1950). Relations between the size of the group and the behavior of "superior" leaders. *Journal of Social Psychology*, 32, 11–22.

Hemphill, J. K. (1959). Job descriptions for executives. *Harvard Business Review*, 37 (September–October), 55–67.

Hemphill, J. K., & Coons, A. E. (1957). Development of the leader behavior description questionnaire. In R. M. Stogdill & A. E. Coons (Eds.), *Leader behavior: Its description and measurement*. Columbus: Bureau of Business Research, Ohio State University, pp. 6–38.

Heneman, R. L., Greenberger, D. B., & Anonyuo, C. (1989). Attributions and exchanges: The effects of interpersonal factors on the diagnosis of employee performance. *Academy of Management Journal*, 32, 466–476.

Herold, D. (1977). Two way influence processes in leader-follower dyads. *Academy of Management Journal*, 20, 224–237.

Hersey, P., & Blanchard, K. H. (1977). *The management of organizational behavior*, 3rd ed. Englewood Cliffs, NJ: Prentice Hall.

Hersey, P., & Blanchard, K .H. (1984). *The management of organizational behavior*, 4th ed. Englewood Cliffs, NJ: Prentice Hall.

Hewett, T. T., O'Brien, G. E., & Hornik, J. (1974). The effects of work organization, leadership, and member compatibility of small groups working on a manipulative task. *Organizational Behavior and Human Performance*, 11, 283–301.

Hickman, C. F. (1990). *Mind of a manager, soul of a leader*. New York: John Wiley.

Hickson, D. J., Hinings, C. R., Lee, C. A., Schneck, R. S., & Pennings, J. M. (1971). A strategic contingencies theory of intra-organizational power. *Administrative Science Quarterly*, 16, 216–229.

Higgans, C. A., Judge, T. A., & Ferris, G. R. (2003). Influence tactics and work outcomes: A meta-analysis. *Journal of Occupational Behavior*, 24, 89–106.

Hill, G. W. (1982). Group versus individual performance: Are N + 1 heads better than one? *Psychology Bulletin*, 91, 517–539.

Hillman, L. W., Schwandt, D. R., & Bartz, D. E. (1990). Enhancing staff member's performance through feedback and coaching. *Journal of Management Development*, 9, 20–27.

Hills, F. S., & Mahoney, T. A. (1978). University budgets and organizational decision making. *Administrative Science Quarterly*, 23, 454–465.

Hinings, C. R., & Greenwood, R. (1988). *The dynamics of strategic change*. Oxford, England: Blackwell.

Hinings, C. R., Hickson, D. J., Pennings, J. M., & Schneck, R.E. (1974). Structural conditions of intra-organizational power. *Administrative Science Quarterly*, 19, 22–44.

Hinkin, T. R., & Schriesheim, C. A. (1989). Development and application of new scales to measure the French and Raven bases of social power. *Journal of Applied Psychology*, 74, 561–567.

Hinkin, T. R., & Schriesheim, C. A. (1990). Relationships between subordinate perceptions of supervisor influence tactics and attributed bases of supervisory power. *Human Relations*, 43, 221–237.

Hinkin, T. R., & Tracey, J. B. (1999). The relevance of charisma for transformational leadership in stable organizations. *Journal of Organizational Change Management*, 12 (2), 105–119.

Hitt, M.A., & Tyler, B.B. (1991). Strategic decision models: Integrating different perspectives. *Strategic Management Journal*, 12, 327–352.

Hochwarter, W. A., Pearson, A. W., Ferris, G. R., Perrewe, P. A., & Ralston, D. A. (2000). A re-examination of Schriesheim and Hinkin's measure of upward influence. *Educational and Psychological Measurement*, 60, 755–771.

Hofstede, G. (1980). *Culture's consequences: International differences in work-related values*. London: Sage.

Hofstede, G. (1993). Cultural constraints in management theories. *Academy of Management* Executive, 7, 81–90.

Hofstede, G. (2001). *Culture's consequences: Comparing values, behaviors, institutions, and organizations across nations*. Thousand Oaks, CA: Sage.

Hogan, R. J., Curphy, G. J., & Hogan, J. (1994). What we know about personality: Leadership and effectiveness. *American Psychologist*, 49, 493–504.

Hogan, R.J., Raskin, R., & Fazzini, D. (1990). The dark side of charisma. In K.E. Clark & M.B. Clark (Eds.), *Measures of leadership*. West Orange, NJ: Leadership Library of America, pp. 343–354.

Holladay, S. J., & Coombs, W. T. (1993). Speaking of visions and visions being spoken: An exploration of the effects of content and delivery on perceptions of leader charisma. *Management Communication Quarterly*, 8, 165–189.

Holladay, S. J., & Coombs, W. T. (1994). Communicating visions: An exploration of the role of delivery in the creation of leader charisma. *Management Communication Quarterly*, 6, 405–427.

Hollander, E. P. (1958). Conformity, status, and idiosyncrasy credit. *Psychological Review*, 65, 117–127.

Hollander, E. P. (1960). Competence and conformity in the acceptance of influence. *Journal of Abnormal and Social Psychology*, 61, 361–365.

Hollander, E. P. (1961). Some effects of perceived status on responses to innovative behavior. *Journal of Abnormal and Social Psychology*, 63, 247–250.

Hollander, E. P. (1980). Leadership and social exchange processes. In K. J. Gergen, M. S. Greenberg, & R. H. Willis (Eds.), *Social exchange: Advances in theory and research*. New York: Plenum Press, pp. 343–354.

Hollander, E. P. (1995). Ethical challenges in the leader-follower relationship. *Business Ethics Quarterly*, 5, 54–65.

Hollander, E. P., & Julian, J. W. (1970). Studies in leader legitimacy, influence, and innovation. In L. Berkowitz (Ed.), *Advances in experimental social psychology*, vol. 5. New York: Academic Press, pp. 33–69.

Hollander, E. P., & Julian, J. W. (1978). A further look at leader legitimacy, influence, and innovation. In L. Berkowitz (Ed.), *Group processes: Papers from Advances in Experimental Social Psychology*. New York: Academic Press, pp. 153–165.

Homans, G. C. (1958). Social behavior as exchange. *American Journal of Sociology*, 63, 597–606.

Hooijberg, R., Hunt, J. G., & Dodge, G. E. (1997). Leadership complexity and the development of the leaderplex model. *Journal of Management*, 23, 375–408.

Horner-Long, P., & Schoenberg, R. (2002). Does e-business require different leadership characteristics? An empirical investigation. *European Management Journal*, 20 (96), 611–619.

Hosking, D. M. (1988). Organizing, leadership, and skillful process. *Journal of Management Studies*, 25, 147–166.

Hough, L. M. (1992). The "Big Five" personality variables—Construct confusion: Description versus prediction. *Human Performance*, 5, 139–155.

House, R. J. (1971). A path-goal theory of leader effectiveness. *Administrative Science Quarterly*, 16, 321–339.

House, R. J. (1977). A 1976 theory of charismatic leadership. In J. G. Hunt and L. L. Larson (Eds.), *Leadership: The cutting edge*. Carbondale: Southern Illinois University Press, pp. 189–207.

House, R. J. (1988a). Leadership research: Some forgotten, ignored, or overlooked findings. In J. G. Hunt, B. R. Baliga, H. P. Dachler, & C. A. Schriesheim (Eds.), *Emerging leadership vistas*. Lexington, MA: Lexington Books, pp. 245–260.

House, R. J. (1988b). Power and personality in organizations. *Research in Organizational Behavior*, 10, 305–357.

House, R. J. (1996). Path-goal theory of leadership: Lessons, legacy, and a reformulated theory. *Leadership Quarterly*, 7, 323–352.

House, R. J., & Aditya, R. N. (1997). The social scientific study of leadership: Quo Vadis? *Journal of Management*, 23, 409–473.

House, R. J., & Dessler, G. (1974). The path-goal theory of leadership: Some post hoc and a priori tests. In J. Hunt & L. Larson (Eds.), *Contingency approaches to leadership*. Carbondale: Southern Illinois University Press, pp. 29–55.

House, R. J., & Howell, J. M. (1992). Personality and charismatic leadership. *Leadership Quarterly*, 3 (2), 81–108.

House, R. J., Hanges, P. J., Javidan, M., Dorfman, P. W., Gupta, V., & Associates. (2004). *Leadership, culture, and organizations: The GLOBE study of 62 societies*. Thousand Oaks, CA: Sage.

House, R. J., & Mitchell, T. R. (1974). Path-goal theory of leadership. *Contemporary Business*, 3 (Fall), 81–98.

House, R. J., & Singh, J. V. (1987). Organizational behavior: Some new directions for I/O psychology. *Annual Reviews of Psychology*, 38, 669–718.

House, R. J., Spangler, W. D., & Woycke, J. (1991). Personality and charisma in the U.S. presidency: A psychological theory of leadership effectiveness. *Administrative Science Quarterly*, 36, 364–396.

House, R. J., Wright, N. S., & Aditya, R. N. (1997). Cross-cultural research on organizational leadership: A critical analysis and a proposed theory. In P.C. Earley & M. Erez (Eds.), *New perspectives on international/organizational psychology*. San Francisco: New Lexington Press, pp. 535–625.

Howard, A. (1998). The empowering leader: Unrealized opportunities. In G. R. Hickman (Ed.), *Leading organizations: Perspectives for a new era*. Thousand Oaks, CA: Sage Publications, pp. 202–213.

Howard, A., & Bray, D. W. (1988). *Managerial lives in transition: Advancing age and changing times*. New York: Guilford Press.

Howard, A., & Wellins, R. S. (1994). *High-involvement leadership: Changing roles for changing times*. Pittsburgh, PA: Developmental Dimensions International.

Howell, J. M. (1988). Two faces of charisma: Socialized and personalized leadership in organizations. In J. A. Conger & R. N. Kanungo (Eds.), *Charismatic leadership: The elusive factor in organizational effectiveness*. San Francisco: Jossey-Bass, pp. 213–236.

Howell, J. M., & Avolio, B. J. (1992). The ethics of charismatic leadership: Submission or liberation? *Academy of Management Executive*, 6 (2), 43–54.

Howell, J. M., & Avolio, B. J. (1993). Transformational leadership, transactional leadership, locus of control, and support for innovation: Key predictors of consolidated business unit performance. *Journal of Applied Psychology*, 78, 891–902.

Howell, J. M., & Frost, P. (1989). A laboratory study of charismatic leadership. *Organizational Behavior and Human Decision Processes*, 43, 243–269.

Howell, J. M., & Higgins, C. A. (1990). Leadership behaviors, influence tactics, and career experiences of champions of technological innovation. *Leadership Quarterly*, 1, 249–264.

Howell, J. P., Bowen, D. E., Dorfman, P. W., Kerr, S., & Podsakoff, P. M. (1990). Substitutes for leadership: Effective alternatives to ineffective leadership. *Organizational Dynamics*, 19, 21–38.

Howell, J. P., & Dorfman, P. W. (1981). Substitutes for leadership: Test of a construct. *Academy of Management Journal*, 24, 714–728.

Howell, J. P., & Dorfman, P. W. (1986). Leadership and substitutes for leadership among professional and nonprofessional workers. *Journal of Applied Behavioral Science*, 22, 29–46.

Howell, W. C., & Cooke, N. J. (1989). Training the human information processor: A review of cognitive models. In I. L. Goldstein (Ed.), *Training and development in organizations*. San Francisco: Jossey-Bass, pp. 121–182.

Huber, G. P. (1991). Organizational learning: The contributing processes and the literatures. *Organization Science*, 2, 88–115.

Huczynski, A. A., & Lewis, J. W. (1980). An empirical study into the learning transfer process in management training. *Journal of Management Studies*, 17, 227–240.

Humes, S. (1993). *Managing the multinational*. Englewood Cliffs, NJ: Prentice Hall.

Hundal, P. S. (1971). A study of entrepreneurial motivation: Comparison of fast and slow progressing small scale industrial entrepreneurs in Punjab, India. *Journal of Applied Psychology*, 55, 317–323.

Hunt, D. M., & Michael, C. (1983). Mentorship: A career training and development tool. *Academy of Management Review*, 8, 475–485.

Hunt, J. G. (1991). *Leadership: A new synthesis*. Newbury Park, CA: Sage.

Hunt, J. G., Baliga, B. R., & Peterson, M. F. (1988). Strategic apex leadership scripts and an organizational life cycle approach to leadership. *Journal of Management Development*, 7 (5), 61–83.

Hunt, J. G., Boal, K. B., & Dodge, G. E. (1999). The effects of visionary and crisis-responsive charisma on followers: An experimental examination of two kinds of charismatic leadership. *Leadership Quarterly*, 10, 423–448.

Hunt, J. G., & Osborn, R. N. (1982). Toward a macro-oriented model of leadership: An odyssey. In J. G. Hunt, U. Sekaran, & C. Schriesheim (Eds.), *Leadership: Beyond establishment views*. Carbondale: Southern Illinois University Press, pp. 196–221.

Hunt, J. G., & Ropo, A. (1995). Multi-level leadership: Grounded theory and mainstream theory applied to the case of General Motors. *Leadership Quarterly*, 6 (3), 379–412.

Iacocca, L. (1984). *Iacocca: An autobiography*. New York: Bantam.

Ilgen, D. R., Mitchell, T. R., & Fredrickson, J. W. (1981). Poor performers: Supervisor's and subordinate's responses. *Organizational Behavior and Human Performance*, 27, 386–410.

Ilgen, D. R., & Youtz, M. S. (1986). Factors influencing the evaluation and development of minorities. *Research in Personnel and Human Resource Management*, 4, 307–337.

Isenberg, D. J. (1984). How senior managers think. *Harvard Business Review*, (November–December), 81–90.

Jacobs, T. O. (1970). *Leadership and exchange in formal organizations*. Alexandria, VA: Human Resources Research Organization.

Jacobs, T. O., & Jaques, E. (1987). Leadership in complex systems. In J. Zeidner (Ed.), *Human productivity enhancement: Organizations, personnel, and decision making*, vol. 2. New York: Praeger, pp. 7–65.

Jacobs, T. O., & Jaques, E. (1990). Military executive leadership. In K. E. Clark & M. B. Clark (Eds.), *Measures of leadership*. West Orange, NJ: Leadership Library of America pp. 281–295.

Jacobs, T. O., & Lewis, P. (1992). Leadership requirements in stratified systems. In R. L. Phillips & J. G. Hunt (Eds.), *Strategic leadership: A multiorganizational-level perspective.* Westport, CT: Quorum Books, pp. 121–137.

Jacobsen, C., & House, R. J. (2001). Dynamics of charismatic leadership: A process theory, simulation model, and tests. *Leadership Quarterly,* 12, 75–112.

Jago, A. G., & Vroom, V. H. (1980). An evaluation of two alternatives to the Vroom/Yetton normative model. *Academy of Management Journal,* 23, 347–355.

Jain, S. C. (1984). Environmental scanning in U.S. corporations. *Long Range Planning,* 17, 117–128.

James, C. R. (2002). Designing learning organizations. *Organizational Dynamics,* 32 (1), 46–61.

James, L. R., & White, J. F. (1983). Cross-situational specificity in manager's perceptions of subordinate performance, attributions, and leader behaviors. *Personnel Psychology,* 36, 809–856.

Janda, K. F. (1960). Towards the explication of the concept of leadership in terms of the concept of power. *Human Relations,* 13, 345–363.

Janis, I. L. (1972). *Victims of groupthink.* Boston: Houghton-Mifflin.

Janis, I. L., & Mann, L. (1977). *Decision making: A psychological analysis of conflict, choice, and commitment.* New York: Free Press.

Jaques, E. (1989). *Requisite organization.* Arlington, VA: Cason Hall.

Jaussi, K. S., & Dionne, S. D. (2003). Leading for creativity: The role of unconventional leader behavior. *Leadership Quarterly,* 14, 475–498.

Javidan, M. (1992). Managers as leaders: Developing a profile of effective leadership in top management. In K. Clark, M. B. Clark, & D. P. Campbell (Eds.), *Impact of Leadership.* Greensboro, NC: Center for Creative Leadership, pp. 47–58.

Jay, A. (1976). How to run a meeting. *Harvard Business Review,* March–April, 43–57.

Jenster, P. V. (1987). Using critical success factors in planning. *Long Range Planning,* 20, 102–109.

Jick, T. D. (1979). Mixing qualitative and quantitative methods: Triangulation in action. *Administrative Science Quarterly,* 24, 602–611.

Jick, T. D. (1993). *Implementing change.* Burr Ridge, IL: Irwin.

Johnson, G. (1992). Managing strategic change—Strategy, culture, and action. *Long Range Planning,* 25, 28–36.

Johnson, M., & Moran, R. T. (1992). *Cultural guide to doing business in Europe.* Oxford: Butterworth-Heinemann.

Johnston, M. A. (2000). Delegation and organizational structure in small businesses: Influences of manager's attachment patterns. *Group and Organization Management,* 25, 4–21.

Jones, E. E., & Pitman, T. S. (1982). Toward a general theory of strategic self presentation. In J. Suls (Ed.), *Psychological perspectives on the self.* Hillsdale, NJ: Lawrence Erlbaum, pp. 231–262.

Judge, T. A., Bono, J. E., Illies, R., & Gerhardt, M. W. (2002). Personality and leadership: A qualitative and quantitative review. *Journal of Applied Psychology,* 87, 765–780.

Jung, D. I., & Avolio, B. J. (1999). Effects of leadership style and followers' cultural orientation on performance in group and individual task conditions. *Academy of Management Journal,* 42, 208–218.

Jung, D. I., Chow, C., & Wu, A. (2003). The role of transformational leadership in enhancing organizational innovation: Hypotheses and some preliminary findings. *Leadership Quarterly,* 14, 525–544.

Kabanoff, B. (1991). Equity, equality, power, and conflict. *Academy of Management Review,* 16, 416–441.

Kacmar, K. M., & Baron, R. A. (1999). Organizational politics: The state of the field, links to related processes, and an agenda for future research. In G. R. Ferris (Ed.), *Research in personnel and human resources management,* vol. 17, pp. 1–39. Stamford, CT: JAI Press.

Kahn, R. L., Wolfe, D. M., Quinn, R. P., & Snoek, J. D. (1964). *Organizational stress: Studies in role conflict and ambiguity*. New York: John Wiley.

Kahn, W. A. (1990). Toward an agenda for business ethics research. *Academy of Management Review*, 15, 311–328.

Kanter, R. M. (1982). The middle manager as innovator. *Harvard Business Review,* July–August, 95–105.

Kanter, R. M. (1983). *The change masters*. New York: Simon & Schuster.

Kanungo, R. N., & Mendonca, M. (1996). *Ethical dimensions in leadership*. Beverly Hills, CA: Sage.

Kaplan, E. M., & Cowen, E. L. (1981). Interpersonal helping behavior of industrial foremen. *Journal of Applied Psychology*, 66, 633–638.

Kaplan, R. E. (1984). Trade routes: The manager's network of relationships. *Organizational Dynamics,* Spring, 37–52.

Kaplan, R. E. (1988). The warp and woof of the general manager's job. In F. D. Schoorman & B. Schneider (Eds.), *Facilitating work effectiveness*. Lexington, MA: Lexington Books, pp. 183–211.

Kaplan, R. E. (1990). Character change in executives as reform in the pursuit of self-worth. *Journal of Applied Behavioral Science*, 26 (4), 461–481.

Kaplan, R. E. (1993). 360-degree feedback PLUS: Boosting the power of co-worker ratings for executives. *Human Resource Management*, 32 (2/3), 299–314.

Kaplan, R. E., Kofodimos, J. R., & Drath, W. H. (1987). Development at the top: A review and prospect. In W. Pasmore & R. W. Woodman (Eds.), *Research in organizational change and development*, vol. 1. Greenwich, CT: JAI Press, pp. 229–273.

Kaplan, R. E., Lombardo, M. M., & Mazique, M. S. (1985). A mirror for managers: Using simulation to develop management teams. *Journal of Applied Behavioral Science*, 21, 241–253.

Kaplan, R. E., & Palus, C. J. (1994). *Enhancing 360-degree feedback for senior executives*. Technical Report #160. Greensboro, NC: Center for Creative Leadership.

Kapoor, A., & Ansari, M. A. (1988). Influence tactics as a function of personal and organizational characteristics. *Management and Labour Studies*, 13, 229–239.

Kark, R., Shamir, B., & Chen, G. (2003). The two faces of transformational leadership: Empowerment and dependency. *Journal of Applied Psychology*, 88, 246–255.

Karmel, B. (1978). Leadership: A challenge to traditional research methods and assumptions. *Academy of Management Review*, 3, 475–482.

Katz, D., & Kahn, R. L. (1952). Some recent findings in human-relations research in industry. In E. Swanson, T. Newcomb, & E. Hartley (Eds.), *Readings in social psychology*. New York: Holt, pp. 650–665.

Katz, D., & Kahn, R. L. (1978). *The social psychology of organizations,* 2nd ed. New York: John Wiley.

Katz, D., Maccoby, N., Gurin, G., & Floor, L. (1951). *Productivity, supervision, and morale among railroad workers*. Ann Arbor: Survey Research Center, University of Michigan.

Katz, D., Maccoby, N., & Morse, N. (1950). *Productivity, supervision, and morale in an office situation*. Ann Arbor, MI: Institute for Social Research.

Katz, D., & Tushman, M. (1979). Communication patterns, project performance, and task characteristics: An empirical evaluation and integration in an R & D laboratory. *Organizational Behavior and Human Performance*, 23, 139–162.

Katz, R. (1982). The effects of group longevity on project communication and performance. *Administrative Science Quarterly*, 27, 81–104.

Katz, R. L. (1955). Skills of an effective administrator. *Harvard Business Review* January–February, 33–42.

Katzell, R. A., Barrett, R. S., Vann, D. H., & Hogan, J. M. (1968). Organizational correlates of executive roles. *Journal of Applied Psychology*, 52, 22–28.

Katzenbach, J. R., & Smith, D. K. (1993). *The wisdom of teams*. Boston: Harvard Business School Press.

Kay, B. R. (1959). Factors in effective foreman behavior. *Personnel*, 36, 25–31.

Keck, S., & Tushman, M. (1993). Environmental and organizational context and executive team structure. *Academy of Management Journal*, 36 (6), 1314–1344.

Kefalas, A. G., & Schoderbek, P. P. (1973). Scanning the business environment: Some empirical results. *Decision Sciences*, 4, 63–74.

Kelleher, D., Finestone, P., & Lowy, A. (1986). Managerial learning: First notes from an unstudied frontier. *Group and Organization Studies*, 11, 169–202.

Keller, R. T. (2001). Cross-functional project groups in research and new product development: Diversity, communications, job stress, and outcomes. *Academy of Management Journal*, 44 (3), 547–555.

Keller, R. T., & Szilagyi, A. D. (1976). Employee reactions to leader reward behavior. *Academy of Management Journal*, 19, 619–627.

Keller, T. (1999). Images of the familiar: Individual differences and implicit leadership theories. *Leadership Quarterly*, 10, 589–607.

Kelley, R. E. (1992). *The power of followership: How to create leaders people want to follow and followers who lead themselves*. New York: Doubleday/Currency.

Keller, R. T. (1992). Transformational leadership and the performance of research and development product groups. *Journal of Management*, 18 (3), 489–501.

Kelman, H. C. (1958). Compliance, identification, and internalization: Three processes of attitude change. *Journal of Conflict Resolution*, 2, 51–56.

Kelman, H. C. (1974). Further thoughts on the process of compliance, identification, and internalization. In J. T. Tedeschi (Ed.), *Perspectives on social power*. Chicago: Aldine, pp. 125–170.

Kennedy, J. K., Jr. (1982). Middle LPC leaders and the contingency model of leadership effectiveness. *Organizational Behavior and Human Performance*, 30, 1–14.

Kepner, C., & Tregoe, B. (1965). *The rational manager*. New York: McGraw-Hill.

Kepner, C., & Tregoe, B. (1981). *The new rational manager*. Princeton, NJ: Kepner-Tregoe.

Kerr, J. L. (2004). The limits of organizational democracy. *Academy of Management Executive*, 18 (3), 81–97.

Kerr, S. (1975). On the folly of rewarding A while hoping for B. *Academy of Management Journal*, 18, 769–783.

Kerr, S., Hill, K. D., & Broedling, L. (1986). The first-line supervisor: Phasing out or here to stay? *Academy of Management Review*, 11, 103–117.

Kerr, S., & Jermier, J. M. (1978). Substitutes for leadership: Their meaning and measurement. *Organizational Behavior and Human Performance*, 22, 375–403.

Kessler, R. C., Price, R. H., & Wortman, C. B. (1985). Social factors in psychopathology: Stress, social support, and coping processes. *Annual Review of Psychology*, 36, 531–572.

Kets de Vries, M. F. R. (1988). Prisoners of leadership. *Human Relations*, 41 (3), 261–280.

Kets de Vries, M.F.R., & Miller, D. (1984). *The neurotic organization: Diagnosing and changing counter-productive styles of management*. San Francisco: Jossey-Bass.

Kets de Vries, M. F. R., & Miller, D. (1985). Narcissism and leadership: An object relations perspective. *Human Relations*, 38, 583–601.

Keys, B. & Wolfe, J. (1990). The role of management games and simulation in education and research. *Journal of Management*, 16, 307–336.

Kilburg, R. R. (1996). Toward a conceptual understanding and definition of executive coaching. *Consulting Psychology Journal: Practice and Research*, 48, 134–144.

Kim, H., & Yukl, G. (1995). Relationships of self-reported and subordinate-reported leadership behaviors to managerial effectiveness and advancement. *Leadership Quarterly*, 6, 361–377.

Kim, K. I., & Organ, D. W. (1982). Determinants of leader-subordinate exchange relationships. *Group and Organization Studies*, 7, 77–89.

Kipnis, D. (1972). Does power corrupt? *Journal of Personality and Social Psychology*, 24, 33–41.

Kipnis, D. (1976). *The powerholders*. Chicago: University of Chicago Press.

Kipnis, D., & Cosentino, J. (1969). Use of leadership powers in industry. *Journal of Applied Psychology*, 53, 460–466.

Kipnis, D., & Lane, W. P. (1962). Self-confidence and leadership. *Journal of Applied Psychology*, 46, 291–295.

Kipnis, D., Schmidt, S. M., Price, K., & Stitt, C. (1981). Why do I like thee: Is it your performance or my orders? *Journal of Applied Psychology*, 66, 324–328.

Kipnis, D., Schmidt, S. M., & Wilkinson, I. (1980). Intra-organizational influence tactics: Explorations in getting one's way. *Journal of Applied Psychology*, 65, 440–452.

Kirby, P. C., King, M. I., & Paradise, L. V. (1992). Extraordinary leaders in education: Understanding transformational leadership. *Journal of Educational Research*, 85, 303–311.

Kirkman, B. L., & Rosen, B. (1999). Beyond self-management: Antecedents and consequences of team empowerment. *Academy of Management Journal*, 42, 58–74.

Kirkpatrick, S. A., & Locke, E. A. (1996). Direct and indirect effects of three core charismatic leadership components on performance and attitudes. *Journal of Applied Psychology*, 81, 36–51.

Klein, K. J., Dansereau, F., & Hall, R. J. (1994). Levels issues in theory development, data collection, and analysis. *Academy of Management Review*, 19 (2), 195–229.

Klein, K. J., & House, R. J. (1995). On fire: Charismatic leadership and levels of analysis. *Leadership Quarterly*, 6, 183–198.

Klimoski, R., & Jones, R. G. (1995). Staffing for effective group decision making: Key issues in matching people and teams. In R. A. Guzzo & E. Salas (Eds.), *Team effectiveness and decision making in organizations*. San Francisco: Jossey-Bass.

Kluger, A. N., & DeNisi, A. (1996). The effects of feedback interventions on performance: A historical review, a meta-analysis, and a preliminary feedback intervention theory. *Psychological Bulletin*, 119, 254–284.

Kobe, L. M., Reitter-Palmon, R., & Rickers, J. D. (2001). Self-reported leadership experiences in relation to inventoried social and emotional intelligence. *Current Psychology*, 20 (2), 154–163.

Koberg, C. S., Boss, R. W., Senjem, J. C., & Goodman, E. A. (1999). Antecedents and outcomes of empowerment. *Group and Organization Management*, 24, 71–91.

Kohlberg, L. (1984). *The psychology of moral development*. New York: Harper & Row.

Komaki, J. (1986). Toward effective supervision: An operant analysis and comparison of managers at work. *Journal of Applied Psychology*, 71, 270–278.

Komaki, J., Desselles, M. L., & Bowman, E. D. (1989). Definitely not a breeze: Extending an operant model of effective supervision to teams. *Journal of Applied Psychology*, 74, 522–529.

Komaki, J. L., & Minnich, M. R. (2002). Crosscurrents at sea: The ebb and flow of leaders in response to the shifting demands of racing sailboats. *Group and Organization Management*, 27 (1), 113–141.

Konst, D., Vonk, R., & Van der Vlist, R. (1999). Inferences about causes and consequences of behavior of leaders and subordinates. *Journal of Organizational Behavior*, 20, 261–271.

Konczak, L. J., Stelly, D. J., & Trusty, M. L. (2000). Defining and measuring empowering leader behavior: Development of an upward feedback instrument. *Educational and Psychological Measurement*, 60, 301–315.

Korda, M. (1975). *Power! How to get it, how to use it*. New York: Ballantine Books.

Korman, A. K., & Tanofsky, R. (1975). Statistical problems of contingency models in organizational behavior. *Academy of Management Journal*, 18, 393–397.

Korsgaard, M. A., Schweiger, D. M., & Sapienze, H. J. (1995). Building commitment, attachment, and trust in strategic decision making: The role of procedural justice. *Academy of Management Journal*, 38, 60–84.

Kotter, J. P. (1982). *The general managers*. New York: Free Press.

Kotter, J. P. (1985). *Power and influence: Beyond formal authority*. New York: Free Press.

Kotter, J. P. (1988). *The leadership factor*. New York: Free Press.

Kotter, J. P. (1990). *A force for change: How leadership differs from management*. New York: Free Press.

Kotter, J. P. (1996). *Leading change*. Boston: Harvard Business School Press.

Kotter, J. P., & Heskett, J. L. (1992). *Corporate culture and performance*. New York: Free Press.

Kotter, J. P., & Lawrence, P. (1974). *Mayors in action: Five studies in urban governance*. New York: John Wiley.

Kouzes, J. M., & Posner, B. Z. (1987). *The leadership challenge: How to get extraordinary things done in organizations*. San Francisco: Jossey-Bass.

Kouzes, J. M., & Posner, B. Z. (1993). *Credibility: How leaders gain and lose it, why people demand it*. San Francisco: Jossey-Bass.

Kouzes, J. M., & Posner, B. Z. (1995). *The leadership challenge: How to keep getting extraordinary things done in organizations*, 2nd ed. San Francisco: Jossey-Bass.

Kovach, B. E. (1989). Successful derailment: What fast-trackers can learn while they're off the track. *Organizational Dynamics*, 18, 33–47.

Kozlowski, S. W. J., & Hults, B. M. (1987). An exploration of climates for technical updating and performance. *Personnel Psychology*, 40, 539–564.

Kram, K. E. (1985). *Mentoring at work: Developmental relationships in organizational life*. Glenview, IL: Scott Foresman.

Kram, K. E., & Hall, D. T. (1989). Mentoring as an antidote to stress during corporate trauma. *Human Resource Management*, 28, 493–510.

Kram, K. E., & Isabella, L. A. (1985). Mentoring alternatives: The role of peer relationships in career development. *Academy of Management Journal*, 28, 110–132.

Kramer, M. W. (1995). A longitudinal study of superior-subordinate communication during job transfers. *Human Communications Research*, 22, 39–64.

Krause, D. E. (2004). Influence-based leadership as a determinant of the inclination to innovate and of innovation-related behaviors: An empirical investigation. *Leadership Quarterly*, 15, 79–102.

Kraut, A. I., Pedigo, P. R., McKenna, D. D., & Dunnette, M. D. (1989). The role of the manager: What's really important in different management jobs. *Academy of Management Executive*, 3 (4), 286–293.

Kreutzer, W. B. (1993). A buyer's guide to off-the-shelf microworlds. In P. M. Senge, C. Roberts, R. B. Ross, B. J. Smith, & A. Kleiner (Eds.), *The fifth discipline fieldbook: Strategies and tools for building a learning organization*. New York: Currency-Doubleday, pp. 536–537.

Kuhn, A. (1963). *The study of society: A unified approach*. Homewood, IL: Irwin.

Kuhnert, K. W., & Lewis, P. (1987). Transactional and transformational leadership: A constructive/developmental analysis. *Academy of Management Review*, 12, 648–657.

Kurke, L., & Aldrich, H. (1983). Mintzberg was right: A replication and extension of the nature of managerial work. *Management Science*, 29, 975–984.

Lant, T. K., Milliken, F. J., & Batra, B. (1992). The role of managerial learning and interpretation in strategic persistence and reorientation: An empirical investigation. *Strategic Management Journal*, 13, 585–608.

Larson, J. R., & Callahan, C. (1990). Performance monitoring: How it affects productivity. *Journal of Applied Psychology*, 75, 530–538.

Larson, L. L., Hunt, J. G., & Osborn, R. N. (1976). The great hi-hi leader behavior myth: A lesson from Occam's razor. *Academy of Management Journal*, 19, 628–641.

Larwood, L., Falbe, C. M., Kriger, M. P., & Miesing, P. (1995). Structure and meaning of organizational vision. *Academy of Management Journal*, 38, 740–769.

Latham, G. P. (1988). Human resource training and development. *Annual Review of Psychology*, 39, 545–582.

Latham, G. P. (1989). Behavior approaches to the training and learning process. In I. L. Goldstein (Ed.), *Training and development in organizations*. San Francisco, CA: Jossey-Bass, pp. 256–295.

Latham, G. P., Erez, M., & Locke, E. A. (1988). Resolving scientific disputes by the joint design of crucial experiments: Application to the Erez-Latham dispute regarding participation in goal setting. *Journal of Applied Psychology*, 73, 753–777.

Latham, G. P., & Saari, L. (1979). The application of social learning theory to training supervisors through behavioral modeling. *Journal of Applied Psychology*, 64, 239–246.

Latham, G. P., & Wexley, K. N. (1977). Behavioral observation scales for performance appraisal purposes. *Personnel Psychology*, 30, 255–268.

Lauterbach, B., Vu, J., & Weisberg, J. (1999). Internal versus external successions and their effect on firm performance. *Human Relations*, 12, 1485–1504.

Lawler, E. E. (1986). *High involvement management*. San Francisco, CA: Jossey-Bass.

Lawler, E. E. (1988). Substitutes for hierarchy. *Organizational Dynamics*, 17 (Summer), 5–15.

Lawler, E. E., Mohrman, S. A., & Ledford, G. E., Jr. (1992). *Employee involvement and total quality management*. San Francisco: Jossey-Bass.

Lawrence, P. R., & Lorsch, J. W. (1967). New management job: The integrator. *Harvard Business Review*, 45 (November–December), 142–151.

Lawrence, P., & Lorsch, J. (1969). *Organization and environment: Managing differentiation and integration*. Homewood, IL: Richard D. Irwin.

Lazarus, R. S. (1991). *Emotion and adaptation*. New York: Oxford University Press.

Leadbeater, C. (2000). *The weightless society*. London: Texere.

Leana, C. R. (1986). Predictors and consequences of delegation. *Academy of Management Journal*, 29, 754–774.

Leana, C. R. (1987). Power relinquishment versus power sharing: Theoretical clarification and empirical comparison of delegation and participation. *Journal of Applied Psychology*, 72, 228–233.

Leana, C. R., Locke, E. A., & Schweiger, D. M. (1990). Fact and fiction in analyzing research on participative decision making: A critique of Cotton, Vollrath, Froggatt, Lengnick-Hall, and Jennings. *Academy of Management Review*, 15, 137–146.

Leary, M. R., & Kowalski, R. M. (1990). Impression management: A literature review and two-component model. *Psychological Bulletin*, 107, 34–47.

Lester, S. W., Meglino, B. M., & Korsgaard, M. A. (2002). The antecedents and consequences of group potency: A longitudinal investigation of newly formed work groups. *Academy of Management Journal*, 45 (2), 352–368.

Lewis, M. W., Welsh, M. A., Dehler, G. E., & Green, S. G. (2002). Product development tensions: Exploring contrasting styles of product management. *Academy of Management Journal*, 45 (3), 546–564.

Levitt, B., & March, J. G. (1988). Organizational learning. *Annual Review of Sociology*, 14, 319–340.

Lee, J. A. (1977). Leader power for managing change. *Academy of Management Review*, 2, 73–80.

Lefkowitz, J. (1994). Sex-related differences in job attitudes and dispositional variables: Now you see them... *Academy of Management Journal*, 37, 323–349.

Lepsinger, R., & Lucia, A. D. (1997). *The art and science of 360° feedback*. San Francisco: Pfeiffer.

Levinson, H., & Rosenthal, S. (1984). *CEO: Corporate leadership in action*. New York: Basic Books.

Levitt, B., & March, J. G. (1988). Organizational learning. *Annual Review of Sociology*, 14, 319–340.

Lewin, K. (1951). *Field theory in social science*. New York: Harper & Row.

Lewin, K., Lippitt, R., & White, R. K. (1939). Patterns of aggressive behavior in experimentally created social climates. *Journal of Social Psychology*, 10, 271–301.

Liddell, W. W., & Slocum, J. W., Jr. (1976). The effects of individual role compatibility upon group performance: An extension of Shutz's FIRO theory. *Academy of Management Journal*, 19, 413–426.

Liden, R. C., & Maslyn, J. M. (1998). Multidimensionality of leader-member exchange: An empirical assessment through scale development. *Journal of Management*, 24, 43–72.

Liden, R. C., & Mitchell, T. R. (1988). Ingratiatory behaviors in organizational settings. *Academy of Management Review*, 13, 572–587.

Liden, R. C., Sparrowe, R. T., & Wayne, S. J. (1997). Leader-member exchange theory: The past and potential for the future. *Research in Personnel and Human Resource Management*, 15, 47–119.

Liden, R. C., Wayne, S. J., & Stilwell, D. (1993). A longitudinal study on the early development of leader-member exchanges. *Journal of Applied Psychology*, 78, 662–674.

Lieberson, S., & O'Connor, J. F. (1972). Leadership and organizational performance: A study of large corporations. *American Sociological Review*, 37, 117–130.

Likert, R. (1961). *New patterns of management*. New York: McGraw-Hill.

Likert, R. (1967). *The human organization: Its management and value*. New York: McGraw-Hill.

Lind, E. A., & Tyler, T. R. (1988). *The social psychology of procedural justice*. New York: Plenum.

Lindholm, C. (1988). Lovers and leaders: Comparative models of romance and charisma. *Social Science Information*, 27 (1), 3–45.

Lindsey, E., Homes, V., & McCall, M. W. Jr. (1987). *Key events in executive lives*. Technical Report #32. Greensboro, NC: Center for Creative Leadership.

Litwin, G. H., & Stringer, P. A. (1966). *Motivation and organizational climate*. Boston: Division of Research, Harvard Business School.

Locke, E. A., & Latham, G. P. (1990). *A theory of goal setting and task performance*. Englewood Cliffs, NJ: Prentice Hall.

Locke, E. E., & Becker, T. E. (1998). Rebuttal to a subjectivist critique of an objectivist approach to integrity in organizations. *Academy of Management Review*, 23, 170–175.

Lombardo, M. M., & Eichinger, R. W. (1989). *Eighty-eight assignments for development in place: Enhancing the developmental challenge of existing jobs*. Technical Report #136. Greensboro, NC: Center for Creative Leadership.

Lombardo, M. M., & McCall, M. W., Jr. (1978). Leadership. In M. W. McCall Jr. and M. M. Lombardo (Eds.), *Leadership: Where else can we go?* Durham, NC: Duke University Press, pp. 1–12.

Lombardo, M. M., & McCauley, C. D. (1988). *The dynamics of management derailment*. Technical Report No. 34. Greensboro, NC: Center for Creative Leadership.

London, M. (1989). *Managing the training enterprise*. San Francisco, CA: Jossey-Bass.

London, M. (2002). *Leadership development: Paths to self-insight and professional growth.* Mahwah, NJ: Lawrence Erlbaum.

London, M., & Mone, E. M. (1987). *Career management and survival in the workplace.* San Francisco, CA: Jossey-Bass.

London, M., & Smither, J. W. (1995). Can multi-source feedback change perceptions of goal accomplishment, self-evaluations, and performance-related outcomes? Theory-based applications and directions for research. *Personnel Psychology, 48,* 803–839.

London, M., Wohler, A. J., & Gallagher, P. (1990). A feedback approach to management development. *Journal of Management Development, 9* (6), 17–31.

Lord, R. G. (1977). Functional leadership behavior: Measurement and relation to social power and leadership perceptions. *Administrative Science Quarterly, 22,* 114–133.

Lord, R. G., Binning, J. F., Rush, M. C., & Thomas, J. C. (1978). The effect of performance cues and leader behavior on questionnaire ratings of leader behavior. *Organizational Behavior and Human Performance, 21,* 27–39.

Lord, R. G., Brown, D. J., Harvey, J. L., & Hall, R. J. (2001). Contextual constraints on prototype generation and their multilevel consequences for leadership perceptions. *Leadership Quarterly, 12,* 311–338.

Lord, R. G., DeVader, C. L., & Alliger, G. M. (1986). A meta-analysis of the relation between personality traits and leadership: An application of validity generalization procedures. *Journal of Applied Psychology, 71,* 402–410.

Lord, R. G., Foti, R. J., & DeVader, C. L. (1984). A test of leadership categorization theory: Internal structure, information processing, and leadership perceptions. *Organizational Behavior and Human Performance, 34,* 343–378.

Lord, R. G., & Maher, K. J. (1991). *Leadership and information processing: Linking perceptions and performance.* Boston: Unwin-Hyman.

Lourenco, S. V., & Glidewell, J. C. (1974). A dialectical analysis of organizational conflict. *Administrative Science Quarterly, 20,* 489–508.

Lowe, K. B. & Gardner, W. L. (2001). Ten years of the Leadership Quarterly: Contributions and challenges for the future. *Leadership Quarterly, 11* (4), 459–514.

Lowe, K. B., Kroeck, K. G., & Sivasubramaniam, N. (1996). Effectiveness of correlates of transformational and transactional leadership: A meta-analytic review of the MLQ literature. *Leadership Quarterly, 7,* 385–425.

Lowin, A., & Craig, J. R. (1968). The influence of level of performance on managerial style: An experimental object lesson in the ambiguity of correlational data. *Organizational Behavior and Human Performance, 3,* 440–458.

Lowin, A., Hrapchak, W. J., & Kavanagh, M. J. (1969). Consideration and initiating structure: An experimental investigation of leadership traits. *Administrative Science Quarterly, 14,* 238–253.

Lucas, K. W., & Markessini, J. (1993). *Senior leadership in a changing world order: Requisite skills for U. S. Army one- and two-star generals.* Alexandria, VA: U. S. Army Research Institute for the Behavioral and Social Sciences, Technical Report #976.

Luthans, F., & Kreitner, R. (1985). *Organizational behavior modification and beyond.* Glenview, IL: Scott Foresman.

Luthans, F., & Lockwood, D. L. (1984). Toward an observation system for measuring leader behavior in natural settings. In J. G. Hunt, D. Hosking, C. A. Schriesheim, and R. Stewart (Eds.), *Leaders and managers: International perspectives on managerial behavior and leadership.* New York: Pergamon Press.

Luthans, F., Rosenkrantz, S. A., & Hennessey, H. W. (1985). What do successful managers really do? An observational study of managerial activities. *Journal of Applied Behavioral Science, 21,* 255–270.

Mahoney, T. A., Jerdee, T. H., & Carroll, S. J., Jr. (1963). *Development of managerial performance: A research approach.* Cincinnati: South-Western.

Mahoney, T. A., Jerdee, T. H., & Carroll, S. J., Jr. (1965). The jobs of management. *Industrial Relations*, 4, 97–110.

Maier, N. R. F. (1963). *Problem-solving discussions and conferences: Leadership methods and skills.* New York: McGraw-Hill.

Main, J. (1992). How to steal the best ideas around. *Fortune*, October 19, 102–106.

Major, D. A., Kozlowski, S. W., Chao, G. T., & Gardner, P. D. (1995). A longitudinal investigation of newcomer expectations, early socialization outcomes, and the moderating effects of role development. *Journal of Applied Psychology*, 80, 418–431.

Mann, F. C. (1965). Toward an understanding of the leadership role in formal organization. In R. Dubin, G. C. Homans, F. C. Mann, and D. C. Miller (Eds.), *Leadership and productivity.* San Francisco: Chandler.

Mann, F. C., & Dent, J. (1954). The supervisor: Member of two organizational families. *Harvard Business Review*, 32 (6), 103–112.

Mann, F. C., & Hoffman, L. R. (1960). *Automation and the worker: A study of social change in power plants.* New York: Holt, Rinehart & Winston.

Manz, C. C. (1992). *Mastering self-leadership: Empowering yourself for personal excellence.* Englewood Cliffs, NJ: Prentice Hall.

Manz, C. C., & Sims, H. P. Jr. (1980). Self-management as a substitute for leadership: A social learning perspective. *Academy of Management Review*, 5, 361–367.

Manz, C. C., & Sims, H. P., Jr. (1981). Vicarious learning: The influence of modeling on organizational behavior. *Academy of Management Review*, 6, 105–113.

Manz, C. C., & Sims, H. P., Jr. (1987). Leading workers to lead themselves: The external leadership of self-managing work teams. *Administrative Science Quarterly*, 32, 106–128.

Manz, C., & Sims, H. P. (1989). *Superleadership: Leading others to lead themselves.* Englewood Cliffs, NJ: Prentice Hall.

Manz, C. C., & Sims, H. P. Jr. (1991). Superleadership: Beyond the myth of heroic leadership. *Organizational Dynamics*, 19, 18–35.

Manz, C. C., & Sims, H. P., Jr. (1993). *Business without bosses.* New York: Wiley.

March, J. G., & Simon, H. A. (1958). *Organizations.* New York: John Wiley.

Margerison, C. J. (1988). Action learning and excellence in management development. *Journal of Management Development*, 7, 43–54.

Margerison, C., & Glube, R. (1979). Leadership decision making: An empirical test of the Vroom and Yetton Model. *Journal of Management Studies*, 16, 45–55.

Marion, R., & Uhl-Bien, M. (2001). Leadership in complex organizations. *Leadership Quarterly*, 12, 389–418.

Marks, M. A., Zaccaro, S. J., & Mathieu, J. E. (2000). Performance implications of leader briefings and team-interaction training for team adaptation to novel environments. *Journal of Applied Psychology*, 85, 971–986.

Marsh, H. W., Richards, G. E., & Barnes, J. (1987). A long-term follow-up of the effects of participation in an Outward Bound program. *Personality and Social Psychology Bulletin*, 12, 475–492.

Marshall-Mies, J. C., Fleishman, E. A., Martin, J. A., Zaccaro, S. J., Baughman, W. A., & McGee, M. L. (2000). Development and evaluation of cognitive and metacognitive measures for predicting leadership potential. *Leadership Quarterly*, 11, 135–153.

Marsick, V. (1990). Experience-based learning: Executive learning outside the classroom. *Journal of Management Development*, 9, 50–60.

Marson, P. P., & Bruff, C. D. (1992). The impact of classroom leadership training on managerial/supervisory job performance. In K. E. Clark, M. B. Clark, and D. P. Campbell (Eds.), *Impact of leadership*. Greensboro, NC: Center for Creative Leadership.

Martinko, M. J., & Gardner, W. L. (1985). Beyond structured observation: Methodological issues and new directions. *Academy of Management Review*, 10, 676–695.

Martinko, M., & Gardner, W. L. (1987). The leader/member attribution process. *Academy of Management Review*, 12, 235–249.

Maslow, A. (1954). *Motivation and personality*. New York: Harper & Row.

Mathews, S. (2003). About Home Depot. *Bloomberg News*.

Maurer, R. (1996). *Beyond the wall of resistance: Unconventional strategies that build support for change*. Austin, TX: Bard Books.

Mayer, J. D., & Salovey, P. (1995). Emotional intelligence and the construction and regulation of feelings. *Applied and Preventive Psychology*, 4, 197–208.

Mayer, J. D., & Salovey, P. (1997). What is emotional intelligence: Implications for educators. In P. Salovey and D. Sluyter (Eds.), *Emotional development, emotional literacy, and emotional intelligence*. New York: Basic Books, pp. 3–31.

Mayer, S. J., & Russell, J. S. (1987). Behavior modeling training in organizations: Concerns and conclusions. *Journal of Management*, 13, 21–40.

McCall, M. W., Jr. (1977). Leaders and leadership: Of substance and shadow. In J. Hackman, E. E. Lawler Jr., L. W. Porter (Eds.), *Perspectives on behavior in organizations*. New York: McGraw-Hill.

McCall, M. W., Jr. (1992). Executive development as a business strategy. *The Journal of Business Strategy*, 3 (January–February), 25–31.

McCall, M. W., Jr. (1994). Identifying leadership potential in future international executives: Developing a concept. *Consulting Psychology Journal Practice and Research*, 46 (1), 49–63.

McCall, M. W. Jr. (1998). *High flyers: Developing the next generation of leaders*. Boston, MA: Harvard Business School Press.

McCall, M. W., Jr., & Kaplan, R. E. (1985). *Whatever it takes: Decision makers at work*. Englewood Cliffs, NJ: Prentice Hall.

McCall, M. W., Jr., & Lombardo, M. M. (1983a). *Off the track: Why and how successful executives get derailed*. Technical Report No. 21. Greensboro, NC: Center for Creative Leadership.

McCall, M. W. Jr., & Lombardo, M. M. (1983b). What makes a top executive? *Psychology Today*, February, 26–31.

McCall, M. W. Jr., Lombardo, M. M., & Morrison, A. (1988). *The lessons of experience*. Lexington, MA: Lexington Books.

McCall, M. W. Jr., Morrison, A. M., & Hannan, R. L. (1978). *Studies of managerial work: Results and methods*. Technical Report No. 9. Greensboro, NC: Center for Creative Leadership.

McCall, M. W. Jr., & Segrist, C. A. (1980). *In pursuit of the manager's job: Building on Mintzberg*. Technical Report No. 14. Greensboro, NC: Center for Creative Leadership.

McCauley, C. D. (1986). *Developmental experiences in managerial work*. Technical Report No. 26. Greensboro, NC: Center for Creative Leadership.

McCauley, C. D. (2001). Leader training and development. In S. J. Zaccaro and R. J. Klimoski, (Eds.), *The nature of organizational leadership*. San Francisco: Jossey-Bass, pp. 347–383.

McCauley, C. D., & Douglas, C. A. (1998). Developmental relationships. In C. D. McCauley, R. S. Moxley, and E. Van Velsor (Eds.), *The Center for Creative Leadership handbook of leadership development*. San Francisco: Jossey-Bass.

McCauley, C. D., Eastman, L. J., & Ohlott, P. J. (1995). Linking management selection and development through stretch assignments. *Human Resource Management*, 34 (1), 93–115.

McCauley, C. D., & Hughes-James, M. W. (1994). *An evaluation of the outcomes of a leadership development program.* Greensboro, NC: Center for Creative Leadership.

McCauley, C. D., & Lombardo, M. M. (1990). Benchmarks: An instrument for diagnosing managerial strengths and weaknesses. In K. E. Clark and M. B. Clark (Eds.), *Measures of leadership.* West Orange, NJ: Leadership Library of America. pp. 535–545.

McCauley, C. D., Lombardo, M. M., & Usher, C. J. (1989). Diagnosing management development needs: An instrument based on how managers develop. *Journal of Management*, 15, 389–403.

McCauley, C. D., Ruderman, M. N., Ohlott, P. J., & Morrow, J. E. (1994). Assessing the developmental components of managerial jobs. *Journal of Applied Psychology*, 79, 544–560.

McClane, W. E. (1991). Implications of member role differentiation: Analysis of a key concept in the LMX model of leadership. *Group & Organization Studies*, 16, 102–113.

McClelland, D. C. (1965). N-achievement and entrepreneurship: A longitudinal study. *Journal of Personality and Social Psychology*, 1, 389–392.

McClelland, D. C. (1975). *Power: The inner experience.* New York: Irvington.

McClelland, D. C. (1985). *Human motivation.* Glenview, IL: Scott Foresman.

McClelland, D. C., & Boyatzis, R. E. (1982). Leadership motive pattern and long-term success in management. *Journal of Applied Psychology*, 67, 737–743.

McClelland, D. C., & Burnham, D. H. (1976). Power is the great motivator. *Harvard Business Review*, March–April, 100–110.

McClelland, D. C., & Winter, D. G. (1969). *Motivating economic achievement.* New York: Free Press.

McColl-Kennedy, J. R., & Anderson, R. D. (2002). Impact of leadership style and emotions on subordinate performance. *Leadership Quarterly*, 13, 545–559.

McFillen, J. M., & New, J. R. (1979). Situational determinants of supervisor attributions and behavior. *Academy of Management Journal*, 22, 793–809.

McGill, M. E., Slocum, J. W. Jr., & Lei, D. (1993). Management practices in learning organizations. *Organizational Dynamics*, 22 (1), 5–17.

McGrath, J. E. (1984). *Groups: Interaction and performance.* Englewood Cliffs, NJ: Prentice Hall.

McGregor, D. (1960). *The human side of enterprise.* New York: McGraw-Hill.

McIntosh, N. J. (1988). *Substitutes for leadership: Review, critique, and suggestions.* Paper presented at the Academy of Management Meeting, August.

McLennan, K. (1967). The manager and his job skills. *Academy of Management Journal*, 3, 235–245.

McMahon, J. T. (1972). The contingency theory: Logic and method revisited. *Personnel Psychology*, 25, 697–711.

McNatt, D. B. (2000). Ancient pygmalion joins contemporary management: A meta-analysis of the result. *Journal of Applied Psychology*, 85, 314–322.

Mechanic, D. (1962). Sources of power of lower participants in complex organizations. *Administrative Science Quarterly*, 7, 349–364.

Meindl, J. R. (1990). On leadership: An alternative to the conventional wisdom. In B. M. Staw and L. L. Cummings (Eds.), *Research in organizational behavior*, vol. 12. Greenwich, CT: JAI Press, pp. 159–203.

Meindl, J. R., Ehrlich, S. B., & Dukerich, J. M. (1985). The romance of leadership. *Administrative Science Quarterly*, 30, 78–102.

Meister, J. C. (1994). *Corporate Quality Universities.* New York: Richard D. Irwin.

Meredith, J. R., & Mantel, S. J., Jr. (1985). *Project management: A managerial approach.* New York: John Wiley.

Meyer, A. (1982). How ideologies supplant formal structures and shape responses to environments. *Journal of Management Studies*, 19 (1), 45–61.

Michael, J., & Yukl, G. (1993). Managerial level and subunit function as determinants of networking behavior in organizations. *Group and Organizational Management*, 18. 328–351.

Miller, C. C., & Cardinal, L. B. (1994). Strategic planning and firm performance: A synthesis of more than two decades of research. *Academy of Management Journal*, 37, 1649–1665.

Miller, D. (1990). *The Icarus paradox*. New York: Harper-Collins.

Miller, D. (1993). Some organizational consequences of CEO succession. *Academy of Management Journal*, 36, 644–659.

Miller, D., & Chen, M-J. (1994). Sources and consequences of competitive inertia. *Administrative Science Quarterly*, 39, 1–23.

Miller, D., & Friesen, P. H. (1984). *Organizations: A quantum view*. Englewood Cliffs, NJ: Prentice Hall.

Miller, D., Kets de Vries, M. F. R. & Toulouse, J. (1982). Locus of control and its relationship to strategy, environment, and structure. *Academy of Management Journal*, 25, 237–253.

Miller, D., Lack, E. R., & Asroff, S. (1985). Preferences for control and the coronary-prone behavior pattern: "I'd rather do it myself." *Journal of Personality and Social Psychology*, 49, 492–499.

Miller, D., & Toulouse, J. (1986). Chief executive personality and corporate strategy and structure in small firms. *Management Science*, 32, 1389–1409.

Miller, K. I., & Monge, P. R. (1986). Participation, satisfaction, and productivity: A meta-analytic review. *Academy of Management Journal*, 29, 727–753.

Milliken, F. J., & Martins, L. L. (1996). Searching for common threads: Understanding the multiple effects of diversity in organizational groups. *Academy of Management Review*, 21, 402–433.

Milliken, F. J., & Vollrath, D. A. (1991). Strategic decision-making tasks and group effectiveness: Insights from theory and research on small group performance. *Human Relations*, 44, 1229–1253.

Miner, J. B. (1965). *Studies in management education*. Atlanta: Organizational Measurement Systems Press.

Miner, J. B. (1967). *The school administrator and organizational character*. Eugene, OR: Center for the Advanced Study of Educational Administration.

Miner, J. B. (1975). The uncertain future of the leadership concept: An overview. In J. G. Hunt and L. L. Larson (Eds.), *Leadership frontiers*. Kent, OH: Kent State University Press.

Miner, J. B. (1977). *Motivation to manage: A ten-year update on the "studies in management education" research*. Atlanta: Organizational Measurement Systems Press.

Miner, J. B. (1978). Twenty years of research on role motivation theory of managerial effectiveness. *Personnel Psychology*, 31, 739–760.

Miner, J. B. (1985). Sentence completion measures in personnel research: The development and validation of the Miner Sentence Completion Scales. In H. J. Bernardin and D. A. Bownas (Eds.), *Personality assessment in organizations*. New York: Praeger, pp. 145–176.

Miner, J. B. (1986). Managerial role motivation training. *Journal of Management Psychology*, 1 (1), 25–30.

Mintzberg, H. (1973). *The nature of managerial work*. New York: Harper & Row.

Mintzberg, H. (1979). *The structuring of organizations*. Englewood Cliffs, NJ: Prentice Hall.

Mintzberg, H. (1983). *Power in and around organizations*. Englewood Cliffs, NJ: Prentice Hall.

Mintzberg, H., Raisinghani, D., & Theoret, A. (1976). The structure of unstructured decision processes, *Administrative Science Quarterly*, 21, 246–275.

Miron, E., Erez, M., & Naveh, E. (2004). Do personal characteristics and cultural values that promote innovation, quality, and efficiency compete or complement each other? *Journal of Organizational Behavior*, 25, 175–199.

Misumi, J. (1985). *The behavioral science of leadership: An interdisciplinary Japanese research program.* Ann Arbor, MI: The University of Michigan Press.

Misumi, J., & Peterson, M. (1985). The performance-maintenance (PM) theory of leadership: Review of a Japanese research program. *Administrative Science Quarterly*, 30, 198–223.

Misumi, J., & Shirakashi, S. (1966). An experimental study of the effects of supervisory behavior on productivity and morale in a hierarchical organization. *Human Relations*, 19, 297–307.

Mitchell, R. (1986). Team building by disclosure of internal frames of reference. *Journal of Applied Behavioral Science*, 22, 1, 15–28.

Mitchell, T. R. (1973). Motivation and participation: An integration. *Academy of Management Journal*, 16, 660–679.

Mitchell, T. R. (1974). Expectancy models of job satisfaction, occupational preference, and effort: A theoretical, methodological, and empirical appraisal. *Psychological Bulletin*, 81, 1053–1077.

Mitchell, T. R., Green, S. C., & Wood, R.E. (1981). An attributional model of leadership and the poor performing subordinate: Development and validation. In L. L. Cummings and B. M. Staw (Eds.), *Research in organizational behavior,* vol. 3, Greenwich, CT: JAI Press.

Mitchell, T. R., & Kalb, L. S. (1981). Effects of outcome knowledge and outcome valence on supervisor's evaluation. *Journal of Applied Psychology*, 66, 604–612.

Mitchell, T. R., & Kalb, L. S. (1982). Effects of job experience on supervisor attributions for a subordinate's peer performance. *Journal of Applied Psychology*, 67, 181–188.

Mitchell, T. R., Larson, J. R. Jr., & Green, S. G. (1977). Leader behavior, situational moderators, and group performance: An attributional analysis. *Organizational Behavior and Human Performance*, 18, 254–268.

Mitchell, T. R., & Liden, R. C. (1982). The effects of social context on performance evaluations. *Organizational Behavior and Human Performance*, 29, 241–256.

Mitchell, T. R., & Wood, R. E. (1980). Supervisor's responses to subordinate poor performance: A test of an attributional model. *Organizational Behavior and Human Performance*, 25, 123–138.

Mitroff, I. I., Barabba, V. P., & Kilmann, R. H. (1977). The application of behavioral and philosophical technologies to strategic planning: A case study of a large federal agency. *Management Science*, 24, 44–58.

Morgan, G., & Smircich, L. (1980). The case for qualitative research. *Academy of Management Review*, 5, 491–500.

Morrison, A. M., Ruderman, M. N., & Hughes-James, M. W. (1993). *Making diversity happen: Controversies and solutions.* Greensboro, NC: Center for Creative Leadership.

Morse, J. J., & Wagner, F. R. (1978). Measuring the process of managerial effectiveness. *Academy of Management Journal*, 21, 23–35.

Morse, N. C., & Reimer, E. (1956). The experimental change of a major organizational variable. *Journal of Abnormal and Social Psychology*, 52, 120–129.

Moses, J., Hollenbeck, G., & Sorcher, M. (1993). Other people's expectations. *Human Resource Management*, 32 (2/3), 283–297.

Mott, P. E. (1972). *The characteristics of effective organizations.* New York: Harper & Row.

Nadler, D. A. (1998). Leading executive teams. In D. Nadler, J. Spencer, & Associates (Eds.), *Executive teams.* San Francisco: Jossey-Bass, pp. 3–20.

Mowday, R. (1978). The exercise of upward influence in organizations. *Administrative Science Quarterly*, 23, 137–156.

Moxley, R. S., & O'Connor-Wilson, P. (1998). A systems approach to leadership development. In C. D. McCauley, R. S. Moxley, and E. Van Velsor (Eds.), *Center for Creative Leadership handbook of leadership development.* San Francisco: Jossey-Bass, pp. 217–241.

Mulder, M., DeJong, R. D., Koppelaar, L., & Verhage, J. (1986). Power, situation, and leaders' effectiveness: An organizational study. *Journal of Applied Psychology*, 71, 566–570.

Mulder, M., Ritsema van Eck, J. R., & de Jong, R. D. (1970). An organization in crisis and non-crisis conditions. *Human Relations*, 24, 19–41.

Mulder, M., & Stemerding, A. (1963). Threat, attraction to group, and need for strong leadership. *Human Relations*, 16, 317–334.

Mulvey, P. W., & Klein, H. J. (1998). The impact of perceived loafing and collective efficacy on group goal processes and group performance. *Organizational Behavior and Human Decision Processes*, 74 (1), 62–87.

Mumford, M. D. (1986). Leadership in the organizational context: Some empirical and theoretical considerations. *Journal of Applied Psychology*, 16, 508–531.

Mumford, M. D., & Connelly, M. S. (1991). Leaders as creators: Leader performance and problem solving in ill-defined domains. *Leadership Quarterly*, 2, 289–315.

Mumford, M. D., Gessner, T. L., Connelly, M. S., O'Connor, J. A., & Clifton, T. C. (1993). Leadership and destructive acts: Individual and situational influences. *Leadership Quarterly*, 4, 115–147.

Mumford, M. D., Marks, M. A., Connelly, M. S., Zaccaro, S. J., & Reiter-Palmon, R. (2000). Development of leadership skills: Experience and timing. *Leadership Quarterly*, 11, 87–114.

Mumford, M. D., Scott, G. M., Baddis, B., & Strange, J. M. (2002). Leading creating people: Orchestrating expertise and relationships. *Leadership Quarterly*, 13, 705–750.

Mumford, M. D., & Van Doorn, J. R. (2001). The leadership of pragmatism: Reconsidering Franklin in the age of charisma. *Leadership Quarterly*, 12, 279–309.

Munchus, G. III, & McArthur, B. (1991). Revisiting the historical use of the assessment center in management selection and development. *Journal of Management Development*, 10 (1), 5–13.

Murphy, S. E., Blyth, D., & Fiedler, F. E. (1992). Cognitive resources theory and the utilization of the leader's and group member's technical competence. *Leadership Quarterly*, 3, 237–255.

Murray, A. I. (1989). Top management group heterogeneity and firm performance. *Strategic Management Journal*, 10, 125–141.

Musser, S. J. (1987). *The determination of positive and negative charismatic leadership.* Working paper, Grantham, PA: Messiah College.

Nadler, D. A. (1988). Organizational frame bending: Types of change in the complex organization. In R. H. Kilmann and T. J. Covin (Eds.), *Corporate transformation: Revitalizing organizations for a competitive world.* San Francisco: Jossey-Bass, pp. 66–83.

Nadler, D. A., Shaw, R. B., Walton, A. E., & Associates. (1995). *Discontinuous change: Leading organizational transformation.* San Francisco, Jossey-Bass.

Nahavandi, A., Mizzi, P. J., & Malekzadeh, A. R. (1992). Executive's Type A personality as a determinant of environmental perception and firm strategy. *Journal of Social Psychology*, 132, 59–68.

Nanus, B. (1992). *Visionary leadership: Creating a compelling sense of direction for your organization.* San Francisco: Jossey-Bass.

Narchal, R. M., Kittappa, K., & Bhattacharya, P. (1987). An environmental scanning system for business planning. *Long Range Planning*, 20, 96–105.

Nemeroff, W., & Cosentino, J. (1979). Utilizing feedback and goal setting to increase performance appraisal interviewer skills of managers. *Academy of Management Journal*, 22, 566–576.

Nemetz, P. L., & Christensen, S. L. (1996). The challenge of cultural diversity: Harnessing a diversity of views to understand multiculturalism. *Academy of Management Review*, 21, 434–462.

Neustadt, R. E. (1960). *Presidential power.* New York: John Wiley.

Nevis, E. C., Dibella, A. J., & Gould, J. M. (1995). Understanding organizations as learning systems. *Sloan Management Review*, Winter, 73–85.

Newman, W. H., & Warren, K. (1977). *The process of management*. Englewood Cliffs, NJ: Prentice Hall.

Nielsen, R. P. (1989). Changing unethical organizational behavior. *Academy of Management Executive*, 3 (2), 123–130.

Noe, R. A. (1988). An investigation of the determinants of successful assigned mentoring relationships. *Personnel Psychology*, 41, 457–479.

Noe, R. A. (1991). Mentoring relationships for employee development. In J. W. Jones, B. D. Steffy, and D. W. Bray (Eds.), *Applying psychology in Business: The manager's handbook*. Lexington, MA: Lexington Press, pp. 475–482.

Noe, R. A., & Ford, J. K. (1992). Emerging issues and new directions for training research. In K. Rowland and G. Ferris (Eds.), *Research in Personnel and Human Resource Management*. Greenwich, CT: JAI Press.

Noe, R. A., & Schmitt, N. (1986). The influence of trainee attitudes on training effectiveness: Test of a model. *Personnel Psychology*, 39, 497–523.

Norris, W. R., & Vecchio, R. P. (1992). Situational leadership theory: A replication. *Group and Organization Management*, 17 (3), 331–342.

Nunamaker, J. F., Briggs, R. O., & Mittleman, D. D. (1995). Electronic meeting systems: Ten years of lessons learned. In D. Coleman and R. Khanna (Eds.), *Groupware: Technology and application*. Upper Saddle River, NJ: Prentice Hall, pp. 149–193.

Nutt, P. C. (1993). Flexible decision styles and the choices of top exeuctives. *Journal of Management Studies*, 30, 695–721.

Nystrom, P. C., & Starbuck, W. H. (1984). To avoid organizational crises, unlearn. *Organizational Dynamics*, Spring, 53–65.

O'Brien, G. E., & Kabanoff, B. (1981). The effects of leadership style and group structure upon small group productivity: A test of a discrepancy theory of leader effectiveness. *Australian Journal of Psychology*, 33 (2), 157–158.

O'Connor, J., Mumford, M. D., Clifton, T. C., Gessner, T. L., & Connelly, M. S. (1995). Charismatic leaders and destructiveness: A historiometric study. *Leadership Quarterly*, 6, 529–555.

Offermann, L. R., Kennedy, J. K., & Wirtz, P. W. (1994). Implicit leadership theories: Content, structure, and generalizability. *Leadership Quarterly*, 5, 43–58.

Offermann, L. R., Schroyer, C. J., & Green S. K. (1998). Leader attributions for subordinate performance: Consequences for subsequent leader interactive behaviors and ratings. *Journal of Applied Social Psychology*, 28, 1125–1139.

O'Hair, M. J., Cody, M. J., & O'Hair, D. (1991). The impact of situational dimensions on compliance-resistance strategies: A comparison of methods. *Communication Quarterly*, 39, 226–240.

Ohlott, P. J. (1998). Job assignments. In C. D. McCauley, R. S. Moxley, & E. Van Velsor (Eds.), *Center for Creative Leadership handbook of leadership development*. San Francisco: Jossey-Bass, pp. 127–159.

Ohlott, P. J., Ruderman, M. N., & McCauley, C. D. (1994). Gender differences in manager's developmental job experiences. *Academy of Management Journal*, 37, 46–67.

Oldham, G. R. (1976). The motivational strategies used by supervisors: Relationships to effectiveness indicators. *Organizational Behavior and Human Performance*, 15, 66–86.

Olivero, G., Bane, D. K., & Kopelman, R. E. (1997). Executive coaching as a transfer of training tool: Effects on productivity in a public agency. *Public Personnel Management*, 26, 461–469.

Orsburn, J. D., Moran, L., Musselwhite, E., & Zenger, J. H. (1990). *Self-directed work teams: The new American challenge*. Homewood, IL: Business One Irwin.

Osborn, R. N. (1974). Discussant comments. In J. G. Hunt & L. L. Larson (Eds.), *Contingency approaches to leadership*. Carbondale: Southern Illinois University Press, pp. 56–59.

Osborn, R. N., Hunt, J. G., & Jauch, L. R. (2002). Toward a contextual theory of leadership. *Leadership Quarterly*, 13, 797–837.

O'Toole, J. (1995). *Leading change: Overcoming the ideology of comfort and the tyranny of custom*. San Francisco: Jossey-Bass.

O'Toole, P. (1985). *Corporate messiah*. New York: New American Library.

Page, R. (1985). *The position description questionnaire*. Unpublished paper. Minneapolis: Control Data Business Advisors.

Page, R., & Tornow, W. W. (1987). *Managerial job analysis: Are we farther along?* Paper presented at the Second Annual Conference of the Society for Industrial and Organizational Psychology, Atlanta (April).

Paglis, L. L., & Green, S. G. (2002). Leadership self-efficacy and managers' motivation for leading change. *Journal of Organizational Studies*, 23, 215–235.

Paolillo, J. G. (1981). Role profiles for managers at different hierarchical levels. *Proceedings of the Academy of Management Meetings*, August, 91–94.

Papa, M. J., & Graham, E. E. (1991). The impact of diagnosing skill deficiencies and assessment-based communication training on managerial performance. *Communication Education*, 40, 368–384.

Parry, S. B., & Reich, L. R. (1984). An uneasy look at behavior modeling. *Training and Development Journal*, March, 57–62.

Pascale, R. T. (1990). *Managing on the edge*. New York: Simon & Schuster.

Pasmore, W. A. (1978). The comparative impacts of sociotechnical systems, job redesign, and survey feedback interventions. In W. A. Pasmore & J. J. Sherwood (Eds.), *Sociotechnical systems: A sourcebook*. La Jolla, CA: University Associates, pp. 291–301.

Patchen, M. (1974). The locus and basis of influence on organizational decisions. *Organizational Behavior and Human Performance*, 11, 195–221.

Paul, R. J., & Ebadi, Y. M. (1989). Leadership decision making in a service organization: A field test of the Vroom-Yetton model. *Journal of Occupational Psychology*, 62, 201–211.

Paulus, P. B., & Yang, Huei-Chuan. (2000). Idea generation in groups: A basis for creativity in organizations. *Organizational Behavior and Human Decision Processes*, 82 (1), 76–87.

Pavett, C., & Lau, A. (1983). Managerial work: The influence of hierarchical level and functional specialty. *Academy of Management Journal*, 26, 170–177.

Pawar, B. S., & Eastman, K. K. (1997). The nature and implications of contextual influences on transformational leadership: A conceptual examination. *Academy of Management Review*, 22, 80–109.

Pearce, C. L., Gallagher, C. A., & Ensley, M. D. (2002). Confidence at the group level of analysis: A longitudinal investigation of the relationship between potency and team effectiveness. *Journal of Occupational and Organizational Psychology*, 75, 115–119.

Pearce, C. L., & Sims, H. P. (2000). Shared leadership: Toward a multi-level theory of leadership. *Advances in interdisciplinary studies of work teams*, vol. 7. Greenwich, CT: JAI Press.

Pearce, J. H., II, & Ravlin, E. C. (1987). The design and activation of self-regulating work groups. *Human Relations*, 40, 751–782.

Pearson, C. L. (1992). Autonomous workgroups: An evaluation at an industrial site. *Human Relations*, 45, 905–936.

Peng, T. K., Peterson, M. F., & Shyi, Y. (1991). Quantitative methods in cross-national management research: Trends and equivalence issues. *Journal of Organizational Behavior*, 12, 87–107.

Perry, E. L., Davis-Blake, A., & Kulik, C. T. (1994). Explaining gender-based selection decisions: A synthesis of contextual and cognitive approaches. *Academy of Management Review*, 19, 786–820.

Peters, L. H., Hartke, D. D., & Pohlmann, J. T. (1985). Fiedler's contingency theory of leadership: An application of the meta-analysis procedures of Schmidt and Hunter. *Psychological Bulletin*, 97, 274–285.

Peters, L. H., O'Connor, E. J., & Eulberg, J. R. (1985). Situational constraints: Sources, consequences, and future considerations. *Research in Personnel and Human Resource Management*, 3, 79–114.

Peters, L. H., O'Connor, E. J., Eulberg, J. R., & Rudolf, C. J. (1980). The behavioral and affective consequences of performance-relevant situational variables. *Organizational Behavior and Human Performance*, 25, 79–96.

Peters, T. J. (1987). *Thriving on chaos*. New York: Harper Collins.

Peters, T. J., & Austin, N. (1985). *A passion for excellence: The leadership difference*. New York: Random House.

Peters, T. J., & Waterman, R. H., Jr. (1982). *In search of excellence: Lessons from America's best-run companies*. New York: Harper & Row.

Peterson, D. B. (1966). Executive coaching at work: The art of one-on-one change. *Consulting Psychology Journal: Practice and Research*, 48, 78–86.

Pettigrew, A. M. (1972). Information control as a power resource. *Sociology*, 6, 187–204.

Pettigrew, A. M. (1988). Context and action in the transformation of firms. *Journal of Management Studies*, 24, 649–670.

Pettigrew, A. M. (1992). On studying managerial elites. *Strategic Management Journal*, 13, 163–182.

Pettigrew, A. M., Ferlie, E., & McKee, L. (1992). *Shaping strategic change in large organizations: The case of the national health service*. London: Sage.

Pettigrew, A. M., & Whipp, R. (1991). *Managing change for competitive success*. Oxford, England: Blackwell.

Pfeffer, J. (1977a). Power and resource allocation in organizations. In B. Staw & G. Salancik (Eds.), *New directions in organizational behavior*. Chicago: St. Clair Press, pp. 235–265.

Pfeffer, J. (1977b). The ambiguity of leadership. *Academy of Management Review*, 2, 104–112.

Pfeffer, J. (1981). *Power in organizations*. Marshfield, MA: Pittman.

Pfeffer, J. (1992). *Managing with power: Politics and influence in organizations*. Boston, MA: Harvard Business School Press.

Pfeffer, J, Cialdini, R. B., Hanna, B., & Knopoff, D. (1998). Faith in supervision and the self-enhancement bias: Two psychological reasons why managers don't empower workers. *Basic and Applied Social Psychology*, 20, 313–321.

Pfeffer, J., & Davis-Blake, A. (1986). Administrative succession and organizational performance: How administrator experience mediates the succession effect. *Academy of Management Journal*, 29, 72–83.

Pfeffer, J., & Moore, W. L. (1980). Average tenure of academic department heads: The effects of paradigm, size and department demography. *Administrative Science Quarterly*, 25, 387–406.

Pfeffer, J., & Salancik, G. R. (1974). Organizational decision making as a political process: The case of a university budget. *Administrative Science Quarterly*, 19, 135–151.

Pfeffer, J., & Salancik, G. R. (1975). Determinants of supervisory behavior: A role set analysis. *Human Relations*, 28, 139–153.

Philips, A. S., & Bedeian, A. G. (1994). Leader-follower exchange quality: The role of personal and interpersonal attributes. *Academy of Management Journal*, 37, 990–1001.

Pillai, R. (1996). Crisis and the emergence of charismatic leadership in groups: An experimental investigation. *Journal of Applied Social Psychology*, 26, 143–163.

Pillai, R., & Meindl, J. R. (1998). Context and charisma: A "meso" level examination of the relationship of organic structure, collectivism, and crisis to charismatic leadership. *Journal of Management*, 24, 643–671.

Pirola-Merlo, A, Hartel, C., Mann, L., & Hirst, G. (2002). How leaders influence the impact of affective events on team climate and performance in R&D teams. *Leadership Quarterly*, 13, 561–581.

Pitner, N.J. (1986). Substitutes for principal leader behavior: An exploratory study. *Educational Administration Quarterly*, 22, 23–42.

Podsakoff, P.M. (1982). Determinants of a supervisor's use of rewards and punishments: A literature review and suggestions for future research. *Organizational Behavior and Human Performance*, 29, 58–83.

Podsakoff, P. M., Dorfman, P. W., Howell, J. P., & Todor, W. D. (1986). Leader reward and punishment behaviors: A preliminary test of a culture-free style of leadership effectiveness. In R. N. Farmer (Ed.), *Advances in International comparative management*, vol. 2. Greenwich, CT: JAI Press, pp. 95–138.

Podsakoff, P. M., MacKenzie, S. B., & Ahearne, M. (1997). Moderating effects of goal acceptance on the relationship between group cohesiveness and productivity. *Journal of Applied Psychology*, 82 (6), 974–983.

Podsakoff, P. M., MacKenzie, S. B., Ahearne, M., & Bommer, W. H. (1995). Searching for a needle in a haystack: Trying to identify the illusive moderators of leadership behaviors. *Journal of Management*, 21, 423–470.

Podsakoff, P. M., MacKenzie, S. B., & Bommer, W. H. (1996). Transformational leader behaviors and substitutes for leadership as determinants of employee satisfaction, commitment, trust, and organizational citizenship behaviors. *Journal of Management*, 22, 259–298.

Podsakoff, P. M., MacKenzie, S. B., Morrman, R. H., & Fetter, R. (1990). Transformational leader behaviors and their effects on follower's trust in leader, satisfaction, and organizational citizenship behaviors. *Leadership Quarterly*, 1, 107–142.

Podsakoff, P. M., MacKenzie, S. B., & Bommer, W. H. (1996). Transformational leader behaviors and substitutes for leadership as determinants of employee satisfaction, commitment, trust, and organizational citizenship behaviors. *Journal of Management*, 22, 259–298.

Podsakoff, P. M., Niehoff, B. P., MacKenzie, S., & Williams, M. L. (1993). Do substitutes for leadership really substitute for leadership? An examination of Kerr and Jermier's situational leadership model. *Organizational Behavior and Human Decision Processes*, 54, 1–44.

Podsakoff, P. M., & Schriesheim, C. A. (1985). Field studies of French and Raven's bases of power: Critique, reanalysis, and suggestions for future research. *Psychological Bulletin*, 97, 387–411.

Podsakoff, P. M., & Todor, W. D. (1985). Relationships between leader reward and punishment behavior and group processes and productivity. *Journal of Management*, 11, 55–73.

Podsakoff, P. M., Todor, W. D., Grover, R. A., & Huber, V. L. (1984). Situational moderators of leader reward and punishment behavior: Fact or fiction? *Organizational Behavior and Human Performance*, 34, 21–63.

Podsakoff, P. M., Todor, W. D., & Skov, R. (1982). Effects of leader contingent and noncontingent reward and punishment behaviors on subordinate performance and satisfaction. *Academy of Management Journal*, 25, 810–821.

Popper, M., & Lipshitz, R. (1998). Organizational learning mechanisms: A structural and cultural approach to organizational learning. *Journal of Applied Behavioral Science*, 34 (2), 161–179.

Porras, J. I., & Anderson, B. (1981). Improving managerial effectiveness through modeling-based training. *Organizational Dynamics*, Spring, 60–77.

Porter, L. W., Allen, R. W., & Angle, H. L. (1981). The politics of upward influence in organizations. *Research in Organizational Behavior*, 3, 109–149.

Porter, L. W., & Lawler, E. E. (1968). *Managerial attitudes and performance*. Homewood, IL: Irwin-Dorsey.

Porter, M. E. (1980). *Competitive strategy*. New York: Free Press.

Potter, E. H., & Fiedler, F. E. (1981). The utilization of staff member intelligence and experience under high and low stress. *Academy of Management Journal*, 24, 361–376.

Powell, G. N. (1990). One more time: Do female and male managers differ? *Academy of Management Executive*, 4, 68–75.

Powell, G. N. (1993). *Women and men in management*, 2nd ed. Newbury Park, CA: Sage.

Powell, G. N.., Butterfield, A. D., & Parent, J. D. (2002). Gender and managerial stereotypes: Have the times changed? *Journal of Management*, 28, 177–193.

Prahalad, C. K., & Hamel, G. (1990). The core competence of the corporation. *Harvard Business Review*, May–June, 79–91.

Preston, P., & Zimmerer, T. W. (1978). *Management for supervisors*. Englewood Cliffs, NJ: Prentice Hall.

Price, T. L. (2003). The ethics of authentic transformational leadership. *Leadership Quarterly*, 14, 67–81.

Prideaux, G., & Ford, J. E. (1988). Management development: Competencies, teams, learning contracts, and work experience-based learning. *Journal of Management Development*, 7, 13–21.

Priem, R. L. (1990). Top management team group factors, consensus, and firm performance. *Strategic Management Journal*, 11, 469–478.

Priem, R. L., Lyon, D. W., & Dess, G. G. (1999). Inherent limitations of demographic proxies in top management team heterogeneity research. *Journal of Management*, 25 (6), 935–953.

Prince, G. M. (1969). How to be a better meeting chairman. *Harvard Business Review*, January–February, 98–108.

Prince, G. M. (1970). *The practice of creativity*. New York: Harper & Row.

Pruitt, D. G. (1972). Methods for resolving differences of interest: A theoretical analysis. *Journal of Social Issues*, 28, 133–154.

Pryor, A. K., & Shays, M. (1993). Growing the business with intrepreneurs. *Business Quarterly*, 57 (3), 42.

Quinn, J. B. (1980). Formulating strategy one step at a time. *Journal of Business Strategy*, 1, 42–63.

Quinn, J. B. (1992). *The intelligent enterprise*. New York: Free Press.

Quinn, R. E. (1988). *Beyond rational management: Mastering the paradoxes and competing demands of high performance*. San Francisco: Jossey-Bass.

Quinn, R. E., & Cameron, K. (1983). Organizational life cycles and the criteria of effectiveness. *Management Science*, 29, 63–77.

Quinn, R. E., & Rohrbaugh, J. (1983). A spatial model of effectiveness criteria: Toward a competing values approach to organizational analysis. *Management Science*, 29, 363–377.

Raelin, J. A. (1989). An anatomy of autonomy: Managing professionals. *Academy of Management Executive*, 3, 216–228.

Ragins, B. R., & Cotton, J. L. (1991). Easier said than done: Gender differences in perceived barriers to gaining a mentor. *Academy of Management Journal*, 34, 939–951.

Ragins, B. R., & Cotton, J. L. (1993). Gender and willingness to mentor in organizations. *Journal of Management*, 19, 97–111.

Ragins, B. R., & McFarlin, D. B. (1990). Perceptions of mentoring roles in cross-gender mentoring relationships. *Journal of Vocational Behavior*, 37, 321–339.

Ragins, B. R., Townsend, B., & Mattis, M. (1998). Gender gap in the executive suite: CEOs and female executives report on breaking the glass ceiling. *Academy of Management Executive*, 12, 28–42.

Rahim, M. A. (1989). Relationships of leader power to compliance and satisfaction: Evidence from a national sample of managers. *Journal of Management*, 15, 545–556.

Rahim, M. A. (1992). *Managing conflict in organizations*. Westport, CT: Praeger.

Ralston, D. A., & Elsass, P. M. (1989). Ingratiation and impression management in the organization. In R. A. Giacalone & P. Rosenfeld (Eds.), *Impression management in the organization*. Hillsdale, NJ: Erlbaum, pp. 235–247.

Randolph, W. A. (1995). Navigating the journey to empowerment. *Organizational Dynamics*, 23 (4), 19–31.

Raskin, R., & Hall, C. S. (1981). The narcissistic personality inventory: Alternate form reliability and further evidence of construct validity. *Journal of Personality Assessment*, 45, 159–162.

Raskin, R., Novacek, J., & Hogan, R. (1991). Narcissistic self-esteem management. *Journal of Personality and Social Psychology*, 60, 911–918.

Rauch, C. F., & Behling, O. (1984). Functionalism: Basis for an alternate approach to the study of leadership. In J. G. Hunt, D. M. Hosking, C. A. Schriesheim, & R. Stewart (Eds.), *Leaders and managers: International perspectives on managerial behavior and leadership*. Elmsford, NY: Pergamon Press, pp. 45–62.

Rayner, T., & Goodge, P. (1988). New techniques in assessment centres: LRT's experience. *Journal of Management Development*, 7 (4), 21–30.

Reilly, R. R., Smither, J. W., & Vasilopoulos, N. L. (1996). A longitudinal study of upward feedback. *Personnel Psychology*, 49, 599–612.

Reitz, H. J. (1977). *Behavior in organizations*. Homewood, IL: Irwin.

Revans, R. W. (1982). *The origin and growth of action learning*. Hunt, England: Chatwell-Bratt.

Reynolds, P. C. (1987). Imposing a corporate culture. *Psychology Today*, March, 32–38.

Rice, R. W. (1978). Construct validity of the least preferred coworker score. *Psychological Bulletin*, 85, 1199–1237.

Richards, D., & Engle, S. (1986). After the vision: Suggestions to corporate visionaries and vision champions. In J. D. Adams (Ed.), *Transforming leadership*. Alexandria, VA: Miles River Press, pp. 199–214.

Robbins, S. P. (1996). *Organizational behavior: Concepts, controversies, applications*. Englewood Cliffs, NJ: Prentice Hall.

Roberson, Q. M., Moye, N. A., & Locke, E. A. (1999). Identifying a missing link between participation and satisfaction: The mediating role of procedural justice perceptions. *Journal of Applied Psychology*, 84, 585–593.

Roberts, N. C. (1985). Transforming leadership: A process of collective action. *Human Relations*, 38, 1023–1046.

Roberts, N. C., & Bradley, R. T. (1988). Limits of charisma. In J. A. Conger & R. N. Kanungo (Eds.), *Charismatic leadership: The elusive factor in organizational effectiveness*. San Francisco: Jossey-Bass, pp. 253–275.

Robertson, I. T. (1990). Behavioral modeling: Its record and potential in training and development. *British Journal of Management*, 1, 117–125.

Robertson, P. J., Roberts, K. R., & Porras, J. I. (1993). An evaluation of a model of planned organizational change: Evidence from a meta-analysis. In R. W. Woodman and W. A. Pssmore (Eds.), *Research in organizational change and development*, vol. 7. Greenwich, CT: JAI Press, pp. 1–39.

Rojahn, K. M., & Willemsen, T. (1994). The evaluation of effectiveness and likability of gender-role congruent and gender-role incongruent leaders. *Sex Roles*, 30, 109–119.

Romanelli, E., & Tushman, M. L. (1994). Organizational transformation as punctuated equilibrium: An empirical test. *Academy of Management Journal*, 37, 1141–1186.

Rosener, J. (1990). Ways women lead. *Harvard Business Review*, 68 (6), 119–125.

Rost, J. C. (1991). *Leadership for the twenty-first century*. Westport, CT: Greenwood.

Rothwell, W. J., & Kazanas, H. C. (1994). Management development: The state of the art as perceived by HRD professionals. *Performance Improvement Quarterly*, 4 (1), 40–59.

Rotter, J. B. (1966). Generalized expectancies for internal versus external control of reinforcement. *Psychological Monographs*, 80 (609).

Rouiller, J. S., & Goldstein, I. L. (1993). The relationship between organizational transfer climate and positive transfer of training. *Human Resource Development Quarterly*, 4, 377–390.

Rousseau, D. M. (1985). Issues of level in organizational research: Multi-level and cross-level perspectives. *Research in Organizational Behavior*, 7, 1–38.

Ruderman, M. N., & Ohlott, P. J. (1994). *The realities of management promotion.* Technical Report #157. Greensboro, NC: Center for Creative Leadership.

Ruderman, M. N., Ohlott, P. J., & McCauley, C. D. (1990). Assessing opportunities for leadership development. In K. E. Clark & M. B. Clark (Eds.), *Measures of leadership.* West Orange, NJ: Leadership Library of America, pp. 547–562.

Rush, M. C., Thomas, J. C., & Lord, R. G. (1977). Implicit leadership theory: A potential threat to the internal validity of leader behavior questionnaires. *Organizational Behavior and Human Performance*, 20, 93–110.

Saari, L. M., Johnson, T. R., McLaughlin, S. D., & Zimmerle, D. M. (1988). A survey of management training and education practices in U.S. companies. *Personnel Psychology*, 41, 731–743.

Sandowsky, D. (1995). The charismatic leader as narcissist: Understanding the abuse of power. *Organizational Dynamics*, 23 (4), 57–71.

Sagie, A., & Koslowsky, M. (2000). *Participation and empowerment in organizations.* Thousand Oaks, CA: Sage.

Salancik, G. R., Calder, B. J., Rowland, K. M., Leblebici, H., & Conway, M. (1975). Leadership as an outcome of social structure and process: A multidimensional analysis. In J. C. Hunt & L. L. Larson (Eds.), *Leadership frontiers.* Kent, OH: Kent State University Press, pp. 81–101.

Salancik, G. R., & Meindl, J. R. (1984). Corporate attributions as strategic illusions of management control. *Administrative Science Quarterly*, 29, 238–254.

Salancik, G. R., & Pfeffer, J. (1977a). Who gets power and how they hold on to it: A strategic contingency model of power. *Organizational Dynamics*, 5, 3–21.

Salancik, G. R., & Pfeffer, J. (1977b). Constraints on administrative discretion: The limited influence of mayors on city budgets. *Urban Affairs Quarterly*, 12, 474–498.

Salas, E., & Cannon-Bowers, J. A. (2000) . The science of training: A decade of progress. *Annual Review Psychology, 52, pp. 471–499.*

Salovey, P. & Mayer, J. (1990). Emotional intelligence. *Imagination, Cognition, and Personality*, 9, 185–211.

Samuelson, B. A., Galbraith, C. S., & McGuire, J. W. (1985). Organizational performance and top-management turnover. *Organizational Studies*, 6, 275–291.

Sandowsky, D. (1995). The charismatic leader as narcissist: Understanding the abuse of power. *Organizational Dynamics*, 24 (4), 57–71.

Sashkin, M., & Fulmer, R. M. (1988). Toward an organizational leadership theory. In J. G. Hunt, B. R. Baliga, H. P. Dachler, & C. A. Schriesheim (Eds.), *Emerging leadership vistas.* Lexington, MA: Heath, pp. 51–65.

Savard, C. J., & Rogers, R. W. (1992). A self-efficacy and subjective expected utility theory analysis of the selection and use of influence strategies. *Journal of Social Behavior and Personality*, 7, 273–292.

Sayles, L. R. (1979). *What effective managers really do and how they do it.* New York: McGraw-Hill.

Scandura, T. A. (1992). Mentorship and career mobility: An empirical investigation. *Journal of Organizational Behavior*, 13, 169–174.

Scandura, T. A. (1999). Rethinking leader-member exchange: An organizational justice perspective. *Leadership Quarterly*, 10, 25–40.

Scandura, T. A., & Graen, G. B. (1984). Moderating effects of initial leader-member exchange status on the effects of leadership intervention. *Journal of Applied Psychology*, 69, 428–436.

Scandura, T. A., & Schriesheim, C. A. (1994). Leader-member exchange and supervisor career mentoring as complementary constructs in leadership research. *Academy of Management Journal*, 37, 1588–1602.

Scandura, T. A., Von Glinow, M. A., & Lowe, K. B. (1999). When East meets West: Leadership "best practices" in the United States and Middle East. In W. H. Mobley, M. J. Gessner, & V. Arnold (Eds.), *Advances in global leadership*. Stamford, CT: JAI Press, pp. 235–248.

Schein, E. H. (1969). *Process consultation: Its role in management development*. Reading, MA: Addison-Wesley.

Schein, E. H. (1992). *Organizational culture and leadership*, 2nd ed. San Francisco: Jossey-Bass.

Schein, E. H. (1993a). How can organizations learn faster? *Sloan Management Review*, 34, 85–90.

Schein, E. H. (1993b). On dialogue, culture, and organizational learning. *Organizational Dynamics*, 22 (2), 40–51.

Schein, V. E. (1975). Relationships between sex role stereotypes and requisite management characteristics among female managers. *Journal of Applied Psychology*, 75 (60), 340–344.

Schilit, W. K., & Locke, E. A. (1982). A study of upward influence in organizations. *Administrative Science Quarterly*, 27, 304–316.

Schlesinger, L., Jackson, J. M., & Butman, J. (1960). Leader-member interaction in management committees. *Journal of Abnormal and Social Psychology*, 61, 360–364.

Schmidt, S. M., & Kipnis, D. (1984). Manager's pursuit of individual and organizational goals. *Human Relations*, 37, 781–794.

Schneier, C. E. (1974). Behavior modification in management: A review and critique. *Academy of Management Journal*, 17, 528–548.

Schoen, S. H., & Durand, D. E. (1979). *Supervision: The management of organizational resources*. Englewood Cliffs, NJ: Prentice Hall.

Schriesheim, C. A., Castro, S., & Cogliser, C. C. (1999). Leader-member exchange research: A comprehensive review of theory, measurement, and data-analytic procedures. *Leadership Quarterly*, 10, 63–113.

Schriesheim, C. A., & Hinkin, T. R. (1990). Influence tactics used by subordinates: A theoretical and empirical analysis and refinement of the Kipnis, Schmidt, and Wilkinson subscales. *Journal of Applied Psychology*, 75, 246–257.

Schriesheim, C. A., Hinkin, T. R., & Podsakoff, P. M. (1991). Can ipsative and single-item measures produce erroneous results in field studies of French and Raven's five bases of power? An empirical examination. *Journal of Applied Psychology*, 76, 106–114.

Schriesheim, C. A., & Kerr, S. (1977a). Theories and measures of leadership: A critical appraisal. In J. G. Hunt & L. L. Larson (Eds.), *Leadership: The cutting edge*. Carbondale: Southern Illinois University Press, pp. 9–45.

Schriesheim, C. A., & Kerr, S. (1977b). R.I.P. LPC: A response to Fiedler. In J. G. Hunt and L. L. Larson (Eds.), *Leadership: The cutting edge*. Carbondale, IL: Southern Illinois University Press, pp. 51–56.

Schriesheim, C. A., Kinicki, A. J., & Schriesheim, J. F. (1979). The effect of leniency on leader behavior descriptions. *Organizational Behavior and Human Performance*, 23, 1–29.

Schriesheim, C. A., Neider, L. L., & Scandura, T. A. (1998). Delegation and leader-member exchange: Main effects, moderators, and measurement issues. *Academy of Management Journal*, 41, 298–318.

Schriesheim, C. A., Neider, L. L., Scandura, T. A., & Tepper, B. J. (1992). Development and preliminary validation of a new scale (LMX-6) to measure leader-member exchange in organizations. *Educational and Psychological Measurement*, 52, 135–147.

Schriesheim, C. A., & Stogdill, R. M. (1975). Differences in factor structure across three versions of the Ohio State leadership scales. *Personnel Psychology*, 28, 189–206.

Schwartz, K. B., & Menon, K. (1985). Executive succession in failing firms. *Academy of Management Journal*, 26, 680–686.

Schwartz, S. H. (1992). Universals in the content and structure of values: Theoretical advances and tests in 20 countries. *Advances in Experimental Social Psychology*, 25, 1–65.

Schweiger, D. M. (1983). Is the simultaneous verbal protocol a viable method for studying managerial problem solving and decision making? *Academy of Management Journal*, 26, 185–192.

Schweiger, D. M., Anderson, C. R., & Locke, E. A. (1985). Complex decision making: A longitudinal study of process and performance. *Organizational Behavior and Human Decision Processes*, 36, 245–272.

Schweiger, D. M., & Sandberg, W. R. (1991). A team approach to top management's strategic decisions. In H. E. Glass (Ed.), *Handbook of business strategy*. New York: Warren, Gorham & Lamont, pp. 1–20.

Schweiger, D. M., Sandberg, W. R., & Ragan, J. W. (1986). Group approaches for improving strategic decision making: A comparative analysis of dialectical inquiry, devil's advocacy, and consensus. *Academy of Management Journal*, 29, 51–71.

Seers, A., Petty, M. M., & Cashman, J. F. (1995). Team member exchange under team and traditional management: A naturally occurring quasi-experiment. *Group and Organization Management*, 20, 18–38.

Seifert, C., Yukl, G., & McDonald, R. (2003). Effects of multisource feedback and a feedback facilitator on the influence behavior of managers toward subordinates. *Journal of Applied Psychology*, 88, 561–569.

Semler, R. (1989). Managing without managers. *Harvard Business Review*, September–October, 76–84.

Senge, P. M. (1990). *The fifth discipline: The art and practice of the learning organization*. New York: Doubleday/Currency.

Senge, P. M., Roberts, C., Ross, R., Smith, B., & Kleiner, A. (1993). *The fifth discipline fieldbook*. New York: Doubleday.

Shamir, B. (1991). Meaning, self, and motivation in organizations. *Organization Studies*, 12, 405–424.

Shamir, B. (1995). Social distance and charisma: Theoretical notes and an exploratory study. *Leadership Quarterly*, 6, 19–47.

Shamir, B., House, R. J., & Arthur, M. B. (1993). The motivational effects of charismatic leadership: A self–concept based theory. *Organization Science*, 4, 1–17.

Shamir, B., & Howell, J. M. (1999). Organizational and contextual influences on the emergence and effectiveness of charismatic leadership. *Leadership Quarterly*, 10, 257–283.

Shamir, B., Zakay, E., & Popper, M. (1998). Correlates of charismatic leader behavior in military units: Subordinates' attitudes, unit characteristics, and superiors' appraisals of leader performance. *Academy of Management Journal*, 41, 387–409.

Sharp-Paine, L. (1994). Managing for organizational integrity. *Harvard Business Review*, March–April, 106–117.

Shea, C. M., & Howell, J. M. (1999). Charismatic leadership and task feedback: A laboratory study of their effects on self-efficacy and task performance. *Leadership Quarterly*, 10, 375–396.

Sherman, H. (1966). *It all depends: A pragmatic approach to delegation*. Birmingham: University of Alabama Press.

Shetty, Y. K., & Peery, N. S. (1976). Are top executives transferable across companies? *Business Horizons*, 19 (3), 23–28.

Shiflett, S. C. (1973). The contingency model of leadership effectiveness: Some implications of its statistical and methodological properties. *Behavioral Science*, 18 (6), 429–440.

Shiflett, S. C. (1979). Toward a general model of small group productivity. *Psychological Bulletin*, 86, 67–79.

Shipper, F. (1991). Mastery and frequency of managerial behaviors relative to subunit effectiveness. *Human Relations*, 44, 371–388.

Shipper, F., & Manz, C. (1992). Employee self management without formally designated teams: An alternative road to empowerment. *Organizational Dynamics*, Winter, 48–61.

Shipper, F., & Wilson, C. L. (1992). The impact of managerial behaviors on group performance, stress, and commitment. In K. Clark, M. B. Clark, & D. P. Campbell (Eds.), *Impact of leadership*. Greensboro, NC: Center for Creative Leadership, pp. 119–129.

Shull, F. A., Delbecq, A. L., & Cummings, L. L. (1970). *Organizational decision making*. New York: McGraw-Hill.

Shutz, W. C. (1955). What makes groups productive? *Human Relations*, 8, 429–465.

Simon, H. (1987). Making managerial decisions: The role of intuition and emotion. *Academy of Management Executive*, 1, 57–64.

Sims, H. P., Jr. (1977). The leader as a manager of reinforcement contingencies: An empirical example and a model. In J. G. Hun & L. L. Larson (Eds.), *Leadership: The cutting edge*. Carbondale: Southern Illinois University Press, pp. 121–137.

Sims, H. P., Jr., & Lorenzi, P. (1992). *The new leadership paradigm: Social learning and cognition in organizations*. Newbury Park, CA: Sage.

Sims, H. P., Jr., & Manz, C. C. (1984). Observing leader verbal behavior: Toward reciprocal determinism in leadership theory. *Journal of Applied Psychology*, 69, 222–232.

Sinclair, A. (1992). The tyranny of a team ideology. *Organization Studies*, 13, 611–626.

Sivasubramaniam, N., Murry, W. D., Avolio, B. J., & Jung, D. I. (2002). A longitudinal model of the effects of team leadership and group potency on group performance. *Group & Organization Management*, 27 (1), 66–96.

Skinner, E. W. (1969). Relationships between leadership behavior patterns and organizational-situational variables. *Personnel Psychology*, 22, 489–494.

Slater, P. E. (1955). Role differentiation in small groups. In A. P. Hare, E. F. Borgatta, & R. F. Bales (Eds.), *Small groups: Studies in social interactions*. New York: Knopf, pp. 498–515.

Smith, B. (1990). Mutual mentoring on projects: A proposal to combine the advantages of several established management development methods. *Journal of Management* Development, 9, 51–57.

Smith, B. J. (1982). *An initial test of a theory of charismatic leadership based on the response of subordinates*. Unpublished doctoral dissertation. University of Toronto, Canada.

Smith, C. G., & Tannenbaum, A. S. (1963). Organizational control structure: A comparative analysis. *Human Relations*, 16, 299–316.

Smith, J. E., Carson, K. P., & Alexander, R. A. (1984). Leadership: It can make a difference. *Academy of Management Journal*, 27, 765–776.

Smith, P. B., Misumi, J., Tayeb, M., Peterson, M., & Bond, M. (1989). On the generality of leadership styles across cultures. *Journal of Occupational Psychology*, 62, 97–107.

Smith-Jentsch, K., Salas, E., & Baker, D. P. (1996). Training team performance-related assertiveness. *Personnel Psychology*, 49, 110–116.

Smither, J. W., London, M., Vasilopoulos, N. L., Reilly, R. R., Millsap, R. E., & Salvemini, N. (1995). An examination of the effects of an upward feedback program over time. *Personnel Psychology*, 46, 1–34.

Snyder, M. (1974). Self-monitoring of expressive behavior. *Journal of Personality and Social Psychology*, 30, 526–537.

Snyder, N., & Glueck, W. F. (1980). How managers plan: The analysis of managers' activities. *Long Range Planning*, 13, 70–76.

Sosik, J. J., Kahai, S. S., & Avolio, B. J. (1998). Transformational leadership and dimensions of creativity: Motivating idea generation in computer-mediated groups. *Creativity Research Journal*, 11, 111–121.

Sparrowe, R. T., & Liden, R. C. (1997). Process and structure in leader-member exchange. *Academy of Management Review*, 22, 522–552.

Spector, P. E. (1986). Perceived control by employees: A meta-analysis of studies concerning autonomy and participation at work. *Human Relations*, 39, 1005–1016.

Spreitzer, G. M. (1995). Psychological empowerment in the workplace: Dimensions, measurement, and validation. *Academy of Management Journal*, 38, 1442–1465.

Spreitzer, G. M. (1996). Social structural characteristics of psychological empowerment. *Academy of Management Journal*, 39, 483–504.

Spreitzer, G. M., Cohen, S. G., & Ledford, G. E., Jr. (1999). Developing effective self-managing work teams in service organizations. *Group and Organization Management*, 24, 340–365.

Spreitzer, G. M., Kizilos, M. A., & Nason, S. W. (1997). A dimensional analysis of the relationship between psychological empowerment and effectiveness, satisfaction, and strain. *Journal of Management*, 23, 679–704.

Spreitzer, G. M., McCall, M. W., Jr., & Mahoney, J. D. (1997). Early identification of international executive potential. *Journal of Applied Psychology*, 82, 6–29.

Stahl, M. J. (1983). Achievement, power and managerial motivation: Selecting managerial talent with the job choice exercise. *Personnel Psychology*, 36, 775–789.

Stamp, G. (1988). *Longitudinal research into methods of assessing managerial potential*. Alexandria, VA: U.S. Army Research Institute.

Staw, B. M., McKechnie, P. I., & Puffer, S. M. (1983). The justification of organizational performance. *Administrative Science Quarterly*, 28, 582–600.

Staw, B. M., & Ross, J. (1987). Behavior in escalation situations: Antecedents, prototypes, and solutions. In B. M. Staw and L. L. Cummings (Eds.), *Research in Organizational Behavior*, vol. 9. Greenwich, CT: JAI Press, pp. 39–78.

Steiner, D. D. (1997). Attributions in leader-member exchanges: Implications for practice. *European Journal of Work and Organizational Psychology*, 6, 59–71.

Stephens, C. W., D'Intino, R. S. & Victor, B. (1995). The moral quandary of transformational leadership. *Research in Organizational Change and Development*, 8, 123–143.

Stern, A. (1993). Managing by team is not always as easy as it looks. *New York Times*, July 18, B-14.

Stevenson, W. B., Pearce, J. L., & Porter, L. W. (1985). The concept of coalition in organization theory and research. *Academy of Management Review*, 10, 256–268.

Stewart, R. (1967). *Managers and their jobs*. London: MacMillan.

Stewart, R. (1976). *Contrasts in management*. Maidenhead, Berkshire, England: McGraw-Hill UK.

Stewart, R. (1982). *Choices for the manager: A guide to understanding managerial work*. Englewood Cliffs, NJ: Prentice Hall.

Stogdill, R. M. (1948). Personal factors associated with leadership: A survey of the literature. *Journal of Psychology*, 25, 35–71.

Stogdill, R. M. (1974). *Handbook of leadership: A survey of the literature*. New York: Free Press.

Stogdill, R. M., Goode, O. S., & Day, D. R. (1962). New leader behavior description subscales. *Journal of Psychology*, 54, 259–269.

Strange, J. M., & Mumford, M. D. (2002). The origins of vision: Charismatic versus ideological leadership. *Leadership Quarterly*, 13, 343–377.

Strauss, G. (1962). Tactics of lateral relationship: The purchasing agent. *Administrative Science Quarterly*, 7, 161–186.

Strauss, G. (1963). Some notes on power equalization. In H. J. Leavitt (Ed.), *The social science of organizations: Four perspectives*. Englewood Cliffs, NJ: Prentice Hall, pp. 39–84.

Strauss, G. (1977). Managerial practices. In J. R. Hackman & J. L. Suttle (Eds.), *Improving life at work: Behavioral science approaches to organizational change*. Santa Monica, CA: Goodyear, pp. 297–363.

Strong, P. M. (1984). On qualitative methods and leadership research. In J. G. Hunt, D. M. Hosking, C. A. Schriesheim, & R. Stewart (Eds.), *Leaders and managers: An international perspective on managerial behavior and leadership*. New York: Pergamon Press, pp. 204–208.

Strube, M. J., & Garcia, J. E. (1981). A meta-analytic investigation of Fiedler's contingency model of leadership effectiveness. *Psychological Bulletin*, 90, 307–321.

Strube, M. J., Turner, C. W., Cerro, D., Stevens, J., & Hinchey, F. (1984). Interpersonal aggression and the type A coronary-prone behavior pattern: A theoretical distinction and practical implications. *Journal of Personality and Social Psychology*, 47, 839–847.

Sundstrom, E., DeMeuse, K. P., & Futrell, D. (1990). Work teams: Applications and effectiveness. *American Psychologist*, 45, 120–133.

Sutcliffe, K. M. (1994). What executives notice: Accurate perception in top management teams. *Academy of Management Journal*, 5, 1360–1378.

Sutton, C., & Woodman, R. (1989). Pygmalion goes to work: The effects of supervisor expectations in a retail setting. *Journal of Applied Psychology*, 74, 943–950.

Tannenbaum, R., & Schmidt, W. H. (1958). How to choose a leadership pattern. *Harvard Business Review*, 36 (March–April), 95–101.

Tannenbaum, S. I., Beard, R. L., & Salas, E. (1992). Team building and its influence on team effectiveness: An examination of conceptual and empirical developments. In K. Kelley (Ed.), *Issues, theory, and research in industrial/organizational psychology*. New York: Elsevier Science Publishers B.V., pp. 117–153.

Tannenbaum, S. I., Smith-Jentsch, K., & Behson, S. J. (1998). Training team leaders to facilitate team learning and performance. In J. A. Cannon-Bowers & E. Salas (Eds.), *Making decisions under stress: Implications for individual and team training*. Washington, DC: American Psychological Association, pp. 247–270.

Tannenbaum, S. I., & Yukl, G. (1992). Training and development in work organizations. *Annual Review of Psychology*, 43, 399–441.

Taylor, J., & Bowers, D. (1972). *The survey of organizations: A machine-scored standardized questionnaire instrument*. Ann Arbor: Institute for Social Research, University of Michigan.

Tedeschi, J. T., & Melburg, V. (1984). Impression management and influence in the organization. In S. B. Bacharach & E. J. Lawler (Eds.), *Research in the sociology of organizations*, vol. 3. Greenwich, CT: JAI Press, pp. 31–58.

Tejeda, M. J., Scandura, T. A., & Pillai, R. (2001). The MLQ revisited: Psychometric properties and recommendations. *Leadership Quarterly*, 12, 31–52.

Tepper, B. J., Eisenbach, R. J., Kirby, S. L., & Potter, P. W. (1998). Test of a justice-based model of subordinates' resistance to downward influence attempts. *Group & Organization Management*, 23, 144–160.

Tepper, B. J., Nehring, D., Nelson, R. J., & Taylor, E. C. (1997). *Resistance to downward influence attempts*. Paper presented at the Academy of Management meetings, Boston.

Tepper, B. J., & Percy, P. M. (1994). Structural validity of the multifactor leadership questionnaire. *Educational and Psychological Measurement*, 54, 734–744.

Terry, P. T. (1977). Mechanisms for environmental scanning. *Long Range Planning*, 10, 2–9.

Tesluk, P. E., & Mathieu, J. E. (1999). Overcoming roadblocks to effectiveness: Incorporating management of performance barriers into models of work group effectiveness. *Journal of Applied Psychology*, 84, 200–217.

Tesluk, P. E., & Mathieu, J. E. (1999). Overcoming roadblocks to effectiveness: Incorporating management of performance barriers into models of work group effectiveness. *Journal of Applied Psychology*, 84 (2), 200–217.

Tesluk, P. E., Zaccaro, S. J., Marks, M., & Mathieu, J. E. (1997). Task and aggregation issues in the analysis and assessment of team performance. In M. Brannick & E. Salas (Eds.), *Assessment and measurement of team performance: Theory, research, and applications*. Greenwich, CT: JAI Press, pp. 197–224.

Tetrault, L. A., Schriesheim, C. A., & Neider, L. L. (1988). Leadership training interventions: A review. *Organizational Development Journal*, 6 (3), 77–83.

Thacker, R. A., & Wayne, S. J. (1995). An examination of the relationship between upward influence tactics and assessments of promotability. *Journal of Management*, 21, 739–756.

Thambain, H. J., & Gemmill, G. R. (1974). Influence styles of project managers: Some project performance correlates. *Academy of Management Journal*, 17, 216–224.

Tharenou, P., Latimer, S., & Conroy, D. (1994). How do you make it to the top? An examination of influences on women's and men's managerial advancement. *Academy of Management Journal*, 37, 899–931.

Thibaut, J. W., & Kelley, H. H. (1959). *The social psychology of groups*. New York: John Wiley.

Thomas, A. B. (1988). Does leadership make a difference to organizational performance? *Administrative Science Quarterly*, 33, 388–400.

Thomas, B. (1976). *Walt Disney: An American tradition*. New York: Simon & Schuster.

Thomas, D. A. (1990). The impact of race on manager's experiences of developmental relationships (mentoring and sponsorship): An intra-organizational study. *Journal of Organizational Behavior*, 11, 479–492.

Thomas, J. B., & McDaniel, R. R., Jr. (1990). Interpreting strategic issues: Effects of strategy and the information processing structure of top management teams. *Academy of Management Journal*, 33, 286–306.

Thomas, K. W. (1992). Conflict and negotiation processes in organizations. In M. D. Dunnette & L. M. Hough (Eds.), *Handbook of industrial and organizational psychology*, vol. 3. Palo Alto: Consulting Psychologists Press, pp. 651–718.

Thomas, K. W., & Velthouse, B. A. (1990). Cognitive elements of empowerment: An interpretive model of intrinsic task motivation. *Academy of Management Review*, 15, 666–681.

Thomason, G. F. (1967). Managerial work roles and relationships (Part 2). *Journal of Management Studies*, 4, 17–30.

Thornton, G. C., III, & Cleveland, J. N. (1990). Developing managerial talent through simulation. *American Psychologist*, 45, 190–199.

Tichy, N. M. & Devanna, M. A. (1986). *The transformational leader*. New York: John Wiley.

Tjosvold, D., Wedley, W. C., & Field, R. H. G. (1986). Constructive controversy: The Vroom-Yetton model and managerial decision making. *Journal of Occupational Behavior*, 7, 125–138.

Tornow, W. W., & London, M., Eds. (1998). *Maximizing the value of 360-degree feedback: A process for successful individual and organizational development*. San Francisco: Jossey-Bass.

Tornow, W. W., & Pinto, P. R. (1976). The development of a managerial job taxonomy: A system for describing, classifying, and evaluating executive positions. *Journal of Applied Psychology*, 61, 410–418.

Torrance, E .P. (1954). The behavior of small groups under stress conditions of survival. *American Sociological Review*, 19, 751–755.

Tosi, H. L., Misangyi, V. F., Fanelli, A., Waldman, D. A., & Yammarino, F. J. (2004). CEO charisma, compensation, and firm performance. *Leadership Quarterly*, 15, 405–420.

Townsend, A. M., DeMarie, S. M., & Hendrickson, A. R. (1998). Virtual teams: Technology and the workplace of the future. *Academy of Management Executive*, 12(3), 17–29.

Tracey, J. B., & Hinkin, T. R. (1998). Transformational leadership or effective managerial practices. *Group and Organization Management*, 23, 220–236.

Tracey, J. B., Tannenbaum, S. I., & Kavanagh, M. J. (1995). Applying trained skills on the job: The importance of the work environment. *Journal of Applied Psychology*, 80, 239–252.

Trahan, W. A., & Steiner, D. D. (1994). Factors affecting supervisors' use of disciplinary actions following peer performance. *Journal of Organizational Behavior*, 15, 129–139.

Trevino, L. K. (1986). Ethical decision making in organizations: A person-situation interactionist model. *Academy of Management Review*, 11, 601–617.

Trevino, L. K., Butterfield, K. D. & McCabe, D. L. (1998). The ethical context in organizations: Influences on employee attitudes and behaviors. *Business Ethics Quarterly* 8 (3), 447–476.

Trevino, L. K., & Youngblood, S. A. (1990). Bad apples in bad barrels: A causal approach. *Journal of Applied Psychology*, 75, 378–385.

Triandis, H. C., Kurowski, L. L., & Gelfand, M. J. (1994). Workplace diversity. In H. C. Triandis, M. D. Dunnette, & L. M. Hough (Eds.), *Handbook of industrial and organizational psychology*, vol. 4. Palo Alto: Consulting Psychologists Press, pp. 769–827.

Trice, H. M., & Beyer, J. M. (1986). Charisma and its routinization in two social movement organizations. In L. L. Cummings & B. M. Staw (Eds.), *Research in organization behavior*, vol. 8. Greenwich, CT: JAI Press, pp. 113–164.

Trice, H. M., & Beyer, J. M. (1991). Cultural leadership in organizations. *Organization Science*, 2, 149–169.

Trice, H. M., & Beyer, J. M. (1993). *The cultures of work organizations*. Englewood Cliffs, NJ: Prentice Hall.

Trimble, S. K., Nathan, B. R., & Decker, P. J. (1991). The effect of positive and negative models on learning in behavior modeling training: Testing for proactive and retroactive interference. *Journal of Human Behavior and Learning*, 7 (2), 1–12.

Trompenaars, F. (1993). *Riding the waves of culture*. London: Brealey.

Tropman, J. E. (1996). *Making meetings work: Achieving high quality group decisions*. Thousand Oaks, CA: Sage.

Tsui, A. (1984). A role set analysis of managerial reputation. *Organizational Behavior and Human Performance*, 34, 64–96.

Turban, D. B., & Dougherty, T. W. (1994). Role of protégé personality in receipt of mentoring and career success. *Academy of Management Journal*, 37, 688–702.

Turnley, W. H., & Bolino, M. C. (2001). Achieving desired images while avoiding undesirable images: Exploring the role of self-monitoring in impression managment. *Journal of Applied Psychology*, 86, 351–360.

Tushman, M. L., & Anderson, P. (1986). Technological discontinuities and organizational environments. *Administrative Science Quarterly*, 31, 439–465.

Tushman, M. L., Newman, W. H., & Romanelli, E. (1986). Convergence and upheaval: Managing the unsteady pace of organizational evolution. *California Management Review*, 29 (1), 29–44.

Tushman, M. L., & O'Reilly, C. A. III. (1996). Ambidextrous organizations: Managing evolutionary and revolutionary change. *California Management Review*, 38 (4), 8–30.

Tushman, M.L., & Romanelli, E. (1985). Organizational evolution: A metamorphosis model of convergence and reorientation. *Research in Organizational Behavior*, 7, 171–222.

Uleman, J. S. (1991). Leadership ratings: Toward focusing more on specific behaviors. *Leadership Quarterly*, 2, 175–187.

Ulrich, D., Jick, T., & Von Glinow, M. A. (1993). High impact learning: Building and diffusing learning capability. *Organizational Dynamics*, 22 (1), 52–79.

Urwick, L. F. (1952). *Notes on the theory of organization.* New York: American Management Association.

Vaill, P. B. (1978). Toward a behavior description of high-performing systems. In M. W. McCall, Jr. & M. M. Lombardo (Eds.), *Leadership: Where else can we go?* Durham, NC: Duke University Press, pp. 103–125.

Valerio, A. M. (1990). A study of the developmental experiences of managers. In K. E. Clark & M. B. Clark (Eds.), *Measures of leadership.* West Orange, NJ: Leadership Library of America, pp. 521–534.

Valle, M., & Perrewe, P. L. (2000). Do politics perceptions relate to political behaviors? *Human Relations,* 53, 359–386.

Van der Heijden, K. (1996). *Scenarios: The art of strategic conversation.* New York: John Wiley.

Vanderslice, V. J. (1988). Separating leadership from leaders: An assessment of the effect of leader and follower roles in organizations. *Human Relations,* 41, 677–696.

Van Fleet, D. D., & Yukl, G. (1986a). A century of leadership research. In D. A. Wren (Ed.), *One hundred years of management.* Chicago: Academy of Management, pp. 12–23.

Van Fleet, D. D., & Yukl, G. (1986b). *Military leadership: An organizational perspective.* Greenwich, CT: JAI Press.

Van Velsor, E., & Hughes, M. W. (1990). *Gender differences in the development of management: How women managers learn from experience.* Technical Report #145. Greensboro, NC: Center for Creative Leadership.

Van Velsor, E., & Leslie, J. B. (1991). *Feedback to managers / Vol. 2: A review and comparison of sixteen multi-rater feedback instruments.* Technical Report #150. Greensboro, NC: Center for Creative Leadership.

Van Velsor, E., & Leslie, J. B. (1995). Why executives derail: Perspective across time and cultures. *Academy of Management Executive,* 9 (4), 62–72.

Van Velsor, E., Leslie, J. B., & Fleenor, J. W. (1997). *Choosing 360: A guide to evaluating multi-rater feedback instruments for management development.* Greensboro, NC: Center for Creative Leadership.

Van Velsor, E., Ruderman, E., & Phillips, A. D. (1989). The lessons of the looking glass. *Leadership and Organizational Development Journal,* 10, 27–31.

Varga, K. (1975). N-achievement, n-power and effectiveness of research development. *Human Relations,* 28, 571–590.

Vecchio, R. P. (1983). Assessing the validity of Fiedler's contingency model of leadership effectiveness: A closer look at Strube and Garcia. *Psychological Bulletin,* 93, 404–408.

Vecchio, R. P. (1987). Situational leadership theory: An examination of a prescriptive theory. *Journal of Applied Psychology,* 72, 444–451.

Vecchio, R. P. (1990). Theoretical and empirical examination of cognitive resource theory. *Journal of Applied Psychology,* 75, 141–147.

Vecchio, R. P. (2002). Leadership and the gender advantage. *Leadership Quarterly,* 13, 643–671.

Vecchio, R. P. (2003). In search of the gender advantage. *Leadership Quarterly,* 14, 835–850.

Vecchio, R. P., & Gobdel, B. C. (1984). The vertical dyad linkage model of leadership: Problems and prospects. *Organizational Behavior and Human Performance,* 34, 5–20.

Vera, D., & Crossan, M. (2004). Strategic leadership and organizational learning. *Academy of Management Review,* 29, 222–240.

Vicere, A. A. & Fulmer, R. M. (1997). *Leadership by design.* Boston: Harvard Business School Press.

Virany, B., Tushman, M. L., & Romanelli, E. (1992). Executive succession and organization outcomes in turbulent environments: An organization learning approach. *Organization Science,* 3, 72–91.

Vroom, V. H. (1964). *Work and motivation*. New York: John Wiley.

Vroom, V. H., & Jago, A. G. (1978). On the validity of the Vroom-Yetton model. *Journal of Applied Psychology*, 63, 151–162.

Vroom, V. H., & Jago, A. G. (1988). *The new leadership: Managing participation in organizations*. Englewood Cliffs, NJ: Prentice Hall.

Vroom, V. H., & Yetton, P. W. (1973). *Leadership and decision making*. Pittsburgh: University of Pittsburgh Press.

Wagner, J. A., & Gooding, R. Z. (1987). Shared influence and organizational behavior: A meta-analysis of situational variables expected to moderate participation-outcome relationships. *Academy of Management Journal*, 30, 524–541.

Wainer, H. A., & Rubin, I. M. (1969). Motivation of research and development entrepreneurs: Determinants of company success. *Journal of Applied Psychology*, 53, 178–184.

Wakabayashi, M., & Graen, G. B. (1984). The Japanese career progress study: A seven-year follow-up. *Journal of Applied Psychology*, 69, 603–614.

Waldman, D. A., Atwater, L. E., & Antonioni, D. (1998). Has 360-degree feedback gone amok? *Academy of Management Executive*, 12, 86–94.

Waldman, D. A., Javidan, M., & Varella, P. (2004). Charismatic leadership at the strategic level: A new application of upper echelons theory. *Leadership Quarterly*, 15, 355–380.

Waldman, D. A., Ramirez, G. R., House, R. J., & Puranam, P. (2001). Does leadership matter? CEO leadership attributes and profitability under conditions of perceived environmental uncertainty. *Academy of Management Journal*, 44, 134–143.

Waldman, D. A., & Yammarino, F. J. (1999). CEO charismatic leadership: Levels of management and levels of analysis effects. *Academy of Management Review*, 24 (2), 266–285.

Waldron, V. R. (1991). Achieving communication goals in superior-subordinate relationships: The multifunctionality of upward maintenance tactics. *Communication Monographs*, 58, 289–306.

Walker, A. G., & Smither, J. W. (1999). A five-year study of upward feedback: What managers do with their results matters. *Personnel Psychology*, 52, 393–423.

Walker, C. R., Guest, R. H., & Turner, A. N. (1956). *The foreman on the assembly line*. Cambridge, MA: Harvard University Press.

Wall, J. (1986). *Bosses*. Lexington, MA: Lexington Books.

Wall, S. J., & Wall, S. R. (1995). *The new strategists: Creating leaders at all levels*. New York: Free Press.

Wall, T. D., Kemp, N. J., Jackson, P. R., & Clegg, C. W. (1986). Outcomes of autonomous workgroups: A long-term field experiment. *Academy of Management Journal*, 29, 280–304.

Walton, R. E. (1977). Work innovations at Topeka: After six years. *Journal of Applied Behavioral Science*, 13, 422–433.

Walton, R. W. (1987). *Managing conflict: Interpersonal dialogue and third-party roles*. Reading, MA: Addison-Wesley.

Warren, D. I. (1968). Power, visibility, and conformity in formal organizations. *American Sociological Review*, 6, 951–970.

Watson, W. E., Kumar, K., & Michaelsen, L. L. (1993). Cultural diversity's impact on interaction process and performance: Comparing homogeneous and diverse task groups. *Academy of Management Journal*, 36, 590–602.

Wayne, S. J., & Ferris, G. R. (1990). Influence tactics, affect, and exchange quality in supervisor-subordinate interactions: A laboratory experiment and field study. *Journal of Applied Psychology*, 75, 487–499.

Wayne, S. J., & Kacmar, M. K. (1991). The effects of impression management on the performance appraisal process. *Organizational Behavior and Human Decision Processes*, 48, 70–88.

Wayne, S. J., & Liden, R. C. (1995). Effects of impression management on performance ratings: A longitudinal study. *Academy of Management Journal*, 38, 232–260.

Webber, R. A. (1972). *Time and management*. New York: Van Nostrand-Reinhold.

Webber, R. A. (1975). *Management: Basic elements of managing organizations*. Homewood, IL: Irwin.

Webber, R. A. (1980). *Time is money: The key to managerial success*. New York: Free Press.

Webber, R. A. (1981). *To be a manager*. Homewood, IL: Irwin.

Weber, M. (1947). *The theory of social and economic organizations*. Translated by T. Parsons. New York: Free Press.

Weed, F. J. (1993). The MADD queen: Charisma and the founder of mothers against drunk driving. *Leadership Quarterly*, 4, 329–346.

Weimann, J. M. (1977). Explication and test of a model of communicative competence. *Human Communication Research*, 3, 195–213.

Weiner, N., & Mahoney, T. A. (1981). A model of corporate performance as a function of environmental, organizational, and leadership influences. *Academy of Management Journal*, 24, 453–470.

Wellins, R. S., Byham, W. C., & Wilson, J. M. (1991). *Empowered teams: Creating self-directed work groups that improve quality, productivity, and participation*. San Francisco: Jossey-Bass.

Westley, F., & Mintzberg, H. (1989). Visionary leadership and strategic management. *Strategic Management Journal*, 10, 17–32.

Wexley, K. N., & Latham, G. P. (1991). *Developing and training human resources in organizations*. Glenview, IL: Scott Foresman.

Wexley, K. N., & Nemeroff, W. F. (1975). Effects of positive reinforcement and goal setting as methods of management development. *Journal of Applied Psychology*, 60, 446–450.

Wexley, K. N., & Yukl, G. (1984). *Organizational behavior and personnel psychology*. Homewood, IL: Irwin.

Whetton, D. A., & Cameron, K. S. (1991). *Developing management skills*. New York: Harper-Collins.

White, L. P., & Wooten, K. C. (1986). *Professional ethics and practice in organizational development: A systematic analysis of issues, alternatives, and approaches*. New York: Praeger.

White, S. E., Dittrich, J. E., & Lang, J. R. (1980). The effects of group decision-making process and problem-situation complexity on implementation strategies. *Administrative Science Quarterly*, 25, 428–440.

Whitely, W. T., & Coetsier, P. (1993). The relationship of career mentoring to early career outcomes. *Organization Studies*, 14 (3), 419–441.

Whyte, W. F. (1969). *Organizational behavior: Theory and applications*. Homewood, IL: Irwin.

Wikoff, M., Anderson, D. C., & Crowell, C. R. (1983). Behavior management in a factory setting: Increasing work efficiency. *Journal of Organizational Behavior Management*, 4, 97–128.

Wilbur, J. (1987). Does mentoring breed success? *Training and Development Journal*, November, 38–41.

Williams, M. L., Podsakoff, P. M., Todor, W. D., Huber, V. L., Howell, J., & Dorfman, P. W. (1988). A preliminary analysis of the construct validity of Kerr and Jermier's substitutes for leadership scales. *Journal of Occupational Psychology*, 61, 307–333.

Willner, A. R. (1984). *The spellbinders: Charismatic political leadership*. New Haven: Yale University Press.

Wilson, C. L., O'Hare, D., & Shipper, F. (1990). Task cycle theory: The processes of influence. In K. E. Clark & M. B. Clark (Eds.), *Measures of leadership*. West Orange, NJ: Leadership Library of America, pp. 185–204.

Winter, D. G. (1973). *The power motive*. New York: Free Press.

Winter, D. G. (1979). *Navy leadership and management competencies: Convergence among tests, interviews, and performance ratings.* Boston: McBer.

Wofford, J. C. (1982). An integrative theory of leadership. *Journal of Management, 8,* 27–47.

Wofford, J. C. (1999). Laboratory research on charismatic leadership: Fruitful or futile? *Leadership Quarterly, 10,* 523–529.

Wofford, J. C., & Liska, L. Z. (1993). Path-goal theories of leadership: A meta analysis. *Journal of Management, 19,* 858–876.

Wolfe, J., & Roberts, C. R. (1993). A further study of the external validity of business games: Five-year peer group indicators. *Simulation and Gaming,* 24 (1), 21–33.

Wong, C-S, & Law, K. S. (2002). The effects of leader and follower emotional intelligence on performance and attitude: An exploratory study. *Leadership Quarterly, 13,* 243–274.

Wood, R. E., & Mitchell, T. R. (1981). Manager behavior in a social context: The impact of impression management on attributions and disciplinary actions. *Organizational Behavior and Human Performance, 28,* 356–378.

Woodruff, D. (1993). Chrysler's neon: Is this the small car Detroit couldn't build? *Business Week,* May 3, 464–476.

Woodward, H., & Bucholz, S. (1987). *Aftershock.* New York: John Wiley.

Worley, C. G., Hitchin, D. E., & Ross, W. L. (1996). *Integrated strategic change: How OD builds competitive advantage.* Reading, MA: Addison-Wesley.

Wortman, C. B., & Linsenmeier, J. A. (1977). Interpersonal attraction and techniques of ingratiation in organizational settings. In B. M. Staw & G. R. Salancik (Eds.), *New directions in organizational behavior.* Chicago: St. Clair Press, pp. 133–178.

Xin, K. R., & Tsui, A. S. (1996). Different strokes for different folks? Influence tactics by Asian-American and Caucasian-American managers. *Leadership Quarterly, 7,* 109–132.

Yagil, D. (1998). Charismatic leadership and organizational hierarchy: Attribution of charisma to close and distant leaders. *Leadership Quarterly, 9,* 161–176.

Yammarino, F. J. (1990). Individual and group directed leader behavior descriptions. *Educational and Psychological Measurement, 50,* 739–759.

Yammarino, F. J. (1994). Indirect leadership: Transformational leadership at a distance. In B. M. Bass & B. J. Avolio (Eds.), *Improving organizational effectiveness through transformational leadership.* Thousand Oaks, CA: Sage, pp. 26–47.

Yammarino, F. J., & Bass, B. M. (1990). Long-term forecasting of transformational leadership and its effects among naval officers. In K. E. Clark & M. B. Clark (Eds.), *Measures of leadership.* West Orange, NJ: Leadership Library of America, pp. 151–170.

Yammarino, F. J., Dionne, S., & Chun, J. U. (2002). Transformational and charismatic leadership: A levels-of-analysis review of theory, measurement, data analysis, and inferences. In L. L. Neider and C. A. Schriesheim (Eds.), *Leadership.* Greenwich, CT: New Information Age Publishing, pp. 23–63.

Yammarino, F. J., Spangler, W. D., & Dubinsky, A. J. (1998). Transformational and contingent reward leadership: Individual, dyad, and group levels of analysis. *Leadership Quarterly, 9,* 27–54.

Yang, D. J. (1992). Nordstrom's gang of four. *Business Week,* June 15, 122–123.

Yanouzas, J. N. (1964). A comparative study of work organization and supervisory behavior. *Human Organization, 23,* 245–253.

Yeung, A. K., Ulrich, D. O., Nason, S. W., & Von Glinow, M. A. (1999). *Organizational learning capability: Generating and generalizing ideas with impact.* New York: Oxford University Press.

Young, D., & Dixon, N. (1996). *Helping leaders take effective action: A program evaluation.* Greensboro, NC: Center for Creative Leadership.

Yorges, S. L., Weiss, H. M., & Strickland, O. J. (1999). The effect of leader outcomes on influence, attributions, and perceptions of charisma. *Journal of Applied Psychology*, 84, 428–436.

Yukl, G. (1970). Leader LPC scores: Attitude dimensions and behavioral correlates. *Journal of Social Psychology*, 80, 207–212.

Yukl, G. (1971). Toward a behavioral theory of leadership. *Organizational Behavior and Human Performance*, 6, 414–440.

Yukl, G. (1981). *Leadership in organizations*. Englewood Cliffs, NJ: Prentice Hall.

Yukl, G. (1989). *Leadership in organizations,* 2nd ed. Englewood Cliffs, NJ: Prentice Hall.

Yukl, G. (1990). *Skills for managers and leaders*. Englewood Cliffs, NJ: Prentice Hall.

Yukl, G. (1997). *Effective leadership behavior: A new taxonomy and model*. Paper presented at the Eastern Academy of Management International Conference, Dublin, Ireland.

Yukl, G. (1999a). An evaluative essay on current conceptions of effective leadership. *European Journal of Work and Organizational Psychology*, 8, 33–48.

Yukl, G. (1999b). An evaluation of conceptual weaknesses in transformational and charismatic leadership theories. *Leadership Quarterly*, 10, 285–305.

Yukl, G., & Chavez, C. (2002). Influence tactics and leader effectiveness. In L. L. Neider and C. A. Schriesheim (Eds.), *Leadership*. Greenwich, CT: New Information Age Publishing, pp. 139–165.

Yukl, G., & Clemence, J. (1984). A test of path-goal theory of leadership using questionnaire and diary measures of behavior. *Proceedings of the Eastern Academy of Management Meetings*, 174–177.

Yukl, G., & Falbe, C. M. (1990). Influence tactics in upward, downward, and lateral influence attempts. *Journal of Applied Psychology*, 75, 132–140.

Yukl, G., & Falbe, C. M. (1991). The importance of different power sources in downward and lateral relations. *Journal of Applied Psychology*, 76, 416–423.

Yukl, G., Falbe, C. M., & Youn, J. Y. (1993). Patterns of influence behavior for managers. *Group and Organization Management*, 18, 5–28.

Yukl, G., & Fu, P. (1999). Determinants of delegation and consultation by managers. *Journal of Organizational Behavior*, 20, 219–232.

Yukl, G., Fu, P. P., & McDonald, R. (2003). Cross-cultural differences in perceived effectiveness of influence tactics for initiating or resisting change. *Applied Psychology: An international review,* 52, 68–82.

Yukl, G., Gordon, A., & Taber, T. (2002). A hierarchical taxonomy of leadership behavior: Integrating a half century of behavior research. *Journal of Leadership and Organization Studies*, 9, 15–32.

Yukl, G., Guinan, P. J., & Sottolano, D. (1995). Influence tactics used for different objectives with subordinates, peers, and superiors. *Group and Organization Management*, 20, 272–296.

Yukl, G., Kim, H., & Chavez, C. (1999). Task importance, feasibility, and agent influence behavior as determinants of target commitment. *Journal of Applied Psychology*, 84, 137–143.

Yukl, G., Kim, H., & Falbe, C. M. (1996). Antecedents of influence outcomes. *Journal of Applied Psychology*, 81, 309–317.

Yukl, G., & Lepsinger, R. (1991). An integrating taxonomy of managerial behavior: Implications for improving managerial effectiveness. In J. W. Jones, B. D. Steffy, & D. W. Bray (Eds.),

Applying psychology in business: The manager's handbook. Lexington, MA: Lexington Press, pp. 563–572.

Yukl, G., & Lepsinger, R. (1995). 360-degree feedback: What to put into it to get the most out of it. *Training,* December, 45–50.

Yukl, G., & Lepsinger, R. (2004). *Flexible leadership: Creating value by balancing multiple challenges and choices.* San Francisco, CA: Jossey-Bass.

Yukl, G., Lepsinger, R., & Lucia, A. (1992). Preliminary report on development and validation of the influence behavior questionnaire. In K. Clark, M. B. Clark, & D. P. Campbell (Eds.), *Impact of leadership.* Greensboro, NC: Center for Creative Leadership, pp. 417–427.

Yukl, G., & Nemeroff, W. (1979). Identification and measurement of specific categories of leadership behavior: A progress report. In J. G. Hunt & L. L. Larson (Eds.), *Crosscurrents in leadership.* Carbondale: Southern Illinois University Press, pp. 164–200.

Yukl, G., & Seifert, C. (2002). *Preliminary validation research on the extended version of the influence behavior questionnaire.* Poster at the Society for Industrial and Organizational Psychology meetings, Toronto, Canada.

Yukl, G., & Tracey, B. (1992). Consequences of influence tactics used with subordinates, peers, and the boss. *Journal of Applied Psychology,* 77, 525–535.

Yukl, G., & Van Fleet, D. (1982). Cross-situational, multi-method research on military leader effectiveness. *Organizational Behavior and Human Performance,* 30, 87–108.

Yukl, G., Wall, S., & Lepsinger, R. (1990). Preliminary report on validation of the managerial practices survey. In K. E. Clark & M. B. Clark (Eds.), *Measures of leadership.* West Orange, NJ: Leadership Library of America, pp. 223–238.

Zacarro, S., Foti, R. J., & Kenny, D. A. (1991). Self-monitoring and trait-based variance in leadership: An investigation of leader flexibility across multiple group situations. *Journal of Applied Psychology,* 76 (2), 308–315.

Zacarro, S. J., Gilbert, J. A., Thor, K. K., & Mumford, M. D. (1991). Leadership and social intelligence: Linking social perspectiveness and behavioral flexibility to leader effectiveness. *Leadership Quarterly,* 2, 317–342.

Zacarro, S. J., Mumford, M. D., Marks, M. A., Connelly, M. S., Threlfall, K. V., Gilbert, J. A., et al. (1997). *Cognitive and temperament determinants of army leadership.* Technical Report MRI 97–2. Bethesda, MD: Management Research Institute.

Zaccaro, S. J., Rittman, A. L., & Marks, M. A. (2001). Team leadership. *Leadership Quarterly,* 12, 451–484.

Zajac, E. J., Kraatz, M. S., & Bresser, R. K. F. (1999). Modeling the dynamics of strategic fit: A normative approach to strategic change. *Strategic Management Journal,* 21, 429–453.

Zaleznik, A. (1970, May–June). Power and politics in organizational life. *Harvard Business Review,* 47–60.

Zaleznik, A. (1977). Managers and leaders: Are they different? *Harvard Business Review,* 55 (5), 67–78.

Zanzi, A., & O'Neil, R. M. (2001). Sanctioned versus non-sanctioned political tactics. *Journal of Management Issues,* 13, 245–262.

Zey, M. G. (1988). A mentor for all reasons. *Personnel Journal,* January, 46–51.

Zumwalt, E. R. (1976). *On watch: A memoir.* New York: Times.

Author Index

Subject Index